AKDENİZ ÜNİVERSİTESİ
AKDENİZ DİLLERİNİ VE KÜLTÜRLERİNİ ARAŞTIRMA MERKEZİ

FORSCHUNGSZENTRUM FÜR SPRACHEN UND KULTUREN DES MITTELMEERRAUMES
AN DER AKDENİZ UNIVERSITÄT

Araştırma Merkezi GEPHYRA Bilimsel Çalışma Grubu
Wissenschaftliche Arbeitsgruppe GEPHYRA beim Forschungszentrum

Prof. Dr. N. Eda AKYÜREK ŞAHİN (Antalya), Prof. Dr. Feriştah ALANYALI (Eskişehir), Prof. Dr. Hüseyin ALANYALI (Eskişehir), Dr. Öğr. Üyesi Mehmet ALKAN (Karaman), Arş. Gör. Fatma AVCU (Antalya), Prof. Dr. Alexandru AVRAM (Le Mans), Prof. Dr. Jan BREMMER (Groningen), Prof. Dr. Kostas BURASELIS (Atina), Prof. Dr. Burcu CEYLAN DUGGAN (Antalya), Öğr. Üy. T. Michael P. DUGGAN (Antalya), Dr. Victor COJOCARU (Iaşi), Prof. Dr. A. Vedat ÇELGİN (İstanbul), Yadigâr DOĞAN (Antalya), Prof. Dr. Boris DREYER (Erlangen), Prof. Dr. Serra DURUGÖNÜL (Mersin), Prof. Dr. Denis FEISSEL (Paris), Prof. Dr. Michaela FUCHS (München), Selçuk GÜR (Antalya), Prof. Dr. Bülent İPLİKÇİOĞLU (Ankara), Prof. Dr. Andreas KÜLZER (Wien), Doç. Dr. Dinçer Savaş LENGER (Antalya), Prof. Dr. Katerini LIAMPI (Janina), Prof. Dr. Stephen MITCHELL (Berlin), Prof. Dr. Johannes NOLLÉ (München), Dr. Marta OLLER GUZMÁN (Barcelona), Doç. Dr. Fatih ONUR (Antalya), Prof. Dr. Andreas RHOBY (Wien), Prof. Dr. Marijana RICL (Belgrad), Prof. Dr. Kent J. RIGSBY (Durham), Prof. Dr. Charlotte ROUECHÉ (London), Prof. Dr. Mustafa Hamdi SAYAR (İstanbul), Dr. Hertha SCHWARZ (München), Arş. Gör. Erkan TAŞDELEN (Antalya), Prof. Dr. Oğuz TEKİN (İstanbul), Berfu TÜZÜN (Antalya), Dr. Hüseyin UZUNOĞLU (Antalya), Dr. Hans-Christoph VON MOSCH (München), Prof. Dr. Emmanouil VOUTIRAS (Thessaloniki), Dr. Bernhard WOYTEK (Wien), Dr. Öğr. Üyesi M. Ertan YILDIZ (Antalya)

GEPHYRA

DOĞU AKDENİZ BÖLGESİ ESKİÇAĞ TARİHİ VE KÜLTÜRLERİNİ ARAŞTIRMA DERGİSİ
ZEITSCHRIFT FÜR DIE GESCHICHTE UND KULTUREN DES ANTIKEN ÖSTLICHEN MITTELMEERRAUMS

SAYI / BAND

17, 2019

YAYIMLAYANLAR / HERAUSGEBER

N. Eda AKYÜREK ŞAHİN

Boris DREYER

Stephen MITCHELL

Johannes NOLLÉ

Fatih ONUR

Charlotte ROUECHÉ

Mustafa H. SAYAR

GEPHYRA

Doğu Akdeniz Bölgesi Eskiçağ Tarihi ve Kültürlerini Araştırma Dergisi

Sencer ŞAHİN ve Johannes NOLLÉ tarafından kurulmuştur

Zeitschrift für die Geschichte und Kulturen des antiken östlichen Mittelmeerraums

begründet von Johannes NOLLÉ und Sencer ŞAHİN

Bilimsel Danışma Kurulu | *Wissenschaftlicher Beirat*

Feriştah ALANYALI, Hüseyin ALANYALI,
Jan BREMMER, A. Vedat ÇELGİN,
Angelos CHANIOTIS, Victor COJOCARU,
Serra DURUGÖNÜL, Denis FEISSEL,
Andreas KÜLZER, Christian MAREK,
Marta Oller GUZMÁN, Andreas RHOBY,
Marijana RICL, Kent J. RIGSBY, Oğuz TEKİN,
Emmanouil VOUTIRAS, Bernhard WOYTEK

GEPHYRA

hakemli bir dergidir.	ist eine peer-reviewed Zeitschrift.
2017 itibari ile SCOPUS tarafından taranmaktadır.	wird seit 2017 von SCOPUS indexiert.

Baskı | *Druck*

Prime Rate Kft.
1044 Budapest / Hungary

İletişim | *Kontakt*

Akdeniz Üniversitesi
Akdeniz Dillerini ve Kültürlerini Araştırma Merkezi
Edebiyat Fakültesi
Eskiçağ Dilleri ve Kültürleri Bölümü
Kampüs 07058
Antalya / TÜRKİYE
Tel: (+9) 0 242 310 61 84/97
Fax: (+9) 0 242 310 22 87
http://edergi.akdeniz.edu.tr/index.php/Gephyra
E-mail: gephyra@akdeniz.edu.tr;
n.eda.akyurek@gmail.com; nolle@gmx.de

Yayıncı | *Verlag*

Phoibos Verlag
Mag. Roman Jacobek
Anzengrubergasse 16/4
1050 Wien / AUSTRIA
Tel.: (+43) 1 544 03 191
Fax: (+43) 1 544 03 199
https://phoibos.at
E-mail: office@phoibos.at
ISBN 978-3-85161-222-6 | ISSN 1309-3924
Copyright 2020 © All Rights reserved

İçindekiler / Inhaltsverzeichnis

Zsolt SIMON
    Kar. *sδisa* und ein lykischer Ortsname..1

Diether SCHÜRR
    Ein Königssohn, der Mops hieß (oder Mucks?): von Phantasie-Inschriften, antiken
    Fabeleien und Namenbelegen zwischen Pylos und Karatepe...11

Max GANDER
    Eine bisher unbekannte Alyattes-Münze..25

Wilhelm MÜSELER
    Opponents and successors of the Xanthian dynasty in Western Lycia: The Weχssere
    questions reconsidered...29

Jürgen BORCHHARDT
    Χρυσᾶ τῶν Ἡλιάδων τὰ δάκρυα. „Golden strömen die Tränen der Heliaden" oder Die
    mithrische Interpretation des Phaëton-Mythos..83

Terrance Michael Patrick DUGGAN
    On early antiquarians in Asia Minor to the start of the 19th century....................................115

Hans KLOFT
    Rom im Norden...169

Aygün EKİN MERİÇ – Boris DREYER
    Eine Statuenbasis mit Ehreninschrift für den Asklepiospriester
    P. Claudius Calpurnianus..183

Helmuth SCHNEIDER
    Innovationen und wirtschaftliche Entwicklung im Imperium Romanum............................189

Katharina MARTIN
    Was macht Skylla im lydischen Hinterland? Zu einer Homonoia-Prägung von
    Philadelpheia und Smyrna..223

N. Eda AKYÜREK ŞAHİN – Hüseyin UZUNOĞLU
    New inscriptions from the Museum of Bursa...239

Kar. *sδisa* und ein lykischer Ortsname

Zsolt SIMON*

1. Einführung

Im Glossar des Handbuchs zum Karischen findet sich der folgende Eintrag (Adiego 2007, 412, Umschrift und Siglen folgen Adiego 2007):

„*sδi* (C.Tr 1, C.Al 1)

sδisas (C.Ka 1)

sδisas? (C.Kr 1)

Noun used in funerary contexts (therefore 'tomb', 'stela' or sim.). The morphological analysis of these forms remains unclear. Cf. the variant form *siδi*."[1]

Im Einklang mit dieser Analyse Adiegos wird allgemein angenommen, dass diese Formen zu einem einzigen Wort gehören,[2] auch wenn Duhoux 2007, 70-71 und Henry 2007, 100-101 anhand von kontextuellen Argumenten die Bedeutung als ‚Grab' präzisieren. Neuere Erkenntnisse erfordern allerdings eine Neubetrachtung dieses Wortes, der dieser Aufsatz gewidmet ist. §2 bespricht *sδi*, §3 *siδi* und schließlich §4 *sδisas*.

2. C.Tr 1, C.Al 1: *sδi*

Vor der Besprechung der Bedeutung müssen einige Fragen zur Lesung erörtert werden. Die Inschrift C.Al 1 wurde in *scriptio continua* geschrieben („*sδiaxmob*"), in der ein beschädigtes Zeichen nach *sδia*° steht, von dem nur der untere Teil, ein vertikaler Strich erhalten ist. Es wurde von Schürr 2001, 109 Anm. 12 und Henry 2007, 98 (mit Fragezeichen) als Worttrenner rekonstruiert. Wenn diese Rekonstruktion zutrifft, lautet das Wort *sδia* und nicht *sδi* (Henry 2007, 100 erwog eine Abtrennung von °*a* als Demonstrativpronomen, was Duhoux 2007, 62 mit Anm. 49 allerdings zu Recht ablehnte). Die geographische Verteilung der karischen Worttrenner ist hier nicht hilfreich: zwar ist die senkrechte Linie bisher nur in Euromos und Iasos belegt, dies schließt die Verwendung des gleichen Zeichens in Alabanda aber noch nicht aus. Ein Grund dafür ist, dass keine weiteren Inschriften aus Alabanda zur Verfügung stehen und man deshalb nicht beurteilen kann, ob Worttrenner in Alabanda immer verwendet wurden bzw. welche(r) Worttrenner in der Region von Alabanda gebräuchlich waren, wenn überhaupt (vgl. Simon 2018). Dagegen rekonstruiert Duhoux 2007, 62 das beschädigte Zeichen als <n>, was aus epigraphischer Sicht ebenfalls

---

* Zsolt Simon, Institut für Assyriologie und Hethitologie, Ludwig-Maximilians-Universität München, Deutschland (zsltsimon@gmail.com).

[1] Unter *siδi* steht nur die Belegstelle (C.Tr 2) sowie die Bemerkung: „A variant form of *sδi*, q.v." (Adiego 2007, 412).

[2] Schürr 2001, 109 mit Anm. 12, Schürr 2013, 25-27; Duhoux 2007, 56-72; Henry 2007, 94-100 mit Anm. 17; Kloekhorst 2008, 139-143. Dazu gehört auch eine(r) Gutachter(in), der/dem zufolge „man sollte [sic] schon einen Zusammenhang zwischen allen diesen Wortformen annehmen", auch wenn ihre/seine Auffassung schon 2008 (mit dem Aufsatz von Kloekhorst 2008, vgl. unten §3) obsolet wurde.

möglich ist. In diesem Fall würde das Wort nur *sδi* lauten, insbesondere wenn die Deutung Duhouxs als *sδi an* ‚dieses Grab' zutrifft. Schließlich zweifelt Henry 2007, 98 die Lesung des dritten Zeichens als <i> und des vierten Zeichens als <a> an. Allerdings ist das dritte Zeichen auf dem Foto des Abklatsches (Henry 2007, 99 Planche III) klar erkennbar. Dagegen ist das vierte Zeichen tatsächlich problematisch.

Im Falle von C.Tr 1 behauptet Adiego 2007, 130 (Schürr 2001, 109 Anm. 12 folgend), der dritte Buchstabe sei „definitely" ein <i>, aber das Foto des Abklatsches (Deroy 1955, Planche I) und die veröffentlichten Zeichnungen (Deroy 1955, 307 [anhand des Abklatsches] und Kubitschek *apud* Adiego 2007, 130 [anhand des verschollenen Originals]) unterstützen diese Behauptung nicht. Allerdings bietet sich kein passenderes karisches Zeichen an. Deshalb und auch weil das Wort *sδi* hervorragend zum Kontext passt, scheint es die bessere Lösung zu sein, die Lesung *sδi* beizubehalten. Unklar ist des Weiteren die Segmentierung der erste Zeile <sδimτ[>. Adiego 2007, 130 gibt *sδi amτ*[an (räumt jedoch sofort ein, dass es sich dabei um eine unsichere Interpretation handelt), Schürr 2001, 109 Anm. 12 liest dagegen *sδia mτ*[. Beide Interpretationen sind möglich und da die Inschrift in *scriptio continua* erscheint und (*a*)*mτ*[sonst unbekannt ist (Adiego 2007, 351), lässt sich momentan keine Entscheidung fällen.[3]

Was die Bedeutung betrifft, schränkt Adiego 2007, 292 den Bedeutungsansatz ‚tomb, stela *vel sim*.' dadurch ein, dass diese Inschriften für eine Interpretation zu fragmentarisch sind. Duhoux 2007, 62-63, 70-71 und Henry 2007, 100-101 würden die Bedeutung auch hier genauer und zwar als ‚Grab' angeben. All diese Vorschläge passen zweifellos zum Kontext.

Kloekhorst 2008, 143 schlägt allerdings anhand seiner Übersetzung von *siδi* in C.Tr 2 als ‚sie liegen' (vgl. §3) vor, dass dieses Verb auch in der Form *sδi* von C.Tr 1 vorliegt (der Ø/i-Wechsel vor nasalisierten Konsonanten ist im Karischen gut belegt), weil die nachfolgenden Wörter der Inschrift (¹*sδiamτ*[²*pauś* ³*art mon*) auf zwei verstorbene Personen hinweisen können: „Amτ[...], (son) of Pau [and]² Artmon". Obwohl dies möglich ist, bleibt das deutliche, große Spatium zwischen <art> und <mon>, das eventuell Worttrennung anzeigt, problematisch (für verschiedene Möglichkeiten s. Duhoux 2007, 57-58). Falls sie sich nicht auf eine Person namens Artmon beziehen, würde dann nur ein Verstorbener genannt werden anstatt (zumindest) zwei, deren Anwesenheit das angebliche Verb verlangt. Allerdings ist zu betonen, dass das Spatium so gut wie nie zur Worttrennung in den karischen Inschriften verwendet wurde, die einzige Ausnahme bildet C.My 1, wo es nur selten und inkonsistent gebraucht wurde (Simon 2018). Zudem könnte hier auch eine Form *sδia* zu segmentieren sein (wie vielleicht in C.Al 1), die dann nichts mit dem Verb *si*- zu tun hat. Diese Lösung kann ggf. durch den gewissermaßen größeren Raum nach °*a* unterstützt werden, wie Duhoux 2007, 68 anmerkt, der, allerdings, zu Recht betont, dass das Original verschollen ist, weshalb sich dieser größere Abstand nicht mehr nachweisen lässt. Das größte Problem des Vorschlags Kloekhorsts besteht darin, dass in der Inschrift C.Tr 1 es kein (identifiziertes)

---

[3] Die Zeichnung Kubitscheks (*apud* Adiego 2007, 130), die ein Spatium nur nach dem *a* zeigt, ist aus dieser Sicht irreführend, da, wie die Aufnahme des Abklatsches (Deroy 1955, Planche I) zeigt, ein ebenso großes Spatium auch nach dem *δ* steht. – Trotz dieser Erörterungen glaubt eine(r) Gutachter(in), dass die Struktur dieser Inschriften nicht erklärt wurde.

Adverb mit der Bedeutung ‚hier', ‚unten' o.ä. vorhanden ist und die Übersetzung dadurch unvollständig wirkt.[4]

Schließlich soll Schürr erwähnt werden, der *sδi(a)* zunächst noch nicht übersetzte (2001, 109 Anm. 12), später aber (2013, 26) ein Verb oder eine „Personenbezeichnung" vorschlug (die dem *sδisa* in C.Ka 1 entsprechen würde, s. §4). Obwohl theoretisch beide Vorschläge möglich sind, lassen sie sich nicht nachweisen.

Zusammenfassend kann man feststellen, dass bisher der Bedeutungsansatz ‚Grab' von Duhoux und Henry am besten zu diesen Inschriften passt und die Form des Wortes kann momentan nur als *sδi(a)* angegeben werden.

3. C.Tr 2: *siδi*

Adiego 2007, 412 zufolge stellt das Wort *siδi* der Inschrift C.Tr 2 eine Variante von *sδi(sas)* ‚tomb, stela *vel. sim.*' dar, die in diesem Fall ‚tomb' bedeuten würde (Adiego 2007, 290; vgl. schon Hajnal 1995, 20 [‚Grab, Grabteil, Grabstätte o.ä.']). Im Grunde genommen schließen sich dieser Interpretation auch Duhoux 2007, 70-71 und Henry 2007, 100-101 an, die die Bedeutung eher als ‚Grab' angeben. Kloekhorst 2008, 139-141 argumentiert allerdings aus kontextuellen und formalen Gründen überzeugend dafür, dass die Inschrift C.Tr 2 *an siδi artmi pauś parŋaq* (zur Lesung des letzten Wortes s. Adiego 2007, 131 mit Lit. und Kloekhorst 2008, 140) folgendermaßen zu übersetzen ist: ‚here/underneath lie Artmi, (son) of Pau, and Parŋa' (*contra* Hajnal 1995, 20; Adiego 2007, 289-290; Duhoux 2007, 60-61).[5] Dementsprechend handelt es sich hier um ein Verb *si-* ‚liegen' in 3. Pl. Präsens.

4. C.Ka 1 und C.Kr 1: *sδisa(s)*

Schürr schlug schon in 2001, 109 vor, dass die korrekte Segmentierung dieser Wörter *sδisa* (C.Kr 1) und *sδisas* (C.Ka 1) lautet, und gab deren Bedeutung als „Bezeichnung des Toten" an, allerdings ohne Argumente (seine Auffassung ließen die oben zitierten Forscher außer Acht, ihm schloss sich aber Marek 2006, 124-125 an). Mithilfe des Parallelismus der beiden Texte C.Ka 1 und C.Kr 1 konnte Schürr 2013, 25-26 schließlich beweisen, dass diese in der Tat die richtige Segmentierung ist und dass das Wort sich auch auf den Verstorbenen bezieht:

C.Kr 1	C.Ka 1	
qoΩomu	sñis:	‚Personenname (Nom./Dat. Sg.)'
sδisa	sδisas:	*s.* (kongruiert mit dem vorangehenden Personennamen)

---

[4] Kloekhorst 2008, 143 ließ die Inschrift C.Al 1 außer Acht, weil sie „badly broken" sei. Dies ist allerdings abgesehen von dem oben genannten bruchstückhaften Zeichen nicht der Fall, vgl. Duhoux 2007, 63 und Schürr 2013, 26 Anm. 22.

[5] Hajnals Übersetzung (wiederholt in Hajnal – Zipser 2017, 277 Anm. 5, ohne Kloekhorsts Interpretation zu erwähnen) beruht auf seiner Fehlinterpretation von *parŋa-q* als ‚ich errichtete' aus *párnewā-ha*, was phonologisch nicht möglich ist, weil ŋ *nk (aber jedenfalls eine mit [n] anlautende Konsonantengruppe) fortsetzt (Adiego 2007, 251; Kloekhorst 2008, 139). Ein(e) Gutachter(in) behauptet fälschlicherweise, dass es nicht erklärt wird, worauf die Deutung Kloekhorsts stützt. Des Weiteren behauptet sie/er, dass die Trennung von sδi und siδi aus semantischer Sicht „wenig wahrscheinlich" ist, was selbstverständlich nur eine subjektive Meinung darstellt und den formalen Unterschied beider Wortformen außer Acht lässt.

snś	psuśoλś:	‚Patronym (Gen. Sg.)'
šoδubrś	malś:	‚Personenname (Gen. Sg.)'
sbmnoś	mnoś	‚Berufsbezeichnung / Verwandtschaftsbegriff'[6]

(…)

Dieser Parallelismus schließt die früheren Vorschläge aus: Adiego 2007, 291-292 (dem sich Melchert 2010, 180-181 mit Anm. 18 anschloss) schlug sehr vorsichtig vor, C.Ka 1 als „These (sñi-s) (are) the burials (sδisas) / These (sñi-s) burials (sδi-s) (are) those (a-s) of Psuśoλ (son) of Mal (and) the son" zu übersetzen (ähnlich Henry 2007, 98, 100-101: „sñis: ces sδi/tombe de Psuśoλ (fils) de Mal (et) du fils") und C.Kr 1 als „Qoτ₂omu. These tombs (sδi-s a-s) (are) of him (nś), of Šoδubr, and of the son (…)" (ähnlich wiederum Henry 2007, 96, 100-101: „QoΩomu (a fait) ces sδi/tombe pour lui, pour šoδubr et pour le fils (…)"). Obwohl diese Übersetzungen formal nicht unmöglich sind (wobei zu beachten ist, dass Sn sonst als Personenname belegt ist und dass Sñi vermutlich eine Ableitung dazu darstellt, Schürr 2013, 27), erfordern sie die Anwesenheit eines bisher unbelegten Pronomens (was angesichts des äußerst knappen karischen Sprachmaterials offensichtlich kein schwerwiegendes Problem darstellt). Zudem gibt es gute Gründe anzunehmen, dass die Endung des Nom. Pl. -š und nicht -s lautete.[7] Schließlich kritisiert Schürr 2013, 25 zu Recht, dass die Ergänzung mit „(a fait)" willkürlich ist, ohne die die vorgeschlagene Übersetzung nicht funktioniert.

Die Lösung von Duhoux (2007, 64-65, 70-71) ist grammatikalisch gesehen besser als diese Übersetzungen im Falle von C.Ka 1: „sδi/tombe appartenant à Sñi, sas de Psuśoλ, fils de Mal". Dementsprechend übersetzt er C.Kr 1 als „sδi/tombe appartenant à Qoτ₂omu. Celui-ca [sa] (est) le mᵋnś/sᵋnś de Šoδubr et de (son) fils". Um QoΩomu als Dativ identifizieren zu können muss er allerdings annehmen, dass die in *scriptio continua* geschriebene Sequenz <qoΩomusδi…> „qoΩomus sδi…" mit „simplification graphique" darstellt (2007, 65-67, 70-71). Ein solcher Gebrauch wurde allerdings bisher in den karischen Inschriften nicht beobachtet (auch Duhoux selbst konnte nur griechische Parallelen zitieren) und die Annahme eines Schreiberfehlers wäre *petitio principii*.[8]

Des Weiteren möchte Kloekhorst 2008, 142-143 in beiden Inschriften das Verb siδi ‚they lie' sehen (zum Ø/i-Wechsel vgl. oben). Dementsprechend muss er in beiden Inschriften sas segmentieren (er tut dies im Falle von C.Kr 1 nur implizit), das in beiden Sätzen das Subjekt wäre: ‚… lie the sas of (the persons mentioned)'. Dabei bleibt allerdings das erste Wort ungeklärt: obwohl man im Falle von C.Ka 1 wie Kloekhorst argumentieren könnte, dass sñis eine Art Adverb (z.B. ‚hier') aus dem Demonstrativpronomen sa-/sn- ‚dieser/e/s' darstellt, ist dies im Falle von der Inschrift C.Kr 1 nicht möglich, da sie mit qoΩomu beginnt, was offensichtlich ein komponierter Personenname

---

[6] Das Wort mno wird traditionell als ‚Sohn' übersetzt, was Schürr 2013, 28-29 mit guten Gründen in Zweifel zog und stattdessen die Bedeutung ‚eine Person in persönlicher Abhängigkeit', etwa ‚Knecht' vorschlug. Diese Frage ist hier allerdings nicht weiter relevant.

[7] Vgl. schon Duhoux 2007, 64 und sogar Adiego 2007, 318 (der über dialektale Unterschiede spekuliert); für einen Überblick mit Lit. s. Melchert 2010, 178, aber s. schon Hajnal 1995, 14 Anm. 7; Schürr 1998, 146, Schürr 2001, 111, 117; und Adiego 2007, 306-307, 318 mit Lit.

[8] Schürr 2013, 25 geht davon aus, dass die Ergänzung mit „appartenant à" willkürlich ist. Dies ist aber nicht der Fall, weil es sich dabei einfach nicht um die wörtliche Wiedergabe des Dativs handelt.

mit -*muwa*- im Hinterglied ist. Der andere Vorschlag Kloekhorsts, *sas* sei ein Adverb aus dem gerade erwähnten Pronomen („the *sñi*-s of Psuśoλ, son of Mal, lie here"), könnte zu C.Ka 1 passen (abgesehen von der *s*-Endung des Nom. Pl. statt -*š*, vgl. oben), nicht aber zu C.Kr 1, wo es, obwohl das Verb dieser Interpretation zufolge im *Plural* steht, nur einen Verstorbenen gibt: QoΩomu, der in diesem Fall das Subjekt sein muss.[9]

Wenn aber mit Schürr tatsächlich ein *sδisa* zu segmentieren ist, muss noch dessen Bedeutung bestimmt werden. Schürr (2013, 26-27 mit Lit., vgl. schon 2001, 109) verglich es mit dem lykischen Personennamen *Hñtihāma* (TL 75, Tyberissos) von unbekannter Bedeutung. Er schlug vor, diesen Namen aus einem Verb **hñti-ha-* (Stamm *ha-* ‚haben') herzuleiten, das die lykische Entsprechung von *sδisa-* wäre und „Besitz besitzen" bedeuten würde. Demnach würde *sδisa* „Besitzbesitzer" bedeuten. Abgesehen davon, dass die Bedeutung des lykischen Verbs kontrovers diskutiert wird (vgl. Melchert 2004, 21 und Neumann 2007, 88-89: ‚(los)lassen') und somit auch die Bedeutung von *Hñtihāma* unklar ist (vgl. auch Neumann 2007, 96), macht die vorgeschlagene Bedeutung „Besitzbesitzer" schon an sich wenig Sinn, insbesondere nicht für *sδisa* in dieser Inschrift (wäre es ein Rang? ein Titel?), außerdem bleibt unklar, wie ein Nomen agentis *sδisa* aus einem angeblichen Verb *sδisa-* abgeleitet wird.

Der gängigen Forschungsmeinung zufolge, die dieses Wort mit *sδi(a)* verknüpft (s. die Literatur in der Einführung, zu der Möglichkeit mit einer Verbindung mit dem Verb *si-* vgl. oben), stehen verschiedene Probleme gegenüber. Die Ableitung ist unklar, aber man könnte argumentieren, dass es sich um ein ethnisches oder um ein Possessivadjektiv mit -*s*- handelt (zu diesem karischen Suffix vgl. Adiego 2007, 392 mit Lit.). Dieses würde perfekt passen, allerdings nur, wenn der Stamm *sδi-* lautet. Wenn der Stamm *sδia-* heißt, was genauso möglich ist (vgl. oben), muss der Schwund des [a] erklärt werden, was jedoch wegen unserer begrenzten Kenntnisse über die zumindest graphisch nicht vorhandenen karischen Vokale nicht unbedingt fatal ist. Letztlich führt diese Erklärung, auch wenn sich die Verknüpfung morphologisch aufrechterhalten lässt, aus semantischer Sicht zu keinem befriedigendem Ergebnis: da *sδi(a)* vermutlich ‚Grab' bedeutet (vgl. oben), würde *sδisa* etwa ‚Grabherr' bedeuten – eine solche Bezeichnung scheint allerdings bei Grabinschriften völlig unnötig zu sein. Vorsichtshalber sollten daher beide Wörter bis zum Auftreten neuer Beweise getrennt behandelt werden.

Da *sδisa* unmittelbar hinter dem Namen des Verstorbenen steht und dies das einzige Wort ist, das den Verstorbenen beschreibt (abgesehen von den genealogischen Angaben), erwartet man einen Titel, eine Berufsbezeichnung oder ein (ethnisches) Adjektiv. Ein Titel oder eine Berufsbezeichnung passen semantisch nicht zu dem belegten Stamm *sδi-* (vgl. oben). Es gibt allerdings mehrere Kandidaten für ein Toponym (für eine ausführliche Liste der karischen Toponyme s. Adiego 2007, 456-459): Erstens, Σίνδα (Adiego 2007, 458), aber man erwartet †*sδasa* mit dem Ethnikonsuffix -*s*- (man beachte auch, dass die Form des Toponyms unklar ist, vgl. die Diskussion in Zgusta 1984, 571 §1219-2, zum Suffix vgl. unten). Zweitens, Σινδησσός (Adiego 2007, 458), mit dem Ethnikonsuffix, das zumindest graphisch als Nullmorphem erscheint (wie in *ksolb* ‚von Κασωλαβα', vgl. Adiego 2007, 269-270, 2010, 165-166 und Janda 1994, 176), aber man erwartet in diesem Falle †*sδesa*, weil das Eta karisches <e> umschreibt (Adiego 2007, 236). Es gibt, allerdings, auch eine Stadt Σινδία in Lykien (Zgusta 1984, 572 §1219-5, genaue Lokalisierung ist

---

[9] Nur der Vollständigkeit halber sei Schürr 2013, 25 erwähnt, weil er die Interpretation Kloekhorsts ohne Argumente ablehnte („scheint mir nicht möglich").

unbekannt). Wenn man in Betracht zieht, dass beide Inschriften mit *sδisa* aus dem karisch-lykischen Grenzland stammen, würde es nicht überraschen, wenn die Verstorbenen aus einer Stadt stammten oder in einer Stadt lebten, die in Lykien liegt.[10] Obwohl Psuśoλ eindeutig ein karischer Name ist, kann man einerseits nicht die Möglichkeit lykischer Namen unter den übrig gebliebenen ausschließen (die Herkunft von Mal, QoΩomu, Sn / Sñi, und Šoδubr ist unbekannt [zum letzteren s. Schürr 2013, 28]), schließt dies andererseits eine Verknüpfung mit einer lykischen Stadt natürlich noch nicht aus.[11] Die übrig gebliebene Frage ist die nach dem °*a*: Man muss bedenken, dass bisher nur der Akk. Sg. aus dem Paradigma des Ethnikonsuffixes -*s*- belegt ist (*otonosn*, C.Ka 5, 4.6), weshalb nicht auszuschließen ist, dass der Nom. Sg. -*sa* und der Dat. Sg. -*sas* lautete (es überrascht nicht, dass ein Vokal zwischen dem Sibilanten des Suffixes und dem des Dativs erscheint), insbesondere, weil es das luwo(i)de („Luwic") Suffix *-*e*/*osso*- fortsetzt (Melchert 2012, 276).[12]

5. Zusammenfassung

Der anfangs erwähnte Eintrag aus Adiegos Glossar ist daher in die folgenden drei Lexeme zu trennen:

1. **sδi(a)** ‚Grab':   *sδi(a)* (Nom. Sg., C.Tr 1), *sδi(a?)* (Nom. Sg., C.Al 1)

2. **sδisa** ‚aus Sindia':   *sδisa* (Nom. Sg., C.Kr 1), *sδisas* (Dat. Sg., C.Ka 1)

3. **si-** ‚liegen':   *siδi* (3.Pl. Präsens, C.Tr 2)

Danksagung

Dieser Aufsatz entstand im Rahmen des durch das spanische Ministerium für Wirtschaft und Wettbewerbsfähigkeit geförderten Forschungsprojekts *Los dialectos lúvicos de transmisión alfabética en su contexto lingüístico, geográfico e histórico* (FFI2015-68467-C2-1-P). Ich bedanke mich bei Anja Busse für sprachliche Verbesserungen.

---

[10] Eine(r) Gutachter(in) behauptet, die Existenz dieses Ortes sei „zweifelhaft", weil der Name nur bei Stephanos von Byzanz (mit Hinweis auf Hekataios) belegt ist. Eine solche Skepsis ist selbstverständlich nicht begründet. Zu Recht weist dagegen der/die andere Gutachter(in) auf die These hin, die Σινδία mit der inschriftlich belegten Siedlung Isindia identifiziert (French 1994, 86, mit einem Überblick zu den ähnlich lautenden Ortsnamen), auch wenn mich diese Gleichung wegen des ungeklärten Unterschieds im Anlaut nicht überzeugt.

[11] Man beachte, dass die wiederholte Behauptung Melcherts (2003, 15 Anm. 9, 2004, 108), die Namen der lykischen Dynasten Xereî und Xeriga würden ‚Karer' o.ä. bedeuten, jeder Grundlage entbehrt, vgl. schon Simon 2015, 795 Anm. 15.

[12] *Contra* Adiego 2007, 319, 351, 2013, 21 mit Lit. (dem auch Yakubovich 2015, 44 folgt [„likely"]) kann der Ausdruck *alos karnos* / *alosδ karnosδ* kein ethnisches Adjektiv aus dem Stadtnamen Halikarnassos darstellen, s. schon Simon 2008, 459, 462. Ein(e) Gutachter(in) glaubt, der Nom. Sg. von *otonosn* *otonos* (und daher in diesem Fall **sδis*) „solchen Ethnika im Lykischen entsprechend" lauten sollte: es ist allerdings ein schwerwiegender methodologischer Fehler, die Morphologie einer Sprache anhand der Morphologie einer *anderen* Sprache zu bestimmen.

Bibliographie

Adiego 2007 — I.-X. Adiego, The Carian Language (Handbuch der Orientalistik 86), Leiden-Boston 2007.

Adiego 2010 — I.-X. Adiego, Recent Developments in the Decipherment of Carian, in: R. van Bremen – J.-M. Carbon (Hg.), Hellenistic Karia. Proceedings of the First International Conference on Hellenistic Karia-Oxford, 29 June - 2 July 2006, Bordeaux 2010, 147-176.

Adiego 2013 — I.-X. Adiego, Unity and Diversity in the Carian Alphabet, in: P. Brun et al. (Hg.), Euploia. La Lycie et la Carie antiques. Dynamiques des territoires, échanges et identités. Actes du colloque de Bordeaux, 5, 6, et 7 novembre 2009, Bordeaux 2013, 17-28.

Deroy 1955 — L. Deroy, Les inscriptions cariennes de Carie (L'Antiquité Classique 24), 1955, 305-335.

Duhoux 2007 — Y. Duhoux, Le vocabulaire carien de la „tombe". À propos d'une possible isoglosse étrusco-carienne (suθi/śuθi, "tombeau" ~ carien sδi/siδi, "tombe"), Kadmos 46, 2007, 53-107.

French 1994 — D. French, Isinda and Lycia, in: id. (Hg.), Studies in the History and Topography of Lycia and Pisidia in memoriam A. S. Hall, Ankara 1994, 53-92.

Hajnal 1995 — I. Hajnal, Das Vokalsystem des Karischen. Eine provisorische Bestandsaufnahme, Die Sprache 37, 1995 [1997], 12-30.

Hajnal – Zipser 2017 — I. Hajnal – K. Zipser, Lykisch me- versus hethitisch -ma: Ein Beitrag zur vergleichenden Syntax der anatolischen Sprachen, in: I. Hajnal – D. Kölligan – K. Zipser (Hg.), Miscellanea Indogermanica. Festschrift für José Luis García Ramón zum 65. Geburtstag, Innsbruck 2017, 275-293.

Henry 2007 — O. Henry, Quelques remarques sur des inscriptions funéraires cariennes de Carie, in: P. Brun (Hg.), Scripta anatolica. Hommages à Pierre Debord, Bordeaux 2007, 93-101.

Janda 1994 — M. Janda, Beiträge zu Karischen, in: M. E. Giannotta et al. (Hg.), La decifrazione del cario. Atti del 1° Simposio Internazionale. Roma, 3-4 maggio 1993, Roma 1994, 171-190.

Kloekhorst 2008 — A. Kloekhorst, Studies in Lycian and Carian Phonology and Morphology, Kadmos 47, 2008, 117-146.

Marek 2006 — Chr. Marek, Die Inschriften von Kaunos (Vestigia 55), München 2006.

Melchert 2003 — H. C. Melchert, Prehistory, in: id. (Hg.), The Luwians (Handbuch der Orientalistik 68), Leiden-Boston, 8-26.

Melchert 2004 — H. C. Melchert, A Dictionary of the Lycian Language, Ann Arbor-New York 2004.

Melchert 2010 — H. C. Melchert, Further Thoughts on Carian Nominal Inflection, in: R. van Bremen – J.-M. Carbon (Hg.), Hellenistic Karia.

	Proceedings of the First International Conference on Hellenistic Karia – Oxford, 29 June - 2 July 2006, Bordeaux 2010, 177-186.
Melchert 2012	H. C. Melchert, Genitive Case and Possessive Adjective in Anatolian, in: V. Orioles (Hg.), Per Roberto Gusmani. Studi in ricordo. Linguistica storica e teorica II/1, Udine 2012, 273-286.
Neumann 2007	G. Neumann, Glossar des Lykischen. Überarbeitet und zum Druck gebracht von Johann Tischler (Dresdner Beiträge zur Hethitologie 21), Wiesbaden 2007.
Schürr 1998	D. Schürr, Kaunos in lykischen Inschriften, Kadmos 37, 1998, 143-162.
Schürr 2001	D. Schürr, Karische und lykische Sibilanten, Indogermanische Forschungen 106, 2001, 94-121.
Schürr 2013	D. Schürr, Kaunisch-Karisches in Krya: Revision der Grabinschrift und Vergleiche, in: O. Henry (Hg.), 4th Century Karia. Defining a Karian Identity under the Hekatomnids, Istanbul-Paris, 21-31 (Varia Anatolica XXVIII).
Simon 2008	Zs. Simon, Rezension zu Adiego 2007, Acta Antiqua Academiae Scientiarum Hungaricae 48, 2008, 457-463.
Simon 2015	Zs. Simon, Against the identification of Karkiša with Carians, in: N. Chr. Stampolidis – Ç. Maner – K. Kopanias (Hg.), Nostoi. Indigenous Culture, Migration and Integration in the Aegean Islands and Western Anatolia during the Late Bronze and Early Iron Age, Istanbul 2015, 791-809.
Simon 2018	Zs. Simon, Die karischen Worttrennungszeichen, Unveröffentlichter Vortrag gehalten auf der Arbeitstagung der Indogermanischen Gesellschaft „Schriftkonventionen in pragmatischer Perspektive". Brüssel, 13. September 2018.
Yakubovich 2015	I. Yakubovich, Phoenician and Luwian in Early Iron Age Cilicia, Anatolian Studies 65, 2015, 35-53.
Zgusta 1984	L. Zgusta, Kleinasiatische Ortsnamen (BNF Beiheft 21), Heidelberg 1984.

Karca *sδisa* ve Lykia'da bir yer ismi
Özet

Bu makale, geleneksel olarak bir mezarı ya da mezarın bir kısmını tanımladığı düşünülen Karca bir sözcüğün kritik bir incelemesini sunmaktadır. Makalede yakın zamanlardaki filolojik gelişmeler, ilgili yazıtların detaylı analizi ve bunların beraber değerlendirilmesi temelinde aslında üç ayrı sözcük ile karşı karşıya olduğumuz tartışılmaktadır. Bir tanesi gerçekten "mezar"ı ifade ederken, diğer ikisinden bir tanesi bir fiil ve diğeri de Lykia'daki bir yer isminden türetilmiş ek bir sıfattır.

Anahtar sözcükler: Karca, epigrafi, mezar terminolojisi, Anadolu coğrafyası.

Carian *sδisa* and a Lycian toponym
Abstract

This article offers a critical account of a Carian word traditionally assumed to refer to the tomb or to one of its parts. Based on recent philological improvements, on a detailed analysis of the relevant inscriptions as well as on the combinatory method it will be argued in this paper that in fact we are dealing with three different words. One of them indeed refers to the tomb, but the other two are a verb and an appurtenance adjective based on a Lycian toponym.

Keywords: Carian, Epigraphy, Sepulchral Terminology, Anatolian Geography.

Ein Königssohn, der Mops hieß (oder Mucks?): von Phantasie-Inschriften, antiken Fabeleien und Namenbelegen zwischen Pylos und Karatepe

Diether SCHÜRR*

Dem Historiker Xanthos, der Lyder genannt und im 5. Jh. v. Chr. lebend, wurde eine seltsame Geschichte zugeschrieben, die einen Lyder namens Mopsos mit der Stadt Askalon, dem heutigen Aschkelon im Süden Israels, verbindet. Er habe da wegen ihrer Hybris die Atargatis [eigentlich eine Göttin] zusammen mit ihrem Sohn Ichthys [Fisch] in einem See ertränkt, und sie sei von Fischen gefressen worden – offenbar eine krude euhemeristische Erfindung. Athenaios führt sie – nicht mehr als zwei Sätze – in den ‚Deipnosophistai' (VIII 37) nach dem Historiker Mnaseas an. Da Mopsos ein griechischer Name (vor allem von zwei sagenhaften Sehern) ist[1], dürfte er hier an die Stelle des gräzisierten lydischen Namens Moxos getreten sein: Nikolaos von Damaskus berichtet von einem Lyderkönig dieses Namens, und er hat mit dem Mopsos des Xanthos das Ertränken in einem See gemeinsam[2].

Dieser kleine Splitter aus dem riesigen Schutthaufen antiker Überlieferungen[3] war bis vor kurzem nicht weiter bemerkenswert, aber Ende 2017 veröffentlichten Eberhard Zangger und Fred Woudhuizen eine ellenlange hieroglyphen-luwische Inschrift, worin es heißt, „the Great King's son, Mukusus, king and lord of the Land Amiwina; son of Kuwadna-ziti, Great King; son of Asuwati, Great King; son of Piyama-Kurunta, Great king....[Reached] / the frontier(s) of the land Mizri (Egypt); the city Asakuluna and the city Gazi a fortress [with] infantry, chariotry, navy"[4].

---

* Diether Schürr, Katharina-Belgica-Str. 22b, D-63450 Hanau/Deutschland (diether.schuerr@freenet. de).

Siehe: Ein bisher unbekanntes Lied Victor von Scheffels (mit englischer Übersetzung), das ich bei academia.edu eingestellt habe. Sehr herzlich danke ich Max Gander für kritische Bemerkungen, Michael Janda für Auskünfte, Zsolt Simon für das Skript seines Mopsos-Artikels, Auskünfte und weitere Literatur, Aslı Özyar für eine Auskunft, Rostislav Oreshko für seinen neuesten Aufsatz und Literatur, Stephen Durnford für die Verbesserung des Abstracts und auch einem der Peer-Reviewer für Kritik und Anregungen.

[1] Eine ausführliche und kritische Darstellung der diversen Mopsos-Überlieferungen einschließlich der anderen mit ihm assoziierten Sagenfiguren bietet Scheer 1993, 153-271 (Hinweis Michael Jandas).

[2] Siehe Abschnitt 4. „Muksu, Muksa, Mpš, Muksos, Moxos und Mopsos" in Gander 2012, 297ff., wo die Belege für diese Namen und viel weitere Literatur zu finden sind, allerdings mit der Namenform Moxos bei Xanthos, die auf eine Emendation Jacobys nach Nikolaos zurückgeht. Bei diesem heißt die Stadt übrigens Krabos.

[3] Hekataios (um 500 v. Chr.) begründete mit der Feststellung: οἱ γὰρ Ἑλλήνων λόγοι πολλοί τε καὶ γελοῖοι, „denn die Erzählungen der Griechen sind viele und lächerlich", den Beginn der Geschichtsschreibung.

[4] Zangger – Woudhuizen 2018, 12 Zeichnung Block 17 (9) - 18 (10), S. 17 Übersetzung Block 9.-10., von Woudhuizen S.24f. § 26-28 modifiziert.

Im folgenden tritt er auch noch als Großkönig von Arzawa auf, und in einer weiteren hieroglyphen-luwischen Inschrift erscheint gleich zu Beginn als Urheber der „Great prince Muksas"[5]. So eindrucksvoll dürfte der geschichtliche Kern einer (Pseudo-)Sage noch nie bestätigt worden sein.

Allerdings ist das auch kein Wunder: Die Zeichnungen der Inschriften wie die Übersetzung der längsten stammen von James Mellaart, der nicht nur ein bedeutender Archäologe war, sondern auch ein skrupelloser Erfinder von Artefakten wie dem Schatz von Dorak und von kelimartigen Wandmalereien in Çatal Hüyük, die alle nur in seinen Zeichnungen existieren. Und bereits 1954 hatte er die Zeichnung eines Siegelabdrucks mit dem hieroglyphen-luwischen Namen eines Königssohns publiziert, dessen Schreibung wie die Lesung offenkundig von ihm selbst stammte[6]. Bei den von ihm hinterlassenen Inschriftenzeichnungen[7] verwertete er eine Vielzahl von Informationen. In der Form imitieren sie die Inschrift von Yalburt, inhaltlich kombinierte er aus hethitischen Quellen bekannte Königs- und Ländernamen mit Seevölkernamen (*Pulasati, Luka, Sakarasa*), später belegten Städtenamen und auch der Xanthos zugeschriebenen Fabelei, wobei er mit Mopsos alias Moxos den in einem bronzezeitlichen, hethitischen Text belegten Namen *Muksus* (*Mu-uk-šu-uš* geschrieben) beziehungsweise den in der eisenzeitlichen hieroglyphen-luwischen Doppel-Inschrift vom Karatepe in Kilikien belegten Namen *Mu-ka-sa-* gleichsetzte, wie das andere schon lange vor ihm getan hatten. So verwendete er auch beide Namenformen (*Mu-ku-su-sa* und *Mu-ka-sa*). Mellaarts gewaltsame Historisierungen basieren also auf einer gängigen Praxis von Gelehrten, die mit griechischen Sagen – und Pseudo-Sagen – vertraut sind und schnell bereit, Sagennamen anderswo wiederzuerkennen. Das ist das eigentliche, perennierende Problem – obwohl es ja eigentlich keine neue Erkenntnis ist, daß die Unzahl von Wander- und Gründungssagen, die im Laufe der Zeit angehäuft wurden, in erster Linie als Produkte zu verstehen sind, die den Bedarf nach Tradition und damit Identitätsversicherung stillten.

Am Karatepe ist vom „(Herrscher-)Haus des *Mu-ka-sa-*" die Rede (Hawkins 2000, 51 § XXI und 56 § LVIII), und genaugenommen ist unklar, ob dieser Name [Muksa-] zu lesen ist, der zweite Silbenvokal also ausgelassen werden darf und keine silbenschließenden Nasale – die stets ungeschrieben blieben – einzufügen sind. Es gibt aber auch drei phönizische Fassungen der Inschrift, und da erscheint „Haus (des) MPŠ" (Hawkins 2000, 51 § XXI, 54 § XLII und 56 § LVIII), worin man bald nach der Entdeckung den griechischen Seher Mopsos erkennen wollte, weil den der ein oder andere antike Autor auch nach Kilikien kommen und dort sogar regieren ließ. So reichte das Karatepe-Zeugnis beispielsweise Houwink ten Cate 1961, 44 schon, um zu erklären: „Mopsus can justifiably be considered and treated as an historical figure", was bis heute viele Anhänger hat –

---

[5] Zangger – Woudhuizen 2018, 48 Fig. 3 Zeichnung, S. 46 Woudhuizens Übersetzung.

[6] Siehe Schürr, im Druck.

[7] Außerdem erfand er auch noch Keilschrifttexte, in diesem Fall aber natürlich nur Übersetzungen: von einem noch viel längeren hethitischen Text auf Bronzetafeln und einem Brief des Assyrerkönigs Assurbanipal an den Lyderkönig Ardys. Diese Texte erwähnte Mellaart (neben „rock monuments in Hittite 13th-century style") bereits in einer Buchbesprechung von 1992, und da spricht er S. 38 auch schon von einem Königssohn namens Muksus, der nach dem ersten Text die Seevölkerflotte 1175 v. Chr. bis nach Askalon geführt hätte. Der Editor bemerkte dazu im nächsten Band S. 82: "Clearly, unless the authenticity of documents can be established, they should not be cited as valid source material." Zangger, zu dessen Theorien all diese Texte so schön passen, hat immerhin kurz nach der Veröffentlichung der hieroglyphischen eingeräumt, daß Mellaart zumindest den ersten Text selbst erfunden hat.

offenbar mehr als die Gegenposition: „Les sources orientales ne fournissent pas, en tout cas, la moindre preuve favorable à l'éventuelle consistance historique des pérégrinations du Mopsos de Colophon" (Vanschoonwinkel 1990, 198). Mellaart war, was den Nachweis der Geschichtlichkeit betrifft, also anspruchsvoller als die meisten, und er zog den lydischen Sagenkönig dem griechischen Seher vor.

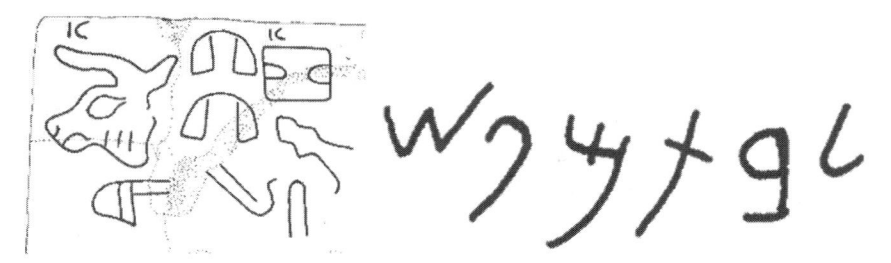

Abb.1) KARATEPE 1: ᴵᶜ*Mu-ka-sá-sá-na* ᴵᶜDOMUS-*ní-i* „dem Hause des *Mu-ka-sa-*" (nach Hu 4b, Çambel 1999, Pl. 66), linksläufig L-BT MPŠ „dem Hause (des) MPŠ" (nach Phu/A I, 16, Çambel 1999, Pl. 9).

Nun geht Μόψος auf den in Linear B, in Knossos wie in Pylos belegten Männernamen *Mo-qo-so* zurück, falls dieser [Mokʷsos] zu lesen ist (ohne Etymologie). Und so konnte man annehmen, daß dieser Name in der Bronzezeit in Anatolien zu *Muksus* vereinfacht oder wenigstens so von hethitischen Schreibern wiedergegeben wurde[8]. Dieser Name kommt in dem mittelhethitischen Madduwatta-Text (Rs 75 bei Götze 1927, 36f.) vor, in nicht rekonstruierbarem Zusammenhang. Zuvor wird Rs 71 die ansonsten unbekannte Stadt Maharmaha genannt, danach Rs 81 das Land Karakiša, das in Westkleinasien zu suchen ist. Die Person mag also nach Westkleinasien gehören, aber sicher ist das keineswegs. An *Muksus* ließen sich jedenfalls das gräko-lydische Μοξος[9] und *Mu-ka-sa-* am Karatepe anschließen, zumal seit 2009 auch ein ca. 740 v. Chr. datierter phrygischer Beleg *Muksos* in Gordion bekannt ist (Brixhe – Liebhart 2009, 147f. und 156, Fig. 7), der das Bild von der Namenverbreitung merklich verändert. Denn dieser vermittelt zwischen Lydien und Kilikien, so daß der Name in der Eisenzeit quer durch Anatolien gewandert sein kann – statt eines griechischen Sehers oder eines lydischen Königs in grauer Vorzeit. Und die anderen Namenbelege, vor allem das etwa zeitgleiche *Muksos*, sprechen dafür, daß am Karatepe tatsächlich [Muksa-] zu lesen ist.

Allerdings wäre eine solche Ostwanderung eines Personennamens höchst ungewöhnlich. Es ist also als Alternative immerhin zu erwägen, daß ein Mykener namens [Mokʷsos] tatsächlich nach Kilikien gelangt sein könnte (dann eher auf dem Seeweg), Dynastiegründer wurde und sein Name dort zu [Muksas] wurde. Diese Form konnte dann viel später auch zu den Phrygern gelangt sein – aber dann sollte man dort statt *Muksos* den Ausgang *-as* wie bei *Midas* erwarten. Und es ist ja für Lydien Μοξος bezeugt, und nicht so vereinzelt wie *Muksus*, *Muksos* und [Muksa-]. Daher ist es plausibler, daß das altphrygische *Muksos* auf die lydische Form zurückgeht, die zu dem gräzisierten Μοξος geführt hat (s. u.). Übernahme von lydischen Namen ins Altphrygische ist auch

---

[8] Simon (demnächst) wendet gegen letzteres ein, daß im Hethitischen /kʷs/ existierte, [Mokʷsos] also durch †*Mukkušu-* hätte wiedergegeben werden können.

[9] Bereits Götze 1927, 140 verglich Μοξου πόλις im Süden Phrygiens (Zgusta 1984, § 835-2 mit Karte 303). Μοξος ist auch Name mehrerer Männer aus Sardes im 4. Jh. v. Chr. (Zgusta 1964, § 960-1). In Phrygien sind außerdem auch Μοξο/εανοι belegt (Zgusta 1984, § 835-1 mit Karte 303).

sonst zumindest möglich, vor allem bei Namen auf -es wie *Manes*, *Ates*, und m. E. sehr wahrscheinlich bei lydisch *Śrkaśtus* – altphrygisch *Surgastos* (s. Obrador Cursach 2018, 119f. und Schürr 2006, 1583f.). Und was die Übernahme eines Namens aus dem Altphrygischen ins Hieroglyphen-Luwische angeht, hat Simon 2017 überzeugend gezeigt, daß der in vier hieroglyphen-luwischen Inschriften Kappadokiens für Kleinkönige und andere Personen belegte Name *Ku+ra/i-ti(-ia)-* auf den phrygischen Namen zurückgeht, der gräzisiert als Γορδιος/ης und in neuassyrischen Quellen als *Gurdî* belegt ist. So ist die etappenweise Wanderung eines Namens von den Lydern zu den Phrygern und von den Phrygern zu den Kilikern auch denkbar.

Aber in jedem Fall ist sehr merkwürdig, daß diesem *Mu-ka-sa-* im 8. Jh. v. Chr. phönizisch MPŠ zur Seite tritt, als ob in Kilikien bekannt gewesen wäre, daß [Muksa-] einem griechischen Μόψος entspricht, d. h. beide Namenformen einen gemeinsamen, weit zurückliegenden Ursprung hätten. Nach dem Lautwandel [Mok^wsos] > Μόψος hätte diese neue Namenform auch nach Kilikien gelangt und dort aus irgendeinem Grund mit [Muksa-] gleichgesetzt worden sein müssen. Und es wäre dann auch merkwürdig, daß Μόψος nur in der phönizischen Version aufgenommen worden wäre. Falls der irgendwie erinnerte mykenische Ursprung des Namens durch das Aufgreifen der nachmykenischen Lautform hätte unterstrichen werden sollen, wäre ja auch hieroglyphen-luwisch †*Mu-pa-sa-* oder konsequenter †*Mu-pu-su-* oder gar †*Ma-pa-sa-* zu erwarten. Das Nebeneinander der beiden Namenformen ist kaum zu verstehen, wenn sie tatsächlich gleichen Ursprungs wären: „Aucune explication satisfaisante n'a été apportée à ce phènomène" (Vanschoonwinkel 1990, 197).

Und natürlich ist auch die Annahme eines gemeinsamen Ursprungs der beiden Namenformen nicht zwingend. [Muksa-] ist offenbar keine tragfähige Stütze für die Annahme, daß MPŠ auf Μόψος zurückgeht. Es läßt sich viel leichter vorstellen, daß MPŠ erst später von Griechen mit ihrem Μόψος gleichgesetzt wurde, ebenso wie das gräko-lydische Μοξος durch irgendeinen Euhemeristen oder Abschreiber. Die alten Griechen hatten ja einen starken Hang, die gleichen Sagenfiguren an vielen Orten als Gründerfiguren auftreten zu lassen, und auch dazu, fremde Namen gewaltsam zu gräzisieren[10]. Wenn der Kirchenvater Hieronymus in seiner Übersetzung der Chronik des Eusebius von Caesarea zum Jahr 1184 v. Chr. vermerkt: *Mopsus regnavit in Cilicia, a quo Mopsicrene et Mopsistiae*, dann geht das auf eine regionale Tradition zurück, wie die beiden Städtenamen zeigen. Und dafür ist der Dynastiegründer MPŠ ein plausibler Ausgangspunkt, nicht aber der Seher Μόψος oder der Lyderkönig Μόψος/Μοξος: „Die Karriere des Mopsos im Süden entsprang der interessegeleiteten Interpretation von Griechen, unter anderem auch Euböern, die von den Namen beeindruckt waren, die sie von den Kilikern hörten" (Lane Fox 2011, 271).

Daß die Chronik diese Herrschaft knapp vor dem Fall Trojas ansetzt (andere Quellen lassen Mopsos erst danach wandern[11]), taugt auch nicht als Argument, den Dynastiegründer so weit zurückzudatieren. Und dagegen spricht die hieroglyphen-luwische Inschrift von Çineköy, ebenfalls in

---

[10] Um nur ein lykisches Beispiel anzuführen: In einer Bilingue in Tlos wurde aus *Purihimeti* ein pseudo-griechischer Πυριβάτης, ein 'Feuergänger', gemacht (Zgusta 1964, § 1292-5).

[11] So der Alexanderhistoriker Kallisthenes bei Strabon XIV 4, 3, der Leute mit dem Seher Mopsos den Tauros überschreiten ließ, von denen ein Teil in Pamphylien blieb, während der andere sich über Kilikien und Syrien bis Phönizien verbreitete – wohin dann in den ‚Deipnosophistai' auch der Lyder Mopsos gelangt. Herodot VII 91 führte die Pamphyler dagegen auf die Seher Amphilochos und Kalchas zurück und

Kilikien: Da ist *Wa/i+ra/i-i-ka-sá*, der König der Stadt Hiyawa, der Sohn einer Person, deren Name nicht erhalten ist, und der Enkel des [*Mu-ka*]-*sa*-. Vom Beginn der phönizischen Version ist nur „Moi, je suis" W[und in Z.2 „de la lignée de" MPŠ erhalten, offenbar gleichbedeutend mit „Haus (des) MPŠ"[12]: Dieser Ahnherr scheint also nach der ersten Version der Großvater gewesen zu sein, auch wenn schon in der Erstpublikation Recai Tekoğlu unter dem Eindruck der Mopsos-Spekulationen das luwische [hamsis] hier mit „descendant" statt ‚petit-fils' übersetzte (Tekoğlu et al. 2000, 970)[13]. Man könnte annehmen, daß der Großvater nur den gleichen Namen wie der Ahnherr trug, aber dann sollte man schon die Nennung weiterer Vorfahren erwarten. Aller Wahrscheinlichkeit war die Dynastie also erst um 800 gegründet worden.

Es bleibt auf jeden Fall unklar, warum *Mu-ka-sa-* MPŠ entspricht. Es kommt aber vor, daß die gleiche Person in unterschiedlichen Sprachen mit lediglich lautlich ähnlichen Namen bezeichnet wird. Daß die französischen Könige namens Louis deutsch hartnäckig als Ludwige bezeichnet werden, geht zwar auf das überlieferte Wissen von der Namenidentität zurück, aber ein solches Wissen über die dunklen Jahrhunderte nach 1200 v. Chr. und vermutlich eine Reihe verschiedener Völker hinweg ist schwer vorstellbar. Ein Beispiel aus Lykien für lautähnliche Namen einer Person wäre Κτησικλῆς, der auch Κτασαδας hieß, in Idebessos (Zgusta 1964, § 759): Da ist der erste Name griechisch, der zweite wahrscheinlich lykisch, von *χddaza* ‚Sklave' abgeleitet (Lebrun 1983, 68). Allerdings muß dann offenbleiben, aus welcher Sprache MPŠ stammt und wie es vokalisiert wurde.

Die vielleicht von den Hethitern aus Westanatolien übernommene Namenform *Muksus* könnte dort durch das lydische, aber gräzisierte Μοξος fortgesetzt worden sein. Wie eine lydische Zwischenform lauten müßte, ist erst einmal unklar. Es ist aber gut möglich, daß sie sich gar nicht verändert hatte: Namen und Wörter auf -*u*- sind im Lydischen nicht selten, und zur Wiedergabe von lydischem *u* durch griechisches Omikron läßt sich etwa der Ortsname *Kulu*-, gräzisiert Κολοη (Zgusta 1984, § 554), vergleichen. Vielleicht ist daher *Muksus* sogar dem Proto-Lydischen zuzuordnen[14]. Und es wäre auch dann möglich, daß es tatsächlich auf ein mykenisches [Mok^{w}sos] zurückging: Wenn das Proto-Lydische schon kein kurzes *o mehr kannte (das lydische *o* ist sekundär, siehe hier auch Anm. 14), wäre die Substitution durch *u plausibel, so, wie später Ἀλέξανδρος durch *Alikšā/antrus* wiedergegeben wurde. Und eine Vereinfachung der Lautfolge $k^w s$ zu ks ist gut möglich; zumindest ist das auf *k^w zurückgehende lydische *q* vor *s* oder *š* nicht

---

III 91 die Stadt Poseideion an der kilikisch-syrischen Grenze auf Amphilochos allein; Mopsos spielt bei ihm noch keine Rolle.

[12] Siehe auch die Inschrift von İncirli (Kaufman 2007), ebenfalls in Kilikien, wo W<u>RYKS</u>, der König von QW, zweimal diesem Haus zugeordnet wird.

[13] Yakubovich 2015, 46 nimmt sogar eine falsche Übersetzung des phönizischen Textes an: „Since the Anatolian rendering of his name as Muksa goes back to the time when the Greek labiolvelar stops were still in place, this Mopsus could hardly be the grandfather of the late eighth-century king Waraika."

[14] Simon (demnächst) nimmt auch an, daß *Muksus* eine proto-lydische Namenform reflektiert, für die er aber *Moksos* ansetzt, so daß die phrygische Form *Muksos* aus dem Hieroglyphen-Luwischen entlehnt worden sein müßte. Im belegten Lydischen ist eine solche Form jedenfalls nicht möglich, da auf *o* immer der Akzent fällt, vergleiche dazu auch die Wiedergabe von lydisch *Karos* durch Καρους (Zgusta 1964, § 542), in der gleichen Inschrift wie Μοξος. Es wäre, wenn man mit Simon von einem vorlydischen *Mé/á/ówkso*- ausginge, ein lydisches *Moksas* zu erwarten.

belegt. Ein lydisches *Muksus wäre dann auch eine plausible Ausgangsform für das phrygische *Muksos*, und dieses für das hieroglyphen-luwische [Muksas].

Wir haben also, wenn man an dem möglichen mykenischen Ursprung der in Kleinasien belegten Namenformen festhält, vielleicht folgendes Szenario:

myk. [Mokʷsos] → *Muksus? → heth. *Muksus*

    ↓   ↓

    ↓   lyd. *Muksus? → phryg. *Muksos* → h.-luw. [Muksa-] = phön. MPŠ

gr. Μόψος ←————↓

               Μόξος

Aber eine vom Griechischen unabhängige Verbreitung in Anatolien ist sicher auch möglich. So nimmt Gander 2012, 300 an, „daß ein ähnlicher Name in Griechenland und in Kleinasien bekannt war", und Simon (demnächst) ist noch entschiedener dieser Ansicht. Ohne den Klebstoff der Sage ist der Zusammenhang der Namen ja nicht mehr so einfach herzustellen.

Der Glaube an die Mopsos-Sage hat noch weitere griechische Namendeutungen nach sich gezogen. So sind die in beiden Sprachen konstant verschieden geschriebenen und daher sicher zu unterscheidenden[15] Königsnamen (a) *Wa/i+ra/i-i-ka-sá* = W[Çineköy, WRYKS İncirli (sehr unsichere Lesung), WRYK Cebelireis (im Rauhen Kilikien) und (b) *Á-wa/i+ra/i-ku-sa* = 'WRK (Karatepe: König der Stadt Adanawa, Hassanbeyli: König von DN) auch griechisch gedeutet worden, aber wenn der erste mit mykenisch *Wo-ro-ko*, kyprisch *Wo-ro-i-ko* bzw. Ῥοῖκος gleichgesetzt wird, der zweite mit Εὔαρχος, wäre die griechische Endung -ος in den hieroglyphen-luwischen Schreibungen verschieden wiedergegeben[16]. Simon 2014 hält daher nur die erste Gleichung für überzeugend, freilich davon ausgehend, daß MPŠ tatsächlich auf Μόψος zurückgeht (aber unabhängig von der Sage). Wenn man diese Annahme nicht akzeptiert, entfällt auch das Motiv für eine griechische Deutung dieser Namen. Möglich wären ja beide Deutungen, zwingend ist aber keine von ihnen, und so stützen sie die Deutung von MPŠ nicht, sondern stehen und fallen mit ihr.

Es scheint mir übrigens möglich, daß der König *Á-wa/i+ra/i-ku-sa* gar nicht zum „Haus des [Muksa-]" gehörte, denn am Karatepe ist zuerst vom „Haus meines Herrn" die Rede (§ XIV, Hawkins 2000, 50), und später wird das „Haus des [Muksa-]" in einem Atemzug mit Azatiwadas, den dieser König ‚großgemacht' hatte, genannt (§ LVIII, Hawkins 2000, 56): „Dienen mögen sie [parnawantu] dem Azatiwadas und dem Haus [parni] des [Muksa-]!"[17] Das klingt eher so, als hätte sich Azatiwadas, der einen gut luwischen Namen hat, selbst diesem Haus zugerechnet.

Außerdem ist auch KRNTRYŠ, der Beiname des Baal in Karatepe, auf ein griechisches Wort zurückgeführt worden: Während Bossert 1953, 183 an eine Ableitung von κράντωρ ‚Herrscher'

---

[15] Siehe Simon 2014.

[16] Dazu kommt neu-assyrisch *Uriyaikki/Urikki/Urik*, König von Que, der 739/738 - 710/709 v. Chr. genannt wird (Belege bei Simon 2014, 95). Diese Namenform paßt nur zu *Wa/i+ra/i-i-ka-sá* und WRYK.

[17] Eine *figura etymologica*: dienen wie in einem Haushalt.

dachte[18], postulierte Schmitz 2009 ein *κορυνητήριος zu einem ebenfalls nicht belegten *κορυνητηρ statt κορυνήτης ‚Keulenschwinger' (Ilias VII 138 Beiname des Königs Areithoos), wobei dieses Adjektiv ‚mace-bearing' bedeuten sollte. Da wäre also die griechische Endung anders als bei MPŠ, WRYK und 'WRK wiedergegeben. Und wenn Kaufmans Lesung W<u>R</u>YKS richtig ist, wäre sie da mit einem anderen Zeichen wiedergegeben. Aber in Çineköy und Cebelireis, dazu auch in Sidon (Lawson Younger 2009, 1f.) ist der Beiname nur KR, was die Trennung von KR und NTRYŠ nahelegt (auch von Lawson Younger 2009, 16 erwogen). Und fatal für diese Etymologie ist, daß der Wettergott vom Karatepe und von Çineköy gar keine Keule hat (falls er eine hätte, sollte er auch besser κορυνήτης heißen), auch wenn für Schmitz 2009, 132 Anm. 29 „the object in the right hand (…) probably what remains of a mace handle" ist. So konnte sich Schmitz für seine Hypothese nur auf den Wettergott von Aleppo in der Bronzezeit und drei nordsyrische Wettergottdarstellungen in der Eisenzeit berufen, die nächstgelegene bei Zincirli (Pancarlı 1) – aber dieser Gott schwingt eher eine Axt mit abgerundeten Schneiden (nach Autopsie, vgl. auch Orthmann 1971, 440 Anm. 2) und es ist auch nicht klar, ob es sich wirklich um einen Wettergott handelt. Und sonst schwingen die eisenzeitlichen Wettergötter immer eine Axt. Es spricht nichts dafür, daß die Statue „may well represent the Storm god of Aleppo as a mace bearing god" (S. 134), schon gar nicht ein angeblich griechischer Beiname, dem in § LI übrigens hieroglyphen-luwisch ARHA [usanuwamis] „highly blessed" (Hawkins 2000, 55) entspricht.

Schließlich muß hier wenigstens kurz erwähnt werden, daß seit der Publikation der Inschrift von Çineköy angenommen wird, daß der mykenische [Mokʷsos] in seinem Gepäck auch den Landesnamen mitgebracht hätte, der zuerst im hethitischen Madduwatta-Text (s. o.) durch Attar(is)iya, den „Mann von Āhhiyā", später als Ahhiyawā belegt ist, und daß dieser in Kilikien zu Hiyawa verkürzt worden wäre. Das liegt daran, daß dieser Name seit Forrer 1924 mit Homers Achäern verbunden wird, obwohl das lautlich alles andere als plausibel ist[19]. Und in diesem Rahmen wurde auch eine bereits von Kretschmer 1933 vorgetragenen Kombination wieder aufgegriffen: Herodot VII 91 erwähnt, daß die Kiliker ehemals Ὑπαχαίοι genannt worden wären, erst später nach dem Phönizier Kilix[20]. Kretschmer kombinierte diese völlig obskure Benennung (Sub-Achäer?) mit dem assyrischen Landesnamen Qaue > Que, den er so auf Ahhiyawā = *Ἀχαιϝᾶ zurückführen wollte, das er allerdings ebenfalls in Kilikien vermutete. Dazu schien die Inschrift von Çineköy mit der Stadt Hiyawa zu passen. Eine eingehende Kritik daran hat Gander 2012 vorgelegt, aber es versteht sich fast von selbst, daß diese Kombinationen damit nicht erledigt sind, obwohl es keinen vernünftigen Grund gibt, eine Übertragung von Ahhiyawā nach Kilikien anzunehmen, schon gar nicht die Hypachäer Herodots. Im Gegenteil, mit der Idee, in den Inschriften vom Karatepe Á-*429-wa/i- (URBS) von Á-ta-na-wa/i- (URBS) zu trennen und als Á-HIYA-wa/i- zu interpretieren

---

[18] „Weilte vielleicht um diese Zeit noch ein anderes indoeuropäisches Volk in Kilikien, das den Namen Moxos »Mopsos« aussprach und den Wettergott als »Erfüllenden, Erhörenden« mit *krantoriias bezeichnete?" Κραντήριοι wäre bei Hesych belegt.

[19] Kloekhorst 2018, 78f. führt nun als „Argument 3" für die umstürzende Hypothese, daß die Laryngale *h_2 und *h_3 auf Verschlußlaute zurückgehen würden, die Verbindung von Ahhijawā mit den Achäern an: Sie würde „easier", wenn Ahhijawā auf *[aq:iaw-] zurückginge. Dann müßte der Achäername freilich schon ins Uranatolische gelangt sein. Dagegen sieht etwa Steiner 2011, 277 in Āhhiyā und Ahhiyawā „in der Struktur anatolische Toponyme" und Hajnal 2011, 251 ein „echtanatolisches Toponym".

[20] Darauf folgt die Zurückführung der (griechischen) Pamphyler auf Amphilochos und Kalchas, siehe Anm. 11.

(Oreshko 2013), haben sie eine neue Stufe erreicht. Allerdings sind nun in ARSUZ 1 (Syrien, jetzt Hatay) wesentlich früher *429-*sa* (URBS) und *Hi-ia-wa/i-* (REGIO) belegt (Dinçol et al. 2015, 64). Für eine Kritik der Idee Oreshkos[21] sei auf Simon 2018, 316f. verwiesen (mit weiterer Literatur).

Was die zusammen mit dem griechischen Ursprung der Dynastie angenommene Präsenz von Griechen betrifft[22], wissen die assyrischen Quellen nichts davon, sondern führen die *Jawnāja* (von griechisch Ἰά(ϝ)ονες, Ionier) als eine Bedrohung auch von Que an. So heißt es in den Khorsabad-Annalen Sargons II. im ausgehenden 8. Jh., daß sie „seit fernster [Vergangenheit] die Einwohner [der Stadt] Tyros (und) [des Landes] Que töteten" (zitiert nach Rollinger 2007, 68)[23]. Und griechische Inschriften gibt es im Ebenen Kilikien erst in hellenistischer Zeit, abgesehen von einem angekauften Siegel im Museum von Adana, das in die zweite Hälfte des 8. Jhs. datiert wird und den griechischen Namen Diweiphilos in kyprischer Silbenschrift bietet (M. Egetmeyer in Poncy 2001, 18ff. mit Abb. 79ab S. 35). Aber es muß ja nicht in Kilikien gefunden worden sein. Novák 2010, 408 kommt zu dem Schluß: „Die Anwesenheit von Griechen ist im Ebenen Kilikien für die fragliche Zeit folglich nicht nachweisbar", ebenso Meyer 2011, 94.

Es ließe sich also höchstens eine Dynastie griechischen Ursprungs annehmen, für die das Griechische keine Rolle mehr spielte[24]. Aber mehr als allenfalls mögliche Namengleichungen und das Vertrauen auf Mopsos-Geschichten[25] müßte es dafür schon geben. Eher als ein Grieche könnte der Begründer der Dynastie (um 800?) ein Phryger gewesen sein. Man sollte also auch hier nicht immer nur durch die altgriechische Brille sehen, sondern die Sprachenvielfalt Kleinasiens in Rechnung stellen.

Bibliographie

Bossert 1953   H. Th. Bossert, Die phönizisch-hethitischen Bilinguen vom Karatepe, 4. Fortsetzung, Jahrbuch für kleinasiatische Forschung 2, 1953, 167-188.

Brixhe – Liebhart 2009   C. Brixhe – R. F. Liebhart, The Recently Discovered Inscriptions from Tumulus MM at Gordion. A Preliminary Report, Kadmos 48, 2009, 141-156.

---

[21] Oreshko 2018 greift außerdem die Verbindung der DNNYM, die in den phönizischen Texten Adanawa oder Hiyawa entsprechen, mit den Danaern wieder auf, womit zwei der homerischen Namen für die Griechen in Kilikien vertreten wären.

[22] Im Extremfall ist Kilikien sogar zu „Homers Heimat" geworden (Schrott 2008).

[23] Allerdings wurden die Griechen auf Zypern nicht zu den *Jawnāja* gerechnet. Simon 2018 tritt dafür ein, daß zyprische Griechen vor 850 v. Chr. in Kilikien eingewandert wären und in Ermangelung einer eigenen Schrift die phönizische Schrift und Sprache mitgebracht hätten. Dann sollten sie beide auch auf Zypern verwendet haben.

[24] Das nimmt Özyar 2016 an.

[25] Wie jetzt auch bei Kopanias 2018: „The followers of Mopsos were able to occupy a part of Cilicia and to establish there a kingdom" (S. 84)!

Çambel 1999	H. Çambel, Corpus of Hieroglyphic Luwian Inscriptions. Vol. II: Karatepe-Aslantaş. The Inscriptions: Facsimile Edition (Untersuchungen zur indogermanischen Sprach- und Kulturwissenschaft, NF 8.2), Berlin – New York 1999.
Dinçol et al. 2015	B. Dinçol – A. Dinçol – J. D. Hawkins – H. Peker – Aliye Öztan, Two new inscribed Storm-god stelae from Arsuz (İskenderun): ARSUZ 1 and 2, AnSt 65, 2015, 59-77.
Forrer 1924	E. Forrer, Vorhomerische Griechen in den Keilschrifttexten von Boghazköi, MDOG 63, März 1924, 1-21 nebst 2 Karten.
Gander 2012	M. Gander, Aḫḫiyawa – Ḫiyawa – Que: Gibt es Evidenz für die Anwesenheit von Griechen in Kilikien am Übergang von der Bronze- zur Eisenzeit? SMEA 54, 2012, 281-309.
Götze 1927	A. Götze, Madduwattaš (Mitt. der Vorderasiat.-Aeg. Ges. 32, Heth. Texte III), Leipzig 1927.
Hajnal 2011	I. Hajnal, Namen und ihre Etymologien – als Beweisstücke nur bedingt tauglich? In: Ch. Ulf – R. Rollinger (Hgg.), Lag Troia in Kilikien? Der aktuelle Streit um Homers Ilias, Darmstadt 2011, 241-263.
Hawkins 2000	J. D. Hawkins, Corpus of Hieroglyphic Luwian Inscriptions. Vol. I: Inscriptions of the Iron Age, Part 1, Berlin-New York 2000.
Houwink ten Cate 1961	Ph. H. J. Houwink ten Cate, The Luwian population groups of Lycia and Cilicia Aspera during the hellenistic period (Documenta et monumenta orientis antiqui 10), Leiden 1961.
Kaufman 2007	St. Kaufman, The Phoenician Inscription of the Incirli Trilingual: A Tentative Reconstruction and Translation, Maarav 14, 2007, 7-26.
Kloekhorst 2018	A. Kloekhorst, Anatolian evidence suggests that the Indo-European laryngeals $*h_2$ and $*h_3$ were uvular stops, Indo-European Linguistics 6, 2018, 69-94.
Kopanias 2018	K. Kopanias, Cilicia and Pamphylia during the Early Iron Age: Hiyawa, Mopsos and the Foundation of Greek Poleis, AURA 1, 2018, 69-95.
Kretschmer 1933	P. Kretschmer, Die Hypachäer, Glotta 21, 1933, 213-257.
Lane Fox 2011	R. Lane Fox, Reisende Helden. Die Anfänge der griechischen Kultur im homerischen Zeitalter. Aus dem Englischen von S. Held, Stuttgart 2011.
Lawson Younger Jr. 2009	K. Lawson Younger Jr., The Deity Kur(r)a in the First Millennium Sources, JANER 9, 2009, 1-23.
Lebrun 1983	R. Lebrun, Notes d'onomastique gréco-asianique, Hethitica 5, 1983, 63-74.
Mellaart 1991-92	J. Mellaart, Rezension von P. James et alii, Centuries of Darkness. A Challenge to the Conventional Chronology of Old World Archaeology, London 1991 in Bull. of the Anglo-Israel Arch. Society 11, 1991-1992, 35-38.

Meyer 2011	M. Meyer, Kilikien: örtliche Gegebenheiten und archäologische Evidenzen, in Ch. Ulf – R. Rollinger (Hgg.), Lag Troia in Kilikien? Der aktuelle Streit um Homers Ilias. Darmstadt 2011, 81-114.
Novák 2010	M. Novák, Kizzuwatna - Ḫiyawa – Quwe. Ein Abriss der Kulturgeschichte des Ebenen Kilikien, in: J. Becker et al. (Hgg.), Kulturlandschaft Syrien. Zentrum und Peripherie, Fs J.-W. Meyer (AOAT 371), Münster 2010.
Obrador Cursach 2018	B. Obrador Cursach, Lexicon of the Phrygian Inscriptions (Diss.), Barcelona 2018.
Oreshko 2013	R. Oreshko, 'The Achaean Hides, Caged in Yonder Beams': The Value of Hieroglyphic Luwian Sign *429 Reconsidered and a New Light on the Cilician Ahhiyawa, Kadmos 52, 2013, 19-33.
Oreshko 2018	R. Oreshko, *Ahhiyawa – Danu(na)*. Greek Ethnic Groups in the Eastern Mediterranean in the Light of Old and New Hieroglyphic Luwian Evidence, in: Ł. Niesiołowski-Spano – M. Węcowski (Hgg.), Change, Continuity, and Connectivity. North-Eastern Mediterranean at the turn of the Bronze Age and in the early Iron Age, Wiesbaden 2018, 23-56.
Özyar 2016	A. Özyar, Phoenicians and Greeks in Cilicia? Coining Elite Identity in Iron Age Anatolia, in: J. Aruz – M. Seymour (Hgg.), Assyria to Iberia: Art and Culture in the Iron Age. A Metropolitan Museum of Art Symposia [sic!], New York 2016, 136-146.
Poncy et al. 2001	H. Poncy et al., Sceaux du musée d'Adana: Groupe du "Joueur de lyre" (VIIIe siècle av. J. C) – Sceaux en verre et cachets anépigraphes d'époque achéménide – Scaraboïdes inscrits – Scarabées et sceaux égyptisants, Anatolia Antiqua 9, 2001, 9-37.
Rollinger 2007	R. Rollinger, Überlegungen zur Frage der Lokalisation von Jawan in neuassyrischer Zeit, State Archives of Assyria Bulletin 16, 2007, 63-90.
Scheer 1993	T. S. Scheer, Mythische Vorväter: zur Bedeutung griechischer Heroenmythen im Selbstverständnis kleinasiatischer Städte (Münchener Arbeiten zur Alten Geschichte Bd. 7), München 1993.
Schmitz 2009	Ph. C. Schmitz, Phoenician KRNTRYŠ, Archaic Greek *ΚΟΡΥΝΗΤΗΡΙΟΣ, and the Storm God of Aleppo, KUSATU 11, 2009, 119-160.
Schrott 2008	R. Schrott, Homers Heimat. Der Kampf um Troia und seine realen Hintergründe, München 2008.
Schürr 2006	D. Schürr, Elf lydische Etymologien, in: R. Bombi et al. (Hgg.), Studi linguistici in onore di Roberto Gusmani, Alessandria 2006, 1569-1587.
Schürr, im Druck	D. Schürr, Mellaarts erste Erfindung: ein hieroglyphen-luwisches Siegel, Talanta 50, im Druck.

Simon 2014	Z. Simon, Awarikus und Warikas: Zwei Könige von Hiyawa, Zs Assyriologie 104, 2014, 91-103.
Simon 2017	Z. Simon, Kurtis: A Phrygian Name in the Neo-Hittite World, News from the Land of the Hittites 1, 2017, 113-118.
Simon 2018	Z. Simon, Die Griechen und das Phönizische im späthethitischen Staat Hiyawa: die zyprische Verbindung, in: P. A. Mumm (Hg.), Sprachen, Völker und Phantome: sprach- und kulturwissenschaftliche Studien zur Ethnizität (Münchner Vorlesungen zu Antiken Welten 2), Berlin – Boston 2018, 313-338.
Simon, demnächst	Z. Simon, The *Mopsos* Names and the Prehistory of the Lydians, in: Michele Bianconi (Hg.), Linguistic and Cultural Interactions between Greece and the Ancient Near East: In Search of the "Golden Fleece" (demnächst).
Steiner 2011	G. Steiner, Namen, Orte und Personen in der hethitischen und der griechischen Überlieferung, in: Ch. Ulf – R. Rollinger (Hgg.), Lag Troia in Kilikien? Der aktuelle Streit um Homers Ilias, Darmstadt 2011, 265-291.
Tekoğlu et al. 2000	R. Tekoğlu – A. Lemaire et al., La bilingue royale louvito-phénicienne de Çineköy, CRAI 144, 2000, 961-1007.
Vanschoonwinkel 1990	J. Vanschoonwinkel, Mopsos: Légendes et réalité, Hethitica 10, 1990, 185-211.
Yakubovich 2015	I. Yakubovich, Phoenician and Luwian in Early Iron Age Cilicia, AnSt 65, 2015, 35-53.
Zangger – Woudhuizen 2018	E. Zangger – F. Woudhuizen, Rediscovered Luwian Hieroglyphic Inscriptions from Western Asia Minor (provisional version), Talanta 50, 2018, 9-56.
Zgusta 1964	L. Zgusta, Kleinasiatische Personennamen (Monografie Orientálního ústavu ČSAV 19), Prag 1964.
Zgusta 1984	L. Zgusta, Kleinasiatische Ortsnamen (BNF NF, Beih.21), Heidelberg 1984.

Bir kralın Mops (veya Mucks) adındaki oğlu:
Kurgu yazıtlar, Pylos ile Karatepe arasındaki antik hikaye anlatıcılığı ve isim kayıtları
Özet

Karatepe'de (Kilikya) hanedanlığın kurucusu olarak *Muksas* veya MPŠ'den kesin olarak bahseden, uzun Fenike ve Luvi hiyeroglif yazıtlarının keşfinden sonra, bu isim doğrudan efsanevi Yunan kâhini Mopsos ile ilişkilendirildi. Çünkü bazı yazarlar onun Troya'nın düşüşünden sonra Pamphylia'ya ve sonra Kilikya'ya seyahat ettiğini, hatta Kilikya'da hüküm sürdüğünü bildirirler. Bu isimler diğer erkek adlarıyla da bağlantılıydı: Mykenli Mok^wsos, Hitit metninde *Muksus*, (Yunan uyarlamasında) Lidyalı ismi Moksos ve son olarak Frigyalı *Muksos*. Hatta ünlü arkeolog James Mellaart Büyük Kral'ın Muksus ismindeki oğlunun Ashkelon kentine geldiğini belirttiği ve kısa bir süre önce yayımlanmış olan Bronz Çağı'na ait Luvice bir yazıt kurgulamıştır. Athenaeus'un "Deipnosophistler" eserinde bahsettiği Lydialı Mopsos da aynı şekilde sunulmuştur.

Hikâye anlatıcılığına böylesi bir güven olgusu yerleştirmeden, hem de geç, çok geç ve tam anlamıyla güvenilir olmadan, Kilikyalı MPŠ'nin, çok daha geç bir dönemde Yunan Mopsos ile özdeşleştirilmiş olduğunu varsaymak ve hanedan kurucusunun neden iki benzer, fakat farklı isimlere sahip olduğunu açık bırakmak daha kolay gelmiştir. Bu kurucunun Bronz Çağı'na ait olduğunu gösteren hiçbir şey yoktur. Aksine Adana yakınlarındaki Çineköy'den bir Luvi hiyeroglifindeki bağışçı kral onun "torun"udur ve bu büyük ihtimalle, sadece onun soyundan gelen birisi olarak değil doğrudan doğruya sözcük anlamıyla "torun" olarak anlaşılmalıdır. Mikenli *Mokʷsos* gerçekten Batı Anadolu'da *Muksus* olarak uyarlanmış olabilir ve bu Lidya'ya aktarılmış, sonra ilkin Friglere ve daha sonra ise Friglerden Luvilere aktarılmış olabilir: bu bir ismin yolculuğu olup uydurma bir kâhinin seyahatleri değildir. Ancak Anadolu'da tespit edilen isimlerin Mikenceden türetildiği fikri ikna edici değildir; isimler basit bir şekilde bunlardan bağımsız olabilirlerdi.

MPŠ adının Mopsos'tan türediği fikri sadece Kilikya hanedanlığının Yunan kökenli olmasına değil, aynı zamanda Kilikya'da erken bir Yunan varlığına dair güçlü bir inanca sebep olmuştur. Bununla birlikte bu düşünce için daha fazla dayanak bulunmamaktadır: ne kraliyet isimleri *Á-wa/i+ra/i-ku-sa* (Euarchos?) ve *Wa/i+ra/i-i-ka-sá* (Wroikos?) için bir Yunan kökeni, ne Karatepe'deki Baal isimlendirmesi olan KRNTRYŠ (başka yerde belgelenmemiş olan κορυνητήριος? sıfatı) için bir Yunan kökeni, ne de Homeros'un Akhaialılarının Hiyawa ile ilişkilendirilmesi buna dayanak sayılabilir. Kilikya'da Helenistik Dönem öncesine ait hiçbir Yunanca yazıtın olmaması zaten zayıf olasılığı olan bu türden açıklamaların karşısında durmaktadır ve bu da belirleyicidir.

Anahtar sözcükler: Miken Yunancası, Hititçe, Luvi hiyeroglifi, Lidce, Frigce, Fenikece, Karatepe, Antik hikâye anlatıcılığı, Yunan kâhini Mopsos, Lydia kralı Moksos.

A king's own son, named Mops (or Mucks?):
about fantasy inscriptions, antique storytelling and name records between Pylos and Karatepe
Abstract

After the discovery of the long Phoenician and Hieroglyphic Luwian inscriptions of Karatepe (Cilicia), which mention a certain *Muksas* or MPŠ as the founder of a dynasty, this name was immediately linked with a fabled Greek seer named Mopsos, because some authors tell that he traveled, after the fall of Troy, to Pamphylia and also to Cilicia and even ruled there. These names were linked with other male names too: Mycenaean *Mokʷsos* (?), *Muksus* in a Hittite text, the Lydian name (in Greek adaption) Moxos and, finally, Phrygian *Muksos*. The famous archaeologist James Mellaart even invented a long Bronze Age Hieroglyphic Luwian inscription, published recently, where a Great King's son named *Muksus* came to the city of Ashkelon, as did the Lydian called Mopsos in the 'Deipnosophists' of Athenaeus.

Without placing such confidence in storytelling, late and very late and not altogether trustworthy, it is easier to suppose that the Cilician MPŠ was identified with the Greek Mopsos only much later and to leave open why the founder of the dynasty had two similar but different names. And nothing speaks for a Bronze Age date for this founder – on the contrary, in the Hieroglyphic Luwian inscription from Çineköy near Adana the donating king is his grandchild, and this must probably be taken literally, not merely as 'descendant'. The Mycenaean *Mokʷsos* may indeed have been adapted in West Anatolia as *Muksus*, and this handed down in Lydia and then first taken over by Phrygians and later by Luwians from Phrygians: travels of a name and not travels of the fabled seer. It is however not cogent that the names attested in Anatolia are derived from Mycenaean; they could be easily independent.

The supposed derivation of MPŠ from Mopsos has led to the strong belief, not only in a Greek origin for the Cilician dynasty, but also in an early Greek presence in Cilicia. However, there are no more reliable props for it: neither a Greek origin for the royal names *Á-wa/i+ra/i-ku-sa* (Euarchos?) and *Wa/i+ra/i-i-ka-sá* (Wroikos?), nor one for KRNTRYŠ, an epiclesis of Baal in Karatepe (an otherwise unattested adjective κορυνητήριος?), nor linking *Hiyawa* with the Achaeans of Homer. Against the mere possibility of such explanations stands the total lack of Greek inscriptions in Cilicia before Hellenistic times, and this is decisive.

Keywords: Mycenaean Greek, Hittite, Hieroglyphic Luwian, Lydian, Phrygian, Phoenician, Karatepe, antique storytelling, the Greek seer Mopsos, the Lydian king Moxos.

Received: January 8, 2019 | Accepted: April 7, 2019

Eine bisher unbekannte Alyattes-Münze

Max GANDER*

Ziel der vorliegenden kurzen Nachricht soll es sein, die Forschungswelt auf eine Münze aufmerksam zu machen, die kürzlich im Handel aufgetaucht ist, und die, falls sie echt ist,[1] auf die Deutung der lydischen Münzlegenden Einfluss nehmen wird.

Abb. 1) *Die neue Alyattes-Münze (Roma Numismatics Ltd. www.RomaNumismatics.com)*

Im Katalog Nummer XV, 5. April 2018, der Roma Numismatics wurde eine bisher unpublizierte lydische Trite aus einer deutschen Privatsammlung versteigert, die schon 2012 veräußert werden sollte, damals aber keinen Käufer fand.[2] Zusammen mit der Münze wurden 2012 drei Walwet-

---

* Dr. des. Max Gander, Winterthurerstr. 8, CH-8610 Uster (max.r.gander@googlemail.com).

[1] Verschiedene Personen haben mir gegenüber Zweifel an der Echtheit der Münze geäußert ohne diese aber eingehend erläutern zu können. Es ist in der Tat erstaunlich, dass weder Münzsammler (die Münze wurde 2012 nicht verkauft), noch Forschende auf die Münze aufmerksam wurden. Die Authentizität der Münze zu beurteilen liegt nicht in meiner Kompetenz. Die vorliegende Notiz soll auch die Diskussion darüber anregen.

[2] Roma Numismatics 2012, 79-80 Nr. 277, Roma Numismatics 2018, 78 Nr. 245. Der Wert der Münze wurde damals auf ca. 125'000 £ geschätzt, das Eröffnungsgebot lag bei 100'000 £. Die Münze fand aber zu diesem Preis keinen Abnehmer. Bei der Auktion XV wurde der Wert auf lediglich 30'000 £ geschätzt, das Eröffnungsgebot stand bei 24'000 und die Münze wurde schließlich für 56'000 £ verkauft (Information Alex

Münzen des gleichen Besitzers angeboten.³ Ob die vier Stücke allerdings zusammengehören, bleibt unklar.

Die hier behandelte Trite zeigt einen nach rechts blickenden Löwen mit heraushängender Zunge und deutlich sichtbaren Eckzähnen. Am rechten Rand lässt sich die Schnauze eines zweiten Löwen erkennen. Zwischen den zwei antithetisch angeordneten Köpfen ist eine Inschrift angebracht. In seiner Form steht das Löwenbildnis zweifellos denen der Walwet-Münzen (insbesondere Typ XVI c) nahe,⁴ ist aber mit ihnen nicht identisch.

Abb. 2) *Die neue Alyattes-Münze (Roma Numismatics Ltd. www.RomaNumismatics.com).*

Von besonderem Interesse ist die Münzlegende. Von unten nach oben finden wir rechtsläufig die Inschrift ΑΛΥΑ̣. Alle vier lesbaren Buchstaben sind im lydischen und im griechischen Alphabet in sehr ähnlichen Formen belegt. Die lydischen Münzlegenden sind aber, ebenso wie die meisten lydischen Inschriften hauptsächlich (wenn nicht gar ausschließlich) linksläufig zu lesen. Zudem steht die Form des Y der ionischen Buchstabenform⁵ näher als der lydischen. Der lydische Buchstabe U (Y) findet sich nur ausnahmsweise als symmetrisches Y, so in LW 2 Z.13, LW 44 Z.18 (das erste U) und konsequent nur in LW 117 aus Kelainai (Z.2 und Z.3).⁶ Ansonsten findet sich eine Form bei welcher eine Schräghaste mittig von einer längeren Vertikalhaste seitlich abgeht.⁷ In

---

Morley-Smith, Roma Numismatics, E-Mail vom 20.6.2018, s. auch https://www.sixbid.com/browse.html?auction=4667&category=134487&lot= 3845114).

³ Roma Numismatics 2012, 81-82, Nr. 278-280.

⁴ S. zu den Löwen auf lydischen Münzen allgemein Robinson 1951, 158-163, Weidauer 1975, 21-28, 94-107, Wallace 1988, 203-204, Le Rider 2001, 47-48, Wallace 2006 39-45. Vgl. aber auch Fischer-Bossert 2016, 23. Zu Weidauer Typ c s. Weidauer 1975, 103-106.

⁵ Bestes Beispiel ist eine in die Mitte des 6. Jh. v. Chr. datierte Inschrift auf einer Silberplatte aus Ephesos s. Jeffery 1963, 414-415 Nr. 53, Plate 66. Andere ionische Inschriften zeigen für Y oft die Form V s. Jeffery 1963, 325-345, Plate 63-66.

⁶ Zu LW 2 und LW 44 s. Buckler 1926, Plate II und Plate XVI, zu LW 117 s. s. Ivantchik – Adiego 2016, 291.

⁷ Ich danke Annick Payne und ihrer Mitarbeiterin Carmen Rindlisbacher für die detaillierte Auskunft zu den lydischen Buchstabenformen, die sie im Rahmen des Projekts *Early History of Alphabetic Writing in Anatolia* bearbeitet haben.

lydischen Inschriften ist zudem die Lautfolge *ua* nicht belegt, die Laute *u* und *a* werden durch einen Gleitlaut miteinander verbunden.[8]

Eine griechische Lesung der Legende ist daher vorzuziehen und die Inschrift ist in diesem Fall zweifellos Ἀλυά(ττης) zu ergänzen.

In Parallele zur griechischen Legende wäre dann zu vermuten, dass Walwet tatsächlich die lydische Form des Namens Alyattes darstellt, wie dies von einer Mehrheit der Forschenden mittlerweile angenommen wird.[9]

Ganz anders wäre es, wenn, wie im Auktionskatalog vorgeschlagen, die Legende lydisch zu lesen wäre.[10] Alua[…] wäre dann mit Alyattes zu verbinden und Walwet müsste anders erklärt werden.[11]

Aus den obengenannten Gründen ist diese Deutung jedoch weniger wahrscheinlich.

Bibliographie

Browne 1996	G. M. Browne, Notes on Two Lydian Texts, Kadmos 35, 1996, 49-52.
Buckler 1926	W. H. Buckler, A Lydian Text on an Electrum Coin, JHS 46, 1926, 36-41.
Dale 2015	A. Dale, WALWET and KUKALIM. Lydian Coin Legends, Dynastic Succession, and the Chronology of Mermnad Kings, Kadmos 54, 2015, 151-166.
Fischer-Bossert 2016	W. Fischer-Bossert, Brüllende Löwen. Eine Elektronserie des 6. Jahrhunderts v. Chr., MÖNG 56/1, 2016, 23-29.
Ivantchik – Adiego 2016	A. Ivantchik – I. -X. Adiego-Lajara, Une inscription lydienne de Kelainai, in: A. Ivantchik – L. Summerer – A. von Kienlin (Hrsg.), Kelainai – Apameia Kibotos: eine achämenidische, hellenistische und römische Metropole / Kelainai – Apameia Kibotos: une métropole achéménide, hellénistique et romaine, Bordeaux 2016, 289-299.
Jeffery 1963	L. H. Jeffery, The Local Scripts of Archaic Greece: A Study of the Origin of the Greek Alphabet and its Development from the Eighth to the Fifth centuries B.C., Oxford 1963.
LW	R. Gusmani, Lydisches Wörterbuch mit grammatischer Skizze und Inschriftensammlung (Ergänzungsband Heidelberg 1984), Heidelberg 1964.

---

[8] Ich danke Diether Schürr für diesen Hinweis. Vgl. LW 11 Z. 1 mruwaad, Z. 12 mruwaaλ, LW 26 Z.4 aspluwas, LW 47 Z.2 laduwad und para-lydisch Papkuwas auf dem Siegel Poetto – Salvatori 1981, 44-45, Nr. 40 und 109 Tav. XL.

[9] Zu den lydischen Münzen mit der Legende Walwet s. Six 1890, 202-208, Weidauer 1975, 25-27, 104-107, Wallace 1988, Browne 1996, 50-52, Wallace 2006, 37-45, Dale 2015.

[10] Roma Numismatics 2012, 79-80, Roma Numismatics 2018, 78.

[11] Roma Numismatics 2012, 79-80, Roma Numismatics 2018, 78.

Poetto – Salvatori 1981	M. Poetto – S. Salvatori, La collezione anatolica di E. Borowski in „The Lands of the Bible Archaeology Foundation" – Royal Ontario Museum, Toronto, Canada, Pavia 1981.
Rider 2001	G. Le Rider, La naissance de la monnaie. Pratiques monétaires de l'Orient ancien, Paris 2001.
Robinson 1951	E. S. G. Robinson, The Coins from the Ephesian Artemision Reconsidered, JHS 71, 1951, 156-167.
Roma Numismatics 2012	Roma Numismatics Auction III 31 March 2012, London 2012.
Roma Numismatics 2018	Roma Numismatics Auction XV 5 April 2018, London 2018.
Six 1890	J. P. Six, Monnaies grecques, inédites et incertaines (Suite), Numismatic Chronicle 10, 1890, 185-259.
Wallace 1988	R. W. Wallace, WALWE. and .KALI., JHS 108, 1988, 203-207.
Wallace 2006	R. W. Wallace, KUKALIM, WALWET, and the Artemision Deposit. Problems in Early Anatolian Electrum Coinage, in: P. Van Alfen (Hrsg.), Agoranomia: Studies in Money and Exchange Presented to John H. Kroll, New York 2006, 37-48.
Weidauer 1975	L. Weidauer, Probleme der frühen Elektronprägung, Fribourg 1975.

Daha önceden bilinmeyen bir Alyattes sikkesi
Özet

Bu kısa çalışmada yakın zamanlarda yayımlanan Ἀλυά(ττης) lejandı taşıyan bir sikke tanıtılmaktadır. Eğer sikke orijinal ise, üzerindeki lejand Lydia sikke lejantlarının yorumunda etkili olacaktır.

Anahtar sözcükler: Lidce, nümismatik, Alyattes.

A previously unknown Alyattes coin
Abstract

In this short notice a recently published coin which bears the legend Ἀλυά(ττης) is presented. If the coin is authentic its legend will influence the interpretation of Lydian coin legends.

Keywords: Lydian, Numismatics, Alyattes.

Opponents and successors of the Xanthian dynasty in Western Lycia: The Weχssere questions reconsidered

Wilhelm MÜSELER[*]

Introduction

The publication of the book on Lycian coins in European private collections by the present author is approaching its third anniversary[1]. As expected, it has already sparked a number of interesting discussions regarding some of its central tenets. The attribution of the main text from the famous Xanthos-Stele to *Xerēi*, once more emphasized in a recent article by the author and by his colleague Diether Schürr[2], has found broad support and was strengthened by a new analysis of the *stoichedon* rules applied to the inscription by Helmut Lotz[3].

However, questions regarding the number and the role of the dynasts, who have been issuing coins that carry either the full or abbreviated personal name *Weχssere* or legends of a somewhat related form such as *Waχssebllimi*, *Waχssepddimi* or *Uχssepddimi*, have caused considerable confusion. The original hypothesis, brought forward by Kenneth Jenkins[4] and subsequently accepted by most scholars studying the archaic and classical coins of Lycia, had asserted that there were two individuals called *Weχssere*, possibly father and son, whose issues belonged to two distinct periods of Lycian coinage: The elder and far more numerous group is in several respects related to the light weight coinage of the dynast *Kuprlli* from mints in Western Lycia and therefore has to be dated to the middle of the 5th century BC. The younger, considerably smaller group is mainly formed by a number of heavier coins bearing the name of the dynast in alternation with the name of the mint place Zagaba in Central Lycia in the back[5]. These coins display on their reverses an impressive frontal bust of the goddess Athena wearing a triple crested attic helmet. It was modelled after a spectacular coin signed by the artist Eukleidas from Sicily, which was created during the final years of the 5th century BC in Syracuse and obviously reached quite a wide range of circulation fairly soon[6]. However, the Lycian imitations of this type can hardly have been struck before the end of the 5th or the beginning of the 4th century BC. There is yet another issue from Zagaba bearing the name *Weχssere*, which in accordance with the reformed Eastern Lycian coins

---

[*] Wilhelm Müseler, Wettsteinallee 83, CH-4058 Basel, Switzerland (wilhelmmueseler@gmail.com).

[1] Müseler 2016.

[2] Müseler – Schürr 2018.

[3] Lotz 2017.

[4] Jenkins 1959 had examined an obviously later coin bearing the name *Weχssere* (for the type see Figure 46), which had been acquired by the British Museum at the time, and had excluded its assignment to the issues of the 5th century BC for a number of stylistic and technical reasons.

[5] The word 𐊗𐊀𐊄𐊁𐊀 or abbreviations thereof had long been considered as the personal name of another dynast by many previous scholars. But Kolb – Tietz 2001 has convincingly shown that this legend refers to a place and not to a person.

[6] Rizzo 1946, pl. XLIII, 21; Tudeer 1913, p. 42, 59 – This is not the only case by far, where a coin from Syracuse has been imitated by an issue from the eastern Mediterranean basin: See for example Wahl 2017.

in the names of *Trbbenimi* and *Perikle* shows a lion-mask on the obverse and a triskeles with a monogram in the central ring on the reverse. This can hardly be earlier than the nineties of the 4ᵗʰ century BC. These heavier Central Lycian coinages are complemented by a single light weight issue bearing the full name *Weχssere*: It has a profile-head of Athena turned to the right on the obverses and a bust of Hermes wearing a winged petasos in an incuse circle on the reverses[7]. Since there is quite a number of series of the same or of a similar type, contemporary and later, bearing the name of the southern harbour-town Patara at the mouth of the Xanthos-River in Western Lycia, the latter issue should be attributed to this place as well.

The older coinages with the name *Weχssere* or with abbreviations thereof are supplemented by a small number of issues bearing the name *Waχssebllimi*. Hitherto these series are only known by some isolated specimens, which are partly related to coins of light standard in the name of *Kuprlli* from unidentified places in Western Lycia, but a closer geographical location of the mints in question is not possible. Thus, the material basis is too narrow for definite conclusions regarding the relationship between the earlier *Weχssere*- and the *Waχssebllimi*-issues. But an apparent link between the two coinages can be demonstrated further below.

However, the coinages to be compared with the *Weχssere*-issues of the 4ᵗʰ century BC are far more numerous and varied. In Central Lycia there is mainly the huge number of contemporary coins with the name *Mithrapata*, possibly issued by more than one mint, and the series with the name *Aruwātijesi* from Zagaba, all aligned to the local heavy standard based upon a weight of ca. 9,8 g for the stater. In the area of the Xanthos valley there are even more issues available for comparison, which are all of the lighter western standard with an average stater-weight of ca. 8,4 g only. Some bear the legends *Waχssepddimi*, *Uχssepddimi* and *Ddēñtimi* and can be assigned to Patara and to Tlos. But a considerable number of those coins do not show any personal name; their legends only mention the respective mint place (Patara, Tlos, Pinara, Xanthos, Araxa, Tymnessos) and display various symbols in the fields, probably as references to the issuing dynast. Moreover, there are some minor issues from the same period without any legend at all, which have nothing but symbols in their reverse-fields. A few of those can be identified by their type as coins from the harbour-town Telmessos in the far Northwest. But in any case, it remains the central matter for discussion, to which rulers the different symbols must be attributed[8].

In a paper presented 2015 at the XV. International Numismatic Congress in Taormina[9] the author had claimed that the variously attested appellations *Waχssepddimi* and *Uχsepddimi* would both refer to the younger *Weχssere* combining his personal name with a surname or title of some kind[10]. This was also assumed with regard to the elder *Weχssere* for the legend *Waχssebllimi* on some coins apparently belonging to his period and for the *Waχssepddimi* mentioned on the Inscribed

---

[7] Vismara 1989, p. 98 sq had annexed this issue in disregard of the obvious differences in style and fabric as type XIII to the series of the elder *Weχssere* from the middle of the 5ᵗʰ century BC. That this was a mistake is easy to see and has already been discussed: Cfr. Müseler 2016, p. 22 sq.

[8] For the general importance of monograms or linear symbols on Lycian coins see Müseler 2016, p. 27 sqq.

[9] Müseler 2017 b. Unfortunately, the editors of the Proceedings of this Congress have completely messed up the plate with the illustrations for the article, thus making the central argument of the paper more difficult to understand.

[10] A similar though somewhat different construction had been proposed by Özüdoğru 2007.

Pillar of Xanthos[11]. The author has expressed the same view in his book on Lycian coinage of 2016[12].

This hypothesis has brought forward considerable criticism from several other scholars. Koray Konuk and Diether Schürr have expressed serious doubts regarding the underlying onomastic construction. Instead they have asserted that all the personal names in their various forms and spellings, as they appear on the coins and on the stele, should be seen as referring to separate individuals[13]. Given the formal similarity of all those names Konuk and Schürr have supposed that their bearers might have belonged to one large family[14]. Thus, a whole clan of dynasts was conjectured, whose members – during two distinct periods and with an intermission of almost forty years – ruled more or less at the same time or in close succession to each other at some places in Western Lycia, namely in Patara and in Tlos. However, this construction fails to explain a number of manifest connections such as die-links between the coinages in question and takes the evident significance of the monograms placed on many of the coins not into account as will be shown below. From a numismatic point of view, it leaves too many questions open and is by far not as conclusive as it may appear.

An alternative model, which is actually quite amusing, was presented by Frank Kolb in his recent book on the history and archaeology of Lycia[15]. In the opinion of Kolb all the coins bearing the name *Weχssere* should belong to one and the same dynast[16]. First, he would have been the issuer of all the early series minted in Western Lycia in succession to the rule of *Kuprlli*; then he would have disappeared from the scene for quite a long time[17], only to re-emerge after a couple of decades in Central Lycia and in the Xanthos valley in order to reinstate another (and completely different) coinage in his name there, which would finally last well into the 4th century BC. Under this assumption one and the same person called *Weχssere* would have issued coins in both Western and Central Lycia over a period of approximately fifty years or even longer. Of course, this is not entirely impossible, but it requires at least an explanation for the long intermitting period,

---

[11] Kalinka, TL 44, a 48-50.

[12] Müseler 2016, p. 52 sq.

[13] Konuk 2016 and Schürr 2018.

[14] Carruba 1989 had proposed to see all those dynastic names as a possible Lycian rendering of the Iranian name *Uvaxs(a)t(a)ra*. But such an Iranian root has been rejected clearly by Schürr 2018, p. 98.

[15] Kolb 2018.

[16] Anyhow, Kolb considers *Waχsseblimi* and *Waχssepddimi* / *Uχssepddimi* as separate persons that should neither be identified with *Weχssere* nor with each other.

[17] Kolb strongly opposes the dating of the later series with the legend *Wekhssere* as well as the entire coinage of Mithrapata to the first two decades of the 4th century BC as proposed by Müseler 2016, p. 35 sqq and in particular p. 45. Since at least the later western coinage of *Weχssere* must be subsequent to the invasion of the Xanthos valley by *Erbbina* the crucial question here is the dating of the famous Tissaphernes-stater from the mint at Xanthos (SNG Cop. Suppl. 460) and the reign of *Ddenewele*. But even if this must be dated a couple of years earlier than Müseler has supposed, i.e. to the time between 411 and 407 BC, this does not leave enough space for the reign of the usurper and his ultimate demise to place the beginning of subsequent coinages still in the 5th century BC. Moreover, there is not the slightest evidence whatsoever permitting to make Mithrapata a late member of the Xanthian dynasty and to place his Tloan coins before his Central Lycian issues!!!!

which Kolb unfortunately fails to provide. Even worse is the fact that this construction is in defiance of basic numismatic method as adopted by Jenkins when dividing the coins bearing the name *Weχssere* into two distinct groups: Coinages clearly belonging to two separate periods should be assigned to separate issuers, even if those happen to bear identical names, unless there is substantial proof to the contrary[18].

In fact, none of the hypothetical solutions for the *Weχssere*-problem brought forward up to this point (the one of the authors included) is really satisfactory. As pointed out above there is a considerable number of coins, which bear witness to the time immediately preceding and following the rule of the later part of the "Dynasty of Xanthos", i.e. of *Xeriga* and his successors including the usurper *Erbbina*. The information, which they carry about the identity and the function of the rulers from the alleged *Waχssa*-clan and of others from the same political context is certainly not complete and sometimes not easy to discover or to interpret, but it is still of great significance. Some of the series in question are quite large and well documented, but of others there are only a few examples known and sometimes there is even just one single specimen left. The widely scattered examples must be once again assembled and studied as a whole in order to detect possible interconnections, which are of importance for the sequence of the various coinages and/or for the identity and the political position of their issuers[19]. Therefore, it is the main purpose of this article to gather the relevant numismatic evidence regarding the time and the ambit of the dynasts named *Weχssere* as completely as possible. Particular emphasis will be laid on the study of the various symbols appearing in the fields of most coins, - an additional medium of information, whose importance and function has been widely underestimated so far. Thus, we may possibly gain some valuable clues leading to a better understanding of the role of these agents in the history of Lycia.

The aftermath of *Kuprllis* reign in the West: *Weχssere* and *Waχssebllimi*

The present catalogue of the coin issues attributable to the elder *Weχssere* resumes and amends Novella Vismara's attempt of 1989 to form a corpus of the respective coinage. However, it disregards minor die-variations, which do not serve the purpose of this article, and is only focussed on the principal types[20]. In an appendix at the end the few examples of the coinage with the name *Waχssebllimi* or abbreviations thereof, which are known so far, are listed:

I.1.1. Diobol (Sixth stater), uncertain mint. Lion crouching to l., in field above linear symbol ϒ / Triskeles in incuse square, in field legend FϒѴϟ
Vismara 2; SNG Cop. Suppl. 436* (1,15 g) *(Figure 1)*

---

[18] Presumably Kolbs hypothesis is at least partly indebted to Vismaras erroneous attribution of the Patarean series in the name of the younger *Weχssere* to the coinages of his elder namesake. (See note 8).

[19] In recent times some scholars have deliberately ignored coins of "uncertain provenance" (i.e. from private collections or from trade), even accepting considerable damage done to their own studies by this act. The miserable colleagues suffer from a serious cognitive aberration known as "*DAI-Syndrome*" or "*Morbus Grütters*", - a special form of monophthalmia caused by political prejudice. A particularly sad result of this affliction is the recently published dissertation of Corinna Hoff: Hoff 2017, rec. Müseler – Schürr 2019.

[20] The main references given refer to Vismara 1989 or to Müseler 2016. A few coins, where the attribution to *Weχssere* has been doubted or is not absolutely certain, have been omitted here.

I.1.2.	Stater, uncertain mint. Lion jumping to r. with head reverted / Triskeles in incuse square, in field ⚭ and legend F↑Ѵϟ
	Vismara - ; Müseler V,2* (8,01 g) *(Figure 2)*
I.1.3.a	Tetrobol (Third stater), uncertain mint. Lion crouching to r. on round shield, above ⚭ / Triskeles in incuse square, in field legend F↑Ѵϟϟ↑P↑
	Vismara 4; Winsemann-Falghera Coll. 144* (2,63 g) *(Figure 3)*
I.1.3.b	Obol (Twelfth stater), uncertain mint. Lion crouching to r., in front ⚭ / Triskeles in incuse square, in field legend F↑ϟ (sic!)
	Vismara 7; Winsemann.Falghera Coll. 146 (0,54 g)
I.1.4.	Stater, uncertain mint. Protome of winged lion to l. / Triskeles in incuse square, in field ⚭ and legend F↑Ѵϟ
	Vismara 8; Müseler V,3* (8,50 g) *(Figure 4)*
I.1.5.	Stater, uncertain mint. Protome of winged boar to l. on round shield / Triskeles in incuse square, in field ⚭ and legend F↑Ѵϟϟ↑
	Vismara 13; Auction Roma XVI, 2018, 316* (8,39 g) *(Figure 5)*
I.1.6.a	Stater, uncertain mint. Protome of pegasus to l. on round shield, above ⚭ / Triskeles in incuse square, in field ⚭ and legend F↑Ѵϟϟ
	Vismara 22; Müseler V,4* (8,42 g) *(Figure 6)*
I.1.6.b	Tetrobol (Third stater), uncertain mint. Protome of pegasus to l. on round shield, above ⚭ / Triskeles in incuse square, in field legend F↑Ѵ
	Vismara 25; SNG Cop. Suppl. 435 (2,40g)
I.1.7.a	Stater, uncertain mint (Telmessos?). Herakles walking to l., head reverted, carrying club and tripod / Triskeles in incuse square, in field ⚭ and legend F↑Ѵϟϟ↑P↑
	Vismara29; Müseler V,19* (8,43 g) *(Figure 7)*
I.1.7.b	Diobol (Sixth stater), uncertain mint (Telmessos?). Herakles walking to l., head reverted, carrying club / Triskeles in incuse square, in field legend F↑Ѵ
	Vismara 30; McClean 8869 (1,21 g)
I.1.8.a	Stater, uncertain mint (Tlos?). Head of Athena with korinthian helmet to r./ Diskeles in incuse square, in field legend F↑Ѵϟϟ↑P↑
	Vismara - ; Müseler -; Auction Roma XVI, 2018, 314* (8,54 g) *(Figure 8)*
I.1.8.b	Tetrobol (Third stater), uncertain mint (Tlos ?). Head of Athena with korinthian helmet to r. / Diskeles in incuse square, in field legend F↑Ѵϟϟ↑P↑
	Vismara 48; ANS (New York) 1987.89.8 (2,81 g)
I.1.8.c	Stater, uncertain mint (Tlos?). Head of Athena with korinthian helmet to r. / Triskeles in incuse square, in field ⚭ and legend F↑Ѵϟϟ↑P↑
	Vismara 35; Müseler V,12* (8,24 g) *(Figure 9)*
I.1.8.d	Tetrobol (Third stater), uncertain mint (Tlos?). Head of Athena with korinthian helmet to r. / Triskeles in incuse square, in field ⚭ and legend F↑Ѵ
	Vismara 41; Müseler V,13 (2,68 g)

I.1.8.e   Diobol (Sixth stater), uncertain mint (Tlos?). Head of Athena with korinthian helmet to r. / Triskeles in incuse square, in field ⌀ and legend F↑V
Vismara 44; Müseler V,16 (1,33 g)

I.1.9.a   Stater, uncertain mint (Xanthos?). Head of Athena with attic helmet to r., on the crest (occasionally) legend F↑V / Head of Apollon with laurel-wreath to r. in incuse square, in field ⌀
Vismara 52; Müseler V,7* (8,38 g)   (Figure 10)

I.1.9.b   Tetrobol (Third stater), uncertain mint (Xanthos?). Head of Athena with attic helmet to r. / Head of Apollon with laurel-wreath to r. in incuse square, in field ⌀
Vismara 56; Müseler V,10 (2,87 g)

I.1.9.c   Diobol (Sixth stater), uncertain mint (Xanthos?). Head of Athena with attic helmet to r. / Head of Apollon with laurel-wreath to r. in incuse square, in field ⌀
Vismara 62; Müseler V,11 (1,40 g)

I.1.9.d   Obol (Twelfth stater), uncertain mint (Xanthos?). Head of Athena with attic helmet to r. / Head of Apollon with laurel-wreath to r. in incuse square, in field ⌀
Vismara 63; Winsemann-Falghera Coll. 162 (0,68 g)

I.1.10.   Stater, uncertain mint (Xanthos?). Head of Apollon with laurel-wreath to r. / Triskeles in incuse square, in field ⌀ and legend F↑V⌐⌐
Vismara 66; Auction Hess/Divo 329, 2015, 103* (8,58 g)   (Figure 11)

I.1.11.   Stater, uncertain mint. Head of a Kabeiros (?) with conical cap to r. / Triskeles in incuse square, in field legend F↑V⌐⌐↑ (retrograd)
Vismara 70; Babelon, Traité II/2, 426 = BM 1863,0706.17* (7,90 g)   (Figure 12)

I.2.1.a   Stater, uncertain mint. Mule kneeling to l., head reverted, above linear symbol ϒ / Triskeles in incuse square, in field legend FPV⌐⌐↑B∧∧E/\/\E
Vismara - ; Müseler V,1* (7,88 g)   (Figure 13)

I.2.1.b   Tetrobol (Third stater), uncertain mint. Mule kneeling to l, head reverted, above linear symbol ϒ / Triskeles in incuse square, in field legend FPV⌐⌐↑B∧
Vismara 3; Babelon, Traité II, , 432 = BN btv 1b 8534854p* (2,31 g)   (Figure 14)

I.2.1.c   Diobol (Sixth stater), uncertain mint. Mule kneeling to l., head reverted, above linear symbol ϒ / Triskeles in incuse square, in field legend FPV⌐⌐↑
Auction Naumann (Pecunem) 14, 2014, 363 (1,00 g)

I.2.1.c   Obol (Twelfth stater), uncertain mint. Mule kneeling to l., head reverted, above linear symbol ϒ / Triskeles in incuse square, in field legend FP[V?]
Vismara 4; Winterthur G 4251 (0,42 g)

I.2.2.   Stater, uncertain mint (Patara?). Bearded head of Hermes (?) with winged petasos to r. on round shield / Triskeles in incuse square, in field linear symbol ϒ and legend FPV⌐⌐↑B∧∧E/\/\E
Vismara -; Müseler -; Auction Gemini VII, 2011, 546* (8,65 g)   (Figure 15)

Apart from the enormous difference in their sizes the coinages in the name of *Weχssere* and of *Waχssebllimi* display several parallel features. Regarding iconography both groups contain issues clearly related to types introduced by the Western coinage of *Kuprlli*. This is true for the jumping lion and the winged lion-protome on coins bearing the legend *Weχssere* and the kneeling-running mule on others with the legend *Waχssebllimi* (see Figure A-C). Even so some completely new motifs are introduced as well: The helmeted heads of the goddess Athena on coins in the name *Weχssere*, which are directly copied from contemporary issues of Athens and possibly pointing to an Athenian allegiance of their issuer (Figure D), and the highly unusual bearded head of Hermes on a stater with the legend *Waχssebllimi* are both without precursor in earlier Lycian coinage.

Furthermore, similar to the majority of issues in the name of *Kuprlli* there is no indicator to any specific place of origin provided by the legends on the coins. In some cases possible mints can be inferred by a comparison of certain typological features with those from later series that carry a toponym in addition to or in place of the personal names: References to the myth of Herakles are usually associated with the mint at Telmessos near the Carian border (Figure E-F). An enlarged linear symbol in place of any pictorial reverse-type or of a triskeles can occasionally be found on coins from Tlos (Figure G-H)[21]. The combination of a helmeted head of Athena on the obverse with a head of Apollon in the back appears on later anonymous issues with the toponym of Xanthos (Figure 78). And the head of Hermes with a winged petasos is displayed (though unbearded) on later issues bearing the place-name of Patara and occasionally also that of Tlos (Figure 48 and 125). However, an attribution of coins with the legends *Weχssere* or *Waχssebllimi* to respective mints must remain mostly hypothetical.

An outstanding common feature of both coinages discussed here is the almost uniform addition of certain linear symbols in the fields, either beside the various obverse-types or beside the personal names on the reverses: With only two exceptions all the issues with the name *Weχssere* are adorned with a diskeles (⚭) somewhere in the field, while on the coins with the name *Waχssebllimi* we always find a V-shaped symbol (Υ). On first sight this distinction seems to be continous, but it is not. The issue with the crouching lion to the left, which is only preserved in small denominations so far but which definitely belongs to the *Weχssere*-group, carries the symbol Υ and not the diskeles in the field above the animal[22]. Possibly this issue forms a bridge between the two groups; but as pointed out above with only such a few specimens of the coinage bearing the name *Waχssebllimi* extant the material base is far too narrow to allow valid conclusions regarding the identity of that ruler and his relationship to the issuer of the far larger series of coins with the name *Weχssere*.

An additonal problem is posed yet by the appearance of the name-form *Waχssepddimi* in the account of the deeds of *Xerēi* on the Xanthos-Stele. The person in question is listed among the enemies beaten by the army of *Xerēi* at the same time or soon after the expedition of the Athenian

---

[21] The enlarged monogram ⌘, usually associated with rulers of the Xanthian- dynasty, has been repeatedly set on coin-issues from the mint at Tlos: See Mørkholm – Zahle 1976, p. 52, 47-49 and Babelon, Traité II/2, 412. For the Tloan origin of the latter issue see Müseler 2017 a, p. 6 sqq.

[22] Vismara (communication by letter) considers this as another proof for the basic equivalence of the spelling Ϝϸ… and ϜΥ… in Lycian, quoting as further examples the words *arawzije / erawazije*, *Erkkazuma / Arkkazuma* or *mere- / mara-*.

commander Melesandros into Lycia[23]. This agent must therefore be dated to the same general period, from which the coin-series discussed here originate. In fact, it cannot be thoroughly excluded that we are dealing with three different individuals here, who bear strikingly similar names. But such a solution cannot claim a very high degree of probability in its favour, - in particular since the situation seems to repeat itself some forty years later after the end of *Erbbina's* rule in the Xanthos valley and the extinction of the Xanthian dynasty[24].

Central Lycia during the final years of the Xanthian dynasty and afterwards: Weχssere, Mithrapata and Aruwãtijesi

The coin-production of Central Lycia between the end of the 5th and the early 4th century BC is dominated by the series in the name of two dynasts, accompanied by an issue in the name of a clearly less important third. Moreover, it has to be divided into two distinct phases. Some time after 410 BC, when the Syracusan celator Eukleidas had designed his famous tetradrachm-die with the facing bust of the goddess Athena wearing a triple-crested helmet (Figure I), a new coinage of heavy weight standard was introduced at Zagaba in the eastern highlands of Central Lycia. The issuer was once more named *Weχssere*. The coins display on the obverse an impressive protome of a roaring lion turned to the left. Above there is a small legend consisting of the letters Λ↑, which is yet unexplained. On the reverse there is quite a well-executed imitation of the masterpiece of Eukleidas. A presumably somewhat later issue shows a facing lion mask instead of the protome, while the facing bust of Athena on the reverse is kept. There is no longer any mention of the issuer. Instead the legend refers to Zagaba, the location of the mint. In addition there is the miniature-legend ҒҺ+Ŧ placed on the visor of Athena's helmet, possibly the signature of a die-cutter[25]. On coins from both issues the monogram ☥ is set in the reverse-field.

At about the same time another coinage aligned to the same weight standard was issued by a dynast with the name *Mithrapata*. The coins carry a similar lion-protome (though turned to the right) on the obverse, which is likewise replaced by a frontal lion-mask later on. But instead of the facing bust of Athena there is the bearded head of an elderly man in profile wearing a diadem on the reverse, apparently a portrait of the issuer himself[26]. In contrast to the issues of *Weχssere* the name of *Mithrapata* is never replaced by a toponym on his Central Lycian coinages; therefore the location of the mint cannot be identified with certainty. There are, however, good reasons for the assumption that the place of origin for Mithrapata's portait coinage was the town of Phellos above

---

[23] Kalinka TL 44, a 58-60. The alternative reading of these lines by David Sasseville (Sasseville NN) has been rejected by Müseler – Schürr 2018, p. 390.

[24] See below p. 64.

[25] Olcay – Mørkholm 1971, 11-12. The miniature legend on the helmet can obviously not be a toponym, since the main legend on the pieces already mentions Zagaba as the location of the mint. On the Sicilian model for this Lycian issue this discrete place was in fact reserved for the signature of the artist.

[26] Portraits had been introduced into Lycian coinage (and coinage in general!) by an issue of *Xeriga* from Tymnessos (SNG Cop. Suppl. 441). Later also the other members of the later Xanthian dynasty (with the exception of *Erbbina*) made extensive use of their own image on their coinages. Cfr. Müseler 2016, p. 18 sqq.

the southwestern coast of the central region[27]. The first series in the name of *Weχssere* from Zagaba and of *Mithrapata* from Phellos are probably more or less contemporary with the rule of *Ddenewele* in Western Lycia and the conquest of power by the usurper *Erbbina*[28].

After the introduction of a reformed coinage of similar weight standard but with a simplified iconography by the dynast *Trbbenimi* at Limyra the new coin types were soon adopted in Central Lycia as well, presumably during the late nineties of the 4th century BC. The coins show a facing lion mask on the obverse and just a large triskeles, often accompanied by monograms or various symbols, which will be discussed further below. There are a few issues of this type signed by *Weχssere*, soon to be followed by the small Central Lycian coinage of *Aruwātijesi*. The bulk of this reformed coinage, however, bears the name of *Mithrapata*. Thereby it remains uncertain, whether these coins replaced his earlier issues entirely or whether the production of coins bearing his portrait was nonetheless continued. Possibly the reformed coinage of *Mithrapata* was no longer struck at Phellos but also at Zagaba, which might have passed under his control after the short reign of *Aruwātijesi* at that place.

Moreover there are two isolated issues from the small town of Tymnessos near the mountain-pass between Central Lycia and the Xanthos valley, – one with the monogram of *Weχssere* and the abbreviated toponym and the other in the name of *Mithrapata* together with the full name of the mint-place. The two issues are of similar type but only vaguely related to each other; they are almost certainly produced at different occasions.

Although an approximate chronological sequence can be established for the main-issues the following catalogue of the Central Lycian issues will be arranged by the different mints. Unless stated otherwise this will be maintained as the guiding principle for the order of the material presented in subsequent sections of this article.

II.1.1.a   *Weχssere*. Stater, [Zagaba]
Protome of lion to l., above legend /V↑ / Bust of Athena with triple-crested attic helmet facing in incuse circle, in field legend F↑[V↳↑P↑]
Olçay – Mørkholm 1971, 1 = Müseler VII, 1* (9,89 g)   (Figure 16)

II.1.1.b   *Weχssere*. Tetrobol (Third stater), [Zagaba]
Head of lion to r., above legend F↑V / Head of Athena with triple-cressted attic helmet facing in incuse circle, in field monogram ☸ and legend F↑V↳
Winsemann-Falghera Coll. 186* (2,85 g)   (Figure 17)

II.1.1.c   [*Weχssere*]. Tetrobol (Third stater), [Zagaba]
Head of lion to r. / Head of Athena with triple-crested attic helmet facing in incuse circle, in field monogram ☸
SNG v. Aulock 4211 (2,89 g)

---

[27] Phellos is actually suggested by its subsequent use as the mint for the coinage of *Perikle* displaying his famous frontal-portrait (Müseler 2016, VIII, 35 and below Figure O).

[28] For the date and the importance of the reign of *Ddenewele* see Müseler 2017a.

II.1.2.a	*[Weχssere]*. Stater, Zagaba Lion mask facing / Bust of Athena with triple-crested attic helmet facing in incuse circle on the helmet miniature legend 𐊇𐊀𐊗, in field laurel-branch and legend 𐊈𐊀𐊆𐊁𐊂𐊀𐊗 (monogram ⚛ missing!) SNG Ashmolean 1191* (9,28 g) *(Figure 18)*
II.1.2.b	*[Weχssere]*. Tetrobol (Third stater), Zagaba Lion mask facing / Head of Athena with triple-crested attic helmet facing in incuse circle, in field dolphin and legend 𐊈𐊀𐊆𐊂𐊀𐊗𐊐 (monogram ⚛ missing!) Müseler VII, 4* (3,04 g) *(Figure 19)*
II.1.2.c	*[Weχssere]*. Tetrobol (Third stater), Zagaba Lion mask facing / Head of Athena with triple crested attic helmet facing in incuse circle, in field monogram ⚛ and legend 𐊈𐊀𐊆𐊂𐊀𐊗 Müseler VII, 3 (3,03 g)
II.2.1.a	*Wekhssere*. Tetrobol (Third stater), [Zagaba] Lion mask facing / Triskeles with monogram ⚛ in center in incuse circle, in field legend 𐊇𐊀𐊇𐊏𐊏𐊐 SNG Cop. Suppl. 468* (3,06 g) *(Figure 20)*
II.2.1.b	*Wekhssere*. Tetrobol (Third stater), [Zagaba] Lion mask facing / Triskeles with monogram ⚛ in center in incuse circle, in field Legend 𐊇𐊐𐊇𐊏𐊏𐊐𐊂𐊐 Leu / Winterthur, E-Auction 7, 2019, 399* (3,05 g) *(Figure 21)*
II.3.1.a	*Aruwātijesi*. Stater, [Zagaba] Lion mask facing / Triskeles in incuse square, in field legend 𐊀𐊕𐊐𐊇𐊗𐊁𐊆𐊐𐊏𐊀 Müseler VII, 59* (9,60 g) *(Figure 22)*
II.3.1.b	*Aruwātijesi*. Tetrobol (Third stater), [Zagaba] Lion mask facing / Triskeles in incuse square, in field legend 𐊀𐊕𐊐𐊇𐊗𐊁𐊆𐊐𐊏𐊀 Müseler VII, 60 (3,06 g)
II.3.1.c	*Aruwātijesi*. Diobol (Sixth stater), Zagaba Lion mask facing / Triskeles in incuse square, in field legend 𐊀𐊕𐊐𐊇𐊗𐊁𐊆𐊐𐊏𐊀 and 𐊆 Müseler VII, 61* (1,49 g) *(Figure 23)*
II.3.1.d	*Aruwātijesi*. Obol (Twelfth stater), Zagaba Lion mask facing / Triskeles in incuse square, in field legend 𐊀𐊕𐊐𐊇𐊗𐊁𐊆𐊐𐊏𐊀 and 𐊆 Müseler VII, 64 (0,69 g)
II.3.2.	*Aruwātijesi*. Obol (Twelfth stater), Zagaba Lion mask facing / Triskeles in incuse circle, in field legend 𐊀𐊕𐊐 and 𐊆 Müseler VII, 65 (0,69 g)

III.1.1.a	*Mithrapata*. Stater, uncertain mint (Phellos?) Protome of lion to r. / Bearded, diademed bust of the dynast to l. in incuse square, in field ⚛ and legend 𐊎𐊁𐊭𐊕𐊀𐊓𐊀𐊗𐊀 SNG Ashmolean 1199* (9,75 g) *(Figure 24)*

III.1.1.b   *Mithrapata*. Stater, uncertain mint (Phellos?)
               Protome of lion to r. / Bearded, diademed bust of the dynast to l. in incuse square, in
               field ⚘ and legend ΜΕΧΡΑΓΑΤΑ
               Müseler VII, 69* (9,73 g)   (Figure 25)

III.1.2.a   *Mithrapata*. Stater, uncertain mint (Phellos?)
               Lion mask facing, below ⚘ / Bearded, diademed bust of Dynast to l. in incuse square,
               in field ⚘ and legend ΜΕΧΡΑΓΑΤΑ
               Müseler VII, 72* (9,84 g)   (Figure 26)

III.1.2.b   *Mithrapata*. Stater, uncertain mint (Phellos?)
               Lion mask facing / Bearded, diademed bus of dynast to l. in incuse square, in field ⚘
               and legend ΜΕΧΡΑΓΑΤΑ
               Müseler VII, 73* (9,97 g)   (Figure 27)

III.2.1.   *Mithrapata*. Stater, uncertain mint (Phellos or Zagaba?)
               Protome of lion to r. / Triskeles in incuse square, in field legend ΜΕΧΡΑΓΑΤΑ
               Auction CNG 99, 2015 301* (9,66 g)   (Figure 28)

III.3.1.a   *Mithrapata*. Stater, uncertain mint (Phellos or Zagaba?)
               Lion mask facing / Triskeles in incuse square, in field legend ΜΕΧΡΑΓΑΤΑ
               CNG Mail Auction 57, 2001, 542* (9,49 g)   (Figure 29)

III.3.1.b   *Mithrapata*. Tetrobol (Third stater), uncertain mint (Phellos or Zagaba?)
               Lion mask facing / Triskeles in incuse square, in field legend ΜΕΧΡΑΓΑΤ
               Auction Naumann 57, 2017, 308 (2,56 g)

III.3.1.c   *Mithrapata*. Diobol (Sixth stater), uncertain mint (Phellos or Zagaba?)
               Lion mask facing / Triskeles in incuse square, in field legend ΜΕΧ
               Müseler VII, 90 (1,39 g)

III.3.1.d   *Mithrapata*. Diobol (Sixth stater), uncertain mint (Phellos or Zagaba?)
               Lion mask facing / Triskeles in incuse square, in field ⚘ and legend ΜΕΧ
               CNG E-Auction 427, 2018, 253* (1,46 g)   (Figure 30)

III.3.2.a   *Mithrapata*. Stater, uncertain mint (Phellos or Zagaba?)
               Lion mask facing / Triskeles in incuse square, in (upper) field small head of Athena
               with attic helmet to l. and legend ΜΕΧΡΑΓΑΤΑ
               SNG v. Aulock 4244 (9,79 g)

III.3.2.b   *Mithrapata*. Stater, uncertain mint (Phellos or Zagaba?)
               Lion mask facing / Triskeles in incuse square, in (lower) field small head of Athena
               with attic helmet to l. and legend ΜΕΧΡΑΓΑΤΑ
               Auction Goldberg 26, 2004, 2111* (9,74 g)   (Figure 31)

III.3.3.a   *Mithrapata*. Stater, uncertain mint (Phellos or Zagaba?)
               Lion mask facing / Triskeles in incuse square, in field small dolphin and legend
               ΜΕΧΡΑΓΑΤΑ
               Müseler VII, 75 (9,72 g)   (Figure 32)

III.3.3.b   *Mithrapata*. Diobol (Sixth stater), uncertain mint (Phellos or Zagaba?)
Lion mask facing / Triskeles in incuse square, in field small dolphin and legend ΜEXPP
CNG E-Auction 427, 2018, 248 (1,52 g)

III.3.4.   *Mithrapata*. Stater, uncertain mint (Phellos or Zagaba?)
Lion mask facing / Triskeles in incuse square, in field small bust of Hermes with winged petasos and kerykeion facing and legend ΜEXPPΓPTP
Müseler VII, 79* (9,88 g)   *(Figure 33)*

III.3.5.   *Mithrapata*. Stater, uncertain mint (Phellos or Zagaba?)
Lion mask facing / Triskeles in incuse square, in field small bus of Herakles with club and lions-skin facing and legend ΜEXPPΓPTP
Müseler VII, 78* (9,58 g)   *(Figure 34)*

III.3.6.   *Mithrapata*. Stater, uncertain mint (Phellos or Zagaba?)
Lion mask facing / Triskeles in incuse square, in field barley-corn and legend ΜEXPPΓPTP
Müseler VII, 80* (9,74 g)   *(Figure 35)*

III.3.7.a   *Mithrapata*. Diobol (Sixth stater), uncertain mint (Phellos or Zagaba?)
Lion mask facing / Triskeles in incuse square, in field astragalos and legend ΜEXPPΓPTP
Müseler VII, 82* (1,34 g)   *(Figure 36)*

III.3.7.b   *Mithrapata*. Obol (Twelfth stater), uncertain mint (Phellos or Zagaba?)
Astragalos / Triskeles in incuse square, in field korinthian helmet and legend ΜEX
Müseler VII, 84* (0,55 g)   *(Figure 37)*

III.3.8.   *Mithrapata*. Diobol (Sixth stater), uncertain mint (Phellos or Zagaba?)
Lion mask facing / Triskeles in incuse square, in field bipennis and legend ΜEXPP
CNG E-Auction 408, 2017, 217* (1,37 g)   *(Figure 38)*

III.3.9.   *Mithrapata*. Diobol (Sixth stater), uncertain mint (Phellos or Zagaba?)
Lion mask facing / Triskeles in incuse square, in field arrow and legend ΜEX
Müseler VII, 86* (1,42 g)   *(Figure 39)*

IV.1.1.   *[Weχssere]*. Stater, Tymnessos
Head of Athena with attic helmet to r. / Bull butting to l. in incuse square, in field ⚶ and legend TOM
SNG Cop. Suppl. 437* (8,40 g)   *(Figure 40)*

IV.1.2.   *[Weχssere]*. Obol (Twelfth stater), [Tymnessos]
Head of Athena with triple-crested attic helmet facing / Bull kneeling running to l. in incuse sqare, in field ⚶
Roma E-Auction 55, 2019,, 396* (0,82 g)   *(Figure 41)*

IV.2.1.	*Mithrapata*. Stater, Tymnessos
Head of Athena with korinthian helmet to l., in field ⟨triskeles⟩ / Bull butting to l. in incuse square, in field legend ΜΕΧΡϞΓϞΤϞ ΤΟΜΕΝΤΟ
SNG Keckman II, 492* (8,41 g)   (Figure 42)

On the initial, "pre-reform" issues of *Weχssere* and of *Mithrapata* the usage of monograms and symbols follows the same pattern that can be observed among earlier coinages: The majority of *Weχssere's* coins with the frontal bust of Athena from Zagaba and two of the coins with the bull from Tymnessos carry a monogram composed of the Lycian letters O, V and ч, which is possibly to be understood as a (though somewhat unusual) abbreviation of the beginning of the issuers name. Apparently, it is generally used as a substitute of the dynasts name on issues that bear only a reference to the location of the mint, a peculiar feature that will gain importance in the analysis of the anonymous issues from the Xanthos valley later on[29]. All the earlier coins of *Mithrapata*, that is both groups displaying his portrait from the mint of uncertain identification, but also a fraction from his "post reform" coinage and the single issue in his name from Tymnessos, carry a small triskeles (⟨triskeles⟩) in their fields as a distinctive mark[30]. Although *Mithrapata's* name has been nowhere omitted, this sign seems to have likewise served as some kind of personal emblem, which allowed the identification of the respective issuer by users of the coins, who were not able to read the legends.

A combination of the dynasts name with the monogram ⟨mon⟩ is also applied on *Weχssere's* "post-reform" issues from Zagaba. There are, however, two different variants of the personal name conveyed by the legends of those coins, Ғ↑ѴччTP↑ and ҒѴчч↑ (Figure 26 and 27). Together with the accompanying monogram that can be spelled out as OVч this probably accounts for a basic equivalence in the use of the various spellings rather than for three basically different names born by more than one individual[31]. Anyway, the entire post-reform coinage of *Wekhssere* seems comparatively small. It is followed by the also not exactly numerous issues in the name of *Aruwātijesi*, which do not bear an additional symbol. Instead some of *Aruwātijesi's* coins show the single letter I beside the dynasts name in the field, - the initial of the mint-place Zagaba (Figure 23). Evidently it had become a requirement to underline the provenance of the issues, since this was no longer apparent from the pictorial type of the coins. Later on, this practice would be resumed by the coinage in the name of *Trbbenimi* at Zagaba (Figure J).

But on the post reform coinage of *Mithrapata* the character and the function of the secondary signs, which accompany the principal type of his coins, underwent a fundamental change. After a number of initial issues without any additional mark or with *Mithrapata's* customary emblem of a small triskeles (Figure 30) various miniature images, pictorial representations of human figures, of animals or of inanimate objects, appear in the reverse-fields beside the large triskeles and the issuers name. So far, the purpose of this innovation is not entirely clear. Some of those figures,

---

[29] See below p. 47 sqq.

[30] The distinctive mark ⟨triskeles⟩ had already been used on the coins of *Kuprlli*, apparently for the same purpose.

[31] This assumption has been opposed by Schürr 2018, who would expect to see positive proof from the numismatic or epigraphic record for the usage of the name-forms *Waχssere* or *Uχssere*, which is admittedly not attested so far, before accepting the idea of a basic equivalence of the different spellings suggested here. The author, however, is convinced that the material extant already provides sufficient evidence to permit such a conjecture.

namely the helmeted head of Athena or the facing busts of Hermes and of Heracles (Figure 33 and 35-36), seem to be allusions to images used for the coinages from mints further to the West such as Xanthos, Patara or Telmessos[32]. Given their principal type and their weight standard the coins in question can, however, neither have been struck in the West, nor can they have been meant to supplement or to replace the respective Western issues in any way. Apparently, they have been all made by one and the same mint that is to be located in Central Lycia. The application of such images on otherwise completely regular Central Lycian coins was presumably meant to emphasize the issuers claim to rule over all of Lycia, in particular including the Xanthos valley. The coins might actually have been produced with the intention to finance a larger military operation in the West.

A military background may perhaps also be conjectured for the re-opening of the mint at Tymnessos in the mountains near the eastern border of the Xanthos valley. It was used for the production of some small series adapted to the lighter weight-standard of western Lycia by *Mithrapata* and by *Weχssere* (Figures 40-42), – though presumably not at the same time. Only at the time of the elder *Weχssere* a couple of issues in the name of *Xeriga* had been minted there before, most likely in preparation of the dynasts campaign from his bases at Phellos and at Kandyba against the regions to the West that eventually led him to the capture of Xanthos (Figure K-L)[33]. Perhaps the mint at Tymnessos was only operational in times of war. For the younger *Weχssere* the occasion might well have been a campaign against the tyrant *Erbbina*, which lead to the ultimate demise of the latter[34], while a possible expedition of Mithrapata into the Xanthos valley would have to be dated somewhat later[35].

New rulers in the West (Waχssebddimi, Ddẽñtimi, Weχssere and Aruwãtijesi)

Although it is not possible to fix an absolute chronology for the series listed and discussed in this section an internal sequence of the coinages from the various mints may actually be deduced from properties of the material: Most likely the issues from Patara begin somewhat earlier than the ones from Tlos. The latter might be more or less contemporaneous with those from Telmessos and the few issues that can be attributed either to Xanthos or to Pinara. Inside the respective groups the sequence of series in the name of the different issuers can also be demonstrated, though to a limited extent. At Telmessos it can be proved by shared obverse-dies that the coins of *Aruwãtijesi* (Figures 59-60) immediately succeed and replace the issues in the name of *Erbbina* at the former stronghold of the usurper outside the Xanthos valley (Figures M-N)[36] and are then followed by issues with the respective monograms used by *Waχssepddimi* and by *Ddẽñtimi*. At Tlos the coins with the legend *Waχssepddimi* apparently precede those with the legend *Ddẽñtimi,* as will be shown further below. Only the sequence of the *Waχssepddimi*-, the *Uχssepddimi*- and the *Weχssere*-series from Patara, which certainly precede the various issues with the name of the mint

---

[32] It should be noted that the coinage from Patara with the bust of Hermes must have preceded the respective Central Lycian issues of *Mithrapata*, if this assumption is correct. See below p. 44.

[33] See Zahle 1998, Müseler 2016, p. 53 sq and Müseler 2018, p. 17 sqq.

[34] See Müseler 2016, p. 65 and Müseler 2017a, p. 15.

[35] See further below p. 57.

[36] One of the dies had even been used under *Ddenewele* before being employed for the coinage of *Erbbina* and then – after some repair – for the one of *Aruwãtijesi*: See Müseler 2017a, p. 11 with notes 20-21.

alone, cannot be established by an analysis of the coins themselves and must potentially rely on other evidence.

V.1.1.	*Waχssepddimi*, Stater, Patara	
	Head of Athena with attic helmet to r. / Head of Hermes with winged petasos to r. in incuse circle, in field legends ⌐TT⊦P⊦ and O𐊤𐊾𐊾↑⌐△△E/ᴧE	
	Müseler VII, 49* (8,11 g)	*(Figure 43)*

V.1.2. *Waχssepddimi*, Stater, [Patara]
Head of Athena with attic helmet to r. / Bust of Hermes with winged petasos to r. in incuse circle, in field legend O[𐊤𐊾]𐊾↑⌐△△E/ᴧE
Inv. Waddington 2952 = BN btv1b8534845q (8,07 g) *(Figure 44)*

V.1.3. *Waχssepddimi*, Stater, [Patara]
Head of Athena with attic helmet to r. / Bust of Hermes with winged petasos to r. in incuse circle, in field legend F⊦∀𐊾𐊾↑⌐△△E/ᴧE
SNG Cop. Suppl. 467* (8,36 g) *(Figure 45)*

V.2.1. *Weχssere*, Stater, [Patara]
Head of Athena with attic helmet to r. / Bust of Hermes with winged petasos to r. in incuse circle, in field legend F↑∀𐊾𐊾↑P↑
Vismara 72-76; Müseler VII, 51* (8,44 g) *(Figure 46)*

V.3.1. *Ddēñtimi*, Obol (Twelfth stater), [Tlos?]
Head of Athena with attic helmet to r. / Head of Hermes with unwinged petasos to r., in field legend △△𐊤𐊹TE/ᴧE
Inv. Waddington 2953 =BN btv1b85348464* (0,57 g) *(Figure 47)*

V.4.1. Anonymous, Stater, Patara
Head of Athena with attic helmet to r. / Head of Hermes with winged petasos to r. in incuse circle, in field legend ⌐TT⊦P⊦I𐊤 (?)
Babelon, Traité II/2, 417 = BN btv1b8534843w* (8,10 g) *(Figure 48)*

V.5.1.a Anonymous, Stater, Patara
Head of Athena with attic helmet to r. / Bust of Hermes with winged petasos to r. in incuse circle, in field legend ⌐TT
Auction Roma IX, 2015, 385* (8,28 g) *(Figure 49)*

V.5.1b Anonymous, Trihemiobol (Eighth stater), Patara
Head of Athena with attic helmet to r. / Head of Hermes with winged petasos to r. in incuse circle, in field legend ⌐TT
CNG E-Auction 400, 2017, 274 (0,89 g)

V.6.1. Anonymous, Diobol (Sixth stater), [Patara]
Head of Athena with attic helmet to r. / Head of Hermes with winged petasos to r. in incuse circle
SNG Cop. Suppl. 500* (1,13 g) *(Figure 50)*

V.7.1. Anonymous, Stater, Patara
Head of Athena with attic helmet to r. / Head of Hermes with winged petasos to l. in incuse circle, in field legend ⌐T
Babelon, Traité II/2, 418 = BM 1844,1015.251* (7,71 g) (Figure 51)

VI.1.1.a *Waχssepddimi*, Stater, [Tlos]
Head of Athena with attic helmet to r. / Two lions with raised paws seated opposite to each other, heads turned to front, in incuse circle, in field monogram or linear symbol ☿ and legend FΓѰϟϟ↑Γ, in exergue legend △△E𝖬[E]
Müseler VII, 11* (8,52 g) (Figure 52)

VI.1.1.b *Waχsseppddim*i, Drachm (Half stater), [Tlos]
Head of Athena with attic helmet to r. / Two lions with raised paws seated opposite to each other, heads turned to front, in incuse circle, in field monogram or linear symbol ☿ and legend FΓѰϟϟ↑Γ, in exergue legend △△E𝖬E
CNG Mail Bid Sale 61, 2002, 761* (4,19 g) (Figure 53)

VI.1.1.c *Waχssepddimi*, Tetrobol (Third stater), [Tlos]
Head of Athena with attic helmet to r. / Two lions with raised paws seated opposite to each other, heads turned to front, in incuse circle, in field monogram or linear symbol ☿ and fragmentary legend Ѱϟ – △E
BM 1905,1005.10 (2,56 g)

VI.1.1.d [*Waχssepddimi*], Diobol (Sixth stater), [Tlos]
Head of Athena with attic helmat to r. / Two lions with raised paws seated opposite to each other, heads turned to front, in incuse circle, in field monogram or linear symbol ☿
Müseler VII, 12 (1,35 g)

VI.1.1.e *Waχssepddimi*], Obol (Twelfth stater), [Tlos]
Head of Athena with attic helmet to r. / Two lions with raised paws seated opposite to each other, heads turned to front, in incuse circle, in field monogram or linear symbol ☿
Müseler VII, 13 (0,69 g)

VI.2.1. *Ddẽñtimi*, Stater, [Tlos]
Head of Athena with attic helmet to r. / Two lions with raised paws seated opposite to each other, heads turned to front, in incuse circle, in field monograms or linear symbols ☿ and ⅄ and legend △△Ύ𐊗E𝖬E
SNG Cop. Suppl. 464* (8,12 g) (Figure 54)

VI.2.2. *Ddẽñtimi*, Obol (Twelfth stater), Tlos
Head of Athena with attic helmet to r. / Head of Apollon (with short hair) to l. in incuse circle, in field legends △△Ύ𐊗E𝖬E and T∧Γ
Roma E-Auction 46, 2018, 258* (0,54 g) (Figure 55)

VI.2.3.a   *Ddēñtimi*, Obol (Twelfth stater), Tlos
            Lion mask facing / Head of Apollon (with short hait) to l. in incuse circle, in field legends △△ᛉⲉTE and TᐱP
            Müseler VII, 20* (0,47 g)   *(Figure 56)*

VI.2.3.b   *Ddēñtimi*, Obol (Twelfth stater), [Tlos]
            Lion mask facing / Head of Apollon (with short hair) to r. in incuse circle, in field legend △△ᛉ
            Müseler VII, 21 (0,59 g)

VI.2.3.c   [*Dddēñtimi*], Obol (Twelfth stater), [Tlos]
            Lion mask facing / Head of Apollon (with short hair) to r. in incuse circle, in field monogram or linear symbol Ȣ
            SNG Cop. Suppl. 505* (0,58 g)   *(Figure 57)*

VI.2.4.a   *Ddēñtimi*, Obol (Twelfth stater)), [Tlos]
            Lion mask facing / Head of Apollon (with long hair) to l. in incuse sqare, in field legend △△ᛉⲉTEᛗE
            Inv. Waddington 2990 = BN btv1b8534865g* (0,56 g)   *(Figure 58)*

VI.2.4.b   [*Ddēñtimi*], Obol (Twelfth stater), Tlos
            Lion mask facing / Head of Apollon (with long hair) to l. in incuse circle, in field legend TᐱPFE
            Babelon, Traité II/2, 447 = BN btv1b85348679 (0,56 g)

VII.1.1.a   *Aruwātijesi*, Stater, [Telmessos]
            Head of Athena with attic helmet to l. / Lion jumping to l. in incuse square, in field legend PPOF↓TEIᛏᛉE
            Babelon, Traité II/2, 434 = BN btv1b85348553* (7,92 g)   *(Figure 59)*

VII.1.1.b   *Aruwātijesi*, Stater, [Telmessos]
            Head of Athena with attic helmet to r. / Lion jumping to l. in incuse square, in field legend PPOF↓TEIᛏᛉE
            Müseler VI, 98* (8,23 g)   *(Figure 60)*

VII.2.1.   [*Waχseppddimi*], Hemidrachm (Quarter stater), [Telmessos]
            Head of Athena with attic helmet to l. / Head of Herakles to r. in incuse square, in field monogram or linear symbol Ȣ
            BM 1905, 1005.7* (2,09 g)   *(Figure 61)*

VII.3.1.   [*Ddēñtimi*], Stater, [Telmessos]
            Head of Athena with attic helmet to r. / Head of Herakles to r. in incuse square, in field monogram or linear symbol Ȣ
            Hurter 1979, p. 102, 14[37]; BMC 128 = BM ?? * (8,61 g)   *(Figure 62)*

---

[37] Hurters assertion that staters of *Ddenewele* listed by her under the numbers 15-17 were struck from the same obverse-die can be demonstrated as mistaken.

VIII.1.1.a [*Waχssepddimi*], Stater, uncertain mint (Xanthos?)
Head of Athena with attic helmet to r., below unidentified letters or symbols / Bearded head of dynast with Persian headdress to r. in incuse circle, in field monogram or linear symbol ᛬
Babelon, Traité II/2, 346 = BM 1877,0508.1* (8,37 g) *(Figure 63)*

VIII.1.1.b [*Waχssepddimi*], Obol (Twelfth stater), uncertain mint (Xanthos?)
Head of Athena with attic helmet to r. / Bearded head of dynast with Persian headdress to r. in incuse circle, in field monogram or linear symbol ᛬
Müseler VII, 9* (0,60 g) *(Figure 64)*

VIII.2.1. [*Waχssepddimi*], Obol (Twelfth stater), [Xanthos or Pinara?]
Head of Athena with attic helmet to l. / Female head with taenia to l. in incuse circle, in field monogram or linear symbol ᛬
Roma E-Auction 35, 2017, 310* (0,59 g) *(Figure 65)*

All the coins presented here are adapted to the light weight standard with an average weight of ca. 8,5 g for the stater, which has been customary for all coinages produced in or for western Lycia since the time of *Kuprlli*[38]. In addition the issues generally follow the denominational sequence of the attic system introduced in the Xanthos valley by *Xeriga*.

It is not certain, whether a mint had previously existed at Patara or whether it was a new installation for the production of the coinages in the name of *Waχssepddimi* (or *Uχssepddimi*) and of *Weχssere*[39]. In any case there had been no active mint at this place during the reigns of *Xeriga*, *Xerēi* and *Ddenewele*. The distinctive type chosen for the coinages of Patara, a youthful bust or a head of Hermes turned to the right side wearing a flat and usually winged petasos, resembles in some respect the bearded head of Hermes set upon one earlier coin bearing the legend *Waχssebllimi* (Figure 15), but there no reference is given to any place of minting. The issues from Patara differ significantly from all the other coinages presented in this section: While the legend *Waχssepddimi* is also found on coins from the mint of Tlos, the name-forms *Weχssere* and *Uχssepddimi* appear only here. Moreover, the issue with the legend *Uχssepddimi* is the first example for the appearance of a personal name in combination with a toponym on a coin from Western Lycia since the time of *Xerēi*, – an important exception being the stater in the name of Tissaphernes from Xanthos[40]. This can hardly be seen as a result of mere chance; there must have been a specific reason for this step: Evidently the act of making the responsible dynast together with the place of origin of this coinage known through a clear and unambiguous statement on

---

[38] Despite being situated in the western part of Central-Lycia the coinages from Tymnessos as well as those from Kandyba were aligned to the light weight standard in force in the Xanthos Valley: See Müseler 2018, p. 17 sqq.

[39] For the assumption that *Waχssepddimi* and *Uχssepddimi* have been nothing else than spelling-variants of the same word see above p. 39 and note 31.

[40] SNG Cop.Suppl. 460. Here the joint mention of the satrap's name and of the mint-location clearly served to emphasize the extraordinary character of the issue and to reflect intelligible to all a particular political situation.

one and the same coin had been deemed necessary, which speaks for the new and unprecedented character of these issues[41].

Furthermore no monograms or symbols have been placed on these initial issues struck at Patara. This concerns not only the coins bearing personal names but also those that denote only the place of minting. It is in sharp contrast to the practice of most other mints, where such monograms or symbols are occasionally even applied as the only reference at all to the origin of the coinage and/or the person of the issuer[42]. The apparent lack of such distinctive marks could once more demonstrate that the Patarean coinage was a completely new production, where no reference to visual conventions introduced previously would make sense. Symbols or additional attributes like for example a kerykeion in the field beside the bust of Hermes were only used for later issues from the mint at Patara[43].

There is a significant die-link that is connecting two of the issues from Patara presented above: The obverse die of most known coins in the name of *Weχssere* has also been used for the coin with the legend *Waχssepddimi* (Figures 45 and 46); unfortunately, the die shows in both cases approximately the same grade of wear so that an internal sequence of the respective issues cannot be established. But for the coins in the name of *Weχssere* and for the ones with the legend *Uχssepddimi* more than just one obverse die is known, what indicates a larger overall volume of those two series. However, an internal coherence of all the respective issues is attested by the described die-link.

There is only a small fraction of Patarean type that bears the the name *Ddēñtimi*. No other coins from Patara with the name of that issuer are known so far. This is, however, in line with the main part of the coinage in the name of the same person from Tlos: Although more numerous these coins are also only Obols and Hemiobols. The only known stater with the name *Ddēñtimi* is clearly dependent from a parallel issue of *Waχssepddimi*. This seems to indicate that *Ddēñtimi* and his coinage were only of secondary importance; he might have been just a deputy of another, more powerful ruler.

In contrast to the Patarean coinages the Tloan issues make use of additional monograms or linear symbols: ☿ has been used on a number of issues with the legend *Waχssepddimi*, while ⚒ is set on others usually referring to *Ddēñtimi*. In most cases the symbols are added to the respective legends but on fractions they sometimes stand as single disctinctive marks in the reverse-fields of the coins. On the only known stater-issue from Tlos bearing the legend *Ddēñtimi* the monogram ☿ is even maintained and the mark ⚒ is just added at the side (Figure 54). The obverse die of the said coin had previously been used for staters of the same type in the name of *Waχssepddimi* (see Figures 51 and 54), the sequence proved by the progressive wear of this die. Therefore, the group showing the legend *Ddēñtimi* seems to have been subsequent to the one with the name

---

[41] This becomes once more customary on the initial issues of *Artumpara* at Telmessos, Xanthos and Tlos (see below issues XX.1-4).

[42] See for example the series with the *Waχssepddimi*-symbol beside the portrait of a dynast from Xanthos (Issue VIII.1.1.).

[43] See below p. 57 sqq.

Waχsepddimi, although the chronological connection between the two coinages is obviously rather close. With respect to the very small number of dies known for the staters of both issues the minting-period of all those coins at Tlos has probably not been of a long duration.

The image jointly employed by both series features two opposed lions with raised paws. Those were possibly derived from a Central Lycian issue in the name of the dynast *Xinaχa* datable to the mid 5th century BC and coming from an unidentified mint that is, however, probably to be located at Zagaba (Figure O)[44]. The dynasts making use of this reverse-type may well have been themselves of Central Lycian origin like *Weχssere* and *Aruwātijesi*; at least the coinage appears to be the reflection of a manifest relationship with that region. In any case this new coin type was kept and adopted by the dynast, who subsequently issued the anonymus series with just the toponym and a diskeles-symbol in the reverse-field at Tlos[45].

While the coins that can be assigned to *Waχsepddimi* all seem to belong to one single series the typological range of the issues of *Ddēñtimi* is somewhat larger: Beside the staters closely related to the coinage of *Waχsepddimi* there is another series, which combines a facing lion mask on the obverse with a youthful male head on the reverse and which is struck from a multitude of slightly differing dies. These coins do not only display the issuers name with the monogram 𐊛 but even add the toponym like the issues with the legend *Uχssepddimi* from Patara. Perhaps users from beyond the immediate neighbourhood of Tlos were not very well acquainted with this coinage, which needed therefore to be equipped with multiple identification-marks in order to be acknowledged as a valid mean of trade elsewhere. However, although this issue judging by the number of dies employed for its production must have been massive there are only fractions known so far, and the question is, whether larger denominations of the same type have been existent at all.

At Telmessos the coin-types of *Ddenewele* and *Erbbina* had been temproaryly replaced by a new design launched by *Aruwātijesi*, but this was subsequently once more abandoned. Issues carrying either the linear symbol of *Waχssepddimi* or the monogram of *Ddēñtimi* make again use of the traditional pattern with the head of Herakles on the reverse. In contrast to all the mints in the Xanthos-valley these issues are not followed by any coinage with the name of the mint-location and the symbol ⚯. The overall volume of the coinage from Telmessos seems to have dwindled considerably after the end of *Erbbina*'s rule. From this mint in the far north-western corner of the Lycian peninsula, which had been highly productive once, there are only a very few issues, known for the period under discussion attested by some single specimens left. The next more important coinage from this place seems to be the series in the name of *Artumpara*[46].

But the most remarkable feature of the coinages discussed within the present section is the unusual distribution of the issues among the various mints of Western Lycia. There is just one issue that can be attributed with some certainty to the mint of Xanthos and another one that might as well have come from Pinara. The issue with the portrait of a bearded man wearing a headdress of Persian type that is additionally adorned with a diadem-band corresponds to an issue of *Xerēi*

---

[44] See Müseler 2018, p. 23.

[45] See below issues IX.1-2.

[46] See issue XX.1.1. below.

from Pinara and even more to a Xanthian issue of *Ddenewele* (Figure P-Q)[47]. Although there are some completely illegible signs or letters under the head of Athena on the obverse of the staters belonging to this series[48] the only reference to the identity of the person depicted seems to consist in the linear symbol ᛯ beside the male head on the reverse, which points to the dynast named *Waχssepddimi*. The same symbol is set on the small coin with the female head that is possibly to be assigned to Pinara[49]. But all this is far inferior to what would be expected from mints that had been installed so long ago and had produced coins in such significant numbers under the Xanthian dynasty. At the time of *Erbbina* the minting-activities in the lower Xanthos valley had apparently been interrupted and the production of coins had ceased for some time. When it was finally resumed dynastic names did no longer appear on the issues from Xanthos and Pinara. Only the places of origin continued to be mentioned, always accompanied by a small diskeles (⚯) in the fields. The respective coinages will be presented and discussed on the following pages.

The issuers of the anonymous *"diskelophoric"* coinages

A coinage that displayed just the name of the mint-place and a small diskeles on the reverse was apparently initiated at Tlos at the same time or soon after the issues bearing the names *Waχssepddimi* or *Ddēñtimi*. Other mints in the lower Xanthos valley soon followed suit: At Xanthos and Pinara the traditional designs, which had been used for the coinages of the former Xanthian dynasty, were gradually abandoned and replaced by a variety of new motifs. From that moment onwards all the coins struck at these mints were only marked with the respective place-name and the symbol ⚯ in the field. On some fractions, otherwise clearly related to the same series, the toponym and sometimes even the small diskeles may occasionally be missing, but those cases are rather rare. However, at Patara the application of the symbol ⚯ remained an exception. Here coins showing the head of Athena in combination with the head of Hermes and naming the location while lacking the diskeles in the field, apparently continued to be struck throughout the entire period of the mint's activity and formed the predominant mainstream of its production[50]. But apart from these issues there exist a few series of a different type and endowed with a diskeles-symbol that must nonetheless also be attributed to Patara. The principal image of these coins, a facing head of Athena with a triple crested attic helmet, is clearly related to the Central Lycian coinage of *Weχssere* from Zagaba, although the execution of the design is somewhat coarser here[51].

---

[47] Winsemann-Falghera Coll. 178 and Zahle 1982, Pl. 17, 18. The erroneous reading of the legend on the latter coin as *Krñna* had still been maintained by Zahle but this has meanwhile been proved as obsolete: See Müseler 2016, p. 8 and VI, 67.

[48] The signs or letters under the head of Athena are only visible on the coin from the BM quoted here and are quite heavily damaged; on the specimen from the von Aulock collection this part of the die is not on the flan. Unfortunately, even a close and repeated inspection of the BM piece has not led to a feasible interpretation so far.

[49] For the "diskelophoric" coinage from Xanthos and from Pinara with such a female head see below issues X,1.4-5. as well as issue XI.1.1. and XI.1.3.

[50] See issues V.4-7. above and issues XVI.2.1-3. below.

[51] These western issues with the facing head of Athena do not provide any reference to their place of origin. However, one of the fractions is from the same obverse-die as a coin that carries a head of Hermes with an abbreviation of the toponym for Patara on the reverse. See Figures 98 and 99.

But in comparison with the bulk of the Patarean issues these series appear quite small. They probably belong to some kind of special edition, which had no lasting consequence for the main-coinages struck at Patara.

In any case, the symbol ⌀ remains the common denominator of all the different issues listed in this section. The author has therefore chosen to call those the "diskelophoric" coinages. The chronological frame, which must be assigned to the coinages of this type, is remarkably broad: While early series showing this characteristic property are either parallel or immediately subsequent to the issues discussed in the previous section a similar coinage was still produced towards the very end of dynastic rule in Lycia, – that is as late as the time of *Artumpara*. The latter has made use of the diskeles symbol on some issues from Telmessos, which are otherwise signed with his personal name. Moreover, a later series that carries only a diskeles symbol instead of any legend is connected by die-link to a coin with *Artumpara's* signature[52]. On these coins the diskeles has apparently undergone a change from its original function as a personal identity-marker to a badge of legitimate political power in Western Lycia, similar to the monogram ⩞ first employed by the dynast *Teththiweibi* at Phellos as his personal emblem but later on adopted by *Xeriga* and his successors as a general symbol for their claim to rule in the Xanthos valley[53]. However, *Artumpara* can hardly have been responsible for the entire diskelophoric coinage. After all it had been him, who had re-introduced the application of the issuers personal name on the coins on a large scale. This must probably be seen as an attempt to make his own coinage easier to distinguish from the one of another issuers, who had made use of the same symbol for his coinage but had deemed the utilization of his personal name either not appropriate or not necessary.

The author therefore assumes that the anonymous diskelophoric coinages have to be divided in two different groups: The presumably somewhat earlier one consists of the coins of a powerful though unnamed issuer, who – analogous to the employment of the sign ⴘ by *Waχssepddimi* and the monogram ⩞ by *Ddēñtimi* – made use of the symbol ⌀ as his personal emblem and a label for his coinage. The other one is formed by supplementary anonymous issues related to the series in the name of *Artumpara*. The border-line between the two is not always easy to be drawn. Anyway, such a division will be attempted (with due reserve) in the following list, which is otherwise once again arranged by the respective mint places:

IX.1.1.a   Anonymous, Stater, Tlos
           Head of Athena with attic helmet to r. / Two lions with raised paws seated opposite to each other in incuse circle, in field ⌀, in exergue legend T∧ʀ and in field legend FE
           Müseler VII,15 (7.90 g)   (Figure 66)

IX.1.1.b   Anonymous, Tetrobol (Third stater), Tlos
           Head of Athena with attic helmet to r. / Two lions with raised paws seated opposite to each other in incuse circle, in field legend T∧, in exergue ⌀
           Winsemann-Falghera Coll. 187 (2,73 g)

---

[52] See below Figures 102 and 130.
[53] See Müseler 2016, p. 33 sq.

IX.1.1.c   Anonymous, Diobol (Sixth stater), [Tlos]
            Head of Athena with attic helmet to r. / Two lions with raised paws seated opposite
            to each other in incuse circle, in exergue ⚬
            SNG Cop. Suppl. 499 (1,30 g)

IX.1.1.d   Anonymous, Hemiobol (Twentyfourth stater), [Tlos]
            Head of Athena with attic helmet to r. / Lion with raised paw seated to r. in incuse
            circle
            Müseler VII, 16* (0,25 g)   (Figure 67)

IX.1.1.e   Anonymous, Hemiobol (Twentyfourth stater), Tlos
            Head of Athena with attic helmet to r. / Lion with raised paw seated to l. in incuse
            circle, in field legend TΛF (sic!)
            Solidus E-Auction 15, 2017, 82 (0,35 g)

IX.1.2.   Anonymous, Hemidrachm (Quarter stater), Tlos
            Head of Athena with attic helmet to r., in field legend TΛΡ / Two lions with raised
            paws seated opposite to each other in incuse circle
            Auction Hirsch 343, 2018, 2337* (1,78 g)   (Figure 68)

IX.1.3.a   Anonymous, Obol (Twelfth stater), [Tlos]
            Head of Athena with attic helmet to l. / Two lions with raised paws seated opposite
            to each other in incuse circle, in field letter F (!!)
            Müseler VII, 14* (0,51 g)   (Figure 69)

IX.1.3.b   Anonymous, Obol (Twelfth stater), Tlos
            Head of Athena with attic helmet to l. / Two lions with raised paws seated opposite
            to each other in incuse circle, in exergue legend TΛΡ
            Klein Coll. 612 (0,54 g)

IX.2.1.a   Anonymous, Stater, Tlos
            Lion mask facing / Two lions with raised paws seated opposite to each other in incuse
            circle, in field ⚬, in field legend TΛΡ-FE
            Auction CNG 88, 2011, 387* (8,51 g)   (Figure 70)

IX.2.1.b   Anonymous, Tetrobol (Third stater), Tlos
            Lion mask facing / Two lions with raised paws seated opposite to each other in incuse
            circle, in field legend TΛ, in exergue ⚬
            SNG v. Aulock 4187 (2,77 g)

IX.2.1.c   Anonymous, Diobol (Sixth stater), Tlos
            Lion mask facing / Two lions with raised paws seated opposite to each other in incuse
            circle, in field legend TΛ and ⚬
            Müseler VII, 23 (1,30 g)

IX.2.1.d   Anonymous, Hemiobol (Twentyfourth stater), [Tlos]
            Lion mask facing / Lion with raised paw seated to r. in incuse circle
            Solidus E-Auktion 21, 207 (0,28 g)

IX.3.1.a   Anonymous, Drachm (Halfstater), Tlos
              Beardless head of dynast with Persian headdress to r./ Head of Athena with attic
              helmet to r. in incuse circle, in field ⊂O⊃ and legend T∧ͰF
              Müseler VII, 6* (4,20 g)   (Figure 71)

IX.3.1.b   Anonymous, Trihemiobol (Eighth stater), [Tlos]
              Head of Athena with attic helmet to r. / Beardless head of dynast with Persian
              headdress to r. in incuse circle, in field ⊂O⊃
              Inv. Waddington 3002 = btv1b8534818t (1,00 g)

IX.3.1.c   Anonymous, Hemiobol (Twentyfourth stater), [Tlos]
              Beardless head of dynast with Persian headdress to r. / Lion with raised paw seated
              to r. in incuse circle, in field ⊂O⊃
              Roma E-Live Auction 4, 2018, 327* (0,28 g)   (Figure 72)

IX.4.1.   Anonymous, Trihemiobol (Eighth stater), Tlos
              Lion mask facing / Head of Hermes (or of a Kabeiros) with winged pileos to l. in
              incuse circle, in field legend T∧Ͱ
              Roma E-Auction 26, 2016, 336 * (0,93 g)   (Figure 73)

IX.5.1.a   Anonymous, Trihemiobol (Eighth stater), [Tlos?]
              Rose / Head of Hermes (or of a Kabeiros) with winged pileos to r. in incuse circle, in
              field ⊂O⊃
              SNG Ashmolean 1190* (0,96 g)   (Figure 74)

IX.5.1.b   Anonymous, Hemiobol (Twentyfourth stater), [Tlos?]
              Rose / Head of Hermes (or of a Kabeiros) with winged pileos to l. in incuse circle
              Müseler VII, 55 (0,23 g)

X.1.1.a   Anonymous, Stater, Xanthos
              Head of Athena with attic helmet to r. / Head of Apollon with long hair and laurel
              wreath to r. in incuse circle, in field ⊂O⊃ and legend ͰPƗ∕V+Ͱ (sic!)
              Müseler VII, 31* (8,17 g)   (Figure 75)

X.1.1.b   Anonymous, Tetrobol (Third stater), Xanthos
              Head of Athena with attic helmet to r. / Head of Apollon with long hair and laurel
              wreath to r. in incuse circle, in field ⊂O⊃ and legend ͰPƗ
              BN btv1b8534842g* (2,51 g)   (Figure 76)

X.1.1.c   Anonymous, Trihemiobol (Eighth stater), Xanthos
              Head of Athena with attic helmet to r. / Head of Apollon with long hair and laurel
              wreath to r. in incuse circle, in field legend ͰPƗ∕V V∕∧Ͱ (sic!)
              Müseler VII, 35 (0,86 g)*   (Figure 77)

X.1.2.a   Anonymous, Stater, Xanthos
              Head of Athena with attic helmet to r. / Head of Apollon with shorter hair and laurel
              wreath to r. in incuse circle, in field ⊂O⊃ and legend ͰPƗ∕VͰ+Ͱ
              Müseler VII, 32* (8,10 g)   (Figure 78)

X.1.2.b   Anonymous, Stater, Xanthos
Head of Athena with attic helmet to r. / Head of Apollon with shorter hair and laurel wreath to r. in icuse circle, in field ꙮ and legend 𐊕𐊇𐊏𐊗𐊀[𐊐]
Auction GM 261, 2019, 352 (8,11 g)   (Figure 79)

X.1.2.c   Anonymous, Hemiobol (Twentyfourth stater), Xanthos
Head of Athena with attic helmet to r. / Head of Apollon with long hair and laurel wreath to r. in incuse circle, in field legend 𐊀𐊕𐊎 (?)
Müseler VII, 33 (0,29 g)

X.1.2.d   Anonymous, Hemiobol (Twentyfourth stater), [Xanthos]
Head of Athena with attic helmet to r. / Head of Apollon with long hair and laurel wreath to r. in incuse circle, in field ꙮ
Müseler VII, 34 (0,27 g)

X.1.3.a   Anonymous, Stater, Xanthos
Head of Athena with attic helmet to r. / Bust of Hermes (or of a Kabeiros) with winged pileos to r. in incuse circle, in field ꙮ and legend 𐊕𐊇𐊏𐊗𐊀
Müseler VII, 37* (8,22 g)   (Figure 80)

X.1.3.b   Anonymous, Trihemiobol (Eighth stater), [Xanthos]
Head of Athena with attic helmet to r. / Head of Hermes (or of a Kabeiros) with winged pileos to r. in incuse circle, in field kerykeion and ꙮ
Müseler VII, 38* (1,11 g)   (Figure 81)

X.1.3.c   Anonymous, Stater, [Xanthos]
Head of Athena with attic helmet to r. / Bust of Hermes (or of a Kabeiros) with winged pileos to l. in incuse circle, in field ꙮ
Auction Roma IX, 2015, 376 * (8,29 g)   (Figure 82)

X.1.4.a   Anonymous, Stater, Xanthos
Head of Athena with attic helmet to r. / Female head with taenia to r. in incuse circle, in field ꙮ and legend 𐊕𐊇𐊏𐊗𐊕
Babelon, Traité II/2, 392 = BN btv1b8534820w* (8,19 g)   (Figure 83)

X.1.4.b   Anonymous, Stater, Xanthos
Head of Athena with attic helmet to r. / Female head with taenia to r. in incuse circle, in field ꙮ and legend 𐊕𐊇𐊏𐊗𐊀
Babelon, Traité II/2, 393 – BN btv1b85348219* (8,63 g)

X.1.4.c   Anonymous, Diobol (Sixth stater), Xanthos
Head of Athena with attic helmet to r. / Female head with taenia to r. in incuse circle, in field ꙮ and legend 𐊀𐊕𐊎
Auction Roma XIII, 2017, 350 (1.23 g)   (Figure 84)

X.1.5.   Anonymous, Trihemiobol (Eighth stater) ?, Xanthos
Cockerell to right on round shield, in field ꙮ / Female head with taenia to r. in incuse circle, in field legend 𐊀𐊕𐊎
Auction GM 219, 2014, 252* (0,90 g)   (Figure 85)

X.1.6. Anonymous, Hemidrachme (Quarter stater), Xanthos
Head of Athena with attic helmet to l. / Bearded male head with laurel wreath (Kronos?) to r. in incuse circle, in field legend ⱣP
Müseler VII, 40* (1,95 g) *(Figure 86)*

X.2.1.a Anonymous, Stater, Xanthos
Bearded head of dynast with Persian headdress to r. / Head of Apollon with long hair and laurel wreath to r. in incuse circle, in field ⵙ and legend ⱣPƗ
CNG E-Auction 362, 2015, 182* (8,09 g) *(Figure 87)*

X.2.1.b Anonymous, Stater, [Xanthos]
Bearded head of dynast with Persian headdress to r. / Head of Apollon with long hair and laurel wreath to r. in incuse circle, in field ⵙ
Müseler VII, 42* (8,29 g) *(Figure 88)*

X.2.2. Anonymous, Hemidrachm (Quarterstater) [Xanthos?]
Bearded head of dynast with Persian headdress to r. / Head of Athena with attic helmet to r. in incuse circle, in field ⵙ
Müseler VII, 8* (2,31 g) *(Figure 89)*

X.3.1.a Anonymous, Hemidrachm (Quarterstater), Xanthos
Head of Athena with korinthian helmet to l. / Bearded Head of dynast with Persian headdress to r. in icuse circle, in field legend ⱣPƗ/VⱣ+Ⱬ
CNG E-Auction 249, 2011, 155* (1,77 g) *(Figure 90)*

X.3.1.b Anonymous, Obol (Twelfth stater), Xanthos
Head of Athena with korinthian helmet to l. / Bearded head of dynast with Persian headdress to r. in incuse circle, in field legend ⱣPƗ
Hurter 1979, p. 100, 3 (0,56 g)

XI.1.1.a Anonymous, Stater, Pinara
Eagle with spread wings standing to r., in field ⵙ and letter Γ / Female head with taenia to r. in incuse circle, in field ⵙ and legend ΓΛΛ↑FE
Müseler VII, 24* (8,49 g) *(Figure 91)*

XI.1.1.b Anonymous, Tetrobol (Third stater), Pinara
Eagle with spread wings standing to r, in field ⵙ and letter Γ / Female head with taenia to r. in incuse circle, in field ⵙ and legend ΓE
Müseler VII, 25 (2,61 g)

XI.1.1.c Anonymous, Diobol (Sixth stater), Pinara
Eagle with spread wings standing to r., in field ⵙ and letter Γ / Female head with taenia to r. in incuse circle, in field ⵙ and legend ΓE
Müseler VII, 26 (1,12 g)

XI.2.1. Anonymous, Diobol (Sixth stater), [Pinara]
Head of Athena with attic helmet to r. / Eagle with spread wings standing to l. in incuse circle, in field ⵙ
Müseler VII, 27* (1,17 g) *(Figure 92)*

XI.3.1	Anonymous, Stater, Pinara
	Head of Athena with attic helmet to r. / Female head with taenia to r. in incuse circle, in field letter V and legend ΓΕΛΛΤFE
	SNG Cop. Suppl. 488* (8,25 g) *(Figure 93)*
XI.3.2.a	Anonymous, Hemidrachm (Quarterstater), Pinara
	Head of Athena with attic helmet to r. / Head of Athena with korinthian helmet to l. in incuse circle, in field ⚭ and letters V and Γ
	Babelon, Traité II/2, 395 = BN btv1b85348234* (1,88 g) *(Figure 94)*
XI.3.2.b	Anonymous, Obol (Twelfth stater), Pinara
	Head of Athena with attic helmet to l. / Head of Athena with attic helmet to r. in incuse circle, in field letter Γ
	Auction Roma XIV, 2017, 263 (0,65 g) *(Figure 95)*
XI.3.3.	Anonymous, Obol (Twelfth stater), Pinara
	Lion mask facing / Head of Athena with attic helmet to l. in incuse circle, in field letter Γ
	Auction PN 422, 2018, 95 (0,53 g) *(Figure 96)*

XII.1.1.a	Anonymous, Stater, [Patara?]
	Head of Athena with attic helmet to r. / Bust of Athena with triple-crested attic helmet facing in incuse circle, in field ⚭
	SNG Cop. Suppl. 489 * (8,05 g) *(Figure 97)*
XII.1.1.b	Anonymous, Diobol (Sixth stater), [Patara?]
	Head of Athena with attic helmet to r. / Bust of Athena with triple-crested attic helmet facing in incuse circle
	BN = btv1b85348286*[54] (1,29 g) *(Figure 98)*
XII.1.1.c	Anonymous, Hemiobol (Twentyfourth stater), [Patara?]
	Head of Athena with attic helmet to r. / Bust of Athena with triple-crested attic helmet facing in incuse circle
	Auction PN 368, 2001, 226 (0,21 g)
XII.1.2.a	Anonymous, Trihemiobol (Eighth stater), [Patara]
	Youthful male head with short hair to r., in field uncertain symbol (diskeles?) /Bust of Athena with triple-crested attic helmet facing in incuse circle
	CNG E-Auction 374, 2016, 271* (0,96 g) *(Figure 99)*
XII.1.2.b	Anonymous, Trihemiobol (Eighth stater), Patara
	Youthful male head with short hair to r., in field ⚭ / Head of Hermes with winged petasos to r. 1in incuse circle, in field legend ΓΤΤΓ
	Auction Roma XIV, 2017, 261* (0,76 g) *(Figure 100)*

---

[54] Contrary to the description of Babelon there is no legend to be found on this coin.

XIII.1.1.	Anonymous (*Artumpara*?), Stater, [Xanthos] Head of Athena with attic helmet to r. / Head of Athena with korinthian helmet to r. in incuse circle, in field ⚬ Müseler VII, 43* (8,34 g) *(Figure 101)*
XIII.1.2.a	Anonymous (*Artumpara*?), Hemidachm (Quarterstater), Xanthos Head of Athena with attic helmet to r. / Head of Athena with attic helmet to l. in incuse circle, in field legend ҎPƗ Babelon, Traité II/2, 394 = BN btv1b8534822q* (2,16 g) *(Figure102)*
XIII.1.2.b	Anonymous (*Artumpara*?), Obol (Twelfth stater), [Xanthos] Head of Athena with attic helmet to r. / Head of Athena with attic helmet to r. in incuse circle, in field ⚬ Babelon, Traité II/2, 396 = btv 1b8534324j (0,73 g)
XIII.1.2.c	Anonymous (*Artumpara*?), Obol (Twelfth stater), [Xanthos] Head of Athena with attic helmet to l. / Head of Athena with attic helmet to l. in incuse circle Babelon, Traité II/2, 397 = BM 1869,0703.13 (0,53 g)
XIII.1.2.d	Anonymous (*Artumpara*?), Hemiobol (Twentyfourth stater), [Xanthos] Head of Athena with attic helmet to l. / Head of Athena with attic helmet to l. in incuse circle Auction PN 423, 2018, 79 (0,31 g)
XIII.1.3.a	Anonymous (*Artumpara*?), Stater, [Xanthos] Protome of lion to r. / Head of Athena with Corinthian helmet to r. in incuse circle, in field ⚬ Müseler VII, 47* (8,31 g) *(Figure 103)*
XIII.1.3.b	Anonymous (*Artumpara*?), Obol (Twelfth stater), [Xanthos] Lion mask facing / Head of Athena with Corinthian helmet to r. in incuse circle, in field ⚬ Müseler VII, 48* (0, 58 g) *(Figure 104)*
XIII.1.4.	Anonymous (*Artumpara*?), Stater, [Xanthos] Protome of lion to r. / Head of Athena with attic helmet to r. in incuse circle, in field ⚬ Müseler VII, 45* (8,21 g) *(Figure 105)*

XIV.1.1.	Anonymous (*Artumpara*?), Stater, Kadyanda Head of Athena with attic helmet to r. / Bust of Hermes with winged petasos to l. in incuse square, in field kerykeion, ⚬ and legend ѴҎΔҎFTE+↑ (sic!) Babelon, Traité II/2, 415= BN btv 1b85348412* (8,15 g) *(Figure 106)*

XV.1.1. Anonymous (*Artumpara*?), Stater, [Telmessos]

Head of Herakles to r. / Head of Athena with attic helmet to r. in incuse circle, in field ⚭

Müseler VII, 29* (7,91 g) *(Figure 107)*

The series that have been attributed to the coinage of *Artumpara* will be discussed together with the signed issues of this dynast later in this article[55].

In the present section priority must be given to an analysis of the vast majority of the diskelophoric issues and to an attempt to identify the dynast responsible for their production. The most important mint-place for coins of this type was obviously Xanthos, closely followed by Tlos. Patara, though in possession of a quite active mint of its own, took only a small part in the production of the diskelophoric series, and the mint at Pinara had generally been of lesser weight. This matches the picture that all sources convey regarding the "political geography" of the Xanthos valley during most of 5th and the 4th century BC. Among the various larger and smaller dynastic seats the city of Xanthos had by far the most powerful position, only occasionally rivaled by Tlos. The political primacy of Xanthos was reflected by the leading role of its mint: Since the time of *Kuprlli* but in particular in the second half of the 5th century under *Xeriga* and *Xerēi* the coins struck in Xanthos had set standards and often provided models for the coinages produced at other mints in the region, - at least with regard to the weight standard and the denominational system but sometimes even concerning the choice of specific motifs.

The traditional distribution of power had been temporarily disturbed by the tyranny of *Erbbina*, who had ruled the Xanthos valley primarily from his northwestern stronghold at Telmessos, but Xanthos recovered its former position soon thereafter and in the period of the diskelophoric coinage its mint had once again become the most influential production facility for coins circulating in western Lycia. A most peculiar die-link between a coin from the mint of Xanthos and one nominally coming from the mint of Pinara (Figures 79 and 93) seems to suggest that even some of the coins in the name of Pinara were in fact struck at Xanthos[56].

Tlos with its favourable location in the center of the Xanthos valley and its highly productive mint had evidently kept or regained much of its former importance and remained only second in rank to the city of Xanthos, but it was now rivaled in this position by the growing influence of Patara. The town was located at the southern shore near the mouth of the Xanthos river and was in possession of a good harbour. It also controlled the main road leading from Central Lycia into the Xanthos valley and had therefore a decisive strategical position. All the trade but also every invasion force from the East had to pass through this place first. Since the ultimate demise of *Erbbina* had apparently been brought about by forces of at least one dynast from Central Lycia, *Aruwātijesi,* the role played by Patara in the presumed military operations leading to the conquest of Telmessos by the latter must have been vital[57]. Probably as a result of these events the power of Patara had risen enormously as it is reflected by the substantial output of its mint from the

---

[55] See below p. 61 sqq.

[56] See also Konuk 2017, but besides the fact that Konuk has failed to notice the coin from Copenhagen already published a long time ago, his attempted attribution of the issue to *Xerēi* has no rational foundation whatsoever!

[57] See Müseler 2016, p. 65 and Müseler 2017a, notes 8 and 42.

beginning of the 4th century BC onwards. However, the issues from Patara remained a separate group that differed in more than one respect from the coinages produced by the other mints in the Xanthos valley.

The images set upon several diskelophoric issues provide a number of explicit clues helping to disclose the identity of the powerful ruler, who initiated the respective coinages. One of the main series from Xanthos displays a helmeted head of Athena coupled with a youthful male head, most probably a representation of Apollon (Figures 76-80). The same combination of motifs, though executed in an earlier style, had been chosen by the elder bearer of the name *Weχssere* for one of his largest series (Figure 10)[58]. Other motifs shown by the diskelophoric series from Xanthos like the youthful male head wearing a pileos (though without wings) can likewise be found on coins in the name of the elder *Weχssere* (Figures 82-83 and Figure 12), whose personal emblem had actually been the same diskeles-symbol. Not less revealing is the facing bust of Athena with the triple-crested helmet on the few diskelophoric issues from Patara (Figures 97-99). The models have rather been coins of the younger *Weχssere* from Zagaba (Figures 16-19) than the tetradrachm created by Eukleidas of Syracuse.

All those aspects together with the ubiquitous use of the diskeles-symbol strongly indicate that the majority of the series presented within this section was issued by someone closely related to the dynasts wih the name *Weχssere*. Given the presumable time frame of the coinages in question this was probably no-one else than the younger *Weχssere* himself. Apparently this dynast had expanded the territories under his control from the mountains of Central Lycia into the Xanthos valley, possibly in connection with a military campaign against the usurper *Ebbina*. Following this conquest he had replaced his original emblem, the monogram ☿ on the coins issued by him in Central Lycia, with the symbol ∞, which had been applied by his elder namesake and possible ancestor on the local coinage, – a gesture that was clearly meant to underline the legitimacy of his own rule over the former realm of the latter. The identification of the younger *Weχssere* as the issuer of the earlier diskelophoric coinages also provides a plausible explanation for the fact, that there is no diskeles to be found on nearly all anonymous Patarean series with the head of Hermes: The various series of this type had been introduced by *Weχssere* (and by *Waχssepddimi*, if this dynast has really to be seen as a separate person) as the initial coinage at the (re)opening of the mint. Therefore the type itself was later on connected with this ruler anyway by almost every user and the coins were not in need of any additional mark for the correct identification of their issuer.

Less clear is the role played by the issuers of the various minor coinages belonging more or less to the same period: *Aruwātijesi* had been in control of the mint at Telmessos immediately following the rule of *Erbbina*. But rather soon thereafter he had completely disappeared from western Lycia and remerged only later as the issuer of a coinage succeeding the last known series in the name of *Weχssere* at Zagaba. He may very well have acted as some kind of lieutenant for the more prominent ruler. The same may possibly be true for *Ddēñtimi*, whose Tloan issue with the two seated lions is die-linked to the one with the legend *Waχssepddimi* and closely related to

---

[58] The head of Athena set on the issues of the elder *Weχssere* (Issue I.1.9) is the first appearance of an image of this divinity in Lycian coinage altogether. It is closely copied from the Athenian tetradrachms of the same time and was most probably intended to demonstrate the political allegiance of the issuer at the beginning of the Peloponnesian war. His later defeat by *Xeriga* may eventually have provoked the invasion of the Athenian commander Melesandros in 428 BC: See Müseler 2016, p. 59 sqq.

Weχssere's larger series of the same type showing only the diskeles in the reverse-field[59]. But it cannot be determined, whether the person adressed by the name or the term *Waχssepddimi* had been an independent predecessor or another deputy of *Weχssere*. It is even not clear, whether the word *Waχssepddimi* denotes a separate person at all or whether it is just another form of the name *Weχssere* as previously assumed by the author[60], although the application of a separate symbol (ᛠ) on coins with this legend would rather point to a different individual behind this label. Based on the numismatic material presented here the question cannot be resolved. It will be discussed once again towards the end of this article.

The end of the diskelophoric issues of *Weχssere* and the passage to the respective series of *Artumpara* can not be clearly defined, at least as far as the coinage from Xanthos is concerned. There seem to be no coins from Telmessos that can be attributed to *Weχssere*, and the single diskelophoric series from Kadyanda is so closely related to a complementary issue bearing the signature of *Artumpara* that it can hardly be assigned to someone else. It is to be doubted that *Weχssere's* sphere of influence had included the region north of Tlos for a longer period. In fact *Artumpara* seems to have been in control of Telmessos and the upper Xanthos valley quite early, – that is still during the reign of *Weχssere* in the South. His subsequent accession at Xanthos may actually have been the result of a major conflict that even involved the dynast *Mithrapata* from Central Lycia as well. This will be demonstrated in the following sections.

Monetary footprints of *Mithrapata* in the Xanthos valley

There is a number of differring issues from Tlos and from Patara, which seem also considerably later than the series in the names of *Waχssepddimi*, *Ddēñtimi* and *Weχssere* but which neither belong to the diskelophoric coinages nor to the issues signed with the name of *Artumpara*. The respective coinage of Patara is rather large and varied, while from Tlos only a small number of fractions is known so far. In Patara the traditional coin-types with a helmeted head of Athena combined with a bust of Hermes wearing a winged petasos, though now usually accompanied by a kerykeion and often turned to the other side, have been maintained. But at Tlos completely new types, the facing head of a young man, a murex-shell and a ketos, were introduced. On some of the Patarean coins a new linear symbol (𐊗) is set beside a figurative mark in the reverse-fields, a small dolphin or a murex-shell, which appears also as the principal type on some Tloan issues. Both, murex shell and dolphin, are known as distinctive symbols from Central Lycian coins struck at the mint of Phellos under *Mithrapata* and later on under *Perikle* (Figure 34 and Figures R-S). The known coins from Tlos, however, do not carry any distinctive marks at all. Instead one of the small fractions is signed with the initials of the issuer: ΜΕΧ, which is beyond doubt the beginning of the name *Mithrapata*. All the coins presented within this section are comparatively scarce, though the overall volume of the Patarean coinage seems considerable:

XVI.1.1.a [*Mithrapata*], Trihemiobol (Eighth stater), [Tlos]
Head of Athena with attic helmet facing / Lion with raised paw seated to l. in incuse circle
Müseler VII, 18* (0,85 g) *(Figure 108)*

---

[59] On one fraction (IX.1.3.a) the diskeles is even replaced by the Lycian initial 𐊁!!
[60] Müseler 2017b.

XVI.1.1.b [*Mithrapata*], Hemiobol (Twentyfourth stater), [Tlos]
Youthful male head with short hair facing / Lion with raised paw seated to l. in incuse circle
Müseler VII, 19* (0,34 g) (Figure 109)

XVI.1.2.a [*Mithrapata*], Diobol (Sixth stater), Tlos
Lion mask facing / Youthful male bust facing in incuse circle, in field legend T𐊀𐊐F↑
Müseler VII, 93* (1,32 g) (Figure 110)

XVI.1.2.b *Mithrapata*, Obol (Twelfth stater], [Tlos]
Murex shell / Youthful male bust facing in incuse circle, in field legend ME𐊴
Müseler VII, 94* (0,51 g) (Figure 111)

XVI.1.2.c [*Mithrapata*], Hemiobol (Twentyfourth stater), [Tlos]
Murex shell / Ketos to r. in incuse circle
Müseler VII, 95* (0, 35 g) (Figure 112)

XVI.1.2.d [*Mithrapata*], Bronze, [Tlos]
Lion mask facing / Murex shell
Müseler VII, 96* (0, 83 g) (Figure 113)

XVI.2.1. [*Mithrapata?*], Stater, Patara
Head of Athena with attic helmet to r. / Bust of Hermes with winged petasos to r. in incuse square, in field kerykeion and legend 𐊓𐊗𐊗𐊀𐊓𐊀𐊅𐊊𐊜
Babelon, Traité II/2, 416 = BM BNK,G.672* (8,38 g)

XVI.2.2.a [*Mithrapata?*], Stater, Patara
Head of Athena with attic helmet to r. / Head of Hermes with winged petasos to l. in incuse circle, in field kerykeion and legend 𐊓𐊗𐊗𐊀𐊓𐊀𐊅𐊊𐊜
Müseler VII, 52* (8,56 g) (Figure 114)

XVI.2.2.b [*Mithrapata?*], Tetrobol (Third stater), Patara
Head of Hermes with winged petasos to r. / Head of Hermes with winged petasos to l. in incuse circle, in filed legend 𐊓𐊗𐊗𐊀𐊓𐊀𐊅𐊊𐊜
Auction GM 249, 2017, 318* (2,44 g) (Figure 115)

XVI.2.3. [*Mithrapata?*], Stater, Patara
Head of Athena with attic helmet to r. / Head of Hermes with winged petasos to l. in incuse circle, in field dolphin, linear symbol ? and legend 𐊓𐊗𐊗𐊀
Auction Lanz 164, 2017,96* (8,24 g) (Figure 116)

XVI.2.4.a [*Mithrapata?*], Stater, [Patara]
Head of Athena with attic helmet to r. / Head of Hermes with winged petasos to l. in incuse circle, in field kerykeion, murex shell, and linear symbol ?
Müseler VII, 54* (8,71 g) (Figure 117)

XVI.2.4.b   [*Mithrapata?*], Stater, [Patara]
             Head of Athena with attic helmet to r. / Head of Hermes with winged petasos to r. in incuse circle, in field kerykeion, murex shell and linear symbol ?
             Hurter 1979, p. 106, 33 (8,33 g)

The relationship between the Patarean and the Tloan group can hardly be denied. Both prove the presence of the dynast *Mithrapata* in the Xanthos valley, presumably at the time around the passage from the reign of *Weχssere* to the one of *Artumpara*. But the difference in size between the large and varied series from Patara and the few fractional issues from Tlos is striking. Moreover, there are once again neither any coins from Xanthos or Pinara nor are there corresponding issues from mints further to the North that can be directly associated with this coinage[61]. Evidently *Mithrapata* did not succeed in seizing control of the entire Lycian West, neither in the political center of the lower Xanthos valley nor in the Northwest of the peninsula. Even his grip on Tlos does not appear to have been very firm or of long duration, since during his presence the activity of the once so important Tloan mint decreased considerably and may even have come to an end altogether. But Patara, the harbour near the mouth of the Xanthos river, where the bulk of the issues presented in this section come from, had apparently become *Mithrapata's* principal stronghold in the West. The same strategical situation is reflected by the corresponding coinage of *Artumpara*: There is no issue in his name, which can be attributed to the mint of Patara, while a substantial coin production for him is attested at Xanthos and Telmessos as well as in Kadyanda and also in Tlos. The status of the latter mint during this time is not entirely clear, since it had struck coins in the name of both dynasts and the sequence of the respective issues cannot be established with any certainty: *Artumpara* might even have reconquered Tlos at a certain point, while *Mithrapata* seems to have kept Patara as a bridgehead over the whole period. The place has possibly remained an important vantage point for invasions from Central Lycia into the Xanthos valley apart from Tymnessos, since its harbour provided a base for naval support. The only coin of *Perikle* known so far that can perhaps be assigned to a mint in Western Lycia shows a facing head of Hermes wearing a winged petasos combined with the well-known frontal-portrait of the dynast on the other side (Figure T).

Enigmatic coinages from the upper course and the headwaters of the Xanthos river

Apart from the various series struck in the lower part and in the center of the valley there is a small coinage showing the name of the settlement Araxa at the upper course of the Xanthos river, which obviously belongs to the same period as the varous series discussed previously, – that is to the early 4th century BC. Moreover, there is an issue from the mint at Kadyanda in the highlands between the Xanthos valley and the coastal plain of Telmessos, which has been discovered only recently and whose type forms a link to an up to now rather mysterious coin bearing the toponym of Patara. A relation to Patara is also evident on an otherwise isolated issue with the toponym of Tlos. Neither the series from Araxa nor the other coins carry any personal name. There is also no monogram or linear symbol, which could be associated with any dynast otherwise known[62].

---

[61] However, for indirect connections with the various series from Araxa and a particular issue from Kadyanda see below.

[62] The only symbol employed here is the monogram on issue XVII.1.3., for which no explanation is available.

Because of the strange connection between the coin from Kadyanda and a likewise unique Patarean issue the strict arrangement of the different coinages by mint is for once abolished here:

XVII.1.1.a Anonymous, Stater, Araxa
Lion mask facing / Female bust with radiate diadem facing in incuse circle, in field legend ͰPͰXXE+↑
SNG Cop. Suppl. 490* (8,38 g) (Figure 118)

XVII.1.1.b Anonymous, Diobol (Twelfth stater), Araxa
Lion mask facing / Female bust with radiate diadem facing in incuse circle, in field legend ͰPͰXE[+]↑ (sic!)
Müseler VII, 57* (1,24 g) (Figure 119)

XVII.1.1.c Anonymous, Hemiobol (Twentyfourth stater), Araxa
Lion mask facing / Fish swimming to l. in incuse circle, in field legend ͰPͰXE.
Müseler VII, 58* (0,29 g) (Figure 120)

XVII.1.2. Anonymous, Obol (Twelfth stater), [Araxa]
Beardless head of dynast with Persian headdress to l. / Female bust with radiate diadem (or kalathos) facing in incuse circle
SNG Cop. Suppl. 502* (0,61 g) (Figure 121)

XVII.1.3. Anonymous, Trihemiobol (Eighth stater), [Araxa]
Head of Athena with attic helmet to l. / Female head with radiate diadem to l. in incuse circle, in field monogram formed of the Lycian letters T, ∧ and P or T, Ѵ and P.
Müseler VII, 56* (0, 89 g) (Figure 122)

XVIII.1.1. Anonymous, Stater, Kadyanda
Head of Athena with attic helmet adorned with a running griffon to r., in the field legend ѴͰ∆ͰF↓TE+↑ / Head of Hermes with winged petasos to l. in incuse circle, in field legend Ѵ↑∆↑F↓TE (sic!)
Auction Roma IX, 2015, 369* (8,43 g) (Figure 123)

XVIII.2.1. Anonymous, Drachm (Halfstater), Patara (?)
Head of Athena with attic helmet adorned with a running griffon to r. / Triskeles in incuse circle, in field legend ͰTTͰ+[...?]
Müseler VII, 53* (3,71 g) (Figure 124)

XIX.1.1. Anonymous, Stater, Tlos
Head of Athena with attic helmet to r. / Head of Hermes with winged petasos to r. in incuse circle, in field ⚭ , kerykeion and legend T∧ͰFE
SNG v. Aulock 4194 = BM 1979.0101.749* (8,15 g) (Figure 125)

There is no precursor for the issues from Araxa among the western Lycian coinages of the 5th century BC. The series from this mint all belong to the early 4th century BC and seem to have been struck during a very limited time span. The shortlived activity of the mint may actually have been the direct result of a major military conflict in the Northwest of Lycia. Whoever was not in control of the important stronghold and mint in the northwestern coastal plain might have found it necessary to install a supplementary mint in the upper Xanthos-valley in order to create a logistic base independent from the harbour of Telmessos to take care of the monetary supply for his troops. This would rather point to *Mithrapata*, whose foothold in the center and in the northern part of the valley seems to have been rather precarious, since *Artumpara*, presumably his main rival, was able to threaten his position simultaneously from Xanthos in the South and Telmessos in the Northwest.

On the other hand Kadyanda had been the residence and the mint of a dynast named *Hñtruma*, whose reign was probably contemporaneous with the one of *Ddenewele* (Figures U-V)[63]. Later on the mint had been used by *Artumpara*, but apparently just for a small number of issues[64]. The newly discovered coin from this place (Figure 123) with its curious rendering of the toponym on both obverse and reverse but in two divergent spellings, notably differs from all the other series known from Kadyanda. But the most unusual head of Athena wearing a helmet adorned with a small running griffon corresponds to the obverse-type of another coin, which displays the same, otherwise unknown head of Athena combined with a large triskeles and the toponym of Patara on its reverse (Figure 124). No date can be established yet for those two remarkable coins, but their connection is evident. This makes their attribution to the Western coinage of *Mithrapata* an attractive possibility. But once again the material basis for such a hypothesis is far too narrow and we must wait for the discovery of other specimens or of related issues that may carry more information.

The unique coin of Patarean type but with the toponym of Tlos from the von Aulock collection (Figure 125) seems to be likewise the result of a typological transfer: The images clearly derive from the issues of the harbour town at the southern shore, which apparently had become the main base of *Mithrapata* in the West as demonstrated in the previous section. The type may simply have been "borrowed" from Patara for the first coins struck at Tlos after its conquest through *Mithrapata*. The types with the youthful male head *en face* may have been developed for the Tloan coinage of the new ruler only thereafter. But also in this case more evidence is needed.

The coinages of *Artumpara*

The following catalogue is indebted to Novella Vismara's listing of the coinage attributable to *Artumpara* published some years ago[65]. However, issues that have only become known in the meantime are added and others, where the connection with the coinage of *Artumpara* is dubious, as well as his exile-issue from Side have been left out. Instead references to anonymous diskelophoric series that may be associated to coinages in the name of *Artumpara* have been inserted as well.

---

[63] The only known hoard-context for coins of *Hñtruma* that allows an approximate dating is the so-called "Tissaphernes-Fund": See Hurter 1979, p. 105, 29-30.

[64] See above p. 57 referring to Issues XIV.1.1. and XX.2.1.

[65] Vismara 2014.

64   *Wilhelm MÜSELER*

XX.1.1.a   *Artumpara*, Stater, Telmessos
            Head of Athena with attic helmet to r. / Head of Herakles to r. in incuse square, in field ⸰O⸰ and legend ⴲPTOXⲒⲎPⲎ TⲦⴷⲦBⲦ+
            SNG Cop. Suppl. 458 (8,40 g)   *(Figure 126)*

XX.1.1.b   *Artumpara*, Stater, [Telmessos]
            Head of Athena with attic helmet to r. / Head of Herakles to r. in incuse square, in field legend ⴲPTOXⲒⲎPⲎ+Ⲧ
            Babelon, Traité II/2, 388 (8,21 g)

XX.1.1.c   [*Artumpara*], Diobol (Sixth stater), [Telmessos]
            Head of Athena with attic helmet to r. / Head of Herakles to r. in incuse square, in field ⸰O⸰
            Müseler VII, 30* (1,49 g)   *(Figure 127)*

* Here the anonymous issue XV.1.1 (Figure 107) must probably be added.

XX.2,1.   *Artumpara*, Stater, [Kadyanda]
            Head of Athena with attic helmet to r. / Head of Hermes with winged petasos to l. in incuse square, in field kerykeion and legend ⴲPTTOXⲒⲎP (sic!)
            BMC Suppl. 111 A = BM 1897,0104.297* (8,15 g)   *(Figure 128)*

* Here the anonymous issue XIV.1.1. (Figure 106) must probably be added.

XX.3,1.   *Artumpara*, Stater, Xanthos
            Head of Athena with attic helmet to l. / Athena with spear and shield holding a small owl on her arm seated to l. on rock in incuse circle, in field letter Ⲓ and legend ⴲPTOXⲒⲎPⲎ (sic!)
            Müseler VIII, 28* (8,07 g)   *(Figure 129)*

XX.3.2.   *Artumpara*, Stater, [Xanthos]
            Protome of lion to r. / Head of Athena with attic helmet to r. in incuse circle, in field legend ⴲPTOXⲒⲎPⲎ
            SNG Cop. Suppl. 457* (8,31 g)   *(Figure 130)*

* Here the anonymous issue XIII.1.4. (Figure 105) must definitely be added (die-link!).
  Probable further additions are the issues XIII.1.1-3 (Figures 101-104).

XX.3.3.a   *Artumpara*, Stater, [Xanthos?]
            Head of Athena with attic helmet to r. / Bearded head of dynast with Persian headdress to r. in incuse circle, in field legend ⴲPTOXⲒⲎPⲎ
            Müseler VIII, 30* (8.03 g)   *(Figure 131)*

XX.3.3.b   *Artumpara*, Stater, [Xanthos?]
            Head of Athena with attic helmet to r. / Bearded head of dynast with Persian headdress to r. in incuse circle, in field legend ⴲPTOXⲒⲎPⲎ
            Müseler VIII, 29 (8,15 g)   *(Figure 132)*

XX.3.4.   *Artumpara*, Stater, [Xanthos?]
Head of Athena with attic helmet to l. / Bearded head of dynast with Persian headdress to r. in incuse circle, in field legend ͰPTOͰϜͰPϞ (sic!)
Weber Coll. 7233 (7,89 g)

* Here Vismara wishes to add the anonymous issue X.3.1. (Figure 90)[66]; the attribution is, however, somewhat uncertain.

XX.4.1.   *Artumpara*, Stater, Tlos
Bearded head of dynast with Persian headdress to r., in field legend T∧ͰFE / Head of Athena with attic helmet in incuse circle, in field legend ͰPTOXͰͰPͰ
Müseler VIII, 31* (8,11 g)   (Figure 133)

Coins in the name of *Artumpara* seem to have been struck at Telmessos rather soon after the coinage with the monogram of *Ddẽñtimi* (Figure 62). The anonymous diskelophoric issue from this mint (Figure 107) with the head of Athena moved to the reverse is also with regard to its style and fabric rather in line with Xanthian and Tloan coins of *Artumpara* and probably represents nothing else than a somewhat later series of this dynast from Telmessos. Since the coinage of *Artumpara* from this place apparently comprises series of different periods, it must have been produced over quite a long time. Taken together with his (however temporary) utilization of the mint at Kadyanda this suggests that the Lycian Northwest had been the original base of *Artumpara*.

His accession at Xanthos and at Tlos and the beginning of the coin-production in his name at these places would have to be considered as subsequent. The adoption of the diskeles, originally empoyed by *Weχssere* to legitimize his claim to rule in Xanthos and Tlos, through *Artumpara* does not necessarily point to a regular and peaceful succession; it may very well be that the latter has taken the lower Xanthos valley from his predecesssor by force. Such a course of events appears to be confirmed by *Artumpara's* explicit choice of models from earlier issues of the Xanthian dynasty and in particular from types introduced by *Xeriga* after his capture of Xanthos from the elder *Weχssere* (Figures W-X) for his own local coinage (Figures 130 and 101). Apparently, there was an allusion to a similar political situation intended here.

One coin in the name of *Artumpara* (Figure 130) has made use of the same obverse-die as one belonging to the anonymous diskelophoric issues (Figure 104). This links at least the respective series with the lion-protome and the head of Athena but possibly also the ones with the head of the goddess on obverse and reverse to the Xanthian coinage of this dynast. The overall output of the mint under the rule of *Artumpara* must therefore be considered as substantial. The dynast seems to have defended his rule at Xanthos and at Telmessos until the very end of his reign. Only the date of his control over Tlos that was occupied by *Mithrapata* for some time remains an open question. However, *Artumpara* has evidently outlived both *Weχssere* and *Mithrapata*. He was only ousted from Western Lycia by *Perikle* some time around the end of the seventies[67]. Therefore the transition from the rule of *Weχssere* to the one of *Artumpara* and the presumed quarrels must have taken place well before that time.

---

[66] Vismara 2014, p. 216.

[67] See for example Schürr 2012.

In place of a conclusion

> *"Ourselves, dismayed we stand, concerned in vain*
> *The curtain's drawn, all questions but remain"*
> Berthold Brecht, Der gute Mensch von Sezuan (1943), transl. by Tobias Schwarz

The assemblage of all the available numismatic evidence attempted here has brought to light quite a large number of details that had not been visible before and provided a more accurate view of the political circumstances and the interaction of the various agents in western Lycia between the late 5th and the early 4th century BC. However, a definite solution for a number of questions presented at the beginning of this article concerning the problem of the number of persons named *Weχssere* or the members of an alleged "*Waχssa*-Clan" is not in sight. But a few remarks may still be derived from the study of the numismatic testimonies compiled above.

Frank Kolbs most imaginative interpretation that stylizes *Weχssere* as a true Methusalem among the Lycian dynasts is hardly credible. Following this reconstruction of events the man, who had isssued the first series in his name still during or immediately after the final years of the reign of *Kuprlli* in the West of Lycia, would have had disappeared thereafter for a very long time, – actually the larger part of his alleged long life. Only near the turn from the 5th to the 4th century BC the same man would have resumed to have coins struck in his name at Zagaba in Central Lycia and continued his minting activity after his presumed return to the Xanthos valley deep into the two following decades. This would make *Weχssere* either a mere boy at the beginning or a man of downright biblical age towards the end of his career as a money issuer[68]. Although not completely impossible the weakest point of this hypothesis (as already mentioned above) is its failure to explain, what happened to the dynast during the remarkably long intermission implied thereby. Moreover, it overemphasizes typological parallels but widely ignores the manifest differences between the coinages in question. From a numismatic perspective there is virtually nothing that justifies such a construction against the much more sensible interpretation of the evidence adopted hitherto, – that is the assumption of two separate individuals of the same name but belonging to two different periods. There is also no visible need created by circumstantial evidence for stretching the substance of the numismatic record this far. This hypothesis can therefore be safely discarded as a probably incorrect though amusing proposal.

But the in all respects directly opposite hypothesis brought forward by Koray Konuk and Diether Schürr is also not really conclusive, since it actually causes more problems than it tries to solve. The difficulty is not the alleged existence of homonymous agents belonging to different generations; this is in fact quite a usual phenomenon in Lycian history. But in the present case the assumption of individuals with identical names acting at two otherwise completely separate occasions thirty or even forty years apart from each other implies a nearly exact repetition of events in different historical situations. At both times we would have somebody called *Weχssere* playing the principal part, assisted or opposed by someone with the name *Waχssepddimi* and with

---

[68] Even if an earlier dating of the "Tissaphernes stater" to the time between 411 and 407 BC as recently proposed by John O. Hyland (cfr. Hyland NN) is accepted, the underlying sequence of events remains more or less the same. If, as a consequence of Hyland's chronological model, the tyranny of *Erbbina* would have to be placed rather in the last years of the 5th than in the first decade of the 4th century BC, this would only result in a difference between 5 and 10 years. In any case the impact on the supposed life-span of Frank Kolb's *Weχssere* would be minimal.

the addition of a separate person called *Waχssebllimi* in the earlier and *Uχssepddimi* in the later case. This is definitely a little bit too much of a coincidence, even if we assume that all participants have belonged to one large family-clan. If this would be an account transmitted by the classical literary tradition, one would be tempted to think of an underlying narrative pattern applied by a well meaning interpreter in order to render the reported events easier comparable and thus more "exemplary" in the minds of the recipients. But we are dealing here with numismatic and epigraphic evidence, – that is with much more direct and less corruptible sources. Therefore the utmost caution is called for in the interpretation of the documents at hand, especially when these seem to suggest a duplication of historical events.

That *Waχssebllimi* was somebody else than the elder *Weχssere* seems in fact possible. He might even have been a relative of some sort as proposed by both Konuk and Schürr. But whether the *Waχssepddimi* mentioned on the Xanthos-Stele has really been a third person remains questionable. Also *Ddēñtimi* has probably to be seen as a separate individual against the earlier proposal of the author. Like *Aruwātijesi* he may have acted as a deputy for the younger *Weχssere* after this dynast had established himself as the surperior ruler at Xanthos.

But in the cases of *Weχssere*, *Waχssepddimi* and/or *Uχssepddimi* the hypothesis originally brought forward by Şükrü Özüdoğru and later on endorsed by the present author with different arguments cannot be dismissed that easily: The common point of both authors was the assertion that the three appellations were just variants or composite forms of the same personal name alternately used by no-one else than the younger *Weχssere* in different situations. Admittedly this causes a number of difficulties from a linguistic or onomastic point of view[69]. Moreover, it would imply that the younger *Weχssere* had changed his personal emblem twice in the course of his campaign and the subsequent consolidation of his rule in the West, – once from the original monogram ⚭ to the linear symbol (or just a simplified form of the same monogram) ⚭ and then again to the ⚭ used by his supposed ancestor. But this is well possible and after all not more complicated than the assumption of a multitude of dynasts with the same or with very similar personal names either cooperating or rather jostling for supremacy in the Xanthos valley at two separate occasions[70]. At Tlos and especially at Patara, where the issue with the name *Waχssepddimi* is even linked to the one with the name *Weχssere* through a shared obverse-die, the close relationship between the respective series is evident and the borderline between them seems floating. Before this background the idea of different name-forms referring to one and the same individual still appears the most plausible solution.

Based on the evidence presently available these problems cannot be resolved with ultimate certainty. We have to rely on the discovery of new material possibly carrying more information to answer the main question posed at the beginning of this essay. What can, however, be demonstrated is the predominant role played by the younger *Weχssere* as the principal issuer of

---

[69] Müseler 2018 a, p. 615 has attempted to explain the name *Waχssepddimi* as a composition of the word *waχssa*-and the title *pddēnehmmi* attested on the trilingual inscription found at the Letoon, which is translated there with the Greek term ἄρχων. As quoted by Schürr 2018, p. 98 Heiner Eichner has suggested a similar connection of the name *Waχssebllimi* to the word *urebillaha* from Kalinka, TL 11, which Schürr 2012, p. 22 considers likewise as a title.

[70] After the count of Schürr 2018 not less than seven different members of this alleged clan would thus be attested.

the diskelophoric coinages in the West of Lycia at the beginning of the 4th century BC, as well as the subsequent rivalry between *Mithrapata* and *Artumpara* until the realms of both contenders got finally annexed by *Perikle*[71].

Comparative Plate:

A Kuprlli, Stater. Lion advancing to right, head reverted / Triskeles in incuse square, in field Lycian legend KOΓPΛΛE
   Auction CNG 102, 2016, 544   (8,66 g)

B Kuprlli, Stater. Protome of winged lion to l. / Triskeles in incuse square, in field Lycian legend KOΓ
   SNG Cop. Suppl. 406   (8,42 g)

C Kuprlli, Stater. Mule kneeling to l., head reverted, in the field ↻ / Triskeles in incuse square, in field legend KOΓ
   Müseler IV, 36   (8,29 g)

D Athens, Tetradrachm around 450 BC. Head of Athena with wreathed attic helmet to r. / Owl standing to r., head facing, in field olive-branch, crescent and legend AΘE
   Auction PN 422, 2018, 48   (17,14 g)

E Xerẽi, Stater, Telmessos. Head of Athena with attic helmet to r., in field letter Ѡ / Head of Herakles with lion-skin to r. in incuse square, in field legend Ѡ↑PϒE T↑Λ↑B↑ɈE+↑
   Müseler VI, 64   (8,55 g)

F [Ddenewele or Erbbina], Stater, Telmessos. Head of Athena with attic helmet to r. / Head of Herakles with lion-skin to r. in incuse square, in field legend T↑Λ↑B↑ɈE+↑
   Müseler VI, 90   (8,39 g)

G Xerẽi, Hemidrachm (Quarterstater), Tlos. Head of Athena with attic helmet to r. / Monogram ⚝ in incuse square, in field legend Ѡ↑PϒE TΛↃFE
   Babelon, Traitè II/2, 358 = btv 1b85347921   (1,83 g)

H Ddenewele, Stater, [Tlos]. Bearded head of dynast with Persian headdress to r. / Monogram ⚝ in incuse square.
   Babelon, Traitè II/2, 412 = MzK Berlin 18200165 (8,28 g)

I Syracuse, Tetradrachm 413/399 BC (?), signed by the artist Eukleidas. Head of Athena with triple-crested helmet in ¾-profile, around 4 dolphins, in field legend [ΣΥΡ]ΑΚΟΣΙΩΝ, above the visor signature ΕΥΚΛΕΙΔΑ[Σ] / Female charioteer holding torch in quadriga to l. , above flying Nike with wreath to r. , in exergue ear of barley.
   Auction NAC 59, 2011, 532   (16,99 g)

J Trbbenimi, Stater, Zagaba. Lion mask facing / Triskeles in incuse circle, in center letter T, in field fish and legend IϺ
   Müseler VIII, 19   (9,86 g)

---

[71] Apparently *Perikle* took over the mints at Phellos and Zagaba from *Mithrapata* before driving *Artumpara* out of the Xanthos valley: Cfr. Müseler 2016, VIII, 42-44 and 46.

K   Xeriga, Stater, Tymnessos. Head of Athena with attic helmet to l. / Bearded male head with thracian helmet to r. in incuse square, in field legend 𐊇𐊗𐊓𐊁𐊊 [𐊗]𐊋𐊎𐊁𐊏𐊗𐊫𐊁
SNG Cop. Suppl. 441   (8,48 g)

L   Xeriga, Stater, [Tymnessos?]. Head of Athena with attic helmet to l. / Bearded male head with korinthian helmet to l., in field legend 𐊇𐊗𐊓𐊁𐊊
SNG Cop. Suppl. 442   (8,12 g)

M   Erbbina, Stater, [Telmessos]. Head of Athena with attic helmet to l. / Herakles with lion-skin, club and bow running to l. in incuse square, in field legend 𐊗𐊓𐊂𐊂𐊁𐊏𐊊
Müseler VI, 83   (8,25 g)

N   Erbbina, Stater, [Telmessos]. Head of Athena with attic helmet to r., in field monogram ⤋ / Head of Herakles with lion-skin to r. in incuse circle, in field club and legend 𐊗𐊓𐊂𐊂𐊁𐊏𐊊
Müseler VI, 86   (8,41 g)

O   Xinaχa, Stater, uncertain mint (Zagaba?). Lion with raised paw, turned to front, seated l. / Lion with raised paw, head turned to front, seated r. in incuse square, in field legend [𐊇]𐊁𐊏𐊊𐊇 .....]
Müseler IV, 71   (8,72 g)

P   Xerēi, Stater, [Pinara]. Head of Athena with attic helmet to r. / Bearded head of dynast with diademed Persian headdress to r. in incuse circle, in field legend 𐊇𐊗𐊓𐊉𐊁
Müseler VI, 57   (8,32 g)

Q   Ddenewele, Stater, [Xanthos]. Head of Athena with attic helmet to r. / Bearded head of dynast with diademed Persian headdress to l. in incuse square, in field legend △△𐊉𐊏𐊗𐊁𐊗𐊏𐊗
Winsemann-Falghera Coll. 178   (8,31 g)

R   Perikle, Stater, Phellos. Bust of Dynast facing, in field dolphin / Naked warrior with korinthian helmet, sword and round shield advancing to r., in field ⌇, murex-shell and legend 𐊓𐊗𐊓𐊁𐊋𐊏𐊗 𐊅𐊗𐊋𐊊𐊗[𐊉𐊉]
Müseler VIII, 35   (9,89 g)

S   Perikle, Tetrobol (Third stater), uncertain mint (Phellos?). Lion mask facing / Triskeles in incuse square, in field dolphin, youthful male head with laurel-wreath facing and legend 𐊓𐊗𐊓[𐊁]𐊋𐊏𐊗
Müseler VIII, 43   (3,03 g)

T   Perikle, Obol (Twelfth stater), uncertain mint (Patara?). Head of Hermes with petasos facing / Head of dynast facing
Müseler VIII, 41   (0,58 g)

U   Hñtruma, Stater, Kadyanda. Head of Athena with attic helmet to l. / Hermes with petasos, holding kerykeion and winged pileos in hands and seated on rock in incuse circle, in field linear symbol ⚹ and legend 𐊋𐊗𐊗𐊒𐊎𐊊 𐊇𐊊△𐊉𐊅𐊏𐊗𐊁𐊋𐊗
Müseler VI, 99   (8,44 g)

V   Hñtruma, Stater, [Kadyanda]. Head of Athena with attic helmet to l. / Head of Hermes with winged petasos to l. in incuse square, in field linear symbol ⚵ and legend +ƗPO/\/\Ͱ
    Müseler VI, 101   (8,35 g)

W   Xeriga, Stater, Xanthos. Head of Athena with attic helmet to r. / Athena with spear and round shield holding small owl and seated on rock in incuse square, in field legend ⱽ↑PEϞͰ ͰPƗ/\Ͱ+↑
    Müseler V, 50   (8,17 g)

X   Xeriga, Hemidrachm (Quarterstater), Xanthos. Head of Athena with attic helmet to r. / Head of Athena with attic helmet to r. in incuse square, in field legend ⱽ↑PEϞͰ ͰPƗ/\Ͱ
    Auction PN 422, 2018, 89   (2,10 g)

Auctioneers

CNG	Classical Numismatic Group, Lancaster PA & London
GM	Giessener Münzhandlung Gorny & Mosch, München
Gemini	Harlan J. Berk Ltd., Chicago IL
Goldberg	Ira & Larry Goldberg Coins and Collectibles, Los Angeles CA
Hess / Divo	Hess / Divo AG, Zürich
Hirsch	Gerhard Hirsch Nachfolger, München
Lanz	Numismatik Lanz, München
Leu Winterthur	Leu Numismatik AG, Winterthur
NAC	Numismatica Ars Classica, London & Zürich
Naumann	Numismatik Naumann, Wien
PN	Dr. Busso Peus Nachfolger, Frankfurt/M.
Roma	Roma Numismatics Ltd., London
Solidus	Solidus Numismatik, München

Photo-Copyrights

Archiv Harlan J. Berk Ltd.: 15

Archiv Classical Numismatic Group (Photos: T. Markel): 28, 29, 30, 38, 53, 70, 87, 90, 99, A

Archiv Ira & Larry Goldberg (Photo: L. Eagleson): 31

Archiv Giessener Münzhandlung Gorny & Mosch: 79, 85, 115

Archiv Hess / Divo AG: 11

Archiv Gerhard Hirsch Nachfolger (Photo: H. Baier): 68

Archiv Numismatik Lanz: 116

Archiv Leu Numismatik AG: 21

Archiv Dr. Busso Peus Nachfolger / Wilhelm Müseler: 2, 4, 6, 7, 9, 10, 13, 16, 19, 22, 23, 25, 26, 27, 32, 33, 34, 35, 36, 37, 39, 43, 46, 52, 56, 60, 61, 64, 66, 67, 69, 71, 75, 77, 78, 80, 81, 86, 88, 89, 91, 92, 96, 101, 103, 104, 105, 107, 108, 109, 110, 111, 112, 113, 114, 117, 119, 120, 122, 124, 127, 129, 131, 132, 133; C, D, E, F, J, M, N, O, P, R, S, T, U, V, W, X

Archiv Roma Numismatics: 5, 8, 41, 49, 55, 65, 73, 82, 84, 95, 100, 123

Ashmolean Museum Oxford, Heberden Coin Room (Photos: V. Heuchert): 18, 24, 74

Bibliothéque Nationale de France: 14, 44, 47, 48, 58, 59, 76, 83, 94, 98, 102, 106, G

The trustees of the British Museum: 12, 51, 61, 62, 63, 125, 128

Dansk Nationalmuseet København (Photos: H. Andersen / V. Bizoev): 1, 40, 45, 50, 54, 57, 93, 97, 118, 121, 126, 130; B, K, L

Heinrich-Heine-Universität Düsseldorf, Münzkabinett (Photos: J. Wienand / K. Martin): 3, 17, Q

Kansallis Museo Helsinki (Photo: J. Oravisjärvi): 42

Münzkabinett Staatliche Museen Berlin (Photo L. J. Lübke): H

Bibliography

Babelon, Traité II/2	E. Babelon, Traité des monnaies Grecques et Romaines, 2eme Partie, tome II, Paris 1910.
BMC	G. F. Hill, A catalogue of the Greek coins in the British Museum 18: Catalogue of the Greek coins from Lycia, Pamphylia and Pisidia, London 1897.
Carruba 1989	O. Carruba, Appendice onomastica, in: Vismara 1989, 111-115.
Hoff 2017	C. Hoff, Identität und Politik – Kollektive kulturelle und politische Identität der Lykier bis zur Mitte des 4. Jahrhunderts v. Chr., Wiesbaden 2017.
Hurter 1979	S. Hurter, Der Tissaphernes Fund, in: O. Mørkholm – N. Waggoner (eds.), Greek Numismatics and Archeology - Essays presented to Margaret Thompson, Wetteren 1979, 97-108.
Hyland NN	J. O. Hyland, Between Amorges and Tissaphernes: Lycia and Persia in the Xanthos Stele, Paper presented at the Conference "Beyond all borders: Anatolia in the 1st Millennium BC", Ascona 2018 (forthcoming).
Inv. Waddington	E. Babelon, Inventaire sommaire de la collection Waddington, Paris 1898.
Jenkins 1959	G. K. Jenkins, Recent acquisitions of Greek coins by the British Museum, NC 1959, 23-45.
Kalinka, TL	E. Kalinka, Tituli Asiae Minoris I: Tituli Lyciae, Wien 1901.
Klein Coll.	D. Klein, Sammlung von griechischen Kleinsilbermünzen und Bronzen, Milano 1999.

Kolb 2018	F. Kolb, Lykien. Geschichte einer antiken Landschaft, Darmstadt 2018.
Kolb – Tietz 2001	F. Kolb – W. Tietz, Zagaba: Münzprägung und politische Geographie in Zentrallykien, Chiron 31, 2001, 347-416.
Konuk 2016	K. Konuk, On some new Lycian coin types, Philia 2, 2016, 20-17.
Konuk 2017	K. Konuk, A new Lycian coin type of Pinara, Philia 3, 2017, 97-98.
Lotz 2017	H. Lotz, Xerẽi, der Errichter des Inschriftenpfeilers von Xanthos, Kadmos 2017, 139-172.
McClean 1929	S. W. Grose, Catalogue of the McClean Collection of Greek coins in the Fitzwilliam Museum III, Cambridge 1929.
Mørkholm – Zahle 1976	O. Mørkholm – J. Zahle, The coinages of the Lycian dynasts Kheriga, Kherẽi and Erbbina, Acta Archaeologica XLVII, 1976, 47-90.
Müseler 2016	W. Müseler, Lykische Münzen in europäischen Privatsammlungen, Istanbul 2016.
Müseler 2017 a	W. Müseler, Ddẽnewele. Der vergessene Dynast vom Xanthostal und das Nereiden-Monument, JNG 67, 2017, 13-30.
Müseler 2017 b	W. Müseler, The place of the two Wekhssere in the history of Lycia, in: M. Caccamo-Caltabiano – M. L. Puglisi (eds.), XV. International Congress of Numismatics, Taormina 2015, Proceedings, Roma-Messina 2017, 608-612.
Müseler 2018	W. Müseler, Beyond the Xanthos valley. Rulers and mints in Eastern and Central Lycia at the time of the "dynasty of Xanthos", Gephyra 15, 2018, 11-28.
Müseler – Schürr 2018	W. Müseler – D. Schürr, Zur Chronologie in den Inschriften auf dem Agora-Pfeiler von Xanthos (TL 44) und den betroffenen Dynasten, Klio 100/2, 2018, 381-406.
Müseler – Schürr 2019	W. Müseler – D. Schürr, Rezension zu C. Hoff, Identität und Politik. Kollektive kulturelle und politische Identität der Lykier bis zur Mitte des 4. Jahrhunderts v. Chr., Gnomon 91/1, 2019, 39-46.
Olçay – Mørkholm 1971	N. Olçay – O. Mørkholm, The coin hoard from Podalia, NC 1971, 1-29.
Özüdoğru 2007	Ş. Özüdoğru, Pttara and the dynast Wakhssepddimi (Wekhssere II), Adalya X, 2007, 31-48.
Rizzo 1946	G. E. Rizzo, Monete greche della Sicilia, Roma 1946.
Sasseville NN	D. Sasseville, Die Deutung von Lykisch terñ als Konjunktion und ihre Konsequenz für die Kriegsgeschichte Lykiens, in: Current research on Lycian: International Workshop of the Digital Philological-Etymological Dictionary of the minor ancient Anatolian Corpus Languages, München 16-17 February 2017, Proceedings (forthcoming).

Schürr 2012	D. Schürr, Der lykische Dynast Artumbara und seine Anhänger, Klio 94, 2012, 18-44.
Schürr 2018	D. Schürr, Weχssere und so weiter: Vom zögerlichen Auftauchen einer lykischen Dynastie, Philia 4. 2018, 96-102.
SNG Ashmolean	Sylloge Nummorum Graecorum Britain, Ashmolean Museum Oxford, Part XI, Asia Minor, Caria to Commagene (except Cyprus), publ. by R. Ashston & S. Ireland, Oxford 2013.
SNG v. Aulock	Sylloge Nummorum Graecorum Deutschland, Die Sammlung Hans von Aulock, Heft 10, Lykien, bearb. v. O. Mørkholm, Berlin 1964.
SNG Cop. Suppl.	Sylloge Nummorum Graecorum Danmark, The Royal Collection of Coins and Medals, Danish National Museum, Supplement Acquisitions 1942-1996, publ. by S. Schultz & J. Zahle, Copenhagen 2002.
SNG Keckman II	Sylloge Nummorum Graecorum Finland, The Erkki Keckman Collection in the Skopbank Helsinki, Part II, Asia Minor except Caria, publ. by R. Ashton, Helsinki 1999.
Tudeer 1913	L. Tudeer, Die Tetradrachmenprägung von Syrakus in der Periode der signierenden Künstler, Berlin 1913.
Vismara 1989	N. Vismara, Monetazione arcaica della Lycia I: Il dinasta Wekhssere I, Milano 1989.
Vismara 2014	N. Vismara, Status quaestionis su Artumpara dal punto di vista della numismatica, in: A. Lemaire (ed.), Phéniciens d'orient et d'occident – Mélanges Josette Elayi, Paris 2014, 205-224.
Wahl 2017	M. P. Wahl, Motivwanderungen. Überlegungen zu Übernahme und Verbreitung von Münzmotiven der Westgriechen in der Klassik, Diss., Wien 2017.
Weber Coll.	L. Forrer, The Weber Collection – Greek coins vol. III, London 1925.
Winsemann-Falghera Coll.	N. Vismara, Monetazione arcaica della Lycia II: La collezione Winsemann-Falghera, Milano 1989.
Zahle 1982	J. Zahle, Persian satraps and Lycian dynasts: The evidence of the diadems, in: T. Hackens – R. Weiller (eds.), Proceedings of the 9th International Congress of Numismatics, Bern 1979, Löwen 1982, 101-112.
Zahle 1998	J. Zahle, Den lykiske by Tuminehi, in: Nordisk Numismatisk Unions Medlemsblad 1998, 98-104.

Batı Lykia'da Ksanthos Hanedanlığı'nın karşıtları ve ardılları:
Weχssere'ye ilişkin soruları yeniden ele alış

Özet

Koray Konuk, Diether Schürr ve Frank Kolb tarafından yayımlanan birkaç yeni çalışmaya cevap olarak yazar, Erbbina'nın hâkimiyetinin bitişi ile Perikle'nin yükselişi arasında Ksanthos Vadisi'nin tarihini yeniden kurgulamak ve bu dönemdeki temel politik figürlerin silsilesini oluşturmak için İ. Ö. 4. yy'dan itibaren Orta ve Batı Likya'daki mevcut nümismatik kanıtları bir araya getirmektedir. Yazar Weχssere adında ikiden az (ve aynı zamanda fazla) yönetici olmadığı şeklindeki geleneksel hipotezi savunmaktadır. Bu yöneticilerden ilki, olasılıkla ondan Ksanthos kentini almış olan Kheriga'nın bir çağdaşıydı. Esasen yaşlı adaşının bir oğlu ya da akrabası olması muhtemel olan ikincisi Orta Likya'dan Ksanthos Vadisi'ni işgal etmiş ve İ. Ö. 4. yüzyılın başında tiran Erbbina'nın hâkimiyetine son vermişti. Aynı şekilde belgelenen figürler Aruwãtijesi ve Ddẽñtimi olasılıkla ortak hükümdar ya da onların vekilleriyken, yazar Waχssebllimi, Waχssepddimi ve Uχssepddimi'nin muhtemelen sırasıyla yaşlı ve genç Weχssere tarafından kullanılan birleşik isim formlarından başka bir şey olarak görülemeyeceği düşüncesini taşımaktadır. Ayrıca yazar, nümismatik malzemenin de işaret ettiği gibi, her ikisinin de Perikle tarafından bozguna uğratılmasından önce Mithrapata ve Artumpara arasındaki bir çatışma olabileceği sonucuna ulaşmaktadır.

Anahtar Sözcükler: Lykia, dinastik sikke basımı, yönetici sırası, Weχssere, Ksanthos.

Opponents and successors of the Xanthian dynasty in Western Lycia:
The Weχssere questions reconsidered

Abstract

In response to several recent studies published by Koray Konuk, Diether Schürr and Frank Kolb the author assembles the extant numismatic evidence of the early 4th century BC from Central and Western Lycia in order to reconstruct the history of the Xanthos-Valley between the end of the rule of Erbbina and the rise of Perikle and to establish the sequence of the principal political agents during that period. He is defending the traditional hypothesis that there were not less (but also not more) than two rulers with the name Weχssere. The first one had been a contemporary of Xeriga, who probably had taken the city of Xanthos from him. The second one, who might actually have been a son or a relative of his elder namesake, invaded the Xanthos-Valley from Central-Lycia bringing the reign of the tyrant Erbbina to an end at the beginning of the 4th century BC. While the likewise attested agents Aruwãtijesi and Ddẽñtimi were probably co-rulers or lieutenants, the author holds that Waχssebllimi, Waχssepddimi and Uχssepddimi are possibly to be seen as nothing else than composite name-forms used by the elder and the younger Weχssere respectively. Furthermore, the author comes to the conclusion that the numismatic material might point to a conflict between Mithrapata and Artumpara in Western Lycia before both were finally defeated by Perikle.

Keywords: Lycia, dynastic coinage, sequence of rulership, Weχssere, Xanthos.

Main Series

1

2

3

4

5

6

7

8

9

10

11

12

13

14

15

16

17

18

19

20

21

22

23

24

25

26

27

28

29 30 31

32 33

34 35 36

37 38 39 40

41 42 43

44   45   46

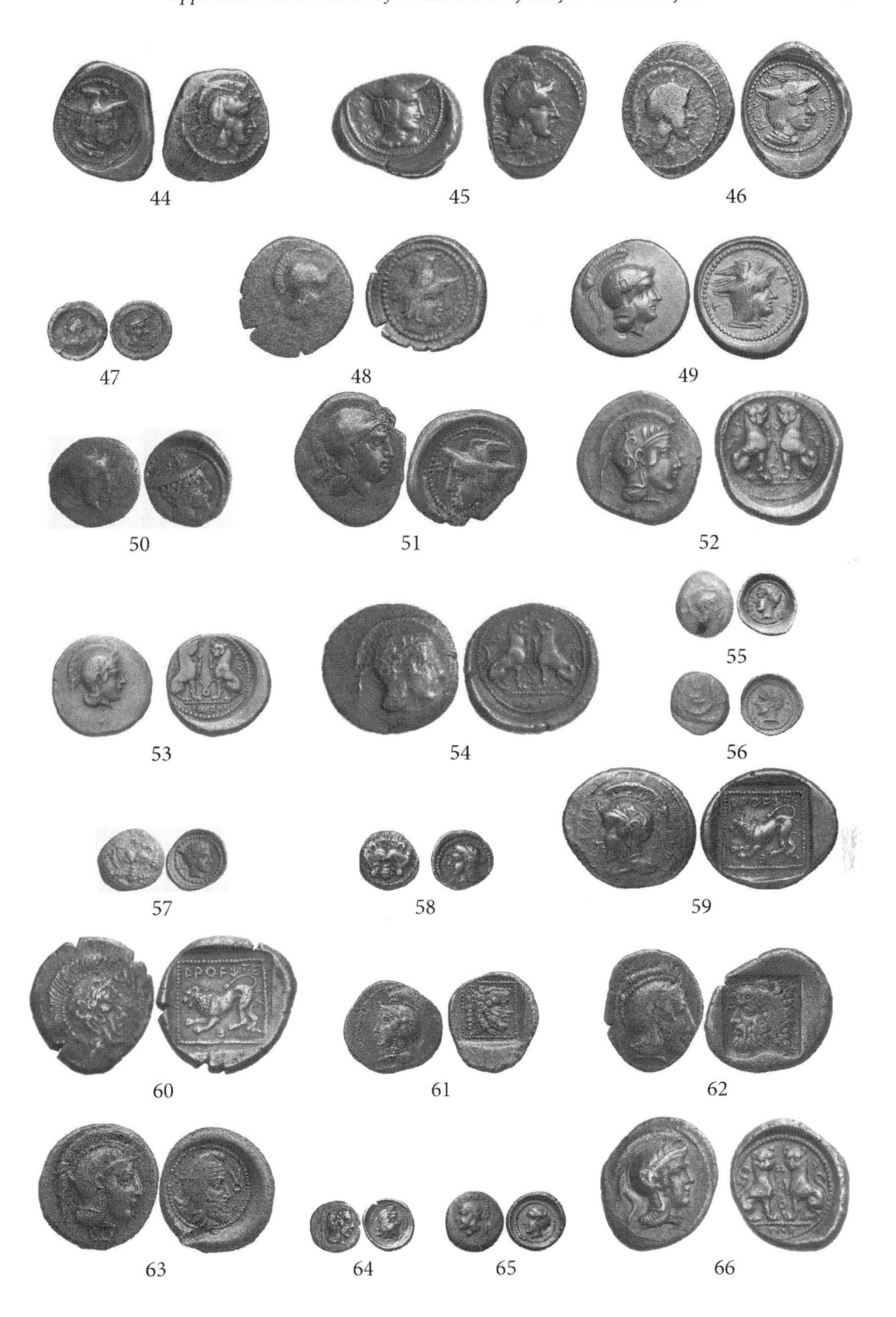

47   48   49

50   51   52

            55
53   54
            56

57   58   59

60   61   62

63   64   65   66

67   68   69   70

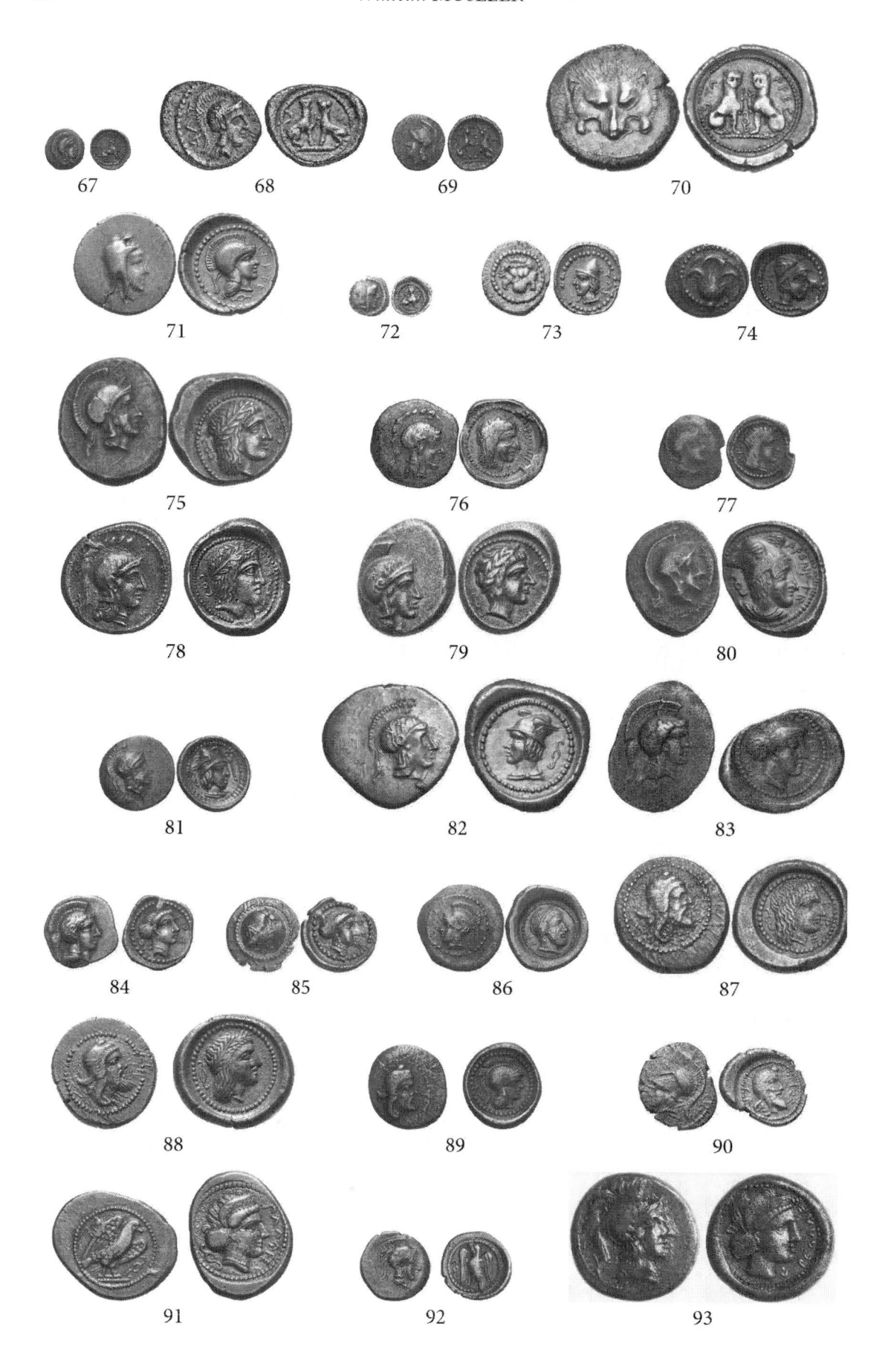

71   72   73   74

75   76   77

78   79   80

81   82   83

84   85   86   87

88   89   90

91   92   93

94 95 96 97

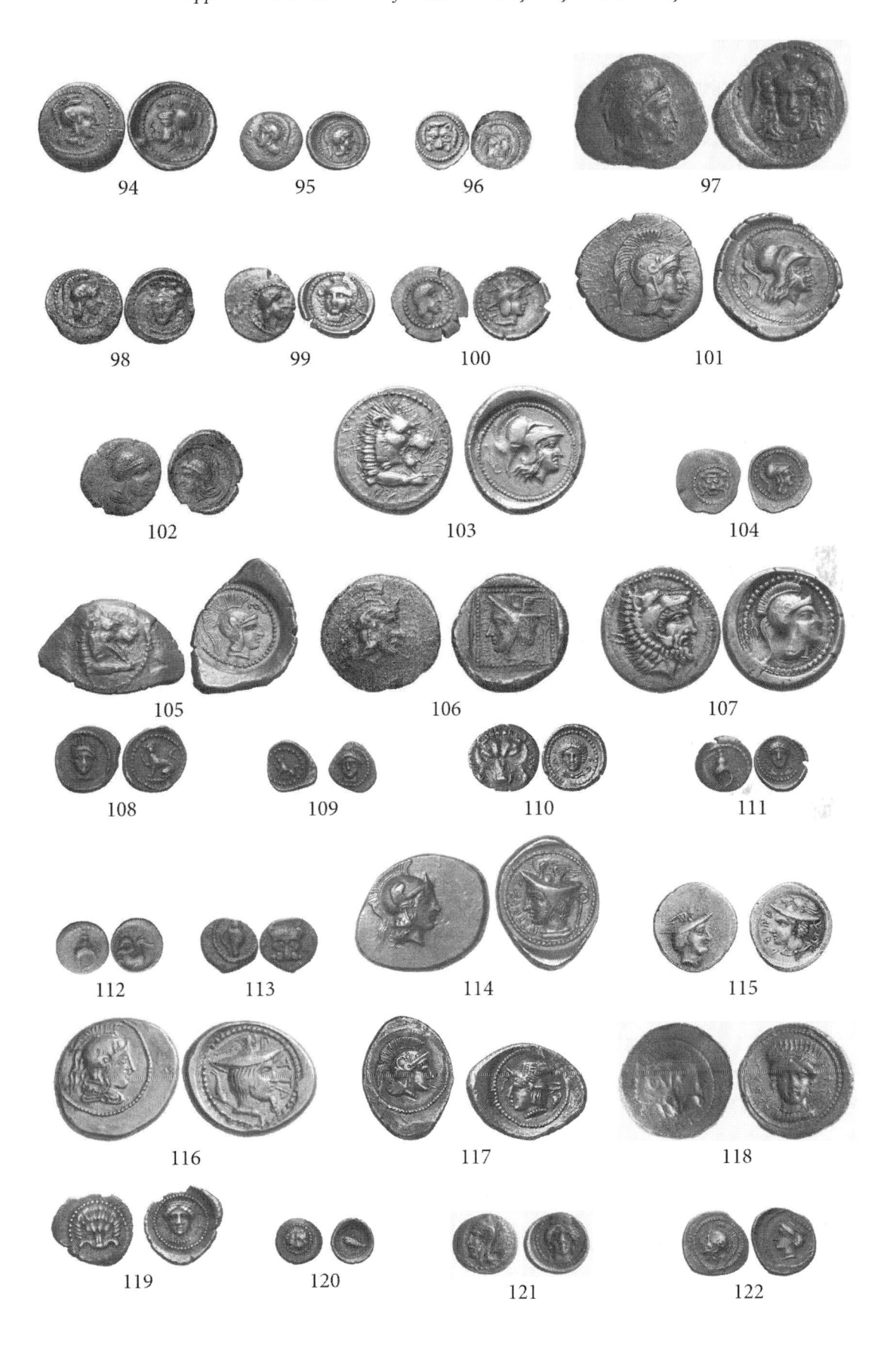

98 99 100 101

102 103 104

105 106 107

108 109 110 111

112 113 114 115

116 117 118

119 120 121 122

123

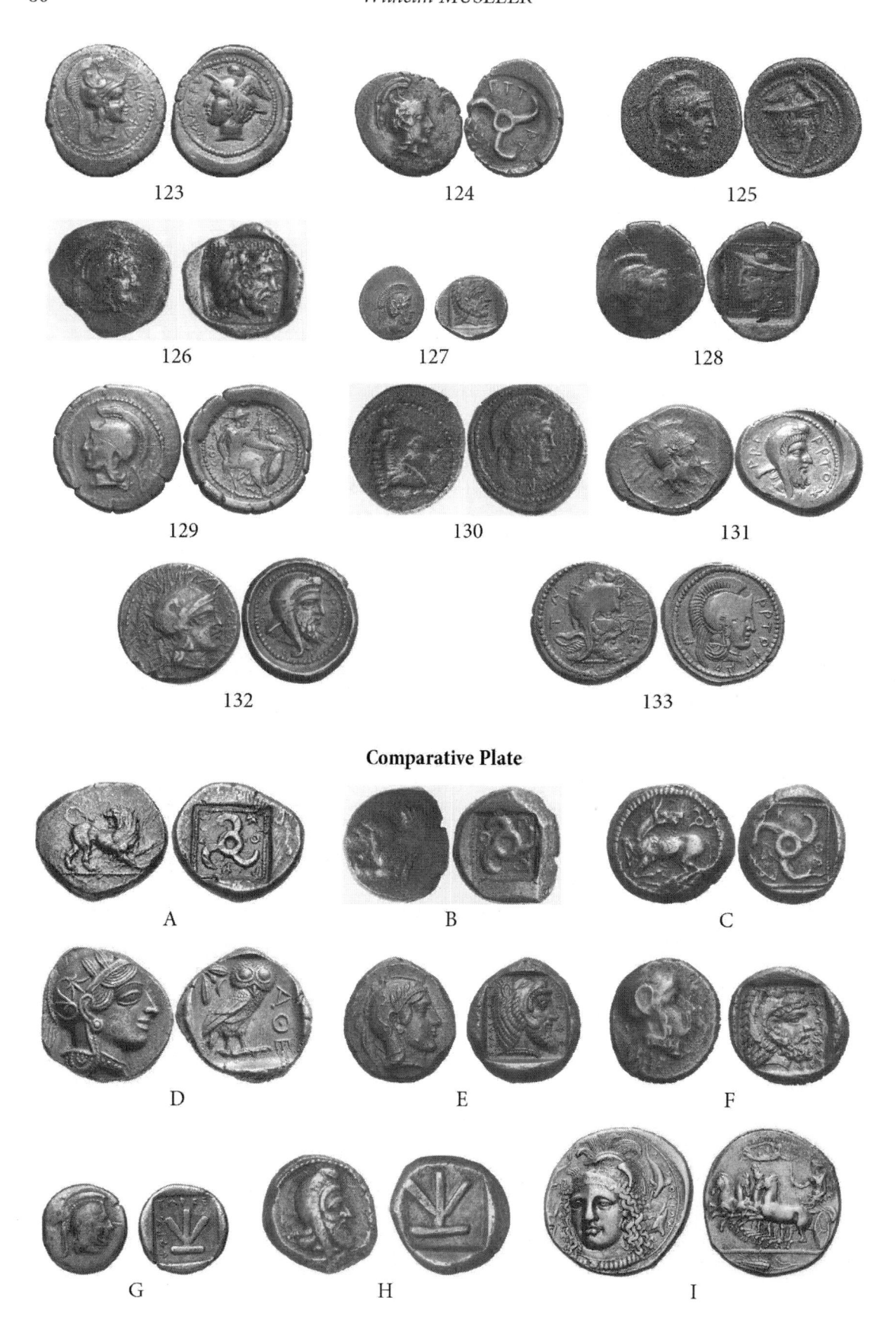

124

125

126

127

128

129

130

131

132

133

Comparative Plate

A

B

C

D

E

F

G

H

I

Opponents and successors of the Xanthian dynasty in Western Lycia

J   K   L

M   N   O

P   Q

R   S   T

U   V   W

X

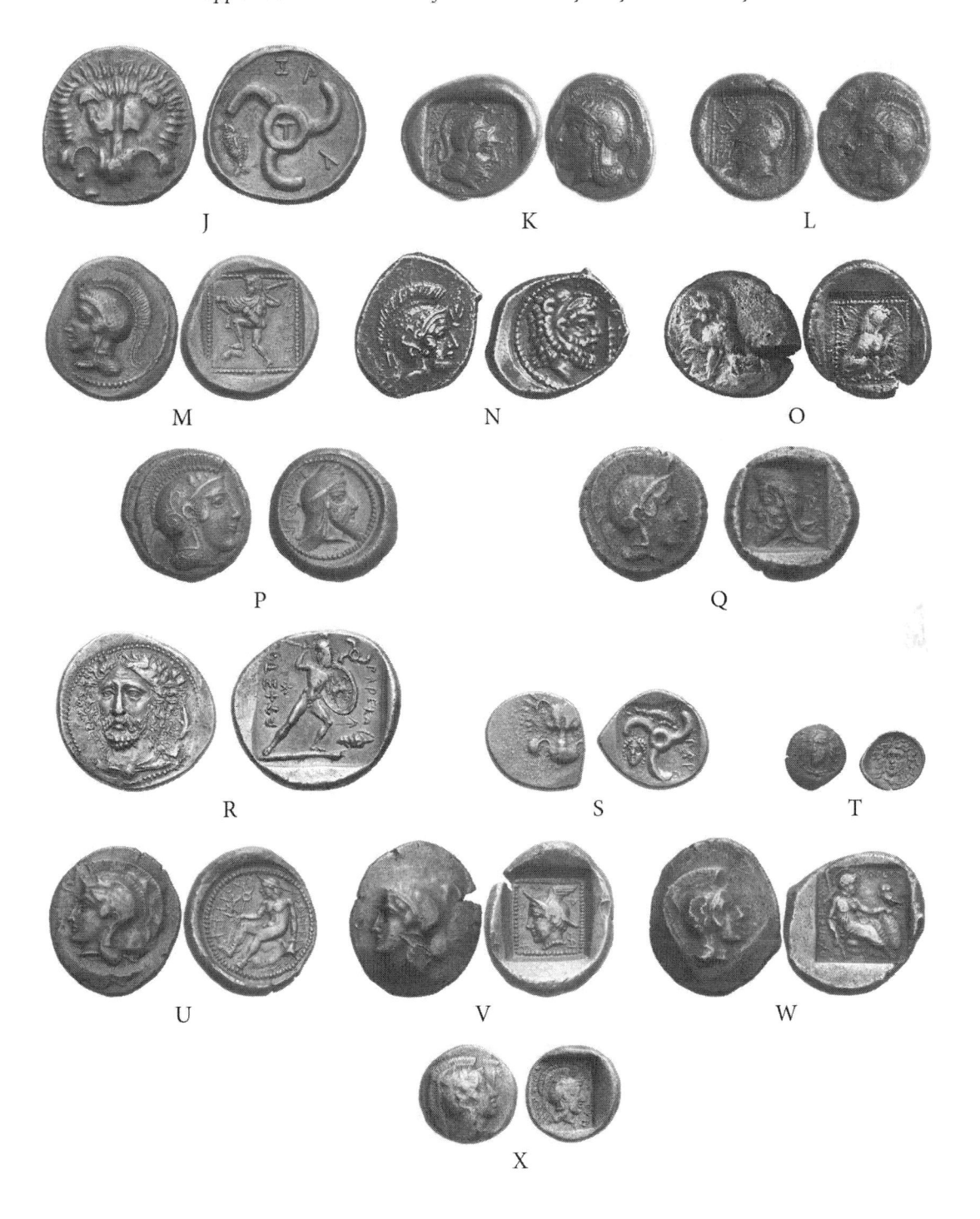

Χρυσᾶ τῶν Ἡλιάδων τὰ δάκρυα
Golden strömen die Tränen der Heliaden
oder Die mithrische Interpretation des Phaëton-Mythos

Jürgen BORCHHARDT*

Der Phaëton-Mythos in der Cella des Mausoleums von Belevi um 300 v. Chr.

In der Bewunderung für die akribisch durchgeführte Nachgrabung im Mausoleum von Belevi mit der umfassenden Würdigung der Bauskulptur[1] sowie in der überzeugenden Beweisführung für Antigonos Monophthalmos als Bauherrn irritiert die durch epigraphische Evidenz nachweisbare, unzweifelhaft bezeugte Existenz des Phaëton-Mythos im Darstellungsprogramm.[2] Warum bezichtigte sich der Bauherr der Hybris? Oder sollte er von späteren Nutzern der Anmaßung bezichtigt werden?[3]

Zwar wissen wir nicht, mit welcher Absicht Aischylos und Euripides[4] den Mythos bearbeitet haben, in der westlichen Rezeption des Phaëton-Mythos, die im „Ovid moralisé en Prose" im 15. Jh. und im Humanismus gipfelt, gilt er aber als Leitmotiv für die Anmaßung, Vermessenheit, den Frevel, den Hochmut; die Hybris des Sohnes dem Vater gegenüber wird gegeißelt.[5] Was könnte Antigonos I. Monophthalmos bewogen haben, an seinem Grabmal einen Zyklus des Phaëton anbringen zu lassen?[6] Sollte er als Verfechter der Reichseinheit in den Diadochenkämpfen als Satrap von Phrygien, Herr über Lykien und Pamphylien, Gründer von Antigoneia am Orontes (306 v. Chr.), König in einem Reich vom Hellespont bis zum Bosporus als Achtzigjähriger vor seinem Tod[7] eingesehen haben, dass er den siegreichen Sonnenwagen Alexanders des

---

* Prof. Dr. Jürgen Borchhardt, Rennweg 89/1/5, 1030 Wien, Österreich (bo.bi@aon.at).

Χρυσᾶ τῶν Ἡλιάδων τὰ δάκρυα: Philostr. imag. I 11.1.

[1] Ruggendorfer 2016a.

[2] Ruggendorfer 2016a, 114ff., Taf. 20.1-2.

[3] Für Anregungen, Literatur und Fotovorlagen sowie Diskussionen habe ich zu danken Brigitte Borchhardt-Birbaumer, Katharina Hasitzka und Peter Ruggendorfer. Für die Textbetreuung danke ich Michaela Golubits, für das Layout der Tafeln Diana Gačić.

[4] Euripides beginnt sein Spätwerk, das Drama *Phaeton* im Palast des Merops im Osten. Der Aithioperkönig will seinen Sohn mit einer Göttin (vermutlich Aphrodite) verheiraten. Phaeton weigert sich. Die Mutter klärt ihn über seinen göttlichen Vater auf und gemahnt ihn, den Vater, an ein Versprechen zu erinnern, das Helios ihr, der Geliebten, einst gegeben habe, einen Wunsch zu erfüllen. Der Sturz erfolgt im Palast des Merops. Klymene versucht, den Leichnam ihres Sohnes im Schatzhaus zu verbergen. Lesky 1963, 433 analysiert die problematische Rekonstruktion des *Phaeton*: „*schwieriger zu fragen ist, wie dies den Anlaß für ihn gab, seine Abstammung von Helios zu erkunden und die verhängnisvolle Fahrt mit dem Sonnenwagen zu verlangen*".

[5] Lücke 2002, 480; Hunger 1988, 412ff. mit Abb. 90.

[6] Nach der Analyse der Bauforschung soll der Phaëton-Mythos in den Nischen der Ostwand im Obergeschoß zur Darstellung gekommen sein: Ruggendorfer 2016b, 117.

[7] Volkmann 1979, 380.

Großen nicht lenken konnte? Eine solche Selbstreflexion passt nicht zu seinem Charakter. Und Ovid konnte er nicht gelesen haben:[8] Die Hesperischen Naiaden im Westen der Welt gewährten dem Frevler ein Tumulus-Grab und stellten eine Stele auf: HIC · SITUS · EST · PHAETON · CURRUS · AURIGA · PATERNI · QUEM · SI · NON · TENUIT · MAGNIS · TAMEN · EXCIDIT · AUSIS. [Hier ruht Phaeton, der Lenker des väterlichen Wagens; zwar konnte er ihn nicht halten, doch fiel er als einer, der Großes gewagt.].[9]

Ikonographisch hat Peter Ruggendorfer die einzelnen Elemente des Ausstattungsprogramms überzeugend in ihre griechischen und orientalischen Teile seziert, die kultischen Ehren des Grabherrn genauso gewürdigt wie die militärischen Leistungen, die Bedeutung des Banquetts und höfische Konventionen.[10] Im hermeneutischen Ansatz wird eine „*Wahrung der menschlichen und göttlichen Sphäre*" attestiert, der bildlichen Wiedergabe des Phaëton-Mythos aber eine „*grundsätzliche Unvereinbarkeit der beiden Ebenen*" bescheinigt. Dennoch wirkt der Schlusssatz erkenntnis-theoretisch resignierend: „*Inwieweit die Anwendung des Phaeton-Mythos durch eine reflektierte Sicht des Stifters auf die eigene Person motiviert war, läßt sich nicht entscheiden*".[11]

I. These: Das Mausoleum von Belevi wurde als Grabstätte der Antigoniden konzipiert

Die anschließenden Überlegungen versuchen die Existenz des Phaeton-Mythos durch folgende Hypothesen zu erklären: I] Das Mausoleum von Belevi wurde nicht von Antigonos I. Monophthalmos allein errichtet, sondern von Vater und Sohn Demetrios Poliorketes konzipiert als Mausoleum der Antigoniden. II] Der Phaëton-Mythos wurde nicht in seiner westlichen Version objektiviert, sondern in einer östlichen Variante ausgestaltet, die man als die mithrische bezeichnen kann. III] Eine Rekonstruktion des Zyklus im Obergeschoß kann vorgeschlagen werden.

Zur Verifizierung können eine Reihe von Argumenten notiert werden:

I 1: Als Stifter können Antigonos Monophthalmos und sein Sohn Demetrios Poliorketes verstanden werden. Sowie das Maussolleion von Halikarnassos nicht für Maussollos als Heroon geplant war[12], sondern als dynastische Grabstätte der Hekatomniden in Karien[13], so konzipier-

---

[8] Ov. met. 2, 327. Nach dem von Knaack 1909, 2180 rekonstruierten Mythos existierte eine auf Hesiod zurückgehende Version, in der Phaëton ohne Wissen des Vaters aber mit Unterstützung der Schwestern den Sonnenwagen bestieg.

[9] Ovid dichtet offensichtlich nicht ohne Empathie.

[10] Ruggendorfer 2016b, 117ff.

[11] Ruggendorfer 2016b, 125. Hans Taueber, der sich nur ungern von der alten Zuschreibung des Mausoleums an Lysimachos zu lösen scheint, hat versucht, durch ein zeitliches Nacheinander der Bauherren die Idee der Hybris zu retten: „*So wäre es theoretisch vorstellbar, Lysimachos in einem zu seinen Lebzeiten weitgehend fertiggestellten Grabmal in der Nähe seiner Residenz Ephesos beizusetzen, sich aber gleichzeitig durch die Anbringung eines (ursprünglich nicht vorgesehenen) Phaeton-Bildes von dem fragwürdigen Charakter und den rücksichtslosen Taten des Verstorbenen zu distanzieren*". Taueber 2016, 320.

[12] Im Gegensatz zur kanonischen Interpretation vgl. z.B. Hoepfner 1997, 48: „*König Maussollos hatte um die Mitte des 4. Jh. v. Chr. die damals berühmtesten Bildhauer und Architekten an seinen Hof geholt, damit sie ihm ein Grabmal errichteten, größer und prächtiger als alles bisher Gebaute und doch ein Ausweis griechischer Kultur*". Der Bau wird als Vorbild spektakulärer Bauwunder gerühmt: „*Sockel und Säulengeschoß, stufenartiger Dachabschluß, reiche Skulpturenausstattung mit Friesen, Figuren zwischen und hinter*

ten Antigonos I. Monophthalmos und sein Sohn Demetrios Poliorketes auf dem Höhepunkt ihrer Macht ein Mausoleum für die Dynastie der Antigoniden.[14] Antigonos gründet 315/314 v. Chr. den Nesiotenbund und garantiert im Erlaß von Tyros die „Freiheit der Griechen". 311 v. Chr. wird er von der Stadt Skepsis vergöttlicht und erhält Temenos, Altar und Kultbild.[15] 307 v. Chr. wurden Vater und Sohn als Eroberer von Athen als Theoi Soteres verehrt.[16] 306 v. Chr., nach dem Seesieg bei Salamis auf Zypern, wurde Demetrios Mitregent seines Vaters und erhielt den Königstitel.[17] 304 v. Chr. wurde er in Athen als Theos Kataibates mit einem Tempel geehrt.[18] Baubeginn des Mausoleums von Belevi könnte vor dem Tode des Vaters bei Ipsos 301 v. Chr. gewesen sein.[19]

I 2: Zur Theorie der Bestattung in der unteren Grabkammer des Mausoleums von Belevi

Die in der Südseite eingeschnittene, tonnengewölbte Grabkammer mit 7,40 m Länge und 4,50 m Breite[20] verfügte über eine Vorkammer (Taf. 1.1, 2.1), die nur Sinn hat, wenn sie funktional auch so genutzt wurde. In der Marmorauskleidung verringerten sich die Maße zu 6,806 m Länge x 3,403 m Breite. Die Stärke der südlichen Außenwand, „die identisch ist mit der Quaderverkleidung des Untergeschosses" wird mit 1,184 m angegeben. Der Bauforscher schloß daraus: *„Sie schloß die Grabkammer nach außen vollständig ab, so daß für den Ununterrichteten nichts an dieser Stelle ihr Vorhandensein verriet. Aber es waren doch Einrichtungen vorhanden, welche auch nach Vollendung des Baues einen Zutritt zur Grabkammer ermöglichten. In der untersten Lage der Wandquader fehlt nämlich ein Stein. Es bleibt eine Öffnung von 1,05 m Breite, 0,794 m Höhe und 1,309 m Tiefe. Ihre untere Fläche ist 16% nach außen geneigt, mit einer kleinen Randschwelle nach innen zu versehen und trägt ein eingegrabenes großes A von 0,15 m Höhe zur besonderen Kennzeichnung."* Für Theuer bestand kein Zweifel, dass der Baubefund durch die „Einrichtung der herausnehmbaren Stufen" eine Öffnung der Grabkammer ermöglichte. *„Es war also auch nach Vollendung des Baues noch möglich, das Grab jederzeit wieder zu öffnen bzw. zu schließen".*[21] In der jüngsten Bearbeitung der Architektur ist das Problem der Schließung der

---

den Säulen und am Dachrand finden sich 70 Jahre später am Grabmal des Königs Lysimachos nahe bei Ephesos.".

[13] Borchhardt 2004, 45ff.

[14] Habicht 1970, 48 rühmt *„die innige Verbundenheit von Vater und Sohn im Kult der Sotere"* als *„einmaliges Phänomen".*

[15] Habicht 1970, 42ff.

[16] Diod. 19,80ff.; 20,45; Plut. Dem. 16; Habicht 1970, 44 diskutiert ausführlich die Vergöttlichung von Vater und Sohn mit Kult und Altar, neuen Phylen Antigonis und Demetrias. Goldene Standbilder der Befreier von der Tyrannis des Demetrios von Phaleron im Wagen wurden neben den Statuen der Tyrannenmörder auf der Agora in Athen aufgestellt, ihre Portraits wurden in den Peplos der Athena eingewoben.

[17] Diod. 20,49ff.; Plut. Dem. 16. Auf Delos wurden Antigoneia und Demetrieia mit Altar, Opfern und Agonen zu Ehren der beiden Könige eingerichtet: Habicht 1970, 58ff.

[18] Habicht 1970, 48f.

[19] Anregungen mögen während der Belagerung von Rhodos 305/04 v. Chr. gekommen sein.

[20] Theuer *in* Praschniker – Theuer 1979, 55ff.

[21] Theuer *in* Praschniker – Theuer 1979, 118. Reinhard Heinz geht 2005, 99ff. auf die Frage der Funktion und Zugänglichkeit der Vorkammer nicht ein.

Grabkammer in der Südaußenwand ausführlich diskutiert worden.[22] Auf Grund der technischen Zurichtung der einzelnen Blöcke vermutet Heinz, dass die Schließung der ersten originalen Bauphase des Mausoleums zugeschrieben werden kann. *„Eine zerstörungsfreie, nochmalige Öffnung des Zugangs und dessen Wiederverschluß waren ohne Spuren zu hinterlassen, nicht durchführbar".* Einschränkend wird aber zugegeben: *„Dies schließt aber dennoch die Möglichkeit nicht aus, daß die bestehende Öffnung nicht sofort, sondern etwa erst Jahrzehnte später verschlossen und in dieser Zeit vielleicht der Zugang nochmals bearbeitet wurde".*[23]

Auf Grund der Schwierigkeiten der Versetzung der Außenblöcke, um den Zugang zu schließen, wird eine zweite Bauphase ebenso für unrealistisch gehalten wie eine Zweitbelegung. *„Ungeachtet dessen muß angemerkt werden, daß der Befund nicht ausschließt, daß die Öffnung über Jahrzehnte oder noch länger offenstand und dann mit dem vorbereiteten Originalsteinmaterial geschlossen wurde".*[24] Übertragen wir den Befund auf die hier vertretene Theorie der Belegung des Sarkophages durch Angehörige der Dynastie der Antigoniden, dann könnte der Zugang während der Nutzung als Mausoleum provisorisch verschlossen worden sein und wurde erst endgültig verschlossen, als unter Antigonos Gonatas (276-239 v. Chr.), dem Sohne des Demetrios, sich der Machtbereich der Antigoniden nach Westen verlagerte, d.h. nach Makedonien und Griechenland.[25]

Als Begründung für diesen Mechanismus habe ich Bestattungssitten der Dynastie postuliert.[26] Die regierenden Mitglieder sollten oben in der Cella in Sarkophagen bestattet werden, während die übrigen Angehörigen im unteren Grabraum in dem großen Klinensarkophag ihre letzte Ruhe finden sollten. Im Kontext dieser Theorie würde das Problem der zwei Zähne einer männlichen 40-45 Jahre alten Leiche, die im Inneren des Sarkophages gefunden wurden, eine natürliche Lösung finden. Deshalb mußte der eine Teil des Deckels nach Norden verschoben werden können (Taf. 2.2). Der Ahnherr wachte bekränzt oder mit dem königlichen Diadem – über die Toten assistiert von dem medisch gekleideten Pagen[27] (Taf. 2.3) über die Mitglieder der Dynastie der Antigoniden – bei jeder Bestattung bereit, die Libation für die Götter der Unterwelt zu entrichten.[28] Wie auf der Langseite A des Marmorsarkophags von Uzun Yuva in Mylasa steht der Mundschenk mit dem Tierkopfrhyton am Fußende der Kline, d.h. der Liegende und der Page waren so im Original arrangiert, dass sie dem Neuzugang entgegenblickten (Taf. 2.2-3).

---

[22] Heinz 2017, 47ff., II 3; 140f., III 2.

[23] Heinz 2017, 58., vgl. besonders Taf. 134.

[24] Heinz 2017, 140.

[25] Ehling – Weber 2014, 29ff.

[26] Borchhardt 2004, 50ff., Abb. 11-12. Während ich dort den Satrapen von Sardis Menandros für den Bauherrn hielt, plädiere ich jetzt für ein dynastisches Grabmal der Antigoniden.

[27] Ruggendorfer 2005, 287ff., Abb. 2, 5; Borchhardt 2012, 143, Abb. 30; Borchhardt – Bleibtreu 2012, 143, Abb. 30.

[28] Ad Libation vgl. Haase 2012, 751-753.

II: These: Nicht die westliche sondern die östliche Version des Phaëton-Mythos wurde gewählt

II 1: Die mithrische Version des Phaëton-Mythos: Nonnos und Dio Chrysostomos

Nach Nonnos (5. Jh. n. Chr.) wurde Mithras als der *„assyrische Phaëton in Persien"* bezeichnet.[29] Dio Chrysostomos XXXVI 39 um 100 n. Chr. überliefert eine Hymne, die den Weltenbrand in ganz ähnlicher Weise wie im Phaëton-Mythos schildert: Die Quadriga von vier Pferden (den Elementen Feuer, Luft, Wasser, Erde) wird von einer höchsten Gottheit gelenkt. Mit glühendem Atem (ἄσθμα ἰσχυρόν) löst das Feuerpferd den Weltenbrand aus und das Wasserpferd die Sintflut. Das Relief von Dieburg (Taf. 6.3a-b) gilt als Beweis, dass Mithras/Phaëton den Weltenbrand entzündet.[30]

II 2: Nero als Mithras-Anhänger

Aus den Begegnungen von Tiridates und Nero läßt sich schließen, dass Nero nicht nur Anhänger des Mithras-Kultes war, sondern sich selbst als Gott Mithras verstand.

1: In Rhandeia treffen Corbulo, der Oberbefehlshaber der römischen Armee und Tiridates, Arsakide, 52 n. Chr. in Armenien eingesetzter König[31], zusammen, um weitreichende diplomatische Pläne zu schmieden. *„Denn sie fanden sich nicht zu bloßer Unterredung zusammen, man errichtete vielmehr eine hohe Bühne und stellte auf ihr Neros Brustbilder auf. Tiridates trat jetzt vor den Augen einer Menge von Armeniern, Parthern und Römern vor diesen hin, beugte ehrfurchtsvoll das Knie vor ihnen, nahm, nachdem er ihnen Opfer und Gelübde dargebracht hatte, sein Diadem vom Haupt und legte es vor sie hin."*[32]

2: In Rom auf dem Forum 63 n. Chr. setzt Nero dem auf den Stufen zur Tribüne knienden Tiridates, dem Arsakiden, dieses Diadem wiederum auf zum Zeichen, dass er als Kaiser und Gott die Macht hat, ihn als König von Armenien zu inthronisieren. Der Mithras-Verehrer Tiridates dankt: *„Ich, des Arsakes Enkel und Bruder der Könige Vologaesus und Pakoros, trete vor dich, mein Gebieter, um dir als dein Sklave zu huldigen. Ich erscheine vor dir, wie dem Mithras, meine Verehrung zu bezeugen, und erwarte das Geschick, das deine Hand mir spinnen wird, denn du bist die Gottheit, die über mein Schicksal gebietet."*[33]

3: Wenn bei den Feierlichkeiten des Empfangs des Tiridates mit seinem großen Gefolge im Theater im Jahre 66. n. Chr. in den purpurnen Vela Nero als Wagenlenker eingestickt war – *„und*

---

[29] Vermaseren 1965, 139f.; Ulansey 1989, 90.

[30] Vermaseren 1965, 141, Abb. 66; Ulansey 1989, 90.

[31] Volkmann 1975, 861 s.v. Tiridates (6).

[32] Cass. Dio LXII 23.3; Tac. ann. 15,29; ausführlich Sonnabend 2016, 194.

[33] Cass. Dio LXII 5.2. Jacobs 1999, 30 übersetzt: *„Und ich kam zu dir als meinem Gott, dich anzubeten wie Mithras, und ich werde sein, was auch immer du beschließt…"*. Nach Sonnabend 2016, 196 inszenierte Nero den Staatsakt als hellenistische Krönung, widerstand aber den Bekehrungsversuchen des Tiridates, der sich nach Plin. nat. 30.16 selbst als Magier, als Priester des Mithras verstand, zur Mithras-Religion. Er ließ im Ornat des Triumphators den armenischen König die Proskynese vollziehen und ließ den Janus-Tempel schließen, zum Zeichen, dass der Krieg mit dem Frieden endete. Wenn sich Nero somit als Kriegskaiser präsentierte, so würde das einer Mithras affinen Haltung Neros nicht widersprechen, denn Mithras war ein Schwertgott. Zur göttlichen Verehrung Neros vgl. Clauss 2001, 98-111, Abb. 5-7.

rings um ihn glänzten goldene Sternchen", dann lässt sich der kosmische Bezug zu Helios, dem Lenker des Sonnenwagens, und seinem Sohn nicht leugnen.[34]

4: Wenn man eine öffentlich nicht deklarierte Symbiose von Mithras und Helios nicht für undenkbar hält, wird man die Willkür von Nero und dem kaiserlichen Freigelassenen Helius nicht für zufällig halten: *„Dieser hatte unumschränkte Vollmacht, ohne vorherige Anzeige bei Nero Güter einzuziehen, gemeine Bürger, Ritter und Senatoren zu verbannen oder zu töten. So stand denn damals Rom unter zwei Kaisern, unter Nero und Helius."*[35]

5: Ein anderer Freigelassener namens Phaon, zuständig für die kaiserlichen Finanzen, war Nero bis zum Suizid ein treuer Gefolgsmann.[36]

II 3: Nero und der Brand von Rom 18.04.-24.04.64 n. Chr.: Die Inszenierung des Weltbrandes und der Geburt eines neuen Zeitalters

Wenn die moderne Forschung dem Kaiser weniger Caesarenwahn als *„bewußte Orientierung an einer Monarchie orientalischer oder hellenistischer Prägung"*[37] attestiert, dann erscheint der Plan, Rom anzuzünden, im Rahmen unserer mithrischen Interpretation in neuem Licht.

„Hierauf kam ihn der Wunsch an, wie er ihn denn auch unverhohlen aussprach, Stadt und Reich noch zu seinen Lebzeiten zugrunde zu richten".[38] Nach Cassius Dio lässt er mit System Rom niederbrennen – über mehrere Tage.[39] Wenn er als Kitharaspieler verkleidet die Zerstörung von Troja besang[40] und Priamos überglücklich pries, dass er den Untergang seiner Vaterstadt und seines Reiches mit ansehen durfte[41], so mag weniger eine pyromanische Wahnvorstellung als Ursache bestimmend gewesen sein, sondern das Wissen um den Untergang der ägäisch-hethitischen Kultur am Ende des 2. Jts., das im Brand von Troja durch Homer im Bewußtsein festgezurrt wurde. Er folgte der religiösen Logik, dass er ein neues Zeitalter heraufführen wollte, das nur durch den Weltenbrand des alten beendet werden konnte. In der modernen althistorischen Forschung findet eine Ehrenrettung statt. Nero als *„verantwortungsbewußten Krisenmanager"* zu interpretieren, der auf einen unglücklichen, zufälligen Brand mit *„dem größten Sicherheits- und Vorsorgepaket"*[42] antwortete, kann vor dem hier vertretenen Szenario nur als Verharmlosung bezeichnet werden. Neropolis sollte die neue Hauptstadt heißen[43], in der er als Mithras, als Kosmokrator herrschen würde.

---

[34] Bergmann 1998, 157ff.; Cass. Dio LXIII 6.2.

[35] Cass. Dio LXIII 12.1-2.

[36] CIL III 14112,2; Sonnabend 2016, 218ff. Zur Macht der Freigelassenen in der kaiserlichen Verwaltung vgl. Alföldy 1975, 96f.

[37] Bergmann 1994, 4.

[38] Cass. Dio LXII 16.1.

[39] Cass. Dio LXII 16.2ff.-18.5; Suet. Nero 38; Tac. ann. 15,38ff.

[40] Cass. Dio LXII 18.1.

[41] Cass. Dio LXII 16.1.

[42] Sonnabend 2016, 116f.

[43] Tac. ann. XV 40.

II 4: Nero als Erbauer der DOMUS AUREA in Rom

Auf Anordnung von Nero konzipierten Severus und Celer, die Baumeister, eine Residenz, die den Prunk und die Ausdehnung orientalischer Paläste mit den Refinements hellenistischer Königspaläste verbinden sollte (Taf. 3.1).[44] Der künstliche See erinnert an das zeitweise überschwemmte Tal zu Füßen des Mausoleums von Belevi (Taf. 3.6). Hier ist die Idee der kaiserlichen Residenz als *instrumentum regni* für eine Politik verwirklicht, die gemäß dem orientalischen Vorbild einer sakralen Vision des Herrschers auf die göttliche Überhöhung des Kaisers hinaus liefen.[45] Grundsätzlich sind wir von der Beurteilung durch Frank Kolb, Rom (1995) 395 überzeugt: *„Als Gott-König war der Kaiser in Gestalt der mit seinen Gesichtszügen ausgestatteten kolossalen Sonnengottstatue im Vestibül des Hauses zu sehen… Die Domus Aurea läßt im übrigen schon in ihrem Namen erkennen, dass sie Symbol eines von Nero inaugurierten neuen Goldenen Zeitalters (aurea aetas) sein sollte."*.

Wenn Nero eine Beziehung zum Mithras-Kult[46] hatte, dann müsste auch im Architektur- oder Ausstattungsprogramm ein Hinweis zu finden sein.

Raum 34 mit der Darstellung des Phaëton-Mythos: Schon L'Orange hatte 1942 die These verfochten, dass Nero sich als Mithras/Sol in der Palastkonzeption mit dem Koloß im Vestibulum als Inkarnation des Sonnengottes als kosmischer Gottherrscher inszenieren wollte.[47] Von der Imitation hellenistischer Paläste war auch Charles-Picard überzeugt. Er betonte dabei den sowohl apollinischen als auch dionysischen Aspekt.[48]

Im Raum 34 war offensichtlich eine Episode des Phaëton-Mythos in der Deckendekoration zur Darstellung gelangt (Taf. 3.3): Eine Audienzszene mit einem jugendlichen, en face thronenden Gott und seiner Entourage sowie den um den Wagen bittenden Phaëton als Mittelemblem und in den Ecken dionysische und mithrische Szenen.[49] *„Le peintures de la Domus Aurea ne sont plus connues qu'à travers les médiocres gravures de Mirri (1), qu'il faut interpréter. Il semble néanmoins quelles correspondent à des cartons sensiblement differents, et offrent ainsi, un demi siècle plus tard, une autre version, des premiers épisodes du mythe élaborée peut-être au début de l'empire (Koch/Sichtermann, Röm. Sark. 181): la rencontre de Phaeton et d'Hélios se fait en présence des Horae; la composition et plus recherchée et plus ample; le dieu de fâce, est assis sous un*

---

[44] L. F. Ball, The Domus Aurea and the Roman Architectural Revolution, 2003.

[45] I. della Portella, Das unterirdische Rom. Katakomben, Bäder, Tempel, 2000, 235. Zu Julian im 4. Jh. n. Chr. als Mithras-Anhänger vgl. J. Bidez, Kaiser Julian. Der Untergang der heidnischen Welt, 1956, s.v. Mithras und Helios.

[46] Zu den Mithräen am Circus Maximus, Barberini, unter San Clemente und unter den Caracalla-Thermen vgl. della Portella 2000, 168ff.

[47] L'Orange 1942; ders., Studies on the Iconography of Cosmic Kingship, 1953, 28ff.

[48] G. Charles-Picard, Auguste et Néron. Le secret de l'empire, 1962, 211.

[49] Y. Perrin, MEFRA 94, 1982, 843ff. lehnt die mithrische Interpretation ab und erklärt die älteren Zeichnungen nach den verloren gegangenen Deckengemälden für unglaubwürdig. Bergmann 1994, 24f. Leider hat Plin. nat. XXXV 120 von dem Maler Famulus oder Fabullus, der für die Malereien in der Domus Aurea verantwortlich war (carcer eius artis Domus Aurea fuit), keine Bildbeschreibungen notiert. F. Coarelli, Rom. Ein archäologischer Führer, 1975, 198 erwähnt zwar die Renaissance-Zeichnungen, geht aber auf das Phaëton-Bild nicht ein.

dais pour accueillir son fils. Sur deux autres tableaux, qui correspondent à la preparation de l'attelagé, les Horae (ou les Héliades: Diggle 210) sont accompagnées par les Vents."[50]

Der Koloss Neros: Im Vestibulum der Domus Aurea stand der bronzene ca. 30 m hohe Koloss Neros mit Portraitzügen und einem siebenstrahligen Kranz.[51] Auf Grund der Berliner Gemme[52] wird er zusätzlich mit Stütze unter dem linken Arm mit Blitzbündel in der Hand und Steuerruder in der rechten Hand rekonstruiert (Taf. 3.4).[53] Wenn unsere Vermutung verifiziert werden könnte und Nero als Mithras dargestellt werden wollte, erweitern sich die Möglichkeiten der Attribute, dann könnte auch Schwert, Globus und Sonnenrad von Zenodoros aus inhaltlichen und statischen Gründen Verwendung gefunden haben, um den Kosmokrator als Weltherrscher zu charakterisieren (Taf. 3.5).[54]

III. Versuch einer Rekonstruktion des Phaëton-Zyklus im Obergeschoß des Mausoleums von Belevi

Kehren wir zum Planungsstab der Bauskulptur des Mausoleums von Belevi zurück und fragen, wie und in welcher Form der Mythos des Phaëton zur Darstellung gebracht werden sollte. Nach den Vorstellungen von Robert Fleischer auf Grund der Inschriften-Fragmente ΗΛΙΑΔΕΣ, ΦΑ[ΕΘΩΝ], Ζ]ΕΥΣ und ·]ΦΙ[· (Taf, 1.3) und seiner Vermutung, dass die Cella im Obergeschoß der Witterung schutzlos ausgeliefert worden wäre, da die Überdachung nicht fertig geworden wäre, Malereien in einer hypäthralen Cella keine Überlebenschance gehabt hätten und die Beischriften für Malerei zu monumental wirken würden, wurde der Mythos in Relief-Technik oder Rundplastik ausgeführt.[55] Unwillkürlich denkt man an den Telephos-Fries im Obergeschoß des Pergamon-Altares.[56] Eine kontinuierende Darstellungsweise[57] könnte man sich auch in Belevi vorstellen. Die gesicherte Evidenz für die Existenz der Visualisierung des Phaëton-Mythos stellen die 4 Fragmente einer (oder mehrerer?) monumentaler Inschriften dar: A: Ἡλιάδες, B: [Ζ?]εύς, C: [...] Φα[έθων?], D: [...] φι [...].[58] Nach palaiographischen Kriterien lassen sich die

---

[50] Baratte 1994, 353f.

[51] Plin. nat. 34,35ff.; Sueton, Nero 31; Martial. epigr. 1, 70.7f.; Notitia urbis regionum XIV 12, regio IV; Bergmann 1994, 7 mit ausführlicher Diskussion der Quellen.

[52] Bergmann 1994, Taf. 2.3.

[53] Bergmann 1994, 17, Abb. 10.

[54] Die Kithara könnte auch allein ohne Altar als Attribut und Stütze des Künstlergottes zur Darstellung gekommen sein, wie eine Apollon-Kleinbronze aus Pompeji beweist: P. Vanags, Glorreiches Pompeji, 1983, 118. Dieses Größenverhältnis von Figur und Instrument zeigt auch das Malereifragment aus Rom: G. Carettoni, Das Haus des Augustus auf dem Palatin, 1983, Farbtaf. X 1 – oder die Kithara spielende Berenike II. der Fürstenbilder von Boscoreale im Metropolitan Museum of Art in New York: G. Grimm, Alexandria. Die erste Königsstadt der hellenistischen Welt, 1998, 136, Abb. 127c. Unsere Rekonstruktion hat sich von der Apollon-Darstellung von der Mainzer Jupitersäule anregen lassen, „die vor 67 n. Chr. pro salute Neronis" aufgestellt wurde: Bergmann 1994, 14, Taf. 4.5.

[55] R. Fleischer *in* Praschniker (+) – Theuer (+) 1979, 148. Nach Hoepfner 2013, 125, Abb. 71-72 gab es keine Stufenpyramide sondern Hallen.

[56] Hoepfner 1997, 48f., Abb. 31.

[57] von Hartel – Wickhoff 1895, 7ff. und 59ff.

[58] Taeuber 2016, 319. Die Fragmente C und D sind offensichtlich verloren gegangen.

Fragmente „*in das letzte Viertel des 4. oder das erste des 3. Jh. v. Chr. datieren*",[59] sie gehören daher zur Originalausstattung des Oberbaues.

In der Neubearbeitung der Architektur wird auf eine Cella verzichtet und der Raum hinter der umlaufenden Kolonnade wird nur noch als Hof interpretiert mit der Funktion eines Entwässerungsareals für das Monument.[60] Durch die besondere Gestaltung der Nordseite im Sockelgeschoß sowie im Obergeschoß erhielt der Bau eine achsiale repräsentative Ausrichtung auf den See. Die Scheintür im Sockel ist aus bauästhetischen Gründen mit funktionalem Anspruch notwendig, in Wirklichkeit verbirgt sie die Grabkammer im Süden, die von außen nicht sichtbar war.

Die Rekonstruktion der Rückwand des Pterons mit einer Blendarchitektur zwischen zwei Antenpfeilern mit vier dorischen Säulen mit Blattkelchkapitellen über einer Sockelzone mit einem vorgelegten Bathron, das nur mittig durch eine sechsstufige Felstreppe unter einer Scheintreppe unterbrochen wird, liefert den Beweis für die Verortung der Inschriften-Architrav-Blöcke: „*Inschriften in den Mauerarchitraven lassen Statuengruppen, vielleicht auch Malereien oder Reliefs in mehreren Jochen wahrscheinlich werden. Einer davon, der Heliades-Block, deutet mit seiner großen Tiefe und dem runden Dübelloch auf der Unterseite auf eine Wandgliederung, etwa mit einer Nische*".[61]

Aber warum sollen diese Blöcke mit dem Phaëton-Mythos die Nordkolonnade geschmückt haben? Einleuchtender und der Planung der Antigoniden näher scheint mir, dass sie über den Darstellungen nach innen blickten aber nicht in den sog. Hof mit den Maßen 14,63 m x 13,80 m, sondern in die Cella unterhalb einer pyramidalen Dachkonstruktion, in der wie im Maussolleion der Hekatomniden Marmorsarkophage und Portraitstatuen der regierenden Antigoniden stehen sollten.[62]

III 1: Die literarische Vorlage von Ovid, Metamorphosen 1.11

Im Mythos des Phaëton lassen sich durchaus mehrere Episoden als darstellungswürdig erweisen.[63] Nehmen wir an, dass Ovid[64] ältere Geschichten für seine Metamorphosen verwendete, dann lassen sich einige Sequenzen eruieren[65]:

1: Der Streit zwischen Phaëton und Epaphus, dem Gründer von Memphis und Sohn des Zeus und der Io.

---

[59] Taeuber 2016, 319.

[60] Heinz 2017, 149ff., 237.

[61] Heinz 2017, 147, Abb. 77, 81, Taf. 103, 123.

[62] Borchhardt 2004, 45.

[63] Wieseler 1857; Heinze 2012, 712.

[64] Ov. met. I, 751ff. Nach Knaack 1909, 2187 hat ein alexandrinischer Dichter, aus dem Ovid, Lukian, Philostratos, Claudian und Nonnos schöpfen, versucht, westliche und östliche Versionen zu verschmelzen und durch den Katasterismos von Phaëton als Fuhrmann (Auriga), Eridanos als himmlischer Fluß, Heliaden als Hyaden, Kyknos als Schwan die verhängten Strafen zu mildern. So soll die Milchstrasse die Bahn des Phaëton nachzeichnen (Claudian).

[65] Die philosophischen Reflexionen wie z.B. bei Plat. Tim. 22c eigneten sich vermutlich weniger zur Darstellung in der bildenden Kunst.

2: Phaëton berichtet seiner Mutter Klymene, der Okeanos-Tochter[66], von dem Streitgespräch mit Epaphos. Der Schwur der Mutter, dass Helios sein Vater ist.

3: Phaëton *„lebt nur noch in Gedanken an den Himmel, durchwandert sein Aethiopien, dann das Gebiet der sonnenverbrannten Inder und geht unverdrossen zum Aufgang seines Vaters".*

4: Im Palast des Helios sitzt Phoebus auf dem Thron mit Entourage, gewährt dem Sohn eine Audienz und gibt seine Vaterschaft zu – und schwört, dem Sohn jede Bitte zu erfüllen. Phaëton bittet *„um den Wagen des Vaters und um das Recht, einen Tag die Rosse lenken zu dürfen."* An seinen Schwur gebunden, rät der Vater dem Sohn zum Widerruf: *„Dein Los ist es, sterblich zu sein; nicht sterblich ist, was du begehrst",* und bittet ihn, einen anderen Wunsch zu äußern.

5: Da Phaëton auf seinem Wunsch beharrt, führt Helios seinen Sohn zum goldenen Wagen, einem Geschenk Vulcans, und gebietet den Horen, die Rosse anzuschirren. Letzte Ratschläge des Vaters, der seinem Sohn den Strahlenkranz aufsetzt.

6: Phaëton besteigt den Wagen, die geflügelten Sonnenrosse Pyrois (Feurig), Eous (Morgenschein), Aethon (Brand) und Phlegon (Lohe) stürmen los und überholen die Ostwinde.

7: Durch das Unvermögen des Phaëton gerät der Sonnenwagen in die Nähe der Erde und erzeugt einen Weltenbrand *„überall dort, wo die Erde am höchsten ist, wird sie vom Feuer ergriffen, bekommt Spalten und Risse... (2, 210)*

„Große Städte gehen mit ihren Mauern unter (2, 215) und der Brand legt ganze Länder mit ihren Völkern in Asche...."

„Wie man glaubt, wurden damals Aethiopiens Völker schwarz" (2, 235)

„Damals ward Libyen trocken" (2, 237)

„Es brannte auch der babylonische Euphrat, es brannte der Orontes, der schnelle Thermodon, der Ganges, der Phasis und die Donau" (2, 248f.)

„Der Nil flüchtete voll Entsetzen ans Ende der Welt...." (2, 254)

8: Der Aufstand von Neptun und die Anrufung der Tellus und Anklage gegen Zeus

„Wenn Meer und Lande vergehen und die Burg des Himmels, dann werden wir wieder ins alte Chaos gewirbelt. Ist noch etwas übrig, so entreiß es den Flammen und sorge für das Wohl der Welt!" (2, 298ff.)

9: Der *pater omnipotent* ruft die Götter und Helios als Zeugen an, dass ohne sein Eingreifen die Welt untergehen würde. (2, 304f.)

„Also donnert er; dann holt er weit aus – bis zum rechten Ohr – und wirft den Blitz auf den Wagenlenker, raubt ihm zugleich den Stand und das Leben und bezähmt mit grausamem Feuer das Feuer. Scheu werden die Rosse springen in verschiedene Richtungen, reißen den Hals aus dem Joch und hinterlassen zerfetzte Riemen. Hier liegt das Zaumzeug, dort von der Deichsel abgebrochen,

---

[66] Bei Euripides, Phaëton ist Klymene Gattin des Merops, des Königs der Aithiopen. von Geisau 1979, 689; Ovid, met. 2.184 lässt Phaëton vor seinem Absturz bereuen: *„Schon hätte er lieber die Rosse des Vaters nie angerührt, schon reut es ihn, seine Herkunft erfahren und seine Bitte durchgesetzt zu haben, schon wünscht er sich sehnlich, ein Sohn des Merops zu heißen".*

die Achse, hier die Speichen geborstener Räder, und weit verstreut sind die Reste des zertrümmerten Wagens.[67]

Aber Phaeton, dessen Haar die verheerende Flamme rötet, wird kopfüber hinabgewirbelt und stürzt in weitem Bogen durch die Luft, wie zuweilen ein Stern von heiterem Himmel zwar nicht fällt, aber zu fallen scheint." (2, 311ff.)

10: Der Sturz des Phaëton im Westen in den Eridanos

Der vom Blitz des Zeus getötete Phaëton fällt *"fern der Heimat am anderen Ende der Welt vom Himmel (2, 323), der gewaltige Eridanos nimmt ihn auf und wäscht sein dampfendes Gesicht. Hesperische Naiaden übergeben den Leib der noch von dem dreizackigen Blitz raucht, dem Grabhügel und sie ritzen in den Stein einen Spruch:* "Hier ruht Phaeton, der Lenker des väterlichen Wagens; zwar konnte er ihn nicht halten, doch fiel er als einer, der Großes gewagt". *Der bejammernswerte Vater hatte in schmerzvoller Trauer sein Antlitz verhüllt und wenn wir es glauben wollen, soll ein Tag ohne Sonne vergangen sein."* (2, 324ff.)

11: Die Suche der Mutter nach dem Sohn

Die Trauer der Clymene, die Suche nach dem toten Sohn und Auffindung des Tumulus mit der Grabinschrift.

12: Die Trauer der Heliaden[68], der Schwestern des Phaëton und ihre Metamorphose am Tumulus-Grab

"Nicht weniger trauern die Sonnentöchter und bringen dem Tod als sinnlose Gaben ihre Tränen dar. Mit der flachen Hand schlagen sie sich an die Brust, rufen Tag und Nacht nach Phaeton, der ihre unglücklichen Klagen nicht hören kann, und werfen sich am Grabe nieder." (2, 340ff.)

"Als eine von ihnen, Phaetusa, die älteste der Schwestern, sich auf die Erde niederwerfen wollte, klagte sie, ihre Füße seien erstarrt. Zu ihr versuchte die strahlende Lampetie zu kommen und wurde von einer plötzlich gewachsenen Wurzel festgehalten. Die dritte wollte sich mit den Händen die Haare raufen und riß Blätter ab. Diese empfindet Schmerz, weil ein Baumstamm ihre Beine umschließt, jene weil ihre Arme zu langen Ästen werden; und während sie sich noch darüber wundern, umfaßt Rinde ihre Weichen und legt sich Schritt für Schritt um den Leib, die Brust, die Schultern, die Hände. Nur noch die Gesichter blickten hervor und der Mund, der nach der Mutter rief." (2, 346ff.)

Die Mutter versucht die Verwandlung ihrer Töchter zu verhindern, und *"bricht mit den Händen die zarten Zweige ab; doch da quellen blutige Tropfen wie aus einer Wunde hervor."* (2, 359ff.)

Die Töchter bitten ihre Mutter sich in das Schicksal zu fügen: *"Bitte, schone mich, Mutter"* ruft eine jede, sobald sie verletzt ist, *"schone mich, bitte! Im Baum verwundest du meinen Leib. Leb wohl!"* und Rinde wuchs über die letzten Worte.

---

[67] Bei einer Rekonstruktionszeichnung würde man sich an elegante Wagen mit großen Rädern halten, wie z.B. bei dem Reliefblock im Museum von Veria um 300 v. Chr.

[68] Nach Knaack 1909, 2180 werden sie schon in der hesiodeischen Version wegen Beihilfe von Zeus bestraft und in Pappeln verwandelt.

"Daraus fließen Tränen; was von den neuentstandenen Zweigen herabtropft, wird an der Sonne hart: Bernstein, den der klare Strom aufnimmt und den Latinerfrauen als Schmuck schickt." (2, 364ff.)[69]

13: Die Metamorphose des Cygnus / Kyknos /: Cygnus, der König der Ligurer, Blutsverwandter über die Mutter, findet ebenfalls das Grabmal des Phaëton am Ufer des Eridanus in dem Wald, *"den die Schwestern vermehrt hatten"* (2, 372) und wird in einen Schwan verwandelt.[70] *"Er vertraut sich dem Himmel und Juppiter nicht an, als erinnere er sich seines ungerechten Blitzschlages. Sümpfe sucht er und weite Seen, und da er das Feuer verabscheut, hat er die Flüsse, die den Flammen feindlich sind, zur Wohnstätte erkoren"*. (2, 373ff.)

14: Die Trauer des Vaters Helios

Vater Helios in seiner Trauer um den Sohn verweigert *"der Welt seinen Dienst"* und zürnt mit dem Göttervater, er solle doch einmal selbst den Sonnenwagen fahren und seine Blitze ruhen lassen, die andere Väter kinderlos machen. (2, 381ff.)

"Hat er einmal die Kraft der feuerfüßigen Rosse zu spüren bekommen, wird er wissen, daß der den Tod nicht verdient hat, der sie nicht gut lenkte". (2, 392ff.)

Nachdem Juppiter sich entschuldigt und *"nach Königsart die Bitten mit Drohungen gewürzt hat"* (2, 396f.), wird Helios von allen Göttern gebeten, seine Arbeit wieder aufzunehmen.

Für unsere Interpretation nicht uninteressant ist die Version, die der augustinische Polyhistor Hyginus[71] in seinen auf alten griechischen Quellen basierenden Genealogiae oder Fabulae überliefert.[72] Phaëton wird nicht als Sohn des Helios deklariert, sondern als Enkel, der auch nicht die Zustimmung zur Wagenfahrt ertrotzt auf Grund des Gelübdes der Mutter gegenüber, sondern heimlich als Dieb die Sonnenquadriga mit Hilfe der Heliaden entwendet. Zeus selbst habe den Weltenbrand durch seinen den Phaëton tötenden Blitz ausgelöst. Die rettende Flut habe nur Deukalion und Pyrrha überleben lassen. Als Strafe ihrer Mitwirkung beim Raub des Sonnenwagens wird die Verwandlung der Heliaden in Pappeln gedeutet. Wer wollte leugnen, dass die Raubszene nicht eine vorzügliche literarische Vorlage für eine künstlerische Visualisierung lieferte.

Wenn es für Ovid und Literaten vor und nach ihm auch Bildhauer und Maler in den gleichen Zeiträumen gab, dann konnten sie daher in 14 Sequenzen in continuierendem Stil[73] den Phaëton-Mythos erzählen. Wenn man die Vorgeschichte 1 + 2 zusammenzieht und die Trauer von Mutter und Töchtern als Einheit auffasst oder 14 für eine spätere Erfindung hält, dann kommt man auf 12 Titel der Narration.[74]

---

[69] So auch Plin. nat. 37, 31. Auch wenn von der dramatischen Bearbeitung der Heliaden durch Aischylos nur wenig erhalten ist, so sind doch die Bernsteintränen nachweisbar: Knaack 1909, 2184.

[70] Nach Knaack 1909, 2181 erfolgt die Metamorphose in einen Singschwan aus verwandtschaftlichem Interesse. Neschke 1986, 133ff., 150, Anm. 52.

[71] Schmidt 1998, 778-779, I c.

[72] Hygin, fab. 152, 154; Taeuber 2016, 319.

[73] Schönberger 1995, 163.

[74] Kanonisch z.B. für Herakles und Theseus.

III 2: Die Bildbeschreibung (Ekphrasis) zum Gemälde „Phaeton" in einer Galerie in einem Vorort von Neapel durch Philostrat, Eikones 1.11,k: 170-220 n. Chr.

Phaeton und die Würdigung durch Johann Wolfgang von Goethe

In der älteren Forschung hat man der Bildbeschreibung nur fiktiven Wert beigemessen.[75] Die Ekphrasis kann jedoch ernst genommen werden[76], deshalb wurde der erste Satz als Titel genommen. Philostratos fordert den Betrachter auf:[77] „*Sieh nur! Am Himmel gerät alles in Aufruhr. Nacht verjagt den Tag vom Mittagshimmel, die Sonnenscheibe sinkt zur Erde und reißt die Gestirne mit sich. Die Horen aber verlassen die Himmelstore und fliehen in das Dunkel, das vor ihnen aufsteigt*".

Bei einem Rekonstruktionsversuch (Taf. 5.2) wird man daher im oberen Drittel links Helios als Sonnenscheibe vermuten; rechts erscheint Nyx als geflügelte Gestalt wie auf dem aretinischen Becher (Taf. 6.1). In der Mitte verlassen die Horen die Tore des Himmels in Richtung der Nacht. Unten hat der Maler die Erde wiederum als Personifikation gestaltet: „*Die Erde aber reckt verzweifelt ihre Hände empor, weil der Feuerregen auf sie niederprasselt*".[78] Der Eridanos, der zweimal genannt wird, mag als Landschaftselement z. T. zu sehen gewesen sein, als Flußpersonifikation[79] agiert er unmißverständlich: „*Auch der Flußgott klagt, taucht aus der wirbelnden Flut empor und bietet Phaeton Brust und Arme dar, denn seine Haltung zeigt, daß er ihn auffangen will.*" Die Mitte wurde von dem Sturz eingenommen: „*Der Jüngling aber fällt aus dem Wagen und stürzt herab – sein Haar steht in Flammen, seine Brust raucht.*" Nach einem hellenistischen Vorbild mögen Schwäne über den Eridanos und Ge geflogen sein: „*Denn Schwäne, die hier und dort eine süße Weise tönen, werden sogar den Fall des Knaben besingen, und Schwärme von ihnen werden aufsteigen und dies dem Kaystros und Istros künden, und kein Teil solcher Kunde wird ungehört verhallen, und sie werden ihr Lied vom West begleiten lassen, der flink ist und ein Wegegott; denn er soll den Schwänen seine Hilfe beim Klagelied zugesagt haben. Deshalb ist er auch bei den Vögeln, schau nur hin, und spielt auf ihnen wie auf Instrumenten.*"[80]

Der oberen dreifigurigen Komposition antwortet unten ebenfalls eine Darstellung aus drei Elementen. Wenn links und rechts die Personifikationen Eridanos und Tellus/Ge das Bild beherrschen, dann nehmen die Heliaden die Mitte ein: „*Die jungen Frauen aber am Ufer, die noch nicht ganz Bäume geworden sind, die Heliaden, sollen sich um ihres Bruders willen verwandelt haben, seien Bäume geworden und vergössen Tränen. Auch das Bild weiß davon: es läßt ja ihre Zehen Wurzeln schlagen, und so sind sie bis zum Nabel hinauf Bäume, während ihre Hände schon in Zweige auslaufen. Ach, und das Haar! Wie ganz Pappellaub! Ach ihre Tränen! Wie ganz aus*

---

[75] Knaack 1909, 2195.

[76] Zum archäologischen Nachweis solcher Galerien vgl. H. Vetters, Die Neapler ‚Galeria' (zu Philostrat, Eikones I 4), ÖJh 50, 1972/73, 223-228.

[77] Philostr. imag. 1, 11.2.

[78] Philostr. imag. 1, 11.2.

[79] Philostr. imag. 1, 11.5.

[80] Philostr. imag. 1,11.3. Bei einer Rekonstruktion wird man den Schwan der Aura vom Tellus-Relief der Ara Pacis in Rom zitieren: Simon 2012, 22-23, Abb. 15, 19. Nach Taeuber 2016, 319f. würde die Nennung der beiden Schicksalsströme Istros (Donau) und Kaystros (bei Ephesos) aus historischen Gründen einem Grabherrn Lysimachos mühelos zugeordnet werden können.

Gold und die Flut in den Augen wirft ihren Glanz auf die strahlenden Augensterne und zieht gleichsam einen Lichtstrahl auf sich; was über die Wangen rinnt, leuchtet in ihrem Rot, was aber auf den Busen tropft ist schon Gold."[81] In der Interpretation von Otto Schönberger verbinden sich im Absturz des Phaëton und der Metamorphose der *„im Leid um den Toten vergossenen Tränen … zu golden schimmerndem Bernstein"*, Trauer und Klage *„zu einem tröstenden Gebilde"*.[82]

„Das Wahre ist eine Fackel, aber eine ungeheure; deswegen suchen wir alle nur blinzelnd so daran vorbeizukommen, in Furcht sogar, uns zu verbrennen".

Goethe, Maximen und Reflexionen Nr. 3236

Johann Wolfgang Goethe hat sich intensiv mit Philostrats Eikones beschäftigt.[83] Unter der Prämisse, *„daß die Gemäldegalerie wirklich existiert habe"*, versucht er, *„die Verworrenheit, in welcher diese Bilder hintereinander aufgeführt werden"*, dadurch aufzulösen, indem er sie thematisch ordnete. Zur ersten Gruppe *„Hochheroischen tragischen Inhalts"* zählte er unter Nr. 11 *„Phaeton; verwegener Jüngling, sich durch Übermut den Tod zuziehend"*. Bedauerlicherweise hat Goethe die Ekphrasis des Phaëton-Gemäldes nicht ausgearbeitet. Nr. 3 Skamander zeigt aber, mit welcher Empathie er die entfesselten Elemente Feuer und Wasser in diesem Landschaftsgemälde gewürdigt hätte.[84]

III.3: Die Illustration des Phaëton-Mythos durch Michelangelo

Natürlich hat Michelangelo Ovid aufmerksam gelesen und die Metamorphose der Heliaden schrittweise in Szene gesetzt: *„Nicht weniger [als die Mutter Clymene] trauern die Sonnentöchter und bringen dem Tod als sinnlose Gaben ihre Tränen dar"*.[85]

In der Windsor-Fassung (Taf. 4.1) schlagen sie sich nicht mit der flachen Hand an die Brust, sondern zeigen nackt mit erhobenem Haupt in Gesten und Gebärden ihre Erschütterung und Trauer. Natürlich kannte Michelangelo die römische Personifikation des Flussgottes mit dem wasserausgießenden Krater.[86] In der zweiten Fassung in Harlem rückt der Künstler die Heliade mit den ausgebreiteten Armen in die Mitte (Taf. 4.2) und illustriert den Beginn der Verwandlung: *„als eine von ihnen, Phaethusa, die älteste der Schwestern, sich auf die Erde niederwerfen wollte, klagte sie, ihre Füße seien erstarrt. Zu ihr versuchte die strahlende Lampetie zu kommen*

---

[81] Philostr. imag. 1, 11.4.

[82] Schönberger 1995, 168.

[83] Goethe, in Beutler 1965, 792ff.

[84] Philostrat, I 1; Schönberger 1968, 89.

[85] Ovid, met. 2, 304f.; in der dritten Fassung (Taf. 4.3) sind die Schwestern ebenfalls noch nackt und umringen klagend den übermächtigen Flußgott Eridanos. Brinkmann 1925, 45 erkennt *„eine fast architektonische Bindung der stürzenden Gruppe"* und notiert eine psychologische Wahrnehmung: *„auch Eridanus ist aus seiner Gleichgültigkeit aufgeschreckt und ringt in mächtiger Gebärde die Arme."* Hier scheinen die Heliaden zum Beiwerk zu verkümmern zu Gunsten einer homoerotischen Gebärde.

Erst Giovanni Bernardi (Taf. 5.1) und der Stecher Nicola Beatrizet (Taf. 4.4) variieren die Metamorphose durch die nach oben erhobenen Arme, denen Zweige entwachsen.

[86] Gnann 2010, 281, Kat. 85 hält diese Fassung für die beste und vermutet, dass Michelangelo römische Sarkophage kannte. Schmidt 1979, 585-587.

und wurde von einer plötzlich gewachsenen Wurzel festgehalten. Die dritte wollte sich mit den Händen die Haare raufen und riß Blätter ab. Diese empfindet Schmerz, weil ein Baumstamm ihre Beine umschließt, jene weil ihre Arme zu langen Ästen werden."[87]

Der Stecher Nicolas Beatrizet (1540-1565) fügt eine vierte Fassung hinzu.[88] Er hält sich bei den *dramatis personae* an die Vorlage der Kohlezeichnung von Michelangelo (Taf. 4.1). Episoden werden hinzugefügt, wie der kniefällig bittende Phaeton vor dem thronenden Helios mit Strahlenkrone oben rechts (Taf. 4.4). Unten links werden die pathetisch jammernden Schwestern in Bäume verwandelt nach Ovid, met. 1, 750-2, 400. Landschaftliche Elemente und Figuren füllen den Hintergrund bis zum Horizont. Bei der 5. Fassung nach Michelangelo (Taf. 5.1) fällt Phaeton nicht zwischen oder unter den Pferden vom Himmel, sondern er nimmt fast die Position des Göttervaters ein, auf den Giovanni Bernardi auf seiner Bronze-Plaquette ebenso verzichtet wie auf Kyknos. Eridanos aber verfolgt das tragische Geschehen am Himmel und die drei Hesperiden erleiden ihre Metamorphose.

Auffallend ist, dass in der dritten Fassung von Venedig (Taf. 4.3) der Schwan fehlt. Entweder meinte Michelangelo als Ortsbestimmung des Sturzes den Eridanus oder wahrscheinlicher skizziert er Kyknos in seiner homoerotischen Verzweiflung über den Tod des Freundes Phaëton.[89]

Kyknos war der Sohn des Königs von Ligurien, Sthenelos, Verwandter und Freund des Phaeton. In tiefer Trauer um Phaeton gab er seine Herrschaft auf. Zeus verwandelte ihn in einen Schwan.[90] Wenn man die Dichter großzügig auslegt, dann wollen sie den Mythos im Westen lokalisieren. Unter Ligurien kann man von der iberischen Halbinsel bis nach Norden das westliche Europa verstehen.[91] Mit dem mythischen Strom Eridanos muß man daher nicht den Rhein, die Rhone auch nicht den Po identifizieren, sondern den Golfstrom im Atlantik, der nach Verg. Aen. 6, 659 aus dem unterirdischen Elysium nach oben fließt.[92]

Wenn er die Küsten im Norden Europas begünstigt, dann darf man vermuten, dass man in der Ägäis und im Vorderen Orient wußte, woher die Tränen der Heliaden stammen. Aus balti-

---

[87] Ovid, met. 2, 342ff.

[88] „*Der Sturz Phaetons*", Radierung, Bibliothek Göttweig, Inv. Nr. XLII Ja7, Stich von Nicolas Beatrizet (1540-1565) nach Michelangelo als Inventor. Thieme-Becker 3, 1909, 113, 24, 1930, 515-526; 12, 1916, 365f.; Lechner – Telesko 1991, 17 Abb., Kat. Nr. 6b; de Tolnay et al. 1966, 466, Abb. 179.

[89] Brinckmann 1925, 45ff.: „*auch Eridanus ist aus seiner Gleichgültigkeit aufgeschreckt und ringt in mächtiger Gebärde die Arme*". Chapman 2005, 224ff. verweist auf die enge Beziehung des homosexuellen Künstlers zu dem römischen Aristokraten Tommaso de' Cavalieri, dem er vermutlich die Windsor-Fassung schenkte. Das Dankschreiben vom 6. Sept. 1533 ist erhalten. Mackowsky 1921, 251 interpretiert: „*Namentlich der Liebling Cavalieri wird wie mit Gedichten so mit sorgfältig erwogenen Kompositionen .... reichlich bedacht. Ihre Motive sind der antiken Mythologie entnommen: Ganymed, vom Adler geraubt, Tityos, dem der Geier das Herz zerfleischt, Phaetons Sturz aus dem Sonnenwagen und leicht erkennbar klingt in dieser Wahl der tragische Grundgedanke ihres Schöpfers vom Himmelsflug und Himmelssturz der Schönheit wider*".

[90] Ov. met. 2, 367ff.; Verg. Aen. 10, 189; Paus. I 30.3; Hyg. fab. 154; von Geisau 1969, 395 (Kyknos 3).

[91] Jetzt versteht man, warum Michelangelo in der Bucht der Küstenlandschaft die Entführungsszene „*Europa auf dem Rücken des Stieres*" von Osten nach Westen einfügt.

[92] von Geisau 1969, 357.

schem Bernstein (Succinit) wurde z.B. das kleine, nur 6 cm hohe Löwenkopfgefäß[93] mit Deckel aus der Königsgruft im syrischen Qatna gearbeitet, ebenso weitere Schmuckobjekte.[94] Während das Rohmaterial als prestigeträchtiges Handelsgut über Griechenland in den Vorderen Orient gelangte, wurde die Bearbeitung in einer syrisch-levantinischen Werkstatt vorgenommen.

III 4: Die Zeugnisse der bildenden Kunst in der Antike

Auffallend ist, dass weder in der archaischen noch in der klassischen Kunst der Griechen der Mythos bildwürdig geworden ist. Dabei hätte sich das Thema in westlicher Botschaft als Geißelung von Hybris und Frevel gegenüber den Göttern doch vorzüglich geeignet.[95]

Die literarische Verortung des Sturzes des Phaëton im Westen „*am anderen Ende der Welt*" (Ov. met. 2, 323) folgt logischen Gesetzen. Die Sonne geht im Westen unter. Der Eridanos in der griechischen Überlieferung gewinnt dabei die Gestalt des Golfstromes.[96] An dessen östlichem Ufer errichteten die Heliaden ihrem Bruder das Tumulus-Grab und mußten ihre Metamorphose in Pappeln erleiden. Johannes Antiochenus Malalas (F.H.G. 4, 540) interpretiert, dass „*Gott zur Zeit der Giganten eine Feuerkugel in das Keltenland habe hinabfallen lassen, die, nachdem das Land verheert und die Riesen verbrannt waren, im Eridanos erloschen sei. Daraus hätten die Griechen die Sage von Phaeton geschaffen.*"[97]

Landschaftliche Elemente dürfen wir für die Rekonstruktion sicherlich in Anspruch nehmen. Denn auch die augusteische Malerei wird hellenistische Vorbilder gehabt haben. Sehr verwandt im Thema und in der Ausführung und in der Botschaft zur Bestrafung der Hybris/Superbia wirkt das Wandgemälde mit Dädalus und Ikarus in der Villa Imperiale um die Zeitenwende.[98]

III 4.1: Aretinischer Becher, Boston, Museum of Fine Arts Taf. 6.1

Auf dem aretinischen Becher[99] mit dem Phaëton-Mythos wird von rechts nach links erzählt: Zeus läßt Artemis mit dem Bogen das Urteil vollziehen unter den weit ausgestreckten Flügeln der Nyx.[100] Tethys, Schwester des Okeanos, rettet ein Rad des Sonnenwagens, denn ihre Aufgabe ist es, morgens die Sonnenrosse zu entlassen.[101] Links davon fängt Helios reitend die Pferde mit einem Lasso ein. Bei einer der Heliaden ist die vollständige Verwandlung erfolgt, bei den anderen wachsen Zweige aus den Köpfen. Die auf sie einschlagenden Jünglinge sind nicht gedeutet.[102]

---

[93] Das Objekt erinnert an Salbgefäße z.B. im englischen Krönungs-Zeremoniell.

[94] P. Pfälzner – E. Roßberger, Das Gold des Nordens – Die Bernsteinobjekte, *in*: Landesmuseum Württemberg, Stuttgart (Hrsg.), Schätze des Alten Syrien. Die Entdeckung des Königreichs Qatna, 2009, 213ff.

[95] Vgl. z.B. den Aktaion-Mythos in der Deutung von Hölscher 2001, 123-130, Abb. 1-6.

[96] Zur Verortung des Eridanos vgl. R. Rollinger (Hrsg.), Die Sicht auf die Welt zwischen Ost und West (750 v. Chr. - 550 n. Chr.), 2017, s.v. Eridanos A 1; 19, 28.

[97] Nach Knaack 1909, 2194.

[98] Simon 1986, 198ff., Abb. 255, Taf. 17.

[99] Knaack 1909, 2195f., Abb. 1.

[100] Zum Typus 2 der geflügelten Personifikation der Nacht vgl. Borchhardt-Birbaumer, Imago noctis 2003, 106ff.

[101] Ov. met. 2, 156.

[102] Baratte 1994, 353, Kat. 24.

III 4.2: Der Sarkophag aus Ostia in der Ny Carlsberg Glyptothek, Kopenhagen 847: 3. Jh. n. Chr. Taf. 5.3

Phaëton bittet den thronenden Helios, der von vier Horen links begleitet wird, um den Wagen.[103] Diese Figuration wird abgeschlossen durch vier Jünglinge, Personifikationen der Winde, die Pferde vorführen. In der Mitte stürzt Phaëton aus dem Wagenkorb, die Pferde stieben auseinander. Die reitenden Dioskuren versuchen sie einzufangen.[104]

Nach Nonn. 217 „αὐταρ ὅ (Helios) θυμῷι ἔμπεδα γινώσκων, ἀμετάτροπα νήματα Μοίρης *im Herzen unerschütterlich wissend die nicht abwendbaren Fäden der Moira*" hockt die Schicksalsgöttin lesend hinter Kyknos, der in einen Schwan verwandelt wird. Die drei Heliaden trauern stehend und sitzend. Eridanos blickt auf den fallenden Phaëton. Das Rad rechts unten verweist auf Thetis, die Schwester des Okeanus. In der Zweiergruppe rechts wird wiederum der trauernde Vater Helios erkannt, den Hermes zu trösten versucht. In der stehenden Frauengestalt wird man die Okeanide Klymene, die Mutter, erkennen.

III 4.3: Der stadtrömische Sarkophag in der Villa Borghese, Rom: um 300 n. Chr.

Mit der Audienzgruppe Phaëton vor Helios, den reitenden Dioskuren, den herrenlosen Gespannpferden sowie der Metamorphose des Kyknos und dem auf den stürzenden Phaëton fixierten Eridanos und den knieenden, sich verwandelnden Hesperiden ist die Szene sehr ähnlich aufgebaut.[105] Die nachdenkliche Geste des bärtigen Göttervaters offenbart stärker als die Moira, warum das Thema bildwürdig wurde: „*Sein Nachdenken zeigt, daß ihm der Tod des Phaeton leid tut*".[106] Neu und fruchtbar ist die Interpretation durch Erika Simon der übrigen männlichen und weiblichen Figuren als Allegorien der Elemente Erde, Wasser, Luft und Feuer als *continua metaphora* im Sinne Quintilians.[107]

III 4.4: Gemme mit dem Sturz des Phaëton, Florenz Taf. 6.2

Nach Furtwängler lassen sich sowohl die Gemme und die Sarkophag-Darstellungen auf ein Gemälde zurückführen.[108] Der Wagen, die vier Gespannpferde und der kopfüber fallende Phaëton sind klar zu erkennen. Bei dem Reiter mit der Fackel darf man an einen der Dioskuren denken oder an den Ostwind. Eridanus ist durch den wasserströmenden Krater präsent und der Liebhaber Cygnus singt als Schwan Trauerlieder.[109]

III 4.5: Das amphiglyphe Weihrelief von Dieburg Taf. 6.3a-b

Im Mithraeum von Dieburg in Hessen konnte ein Weihrelief geborgen werden, eine Stiftung von den Brüdern Silvestrius Silvinus und Silvestrius Perpetus sowie dem Enkel Silvinus Aurelius Cumont und Vermaseren beziehen sich auf Nonnos am Ende des 4. Jhs. n. Chr., der Mithras

---

[103] Knaack 1909, 2198, Abb. 2; Baratte 1994, 352, Kat. 19.

[104] Ikonographisch verwandt ist der stark ergänzte Sarkophag in der Ermitage in St. Petersburg: Saverkina 1979, 45ff., Kat. 19, Taf. 44-47.

[105] Sichtermann – Koch 1975, 61f., Kat. 66, Taf. 159; Baratte 1994, 352, Nr. 15.

[106] Simon 2011, 130 deutet die parallel zu Phaëton aus dem Äther stürzende kleine Gestalt des Fackelträgers als personifizierten Blitz, d.h. als Tatwaffe, „*feurigen Gehilfen Jupiters*".

[107] Quint. inst. 8, 6, 44.

[108] Furtwängler 1900, 1, 263, Taf. LVIII 2.

[109] Knaack 1909, 2199f., Abb. 3.

als den „*assyrischen Phaëton in Persien*" bezeichnet und Dio Chrysostomos XXXVI 39, der auf Reisen in Kleinasien um 100 n. Chr. mit den Magoi bekannt wurde und von ihnen einen alten Hymnus lernte, der von den Magiern in den „*geheimen Mysterien*" gesungen worden sein soll:[110] Hier ist es die oberste Gottheit, die die Quadriga lenkt. Die Pferde symbolisieren Feuer, Luft, Wasser und umrunden das vierte Pferd, die Erde, das sich um die eigene Achse dreht. Das schnellste der Rosse steckt das Erdroß mit seinem glühenden Atem ἄσθμα ἰσχυρόν in Brand, das Wasserpferd bewirkt die Sintflut. Der Weltenbrand ἐκπύρωσις wird durch die Sintflut zum Weltuntergang führen, ohne den kein neues Zeitalter geboren werden kann. „*Im Relief von Dieburg haben wir einen sicheren Anhaltspunkt, daß die Mithrasdiener ihren Gott zum Verursacher des Weltenbrandes erhoben haben; sie folgten darin nur der Tradition der kleinasiatischen Magier, die schon zur Zeit des Hellenismus Mithras mit Phaëton identifizierten*".[111]

Im Tondo gibt es nur eine Hauptperson, den thronenden Helios. Im Hintergrund ragt eine Tempel- oder Palast-Architektur auf.[112] Die hinter und neben dem Thron stehenden vier Frauengestalten werden als Personifikation der Jahreszeiten verstanden.[113] In dem nackten, nur mit einem Mantel bekleideten Jüngling ist zweifellos Phaëton zu identifizieren, der auf der Erfüllung seiner Bitte beharrt. Vier nackte, nur mit einem Mantel bekleidete, bartlose, junge Männer führen am Kopfzeug die vier Pferde des Sonnenwagens. Sie werden für die vier Windgötter gehalten, die in den Zwickeln der hochkant stehenden amphiglyphen Platte als Büsten ihren Auftrag erfüllen. „*Unten sitzt Oceanus mit zwei Göttinnen, von denen die eine, mit einem Krug, das Element Wasser, die andere, mit dem Füllhorn, das Element Erde verkörpert*".[114] Eine neuere Interpretation vermutet „*Caelus unter einem Tuch, Tellus und Oceanus..., Symbole der Elemente Luft, Erde, Wasser; das Feuer als viertes ist in Sol gegenwärtig*".[115]

Mit der Erkenntnis: „*Letztlich läßt sich bei diesem singulären Stück nicht klären, welche Vorstellungen die Stifter gerade mit dieser Darstellung verbanden*",[116] wollen wir uns nicht begnügen. Das amphiglyphe Relief diente der Illustration wichtiger Lehren in einem Mithraeum, da es gedreht werden konnte. Der Sturz ist nicht Thema. Phaëton ist Teil der Erzählung. Er bereitet die *unio mystica* als Mithras mit Sol vor. Nach dem Weltenbrand wird vom Kosmokrator ein neues goldenes Zeitalter heraufgeführt mit den Verheißungen großer Freuden wie der Jagd für die Eingeweihten.

Unsere nicht auf Vollständigkeit angelegte Liste legt Zeugnis dafür ab, dass sich die bildenden Künstler in erster Linie an westliche Variationen des Phaëton-Mythos hielten. Mit Hilfe des amphiglyphen Reliefs aus dem Mithraeum von Dieburg läßt sich nachweisen, dass – vermutlich seit hellenistischer Zeit – im Mysterienkult des Mithras auch eine östliche Narration existierte.

---

[110] Vermaseren 1965, 138.

[111] Vermaseren 1965, 141.

[112] Vermaseren 1965, 139 erkennt ein Palastportal.

[113] Vermaseren 1965, 139; so auch Clauss 2012, 147, Abb. 112. Man könnte in der Verhüllten aber auch die Mutter Klymene und in den leicht Bekleideten die Schwestern des Phaëton erkennen, die Heliaden.

[114] Vermaseren 1965, 139.

[115] Clauss 2012, 147, Abb. 112; vgl. auch M. Clauss, Sol Invictus Mithras, Athenaeum 68, 1990, 428ff.

[116] Clauss 2012, 147.

IV. Schlussbetrachtung

„Bei allen [Dingen oder Menschen]

gibt es nur Mutmaßungen"

Xenophanes

Auffallend ist die wiederholte Vater- und Sohn-Beziehung zwischen Helios und Phaëton sowie zwischen Antigonos I. Monophthalmos und Demetrios Poliorketes. Im Christentum opfert Gott seinen Sohn Christus, um die Welt zu retten, wie Helios gezwungen wird, seinen Sohn zu opfern, damit die Erde nicht im Weltenbrand und in der Sintflut untergeht. Helios muß von Ge angestachelt und von Zeus dazu bestimmt, den Tod des Phaëton erdulden. Mithras aber als Kosmokrator als Herr der Präzession steht über den Olympischen Göttern, durch den Sturz des Phaëton und den Tod des Stieres beendet er das Taurus-Zeitalter und führt ein neues goldenes Zeitalter herauf. Sukzessionsvorstellungen überliefert Nonnos in der Spätantike im 5. Jh. n. Chr.: *„ob Kronos, ob Phaeton, Vielnamiger, oder ob du Mithras bist, der babylonische Helios."*[117]

In der Hoffnung, nicht der Ironie Martials 5.53 erlegen zu sein, der einem schlechten Dichter empfahl, einen *„Deukalion"* oder *„Phaeton"* zu schreiben sowie in der gemeinsamen Überzeugung, dass deduktive Methoden legitim sind und in allen Medien der Altertumswissenschaften nach der Wahrheit geforscht werden kann, wünsche ich dem Jäger im luwischen Sprachgürtel „Yeni seneler mutlu olsun".

Kehren wir zurück zu den Thesen. Das Grabmal von Belevi läßt sich zwar weder durch neue Quellen noch durch neue archäologische Fakten als Mausoleum der Antigoniden verifizieren.[118] Aber in weitgehender Übereinstimmung mit den Ergebnissen von Peter Ruggendorfer und Reinhard Heinz läßt sich feststellen, dass der Bau nach 306 v. Chr. konzipiert wurde. Die Bauarbeiten wurden durch den Tod des Vaters 301 v. Chr. nicht unterbrochen, sondern von seinem Sohn fortgesetzt aber nicht beendet.[119]

Sowohl der Baugrund über dem temporären See als auch die unvollendete Terrassierung sowie die Bauskulptur bezeugen, dass zu Ehren der Dynastie, die im Sinne Alexanders des Großen ein

---

[117] Huld – Zetsche 1999, 102; Borchhardt 2012, 102.

[118] Die Publikation des sog. Hekatomnos-Grabbaues in Mylasa könnte Aufschlüsse gewähren. Wurde Uzun Yuva wirklich für einen einzelnen Herrscher errichtet… z.B. für Hekatomnos? Haben Maussollos und Artemisia das Maussolleion in der neuen Hauptstadt wirklich nur für Maussollos errichtet? Logischer wäre doch ein Mausoleum für die Dynastie der Hekatomniden gewesen. Wenn man den Figuren der Wandmalereien sowie des Sarkophages keinen Portraitcharakter sondern idealtypisches Aussehen der Angehörigen der Dynastie der Hekatomniden attestiert, dann könnte die Ikonographie auf das gleiche Strukturprinzip wie in Halikarnassos und Belevi beurteilt werden: In der unteren Grabkammer sollten die Angehörigen der Dynastie bestattet werden. Im Obergeschoß sollten nur die regierenden Dynasten mit ihren Gattinnen in eigenen Sarkophagen ihre letzte Ruhe finden, Statuen wurden ebenfalls nur ihnen aufgestellt. Wie in Mylasa so auch in Belevi hat die historische Entwicklung gegen die Pläne der Errichter entschieden.

[119] Ruggendorfer 2016a, 180. Die Grabungsbefunde können auf Grund der Tierknochen und der Scherben Totenkult am Mausoleum vom Ende des 4. Jh. bis Anfang des 2. Jh. v. Chr. dokumentieren: Ruggendorfer 2016, 65ff.

neues Zeitalter begründen wollte, musische, gymnische, hippische und vermutlich auch nautische Spiele vorgesehen waren.[120]

Die entscheidende Frage stellt sich: Wenn die Antigoniden einen Künstler beauftragten, in der Cella, im oberen Geschoß einen Zyklus des Phaëton-Mythos in einer mithrischen Version darzustellen, gab es Vorbilder oder mußten diese erst erfunden werden? Das amphiglyphe Kult-Relief im hessischen Dieburg (Taf. 6.3a-b) erlaubt doch die Rekonstruktion einer chronologisch konzipierten Biographie des Mithras von der Felsgeburt über das Einfangen des Himmelsstieres bis zu seinem mühevollen Transport in die Höhle. In der mithrischen Version fehlt die Geißelung der Hybris, d.h. der Sturz des Maßlosen, auch die Tötung des Himmelsstieres muß nicht dokumentiert werden. Phaëton muß geopfert werden und in der *ekpyrosis*, dem kosmischen Weltenbrand[121] untergehen, damit ein neues Zeitalter geboren werden kann und damit die *unio mystica* zwischen Helios und Mithras stattfinden kann,[122] die im Kultmahl gefeiert wird und zur gemeinsamen Auffahrt der beiden Gottheiten in den Himmel führt. Die Erlösung findet im Jenseits statt: Cauto und Cautopates begleiten den berittenen Mithras und seine Gefolgschaft mit Pfeil und Bogen auf der ewigen Jagd.

Wenn Nero sich im 1. Jh. n. Chr. als wiedergeborener Mithras gebärdete, dann könnte der Brand von Rom, die Christenverfolgung und der Bau der *domus aurea* mit der auf Phaëton bezogenen Ausmalung von Raum 34 in einem anderen Lichte erscheinen und seinen Beratern in Architektur, Literatur und Kunst war das vor mehr als 300 Jahren konzipierte, unvollendete Projekt der Antigoniden in der Provinz Asia vielleicht nicht verborgen geblieben.

Die Ikonographie dürfen wir uns in beiden Fällen jedenfalls nicht in der westlichen, von Anmaßung, Hybris und Bestrafung diktierten Version vorstellen, wie die Untersuchungen von Ovid und Philostrat gezeigt haben, sondern in einer östlichen mithrischen, kosmischen Deutung, für die der Tod des Phaëton im Weltenbrand die Voraussetzung für das Heraufziehen eines neuen Zeitalters darstellte.

---

[120] Zur temporären Seebildung vgl. Ruggendorfer 2016, 5f.; Heinz 2017, 12ff. mit Frontispiz.

[121] Ulansey 1989, 90.

[122] Borchhardt 2012, 106, Taf. 24.4, 6.

Bibliographie

Alföldy 1975	G. Alföldy, Römische Sozialgeschichte, Wiesbaden 1975.
Baratte 1994	F. Baratte, LIMC VII 1, 1994, 350-355; VII 2, 1994, 311-313.
Bergmann 1994	M. Bergmann, Der Koloß Neros, die Domus Aurea und der Mentalitätswandel im Rom der frühen Kaiserzeit, Trierer Winckelmannsprogramme 13, Mainz 1994.
Bergmann 1998	M. Bergmann, Die Strahlen der Herrscher. Theomorphes Herrscherbild und politische Symbolik im Hellenismus und in der römischen Kaiserzeit, Mainz 1998.
Beutler 1965	E. Beutler (Hrsg.), Johann Wolfgang Goethe, Schriften zur Kunst. Gedenkausgabe der Werke, Briefe und Gespräche, Zurich 1965, 792-840 (= J. W. Goethe, Philostrats Gemälde, in: Johann Wolfgang von Goethe: Über Kunst und Altertum 2, Stuttgart 1818, 27-144).
Borchhardt 2004	J. Borchhardt, Sarkophage der Klassik und ihre Aufstellung in Lykien und Karien, in: J. Gebauer – E. Grabow – F. Jünger – D. Metzler (Hrsg.), Bildergeschichte. Festschrift Klaus Stähler, Möhnesee 2004, 29-58.
Borchhardt 2012	J. Borchhardt, Der Mithras-Code in Limyra/Lykien, in: M. Seyer (Hrsg.), 40 Jahre Grabung Limyra, Akten des internationalen Symposions Wien, 3.-5. Dezember 2009, Wien 2012, 67-132.
Borchhardt-Birbaumer 2003	B. Borchhardt-Birbaumer, Imago Noctis. Die Nacht in der Kunst des Abendlandes. Vom Alten Orient bis ins Zeitalter des Barock, Wien 2003.
Borchhardt – Bleibtreu 2012	J. Borchhardt – E. Bleibtreu, Ein elamischer Page in der Entourage des persischen Großkönigs im Westfries des Heroons von Zẽmuri /Limyra, IstMitt 62, 2012, 119-160.
Brinckmann 1925	A. E. Brinckmann, Michelangelo. Zeichnungen, München 1925.
Chapman 2005	H. Chapman, Michelangelo. Drawings: Closer to the Master, New Haven 2005.
Clauss 2001	M. Clauss, Kaiser und Gott. Herrscherkult im römischen Reich, München – Leipzig 2001.
Clauss 2012	M. Clauss, Mithras. Kult und Mysterium, Darmstadt – Mainz 2012.
de Tolnay et al. 1966	Ch. de Tolnay et al., Michelangelo, Bildhauer – Maler – Architekt – Dichter, Wiesbaden 1966.
Ehling – Weber 2014	K. Ehling – G. Weber (Hrsg.), Hellenistische Königreiche, Stuttgart 2014.
Furtwängler 1900	A. Furtwängler, Die antiken Gemmen: Geschichte der Steinschneidekunst im Klassischen Altertum, Leipzig – Berlin 1900.
Gnann 2010	A. Gnann, Michelangelo. Zeichnungen eines Genies, Berlin 2010.
Haase 2012	M. Haase, Trankopfer, in: DNP 12/1, 2012, 751-753.

Habicht 1970	C. Habicht, Gottmenschentum und griechische Städte, München ²1970.
Heinz 2005	R. Heinz, Bau- und Versatztechnik in der Grabkammer des Mausoleums von Belevi, in: B. Brandt – V. Gassner – S. Ladstätter (Hrsg.), Synergia. Festschrift Friedrich Krinzinger, I, Wien 2005, 99-112.
Heinz 2017	R. Heinz, Das Mausoleum von Belevi. Bauforschung [Forschungen in Ephesos VI 1], Wien 2017.
Heinze 2012	T. Heinze, Phaëton [3], in: DNP 9, 2012, 712.
Hoepfner 1997	W. Hoepfner, Die Architektur von Pergamon, in W.-D. Heilmeyer (Hrsg.), Der Pergamonaltar. Die neue Präsentation nach Restaurierung des Telephosfrieses, Berlin 1997, 24-55.
Hoepfner 2013	W. Hoepfner, Halikarnassos und das Maussolleion, Darmstadt – Mainz 2013.
Hölscher 2001	T. Hölscher, Aktaion, die Perser und Athen, in: N. Birkle – S. Fähndrich (Hrsg.), Macellum. Culinaria Archaeologica. Festschrift Robert Fleischer, Mainz 2001, 123-130.
Huld-Zetsche 1999	I. Huld-Zetsche, Die Stiertötung als Sternenkarte. Astral-mythologische Hintergründe im Mithraskult, AW 30, 1999, 97-103.
Hunger 1988	H. Hunger, Lexikon der griechischen und römischen Mythologie mit Hinweisen auf das Fortwirken antiker Stoffe und Motive in der bildenden Kunst, Literatur und Musik des Abendlandes bis zur Gegenwart, Wien ⁸1988.
Jacobs 1999	B. Jacobs, Die Herkunft und Entstehung der römischen Mithrasmysterien. Überlegungen zur Rolle des Stifters und zu den astronomischen Hintergründen der Kultlegende [Xenia 43], Konstanz 1999.
Knaack 1909	G. Knaack, in: W. H. Roscher, Ausführliches Lexikon der griechischen und römischen Mythologie 3/2, Leipzig 1909, 2175-2202.
L'Orange 1942	H. P. L'Orange, Domus Aurea: der Sonnenpalast [Serta Eitremiana, SymbOslo Suppl. 11], Oslo 1942.
Lechner – Telesko 1991	G. M. Lechner – W. Telesko, Das Wort ward Bild. Quellen der Ikonographie [Katalog der Ausstellung des Graphischen Kabinetts des Stiftes Göttweig/Niederösterreich, nr. 40], Krems/D. 1991.
Lesky 1963	A. Lesky, Geschichte der griechischen Literatur, München ²1963.
Lücke 2002	H.-K. Lücke – S. Lücke, Helden und Gottheiten der Antike. Ein Handbuch. Der Mythos und seine Überlieferung in Literatur und bildender Kunst, Reinbeck 2002.
Mackowsky 1921	H. Mackowsky, Michelangelo, Berlin 1921.
Neschke 1986	A. Neschke, Erzählte und erlebte Götter. Zum Funktionswandel des griechischen Mythos in Ovids „Metamorphosen", in: R. Faber – R. Schlesier (Hrsg.), Die Restauration der Götter. Antike Religion und Neo-Paganismus, Würzburg 1986, 133-152.

Praschniker – Theuer 1979	C. Praschniker – M. Theuer, Das Mausoleum von Belevi [Forschungen in Ephesos VI], Wien 1979.
Rollinger 2017	R. Rollinger (Hrsg.), Die Sicht auf die Welt zwischen Ost und West (750 v. Chr. – 550 n. Chr.), Wiesbaden 2017.
Ruggendorfer 2005	P. Ruggendorfer, Zum Fundkontext der Statue des Orientalen in der Grabkammer des Mausoleums von Belevi, in: B. Brandt – V. Gassner – S. Ladstätter (Hrsg.), B. Brandt – V. Gassner – S. Ladstätter (Hrsg.), Synergia. Festschrift Friedrich Krinzinger, I, Wien 2005.
Ruggendorfer 2016a	P. Ruggendorfer, Das Mausoleum von Belevi. Archäologische Untersuchungen zur Chronologie, Ausstattung und Stiftung [Forschungen in Ephesos VI 2], Wien 2016.
Ruggendorfer 2016b	P. Ruggendorfer, Antigonos I. Monophthalmos und das Mausoleum von Belevi, in: F. Blakolmer – M. Seyer – H. D. Szemethy (Hrsg.), Angekommen auf Ithaka – Festgabe für Jürgen Borchhardt, Wien 2016, 105-126.
Saverkina 1979	I. I. Saverkina, Römische Sarkophage in der Ermitage, Berlin 1979.
Schmidt 1979	G. Schmidt, Flußgötter, in: DKP 2, 1979, 585-587.
Schmidt 1998	P. L. Schmidt, Hyginus, C. Iulius: Leben und Werk, in: DNP 5, 1998, 778-779.
Schönberger 1995	O. Schönberger, Die „Bilder" des Philostratos, in: G. Boehm – H. Pfotenhauer (Hrsg.), Beschreibungskunst – Kunstbeschreibung. Ekphrasis von der Antike bis zur Gegenwart, München 1995, 157-176.
Sichtermann – Koch 1975	H. Sichtermann – G. Koch, Griechische Mythen auf römischen Sarkophagen, Tübingen 1975.
Simon 1986	E. Simon, Augustus. Kunst und Leben in Rom um die Zeitenwende, München 1986.
Simon 2011	E. Simon, Feuer, Wasser, Luft und Erde, in: A. Heil – M. Korn – J. Sauer (Hrsg.), Noctes Sinenses. Festschrift Fritz-Heiner Mutschler, Heidelberg 2011, 129-132.
Simon 2012	E. Simon, Ara Pacis Augustae. Der Altar der Friedensgöttin Pax Augusta in Rom, Dettelbach ²2012.
Smith 1998	R. R. R. Smith, Hellenistic Royal Portraits, Oxford ²1998.
Sonnabend 2016	H. Sonnabend, Nero. Inszenierung der Macht, Darmstadt 2016.
Taeuber 2016	H. Taeuber, Inschriftenfragmente, in: Ruggendorfer 2016a, 319-321.
Ulansey 1989	D. Ulansey, Die Ursprünge des Mithraskults. Kosmologie und Erlösung in der Antike, Theiss 1989.
Vermaseren 1965	M. J. Vermaseren, Mithras. Geschichte eines Kultes, Stuttgart 1965.
Volkmann 1975	H. Volkmann, Tiridates, in: DKP 5, 1975, 860-861.
Volkmann 1979	H. Volkmann, Antigonos – 1. Monophtalmos oder Kyklops, in: DKP 1, 1979, 380-381.
von Geisau 1967	H. von Geisau, Eridanos, in: DKP 2, 1967, 357.

von Geisau 1969	H. von Geisau, Kyknos, in: DKP 3, 1969, 394-395.
von Geisau 1979	H. von Geisau, Phaeton, in: DKP 4, 1979, 689.
von Hartel – F. Wickhoff 1895	W. Ritter von Hartel – F. Wickhoff (Hrsg.), Die Wiener Genesis, Wien 1895.
Wieseler 1857	F. Wieseler, Phaeton. Eine archäologische Abhandlung, Göttingen 1857.

Tafelverzeichnis

Taf. 1.1	Nord-Südschnitt. Rekonstruktion mit Grabkammer und Obergeschoss mit Dachkonstruktion nach Theuer nach Praschniker – Theuer 1979, 59, Abb. 42c
Taf. 1.2	Grundriss der Cella im Obergeschoss sowie Ansicht und Schnitt mit hypothetischer Ausstattung nach Borchhardt 2004, 58, Abb. 11-12
Taf. 1.3	Die Inschriftfragmente, Foto ÖAI Wien
Taf. 1.3a	Inschriftenfragment A: Heliades nach Ruggendorfer 2016a, Taf. 20.1
Taf. 1.3b	Inschriftenfragment B: Z]eus (?) nach Ruggendorfer 2016a, Taf. 20.2
Taf. 1.4	Demetrius I Poliorketes (306-283 v. Chr.) Tetradrachmon, in Amphipolis geprägt nach Franke – Hirmer 1964, Taf. 174
Taf. 2.1	Rekonstruktion der Grabkammer mit Bodenplatten und Wandblöcken Grundriss nach Heinz 2005, 99ff., Abb. 1
Taf. 2.2	Rekonstruktion des Sarkophages mit geöffnetem Deckel nach Ruggendorfer 2016a, Taf. 107.1
Taf. 2.3	Der Page in der Grabkammer. Hauptansicht vom Vestibulum nach Ruggendorfer 2016a, Taf. 104.4
Taf. 2.4	Rekonstruktion des Sarkophages mit geschlossenem Deckel nach Ruggendorfer 2016, 109, Abb. 3
Taf. 3.1	Der Palast des Nero: Domus Aurea vermuteter Grundriss nach Bergmann 1994, 20, Abb. 5
Taf. 3.2	Nero (54-68 n. Chr.) Dupondius mit Strahlenkrone nach Bergmann 1994, Taf. 1.5
Taf. 3.3	Domus Aurea: Raum 34 mit Phaëton-Mythos im Trakt am Oppiushang mit Oktogon nach Bergmann 1994, 21, Abb. 7
Taf. 3.4	Rekonstruktion des Koloss des Nero Skizze von Silvano Bertolin nach Bergmann 1994, 26, Abb. 10
Taf. 3.5	Rekonstruktion des Nero-Koloss mit Kithara und Globus Skizze Jürgen Borchhardt
Taf. 3.6	Arbeiten auf der Plattform des Mausoleums von Belevi 1933. Foto ÖAI
Taf. 4.1	1. Fassung: Schwarze Kreide / 1533. 41,3 x 23,4 cm. Windsor Castle, The Royal Collection nach Brinkmann 1925, Taf. 56
Taf. 4.2	2. Fassung: Rötelzeichnung. Harlem, Teylers Museum Inv. Nr. A 31 nach Brinkmann 1925, Taf. 55
Taf. 4.3	3. Fassung: Galleria dell' Accademia, Venedig nach Brinkmann 1925, Taf. 57

Taf. 4.4	4. Fassung: Radierung 40,8 x 28,7 cm. Stich von Nicolas Beatrizet (1540-1565) nach Michelangelo als inventor. Bibliothek Göttweig, Inv. Nr. XLII J a 7 nach Lechner – Telesko 1991, 17, Abb. Kat. 6b
Taf. 5.1	5. Fassung: gegossene Bronzeplaquette 1540-1550 / 8,5 x 7 cm. London, British Museum. von Giovanni Bernardi (1495-1553) nach Michelangelo nach L. Goldscheider, Michelangelo. Drawings (1951) Abb. 93
Taf. 5.2	Rekonstruktion des Gemäldes nach Philostrat, Eikones I 11.1ff. Jürgen Borchhardt 2017
Taf. 5.3	Die dramatis personae: Helios, Phaëton, Dioskuren, Moira und Kyknos / Cygnus / Heliaden, Eridanos, Klymene, Thetis. Sarkophag aus Ostia, Ny Carlsberg Glyptothek, Kopenhagen nach Knaack 1909, 2198, Abb. 2
Taf. 6.1	Zeus und Artemis retten die Welt durch den Tod des Phaëton, die Dioskuren fangen die Sonnenpferde ein und die Metamorphose der Heliaden aretinischer Becher, Boston, Museum of Fine Arts nach Knaack 1909, 2195, Abb. 1
Taf. 6.2	Der Sturz des Phaëton in den Eridanos und die Metamorphose des Kygnos. Gemme, Sardonyx, Florenz nach Knaack 1909, 2199, Abb. 3
Taf. 6.3a	Phaëton bittet Helios um den Sonnenwagen / oder die Audienz von Phaëton bei Helios. Weihrelief aus Dieburg/Hessen, Kreis- und Stadtmuseum Dieburg nach Ulansey 1989, 91, Abb. 7.8
Taf. 6.3b	Mithras auf der Jagd. Rückseite des Weihreliefs aus Dieburg. Kreis- und Stadtmuseum Dieburg nach Clauss 2012, 75, Abb. 39

Χρυσᾶ τῶν Ἡλιάδων τὰ δάκρυα. Heliadlar'ın gözyaşları altın akar veya Phaethon efsanesinin Mithras Kültü'ne göre yorumu
Özet

Sadece Efes yakınlarındaki Belevi Mausoleumu'nda değil aynı zamanda Roma'daki Nero'nun sarayındaki (= Domus Aurea) döşemelerde Phaethon (Φαέθων) efsanesi işlenmiştir. Bu durum, bunları yapan ustalar tarafından yeni bir altın çağ yaratmak amacıyla yeniden doğmuş Mithras olarak açıklanacaktır. Pergamon altarındaki Telephos frizine benzer şekilde, bu iki yerde de birden fazla bölümde anlatılmak üzere Phaethon ve kız kardeşleri Heliadlar efsanesinin gösterilmesinin planlandığı varsayılmaktadır.

Phaethon'un küstahlıkla suçlanıp, cezasının ve felaketinin Zeus tarafından verildiği batı versiyonu değil de, Mithras kültü inancına göre dünyanın ateş ile harap edilişinde (ἐκπύρωσις) oğulun babası tarafından kurban edilişini benimseyen doğu versiyonu gösteriliyor olmalıdır. Mithras, Kosmokrator, "Persia'daki Asurlu Phaethon" (Nonnos), olarak yeni altın çağı (*aurea aetas*) garantilemektedir. Güzel sanatlarda sanatçıların Antik Çağ'dan Rönesans'a (Michelangelo) ve modern zamana (Goethe) batı edebiyatı örneklerini (Ovidus, Philostratos) takip etmesi şaşırtıcı değildir. Sadece Almanya Dieburg'da bulunan anfiglifik ("her yönden işlemeli") kabartma Mithras kültüne ait bir yorumun var olduğunu kanıtlamaktadır (Nonnos, Dio Chrysostomos). Bu durum Halikarnassos ve aynı şekilde Belevi'de yer alan mezarların sadece bir hükümdar için değil, hanedanlar için inşa edildiği düşüncesine karşıt değildir. Bu sebeple Hekatomnoslar ve Antigonoslar için yapılan anıt mezarlarda, iktidarda olan hükümdarların gömü ve onların kültü için lahitler ve heykeller bulunan üst katında ve hanedanın normal aile üyeleri için podyumunda çeşitli alanlara ihtiyaç vardı.

Anahtar Sözcükler: Halikarnassos, Belevi, anıtlar, Phaethon Efsanesi, Antigonos Monophthalmos, Demetrios Poliorketes, Nero, Mithras.

Χρυσᾶ τῶν Ἡλιάδων τὰ δάκρυα. Golden flow the tears of the Heliades or The mithric interpretation of the Phaeton myth
Abstract

In the furnishing, not only of the Mausoleum of Belevi near Ephesos but also in the palace of Nero (Domus Aurea) in Rome the myth of Phaëton is shown. It will be explained by the builders to be the reborn Mithras in order to create a new golden age. Analogous to the Telephos-Frieze from the Pergamon-Altar it is supposed that in both places it was planned to show the myth of Phaëton and his sisters, the Heliades, narrative in more than one sequence.

But not the western version, which accused Phaëton of presumption and justified his punishment and destruction by Zeus, should be shown but the eastern interpretation, which demanded in Mithraic understanding the sacrifice of the son by his father in the expyrosis, in the decline of the world by fire. Mithras as Kosmokrator, „the Assyrian Phaëton in Persia" (Nonnos) guarantees a new golden era (aurea aetas). It is not astonishing that in fine arts from antiquity to the renaissance (Michelangelo) to modern times (Goethe) artists follow the literary western examples (Ovid, Philostrat). Only the amphiglyphic relief from Dieburg in Germany testifies that the Mithraic interpretation existed (Nonnos, Dio Chrysostomos). This is not contrary to the assumption that the tombs in Halikarnassos as well as in Belevi are not built for one ruler but for dynasties. Therefore, the mausolea for the Hecatomnids and the Antigonids were in need of different places for funerals and cult of the ruling dynasts in the upper floor with sarcophags and statues and the normal family-members of the dynasty in the podium.

Keywords: Mausolea, Halikarnassos, Belevi, the myth of Phaëton, Antigonos Monophthalmos, Demetrios Poliorketes, Nero, Mithras.

TAFEL 1

1.1) *Nord-Südschnitt. Rekonstruktion mit Grabkammer und Obergeschoss mit Dachkonstruktion nach Theuer*

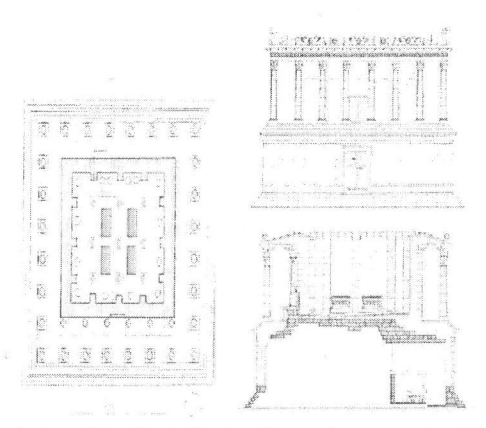

1.2) *Grundriss der Cella im Obergeschoss sowie Ansicht und Schnitt mit hypothetischer Ausstattung*

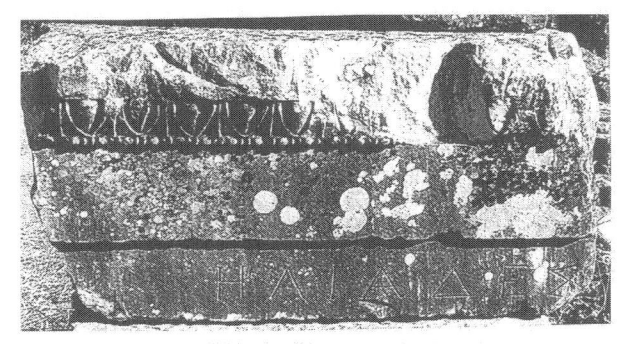

1.3a) *Inschriftfragment A: Heliades*

1.3b) *Inschriftfragment B: Z]eus (?)*

1.4) *Demetrius I Poliorketes (306- 283 v. Chr.) Tetradrachmon, in Amphipolis geprägt*

DAS MAUSOLEUM DER ANTIGONIDEN VON BELEVI IN IONIEN

TAFEL 2

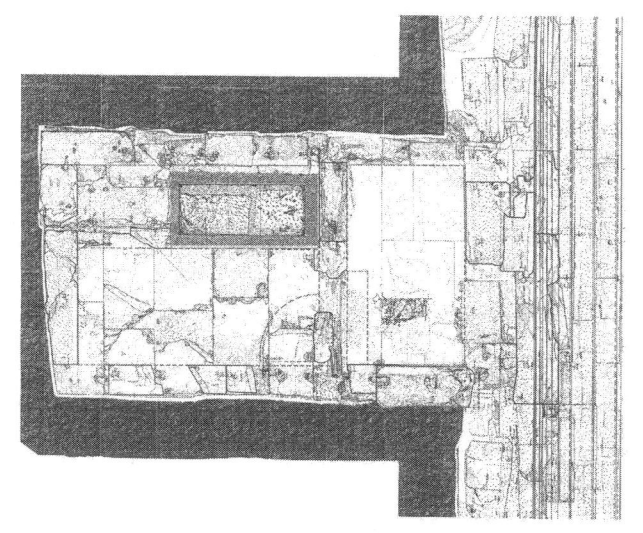

2.1) *Rekonstruktion der Grabkammer mit Bodenplatten und Wandblöcken, Grundriss*

2.2) *Rekonstruktion des Sarkophages mit geöffnetem Deckel*

2.3) *Der Page in der Grabkammer, Hauptansicht vom Vestibulum*

2.4) *Rekonstruktion des Sarkophages mit geschlossenem Deckel*

DAS MAUSOLEUM DER ANTIGONIDEN VON BELEVI IN IONIEN

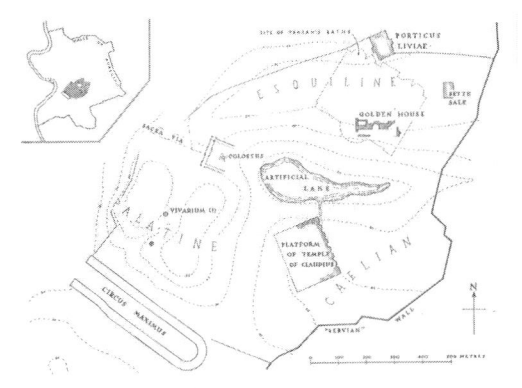

Χρυσᾶ τῶν Ἡλιάδων τὰ δάκρυα. Golden strömen die Tränen der Heliaden oder…

TAFEL 3

3.1) *Der Palast des Nero: Domus Aurea, vermuteter Grundriss*

3.2) *Nero (54-68 n. Chr.) Dupondius mit Strahlenkrone*

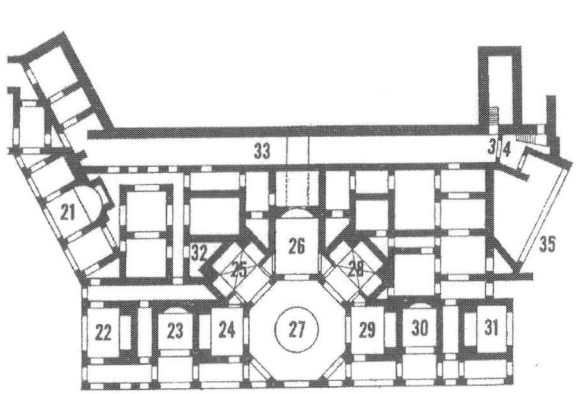

3.3) *Domus Aurea: Raum 34 mit Phaëton-Mythos im Trakt am Oppiushang mit Oktogon*

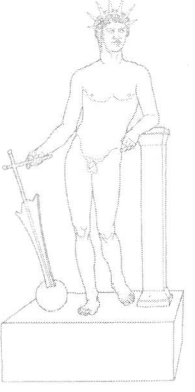

3.4) *Rekonstruktion des Koloss des Nero Skizze von Silvano Bertolin*

3.5) *Rekonstruktion des Nero-Koloss mit Kithara und Globus*

3.6) *Arbeiten auf der Plattform des Mausoleums von Belevi 1933*

DOMUS AUREA IN ROM MIT DEM KOLOSS IM VESTIBULUM UND DEM PHAËTON-MYTHOS IN RAUM 34

TAFEL 4

4.1) *1. Fassung: Schwarze Kreide 1533, 41,3 x 23,4 cm, Windsor Castle, The Royal Collection*

4.2) *2. Fassung: Rötelzeichnung, Harlem, Teylers Museum Inv. Nr. A 31*

4.3) *3. Fassung: Galleria dell' Accademia, Venedig*

4.4) *4. Fassung: Radierung 40,8 x 28,7 cm, Stich von Nicolas Beatrizet (1540-1565) nach Michelangelo als inventor, Bibliothek Göttweig, Inv. Nr. XLII J a 7*

DER STURZ DES PHAËTON von MICHELANGELO BUONAROTTI (1475-1564)

Χρυσᾶ τῶν Ἡλιάδων τὰ δάκρυα. Golden stromen die Tränen der Heliaden oder… 113

TAFEL 5

5.1) 5. Fassung: gegossene Bronzeplaquette 1540-1550
8,5 x 7 cm, London, British Museum
von Giovanni Bernardi (1495-1553) nach Michelangelo

5.2) Rekonstruktion des Gemäldes nach Philostrat,
Eikones I 11.1ff.

5.3) Die dramatis personae: Helios, Phaëton, Dioskuren, Moira und Kyknos / Cygnus / Heliaden,
Eridanos, Klymene, Thetis. Sarkophag aus Ostia, Ny Carlsberg Glyptothek, Kopenhagen

DER PHAËTON-MYTHOS IN DER RÖMISCHEN KUNST
UND IN DER RENAISSANCE

TAFEL 6

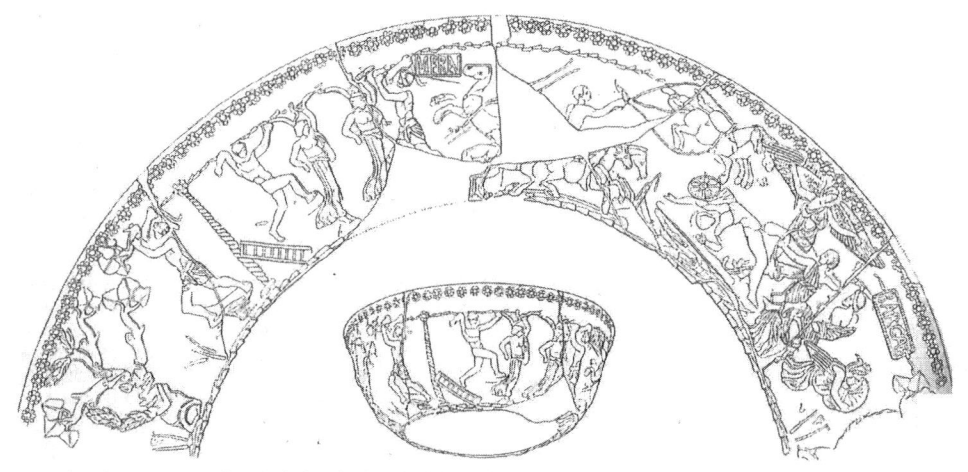

6.1) *Zeus und Artemis retten die Welt durch den Tod des Phaëton, die Dioskuren fangen die Sonnenpferde ein und die Metamorphose der Heliaden, aretinischer Becher, Boston, Museum of Fine Arts*

6.2) *Der Sturz des Phaëton in den Eridanos und die Metamorphose des Kygnos, Gemme, Sardonyx, Florenz*

6.3a) *Phaëton bittet Helios um den Sonnenwagen / oder die Audienz von Phaëton bei Helios, Weihrelief aus Dieburg/Hessen, Kreis- und Stadtmuseum Dieburg*

6.3b) *Mithras auf der Jagd, Rückseite des Weihreliefs aus Dieburg, Kreis- und Stadtmuseum Dieburg*

DER STURZ DES PHAËTON UND DER BEGINN EINES NEUEN ZEITALTERS

On early antiquarians in Asia Minor to the start of the 19th century

Terrance Michael Patrick DUGGAN*

Both the range of this subject and its time span are truly vast.[1] This paper addresses a few of the issues concerning the activities of European antiquarians and the ancient Greek and Roman inscriptions of Asia Minor over the course of four hundred years from 1400 to 1800, touching upon five matters. Firstly, the collection and removal of antiquities including inscriptions by Europeans. Secondly, the varied functions of the visible ancient inscriptions for the Ottoman state and its inhabitants, both talismanic and therapeutic, and of the "non-literal reading" of an ancient inscription, distinct from the European antiquarian interest in the literal text of inscriptions, in establishing record of, and collections of the inscribed historical texts surviving from antiquity. Thirdly, the question of how safe a home was Europe for antiquities, including inscriptions and manuscripts that were brought from Asia Minor, and how much of scholarly importance that had survived was then lost in transit at sea and in Europe in wars and disasters? Fourthly, the problems with the transcriptions made by hand, the content of the record made and its accuracy. Was the inscription regarded simply as a text, prioritised as a text, or, was the text transcribed in its context including the epigraphic surface, its shape and relief carving, if any, its physical location if *in situ*, was it understood as forming a whole, and was it recorded as such? Were the letter forms, the number of lines, the different size of letters and words in an inscription, misspellings, etc., accurately noted or not? And, finally, the problems generated through the printed publication from the 16th c. onwards of the transcriptions that had been made of inscriptions, in particular, those employing a standard font in publication for the study of inscriptions, not least impacting the understanding of orthography. Again, was it a matter of the antiquarian publishing just the text of an inscription, or the text within its context, to scale,

---

* Öğr. Gör. Terrance Michael Patrick Duggan, Mediterranean Civilisations Research Institute, Akdeniz University, Antalya, Turkey (tmpduggan@yahoo.com).

This contribution is the paper from the presentation given at the symposium on the "Epigraphies of Anatolia: their histories and their future", 24-27 April 2018, The Koç University Suna & İnan Kıraç Research Centre for Mediterranean Civilizations (AKMED), Antalya.

[1] Among the more important recent works to address this subject are: *Cyriac of Ancona, Later Travels*, Ed. And Trans. Edward W. Bodnar with Clive Foss, Harvard University Press, 2003, covering the 1440's which provides a broad picture of the quantity at this date of the visible remains of antiquity in the region; and, Michael Greenhalgh, *From the Romans to the Railways: The Fate of Antiquities in Asia Minor*, Brill, Leiden 2013, in part, associating the course of modernisation of the 19th c. Ottoman state with the removal of antiquities, due to the development of improved transportation infrastructure facilitating their removal. See for comparisons, Michael Greenhalgh, *Destruction of Cultural Heritage in 19th-century France: Old Stones versus Modern Identities*, Brill, Leiden 2015, not least, the proposition that modernization and destruction are two sides of the same coin, with museums providing the 'supposed' safeguard. Supposed - as it can be suggested that the exhibition of "deracinated orphans" in museums, itself fuels further collection, and, rather than being a safeguard, it seems evident that collections and museum exhibitions and displays themselves function as an incentive to further collecting.

including the number of lines, the size of letters, the particular letter forms, the presence of guidelines, any remains of applied colour and its support, etc.

It seems to have been the Bishop of Agria (Eger), Antonius Verantius's transcription of the *Res Gestae Divi Augusti* and the copy of it made by Busbecq's servants in Ankara in 1555 which, when circulated and then published[2] (Fig. 5), underlined to European scholars by the end of the 16th c. the importance of the surviving ancient epigraphic record in Asia Minor. However, the search for ancient Greek and Latin inscriptions in Asia Minor, as elsewhere in this period needs to be understood within the context of the importance given to the precedent provided by Roman models, Republican and Imperial, in the ongoing Europe-wide disputes between Emperor and Papacy, of authority for rule, and in Reformation polity formation and justification, in which the precedents adduced or recorded from antiquity played an important role. Busbecq wrote that the hatred for Desiderius Erasmus (1466-1536) derived from the fact that, "*he has sent the world to school with Greece and Rome for its masters.*"[3], rather than Christ, the Apostles and the Popes, and, in this, for Europeans the study and collection of Greek and Latin inscriptions played a role in the attempts at resurrecting the nature of the pre-Christian world, an element in the justification of models for rule, Republican and Imperial, in the Renaissances of Europe. Driven by collectors, humanists and antiquarians, the 16th c. saw the beginning of the attempt by Europeans to understand ancient Roman Asia Minor through both the criticism of the surviving often corrupted literary sources and from the growing range of circulated and published collected epigraphic and numismatic material. Ogier Ghiselin de Busbecq-Busbequius (1522-1592) described his antiquarian mission in Asia Minor in the following words: "*And why should not you help in this work, Ogier? There are manuscripts yet to be discovered, there are inscriptions yet to be copied, there are coins of which no specimen have been gathered.*"[4]

Over this period of 400 years, in *Turchia, Turquia*, the Beylik *bilad ar-rūm*, in Ottoman *Anatolı, Natolia*, Asia Minor/Asia Mineure, there was the transcription of much ancient epigraphic material by antiquarians from Europe, together with the "*gathering,*" selection and the removal where practicable of important epigraphic documents: inscriptions, coins, medals, carved gemstones, as also ancient manuscripts[5], together with the selection and removal of antique "marbles," statues and relief sculptures. A variety of methods and means were employed, with the assistance of merchants, envoys, ambassadors and consular officials, largely Venetian, French, Dutch and English (after 1707) British.[6] In any attempt to place in context the 19th to 21st c. Eu-

---

[2] Joseph Pitton de Tournefort records, "*the inscription is to be found in the Monumentum Ancyranum Gronovii and in Gruter. Leunclave had of it, Clusius (Charles de L'Ecluse, the botanist of tulip fame and antiquary), ...And Faustus Verantius, who communicated this piece to Clusius, had it from his uncle from Venetian Croatia, Antonius Verantius (1504-73), Bishop of Agria (Eger) and Ambassador (in 1553-57 and 1567-1587) of Ferdinand II. to the Porte. This Prelate caused it to be transcribed as he passed by Angora. Busbequius took a Copy of it, ...*" Tournefort 1741, Vol. 111, 286.

[3] Busbecq 1881, 47.

[4] Busbecq 1881, 47.

[5] For example the merchant and dealer in antiquities, Paul Lucas, returned from his 1705-1707 voyage with 22 manuscripts.

[6] For example the Ambassador Extraordinary and Minister Plenipotentiary of His Britannic Majesty to the Sublime Porte from 1775 to 1793, Sir Robert Ainslie collected Greek and Latin inscriptions and other

ropean interest in the epigraphic record surviving from antiquity in Asia Minor, a study of earlier European antiquarian activity in Asia Minor provides us with a range of valuable precedents, not least in the relationship between envoys from European states in Asia Minor and antiquarian activity[7] (Table II), that then precipitated into the various European national archaeological institutes established in Constantinople-Istanbul in the second half of the 19th and early 20th centuries. It also provides some reasons why European antiquarian activity in respect to the ancient inscriptions in Asia Minor had been regarded with suspicion by the Ottoman State and by some of its inhabitants for centuries before Lt. Col. W. M. Leake in his 1824 publication suggested two of the reasons for this suspicion, firstly, the inhabitants thought the foreigners were spying out the land for a future invasion, "*or (that they were in) a search after treasure amongst the ruins of antiquity.*"[8] The latter suspicion was alive two hundred years earlier, as the English Ambassador Sir Thomas Roe related in a letter to the Duke of Buckingham of May 1627, "*From Angory, I had a hal(f)- woman, brought 18 dayes by land, upon change of mules, which wants a hand, a nose, a lip; and is so deformed, that shee makes me remember an hospital. Yet the malicious Turkes brought trouble on the buyers, by a false command, accusing them of a great wealth stolen out of the castle; it hath cost mee money to punish them, and that is all I have for my labor.*"[9] A fuller account not only of the European, but also of the varied Ottoman perspectives, the various views of rulers, *alim*, clerics[10], city dwellers, villagers[11] and nomads, of the members

---

antiquities which were shipped to England in the frigate 'Pearl' in 1789; as also Lord Elgin in 1799 (see below).

[7] This became part of official recognised expected and regular British consular activity by 1864 when a Foreign Office circular was sent out to all acting consuls, making the search for antiquities part of their official duties (on this see Gunning 2016). Hence, for example Alfred Billiotti, British vice-consul on Rhodes between the 1856 and the 1870's, "*who acted as an agent for Charles Newton in acquiring antiquities for the British Museum.*" http://www.britishmuseum.org/research/search_the_collection_database/term_details.aspx?bioId=97427 He was an excavator of antiquities at Halicarnassos with Auguste Salzmann, after Consul Charles Newton left the site, and with Auguste Salzmann at Kameiros in 1852-1864, and at Ialysos from 1868 to 1871, where he excavated the first collection of Mycenean jewellery, at Didyma in 1874, and, again excavated on Crete 1885-1897 in his capacity as British Consul. E.g., "*Mr Albert Billiotti, the British Pro-Consul at Rhodes, who in conjunction with his brother has been carrying out excavations for some years, has sent me the following eight inscriptions which he has noted from time to time and which, so far as I know, are unpublished.*" Smith 1883, 136.

[8] Leake 1824, Preface v.

[9] Hervey 1921, 274.

[10] For example, to what extent did Rum-Greek priests facilitate the removal by European antiquarians of the remains of pagan antiquity from Asia Minor, not only, or solely for the money, but also to protect the orthodox believer, in the centuries prior to the formulation of Greek nationalism in the late 18th c. with its ideological relationship with ancient Greece as it was then understood? To what extent did Augustine of Hippo's charge made in his *City of God*, relating Roman religion to magic and necromancy, serve not just as a call to destroy the Pagan remains, but to remain distant from these remains, or otherwise be associated with the practice of necromancy and other diabolical practices? As also, to what extent were the surviving pagan remains protected from casual pillage by the Rum inhabitants, due to the understood presence of demons recorded in many of the recorded lives of saints, inhabiting the remains of Pagan antiquity. Clive Foss in Byzantine and Ottoman Sardis writes: "*Crosses were carved on the temple of Artemis to nullify the power of the demons who, it was believed, dwelt in the material of pagan edifices.*"

of the various Ottoman millets in respect to these ancient remains, including '*written stones,*' over the course of these four centuries, remains a desideratum.

Table I) *An incomplete list of Asia Minor's ancient sites visited by Europeans between 1400 and 1800 where inscriptions were noted and/or transcribed or removed*

1400-1500   Kyzikos, Nicea, Pergamon, Kyme, Lampsacus, Troy, Didyma, Kyme, Smyrna, Sardis, Phocaea, Miletus, Ephesus

1500-1600   Nicomedie, Ruines de Troye, Tarsus, Adana, Heraclée-Heraclea, Cogne-Iconium-Konya, Achara-Ankara, Nicea

1600-1700   Troy, Lampsacum, Sinope, Ankara, Brussia, Amasia, Pergamo, Assos, Smyrna-İzmir, Ephesus, Magnesia ad Meandrum, Cladie (?), Konya, Eski-Attalie-Side, Satalie-Sattaliya-Antalya, Nice-Nicea-Iznik, Trebisonde, Nicomedia-İzmit, Seliori, Eregli, Sardis, Kyzikos, Eskihisar, Thyatira-Akhisar, Laodicea, Philadelphia, Hierapolis, Panionium, Miletus, Iotan-Didyma, Askem Kalesi, Mylasa-Milas, Manisa (Magnesia ad Sipylum), Bursa, Metropolis, Lampsacus-Lapseki, Clazomene, Angora, Cesarea-Kayseri

1700-1800   Ankara, Sinope, Heraclea, Smyrna-İzmir, Manisa, Eskihisar, Thyatira-Akhisar, Laodicea, Philadelphia, Hierapolis, Sardis, Derrekoy by Sardis, Marmara, Soma, Torbali, Nicomedia, Sigeum-Ilium-Troy, Jeronda-Branchidae-Didyma, Teum, Teos, Tralles, Nissa, Tyria, Aphrodisias, Miletus, Stratonicea-Eskihissar, Vourla, Attourla, Colossae, Iasos, Ephesos, Colophon, Metropolis, Nazilli, Turgutlu, Kuşa-

---

(Foss 1976, 34), as likewise Pococke records in respect to the Augustus temple at Mylasa, "*This building, when Christianity prevailed, was doubtless converted either into a church, or some other public building; for on the stones of the temple I saw several defaced inscriptions, with the cross on them.*" (Pococke 1745, II, 61). And in 1452, with church union, it was thought by the Orthodox that Hagia Sophia in Constantinople, where Procopius relates, Justinian is said to have exclaimed on its completion, Νενίκηκά σε Σολομών, "*Solomon, I have outdone thee!*", had become the abode of demons, becoming a pagan temple, and so the Orthodox left the Great Church unvisited. Likewise, to what extent were Muslim attitudes towards the remains of antiquity shaped by the literary and popular discourse that had repeatedly, over the course of many centuries, associated ancient sites, hidden treasure, the remains of antiquity, inaccessible ravines, and disease, with the malevolent Jinn-Ifrits and ghouls, thereby protecting ancient remains from human disturbance?

[11] To perhaps better understand this other context within which ancient remains and written stones were understood, by both Christian and Muslim populations, it is worth reading Mahmut Makal's *Memleketin Sahipleri* (The Masters of the Country) of 1954, which describes from his own experience as a village school teacher, the local jinn, saints and devils dwelling in caves, tombs, sacred wells and trees, those forces so named that played such an important role in the life of the villager over the past millennia, forces that inhabited the mental landscape in a more proximate manner over the past millennia than is often realised today, and who, from Makal's opinion, an opinion formed by the middle of the last century, are the real "Masters of the Country." as is likewise recorded in Yaşar Kemal's *Yer demir gök bakır* (Iron earth Copper sky) of 1963. See for examples Anderson 2015. In prioritising the importance of the literal text of ancient inscriptions, over the way the written stone was subsequently and differently understood over time by the local inhabitants, our understanding of the more recent past's relationship with these remains may be distorted, while clarifying in places our understanding of the history of antiquity.

dası, Parium, Perinthos, Seluccia, Cilician Gates, Konya, Eskişehir, Mylasa-Milas, Cnidus, Halicarnassos-Bodrum, Çardak Köy facing Gallipoli, Alexander Troas-Assos, Brussa, Cizicus-Cyzique, Nicea-İznik, Telmessos-Makri-Fethiye, Patara, Myra-Andriake, Kekova, Antiphellos-Kaş, Bergamo-Pergamus, Thymbrius, Cymae-Carina-Heraclea, Bithynian Eraclei, Apollonia.

Table I indicates that of the antique sites in Asia Minor, it was largely Troy and the Troad and those cities in Aegean coastal areas and on major trade routes that were visited, where inscriptions were recorded and/or removed. In particular, from the 17th c. onwards, those proximate to Smyrna-Izmir, with its Venetian, French, Dutch and English Consulates. But the majority of Greco-Roman cities-sites in Asia Minor remained unvisited before 1800. The Biblical sites unvisited by antiquarians to 1800 included: Pisidian Antioch, Perge, Lystra, Derbe, and Phaselis; and, amongst those sites known from ancient sources but unvisited by 1800: Aspendos, Xanthus and the Letoon, Side, Termessos, Limyra, Tlos, Pinara-Minare, Rhodiapolis, Caunos, Silenus, Claudiopolis, Ariassos, Apamea, Eumenia, Pessinus, Sagalassos, Cremna, Cibyra, Philomelion, Amorium, Selge, Azanoi, Kelendres, Synnada, Anemorium, etc.

Table II) *An incomplete list of the dates of visits of those Europeans to Natolia-Asia Minor, individual or group, who noted, recorded and/or removed ancient Greek and/or Latin inscriptions. The dates of diplomatic envoys and consular officials recorded as involved in these activities are given in bold*

1400-1500   Italian city states (Florence, Ancona) 1414-1422 & 1430; 1412, 1431, 1435, 1444, 1446, 1447, and acquisitions amongst others for Cardinal Domenico Grimani's (1461-1523) collection donated to the city of Venice, in part from Rome, Crete and almost certainly Asia Minor as some of the sculpture, coins and gems came from the Levant.

1500-1600   French 1546-9.
Austrian 1554-55, 1556-62, 1588-9. Bilingual copy of the *Res Gestae Divi Augusti*, transcribed 1555, published Andreas Schott 1579.

1600-1700   English 1610; 1627-30; 1621-8; 1627-8; 1628-39; 1638, 1670-1678; 1668-71, 1673, 1675-76; 1698-1702. '*Parian Chronicle*,' purchased in 1624 and taken from Smyrna-İzmir to London, published in *Marmora Arundellina*, ed. John Selden in 1628.
French 1624, 1633; 1641; 1675-76; 1699-1707.
Holland-Dutch 1630, 1674-81.

1700-1800   Holland-Dutch 1700-1709; 1703, 1705-06, 1716, 1724-59.
French 1701, 1701-1702; 1716; 1737, 1754; **1757-65**; **1776**; 1784-6, **1786**; 1797.
British 1705-18; 1705; 1709-16, Bilingual *Prices Edict* of Stratonicea copied 1709, 1716; 1718, *Sigaean decree of Antiochus Soter of 278 B.C.* removed by **Amb. Edward Wortley Montague**; 1727, 1732, 1737-38; 1738-9; 1739-1740; 1749; 1764-5; 1792; 1795-6; 1799; 1799-1801. Attic-Ionic '*Sigaean Phanodikos Inscription*,' c. 550 B.C. first transcribed 1716 by Homero, published by Chishull in 1721, removed by William Wittman and Sir Richard Phillips for the **Amb. James Bruce, 7th Earl of Elgin** 1799 with firman from the Porte.
Florence, Naples 1779; 1792

Table II shows rapidly increasing antiquarian interest from the start of the 17th c. onwards in the visible surviving ancient Greek and Latin inscriptions, part of the increasing European interest in the remains of antiquity, in a climate of increasing contacts and trade with Ottoman Asia Minor largely through the

Aegean port of Smyrna-Izmir with the issuance of the Ottoman, so-called capitulations.[12] There were certainly more removals of epigraphic material from Asia Minor to Venice and Genoa than are presently recorded in the modern literature.

Table III) *An incomplete list of antiquarians and those with an interest, scholarly and/or financial in antiquities, who reported on the presence of, transcribed (and at times, collected and removed) ancient inscriptions from Asia Minor*[13].

1400-1500   Ciriaco de Pizzicolli/Cyriacus of Ancona (known to Pope Eugenius IV, to John VIII Paleologus), 1412, 1431, 1435, 1444, 1446, 1447.

1500-1600   Envoy Sieur d'Aramont, with Pierre Gilles and Pierre Belon 1546-49, Petrus Antonius Verantius, Envoy Bishop of Agria (Eger), and Ogier Ghiselin de Busbecq-Busbequius 1554-1555, 1556-1562.

1600-1700   George Sandys 1610, Sir Thomas Roe, English Ambassador to the Porte 1621-1628, Thomas Markham, Rev. William Petty 1620's, French Consul in Smyrna, Sanson Napollon 1624, Sir Peter Wyche, English Ambassador to the Porte 1627-1641, Fra. P. Théophile Minuti 1633, Rev. Thomas Greaves 1637-1638, Rev. Edward Pocock, December 1637 to August 1640, Sieur Du Loir 1641, Dr. John Luke, 1664-9 and 1674-83, Dr. Thomas Smith, Levent Company Chaplain 1668-71, Rev. John Covel 1670-1678, Johann Michael Wansleben 1670, Sir Paul Rycaut 1670-1678, Dr. Pickering 1673, Cornelis de Bruijn 1674-81 (in the Levant), Jacques (Jacob or James) Spon of Lyon and George Wheler 1675-76, Rev. T. Smith chaplain to the English factory at Smyrna 1683, Daniel Cosson, Rev. Edmund Chishull chaplain to the English factory at Smyrna 1698-1702, Sieur Aubry De La Motraye 1699, 1707.

1700-1800   Envoy Johannes Aegidius van Egmond van der Nijenburg, United States of Holland representative Smyrna, and Johannes Wilhelmus Heyman, 1700-1709, Joseph Pitton de Tournefort, Marquis de Nointel 1701-1702, Paul Lucas 1705-Feb. 1706, 1715, Rev. John Tisser 1701-1710, Dr. William Sherard 1705-1717, Rev. Samuel Lisle 1705-1716, with Dr. Antonio Picenini, C. Lockwood, J. Lethieullier (1705 Smryna) and William Sherard's consular dragoman S. Homerus, Rev. Chaplain Bernard Mould 1716-24, Rev. Vandervecht and Jos. Clotterboke, M. L'Abbé Francoise Sevin, Anne Claude Philippe de Tubieres, Comte de Caylus. 1716, Amb. Edward Wortley Montague 1718, Rev. Charles Burdett 1724-1751 chaplain to the

---

[12] Issued to the Genovese 1352, Venetians by 1387, 1403, 1411, 1419, 1430, 1446, 1454; Florentines 1450's, Naples 1498, French 1517, 1569, English 1580, Netherlands 1612, İnalcik 1997, I. 194. These record protection and tax-trade concessions for bearers. They do not record nor grant any permission to remove antiquities.

[13] An extensive list of the names and dates of the Venetian, Genovese, Florentine and, English, French and Dutch merchants and captains of vessels who removed inscriptions from Asia Minor, in addition to the few mentioned here, fn. 50, is certainly a desideratum. It seems probable that some of the inscriptions in the 16th c. collections at Prague Castle and Castle Ambras, came from Asia Minor via Genoa, and, as Krista de Jonge and Koen Ottenheym, remark, "*Apart from real or fake antique statuary, the best way for the elite to dress up their residences in the antique manner was actually to import marble artefacts from Genoa, the main hub in the all'antica luxury trade.*" de Jonge – Ottenheym 2007, 75. For a 12th c. Genovese consignment of coloured antique marble columns from Palestine that sunk in the Gulf of Adalia, Greenhalgh 2009, 386.

English factory at Smyrna, Captain Thomas Morley/Morly 1732, John Montague Earl of Sandwich (with Brabazon Ponsonby, 2nd Viscount Duncannon and Earl of Besborough, Mr Nelthorpe, Mr Mackye and Swiss painter Jean-Étienne Liotard) 1737-1738, Daniel Alexander de Hochepied Consul General of States of Holland at Smyrna 1724-1759, Arthur Pullinger 1733, 1738-9, M. Jean Otter 1737, Richard Pococke 1739-1740, James Caulfield, Lord Charlemont, Mr. Francis Pierpont Burton, Mr. Scott, Rev. Edward Murphy and artist Richard Dalton 1749, M. Le Roy 1754, M. de Paysonnel and M. Le Beau, 1757-1765, Rev. Dr. Richard Chandler, Mr. Revett and Mr Pars, August 1764-August 1765, Sir Robert Ainslie, Ambassador Extraordinary and Minister Plenipotentiary of His Britannic Majesty to the Sublime Porte from 1775 to 1793, Gabriel Florent Auguste de Choiseul-Gouffier and his party of savants 1776, Abbé Domenico Sestini 1779, J. B. Lechevallier 1784-6, Luigi Mayer 1792, Thomas Hope, Mr Edward Lee (Levent Co. Merchant) 1795, John Bacon Sawrey Morritt and Rev. James Dallaway 1795-6, Guillaume-Antoine Olivier, Prof. Rev. Joseph Dacre Carlyle 1799, Thomas Bruce 7th Earl of Elgin and Kincardine, Ambassador Extraordinary and Minister Plenipotentiary of His Britannic Majesty to the Sublime Porte from 1799-1803.

The term *'epigrapher'* appears to have first been used in 1843 in French[14], in 1851 in English[15], the word *'epigraphist'* in English from 1864 onwards; while, *The Saturday Review of Politics, Literature, Science, Art, and Finance*, on the 18th of July, 1863, related, *"The science of epigraphy seems still, as far as Britain is concerned, to be quite in its infancy."*[16] And so, for this period from 1400-1800, antiquarian[17], from the Latin *antiquarius*, or, *antiquary*[18], seem to be the more appropriate terms[19], rather than to use the modern scientific term, 'epigrapher,' or the modern

---

[14] Panciera 2012, 1-10, 2 fn. 4.

[15] s.v. "*epigraphy*" S.O.D.³1969.

[16] Sandys 1919, 1.

[17] s.v. "*antiquarian*" S.O.D.³1969, used from 1610 onwards, "*1. Of, or connected with the study of antiquities.*" The former distinction was between the study of 'antiquities', being the study of the physical 'remains', the 'fragments', archaeological remains, objects, inscriptions or isolated documents, as distinct from 'annals,' on the course of history, historical chronicles. From antiquities, Ar. Antiky/antikât.

[18] s.v. "*antiquary*" S.O.D.³1969, "*B. 2. An official custodian or recorder of antiquities (A title bestowed by Henry VIII upon Leland). 3. A professed student, or collector, of antiquities.*"

[19] The word "antiquary" meaning the study of the ancient, in all its varied aspects, the remains and relics from the past, any form of written text, of customs, architecture, coins and seals, pottery, megaliths and stone circles etc., was first used in English in 1563, the College of Antiquaries was established c. 1585, the Society of Antiquaries of London from 1707, established by Royal Charter in 1751, the Dilettanti Society was founded in 1734; of antiquarians, educated travellers who took an informed interest in, recorded and collected and, at times, published evidence of past civilisations, including ruins, statues, epigraphic material, coins and papyri, and the related recording of views of the ancient site, object or structure, sometimes in plan, elevation and section, work often provided by artists and architects they employed. Francis Bacon (1561-1626) the advancement of learning Bk. II., observed that, *"Antiquities are history defaced, or some remnants of history which have casually escaped the shipwreck of time."* This was then misquoted (PSRL I, 200-201) and subsequently repeated, to read: *"Antiquities may be look'd upon as the*

expression, 'proto-epigrapher,'[20] to describe these people whose education in respect to ancient inscriptions, was often, although not always, simply an ability to read and who at times chose to record ancient Greek and Latin inscriptions. Latin and ancient Greek being an integral part of all European university (and seminary) education from the 16th into the 20th century, as also Hebrew, for those who studied theology, Abbé, Fra. priest, minister, Reverend or chaplain. Those who came to Asia Minor during this period were by profession, merchants, artists, architects, envoys and consuls and wealthy travellers, nobles and gentlemen on tour, some botanising,[21] the collecting of plants and of making copies of ancient inscriptions being closely related in Asia Minor, as elsewhere, educated, able to read ancient Greek and Latin inscriptions, the majority having an antiquarian interest, rather than it being their sole concern. It was understood as early as the 15th c. that the evidence provided through surviving ancient inscriptions could supplement and at times correct the reading of surviving copies of ancient literary texts, shown by the interest generated in Italian humanist circles by the inscriptions transcribed by Cyriacus of Ancona/Ciriaco de Pizzicolli (1391-1453/55), who himself could not read for years the ancient Greek of the inscriptions he transcribed in the *"going backward and forward into Greece, and drawing forth from obscurity the productions of the most enlightened ages of antiquity. Add to all this…the thirst of discovering monuments and remains of a remote antiquity, that animated Ciriacus of Ancona and others to the most laborious researches in Italy, Greece and the East."*[22] In 1670 the German scholar working for the French Minister Colbert, Johann Michael Wansleben, was sent to Asia Minor *"with official instructions, which underline the value of epigraphy to the study of the ancients, as the voice, they supplemented where ancient authors were silent."*[23]

Planks of a Shipwreck, which industrious and wise Men, snatch up and preserve from the deluge of time." Although, rather than '*the planks of a shipwreck*,' perhaps '*deracinated orphans*' is a more accurate term.

[20] Like the term minted in the 20th c., *Proto-archaeology,* sometimes employed to describe the period of excavations from 1860-1914 when a scientific methodology was being developed; but a term which is more often employed by archaeologists today to co-opt into the modern discipline, antiquarianism, as 'proto - archaeology,' although it remains the case that the subjects of antiquarian interest over the course of history, in antiquity, as in the Medieval period, down to the present day, concerns a far wider range of approaches and varieties of material than that studied by the modern discipline of archaeology, and therefore the term proto-archaeology cannot be an accurate synonym for the work undertaken by an antiquarian. The word 'archaeologist' employed to mean a person undertaking the scientific study of ancient peoples and past civilisations, is only recorded in English usage from 1824 onwards, with the Royal Archaeological Institute (RAI) established in 1844, distinct from the related, but different research and documenting activities of antiquarians, such as those who dug at Stonehenge in the 17th century and the cities of Pompeii and Herculaneum in the 18th c., when the digging was not conducted by ordinary treasure hunters, it was not conducted by anybody who thought of themselves or described themselves as archaeologists, such work was carried out by antiquaries into the 19th c.

[21] The botanists who also transcribed inscriptions included: Pierre Belon, Ogier Ghiselin de Busbecq, George Wheler, Joseph Pitton de Tournefort, and W. Sherard.

[22] Review of, "*Storia Della Letteratura Italiana, etc., An History of Italian Literature. By the Abbot Jerome Tiraboshi, Vol. VI.*" 541-533, *The Monthly Review, Or, Literary Journal*, LVI, Art. XIII, 1777, 532.

[23] Greenhalgh 2013, 236, note 20.

There was however almost no European antiquarian interest in this period in inscriptions in Asia Minor as providing *"the voice"* in other languages, little even in the Christian inscriptions in Medieval Greek. It was in the second half of the 17th c. that Dr. John Luke, the Chaplain to the Levant Factory at Smyrna (from 1664 to 1669 and from 1674 to 1683) drew attention to, and was a driving force in investigating the historical remains and record of the early church, of the importance of history and of the historical and epigraphic remains in the *"reading of the plain meaning"* of scripture, and, that, *"the supplying of history was to be found in early Christian texts closest to the time, the practices of Graeco-Roman culture, and perhaps most importantly, 'the poor reliques' of once famous and flourishing churches."*[24] Although in respect to inscriptions, the Society of Dilettanti's Instructions to the mission of the Rev. Dr. Richard Chandler, Mr. Revett and Mr Pars were explicit, as to, *"copying all the Inscriptions you shall meet with,"*[25] it was the case that it was the ancient Greek and Latin inscriptions that were worthy of transcription and publication. The medieval Arabic, Persian, Ottoman and Armenian *in situ* inscriptions in Asia Minor remained in the main clearly visible, and unremarked upon and unrecorded by European antiquarians in this period, as also sculptures that were not, or were thought not to be, *a l'antiqua*.[26] Antiquarian interest in these other inscriptions and their historical and religious content and context, together with the linguistic skills to read them, were largely, although not entirely,[27] lacking. An exception being an anonymous English traveller in 1667 who described the Satalia-Antalya sea-gate and remarked on the presence on it of an inscription in Arabic: *"One of the Gates near the sea, not of the city, but of some outbuildings on the scala (Satalia-Antalya mina), presenteth on each side a statue of stone, in mannar not much unlike those at the gate of Southampton*[28]*, but much less; the right hand statue bearing on his right hand, in fair let-*

---

[24] For the importance of his sermon to the Levant Company board in 1664 on this matter of the remains of Early Christianity, see Cadwallader 2014, 207-9. See also Smith 1678.

[25] Chandler 1776, viii.

[26] The '*newe*' figurative stone statues brought at great cost to Ambassador Thomas Roe, possibly Hittite or Neo-Hittite, but more probably New Roman or Medieval Seljuk sculptures and reliefs, were of no significance, not being *a l'antiqua*. He wrote to the Earl of Arundel from Constantinople on October the 30th 1625, *"I have in my endeavour bad success, by the ignorance of those that I am forced to employ, who send me heavy stones at great chardge, that prove newe images, wher I seeke old idolls; for such also were the Roman statues of their emperors."* (Hervey 1921, 274.) What happened in the 17th c. to these unwanted, *"newe images"* is today of considerable interest, but further information concerning the fate of these unwanted *"newe"* statues seems lacking.

[27] Exceptions in the 17th c. include: the Rev. John Covel who learnt Modern Greek, as also Dr John Luke, Levant Co. chaplain 1664-9 and 1674-83 and then Prof. of Arabic, and Hebrew; Dr. Thomas Smith, Chaplain to Sir Daniel Hervey from 1668 to 1671 the Orientalist, Rev. Edward Pocock, and the Rev. Edmund Chishull who transcribed some medieval Greek inscriptions in Smyrna and Prusia-Bursa, and, in the 18th c., Joseph Pitton de Tournefort, and the Abbé Domenico Sestini, who remarkably transcribed an Ottoman inscription of Sultan Beyazit I. In Aleppo, the Levant Co. Consul 1745-1755, Mr. Pollard employed a Turk to transcribe and another to translate an Arabic inscription that had over the course of more than 840 years been moved from the citadel to the Grand mosque and then to the tomb of the Prophet Zachariah, Drummond 1754, 237.

[28] The medieval Bargate of Southampton (a toll gate) with carved single figure reliefs on either side of the entrance, of 1175 with alterations of c. 1290, which remains *in situ* today.

ters insculpted lillahi (Deus)²⁹. *When I find any images remaining among the Turks, I think it not idle to note them, especially with any sign on them that they are accepted, because known to be generally abhorred by them, more than fire or plague.*"³⁰

The collection and removal of inscriptions from Ottoman Asia Minor: "these may be fetched at charge and secretly; but if we ask leave, it cannot be obtained."

The removal of antiquities, including inscriptions, from Asia Minor seems to have neither a known beginning, preceding the removal of a bronze moving statue automata of Apollo from Didyma to Susa by the Persians in 494 B.C., nor has it any foreseeable end³¹. It is, like it or not, a continuum, an on-going process, spoils, relics, loot, to the powerful ruler, noble collector, director and agents, usually literate at the selection, if not at local collection level, the dealers and the destination, most often to Europe, to the shrine, the palazzo, the cathedral treasury, the mansion and country house, the gallery which is "*an essential part of a magnificent residence and appropriate to a museum of natural and artificial curiosities,*"³² and, latterly, via the dealer and international auction house, to the modern public museum or private collection. After all, there is little that separates the reasons for, the contents of, and the pilgrimage to, a well-stocked ancient temple treasury, the medieval cathedral treasury, the Popes', Emperor's and princes' treasuries and *wunderkammern* of *artificalia* and *naturalia*, the humanists and antiquarian's collections, and modern national and private museums - they are collections of relics, of antiquities, of evidence of wonders, natural and otherwise, of a variety of talisman, being divided over time only by the surrounding discourse and terminology, by the degree of openness of access to these objects and in the forms of presentation employed for these potent symbols - the isolation through removal from its context and objectivisation through possession, the display of cult, - relics, collectively expressing through their subsequent assemblage - religious, individual, corporate, local, national or international power through the display of their possession.

As earlier, from the 15th c. onwards ancient Greek and Roman antiquities, including inscriptions, coins and medals providing evidence of toponyms, cult etc., carved reliefs and statues were removed in some quantity from Asia Minor, largely from coastal sites, to Europe, in larger quantities from the start of the 17th c. onwards, through the activities of merchants, diplomatic envoys, consuls, and networks of travelling antiquarians/factors-agents. These objects were removed whenever possible through purchase and bribes and smuggled abroad without obtaining Ottoman official permission, as it was well known at the time that official permission would not be granted.

---

²⁹ The upper part of this reworked relief is today displayed in the Antalya Archaeological Museum, Inv. No. 156. From the letter sizes and forms, the Arabic inscription dates from the Seljuk period and were added when this relief was re-used in the 13th c., prior to its subsequent re-use in the Lusignan sea-gate, constructed between 1361 and 1373. The sea gate seems to have been demolished in the 19th c. See on this relief, Duggan 2012, 56-61.

³⁰ B. M. Harl. Mss. 1721 anon. Anon 1800, 187-188. Possibly written by the Levant Co. chaplain, Dr. John Luke, or perhaps the Smyrna Levant Co. Consul Richard Baker, 1660, superseded in 1661, and said to have died in 1661 in Settalia-Antalya, the date 1661 of the manuscript, may have been misread as 1667.

³¹ For the recent illegal removal from Lycia to Europe of the inscription in bronze of the Roman-Lycian Treaty of 46 B.C. and its subsequent publication, see Duggan 2015, 59-70.

³² Elmes 1824, s.v. "Gallery".

The English Ambassador to the Porte from 1621-1628, Sir Thomas Roe, himself collected ancient manuscripts and ancient coins and he translated from Latin into English Petrus Gyllius's *Topographia Constantinopoleos et de illius antiquitatibus libri IV*, in 1628[33], his manuscript was published a century later in 1729 by John Ball, who was not the translator as has been rather frequently stated over the past 300 years[34], but who added the explanatory index to Sir Thomas Roe's translation. Ambassador Roe secured *berats* from the Porte for Mr John Markham, "*sent out to collect antiquities*"[35] for the Earl of Arundel, and then for the Rev. William Petty[36] to look for and export antiquities[37] for the Earl. William Petty was indefatigable in his search for antiquities in Asia Minor from 1624, at Pergamo, Smyrna-İzmir, Magnesia, Troy[38] and elsewhere in Aegean coastal areas and obtained "*22 Greek Mss., and raked together 200 pieces.*"[39] He had secured from Asia Minor and the Aegean Islands for the Earl by 1627, "*37 statues, 128 busts, 250 inscriptions, together with a large number of altars, sarcophagi, fragments of sculpture, and an invaluable collection of gems.*"[40] However, the *berat* or fiscal ordinance that the English ambassa-

---

[33] Ball 1729, 317, "*In the Beginning of this MS upon a large Folio Page, are inscribed the following Words, in the Benefactor's own Hand. "Sir John (Sic.) Roe, Bart. Ambassador from His Majesty of Great Britain to the Grand Seignior, as a perpetual Testimony of his Gratitude to the University, (Oxon) gave this Book, which he met with in his Travels, to the Publick Library, 1628.*" It seems John Ball misread a J for a letter T and so misnamed the translator as Sir John Roe, the friend of Shakespeare, Jonson, and Donne, who was in fact the cousin of the Ambassador to the Grand Seignior, Sir Thomas Roe. There was no Ambassador to the Grand Seignior named Sir John Roe and, further Sir John Roe was born the 5th of May 1581 and died a Captain in Ireland in 1608, 20 years before the manuscript was presented to the university by Sir Thomas Roe; see: http://spenserians.cath.vt.edu/BiographyRecord.php?action=GET&bioid=33075.

[34] Modern instances include: E. Thompson, Possession: The Curious History of Private Collectors from Antiquity to the Present, Yale University Press, 2016, "*Pierre Gilles, The Antiquities of Constantinople, trans. John Ball (1729; 2nd ed., New York: Italica, 1988)*"; J. Speake, Literature of Travel and Exploration: An Encyclopedia, Routledge, 2014, 626, "*Gilles, Pierre* [Petrus Gyllius], De topographia Constantinopoleos, et de illius Antiquitatibus libri quatuor, 2 vols., edited by A. *Gilles*, 1562; translated and published by *John Ball* as The Antiquities of Constantinople"; R. Stoneman, Land of Lost Gods: The Search for Classical Greece, Tauris Parke Paperbacks, 2011, 305, "*Pierre Gilles, The Antiquities of Constantinople tr John Ball, 1729, from the original Lyon edition of 1562*"; C. McEvedy, Cities of the Classical World: An Atlas and Gazetteer of 120 centres of Ancient Civilisation, Penguin, 2011, "*There is a translation of sorts appended to John Ball's 1729 version of Pierre Gilles…*"; L. James, A Companion to Byzantium, John Wiley & Sons, 2010, 380, "*Pierre Gilles: Gilles, P. 1988. The antiquities of Constantinople, based on the translation by John Ball 1729.*"; H. C. Evans, Byzantium: Faith and Power (1261-1557), 2004, 618, "*Pierre Gilles. The Antiquities of Constantinople (1729). Translated by John Ball.*", etc. etc.

[35] Hervey 1921, 266, etc.

[36] Hervey 1921, 265-266. Described by John Selden in Marmora Arundellina, Oxford 1628, "*Guilielmi Pettaei, in orientem ad illud negotii non sine honesto commeatu missus, insigni id genus mercium frequentia (ut statuas, figuras insculptas, numismata, & quae sunt ejusmodi caetera selectissima praetermittam) gestionis cui praeficitur sumptus effusisime repensat.*" Selden 1726, 1439.

[37] Hervey 1921, 265-266.

[38] Roe 1740, 495.

[39] Rees 1819, s.v. "*William Pettie-William Petty,*" the presumed translator from Greek into English of the manuscript entitled *The Commentary of George Aeropolita*, dated, 6th February 1644.

[40] Metropolitana 1845, 800; Elmes 1824, s.v. "*Arundelian Marbles.*"

dor secured for these agents did not record any official permission to "*rake together,*" to collect and to remove any antiquities, antiquities such as inscriptions and manuscripts of ancient texts and such are unmentioned in these official documents[41]. This is evident in the Ottoman arrest in 1624 of the French Consul in Smyrna, Sanson Napollon[42], at the same time also factor-agent for the antiquarian Nicolas-Claude Fabri de Peiresc (1580-1637)[43]. He was arrested at Smyrna with a collection of antiquities including inscriptions, for which he had paid 50 crowns,[44] bought from the Ottoman Cyclades and these were confiscated, clearly indicating the immunity provided by Ottoman *berat,* or even in being the Consul of a great European power, did not, in fact, extend to cover the activities of European diplomats, consuls and others collecting antiquities in Ottoman territory, and this was a fact that was certainly well understood at that time by those who undertook the collection and export of antiquities from Ottoman territory.

Sir Thomas Roe himself dispatched many servants to many quarters of the Ottoman State, Greece, the Islands and Asia Minor in the search for 'marbles' for the Duke of Buckingham, but they were repeatedly beaten to the best pieces by the Earl of Arundel's man, the Rev. William Petty. Thomas Roe was assisted in his search by the Scio born titular Roman Catholic Bishop of Smirna, Fra. Pietro de Marchi (d.1645), and Thomas wrote to Sir Isaac Wake, English Agent in Turin in 1626[45], to try and secure for the titular Bishop the vacant post of Bishop of Scio, through soliciting the aid of Bandini, the Cardinal of Savoy (1596-1629). He wrote to Sir Isaac: "*he will and does assist me for marbles for the duke* (of Buckingham), *having been bishop long of St. Errinna in the Arches, and in all those islands of great authority*"[46]. Sir Thomas Roe wrote to the Duke of Buckingham in May 1627, "*I am this day sending a dragoman, and janizarie, with an Italian to Brussia, the antient metropolis of Bythinia, where, I am informed, are many marbles; and I attend a return from Sinope on the Black Sea, in Amasia, Thus your grace will approve my diligence, and accept the success according to your own benignity. The difficulty of carriage, and engines, and expense, is great, and the danger among these more remote habitations greater, some stones weighing about 20 hundred (weight), and brought by hand to the water; yet your grace shall have no cause to repent the charge; for I hope to make you a noble collection. If you please to continue this search, there will be found daily many rare matters, the poor people being set to work, in hope of gain, and all these parts full of the enquiry made by me and Mr Petty; all above*

---

[41] See for example that issued at Constantinople to the French Ambassador in 1604, of 42 articles, not one of which mentions antiquities in any manner whatsoever, but is concerned with trade, customs and taxes, translated, De La Motraye 1723, 387-393; as likewise there is no mention of antiquities in that issued at Constantinople in 1626, translated Roe 1740, 603-605.

[42] The French superintendent of finance's special envoy to the Levant. His nephew, Sanson le Page, Premier Héraut d'Armes de France, au titre de Bourgogne, Secretaire Interprete de sa Majesté, also collected inscriptions for de Peiresc.

[43] Also spelt Peirese, Peiresk; Nichols 1812, Vol. II, 2.

[44] Knight 1866, 596; Gassendus 1657, 33-34.

[45] Sir Issac Wake, the first to plant pines and firs in England in the grounds of his house at Hampstead, had supplied chests of glass from Venice to the Duchess of Buckingham and others in 1625, CSP 1858, 211.

[46] Roe 1740, 513. In 1621 Pope Gregorio XV had nominated Pietro de Marchi apostolic visitor, vescovo di Santorino, the successor to s. Policarp.

*ground being gone to Venice⁴⁷ we must trust, like miners, to chance; but I find, that the old Christians, to prevent the envy of the Turkes, did in all Greece, and the islands, bury their antiquities, which time and diligence will discover."*⁴⁸

Clearly recording the clandestine nature of this activity, Ambassador Roe wrote to the Earl of Arundel from Constantinople May 1624, *"I may also light of some pieces of marble by stealth;"*⁴⁹ He had earlier recorded in a letter to the Duke of Buckingham in January 1623, *"I know as well how to send them,"* meaning he had established a reliable method of smuggling, *"Whatsoever I can collect, having now your graces command, added to mine own desire, shall not go of the way to Venice: I know as well how to send them, and have as much affection to serve your grace as any."*⁵⁰ Thomas Roe's successor as English Ambassador from 1627-1641, Sir Peter Wyche, another London merchant, was also energetic in this clandestine quest for antiquities, *"raking together"* for King Charles I., who related in his letter from Constantinople to Edymion Porter of

---

⁴⁷ D. G. Wright (2004) in her review of Bodnar and Foss 2003, remarks, *"Cyriac's references support the impression one gets from seeing the remarkable but inadequately known antiquities in the Correr Museum in Venice: lovely small pieces chosen for quality, easily carried by one person in a leather bag or small travelling chest,"*. But it would seem from ambassador Roe's repeated remarks concerning the role of Venice in the removal of antiquities from Asia Minor, that many larger works of antiquity were removed by the Venetians in the 16ᵗʰ and into the 17ᵗʰ c., than was the case in the 14ᵗʰ and 15ᵗʰ c., Venice being a major centre of antiquities collecting, as with the 15ᵗʰ c. collections of Cardinal Ludovico Tervisan, friend of Ciriaco of Ancona, of Cardinal Pietro Barbo (later Pope Paul II), of the Grimani, as well as Venetian merchants trafficking and dealing in antiquities from the East and in copies/fakes of them, in Italy and into Northern Europe collections. See also Greenhalgh 1989, 240. It seems to have been a Venetian practice in Turkey and elsewhere, that began before the sack of Constantinople in 1204 with its array of looted antiquities brought to Venice, later for example a group of Greek mid-5ᵗʰ - mid-4ᵗʰ c. B.C. temple statues found their way from Asia Minor, or the islands, to Greece and the Grimani collection in the 16ᵗʰ c. (JHS 1918, Gardner, 4), and which continued into the 18ᵗʰ c. (noted below) and is an issue which raises serious questions concerning the so-called spread of the cult of antiquity from Florence and Rome to Venice, rather than the reverse being perhaps rather more to the point, at least in terms of the influence of collections of ancient objects including inscriptions.

⁴⁸ Roe 1740, 647.

⁴⁹ Roe 1740, 154.

⁵⁰ Roe 1740, 343-344. He knew as well as the Venetians how to smuggle antiquities. It was using the master of certain trade vessels to transport smuggled antiquities, such as Captain Antony Wood of the Rainbow, in the employ of the Levant Company, the company of merchants which also paid the costs of maintaining the English ambassador to the Porte, himself a merchant of the same company. Rev. Thomas Greaves wrote to Edward Pocock in Constantinople to take, *"particular care some marble stones, having inscriptions, which were to be sent by the general ships into England;"* (Twells 1740, 13). Like the Venetian merchants, the Turkey Merchants of the Levant Company removed inscriptions, some were presented to Cambridge University (Dobree – Scholefield 1835, 92, No. VII, was presented by J. Hawkins, who had received it from Mr Edward Lee, a (Levant Co.) Turkey Merchant, it was apparently on Tenos in 1795 and was first transcribed in the 15ᵗʰ c. by Cyriacus). Another Greek inscription, in honour of Crato, the musician of Pergamus, erected in the reign of Eumenes, King of Pergamum, 150 B.C., was brought from the village of Segucque-Segyceque-Teos, between Smyrna and Ephesus, by the Levant Company Captain, Thomas Morley in 1732, and brought to London (Dibdin 1810, 49). In the Levant Co. library in Aleppo there were ancient Greek inscriptions Drummond 1754, 237.

January 1629-30, of the dispatch from Smirna-İzmir on the ship Rainbow, of "*19 statues small and great, some of them I hear are rare pieces, and if they prove so, I shall think my labour well disposed. You will be pleased to give an account hereof unto his majesty, and how these be all I have been able to encompass since my arrival in these parts, and I beseech you let me know how acceptable they be, and whether I shall go on in that service still.*"[51] Cornelis de Bruijn, who removed from Asia Minor Greek and Latin inscriptions, at Ephesus in November 1678 recorded, "*We found there many marble statutes buried in the ground. However, due to the negligence the feet of some of them were outside. I wanted to unearth one of them during the night and to carry it to Smyrna on a carriage. But, I couldn't find anyone to help me even in return for money because they were afraid of our being watched.*"[52] A passage indicating that the local population was aware that this proposed activity was illegal, *berat* or no *berat*, and, that attention was being paid by the Ottoman state to prevent the removal of antiquities. Such clandestine removal by Europeans was, as is noted above, common practice. At Gallipoli in 1699 Sieur Aubry De La Motraye was struck by the fact that important inscriptions that had already been published by Europeans, first in 1678 and again in 1682, were still in place, they had not already in the intervening two decades been removed. He, "*wondered that the Franks had not carried away the stones, whereon were the Inscriptions published by Mr. Spon and Mr Wheeler; one of which ascribes to the Statue of Julia, erected at the Expense of Dyonisus Apollonoteimus, all the Epithets usually given to Ceres; for it lies in a Turk's Garden, who asked me if I would buy it, and sold me some few Paras. I would suppose the Owners of the others, whose Taste does not lie that way, wou'd part as willingly with them for a small matter.*"[53]

Sir Thomas Roe was explicit as to the illegal nature of this activity in his 1624 letter to the Earl of Arundel, concerning the fact that there was no official Ottoman permission for this activity. He wrote:

"*On* (the) *Asia side, about Troy, Zizicum, and all the way to Aleppo, are innumerable pillars, statues, and tombstones of marble, with inscriptions in Greek; these may be fetched at charge and secretly; but if we ask leave, it cannot be obtained; therefore Mr. Markham will use discretion, rather than power, and so the Turks will bring.*"[54] It seems evident therefore that, although there was no written Ottoman antiquities law published until 1869 which forbade the exportation of antiquities, Ottoman law, as recognised in the 17th c. by the English ambassador, firmly objected to the removal of antiquities from Ottoman territory,[55] hence, "*tombstones of marble, with in-*

---

[51] Sainsbury 1859, 353.

[52] de Bruijn 1700, 33. "*Nous y découvrimes encore plusiers statues de marbre ensevelics en terre, mais avec rant de negligence que les pieds de quelques uncs sortoient dehors. J'eusse bien voulu en déterrer quelqu'une pendant la nuit, & la porter à Smyrne en vacherrre, mais je ne pus trouver personne qui m'aidér même pour l'argent, par ce qu'ils craignoient qu'on ne nous epiâr.*" http://gallica.bnf.fr/ark:/12148/bpt6k 85330k/f71.image.

[53] De La Motraye 1723, 303.

[54] Roe 1740, 154. "*Discretion*" meaning in this context, gold. This was stated explicitly by the Rev. Dr. Richard Chandler in his 1776 publication, "*By a proper application of all-prevailing gold,*" see below.

[55] "*Before 1869 the legal status of antiquities was regulated only by Islamic jurisprudence. The first such decree specifically regulating antiquities was adopted on February 13, 1869. This decree required permission, when requested, to search for antiquities. It allowed free trade in antiquities within the Ottoman territory*

scriptions in Greek; these may be fetched at charge and secretly; but if we ask leave, it cannot be obtained." Consequently, *"The premise of Ottoman indifference served as justification for the removal of objects, even entire monuments, from Ottoman territory to western and central European collections"*,[56] was, in fact, simply a useful dishonesty, an unfounded but widely articulated and published self-serving premise that served as justification for the removal of antiquities from Asia Minor and elsewhere in Ottoman territory, addressed to a European audience. In the 17th c. as translated by Ambassador Roe, *"Gilles laments the state of affairs, blaming both the Muslim Ottomans for their uncaring destruction of the ancient city and the "profound ignorance" of their Greek Christian subjects for their indifference to their vanishing antiquities."*[57] And this attitude was echoed more widely in the 18th c. in Europe, not least through Edward Gibbon in Vol. VIII, of his 'Decline and Fall of the Roman Empire,' of 1788, *"The Athenians walk with supine indifference among the glorious ruins of antiquity; and such is the debasement of their character, that they are incapable of admiring the genius of their predecessors."*[58], until the connection between nationalism and the remains of antiquity became ideology[59]. Hence the ongoing search, removal, collection, and illegal export of antiquities, including inscriptions, by Europeans was reinforced and justified through the widespread publication of this self-serving misinformation, an attitude still repeated today in respect to the 18th c.[60] and which is noted in 2015 by Benjamin Anderson in an ethno-archaeological context, concerning the reaction of local populations in Ottoman territory to the removal by Europeans of antiquities.[61] The Rev. Dr. Richard Chandler wrote in 1776, towards the end of these 400 years, concerning his suggested prize for his planned clandestine removal of an inscription from the Troad: *"By a proper application of all-prevailing gold, it is believed they might gain the permission or connivance of the papas and persons concerned. It should be done with secrecy."*[62] He also noted of the three inscribed pedestals he saw at

---

but prohibited exportation. The finder of antiquities on his land was considered the owner. So, the 1869 decree allowed private ownership over antiquities found within the Ottoman territory - within limits." Özel 2010, 178. It is noteworthy that this legislation reiterates that known to Ambassador Roe 250 years earlier, that the exportation of antiquities from Ottoman territory was prohibited.

[56] Anderson 2015, 450.

[57] Matthews 2015, 82.

[58] Gibbon 1788, Ch. LXII, last line. Likewise Ch. LXIV, *"The captivity or ruins of the Seven Churches of Asia was consummated; and the barbarous lords of Ionia and Lydia* (meaning the Ottomans) *still trample on the monuments of classic and Christian antiquity."*

[59] *"German institutions of higher learning in the early nineteenth century, from the Gymnasium to the university, posited ancient Greek language, aesthetics, philosophy, and mythology as the pinnacle of human achievement and as a model for the future. By consequence, the advisers at Otto's court felt themselves in touch with Greek antiquity and predestined to reimport classical ways to the Greeks who had supposedly lost the link to their roots under Byzantine and Ottoman rule."* Langbehn – Salama 2011, 127-128.

[60] See for example, Rosenstein 2009, 94, *"**Since Ottoman rulers were generally indifferent to antiquities of any kind**, the conditions for the future purchase of such antiquities as the Elgin Marbles from the Parthenon were established by good precedent."*

[61] Anderson 2015.

[62] Chandler 1776, 38-39. It seems a similar attitude to that recorded in Oct. 1881 in his journal by Archaeologist Francis H. Bacon at Assos, *"Our plans for the future here at Assos change with every moon. At present are at a standstill for lack of money! There is, however, plenty to do at drawing and measuring. There still remains the disagreeable task of getting the sculptures out of the country and I truly wish that*

Alexander Troas in 1764, that "*A Venetian officer afterwards informed us, that he had removed one of them on board his ship, while they lay at anchor near Tenedos, waiting for the Bailow, whose time of residence at Constantinople was expired.*"[63]

The John Hopkins University Circular of 1884 carried note of the Lectures on Classical Archaeology, the first of which was given by Dr. Charles Waldstein, Director of the Fitzwilliam Museum, Cambridge, and it related: "*Yet the wealth and interest of classic lands two hundred years ago may be judged from the fact that one explorer in the Archipelago returned to Europe with originals and copies of more than two thousand inscriptions*[64]. *Cyriacus, Spon, even Stuart and Revett, saw and described monuments of antiquity which have now entirely disappeared... The weathering of time, and above all the vandalism of man, steadily continue to deprive us of the material remnants of former civilizations. The rapidity of this destruction must be inconceivable to those not acquainted with the recent history of classic monuments from personal experience.*"[65] Yet, more than 250 years earlier Sir Thomas Roe wrote from Constantinople to the Duke of Buckingham in May 1627 concerning the European antiquarian quest for antiquities in Asia Minor, "*If you please to continue this search, there will be found daily many rare matters, **the poor people being set to work, in hope of gain**, and all these parts full of the enquiry made by me and Mr Petty; all above ground being gone to Venice, we must trust, like miners, to chance; but I find, that the old Christians, to prevent the envy of the Turkes, did in all Greece, and the islands, bury their antiquities, which time and diligence will discover.*" (emphasis added).[66] A statement he repeated in a letter to the Duke of April 1628, "***Our search hath made many poor men industrious to rip up old ruins.***" (emphasis added)[67]. In consequence, ironically and most unfortunately it can be suggested that it was the longstanding European interest in, search for, and acquisition of antiquities, the sculptural and epigraphic remains of antiquity in Asia Minor, by Venetians, English,

---

some others than ourselves could take charge of it. . . . We can only do our best! You have the photographs and drawings of the sculptures and you can judge yourselves what you can afford to pay for them [in baksheesh to get them out of the country]!" The Assos Journals of Francis H. Bacon - Archaeology Magazine Archive, Dec. 1st, 2006.

[63] Chandler 1776, 28. This removal related to Chandler by a Venetian officer, may have led to Chandler's suggestion later made in a footnote concerning the removal of the Boustrophedon inscription at Giaurkoi-Sigéum inscribed on a pilaster from the former temple, "*It is to be wished that a Premium (Prize) were offered, and the undertaking recommended to commanders of ships in the Levant trade. They have commonly interpreters to negotiate for them, with men, leavers, ropes, and other requisites, besides instruments or tools, by which the stone might be broken, if necessary. By a proper application of all-prevailing gold, it is believed they might gain the permission or connivance of the papas and persons concerned. It should be done with secrecy. The experiment is easily made, when they are at Tendos, or wind-bound at the mouth of the Hellespont.*"

[64] I have been unable to find record of any 17th c. antiquarian who returned with 2,000 originals and copies of inscriptions, and it's probably a misdated reference to Cyriacus in the 15th c. There are a total of 300-400 transcriptions of inscriptions from Asia Minor in, Sherard Mss. B. M. Harlian No. 7509, which seems to represent the larger quantity collected by an individual.

[65] John Hopkins University Circular, 1880-1884, 1884, 132; a point repeatedly made in Greenhalgh 2013.

[66] Roe 1740, 647.

[67] Roe 1740, 808.

French and Dutch[68], in exchange for gold, it was the increasing European demand from collectors in the period from the end of the 16th century onwards, that generated the supply, the hunt, which had, *"made many poor men industrious to rip up old ruins,"* and it is the fact that, *"the poor people being set to work, in hope of gain,"* was, and it remains today, a factor of major importance in the destruction of ancient sites in Asia Minor, of the remains of antiquity within their cultural context, producing the countless orphans of no secure provenance that are displayed in museums and private collections worldwide. As the Earl of Arundel wrote to Sir Thomas Roe from Whit(e)hall, May 10, 1625 , *"I knowe eyther for some crownes to ye Bashawe* (Pasha), *they may be had, or els stolen for money by ye Turkes, they caring not for them,"*[69]. Travellers themselves at times themselves damaged remains in their search for antiquities[70] and, antiquarian demand also led to the profitable business of counterfeiting, most notably the production of fakes of medals and coins,[71] adding further confusion to the historical record. It can further be suggested that it was, in part, the European financial incentive, provided by European collectors via their agents, which undermined the established cultural and religious taboo's that had, to a considerable extent, previously protected the remains of antiquity in Asia Minor, this, combined with the mistaken assumption that these ancient remains held no meaning for the present inhabitants.

Until the end of the 18th c. there seems to have been no explicit official permission granted by any Ottoman Sultan through the issuance of a *berat*, or a *firman*, which specifically granted permission to remove any type of antiquity, inscriptions, "marbles", ancient coins etc. from Asia Minor[72] or elsewhere in Ottoman territory. At the end of this period there was the issuance of *firmans*, in a most particular set of circumstances, the aftermath of the Battle of the Nile (Aboukir) of the 1st of August 1798 and the ending of the French occupation of Ottoman Egypt in 1801, implied at the head of at least one document, *"That in order to shew their particular respect for the Ambassador of Great Britain, they gave him and his artists the most extensive permission…"* given by the Porte to the British Amb., James Bruce, Earl of Elgin and Kincardine, that

---

[68] In 1639 it was stated: *"Reijnst, an inquisitive man in Amsterdam, has received many antiquities, works of art and beauties from Venice, collected in Turkey, Greece and Italy: statues, tombs, paintings, medals…"* Halbertsma 2003, 8.

[69] Sainsbury 1859, 284.

[70] *"and travellers have enticed soldiers to bring down* (shoot down from the metopes on the Parthenon in Athens) *heads, legs etc. which were injured, and sometimes destroyed by the fall!"* Galignani 1822, fn. 93.

[71] Such as that of *"brass, and very ancient, of a queen of Serbia, with hieroglyphicks now unknown"* Roe 1740, 16. R. P. Dom Bernard de Montfaucon, remarked, *"Pour ce qui est des médailles, on y en pourroit trouver une grande quantité & de sort curieuses; mais il faut être conmnoisseur en ce genre, ou nes'en pas meler. Les Juifs en fabriquent beucoup de fausses qu'ils vendent aux Européens. Il faut d'ailleurs savoir distinguer les rares d'avec les communes, autrement on court risque de faire de la dépense inutilement."* Montfaucon 1761, 153-154.

[72] As noted above: see for example, that issued at Constantinople to the French Ambassador in 1604, of 42 articles, not one of which mentions antiquities in any manner whatsoever, but is concerned with trade, customs and taxes, translated, De La Motraye 1723, 387-393; as likewise no mention in that issued at Constantinople in 1626, translated Roe 1740, 603-605.

explicitly permitted the removal of inscriptions, to *"take away any pieces of stones, with figures or inscriptions, which might be interesting to him."*[73]

The varied functions of visible ancient inscriptions for the Ottoman state and its inhabitants, distinct from European antiquarian interest

Although the suggestion was made repeatedly by Europeans in the past that the *"Turkes, they caring not for them* (the ancient remains),"[74] and on into the 21st century, that the Seljuk, Beylik and Ottoman states did not give importance to, and value the ancient remains, such as ancient statues, reliefs and inscriptions, such allegations, as is noted above, were self-serving, as such was not, in fact, the whole story by any means. The reason why Ottoman permission was not forthcoming for the export of antiquities as recorded by Ambassador Roe in the 17th c. and by Richard Chandler in the 18th c. was because these ancient remains, inscriptions (as also ancient sculptures and reliefs) were at times in Asia Minor, as elsewhere in Ottoman territory[75], understood to carry meaning of considerable relevance and importance to the subsequent inhabitants and to the rulers of different faiths, Christian and Muslim.

Aspects of Late Antique-New Roman attitudes towards the remains of pagan antiquity in Asia Minor are recorded, for example in five chapters of the 7th c. *Life of St. Theodore of Sykeon* (d. 613), monk and bishop of Anastasiopolis in Galatia. It was understood at that time that with the digging up of mounds or of ancient sites to find building stone,[76] and implicitly, or explicitly, treasure hunting in the ruins and disturbing the pagan remains, led to the release of demons. *"He* (Theodore of Sykeon) *also sent a letter to Euphrantas, the governor, and stopped him from proceeding against them* (the villagers) *by satisfying him that the digging in the hillock was not done for the sake of treasure but at the instigation of Satan."*[77] As likewise, *"whether in order to improve the adjoining property which belonged to him or in order to carry off some treasure I cannot say."*[78] And, *"Another time a similar thing happened in the same village. For a marble sarcophagus stood at a certain spot on their boundary and it contained the skeletons of some Greeks (i.e. pagans) of ancient times which were guarded by demons; by the latter's suggestion the follow-*

---

[73] Walsh 1825, 48-49. Or, *"…or in excavating when they find it necessary the foundations in search of inscriptions among the rubbish;…nor hinder them from taking away any pieces of stone with inscriptions and figures…"* Translation of the Italian copy of this *firman* by William St. Clair, St. Clair 1967, 90. The firman issued in 1799 to William Wittman and Sir Richard Phillips who removed the Sigaeum Phanodikos inscription was issued in this climate and may have been equally explicit in respect to the removal of this inscription and the relief, as *"To accomplish this, a firman was procured from the Captain Pacha, who also furnished a chaous to be the bearer of it."* Wittman – Phillips 1803, 66-67. It was seen *in situ* in 1799 by Prof. Rev. Joseph Dacres Carlyle (1758-1804), scholarly advisor to Lord Elgin's party prior to its removal.

[74] Sainsbury 1859, 284.

[75] David Frankfurter notes in respect to Egypt, *"For example, spolia—remnants of pre-Christian iconography—were often recycled as potent apotropaia for the supernatural protection of buildings."* Frankfurter 2017, fn. 54, citing, Saradi 1997, as also Haarman 1996, 612, on the similar uses of hieroglyph-inscribed blocks in medieval mosques.

[76] Dawes – Baynes 1948, Ch. 43, 44, 115, 116.

[77] Dawes – Baynes 1948, Ch. 115.

[78] Dawes – Baynes 1948, Ch. 116.

ing idea occurred to some of the householders of the village; they came and opened the said chest and took off the covering, or lid, and carried it to their village and placed it there to serve as a water trough. Because of this many of the inhabitants of the village were again vexed by demons, and their beasts and properties were likewise injured."[79] It was evidently well understood by the villagers in Galatia in the 6th c. that such activities were liable to cause the release and infestation of unclean spirits-demons, illnesses and trouble to both man and beast of the village and to travellers throughout the region, and such activity, by accident or design, required, at times, the return of that which was taken, the infilling of the diggings-excavations, supplications and exorcisms by a holy man, a wonderworker. It was understood by many of the inhabitants of Ottoman territory both Rum and Muslim that ancient ruins and remains were to be left alone, even if they contained buried treasure. The numerous accounts of Jinn inhabiting old ruins, for Muslims[80]; like the New Roman accounts relating that the ancient temples, ruins and mounds were full of fearful spirits in a variety of forms, likewise unintentionally led to the protection of the remains of antiquity. It was, in part[81], due to these demons and Jinn, understood to inhabit the remains of antiquity within the landscapes inhabited by Muslims and Christians that in the 15th c. European merchant travellers such as Ciriacus of Ancona were able to record after the passage of more than a millennium, so much inscribed and carved material surviving from antiquity.

---

[79] Dawes – Baynes 1948, Ch. 118. See also Saradi 1997, 404-405, and, concerning re-use of pagan material in church construction so that the Christians would walk on the pagan remains, idem, 401, 403.

[80] For examples in *Alf Layla wa-Layla*, The Thousand Nights and One Night, in the Tales of, 'The King's Son and the Ogress,' in 'Ma'aruf the Cobbler', and in 'Qamar az-Zaman' with a Jinn in a Roman well: "It so happened that the chamber and tower were very old, and had been abandoned for many years. There was in the chamber an ancient Roman well in which dwelt a genie, one of the descendants of Iblis, the accursed one. Her name was Maymunah, and she was the daughter of Dimiryat, one of the famous kings of the Jinn. When Qamar az-Zaman had slept through the first watch of the night, the Ifritah rose out of the Roman well, intending to lie in concealment near the heavens in order to eavesdrop. When she reached the rim of the well, she saw a light burning…"; 'Abu Mahomed the Lazy,' "and hath informed me that there is in this city a talisman with which, if he desired to destroy all who are in the city, he could destroy them; and whatsoever he should order his Afrites to do, they would comply with his command; and that talisman is upon a pillar… She answered, 'It is the figure of an eagle, and upon it is an inscription which I know not." "In the name of Solomon," cried he (Habib), "and by virtue of his talisman, I command this bridge to be let down!" In a moment it began to move on its hinges… In the midst of the court stood a lofty column, on top of which was placed an iron cage. This pillar was covered with talismanic inscriptions. On the bottom was written, "Thou canst not be destroyed but by the power of Arabia." Habib struck the talismans with his sword." (Weber 1812, 194). It can also be noted that some Jinn were recorded as being imprisoned in stone columns by the Prophet Süleyman (The Extraordinary Tale of the City of Brass, *Madīnat al-nuhās*) Madrus – Mathers II, 1996, 294. Frederick W. Hasluck (1973, 733) remarked: *"The conception of Arab jinns who guard mysterious buildings, especially castles, or treasures, or both, is partly answerable for the recurring use of Arab in Turkish geographical nomenclature. Arab Hisar ('Castle of the Arab'), the ancient Alabanda, Arab Kulesi ('Arab's Tower') at Rhodes, Arab Euren ('Ruins of the Arab'), and possibly Arabkir are examples."*

[81] Other factors were: the sheer quantity of ancient remains, blocks, slabs, columns, relative to the much reduced population inhabiting the site or in its vicinity following the 542-740 plague pandemic, together with a substantial decrease in the proportion of settled population and an increase in nomads, both factors reducing demand for construction materials; together with the increasing use of wood and lath and plaster in non-state construction.

There were antique protective inscriptions, as well as sculptures and reliefs, some remaining *in situ* from antiquity, others subsequently deliberately placed in city walls, others over city gates. Procopius records that the longer version of the letter of Jesus Christ to Abgar the Black of Edessa was inscribed as a talisman and was placed over each of the city's gates for defence.[82] In 806 the Abbasid Caliph Harun al Rashid is reported to have removed an inscription, a written stone supposedly having talismanic properties[83], from over the gate of Heraclaea Cybistra-Ar. Hiraqlah-Ereğli. The whereabouts of this possibly Hittite inscription is today unknown. If it was removed, it was presumably transported onwards to Tarsus or to Raqqa, removed to be reused because it was understood to possess protective properties. Another source related it dated from 2,000 years earlier and was translated (in a non-literal manner) and was "copied", rather than removed.[84] As late as the 1670's the Rev. John Covel noted that many city walls in Asia Minor still carried the protective inscription in Greek, "*O Virgin, Mother of God, help this city.*"[85]

---

[82] Procopius, Wars 2. 12. 20-30, "*When the Christ saw this message, he wrote in reply to Augarus, saying distinctly that he would not come, but promising him health in the letter. And they say that he added this also that never would the city be liable to capture by the barbarians. This final portion of the letter was entirely unknown to those who wrote the history of that time; for they did not even make mention of it anywhere; but the men of Edessa say that they found it with the letter, so that they have even caused the letter to be inscribed in this form on the gates of the city instead of any other defence.*" Letters inscribed in stone serving like the icon of the Blessed Virgin hung for protection on the gate of Constantinople, at the time of the Avar attack on the city of 626 A.D.

[83] Hasluck 1973, I. 203, citing Hadji Khalfa (katib Çelibi), who mistakenly records *Kal'at al-Salasil* (Castle of the Chains)-Ancyra-Ankara, rather than *Hiraqlah*. Ankara was untouched in the 806 campaign.

[84] Klonsky 1974, 93, "*The poet Chibl* (ibn al-Shibl?), *who served as interpreter in the Caliph's entourage, relates: Heraclea is surrounded by a ditch, with a high front gate that overlooks a ravine. Above this gate I noticed an ornamental stone with an inscription that went back more than 2000 years. I began to translate it aloud, unaware that the Caliph was standing close by watching me do so. Here is what it said: 'O son of man, seize opportunity of the present moment and abandon the vain striving for things that lie beyond you. Be careful lest the excess of your joy precipitate you into sin. Do not let yourself be overwhelmed by care for a day which has not yet come; for if destiny permits you to see that day, and if your life continues, God will provide for you. How many times has a man accumulated possessions for the future husband of his widow, or imposed privations on himself in order to enrich a stranger.' Harun was considerably moved by this inscription, and caused it to be written down in his book.*" The text recorded is a 'non-literal translation' of the inscription, with expressions such as, "*God will provide for you.*", almost certainly not dating from 2000 years earlier. Chibli was giving advice to the Caliph through this 'non-literal' reading of this inscription. A practice that may remind of the several inscriptions in Ionian characters translated by sheikh Abd al Samad in The Extraordinary Tale of the City of Brass, Madrus – Mathers II, 1996, 288-291; 296-297, 300-301; as likewise, "*amongst other things, three round jewels, big as ostrich eggs, from a mine of pure white gems whose like was never seen by man. Upon each were graven characts in Ionian characters, and they have many virtues and properties, amongst the rest that if one of these jewels be hung round the neck of a new-born child, no evil shall befall him and he shall neither wail, nor shall fever ail him as long as the jewel remain without fail.*", likewise, "*and over the doorway was a tablet whereon were graven letters of gold in the old ancient Ionian character.*"

[85] Covel, 1722, 376. His unpublished detailed observations of the walls of Constantinople, Seliori and Eregli and on epigraphy are in the British Library, at Covel Papers, Add. 32,912, 41-72; 75-112; 247-257. New Roman Miletus was also stated to have been protected by a magic inscription, Hasluck 1973, I. 203.

Some inscriptions were understood to serve talismanic functions with telesmatic powers, others reminded of some prophetic association and, together with other objects, were employed to link the contemporary Muslim ruler with the power of antiquity. These understandings were 'reasonable,' valid within their own particular religo-cultural construct, if also quite distinctly different from the European antiquarian's recording of, and literal reading of the text of some of these same inscriptions, insofar as the non-European understandings had their basis in different, non-literal "readings" of ancient inscriptions. In part, these non-literal "readings" were associated with the mysterious inscriptions that were attributed to Balinas (Balīnūs/Balīnās/Abūlūniyūs i.e., Pseudo-Apollonius of Tyana), as for example in the *Kitāb at-Talāsim al-Akbar* (The Great Book of Talismans), a work in part based upon the late 5th c. A.D. Greek pseudo-epigraph entitled, *The Book of Wisdom of Apollonius of Tyana*, translated from Greek into Arabic, *Kitāb ṭalāsim Balīnās al-akbar* (The Great Book of Balinas' talismans) and Ethiopic[86], then into Osmanlija; and also the *Dhakhīrat al-Iskandar* (The Treasury of Alexander), a work said to have been presented by Aristotle to Alexander, and therefore of near prophetic status, given the association of Alexander the Great with the prophetic figure, Dhū'l Qarnayn-Zū'l Karneyn of the Qur'an, and the importance to Islamic rulers from the 12th to the 17th c. of titles such as *İskandar-i Sānī*, the Second Alexander and *Dhū'l Qarnayn al-Zaman*, the Dhū'l Qarnayn of the Age[87]. *The Treasury of Alexander*, was translated from Syriac into Arabic and then into Osmanlija and it included a section on the use of talismans for healing. In the 6th c. John Malalas wrote that in Domitian's reign Apollonius paid a visit Byzantium, where he left many talismans in order to help the Byzantines in their troubles[88] - and the understanding in Asia Minor was - that these talismans, which were usually made out of stone, including inscriptions on columns, or were of metal, were placed in cities and in city walls and on gates[89] to protect the inhabitants against plagues, wild animals, vermin, natural disasters, evil spirits/non-believing jinn and such like, "*with their mysterious inscriptions.*"[90] It was reported that King Qubad (Khusraw I. Anūshirwān

---

[86] Wallis Budge 1896, 355-385, Georgius Elmacinus, written also Elmakin, in his 13th c. *Majmu'-al-Mubarak*. Relates: '*Now there are some who say that Aristotle the sage, the teacher of Alexander, taught the ten Sciences of the earth and established them, and that he composed many treatises on the healing of the body besides other well-known books. And he compiled for Alexander a work, which we have mentioned in a previous place, and entitled it "The Book of the Knowledge of the Laws of Destiny", and in it the Science of talismans and the art of astrology, and he drew therein magical figures which were to be used for frightening and terrifying men and he further gave instructions. . .*' (idem. 382-383) '*And besides this he (Aristotle) wrote the book which is called "The Book of Astamatis" which treateth of the breaching of cities and fortresses and kings' houses and of the submission of kings, and of how men should make use of talismans and of the knowledge derived therefrom, and of the names which will bring down rain and water to them in the desert and in the Waste land, whensoever they utter them.*' (idem. 384).

[87] "*Historians and various Qisas authors relate that al-Iskandar/Dhu'1-Qarnayn went to the ends of the world to demolish pagan temples, spread Islam, and protect the Muslims, as would be expected from a Muslim head of state.*" Milstein – Rührdanz – Schmitz 1999, 148.

[88] Dzielska 1986, 108.

[89] Malalas records that in Antioch he (Apollonius) set a talisman at the East Gate (i.e. north-east) against the north wind.

[90] In 1871, Murray's Handbook for Travellers in Constantinople, p. 85, relates: "*Apollonius of Tyana erected several statues on the Hippodrome, and on the other public places of the city; and their mysterious inscriptions were interpreted as if they referred to the future fate of the city. Others were brought from Ath-*

531-579 A.D., Kisra) had Balinas-Apollonius of Tyana site a stone lion on one of the city gates of Hamadán as a talisman against the cold, and later, the Caliph Muktafi (902-908) wished to transfer it to Bagdad, but he was persuaded to leave it in place.[91] Likewise, presumably to provide protection for the city, a pair of basalt carved stone lions of Hittite workmanship, seem to have been formerly displayed on the Islamic walls of the Harran citadel[92]; and it seems evident that the neo-Hittite stele found built into the top of a minaret of the Ulu Camii two miles to the west of Darende, was understood at the time of the minaret's construction to serve some important protective function;[93] and there is an 8th c. B.C. Hittite inscription carrying a dedication to the Storm-God, which was formerly employed face up, to form a step into the 16th c. Dışarı-Çelebi Hüsamettin Bey mosque at Niğde.[94] The subsequent reuse of these ancient sculptures and of inscriptions in a language then unknown, in these locations in mosques, clearly shows they were understood to carry a variety of meanings of importance for the Muslim inhabitants. Evidence indicating the importance in Ottoman eyes of talisman during the 16th and 17th centuries is recorded, in addition to the numerous talisman reported on and recorded as *in situ* by Evliya Çelibi in his 17th c. *Seyahatnâme;* for example at the Ottoman siege of Oradea in Hungary in 1660, the aim of the Ottoman gunners was to destroy the four 14th c. bronze statues of Hungarian Saint-Kings, understood to have protected the city and which were said to have been responsible for the lifting of the Ottoman siege of Oradea two years earlier. The Ottoman gunners hit their targets in 1660, the talisman and the city fell. The bronze remains of these talismanic statues were then melted down and were cast into cannons that were then described as, *"the gods of the Hungarians."*[95] It can be noted that Ottoman talismanic protective inscriptions were themselves at times carved in relief on marble spolia, with an example from Rhodes dated 987/1579, inscribed to protect Ottoman sailors and ships from dangers such as storms and to ensure safe passage,[96] other talismanic inscriptions, designed to protect Ottoman shipping from bad weath-

---

ens, Cyzicus, Caesarea, Tralles, Sardis, Sebastia, Satalia (Antalya), *Chalcis, Antioch, Cyprus, Crete, Rhodes, Chios, Iconium, and Nicaea, these works of art were destroyed by the Latins, on the capture of Constantinople by Baldwin and Dandolo.*", in the 1204 sack.

[91] Bargebuhr 2011, 126-127. There seems no reason to think the historical Apollonius of Tyana visited Hamadān (Ekbatana) by Mount Alvand and the association with King Qubad is chronologically adrift by more than half a millennium; but then matters of historical accuracy are of little import concerning past and present belief in spiritual connections and associations, as it was understood chronological time could be suspended or compressed to conform and illuminate a different set of chronologies and truths.

[92] Like the Hittite lion reused in the Halep citadel, http://gertrudebell.ncl.ac.uk/photo_ details.php?photo_id=2639.

[93] Garstang – Gurney 1959, 31. Also for example, the 13th c. B.C. Hittite hieroglyphic inscription block built upside down into the Mamlūke mosque of Qaiqan, near the Antioch Gate of Aleppo, photographed *in situ* by Gertrude Bell, http://gertrudebell.ncl.ac.uk/photo_details.php?photo_id=2674.

[94] Hawkins 2000, 526-527. In this position it can be suggested it was employed and understood as marking for the worshipper the victory of Islam, of leaving the polytheist past behind, perhaps following the examples of the reuse of pagan inscriptions as threshold blocks at the entrance to churches, to be trodden on by Early Christian worshippers, e.g. Saradi 1997, 401, 403.

[95] Finkel 2005, 265.

[96] Tütüncü 2018, 13-17.

er, were on-board Ottoman vessels in the 17th c. as recorded by Jacques Gaffarel[97]. The importance over time of what were understood to be ancient talisman, 'written stones,' to Ottoman populations was considerable, as an incident from the 17th c. shows. In May 1626 the English Ambassador to the Porte on behalf of the Levant company from 1621-1628, Sir Thomas Roe, in his final attempt to acquire four of the life-size stone reliefs of the Labours of Hercules still affixed by iron pins to Theodosius the Great's entryway to Constantinople, the "Chrysopule,"- Porta Aurea, for 600 dollars in bribes[98], the reliefs to be lowered and secured by the Great Treasurer, with these reliefs to be divided by lot between his two patrons, the Earl of Arundel and the Duke of Buckingham.[99] But he was prevented from obtaining them after the news leaked, and a mob, possibly informed by the *castellano* of the Seven Towers, gathered preparatory to rioting, preventing their removal on the grounds that they were enchanted (talismans) and their removal would cause the fall of the city to the approaching Cossacks[100] and its collapse into an underground cavern, as was said to be recorded "*in an old book of prophesy.*"[101] In the summer of 1626 the Cossacks raided the shores of the Bosphorus as far as Rumeli Hisar.[102] This event followed a precedent recorded from 1204 by Robert de Clari, that "*an old Greek told Walter the Templar*[103] *that the Latins would conquer Constantinople, because it was written on the Golden Gate, which had not been opened for two hundred years: "When the blond king of the West shall come, I will open of myself."*,"[104] itself a quotation probably recorded in a Greek book of talisman - "*in an old book of prophesy,*" that stated the Latin inscription over the city gate foretold the fall of the city-dynasty, combining the words for, destruction of a tyrant, gold, and golden, into a new non-literal text. The 16th-century traveller Reinhold Lubenau, pharmacist to the Habsburg Imperial mission to the Porte of 1587-1589, related that there was a Byzantine gate in the city walls of

---

[97] See Bulmus 2012, 86, from the Ottoman use of talisman recorded by Jacques Gaffarel, *Concerning the Talismanical Sculpture of the Persians; the Horoscope of the Patriarkes; and the Reading of the Stars*, Trans. Edmund Chilmead, London 1650.

[98] Roe 1740, 444.

[99] Roe 1740 512, states a bribe of 500 dollars over three months, rather than 600 dollars (given in Roe 1740, 444), a possible misreading of the handwritten numerals of these letters.

[100] Roe 1740, 512. Letter, May 1626, to the Duke of Buckingham.

[101] Possibly a reference to *The Great Book of Talismans* or a related work.

[102] Grodz 2016, 5.

[103] Not to be confused with the Templar, Walter of Mesnil, of 1173-4 fame/notoriety.

[104] Clari 1966, 111, also cited by Radulfi de Diceto, Stubbs 1876, 60. However, a transcription of the inscription was published in Rev. Smith 1707, 42, (Inside the main Portal) *Hec loca Theudosius decorat post fata Tyranni*, (Portal exterior) *Aurea secla gerit, qui portam construit aure*, cited from Sirmond, a somewhat different reading of this inscription; although Smith 1707a, 80, gives a related account, "*A certain prophecy of no small authority runs in the minds of all the people, and has gain'd great credit and belief among them, that their empire shall be ruined by a Northern nation, which has white and yellowish hair. The interpretation is as various as their fancy.*", Rev. Smith suggesting Muscovites (incl. Cossacks) and Swedes. It was known in the 1880's that the lost inscription on the portal exterior read: AVREA SAECLA GERIT QVI PORTAM CONSTRVIT AVRO, "*he who builds a gate with gold rules a golden age.*" And inside the main portal, HAEC LOCA THEVDOSIVS DECORAT POST FATA TYRANNI "*After the destruction of a tyrant, Theodosius adorned this place.*", from the location holes for gilded bronze letters, Kelly 2012, 19.

Nicea-Iznik and the inscription on this gate was understood by the Rum population inhabiting Iznik in the 16th c., as recording an ancient prophecy of the forthcoming overthrowal of the ruling dynasty. The inscription over this gateway may in literal fact have recorded the name of the emperor Antoninus.[105] This 16th c. Rum interpretation of this inscription over this gate was brought to the attention of the Ottoman authorities and, in consequence, it was ordered that it be destroyed, and it was, so that the prophecy recorded in this 'non literal reading' of this inscription would be lifted, through the destruction of both the inscription and the gate supporting this inscription.[106] It is therefore evident that the Ottoman state valued both the visible ancient inscriptions and the implications of the contemporary 'non-literal readings' of these ancient inscriptions, of the interpretations that were given to them.

The 'non-literal readings' of the inscription over the gate to Heraclaea Cybistra in the 9th c., on the Golden Gate in the 13th and 17th centuries, as with the 'non-literal reading' of the Greek inscription on a gate at Nicaea in the 16th c., not only indicate the significance and power that was understood to be embodied in any publicly displayed inscription and the respect/fear it generated, quite regardless of its age, script or language, or if it was actually readable in a literal sense by any of the inhabitants or not; as the 'non-literal reading' also reflected the shared understanding of the use of inscriptions in religious contexts, painted or inscribed, employed for protective and prophesying reasons, on and in, both Christian and Muslim structures. It indicated a worldview in which a publicly displayed inscription represented to the inhabitants much more than was simply indicated by reading the literal meaning of the individual words or signs employed in the inscribed text, and, at times, the fact that the script of an inscription was itself no longer literally legible, implicitly suggested it was a magical text, as noted by Hasluck,[107] an inscription to be interpreted. The talismanic function given to both ancient inscriptions and "marbles" was understood and widespread, evinced by the reuse in Seljuk, Beylik and Ottoman structures of remains from antiquity, columns, inscriptions, reliefs, stone lions[108] etc., regarded as evidence of the work of *Balinas*, as of the Prophet Süleyman/Solomon and the wonderworking Jinn, as also of Alexander-İskender, and as such, protective. It is noteworthy for example that the reuse of ancient and of New Roman remains in the construction of Seljuk hans, indicated that in these same locations there were earlier buildings that, given their isolated locations on routes and proximity to water sources, had served related functions, such as Roman *mansio*, and New Roman *pandocheion*, as has been noted, and it can also be suggested, that these remains were deliberately reused, not only because they were a ready source of building material in that location, but perhaps also because when incorporated into the new building they were understood to provide it with protection, both those spolien that may have been visible after construction was

---

[105] Two decades earlier Ogier Ghiselin de Busbecq-Busbequius had recorded at İznik, "*Nicaea lies on the shores of the Lake of Isnik. The walls and Gates of the town are in fairly good condition. There are four gateways in all, and they can be seen from the central market-place. On each of them is an ancient inscription in Latin, stating that the town had been restored by Antoninus. I do not remember which Antoninus it was, but I am quite certain that it was an Antoninus, who was Emperor.*" Busbecq 1881, 136.

[106] Anderson 2015, 457.

[107] Hasluck 1914, 62, "*the fact that it has an inscription not 'understood of the people,' and therefore assumed to be of a magical character.*"

[108] For the re-use of ancient lion sculptures in the Mihaloğlu Mehmed 16th c. extension to shrine of Seyyid Gazi, and of their understood association with the Seljuks in the early 20th c. see, Yürekli 2016, 140.

completed, and those that lay concealed beneath the surfacing of plaster and paintwork,[109] blocks carrying inscriptions pagan and Christian, were not defaced, but often placed face inwards[110], upside down or on their side. Likewise ancient sculptures, reliefs and inscriptions were understood to have served a talismanic function when built into structures such as towers and city gates and city walls, like the ancient reliefs and sculptures built into the Seljuk rebuilt city walls of Konya, Antalya, Alanya, etc., or built into the walls of churches, and mosques, such as the antique lion built into the garden wall of the Arslanhane-Ahi Serafettin mosque in the Ankara citadel, or the Archaic Period lion set in the wall constructed of reused antique masonry blocks of the Aydinoğlu Mehmet Bey Mosque, Birgi of 1312, others built into the bases of minarets, etc. Some sculptures were converted, re-worked[111], re-carved so they would be understood in a different way, while retaining some of their original characteristics, such as the front face of a Late Antique sarcophagus carrying a relief of two angels supporting, one may think, a XI/XI, a *chi-rho* Christogram, or a cross, in a roundel, which, nearly a 1000 years later was built into the outer face of the tower of the Great Citadel Gate in the Muslim Seljuk rebuilding of the city walls of Konya in c. 1221. The roundel with its monogram inscription or cross was infilled and the stucco infill was carved to represent the sun, symbol of the Divine Light, brought by the angels, and the two angels were given stucco haloes. Its employment perhaps served an additional purpose, in marking the tower as that constructed in this building program by the Rum Seljuk Sahib, Şemseddin İsfahânî, Şemseddin meaning the Light of the Religion. It can be suggested that it may also have been read by members of the Rum population of Konya as representing the clause in the Nicean Creed, '*God of God, Light of Light, Very God of God*,' and it remained *in situ* into the 19th c. when it was drawn by Léon Laborde in November 1825.[112] (Figs. 1, 2) On these walls there were not only inscribed quotations from the Holy Qu'ran[113] and the Shahname,[114] but also a talismanic inscription which was said to have been commissioned by Sultan Ala ad-Din

---

[109] Duggan 2008 passim.

[110] For the ancient inscriptions placed face inwards in the Konya walls, the impression of the text remaining in relief on the dried mud in the core of the Seljuk walls, see, Greenhalgh 2013, 377, and references therein. It can be noted that for a talisman to operate, it was not necessary for them to be visible, they could be buried and remain effective, see for an example of this type: "*On this particular case some light is thrown by the peasants' beliefs regarding a 'written stone' buried in a vineyard near Monastir: this was once dug up, but torrents of rain followed. It is now kept buried, because, if any one dug it up again, it would never stop raining.*" Hasluck 1973, I., 211, as in the same way people wore talisman shirts beneath their outer garments and carried talisman hidden in their garments. For examples of talismanic shirts covered in inscriptions worn by Ottoman sultans, see for example, Turks 2005, Z. Tanindi, Cat. Nos. 257, 322.

[111] For examples of the c. 1240 Seljuk reworking of Roman blocks in the facade, on the cornice of the pediment and in the conversion of the Roman relief of Dionysus in the pediment, into the Seljuk stucco relief of the naked Shirin recorded by Charles Texier in 1836 at the Belkis Palace at Aspendos, Duggan 2011. As also Kinnear's 1818 report on the Seljuk walls of Konya, "*that statues and reliefs had missing arms and legs replaced.*" Greenhalgh 2013, 374, presumably in stucco, and presumably altering the meaning conveyed by these sculptures and reliefs to subjects more relevant to 13th c. Seljuk culture, Feridun rather than Hercules, etc.

[112] Published in Laborde 1838, Pl. LXIV.

[113] Perhaps the "protective surahs," *al-Falaq* and *an-Nas* (113, 114).

[114] Ibn Bibi, Vol. I, 1996, 272-3.

Keykubat I. from Jelal ad-Din Rumi, which was composed to protect the city walls[115] and, within this context, it seems most probable that the inscriptions in ancient Greek, both visible and invisible in the reconstructed walls[116] would have implicitly been associated with Balinas.

Fig. 1) *Léon Laborde's November 1825 drawing of an Early Christian sarcophagus relief that had been re-worked and built into a tower of the Seljuk constructed walls of Konya c. 1221.*

Fig. 2) *Christian sarcophagus with XI/XI monogram, Constantinople, c. 400, of the Angels and Christogram type, of the type that was reworked and reused in the tower constructed as part of the Seljuk walls of Konya.*

Sultan Süleyman Kanuni had the title "the Second Solomon" which is recorded on the endowment deed for the Süleymaniye mosque and this association was reinforced through the import for this mosque's construction between 1551 and 1557 of columns removed from Baalbek, a city said to have been built by the Prophet Sulayman's jinn and also from İskanderiyya-Alexandria, a city founded by İskander, and where, it was also related, *"The jinn built an assembly hall for Solomon at Alexandria with 300 columns, each 30 cubits high, of variegated marble polished like mirrors, so that a man could see in them who was walking behind him. In the midst of the hall was a pillar 111 cubits high. The roof was a single block of green marble, square, hewn by the jinn."*[117] Sultan Süleyman, the Sultan-Caliph was understood to be the Second Süleyman, the Alexander of the Age or Time, and so it can be understood that at times the re-used physical remains from antiquity, signified rather more than simply *"old stones to new buildings,"*[118] the reuse of available building material - since some remains, columns[119], were chosen, transported over consider-

---

[115] Hasluck 1973, I. 203.

[116] Leake 1824, 48-49.

[117] Butler – Fraser 1978, 387.

[118] T. S. Eliot, 1940, Four Quartets, "East Coker."

[119] The relationship of columns/pillars in an Islamic context, as also, of columns, Solomon and the jinn has been little explored in the literature. However on the importance of columns-pillars Sahl al-Tustarī (d. 896) related, *"God created from its prostration (sajda) a mighty column (amud) like crystal glass (zujaj) of light that is outwardly (zahir) and inwardly (batin) translucent. It is from this Light of Muhammad, al-Tustarı adds, that the human race originated."* (Akkach 2012, 94), and it may be the quest for ancient columns for reuse was more than simply a search for re-useable building material. It is noteworthy for example that the double-page frontispiece of the 15th c. Ottoman *Sūleymānnāme* painted for Sultan Beyazit II, has at the base, the depiction of jinn and columns, with some jinn shown chained to columns, Chester Beatty Library, Dublin, Ms. No. 406. A variant on the jinn chained to a black stone column by order of the Prophet Süleyman in The Extraordinary Tale of the City of Brass, *"When I myself was taken, after a flight of three months, I was condemned to be fastened to the black pillar until the death of time itself."* (Madrus – Mathers II, 1996, 294). Richard Burton has *"Then they came upon a pillar of black stone like a furnace-chimney wherein was one (Jinn) sunken up to his armpits."* Burton 1959, 445. "So Abdussemed drew near to the pillar and said to him who was therein, 'O creature, what is thy name and what art thou and how camest thou here on this wise?' 'I am an Afrit of the Jinn,' replied he, 'by name Dahish, son of El Aamesh,'" "and this pillar is my prison until judgement day." This relationship between jinn and

able distances and deliberately incorporated into prominent positions in the construction of a new building - due to the understood associations with Süleyman and İskander, Solomon and Alexander, and the precious remains of their constructions, combined with the protection understood to have been afforded through the reuse of these ancient remains and associations, incorporated into the new construction, associations explicitly acknowledged by its 16th c. patron, as being "the Second Süleyman."

Ancient inscriptions were understood to serve therapeutic purposes, when sat upon, healing fevers, malarial and rheumatic, aiding conception, etc.

The ancient Greek inscription on marble carrying a decree of Antiochus Soter of 278 B.C. from Sigeum-Ilium, which had been built into the porch of the church of Yenişehir-Janizari Cape, Giawr-keuy-Giaurkoi, was noted by the British Consul at Smyrna (1705-1715) Dr. William Sherard in 1702.[120] This inscription was bought from the Greek priest by the English Ambassador to the Porte (1717-1718) Mr Edward Wortley Montague in 1718 and shipped to England and was presented by his daughter Lady Bute in 1766 to Trinity College Library, Cambridge, and is today in the Fitzwilliam Museum.

This inscription was regarded by the inhabitants as providing protection and healing and, following its removal, the protection that it was understood to provide was lost and the Rum population was immediately struck by the plague and the majority of the inhabitants died.

Concerning the Phanodikos inscription perhaps from 550 B.C. which was also built into the porch of the church wall of Giaurkoi, Sherard's dragoman Paulo Homero first transcribed it, it was then transcribed by Samuel Lisle and then by Bernard Mould[121], and transcriptions of it and the Monumenta Teïa were sent by Consul Sherard to England, published by Edmund Chishull in 1728.[122] In 1737 John Montague, the Earl of Sandwich remarked:

"In this village is a very valuable inscription, generally allowed to be the most ancient one this day extant. The people, who are proprietors of it, notwithstanding their extreme poverty, are resolved not to part with it upon any consideration whatsoever; having a superstitious tradition among

---

columns/pillars can be related to the hadith, "*Said the Apostle of God (on him be prayers and peace), 'A certain demon of the Jinn attacked me yesterday in order to stop my prayers. But, verily, God gave me victory over him. I was about to tie him to the side of a pillar of the pillars of the Mosque so that ye might get up in the morning and behold him, all of you, when I remembered the prayer of my brother Solomon: "O Lord, forgive me and give me a dominion such as no one ever had,' and after that God set the demon free!*" Columns-jinn are also frequently related to the "dust devils" and desert whirlwinds that carry sand or dust in the form of a column/pillar of prodigious height, said to be inhabited by jinn, "*riding in the whirlwind,*" as in Alf Layla wa-Layla, the 1000 Nights and One Night, as likewise in the related phenomena of waterspouts. While in the course of pilgrimage, at Makkah, one of these pillars, near the Bab-az Ziadah, is known as the pillar of the Jinn, and there is the stoning of the pillars of Satan, while it is known that there are no columns supporting the heavens. The association of Solomon, jinn and columns pre-dates Islam, e.g. the line by the poet, al-Nābigha al-Dhubyānī, addressed to Solomon, "*Exploit the jinn, for I have permitted them/ to build Tadmur [Palmyra] with iron and columns.*" Quoted El-Zein 2009, 41.

[120] On this see Jones 1993, 74.

[121] On this see Crawford 2003, 86.

[122] Chishull 1728, Monumenta TEIA, 102-138.

them that upon the removal of another stone of the same kind (that removed by Edward Wortley Montague's party in 1718), *the village was immediately attacked by a violent plague, which swept away the best part of the inhabitants. Had I imagined that I was likely to have better success than many others, who have endeavoured to tempt the people with considerable sums of money, I would have taken any method of procuring that valuable piece of antiquity."* While Richard Chandler ignored the contemporary function of the inscription, which he described as *"barbarism,"* wrote, *"We copied these inscriptions very carefully, and not without deep regret, that a stone so singularly curious, which has preserved to us a specimen of writing antiquated above two thousand years ago, should be suffered to lie so neglected and exposed. Above half a century has elapsed, since it was first discovered, and it still remains in the open air, a seat for the Greeks, destitute of a patron to rescue it from barbarism, and obtain its removal into the far safer custody of some private museum, or, which is rather to be desired, some public repository."*[123] Later the French Ambassador to the Porte from 1784, Gabriel Florent Auguste de Choiseul-Gouffier attempted to remove the Phanodikos inscription. He sought permission to remove it from the church in Yenişehir-Gavur Kioi, as *"he claimed that the inscription was connected to an ancestor of his who had participated in the crusades,"* as though the inscription on the Phanodikos stele in Ionic and Attic dialects, dated from only 500 earlier, but, *"He failed, notwithstanding the firmans of Hassan Pacha, who had aided him with all his influence over the Greeks:"*[124], due to the Rum inhabitants' opposition to the removal of this "healing" inscription. It was understood to be able to heal fever - malaria, as was known and recorded at the time.[125] W. Wittman and Sir R. Phillips who removed the inscription for the Earl of Elgin relate that the Bey Adamoğlu, *"gave us a very civil reception, and supplied us with horses to proceed to the village of Giawr-keuy, or Janizari Cape, built on the site of ancient Sigaeum, and standing on an eminence which commands the plain of Troy. The purport of our journey thither was to procure a very curious bas-relief, and the celebrated Sigaean inscription, for Lord Elgin, who had seen them, and was desirous to transmit them to England. To accomplish this, a firman was procured from the Captain Pacha, who also furnished a chaous to be the bearer of it. We were not long in coming at these valuable antiquities, which we found at the entrance to a small Greek chapel. The Greeks, by whom the village was exclusively inhabited, were extremely averse to their being taken away. Their reluctance, we were told, arose from a superstition opinion they entertained, that by touching these stones agues were cured."*[126] This inscription was *"resorted to by the people for many miles around, from a belief that it was charmed, and had a power of curing such as sat upon it of the ague. The inscription was consequently in great danger of being rubbed away; when the marble was fortunately procured by Lord Elgin, and brought to England. The whole locality, it is said, was thrown into mourning by*

---

[123] Chandler 1776, 38-39.

[124] Wittman – Phillips 1803, 66-67. It was also seen in place before its removal in 1799 by Prof. Rev. Joseph Dacres Carlyle (1758-1804) scholarly advisor to Lord Elgin's party.

[125] For an example of a similar healing inscription, see the Hittite hieroglyphic inscription built into the corner of a house at Hama, mentioned in 1812 by J. L. Burckhard, which *"they believed, could cure diseases such as rheumatism if the sufferer touched them or rubbed against them."* Morritt 2010, 348.

[126] Wittman – Phillips 1803, 66-67. They write *"that by touching these stones agues were cured,"* while Hasluck 1973, I., 206, records, *"patients were rolled on it, while the priest read an appropriate Christian exorcism."*

the loss of so venerable a relic."[127] It was of course for the inhabitants the loss of the healing properties of this talisman that threw the locality into mourning, not the loss of a venerable relic *per se*. The above clearly shows the different views of the inhabitants and European antiquarians concerning these *grammata*-written stones, respectively, "practical and functional," but described by Europeans as superstition or barbarism, or a "relic", to be copied and removed to the "*safer custody of some private museum, or, which is rather to be desired, some public repository.*" The desire to obtain the original stone with its two inscriptions that had already been transcribed by William Sherard's dragoman Homeros in 1716, by the Rev. Samuel Lisle of the Smyrna factory and then by the subsequent chaplain Rev. Barnard Mould, and which had been published numerous times, not least by E. Chishull in 1728[128], by Richard Chandler in 1775[129], and then by Edmund Fry, in his *Pantographia* of 1799,[130] suggests something more akin to relic hunting, a fetish to possess, rather than simply a scholarly interest in the ancient inscriptions of recording and preserving the textual record from more than two millennia earlier.

There were other views held by Ottoman inhabitants concerning the ancient "written stones," inscriptions, they were not only, or all, regarded as protective and prophetic - talisman[131] by the Muslim and Rum populations; some were healing inscriptions, upon which the sick sat or were laid,[132] others were understood by many Turkish nomads, as still today, to give directions indicating the location of hidden treasure, as was noted by the Rev. James Dallaway c. 1795, "*The Turks assign a singular reason for the curiosity travellers discover to examine all inscribed Stones, but this in particular* (the Sigaean inscription) *that it contains an exact account of the treasures secreted under the different burrows.*"[133]

---

[127] Museum 1850, 366-367, re B. M. No. 107, today, No. 1002, Registration number: 1816,0610.107, Not on display. Today the B. M. catalogue entry, (Object reference number: GAA9341 sigaeum) strangely reports it was "excavated" by William Sherard (1659-1728), not that is was taken from the church porch on behalf of Thomas Bruce, the Earl of Elgin by Wittman and Phillips in 1799, and that it was bought for the British Museum by Act of Parliament, 1st. July 1816 from the Earl, as also the Parthenon marbles, for £35,000, for display in the British Museum, see: Burrow 1817, 167, Inscript. No. 53. See: http://www.britishmuseum.org/research/collection_online/collection_object_details.aspx?objectId=459473&partId=1.

[128] Chishull 1728, "INSCRIPTIO SIGEA," 1-48; C. L. Gr., 3595.

[129] Chandler 1774, 2-3.

[130] Fry 1799, 113-115, Greek 6, 7. "*A splendid and expensive work has just been given to the world by Mr Fry, the letter-founder, under the title of Pantographia, containing accurate copies of all the known alphabets in the world; together with an English explanation of the peculiar force or power of each letter; to which are added specimens of all well authenticated oral languages; forming a comprehensive digest of Phonology. This is a very curious, and to scholars and philosophers a very important work. On the subject of the Greek alphabets and different modes of writing Mr. Fry seems to have bestowed particular attention; and he has in general followed able guides, such as Chishull, Montfaucon, &c.*" The Monthly Magazine: Or, British Register, Feb. 1799, 148-149, 149. Earlier Alexander Drummond had provided examples of Greek orthography, Drummond 1754, npn., before his First Letter.

[131] Being an artificial magical image, or figure.

[132] A practice likewise recorded in Ottoman Syria into the 19th c., "The Hittites," 25-35, Blackwood's Magazine, Edinburgh, Vol. CXLII. July, No. DCCCLXI, 1887, 32.

[133] Dallaway 1797, 349-350.

A further view in respect to an ancient Greek inscription was recorded by the Rev. Edmund Chishull, chaplain to the English factory at Smyrna from 1698-1702[134]. The Muslim, Süleyman effendi's house in Magnesia had a stone staircase, with a reused block carrying an ancient Greek inscription forming one of the steps (Fig. 3). Edmund Chishull related, *"the said effendi not only civilly informed us of the stone, but when we had transcribed the words, he proffered to send it after us to Smyrna; adding, that if it were any piece of sanctity, he was unwilling it should remain there to be trampled underfoot."*[135] With, "*any piece of sanctity*" meaning in this context, if it carried a Christian inscription written by People of the Book, he did not want it to be trodden on, but offered to send it on to the Christians in Smyrna-İzmir, indicating respect for the words of the inscribed Greek text, if these were Christian.

ΣΤΑΤΙΩ ΚΩΔΡΑΤΩ ΑΝΘΥΠΑΤΩ ' ΑΛΕΞΑΝΔΡΟΣ ΔΙΟ-
ΓΝΙΤΟΥ ΕΠΕΣΚΕΥΑΣΕ ΤΟ ΜΝΗΜΕΙΟΝ ΕΑΥΤΩ ΚΑΙ ΤΟΙΣ
ΙΔΙΟΙΣ ΕΚΓΟΝΟΙΣ ΜΗΔΕΝΙ ΔΕ ΕΞΕΣΤΩ ΑΠΑΛΛΟΤΡΙΩΣΑΙ
ΑΥΤΟ ΕΚ ΤΟΥ ΓΕΝΟΥΣ ΜΟΥ ΕΑΝ ΔΕ ΤΙΣ ΑΠΑΛΛΟΤΡΙΩΣΗ
ΥΠΕΥΘΥΝΟΣ ΕΣΤΩ ΕΙΣ ΤΟΝ ΚΑΙΣΑΡΟΣ ΦΙΣΚΟΝ Χ. Ρ. ς.

Fig. 3) *Published transcription by Chishull of the ancient Greek text on the inscribed stone re-employed to form one of the steps of the staircase in Süleyman effendi's house in Magnesia Chishull 1747, 11. How many lines of text were inscribed is unclear, as also the shape of the epigraphic surface.*

This same Muslim respect for sacred texts was recorded in the 18th c. by M. Jean Otter of the Academy Royal of Inscriptions, *"of a conference he had with a learned Persian. The Mahometan said, they reverenced all our sacred writings, except St. Paul's - qu'ils respectent tous, excepté Saint Paul."*[136]

How safe a home was Europe for antiquities, including inscriptions and manuscripts that were brought from Asia Minor, and how much of scholarly importance was lost, at sea and on land?

During this period of 400 years antiquities, including inscriptions, were reused, defaced and destroyed in Asia Minor, some by natural events, earthquakes and tsunami, some due to human intervention, burnt in lime kilns, and reused as building material in construction works for sultans, villagers and others, including, for example, at the start of the 15th c., the destruction of the tomb itself and the reuse of the stone blocks and reliefs of the earthquake damaged Wonder of the World, the Mausoleum of Halicarnassus, to construct the Castle of Petronium/San Pietro (Bodrum) by the Knights of St. John of Jerusalem on Rhodes; the extraction of lead from antique stone clamps to cast bullets, which resulted for example by the 16th c. in the defaced parts of the lower sections of the *Res Gestae Divi Augusti*,[137] and the ongoing reuse, not least of ancient columns for the construction of mosques and churches. But how safe a home was Europe for an-

---

[134] His notebooks are at B. M. Harlian Cat. N. 7509.

[135] Chishull 1747, 11-12.

[136] Warburton 1811, 120, citing, J. Otter, Voyage en Turque et en Perse, Paris 1748, Vol. I, 22.

[137] *"The top lines are nearly perfect; in the middle the gaps begin to present difficulties; the lowest lines are so mutilated with blows of clubs and axes as to be illegible. This is indeed a great literary loss, and one which scholars have much reason to regret; the more so as it is an ascertained fact that Ancyra was dedicated to Augustus as the common gift of Asia."* Busbecq 1881, 142-143.

tiquities, including inscriptions and manuscripts that were brought from Asia Minor, and how much of scholarly importance was lost at sea in transit and on land?

For example, *"In the turbulent reign of Charles I. and the subsequent usurpation, Arundel house was often deserted by the illustrious owners; and in their absence, some of the marbles were defaced and broken, and others either stolen or used for the ordinary purposes of architecture. The chronological marble (The Parian Chronicle[138]) in particular, was unfortunately broken and defaced. The upper part, containing 31 epochas, is said to have been worked up in repairing a chimney in Arundel House."*[139] Only a little over one half of the wisely selected inscriptions assembled by the Earl of Arundel at Arundel House, from Italy, Greece, from the Aegean Islands and from Asia Minor, some through his agent William Petty, 136 of the 250 important Greek, Latin and Hebrew inscriptions collected, including those from Smyrna-Izmir, survived the English Civil War to be presented to Oxford University in 1667.[140] Losses included the upper part, lines 1 to 45 of the Parian Chronicle, an inscribed chronology extending from 1581/0 to 264/3 B.C. covering 1300 years of Hellenic history bought by William Petty in Smyrna-İzmir[141]. This near 50% loss of ancient inscriptions removed from their places of origin was passed over in silence in the ongoing rhetoric concerning securing antiquities in Ottoman territory from any possible destructive activities of the "barbarian" inhabitants. And concerning the Arundel Marbles, *"various other fragments, which were not thought worth removing[142], were buried in the rubbish and foundations of the houses in the lower part of Norfolk Street, and other buildings on the gardens. Several of these, including a few trunks of statues, dug up at a later time, were sent down to the*

---

[138] The lowest section of the chronicle, the base of the inscribed stele was found on Paros in 1897.

[139] s.v. 'Arundel,' Encylopaedia Britannica, Vol. II, 1810, 707. The suggestion it was used in this chimney building work, as also said to have been employed to repair a hearth-stone is quite uncertain, see on this Sandys 1908, 343. Henry Peacham in 1634 had described Arundel House *"as the chief English scene of ancient inscriptions,"* Peacham 1962, 124, and it had been visited by King Charles I. and queen.

[140] Sandys 1908, 343; Tierney 1834, 484. The collection of 'marbles' before the Civil War consisted of 87 statues, 128 busts, and 250 inscribed marbles. The letter from John Evelyn to Henry Howard that resulted in the donation of the surviving inscriptions to Oxford University observed, *"It is not without much regret and more concernment as it regards yr honourable and illustrious family, that I have now so long a time beheld some of the noblest antiquities in the world, and which yr grandfather purchased with so much cost and difficulty, lye abandoned, broken and defaced in divers corner about Arundel House and the gardens belonging to it. I know yr Honour cannot but have thoughts and resolutions of repairing and collecting them together one day; but there are in the meane tyme certain broken inscriptions, now almost obliterated with age, and the ill effects of the weather, which will in a short time utterly be lost and perish, unless they be speedily removed to a more benigne and lesse corrosive ayre..."* Evelyn 1827, 188. The house had been confiscated in the general confiscation made by the parliament, some of the marbles were then sold off to the Spanish ambassador Don Alonzo de Cardenas to The Lord Protector, Oliver Cromwell, and the house was finally returned to Lord Henry Howard in 1660 on the Restoration of the English monarchy.

[141] Several inscriptions brought *in situ* from Smyrna are recorded in Marmora Arundellina of 1628 including the inscribed column from the Temple of Venus Stratonicus.

[142] When Arundel House was demolished in 1678.

Duke of Norfolk's seat at Worksop Manor.",[143] while others, regarded as worthless and buried in the 17th c. were recovered in 1972.[144]

While some of the antiquities including inscriptions that had been removed from Asia Minor to Europe were destroyed in conflict and disaster in Europe; others, including priceless manuscripts, inscriptions and sculptures, were lost in transit to Europe when vessels sank. The precedent was rather well known to antiquarians, being described by Cicero. Gaius Verres the Roman legate, had the shrine of Apollon on Delos looted, including removing its cult statue, and the ship transporting the loot sank[145]. But this precedent was ignored in the quest to obtain the original, for the possession of a venerable relic. Venetian notarial documents, two series of which were studied by Teneti in 1959, show at the end of the 16th and start of the 17th c. there *"were almost 40 shipwrecks along the route Constantinople-Venice in 17 years; that is at least two per year.",*[146] and the total loss of shipping per year throughout this entire period of 400 years on the several routes from Asia Minor to European ports was far greater than on this single route, some of which would have been carrying smuggled antiquities including epigraphic material when they sank. Contributory factors, such as the repeated dangerous overloading of English Levant Co. ships departing from Smyrna-İzmir for the captain's private gain in the 17th century are also recorded.[147] While searching for antiquities the Rev. William Petty in 1625, *"In returning from Samos, he narrowly escaped with his life in a great storm, but lost all his curiosities, and was imprisoned for a spy; but, obtaining his liberty, pursued his searches."*[148] *"he was released on the testimony of some Turks, who knew him, and that he had lost his credentials in the sea. With great industry he recovered his statues..."* [149] he *"is gone to the place he left his boat to fish for his marbles"*[150] and he recovered the sunken marbles,[151] and moved on to Ephesus,[152] but any manuscripts he may have collected were lost, together with his *berat*, when the vessel sank. The Constantinople Patriarch Lucaris, friend of the Rev. Edward Pocock, was executed by strangulation in 1638 and the Patriarch's collection of rare manuscripts was rapidly removed by his longstanding friend, the Dutch resident Cornelius Van Haagen (1611-38), and dispatched to Holland, including the Greek manuscript of Clemens Alexandrinus's *Hypotyposes*, which the patriarch had brought from Alexandria to Constantinople, but the ship sank in a storm on the day of its

---

[143] s.v. 'Arundel Marbles,' Penny Cyclopaedia of the Society for the Diffusion of Useful Knowledge, Vol. II, No. 120, 1833, 427.

[144] Seven classical marbles were found during excavations on the site of Arundel House in the Strand in 1972, see Cook 1974, 247.

[145] Cicero, Against Verres, 2.1.46-48.

[146] Beltrame – Gelichi – Miholjek – Pavao 2014, 151.

[147] CSP 1860, 411.

[148] Caraccioli 1766, 219.

[149] Rees 1819, s.v. William Pettie – William Petty, the presumed translator from Greek of 1644 of *The Commentary of George Aeropolita*.

[150] Roe 1740, 445.

[151] Hervey 1921, 274.

[152] Roe 1740, 445.

arrival in 1638 in Holland and the manuscripts were lost.[153] It can be noted in respect to these losses that these were of collected, carefully selected and illegally removed antiquities. The problem of antiquities in transit shipwrecked continued: a part of the British Minister to the Court of the Two Sicilies in Naples from 1764 to 1800, Sir William Hamilton's collection of South Italian and Greek vases, was lost when it sank with HMS Colossus in 1798 off the Scilly Isles. 30,000 shards were recovered from a part of the wreck in the 1970's.[154] The 'Mentor,' a polacre hired by Lord Elgin sank in 1802, the cargo of Parthenon marbles were recovered with the aid of sponge divers hired by William James Hamilton brought from Syme and Calymno over the course of two years[155], but the collection of ancient Greek papyri scrolls made by Captain Leake was lost, together with his own maps and notebooks from his survey of Egypt.[156] Other works were simply lost at some point in the course of their clandestine removal. For example the English Ambassador, Sir Thomas Roe wrote to the Earl of Arundel from Constantinople, in January 1621: "*I have also a stone taken out of the old Palace of Priam of Troy, cut in a horned shape; but because I neither can tell of what it is, nor hath it any other beauty, but only the antiquity and truth of being a piece of that ruined and famous building, I will not presume to send it you; yet I have delivered it to the same messenger, that your lordship may see it, and throw it away.*"[157] It is perhaps possible this stone cut in the shape of a horn was a work dating from the time of the Trojan War, a cult sculpture, but, whatever it was, it was lost, as the Earl of Arundel wrote in reply from London, Arundell House, December 9th 1622, to Amb. Roe: "*I have received the Medall of Alexander which your Lordship (I thanke you) did send me, and I doe much valewe. For your stone, Your Master of the Shippe* (Antony Wood, captain of the Rainbow) *could not finde it, and I was yet lesse troubled for the wante of it, in respecte your Lordship wrote it had noe engraving upon it.*"[158]

Text and Context: Problems in the transcription by hand of an inscription, of what was to be recorded and in the publication of an inscription in the period from 1550-1800.

Problems with a transcription and in the recording of an inscription

While some European antiquarians over these 400 years, transcribed inscriptions in visits to various parts of Asia Minor, largely in Aegean coastal regions and along major trade routes (Tables I, III), others just noted the presence of inscriptions in their publications. At Nicomedia in 1699 Sieur Aubry De La Motraye wrote, "*As for inscriptions, I met none of them entire; and if Mr. Grelot, who says there are so many, had taken the Pains to communicate them, the Publick had*

---

[153] Twells 1740, 13, from which a synopsis given in, *History of the Works of the Learned for the year One Thousand Seven Hundred and Forty*, Article 29, For June 1740, London, 411. Likewise a bust of Hermes and other collected antiques were removed by the Spanish Amb. to Rome, Don Juan Domingo de Haro y Guzmán, viceroy of Naples 1683-87, but the whole collection is said to have been lost in the wreck of the vessel; while the treasures of the Albani Library in Rome, purchased by the Prussian Government were lost in a shipwreck off the coast of Gibraltar in 1863.

[154] CVA Great Britain 20 (British Museum 10).

[155] Memorandum, 22-23; Galt 1812, 138.

[156] Hamilton 1809, iv; 406; see also Wroth 1893, 324.

[157] Roe 1740, 16.

[158] Hervey 276. Perhaps meaning it was worth less in his eyes for not having any recognisable inscription on it.

been more obliged to him, than for his singly saying so;"¹⁵⁹ Likewise, M. Le Roy in 1754 at Çardak Köy facing Gallipoli remarks, "*et plusieurs inscriptions grecques curieuses,*"¹⁶⁰ but he doesn't record them; as likewise Thomas Hope on his extensive tour of Ottoman territory, who drew in coastal Lycia including the tombs at Antiphellus-Kaş in the early 1790's, wrote, "*on the now almost deserted coast of Lycia, the thousands of sepulchral monuments, of an era apparently preceding its conquest by the Romans, and bearing Greek inscriptions.*",¹⁶¹ but he doesn't transcribe them. There were unsurprisingly both inaccuracies and omissions in the transcriptions of the inscriptions that were published. For example George Sandy in his volume of *Travels relation of a journey begun in 1610,* first published in 1615, mentions Greek and Latin inscriptions on tombs at Troy ,¹⁶² but also provides no transcription of them, but he does provide a transcription of the Latin inscription on "*Pompey's column*" on the Cyanean Rocks at the entrance to the Black Sea.¹⁶³ A later transcription of it was made by Jacques Spon & George Wheler in 1675-6,¹⁶⁴ another by Edmund Chishull on April 22ⁿᵈ 1699¹⁶⁵, another by the Earl of Sandwich in 1738.¹⁶⁶ Each of these published transcriptions of the same Latin inscription, taken over the course of a century differs from the others, and by 1797, G. A. Oliver would write, "*Several travellers have made efforts to read the Latin inscription which is there to be found; but the letters are at present so effaced, that it is difficult, perhaps even impossible, to accomplish that task.*"¹⁶⁷

The problem with transcribing an inscription was not just the light, or its absence, the month and the time of day, the degree of shadow, its degree of visibility, the depth of incision, degree of erosion and encrustation, and time limitations in front of the inscription, as also its accessibility, as with the inaccessible inscriptions high up on the aqueduct by Ephesus, and, at some sites the sheer quantity of inscriptions,¹⁶⁸ which amongst the hundreds needed to be recorded? But also, what the mind of the transcriber read into what he saw, which may not have been exactly what was to be seen on the epigraphic surface, the question of if the actual text of the transcribed inscription was corrected by its transcriber? Even in the copies made by Richard Pococke before 1752 of the careful transcriptions of inscriptions that had been made by Arthur Pullinger¹⁶⁹,

---

[159] De La Motraye 1723, 213-214.

[160] Sevin 1802, 100.

[161] Hope 1835, I, 384.

[162] Sandy 1673, Bk. I, 18.

[163] Sandy 1673, Bk. I, 32: DIVO. CAESARI. AUGUSTO. | L. CLANNIDIUS. | L. F. CLA. PONTO.

[164] Wheler 1682, Bk. II, 206-207, Restitution idem 207: DIVO CAESARI AVGVSTO | E CL. ANNIDIUS | L. F. CL. ARRONTO.

[165] Chishull 1747, 42: DIVO CAESARI AUGVSTO | L. CL. ANNIDIVS | L. F. CLAV. FRONTO.

[166] Sandwich 1807, 137: CAESARI AVGVSTO | CLANNIDIVS LF | CL FRONTO----- | ----CVR------.

[167] Olivier 1802, 78.

[168] Tournefort at Ankara citadel in 1701 writes, "*This whole first enclosure is full of pedestals and inscriptions; but what part of Angora is without them? A good Antiquary would find what would employ a whole year to transcribe. We copied out the following,*" 15 inscriptions in both Latin and Greek" Tournefort, Vol. 111, 283. For other inscriptions transcribed at Ankara, idem, 287-288, in the battlements in Greek and Latin, idem, 291-294.

[169] Pullinger recorded the texts of over 100 Greek inscriptions, BM Mss. H. 4824.

inaccuracies were introduced, which were then published in Pococke's IAGL,[170] such as a single line inscription recorded by Pullinger at Ephesus in 1733, published as four lines by Pococke in 1752.[171] The remarks made in the review by C. Merivale published in *The Academy and Literature* in 1874, concerning Theodore Bergk's 1873 edition entitled, *Augusti rerum a se gestarum indicem cum Graeca metaphrasi*, are to the point, "*Throughout the last century the edition of Chishull (1728) was generally accepted as an adequate representation of the original. The inscription has been frequently examined since, and many emendations have been discovered or suggested.*"[172] Comments also applicable to the slightly later, more accurate transcriptions made at the request of M. le Comte de Pontchartrain for King Louis XIV, by Paul Lucas[173], of the Latin and the Greek texts of the *Res Gestae Divi Augusti* on this same building from 1st to 21st September 1705, published in 1712. In terms of the accuracy of the transcriptions made in this period, of course they varied. W. M. Ramsay noted that ligatures are often misrepresented or ignored in transcriptions, and there is the frequent misreading of: Σ for Ξ, of Λ for A, of Λ for Δ, O for Θ, of Є for C etc.[174] and a late form of Ω mistaken for O, and of K for IC, as by Paul Lucas.[175] Chateaubriand describes this as, Lucas, "*mangles all the inscriptions that he copies,...*"[176] Further, was it simply the inscribed text that was to be recorded? Was the task of the antiquarian simply the noting and collection through transcription of the surviving Greek and Latin texts, and the circulation and publication of these texts as texts, and at times their removal, an adjunct providing data for the more accurate writing of history? When did it begin to become something more than a text, involving the attempt to produce a scientific epigraphic record? Unsurprisingly the aims of individual antiquarians in Asia Minor over this 400 year period varied, the individual's specialities and interests differed, not least in respect to the text of inscriptions. Some mentioned but did not transcribe them, while others transcribed the inscriptions as texts, but a few others went further towards making a careful accurate record of both the text and its context, included recording the shape of the epigraphic surface, the letter forms employed and line breaks. Was the form of the epigraphic surface characteristic of a type, was there any relief carving? Was the epigraphic surface tall and narrow, or wide, or was it a narrow long surface. Was it inscribed on more than one side, on a column, or a post, or on the face of a rock outcrop etc., and were the lines of the text recorded with line breaks, were the different letter forms and sizes and the size of spaces between the letters and between the lines of the text noted? The text was distributed over what area, displayed at what height - were there any remains of surfacing and colour? Carved guidelines, incorrect letters, and other observations? Was any measurement taken? In other words, was only the abstracted transcribed text recorded, a block of text, or, was there an

---

[170] Noted and described, Drew-Bear – Naour – Stroud 1985, Part II, 13ff.

[171] Drew-Bear – Naour – Stroud 1985, Part II, 23.

[172] Merivale 1874, 234. As earlier in the Athenaeum, No. 1335, May 28, 1853, 661, Rev. Beale Poste, Britannic Researches, "*6. The Angora Inscription, part of which relates to Britain. The Latin of this was published by Chishull, the oriental traveller, in 1728, but was without sufficient authenticity,...*"

[173] Paul Lucas relates that, although the text already existed in 'some authors', he had been sent to verify it. *Voyage du Sieur Paul Lucas fait dans la Grèce, l'Asie mineure, la macédoine st l'Afrique, par ordre de Louis XIV*, Paris 1712, I, 138-148, Greek, 308-313, Latin npn. at the end of vol. one.

[174] Ramsay 1918, 126-127.

[175] Ramsay 1918, fn. 76.

[176] Chateaubriand 1812, I., 39.

attempt made to produce an accurate scientific record of the inscription, as an inscription? No publication of inscriptions from Asia Minor into the 19th c., even those that published drawings-engravings of inscriptions, the approximation of a photograph, recorded all of the data expected today as standard: precise location, if *in situ* or not, measured size of object, size and form of epigraphic surface, stone type, spaces, letter size and forms, number of lines, etc.

Publication and problems with the published printed representation of an inscription

Ciriaco de Ancona/Pizzicolli's 15th c. transcriptions of inscriptions were not published but circulated in manuscript copies but they often recorded in a drawing the shape of the epigraphic surface, the relative size of the letters and any relief carving.

> & n'y a que bien peu de vestiges. Nous trouuasmes vn pilier de marbre blanc fiché en terre, mais au demeurant à demi couché, qui auoit ceste inscription ainsi ordonnee, tant d'vn costé que d'autre: *Imperator Cæsar Mar. Aur. Antoninus Pius Felix Particus Maximus, Germanicus Maximus. Trib. P. 1. Imp. Po. XV. Maximus Imp. Cos. III. prouinciam Asiam per viam & flumina pontibus subiugauit.* Toutes lesquelles parolles estoyent d'vn costé du pilier, tãt consumees d'antiquité, qu'à peine les pouuions lire. De l'autre costé du pilier estoyent escrites autres parolles, desquelles le commencement est, *Imp. Cæsar Aug. Diocletiano regnante.* Nous n'en auõs peu lire autre chose.

Fig. 4) *Inscriptions, simply the text? Pierre Belon, Les observations de plusieurs singularitez et choses memorables trouvées en Grèce, Asie, Judée, Egypte, Arabie et autres pays estranges, 1553, T. II, Ch. VI, p. 582.*[177]

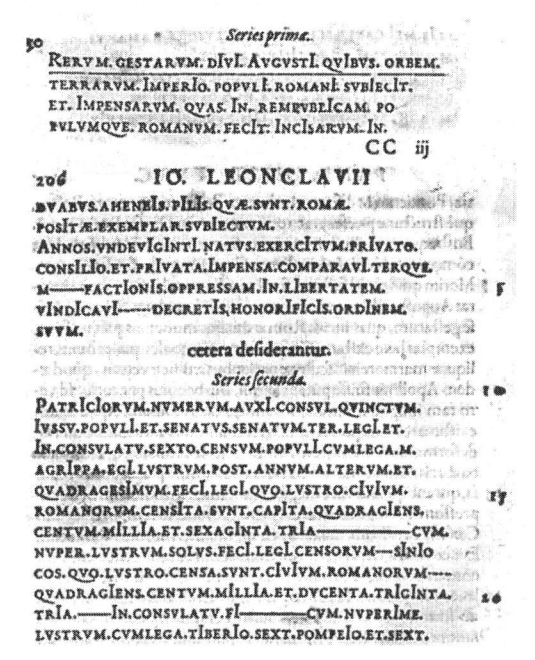

Fig. 5) *Johannes Leunclavius's publication in Annales Sultanorum, A Turcis Sua Lingua Scripti, 1588, of the Res Gestae Divi Augusti, the opening lines, p. 205-6.*

However, the few inscriptions transcribed in Asia Minor by Pierre Belon in 1546-9, were published as a Latin text in a standard font, without visual record of the context of the text of the inscription (Fig. 4), as likewise in publications of the *Res Gestae Divi Augusti* (Fig. 5), and this emphasis on the inscription as text was characteristic for the publication of inscriptions into the 18th c. Strange as it may seem, in terms of the epigraphic information recorded, the drawings made by Ciriaco in the mid-15th c. often provide more accurate information than was practiced a century or two later in the printed publication of an inscription. As W. M. Ramsay stressed: "*Another principal has to be constantly emphasised, that epigraphic copies reproduced in type are dangerous.*";[178] as later, for example with the use by the printer of J. R. S. Sterrett's, *An Epigraphical Journey in Asia Minor*, Papers of the American School of Classical Studies at Athens, II, Boston, 1888, of a typeface ≤

---

[177] Belon 1553, II, Ch. VI, page number typo, 582, should read page 182.

[178] Ramsay 1918, 125.

rather than Σ, suggesting to the reader an earlier date for an inscription than is in fact the case.[179]

Jacques Spon and George Wheler's different approaches and the mischievous Dr. Pickering's remarkable contributions

Michael Werner wrote in 2011: "*Jacques Spon was one of the most effective founders of an epigraphy for the Greek world. He justified the veritas and auctoritas of these new historical sources in the following words: "What is more, it is not as easy to invent or to falsify an antique inscription as it is to falsify a book or to supply it with a different, existing author: it takes great delicacy of spirit to recognize that a work was not written by a specific author. But I do not believe that it is so difficult to tell whether an inscription is not antique, if one has studied the matter a little. The stone that the Ancients chose, the form into which they cut it, and the exact shape of the letters combined with the depth that they gave it, all these things are not easy for the ignorant laborer to imitate.*"[180] However, disregarding the fact that these were not "*new historical sources,*" as the use of epigraphic sources to confirm ancient literary sources, not least in relating antique toponyms to places, was practiced in the 14th and 15th c. by Early Renaissance scholars in Rome, Cola di Rienzo, Giovanni Dondi, Nicola Signorili, Poggio Bracciolini, Niccolo Niccoli, by Ciriaco de Pizzicolli, as by Konrad Peutinger in Augsburg, etc., and that an "*ignorant labourer*" would find it as difficult to imitate an antique text as an antique inscription; there is also at least one ancient Greek inscription from Asia Minor[181] that was published by both Jacques Spon in 1678 and by George Wheler in 1682, that gave the public a non-existent inscription, supposedly inscribed on the façade of the Temple of Augustus at Mylassa-Milas. Wheler writes, "*The first antiquity* (of Mylasa) *was a fair temple of marble, with an inscription on the front, shewing it was built in honour of Augustus Caesar, and to the Goddess of Rome.*"[182] Dr Pickering[183] (Docteur Picrelin[184]) had related his travel with Mr Salter to Mylasa-Milas in 1673 to George Wheler and Jacques Spon in Smyrna, and both then published copies of the drawing made by Dr Pickering showing this inscription (Figs. 6, 7, 9), but there was in fact no inscription in this position on the façade[185]

---

[179] Ramsay 1918, fn. 28.

[180] Cited in translation, Werner 2011, 296.

[181] Spon, 1678, Bk. I, 362-363.

[182] Wheler 1682, Bk. III, 275. In translation, "*The popular assembly* (dedicated) *to imperator Caesar Augustus, son of god, pontifex maximus, and to the Goddess Rome.*" My thanks to F. Onur for this translation.

[183] Medical doctor to the Smyrna factory, recorded inscriptions at Panionium, Miletus, Didyma, Askem Kalesi, Milas. Dr. Pickering was mentioned by William Cave, Smyrna Consul (1662-1667) in a dispatch printed in the Calendar of State Papers of 1st of February, 1667: I "*Fear that Dr. Pickering is drawing the youth of the Smyrna factory into gaming and debauchery, will not feel safe until he, his wife, and other vicious persons there without employment are out of Turkey.*" He was however regarded as a popular, amusing and jolly person by the Levant Co. members at Smyrna in 1675-6, and was thought to be a reliable source by Dr Spon and G. Wheler evinced by their publication of his records.

[184] Spon 1678, 1, 366.

[185] This interpolation of an inscription on the frieze was not of the same order of scholarly manipulation of the evidence as the Abbé Fourmont's destruction of part of the epigraphic record of Sparta and Amyclae in 1730, with the fabrication of new epigraphic records, exposed by Richard Payne Knight in 1791, due to the use of the same orthography on inscriptions supposedly dating from the pre-Homeric

(Fig. 8), it had been inserted by Dr Pickering.[186] The inscription may have been elsewhere on site, perhaps on an altar, or was inspired by Livy 43. 6. 5.[187], put into ancient Greek and added to the drawing of the facade to identify it.

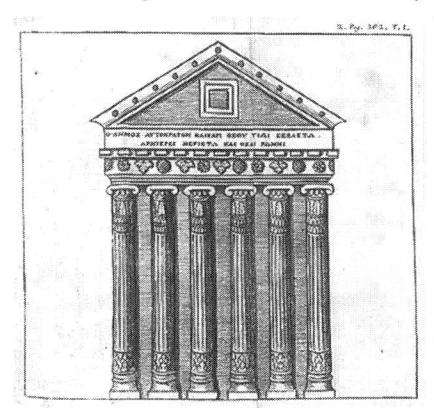

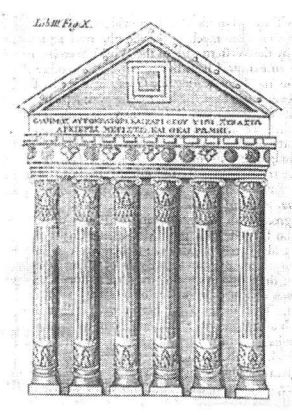

Fig. 6) *Spon 1678, T. I, 362.*

Fig. 7) *Wheler 1682, Vol. III, Fig. X.*

Fig. 8) *R. Pococke's drawing of the temple in 1740, Pococke 1745, Pl. 55.*

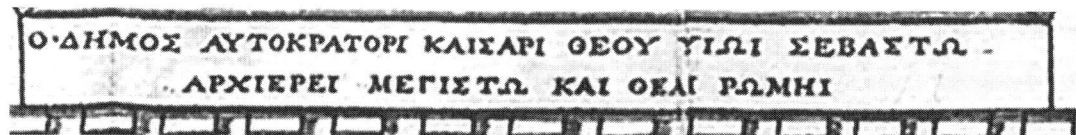

Fig. 9) *Ancient Greek text of the dedicatory inscription placed on the facade by Dr Pickering, from Spon 1678.*

Just the Text, or the Inscription in its Epigraphic Context: Spon and Wheler

Ioli Vingopoulou writes in respect to Jacques Spon of Lyon and George Wheler's works: *"The three-volume account of Spon's voyage was first published in Lyon in 1678… while the third volume is dedicated exclusively to the inscriptions and coins collected by Spon during his journey. Spon's travel account was republished in French and was translated into English. Four years later, George Wheler published his own account of their journey, which is in fact but a mediocre copy of*

---

into the Hellenistic period. See for example Payne Knight 1791, 113-114; Stoneman 2010, 99-106. But report of this "inscription" circulated, e.g. "3. *At Mylassa, (formerly Mylasso in Caria), among other noble remains, are a magnificent marble temple, dedicated to the goddess of Rome, and built in honour of Augustus, as appears from an inscription, still entire, on the front,…*" Sale et al. 1765, 27.

[186] R. Pococke's drawing of 1740, pub 1745, shows no inscription on the facade. It seems worth noting that by the time of J. B. Hilair's fine drawing of 1776, engraved and pub. in 1782, the temple had already been dismantled, "*We were shown the basement, which remains; and we were informed, the ruin had been demolished, and a new Mosque, which we saw on the mountain-side, above the town, raised with the marble.*", stated by Richard Chandler in 1765, Chandler 1776, 187. J. B. Hilair in his drawing simply copied and altered Pococke's drawing of the temple, removing the opening in the face of the pediment, which probably dated from the Late Antique conversion of the building, altering the proportions and the viewpoint of a building which he had not seen himself, in his drawing based on Pococke's, as the temple no longer stood.

[187] "*Alabandenses templum Urbis Romae se fecisse commemoravere ludosque anniversarios ei divae instituisse;*".

Spon's work."[188] However, in respect to the publication of the same epigraphic material presented by both travellers, it was the botanist George Wheler's publication of 1682 that seems to have marked the essential change in the publication of transcriptions of antique inscriptions in Asia Minor, from the transcription of a text, towards the "scientific" recording of antique inscriptions, a novel undertaking, quite different from the usual publication of a transcribed text in the 16th and 17th centuries. Consequently, George Wheler's publication was very far from being "a *mediocre copy of Spon's work,*" as in the publication of the same inscriptions, a great deal more epigraphic data is recorded in Wheler's publication than in the text provided by Spon, in part, it can be suggested, because Spon knew more, and so was concerned with the text and the meaning and commentary on the text itself, not with making a scientific record of the document's actual appearance on the epigraphic surface (see Figs. 10-17 for comparisons). George Wheler however records and shows the reader: the number of lines of the inscription and the relative sizes of the letters employed, with the sequence of letters, words and spaces in any line of an inscription. The shape of the "epigraphic surface' was itself delineated and the inscribed context displayed, as also, if the remains were incomplete through damage or being in part underground, then this was recorded.[189] Unfortunately, no measurement of the epigraphic surface was given by George Wheler in his publication[190].

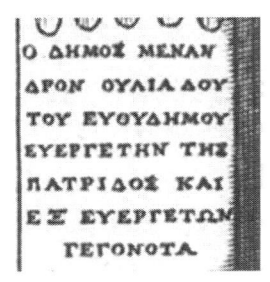

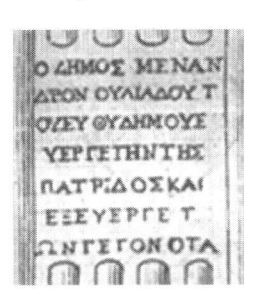

Figs. 10, 11) *Copies of the inscription on the so-called 'pillar of Menander' by Mylasa, from Dr Pickering's original drawing of 1673*[191]*, were published differently by Spon (left) and by Wheler (right). Spon recording the text (Spon 1678, T.I, 362); Wheler recording the inscription, as recorded by Dr Pickering (Wheler 1682, Bk. III, fig. XII).*

---

[188] Ioli Vingopoulou – Aikaterini Laskaridis Foundation, Athens, at: http://eng.travelogues.gr/travelogue.php?view=294&creator=978920&tag=8852.

[189] Wheler 1682, Bk. III, 231, 232.

[190] The publication of the measurement of the epigraphic surface was only remedied in some 19th c. publications, for example M. G. F. A. de Choiseul-Gouffier, *Voyage pittoresque de la Grèce*, II, II, 1822, Pl. 38, both faces of an inscribed marble fragment found in 1814 at Tchiblak (by Troy) by M. Dubois and brought to France, are published drawn to scale, as are two fragmentary inscriptions from Alexandria Troas idem. II, II, 1822, Pl. 44.

[191] The column and inscription was seen and recorded by Richard Chandler, Travels 1817, 216-217, Inscript. Ant. p. 27.

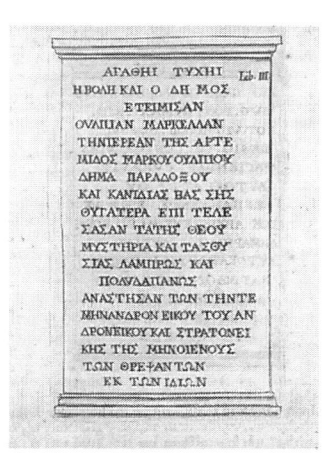

Figs. 12, 13) *Copies of the same inscription at Thyatire/Thyatira/Akhisar by Spon (left) 17 lines and by Wheler (right) 19 lines. Spon recording the inscription as continuous text, first line missing; Wheler's recorded the lines of the inscription as it appeared on the epigraphic surface, with its form.*

Figs. 14, 15) *Copies of the same inscription at Thyatire/Thyatira/Akhisar by Spon (left) 19 lines and by Wheler (right) 16 lines. Spon's publication recording the inscription as text, Wheler's recording the inscription as seem on the epigraphic surface, with its form and with the relative letter sizes shown. All Spon's letters are of the same size.*

Figs. 16, 17) *Copies of the same inscription at Smyrna by Spon (left) 7 lines and by Wheler (right) 5 lines. Spon's publication recording the inscription as text, Wheler recording the inscription as it appeared on the epigraphic surface, with its form, showing the number of lines and relative letter sizes.*

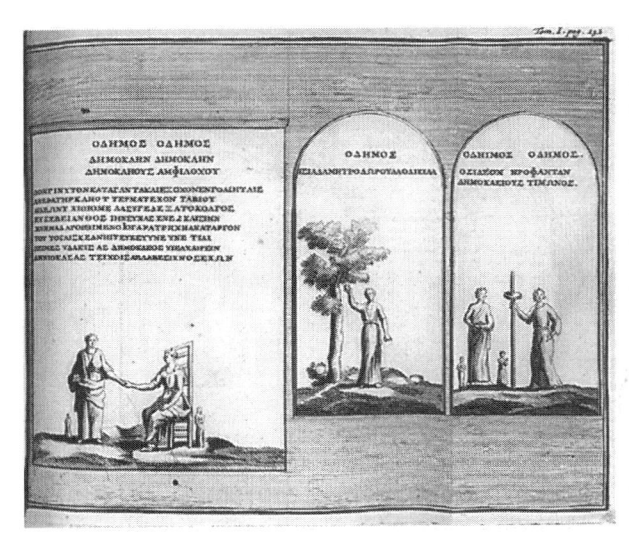

Fig. 18) *The 18th c. publication of three inscribed funerary and votive steles from Smyrna-Izmir. The published depiction of these inscribed steles with relief carving suggests attention was not paid to accurately recording either the inscriptions or the relief carving or the physical shape of these steles. Paul Lucas, Voyage du sieur Paul Lucas fait en MDCCXIV, &c. par ordre de Louis XIV, dans la Turquie, l'Asie, Sourie, Palestine, Haute et Basse Egypte, &c..., Amsterdam, 1720, T.1. p. 252. Paul Lucas collected on instructions from l'abbé Bignon, bibliothécaire du roi, and removed, in part to the French Royal Collection, at least 25 manuscripts,[192] 55 inscriptions and other epigraphic material Greek and Roman medals from Asia Minor.*

Luigi Mayer *Romano* in the gouache drawings he made in Lycia in 1792[193], some of which were published as aquatints in 1803 in his, "*Views in the Ottoman Empire, Chiefly in Caramania, a Part of Asia Minor, hitherto Unexplored. With Some curious Selections from the Islands of Rhodes and Cyprus and the Celebrated Cities of Corinth, Carthage and Tripoli: From the original drawings in the possession of Sir R. Ainslie, taken during his embassy to Constantinople by Luigi Mayer: with Historical Observations, and Incidental Illustrations of the Manners and Customs of the Natives of that Country,*" records on Plate No. 3, entitled, *Ancient Granary at Cacamo*, a quite accurate copy of the Latin inscription extending along the cornice of the facade of the Roman horrea at Andriake[194]. But the transcription of the inscription was added to his drawing of the facade, which was not a measured drawing, and for reasons of legibility extends further along the facade than is actually the case, not least because Luigi Mayer records in his depiction seven, rather than the eight openings in the facade of the horrea, to centre the text and the carved relief Imperial busts over the "middle" door[195].

---

[192] "*Lucas bought only twenty-five manuscripts, but specific ones - those missing from the king's collections.*" McCabe 2008, 131; including Bib. Nat. Paris 3118, a 17th c. manuscript of *Alf Layla wa-Layla* acquired in 1718.

[193] Taylor 2013. It may be worthwhile for an epigrapher to look closely at the inscriptions depicted by Luigi Mayer in Sir Robert Ainslie's set of original gouaches of views of 1792, to determine which carry a legible datable epigraphic text. Recai Tekoğlu kindly looked at one for me depicted on a tabula ansata of a no longer extant sarcophagus at Kekova, and from the letter forms employed for the inscription it was Late Antique.

[194] Recorded in the Catalogue of Plates, description of Plate 3, "*Horrea Imp. Caesaris Divi Trajani Parthici F. Divi Nerva; Nepotis Trajani Hadriani Augusti Cos. III*," L. Mayer, *Views in the Ottoman Empire, Chiefly in Caramania*, …R. Bowyer, London 1803 https://archive.org/details/gri_33125008694883/ page/n21.

[195] The inscription is accurately depicted relative to the eight door openings in the facade in the scale drawing of the elevation drawn by J. P. Gandy, from the sketches and measurements he made on the 1812 Dilettanti mission, today in the RIBA, London, SD140/9, RIBA65811.

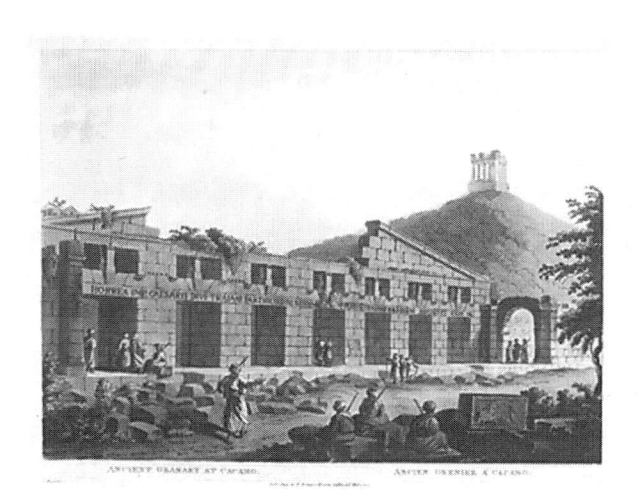

Fig. 19) *Aquatint of Luigi Mayer's drawn record of Hadrian's horrea at Andriake of 1792, published in 1803, Plate 3. The inscription on the facade provides an accurate record of the text.*

Some of the issues concerning the accuracy of the published transcriptions made by antiquarians that are raised above, regarding the works of Belon, Leunclavius, Pickering, Spon and Wheler, Lucas and Mayer, from the 16th to the end of the 18th century were remedied through taking of an epigraphic rubbing and then an epigraphic squeeze in Asia Minor from the late 1830's onwards, and subsequently through photography,[196] in Lycia from 1854 onwards, and today by RTI; although the cleaning of the epigraphic surface to take a squeeze (as also to take a plaster, as later a latex, or a silicone cast of an inscription) could lead to the loss of any remaining traces of colour and the support for it, and the applied surfacing and the colour of inscriptions and epigraphic surface, with very few exceptions,[197] still today remains to be investigated through Raman spectroscopy etc.

Conclusions

Throughout these four centuries epigraphic material including inscriptions, coins, medals, carved gemstones, seals, intaglios and manuscripts, as well as sculptures and architectural elements, were illegally removed from Asia Minor to European collections, utilising for smuggling the numerous merchant vessels trading with Ottoman Asia Minor from Venice, Genoa, France, England and the United Provinces-Holland, some of which sank, while some selected epigraphic material was, after its arrival in Europe, mislaid, ill-used and destroyed. Antiquarian demand and the agents of European dealers and collectors who drove the hunt for antiquities including inscriptions in Asia Minor, as elsewhere in Ottoman territory over this period, and which resulted in incentives given to the poor to dig up ancient ruins and sites, rewarding successful looters, while destroying the context of the *in situ* finds that were made, established a precedent that continues today, and resulted in the collection of isolated relics, like the publication of individual epigraphic documents, isolated from their physical and epigraphic context. It can be stated that the activities of antiquarians in Asia Minor over the course of these four hundred years resulted in the transcription with varying degrees of accuracy and with varying quantities of textual and epigraphic information of some thousands of ancient Greek and Latin inscriptions,

---

[196] French Academician François Arago (1786-1853) endorsed the new medium of photography in 1839 claiming it would provide a labour-saving means "...*all will be struck by this reflection, that if photography had been known in 1798, we should this day have possessed faithful representations of many valuable antiquities now, through the cupidity of the Arabs, and the vandalism of certain travellers, lost for ever to the learned world. To copy the millions and millions of hieroglyphics which entirely cover the great monuments at Thebes, Memphis and Carnac, etc.*" (Daguerre 1839, 15).

[197] Duggan 2016.

some of which remain of considerable importance for our understanding of antiquity and of ancient Greek and Roman epigraphy. The physical whereabouts of many of the inscriptions that were transcribed over these 400 years by antiquarians are today unknown. In the recording and in the publication of epigraphic material from Asia Minor in this period some advances were made, not least by George Wheler, in the change in antiquarian attention from a largely text based approach to an inscription towards a more epigraphic approach. The problems associated with the publication of transcriptions of ancient Greek inscriptions, not least the differences between the letter forms transcribed and the letter font employed in the publication of these transcriptions, formed an impediment at times to dating, correct reading and the understanding of some inscriptions published during this period, as was noted a century ago by W. M. Ramsay.[198] Further, the precedent established by antiquarian practice over the course of these four centuries, of transcribing, publishing and commenting upon individual texts-inscriptions, in part because many had been reused, although valuable of itself, has tended to obscure the wider physical context of these individual documents in antiquity when *in situ*, the importance of the epigraphic context of inscriptions in particular locations within ancient cities and sites and the question of the reasons why epigraphic documents were placed where they were, how they were noticed and read in antiquity, not then being seen as individual inscriptions in isolation from the surrounding epigraphic material and their physical context.

Bibliography

Akkach 2012	S. Akkach, Cosmology and Architecture in Premodern Islam: An Architectural reading of Mystical Ideas, New York 2012.
Anderson 2015	B. Anderson, "An alternative discourse": Local interpreters of antiquities in the Ottoman Empire, Journal of Field Archaeology, 40/4, 2015, 450-460, DOI: 10.1179/2042458215Y.0000000017.
Anon. 1800	Anonymous, Extracts from the Journal of an anonymous Traveller in the Vicinity of Smyrna, preserved in the British Museum. Harl. Mss. 7021, 182-188, in: The Oriental Collections: consisting of Original Essays and Dissertations, Translations, and Miscellaneous Papers, Illustrating the History and Antiquities, the Arts, Sciences, and Literature, of Asia, Vol. III, For January, February, and March, 1799, Debrett, London 1800.
Ball 1729	J. Ball, The Antiquities of Constantinople: With a description of its situation, the conveniencies of its port, its publick buildings, the statuary, sculpture, architecture, and other curiosities of that city. With cuts explaining the chief of them. In four books, London 1729.
Bargebuhr 2011	F. P. Bargebuhr, The Alhambra: A Cycle of Studies on the Eleventh Century in Moorish Spain, (1968) 2011.
Belon 1553	P. Belon, Les observations de plusieurs singularitez et choses memorables trouvées en Grèce, Asie, Judée, Egypte, Arabie et autres pays estranges, II, 1553.
Beltrame – Gelichi –	C. Beltrame – S. Gelichi – I. Miholjek – S. Pavao, Shipwreck: A 16th

---

[198] Ramsay 1918, 125.

Miholjek – Pavao 2014	century Venetian merchantman from Mljet, Croatia 2014.
Bibi 1996	Ibn Bibi, el-Hüseyin b. Muhammed b. Ali el-Ca'feri er-Rugadi. M. Oztürk (çev.), El Evamiru'l-Ale'iye Fi'l-Umuri'l-Ala'iye (Selçukname), Vol. I, Ankara 1996.
Bulmuş 2012	B. Bulmuş, Plague, Quarantines and Geopolitics in the Ottoman Empire, Edinburgh 2012.
Burrow 1817	Rev. E. I. Burrow, The Elgin Marbles: with an Abridged Historical and Topographical Account of Athens ... Vol. I. Illustrated with Forty Plates Drawn and Etched by the Author, London 1817.
Burton 1959	R. Burton, The Arabian Nights: An Adult Selection, New York 1959.
Busbecq 1881	Busbecq 1881, The Life and Letters of Ogier Ghiselin de Busbecq, seigneur of Bousbecque Knight, Imperial Ambassador, C. T. Forster – F. H. Blackburne Daniell, Vol. 1, London 1881.
Butler – Fraser 1978	A. J. Butler – Ed. P. M. Fraser, The Arab conquest of Egypt and the last thirty years of the Roman dominion, Oxford (1902) 1978.
Cadwallader 2014	A. Cadwallader, History as Bulwark, Bridge and Bulldozer: Dei Verbum and Ecumenical, Biblical Endeavour, 207-224, in: Eds. M. O'Brien – C. Monaghan, God's Word and the Church's Council: Vatican II and Divine Revelation, 2014.
Chandler 1774	Rev. Dr. R. Chandler, Inscriptiones Antiquae, Oxford 1774.
Chandler 1776	Rev. Dr. R. Chandler, Travels in Asia Minor, Or an Account of a Tour Made at the Expense of the Society of Dilettanti, London (1775) 1776^2.
Chateaubriand 1812	Travels in Greece, Palestine, Egypt, and Barbary During the Years 1806 and 1807 by F. A. de Chateaubriand; Translated from the French by Frederic Shoberl, in Two Volumes, Vol. I, London 1812.
Chishull 1728	E. Chishull, Antiquitates Asiaticae christianam oram antecedentes, ex primariis monumentis graecis descriptae etc. London 1728.
Chishull 1747	Rev. E. Chishull, Travels in Turkey and Back to England, by the Late Reverend and Learned Edmund Chishull, Chaplain to the Factory of the Worshipfull Turkey Company at Smyrna, London 1747.
Clari 1966	R. de Clari, The Conquest of Constantinople, Ed. E. H. McNeal, 1966.
Cook 1974	B. F. Cook, The Classical Marbles from the Arundel House Site, WC2 in 1972, 209-248 in: London and Middlesex Archaeological Society, Vol. 26, London 1974.
Covel 1722	J. Covel, Some Account of the Present Greek Church, with Reflections on their Present Doctrine and Discipline, Particularly in the Eucharist, And the rest of their Seven Pretended Sacraments, Compared with Jac. Goar's Notes upon Greek Ritual, Euchologion, Cambridge 1722.
Crawford 2003	M. Crawford, William Sherard and the Prices Edict, RN 2003, 83-

	107.
CSP 1858	Calendar of State Papers, Domestic Series, Charles I (1625-1649), Ed. M. A. E. Green, Vol. 1, PRO, London 1858.
CSP 1860	Calendar of State Papers: Of the Reign of Charles II., Domestic series, (1660-1670), Ed. M. A. E. Green, Vol. X, PRO, London 1860.
CVA	Great Britain 20 (British Museum 10).
Daguerre 1839	History and Practice of Photogenic Drawing on the True Principles of the Daguerréotype, with the new method of Dioramic Painting; Published by order of the French Government. By the Inventor L. J. M. Daguerre, with notes and explanations, by M. Arago, etc. Translated by J. S. Memes, London 1839.
Dallaway 1797	J. Dallaway, Constantinople Ancient and Modern: With Excursions to the Shores and Islands of the Archipelago and to the Troad, London 1797.
Dawes – Baynes 1948	E. A. S. Dawes – N. H. Baynes (edd.), Three Byzantine Saints: Contemporary Biographies of St. Daniel the Stylite, St. Theodore of Sykeon and St. John the Almsgiver, trans. Elizabeth Dawes, and introductions and notes by Norman H. Baynes, Basil Blackwell, Oxford 1948. https://sourcebooks.fordham.edu/basis/theodore-sykeon.asp.
de Bruijn 1700	Cornelius de Bruijn, Voyage au Levant, c'est a dire Dans les Principaux endroits de L'Asie Mineure, …, Traduit de Flamand, Delft, Henri de Kroonevelt, 1700 http://gallica.bnf.fr/ark:/12148/bpt6k853 30k/f2. Image.
de Jonge – Ottenheym 2007	K. de Jonge – K. Ottenheym (edd.), Unity and Discontinuity: Architectural Relations Between the Southern and Northern Low Countries 1530-1700, Turnhout 2007.
Dibdin 1810	Typographical Antiquities: Or the History of Printing in England Scotland and Ireland: containing memoirs of our Ancient Printers, An A register of the Books Printed by Them. Begun by the Late Joseph Ames … Considerably Augmented by William Herbert … and Now Greatly Enlarged … by the Rev. Thomas Frognall Dibdin, Vol. 1, London 1810.
Dobree – Scholefield 1835	P. P. Dobree – J. Scholefield, Miscellaneous notes on inscriptions. By Professor Dobree, With some addenda to his Adversaria, Ed. J. Scholefield, Cambridge 1835.
Drew-Bear – Naour – Stroud 1985	T. Drew-Bear – C. Naour – R. S. Stroud, Arthur Pullinger: An Early Traveller in Syria and Asia Minor, Trans. Am. Phil. Soc. New Series, Vol 75. No. 3, 1985, 1-80.
Drummond 1754	A. Drummond, Travels Through Different Cities of Germany, Italy, Greece and Several Parts of Asia, as the Far as the Banks of the Euphrates, in a Series of Letters… by Alexander Drummond, Esq., H.

	M. Consul Aleppo, London 1754.
Duggan 2008	T. M. P. Duggan, The Paintwork and Plaster on Evdir and Kirkgöz Hans by Antalya-and some implications drawn concerning the original appearance of 13th c. Seljuk State Buildings, Adalya XI, 2008, 319-358.
Duggan 2011	T. M. P. Duggan, An interpretation of some unpublished in situ and recorded Rum Seljuk 13th c. external and internal figural relief work on the Belkis (Aspendos) Palace, Antalya, Gephyra 8, 2011, 143-184.
Duggan 2012	T. M. P. Duggan, Liman Kenti Satalya'daki (Antalya), Şeyh Ahmed Bedevi/Vaftizci Yahya ve Başmelek Cebrail Rölyefleri, Toplumsal Tarih, Ağustos 2012, 56-61.
Duggan 2015	T. M. P. Duggan, Due Diligence and the Treaty of 46 B.C., Libri 1, 2015, 59-70.
Duggan 2016	T. M. P. Duggan, Not just the Shadows on the Stone: the Greek, Lycian and Roman Craft of Encaustica (ἔγκαυσις) and the Polishing (γάνωσις) of Coloured Inscriptions, that is, of Graphō (γράφω) and its Study - Epigraphy, Phaselis II, 2016, 269-283.
Dzielska 1986	M. Dzielska, Apollonius of Tyana in Legend and History, Trans. P. Pienkowski, L'erma di Bretschneider, Rome 1986.
Elmes 1824	J. Elmes, A General and Bibliographical Dictionary of the Fine Arts…, Part I., T. Tegg, London 1824.
Evelyn 1827	Memoirs of John Evelyn, Esq. F. R. S., Epistolary Correspondence, Ed. W. Bray, Vol. IV, London 1827.
Finkel 2005	C. Finkel, Osman's Dream: The Story of the Ottoman Empire 1300-1923, London 2005.
Foss 1976	C. Foss, Byzantine and Turkish Sardis, Vol. IV, Archaeological Exploration of Sardis (1958-), Harvard 1976.
Frankfurter 2017	D. Frankfurter, Christianizing Egypt: Syncretism and Local Worlds in Late Antiquity, Princeton 2017.
Fry 1799	E. Fry, Pantographia: Containing Accurate Copies of All the Known Alphabets in the World; Together with an English Explanation of the Peculiar Force or Power of Each Letter: to which are Added, Specimens of All Well-authenticated Oral Languages forming a comprehensive Phonology, London 1799.
Galignani 1822	Ancient Sculptures in the British Museum, Sunday, Jan. 27th, Galignani's Literary Gazette, Vol. XIV, 1822, 92-94.
Galt 1812	J. Galt, Voyages and travels in the years 1809, 1810 and 1811, containing observations on Gibraltar, Sardinia, Sicily, Malta, Scrigo and Turkey, London 1812.
Garstang – Gurney 1959	J. Garstang – O. R. Gurney, The Geography of the Hittite Empire, BIAA, London 1959.
Gassendus 1657	P. Gassendus, Englished by W. Rand, The Mirrour of True Nobility

	and Gentility. Being the Life of The Renowned Nicolaus Claudius Fabricius Lord of Peiresk, Senator of the Parliament at Aix, Bk. IV, London 1657.
Gibbon 1788	E. Gibbon, Decline and Fall of the Roman Empire, Vol. VIII, London 1788.
Greenhalgh 1989	M. Greenhalgh, The Survival of Roman Antiquities in the Middle Ages, Duckworth 1989.
Greenhalgh 2009	M. Greenhalgh, Marble Past, Monumental Present: Building with Antiquities in the Mediaeval Mediterranean, Leiden 2009.
Greenhalgh 2013	M. Greenhalgh, From the Romans to the Railways: The Fate of Antiquities in Asia Minor, Leiden-Boston 2013.
Grodz 2016	S. Grodz, Introduction, 1-15 in, Christian-Muslim Relations. A Bibliographical History, Vol. 8. Northern and Eastern Europe (1600-1700), Leiden 2016.
Gunning 2016	L. P. Gunning, The British Consular Service in the Aegean and the Collection of Antiquities for the British Museum, London 2016.
Haarman 1996	U. Haarman, Medieval Muslim Perceptions of Pharonic Egypt, in: Ancient Egyptian Literature, History and Forms, Ed. A. Loprieno, Leiden 1996, 605-627.
Halbertsma 2003	R. B. Halbertsma, Scholars, Travellers and Trade: The Pioneer Years of the National Museum of Antiquities in Leiden 1818-1840, London-New York 2003.
Hamilton 1809	W. R. Hamilton, Remarks on Several Parts of Turkey: Aegyptiaca, or Some account of the antient and modern State of Egypt, as obtained in the years 1801, 1802. Accompanied with etchings, from original drawings taken on the spot by the late Charles Hayes of the Royal Engineers, Volume 1, London 1809.
Hasluck 1914	F. W. Hasluck, Stone Cults and Venerated Stones in the Graeco-Turkish Area, BSA XXI, 1914, 62-83.
Hasluck 1973	F. W. Hasluck, Christianity and Islam under the Sultans, New York I., II., (1929) 1973.
Hawkins 2000	J. D. Hawkins, Inscriptions of the Iron Age: Part 1: Text, Introduction, Karatepe, Karkamis, Tell Ahmar, Maras, Malatya, Commagene. Part 2: Text, Amuq, Aleppo, Hama, Tabal, Assur Letters, Miscellaneous, Seals, Indices. Part 3: Plates, Berlin 2000.
Hervey 1921	M. F. S. Hervey, The Life, Correspondence & Collections of Thomas Earl of Arundel, Cambridge 1921.
Hope 1835	T. Hope, A Historical Essay on Architecture, Vol. 1, London 1835.
İnalcık 1997	H. İnalcık, An Economic and Social History of the Ottoman Empire, Vol. 1., Cambridge 1997.
Jones 1993	C. P. Jones, The Decree of Ilion in Honor of a King Antiochus, Greek, Roman, and Byzantine Studies 34, 1993, 74-93.

Kelly 2012	C. Kelly, Political History: The Later Roman Empire, 11-23, in: M. Vessey (ed.), A Companion to Augustine, New York 2012.
Klonsky 1974	M. Klonsky, The Fabulous Ego: Absolute Power in History, London 1974.
Knight 1866	Ed. C. Knight, Arts and Sciences: Or, Fourth Division of "The English Encyclopedia", Vol. I, Bradbury, London 1866.
Laborde 1838	L. E. S. J. Laborde, Voyage de l'Asie Mineure par Alexandre de Laborde, Becker, Hall, et L. de Laborde, rédigé et publié par Léon de Laborde, Paris 1838.
Langbehn – Salama 2011	V. Langbehn – M. Salama, German Colonialism: Race, the Holocaust, and Postwar Germany, 2011.
Leake 1824	W. M. Leake, Journal of a tour in Asia Minor, with comparative remarks on the ancient and modern geography of that country, London 1824.
Madrus – Mathers 1996	The Book of the Thousand Nights and One Night, J. C. Madrus – P. Mathers, Vols I-IV, London-New York 1996.
Makal 1954	M. Makal, Memleketin Sahipleri, İstanbul 1954.
Matthews 2015	J. Matthews, The Notitia Urbis Constantinoplitanae, 81-115 Ed. L. Grig – G. Kelly, Two Romes: Rome and Constantinople in Late Antiquity, Oxford 2015.
McCabe 2008	I. B. McCabe, Orientalism in Early Modern France: Eurasian Trade, Exoticism, and the Ancien Régime, Berg, Oxford-New York 2008.
Memorandum	Memorandum on the subject of the Earl of Elgin's pursuits in Greece, London 1815.
Merivale 1874	C. Merivale, Augusti rerum a se gestarum indicem cum Graeca metaphrasi edidit Theodorus Bergk, (Leipzig 1873), The Academy and Literature, No. 95, Feb. 28, 1874, 234-235.
Metropolitana 1845	Encyclopaedia Metropolitana: Eds. E. Smedley – H. J. Rose – H. J. Rose, Vol. XIV, Miscellaneous and Lexicographical, Vol. I. "Arundelian Marbles," London 1845.
Milstein – Rührdanz – Schmitz 1999	R. Milstein – K. Rührdanz – B. Schmitz, Stories of the Prophets: Illustrated Manuscripts of Qiṣaṣ al-anbiyā', Mazda, Costa Mesa, CA 1999.
Montfaucon 1761	R. P. Dom Bernard de Montfaucon, sur des recherches a faire dans le voyage du Constantinople & du Levant (Mercure de France, janvier 1743), 151-166, in Nouveau choix de pièces tirées des anciens Mercures, et des autres journaux par M. De la Place, Tome 68. Paris 1761.
Morritt 2010	R. D. Morritt, Stones that speak, Cambridge 2010.
Motraye 1723	A. De La Mottraye, Travels through Europe, Asia, and into parts of Africa with proper cuts and maps containing: A great variety of Geographical, Topographical and Political Observations on those

parts of the World: especially on Italy, Turky (sic.), Greece, Crim and Noghaian Tartaries, Circassia, Sweden and Lapland. A curious collection of things particularly rare, in both Nature and Antiquity; such as remains of antient Cities and Colonies, Inscriptions, Idols, Medals, Minerals, etc. I, London 1723.

Museum 1850	D. M. Masson, The British Museum, Historical and Descriptive, W. and R. Chambers, Edinburgh 1850.
Olivier 1802	G. A. Olivier, Travels in the Ottoman empire, Egypt, and Persia, undertaken by order of the government of France, during the first six years of the Republic. Transl. Vol.I, II [in 1], Trans. (1800) London 1802.
Özel 2010	S. Özel, Under the Turkish Blanket Legislation: The Recovery of Cultural Property Removed from Turkey, International Journal of Legal Information 38/2, Article 10 (2010) 177-184, 178. Available at: http://scholarship.law. cornell.edu/ijli/vol38/iss2/10. Accessed 12-01-2015.
Panciera 2012	S. Panciera, What is an Inscription? Problems of Definition and Identity of an Historical Source, ZPE 183, 2012, 1-10.
Payne Knight 1791	R. Payne Knight, An Analytical Essay on the Greek Alphabet, London 1791.
Peacham 1962	H. Peacham, The Complete Gentleman: The Truth of Our Times, And, The Art of Living in London Ed. V. B. Heltzel, Folger Documents of Tudor and Stuart Civilisation, New York 1962.
PSRL I	The Present State of the Republic of Letters. For January, 1728, Vol. 1, printed for W. Innys and J. Innys, London 1728.
Ramsay 1918	W. M. Ramsay, The Utilisation of Old Epigraphic Copies, JHS XXXVIII, 1918, 124-192.
Rees 1819	A. Rees, The Cyclopaedia, Or Universal Dictionary of Arts, Sciences and Literature XXVII, Longman, Hurst, Rees, Orme and Brown, London 1819.
Rosenstein 2009	L. Rosenstein, Antiques: the History of an Idea, New York 2009.
Sainsbury 1859	W. N. Sainsbury, Original Unpublished Papers Illustrative of the Life of Sir Peter Paul Rubens: As an Artist and a Diplomatist. Preserved in H. M. State Paper Office. With an Appendix of Documents Respecting the Arundelian Collection; the Earl of Somerset's Collection; the Great Mantuan Collection; the Duke of Buckingham etc., London 1859.
Sale et al. 1765	G. Sale – G. Psalmanazar – A. Bower – G. Shelvocke – J. Swinton (edd.), The Modern Part of an Universal History, from the Earliest Account of Time, Vol. XLIII, London 1765.
Sandwich 1807	J. Montague, Earl of Sandwich, A voyage Performed by the Late Earl of Sandwich Round the Mediterranean, in the Years 1738 and 1739.

	Written by Himself To which are Prefixed Memoirs of the Noble Author's Life, Lackington 1807.
Sandy 1673	G. Sandy, Sandys Travels, Containing an History of the Original and Present State of the Turkish Empire ... the Mahometan Religion and Ceremonies: a Description Of Constantinople ... Also, of Greece ... of Aegypt ... a Voyage on the River Nylvs ... a Description of the Holy-Land; of the Jews ... and What Else Either of Antiquity, or Worth Observation. Lastly, Italy Described, and the Islands Adjoining ... Illustrated with Fifty Graven Maps and Figures, London (1615), 1673.
Sandys 1908	J. E. Sandys, A History of Classical Scholarship: From the Revival of Learning to the End of the Eighteenth Century in Italy, France, England and the Netherlands, Vol. II, Cambridge 1908.
Sandys 1919	J. E. Sandys, Latin Epigraphy: An Introduction to the Study of Latin Inscriptions, Cambridge 1919.
Saradi 1997	H. Saradi, The Use of Ancient Spolia in Byzantine Monuments: The Archaeological and Literary Evidence, International Journal of the Classical Tradition, Vol. 3, No. 4 (Spring, 1997), 395-423.
Selden 1726	J. Selden, Jurisconsulti, Opera omnia, tam edita quam inedita. In tribus voluminibus. Collegit ac recensuit; vitam auctoris, praefationes, & indices adjecit, David Wilkins. In quo continentur, De successionibus in bona defunctorum; & de successionibus in pontificatum Ebraeorum. De diis Syris. Eutychii Ecclesiae suae origines. Uxor ebraica. Analecta anglo-britannica. Janus Anglorum. Dissertatio ad Fletam. Judicium de decem scriptoribus anglicanis. Mare clausum. Vindiciae de scriptione Maris clausi. Marmora Arundelliana. Notae in Eadmerum. Epistolae & poemata. Vol. II, London 1726.
Sevin 1802	F. Sevin, Lettres sur Constantinople. Suivies de plusieurs lettres de m. Peysonnel et d'autres savans. On y a joint la Relation du consulat de m. Anquetil à Surat [&c. Ed. by A. Serieys] revu par l'abbé Bourlet de Vauxcelles, Paris An. X, 1802.
Smith 1678	Dr. T. Smith, Remarks upon the Manners, Religion and Government of the Turks. Together with a Survey of the Seven Churches of Asia as they now lye in their Ruines: and a Brief Description of Constantinople, London 1678.
Smith 1707	T. Smith, Historical Observations relating to Constantinople, 32-48, Miscellanea curiosa. Containing a collection of Curious Travels, Voyages and Natural Histories of Countries, as they have been delivered in to the Royal Society, Royal Society (Great Britain) Vol. III, London 1707.
Smith 1707a	T. Smith, An Account of the City of Prusa in Bithynia, and a continuation of the Historical Observations relating to Constantinople,

	48-83, Miscellanea curiosa. Containing a collection of Curious Travels, Voyages and Natural Histories of Countries, as they have been delivered in to the Royal Society, Royal Society (Great Britain) Vol. III, London 1707.
Smith 1883	C. Smith, Inscriptions from Rhodes, JHS 4, 1883, 136-141.
S.O.D.³ 1969	The Shorter Oxford Dictionary.
Spon 1673	J. Spon, Recherche des Antiquités de la ville de Lyon, Lyon 1673.
Spon 1678	J. Spon, G. Wheler, Voyage d'Italie, de Dalmatie, de Grèce et du Levant: fait és années 1675 & 1676 par Jacob Spon & George Wheler, 1678.
St. Clair 1967	W. St. Clair, Lord Elgin and the Marbles, Oxford 1967.
Stoneman 2010	R. Stoneman, Land of Lost Gods: The Search for Classical Greece, 2010.
Stubbs 1876	Radulfi de Diceto decani Lundoniensis opera historica, The Historical Works of Master Ralph de Diceto, Dean of London Ed. R. Stubbs, Two Vols, Rolls Series, 68, Vol. II, London 1876.
Taylor 2013	B. J. Taylor, Sir Robert Ainslie, Domenico Sestini and Luigi Mayer: A Case of who went where, with Whom and When, Ch. 13, in, Ed. D. Fortenberry, Souvenirs and New Ideas: Travel and collecting in Egypt and the Near East, Oxford 2013.
Tierney 1834	Rev. M. A. Tierney, The Antiquities of Arundel: The peculiar privilege of its castle and Lordship; with an Abstract of the Lives of the Earls of Arundel, from the Conquest to this time, Vol. II, London 1834.
Tournefort 1741	Tournefort A Voyage into the Levant performed by command of the late French King, (1717) Trans. John Ozell, Vol. III, London 1741.
Turks 2005	Turks: A Journey of a Thousand Years, 600-1600, Exh. Cat., Ed. D. J. Roxburgh. Royal Academy of Arts (Great Britain), London 2005.
Tütüncü 2018	M. Tütüncü, Rodos'ta Türk Denizcilerinin Koruyucu (Tılsım) Taşı, Toplumsal Tarih, Şubat 2018, 13-17.
Twells 1740	L. Twells, The theological Works of the Learned Dr. Pocock, containing his porta Mosis and English commentaries on Hosea, Joel, Micah and Malachi: With life and writings of the author by Leonard Twells, Vol. 1., London 1740.
Wallis Budge 1896	E. A. Wallis Budge, The Life and Exploits of Alexander the Great: Being a Series of Translations of the Ethiopic Histories of Alexander by the Pseudo-Callistenes and other Writers, J. Clay and Sons, Cambridge 1896.
Walsh 1825	R. Walsh, Account of the Levant Company, London 1825.
Warburton 1811	The Works of the Right Reverend William Warburton, D. D., Lord Bishop of Gloucester: A New Edition in Twelve Volumes, Vol. IX,

	London 1811.
Weber 1812	H. Weber, Tales of The East; comprising The Most Popular Romances of Oriental Origin; and the best imitations by European authors: with new translations, and additional tales, never before published, Vol. II, Edinburgh 1812.
Werner 2011	M. Werner, Multiple Antiquities-Multiple Modernities: Ancient Histories in Nineteenth Century European Cultures, Frankfurt-New York 2011.
Wheler 1682	George Wheler Esq, Journey into Greece; In Company of Dr. Spon of Lyons, In 6 Books with Variety of Sculptures, London 1682.
Wittman – Phillips 1803	W. Wittman – Sir R. Phillips, Travels in Turkey, Asia-Minor, Syria, and Across the Desert Into Egypt During the Years 1799, 1800, and 1801, in Company with the Turkish Army, and the British Military Mission: To which are Annexed, Observations on the Plague and on the Diseases Prevalent in Turkey, and a Meteorological Journal, London 1803.
Wright 2004	D. G. Wright, Review of E. W. Bodnar, C. Foss, Cyriac of Ancona: Later Travels, 2003, Bryn Mawr Classical Review 2004.07.69 http://bmcr.brynmawr.edu/2004/2004-07-69.html.
Wroth 1893	W. W. Wroth, Leake, William Martin, in: Ed. S. Leslie, DNB 32, London 1893, 323-324.
Yürekli 2016	Z. Yürekli, Architecture and Hagiography in the Ottoman Empire: The Politics of Bektashi Shrines in the Classical Age, London 2016.
El-Zein 2009	A. El-Zein, Islam, Arabs, and the Intelligent World of the Jinn, 2009.

19. yüzyılın başlangıcına kadar Küçük Asya'daki erken dönem antika meraklıları hakkında
Özet

Bu yazı 1400 yılından 1800 yılına kadarki dönem ile, şüphesiz başka isimler de mevcut olmak üzere, antik metinlerin transkripsiyonlarını da yapmış olan 60'tan fazla Avrupalı'nın antik eserlere yönelik etkinliklerini kapsamaktadır. Hikâye ayrıca, onların malzemeyi bulan ve zaman zaman da yazıtların Küçük Asya'dan götürülmesini sağlayan aracılarını, Osmanlı tanıdıklarını, rehberlerini, köylüleri ve Yunan rahiplerini de içermektedir. Aynı zamanda, bununla bağlantılı olarak bu antika meraklıları tarafından "mermer", antik elyazmaları, madalyonlar-sikkeler, yazılı değerli taşlar ve diğer yazılı materyallerin toplanması da konuya dahil edilmiştir. Bu malzemelerin bir kısmı Küçük Asya'dan alındığında taşıma esnasında denizde kaybolurken, bazı antik yazıtlar da hasar görmüş, Avrupa'daki savaşlar esnasında kaybolmuş ya da yok edilmiştir. Yazıtlara ilişkin en erken çalışmalar Ciriaco de Pizzicolli'nin 15. yüzyıldaki transkripsiyonları ve Pierre Belon tarafından 1546-9 yılları arasında yapılan birkaç yazıt transkripsiyonudur. Fakat Avrupalı akademisyenler Küçük Asya'daki günümüze ulaşan antik epigrafik belgelerin önemini, Agria (Eger) Piskoposu Antonius Verantius'un Res Gestae Divi Augusti transkripsiyonu, aynı yazıtın 1555 yılında Busbecq'in Ankara'daki hizmetkârları tarafından yapılan kopyasının yayılması ve bunun 1579 yılından itibaren sürekli yayımlanması sonrasında kavramışlardır. 17. yüzyılın başlarından itibaren sayısı gittikçe artan Avrupalı antika meraklıları, büyük kısmı Troas, Ege'nin kıyı bölgeleri ve Küçük Asya'nın temel ticaret yolları boyunca görülebilen yazıtların kayıt altına alma görevini de üstlenmişlerdir. Söz konusu antik yazıtlara dair kayıtlı Osmanlı görüşlerinin çeşitliliği, yapılan transkripsiyonlar, bu yazıtların zaman zaman berat sahibi Avrupalılarca götürülmeleri; metindeki ya da metnin kontekstindeki sorun, matbu baskı ile birlikte gelen yazıt yayınında oluşan durumlar; epigrafik estampajlardan önceki yüzyıllarda transkripsiyonu gerçekleştirilen yazıtlarda görülen uydurmalar ve hatalara dair bazı örnekler dikkate alınmıştır.

Anahtar Kelimeler: Küçük Asya, antik yazarlar, kolleksiyon, Osmanlı berat sahipleri, transkripsiyonlar.

On early antiquarians in Asia Minor to the start of the 19th century
Abstract

This paper covers a period of 400 years, from 1400 to 1800, and the antiquarian activities of more than 60 named Europeans, there are doubtless others, who were involved in transcribing, and at times, through their agents and Ottoman associates, guides, villagers and Greek priests, those who related the position and at times enabled the physical removal of ancient inscriptions from Asia Minor; as well as the associated antiquarian collecting of "marbles," ancient manuscripts, medals-coins, inscribed gem-stones and other inscription bearing materials. Some of this material was lost at sea, while some ancient inscriptions brought from Asia Minor were damaged, lost or destroyed in warfare in Europe. Following Ciriaco de Pizzicolli's transcriptions in the 15th c. and the few inscriptions transcribed by Pierre Belon in 1546-9, it seems to have been the Bishop of Agria (Eger), Antonius Verantius's transcription of the *Res Gestae Divi Augusti* and the copy made by Busbecq's servants in Ankara in 1555 which, when circulated and then published, underlined to European scholars the importance of the surviving ancient epigraphic record in Asia Minor. From the start of the 17th c. an increasing number of educated European antiquarians undertook the recording of the surviving visible inscriptions, largely in coastal regions and along the major trade routes of Asia Minor. Note is taken of the variety of recorded Ottoman views concerning these ancient inscriptions, of their transcription and, at times, their removal by European *berat* holders; together with some examples of the inaccuracies of the transcriptions of inscriptions that were made.

Keywords: Asia Minor, Ancient inscriptions, collecting, Ottoman *berat* holders, transcriptions.

Rom im Norden

Hans KLOFT*

Für Johannes Nollé
Amico et collegae per multos annos

Jeder, der die Rheinlande und ihre Städte kennt, weiß, welche große Bedeutung die römische Vergangenheit für die urbane Identität spielt, die als Tradition liebevoll gepflegt wird und in Festivitäten aktuelle Dimensionen annehmen kann. Das gilt für Mainz, für Trier und Köln, es gilt für Nijmegen, für Xanten und auch für die alte Kaiserstadt Aachen, wo die heilbringenden warmen Quellen und der Apollo Grannus sich mit dem Erbe aus der Karolingerzeit zu einem eindrucksvollen Stück urbaner Erinnerungskultur verbunden haben. Dies vor unserem Jubilar weiter auszuführen, würde heißen, Eulen nach Athen oder Printen nach Aachen zu tragen, um im heimischen Horizont zu bleiben.

Im Hinblick auf eine urbane römische Tradition hatten es die Städte im Norden und Osten Deutschlands, „In solo barbarico", wie es in einer kürzlich erschienen Publikation hieß,[1] natürlich sehr viel schwerer. Aber erkennbar werden mit dem Spätmittelalter die Bemühungen greifbarer, die Städte in Mitteldeutschland der antiken Welt anzunähern und ihnen im Einzelfall auch eine römische Herkunft zu simulieren. Die Sächsische Weltchronik, kurz vor 1500 zusammengestellt,[2] zählt sieben sogenannte „Planetenstädte" auf, die angeblich Kaiser Julius (Caesar) erbaut haben soll, unter ihnen Hamburg (Hammonia), das Jupiter Hammon, Harzburg (Saterborch), das mit Saturn zusammengebracht, schließlich Lüneburg, welches nach Luna (= Diana) bzw. Lunus, dem Gott des Mondes, benannt wurde.[3] Sein Abbild schmückte eine antike Marmorsäule, die auf vielen Umwegen den Weg in das heutige Museum gefunden hat.

Der Gründungsmythos von Lüneburg führte in den regionalen Überlieferungen der Zeit zu bemerkenswerten Kontroversen, die Klaus Alpers, klassischer Philologe der Universität Hamburg, sorgfältig verzeichnet hat. Sie bezeugen nicht nur den Kampf um eine verlässliche Historiographie, sondern künden auch mit der behaupteten römischen origo vom Streit um den Vorrang im regionalen Städteverband, ein Prestigedenken, das im Kampf um die Neokorie in der römischen Kaiserzeit sattsam bekannt ist.[4]

Für Lüneburg und seine antike Herkunft war der Bezug auf die Göttin Luna und den conditor Caesar maßgebend. Die Mondscheibe findet sich als Stadt- und Herrschaftssymbol auf Lüne-

---

* Prof. Dr. Hans Kloft, Universität Bremen, Fachbereich 8 / Sozialwissenschaften Institut für Geschichtswissenschaft Universitäts-Boulevard 13, 28359 Bremen, Deutschland (hkloft@uni-bremen.de).

[1] Losemann – Ruffing 2018. Karl Christ hatte den Begriff für Marburg geprägt.

[2] Zur sächsischen Weltchronik Schubert 1995, 1242f. mit Lit.

[3] MGH Chron. II 861ff. Alpers 2010, 104. Magdeburg als eine Gründung Caesars, der sie der jungfräulichen Göttin Diana (als „Jungfrauenstadt") gewidmet habe: Claude 1972, 60. Merseburg als römische Gründung unter Caesar, wegen der römischen Kriegstüchtigkeit nach dem Gotte Mars benannt: so Thietmar von Merseburg Chron. I 2.

[4] Zur Neokorie Price 1984; Halfmann 2001, 84ff.

burger Münzen des 17. und 18. Jahrhunderts.[5] Caesar als Gründer eines ansehnlichen Lagers der Mondstadt – *spectabile castrum urbis lunae* – rühmt eine Glasmalerei des 15. Jahrhunderts in der berühmten spät mittelalterlichen Gerichtslaube des Ratshauses, die Caesar als einen der neun guten Helden zeigt mit einem schönen lateinischen Distichon zu seinen Füßen:

Urbis construxi lune spectabile castrum
Et mea pompeiium sincopat ense manus
Der Stadt des Mondes anschauliche Burg habe ich errichtet
Und meine Hand spaltet Pompejus mit dem Schwert.[6]

Die neun guten Helden – das waren seit dem späten Mittelalter die drei Vertreter aus Judentum, Heidentum und Christentum, für die Antike Hektor, Alexander und Caesar, welche vorbildliche weltliche Herrschaft repräsentierten. Die Ikonographie verbindet alttestamentarische mit heidnischen und christlichen Helden und schlägt den Bogen von der ritterlichen zur bürgerlichen Kultur des Mittelalters. In dieser Konstellation schmückten sie bedeutende städtische Rathäuser der Zeit.[7] Caesars Heldentaten: Die Errichtung eines Legionslagers als Kern der späteren Stadt und die persönliche Niederstreckung seines Gegners Pompejus lassen sich mit der Gesamtkomposition zeitlich auf den Beginn des 15. Jahrhunderts festlegen. Dabei mögen historische Vorgaben und literarische Vorlagen für den römischen Horizont existiert haben, die in unserem Zusammenhang nicht weiter interessieren.

I.

Die Referenz auf die Antike, auf Sprache, Kunst und Gesittung gehört in die Zeit des sich ausbreitenden Humanismus in Deutschland zur Bürgerkultur um und nach 1500 und konnte sich auf unterschiedliche Weise aussprechen. Das gilt auch für den Norden, der in der sog. Weserrenaissance eine eigene künstlerische Handschrift besaß, die von einer reichen literarischen Produktion flankiert wurde.[8] Was Lüneburg betrifft, so hat Klaus Alpers in seinem Buch eine außerordentliche Bronzetafel aus der Mitte des 16. Jahrhunderts zitiert, die gut sichtbar am Haus eines einflussreichen Lüneburger Patriziers angebracht war.

Julius Caesar, Gerichtslaube VI

---

[5] Alpers 2010, 105f.

[6] Die Übersetzung nach Beckmann – Koch 1992, 112f. Die Abbildung ebenda Tafel 29.

[7] Zum ikonographischen Programm Beckmann – Koch 1992, 89ff.; Kloft 2017, 355ff.

[8] Zur Weserrenaissance Kreft – Soenke 1986; Grossmann 1990.

Male pereant omnes qui tyrannide gaudent et paucorum imperio in civitate libertatis enim nomen omnibus praeferendum est. Et si quis exiguum habeat in illa multa tamen ha bere sibi videtur.
Euripides 1555

„Elend zugrundegehen sollen alle, die Tyrannenherrschaft und Oligarchie im Staate gutheißen. Denn die Freiheit ist allen Gütern vorzuziehen, und wenn jemand in ihm (d. h. in einem freien Staate) wenig besitzt, so meint er dennoch, viel zu haben".

Das Zitat des griechischen Tragikers Euripides, das von Stobaios überliefert und vom Humanisten Conrad Gessner (1516-1565) ins Lateinische übertragen worden war,[9] versteht sich als ein Bekenntnis zur Freiheit und als eine Absage an die Tyrannei, die Gewaltherrschaft eines Einzelnen wie an die Tyrannei Weniger, die Herrschaft einer aristokratischen Clique. Dieses Bewusstsein der Freiheit war wichtiger, so der Text, als materielle Güter. Hier greift man die Maxime eines städtischen Patriziers, der im Zitat einer antiken Autorität ein allgemeines urbanes Lebensgefühl der Zeit auf den Begriff bringt, das weit über Lüneburg hinaus reicht.

II.

Das bürgerliche Selbstbewusstsein, das sich im Rückgriff auf antike Vorbilder ausspricht, äußert sich in den deutschen Städten zur Zeit des Humanismus vornehmlich an den öffentlichen Bauten, am Rathaus, den Stadttoren, dem Markt. In Bremen wendet die Figur des Ritter Roland auf dem städtischen Forum ihren Schild demonstrativ dem Betrachter zu. Es trägt den Sinnspruch:

Vryheit do ik ju openbar
De karl und mennich vorst vorwar
Desser stede gheheven hat,
Des danket gode, is min radt.

Die Freiheit, die Karl der Große und verschiedene Fürsten der Stadt verliehen haben, verbürgt der mythische Paladin des großen Kaisers, Roland, der in Bremen den Charakter eines Stadtheros besaß.[10] Angesprochen ist über die Marktfreiheit hinaus die Freiheit der Stadtbürgerschaft, die sich als Wehrgemeinde selbst schützt, selbst Recht setzt und Recht spricht.

---

[9] Eurip. frg. 275 Nauck, die Einzelheiten bei Alpers 2010, 45. Dort auch die obige Übersetzung.
[10] Die Abbildung nach Elmshäuser – Kloft 2005, 34; Hempel – Kloft 2004.

Man hat im Zusammenhang mit der Figur des Rolands eine Verbindung von Republikanismus und Kommunalismus angesprochen,[11] die im Rathaus, der domus consulum, in verschiedene Richtungen erweitert wird. Das programmatische salomonische Urteil in der oberen Halle aus der Schule von Bartholomäus Bruyn aus dem Jahre 1532 verbindet die Aufforderung zur Gerechtigkeit mit Sinnsprüchen und Bildern aus dem Alten Testament und Zitaten römischer Autoren. Caesar ist vertreten mit einer Gnome aus seiner Senatsrede anlässlich der Verschwörung des Catilina, die Sallust formuliert:

„*Omnes homines, qui de rebus dubiis consultant,*

ab odio, amicitia, ira atque misericordia vacuos esse decet ..." (Sall. Cat. 51,1).

Der alte Cato macht auf das Vorbild der Vorfahren aufmerksam, welche die Mehrung der Herrschaft verbunden haben mit rechtschaffenem Verhalten im Inneren.

Domi illustria, foris iustum imperium, animus in consulendo liber ...

(nach Sall. Cat. 19 und 21).

Darunter findet sich Ciceros Bekenntnis zur Justitia aus seiner Schrift über die Pflichten:

„*Iustitia ad rem publicam gubernandam necessaria ... omni igitur ratione colenda et retinenda est*" (Off. 2,40).

Gerechtigkeit in der Staatsführung und Unvoreingenommenheit in der Rechtssprechung anders gewendet: Objektivität des Urteils als Verpflichtung werden zentralen römischen Autoren entlehnt. Sie bilden neben dem Alten Testament die moralischen Autoritäten, die den Ratsherren vor Augen stehen.[12]

Die admonitio findet ihre Entsprechung im Ratsgestühl aus dem frühen 15. Jahrhundert. Es war mit Inschriften in niederdeutscher Sprache geschmückt, von denen wir die sogenannte Philosophenbank zitieren wollen, wobei wir einige Verständnisschwierigkeiten bewusst in Kauf nehmen:

Aristoteles	Ein richter sy thovorne recht,
	De richte den heren sampt den knecht
Plato	We im rechte beschonet sinen frund,
	De is der eren unde sinnen blind.
Seneca	Im rade nemande temet,
	De gud vor ere nemet.
Cato	Im torne richte nene sake,
	Hoet dy vor hetischer wrake.
Socrates	Richte nicht eines mannes word,
	De wedderrede sy den gehort.

---

[11] Dilcher 2003, 28. Zur Bedeutung der Rolandstatue weiter V. Paul, ebenda 13f. („Ein allegorisches Rechtszeichen für Markt- und Handelsrechte oder die Rechte der Stadtfreiheit insgesamt").

[12] Die vollständigen Texte bei Börtzler 1952, 23ff. Zur Funktion des Rates als Gericht Isenman 2003, 404ff.

Boetius	Wat magh saken haet unde nid,
	De richte yo in korter tid.
Angelus	Richtet yo in der rechtferdicheit.[13]

Andere Sinnsprüche legen dem Vergil, dem Ovid, dem Horaz, Terenz und dem Julius (Caesar) moralische Empfehlungen in den Mund, die durch Ermahnungen aus dem Alten Testament erweitert werden. Eine sinnvolle Zuordnung der rund 30 Inschriften lässt sich heute kaum noch herstellen. Das Gestühl und seine Botschaft ist mit der Zerstörung im späten 19. Jahrhundert dahin. Trotzdem sind sie als Zeugnisse früh-humanistischer Aneignung antiker Autoren im norddeutschen Raum kaum zu überschätzen, eine Quelle, die aufgrund ihres Verlustes wenig Interesse der landeskundlichen Forschung gefunden hat, aber eben doch auch in ihrer niederdeutschen Form den großen Einfluss antiker Autoren im frühen 15. Jahrhundert bezeugen.

Der kommunale Republikanismus zeigt sich besonders eindrucksvoll im Eingangsportal zur berühmten Güldenkammer in der Oberen Rathaushalle, welche die sogenannte devotio des Marcus Curtius zeigt, flankiert von Sapientia und Concordia und gekrönt von der Göttin Iustitia, die sich über dem bremischen Wappen erhebt.[14]

Umrahmt von überbordenden Schmuckelementen der Spätrenaissance geht die Botschaft der devotio nahezu unter. Sie beschreibt im Römischen das Opfer des Feldherrn, der sich in einer kritischen militärischen Lage den Göttern der Unterwelt weiht und als Gegenleistung den Sieg über die Feinde erbittet.[15] Der Mythos hat im sogenannten Lacus Curtius auf dem Forum Romanum mit einem entsprechenden Relief eine archäologische Lokalität gefunden und war in der Renaissancezeit das Exemplum der Selbstopferung für das Gemeinwesen sehr beliebt.[16]

So fügen sich die römischen virtutes: Fortitudo, Sapientia, Condordia und Iustitia zu einem eindrucksvollem Ensemble zusammen, die der Führungselite des Stadtstaates als Leitlinie dienen sollten. Die römische Republik in ihren Institutionen und ihren Wertvorstellungen bildete nicht nur für Bremen die virtuelle historische Bezugsebene.

Senatur Populusque Bremensis – SPQB, wie sie sich im 16. Jahrhundert vereinzelt auf privaten und öffentlichen Aufschriften findet, nimmt die klassische Hoheitsformel der

---

[13] Zitiert nach Ehmck – Schumacher 1862, 13. Interpretationsangebote bei Gramatzki 1994, 50ff., bes. 56f.

[14] In: Elmshäuser – Kloft 2005, 14.

[15] Vorgang und Formel der devotio bei Liv. XVIII, 11ff., dazu Wissowa 1912, 384f. Rüpke 2006, 117 und 184.

[16] Zum Lacus Curtius auf dem Forum Romanum Freyberger 2009, 18ff. Hendrick Goltzius als Vorbild für die Darstellung der Devotio: Albrecht 1993, 68.

römischen Republik SPQR auf, die in Rom das Zusammenwirken aristokratischer und demokratischer Elemente, von Senatsherrschaft und Entscheidung der Comitien zum Ausdruck bringt[17] – in Rom wie in den frühneuzeitlichen Gemeinden eher eine ideologische Formel, welche das tatsächliche Senatsregiment zu verschleiern hilft, im Stadtstaat Bremen wie in den vergleichbaren Stadtgebilden Hamburg, Lübeck, Lüneburg oder auch Basel, die das Vorbild Rom zitieren.

IV.

Die Stadttore, die den Durchgang von draußen nach drinnen, von drinnen nach draußen regeln, waren Träger von Botschaften, die den geistigen Horizont des Gemeinwesens widerspiegeln. Das berühmte Holstentor in Lübeck trägt in der Außenseite die Inschrift:

Concordia domi – foris pax, welche 1871 die ältere Fassung *Concordia domi et foris pax – sane res est omnium pulcherrima* ersetzte. Äußerer Friede und Eintracht der Bürger bilden, hier wie auch anderswo, höchste Ziele der Stadt.

Die moralische Botschaft in Bremen präsentiert sich durchaus vergleichbar. Das Ansgaritor, das mit seinem Aufbau auch als Schuldturm im Mittelalter diente, schmückte zwei Inschriften:

Justitia et pace crescit respublica pietate conservatur (Stadtseite)
Concordia confirmat, discordia atterit rempublicam (Außenseite)

Das sog. Doventor („taubes Tor"), Anfang des 13. Jahrhunderts erbaut, das aus dem westlichen Stephaniviertel hinaus führte, hebt mit seinen Aufschriften noch stärker auf die Haltung der Bürger ab:

Respublicae post Deum nullo munimento
tutiores sunt quam virtute civium
Civis vero is est, qui sincere patriam diligit
ac bonos omnes salvos incolumesque desiderat.

Der Stadtstaat im Zeichen des Humanismus präsentiert sich ganz wie in der Antike als Verband von Bürgern und hebt auf deren Tugenden ab. Sie lesen sich als moralische Quintessenz aus den Werken eines Cicero, eines Sallust und Livius, eines Valerius Maximus, die auch auf der Schule in Bremen, dem 1528 gegründeten Gymnasium eifrig traktiert wurden (vgl. Anm. 21).

Das Brückentor, durch welche die Straße über die Weser ins Oldenburgische führte, begrüßte die Ankommenden mit dem Spruch

Conserva Domine Hospitium Ecclesiae Tue.
Erhalte, o Herr, die Herberge Deiner Kirche,

---

[17] Zu Rom von Lübtow 1955, 259ff. Zum Ratsregiment in den mittelalterlichen und frühneuzeitlichen Stadtrepubliken Schreiner – Meier 1994. Die Formel SPQB über dem Eingang zum sogenannten Neuen Rathaus zum Jahre 1910 (Foto: P. Heinitz).

eine den unruhigen Zeiten durchaus adäquate Bitte, die Bremen als Hort religiöser Flüchtlinge auswies.[18]

V.

Die theologischen Divergenzen im protestantischen Bereich führten auch den anerkannten Latinisten Nathan Chyträus (1543-1598) von Rostock nach Bremen, wo er Rektor des hiesigen Gymnasium[19] wurde und eine fruchtbare literarische Tätigkeit entfaltete. Aus seiner Sammlung neulateinischer Gedichte, die 1579 noch in Rostock erschienen, seien zwei Epigramme vorgestellt, die wohl kaum Aufnahme in den Unterrichtskanon des Gymnasiums gefunden haben dürften.[20]

Iuvenis et vetula
Sitne, rogas, melius vetulam si ducat ephebus,
aut nubat tremulo si nova nupta seni.
Quaestio digna quidem: cuius me solvere nodum
si iubeas, a me talia dicta feres:
Hoc illo est melius. Vetulae nam iunctus ephebus,
hei miser, in sterili solus arabit agro.
at senior teneram ducens aetate puellam
multorum iuvenum sentiet auxilium.

Jüngling und Greisin
Ist es besser, fragst du, daß ein Jüngling sich nimmt eine Alte
oder sich Jungfrau vermählt mit einem klapprigen Greis?
Wohl ist berechtigt die Frage; und willst du, dass ich dir den Knoten
Lösen soll, ist es dies, was ich zur Antwort dir geb:
Dieses ist besser als jenes, denn ehlicht ein Junger die Alte,
pflügt der Arme allein, ach, in dem fruchtlosen Feld.
Heiratet aber ein Alter ein Mägdlein von zartester Jugend,
wird er merken, dass ihm vielfach ein Jüngerer hilft.

Ein anderes:

Pasiphae
Pasiphae potius formoso nubere tauro
Quam voluit licito regis amore frui;
Credis ab hac stolidas multum differre puellas.
Quae stolidos doctis praeposuere viris?

Pasiphae wollte sich lieber einem wohlgestalteten Stier vermählen
als die gestattete Liebe des Königs genießen.
Glaubst du, dass törichte Mädchen sich (heute) davon sehr unterscheiden,
welche die törichten den gelehrten Männern vorziehen?

---

[18] Die Inschriften nach Börtzler 1952, 11ff. Zu den Stadttoren Bubke 2007, 138ff. Zum religiösen Asyl in Bremen Rudloff 2017, 271f.

[19] Zusammenfassung und Lit. bei Schwarzwälder 2001, 281f.; Elsmann 2005, 71ff. Anm. 8.

[20] Poematum Nathanis Chytraei libri septendecim, Rostock 1579, 141 die beiden Epigramme. Die Übersetzung des ersten bei Schnur – Kößling 1984, 112.

Das sind nun poetische Fingerübungen eines Humanisten, der sich in die epigrammatische Tradition eines Catull oder Martial stellt und sich in der antiken Mythologie auskennt. Hier ist der Vergleich: Die Begattung der verblendeten Königin durch den kretischen Stier (– für den Prometheus das passende Gestell herrichten musste –) mit den beklagenswerten Sitten der damaligen Jugend durchaus gewagt. Chyträus formuliert eine allgemeine betrübliche Einsicht: Gelehrsamkeit, doctrina, und sexuelle Begehrlichkeit gehen selten zusammen.

VI.

Die Wirkung von Bremens hoher Schule, dem Gymnasium Illustre auf die städtische Kultur, die Studenten vor allem aus den Niederlanden in die Hansestadt lockte, wird man kaum überschätzen können. Das Gymnasium hatte 1610 durch die Erweiterung auf vier Fakultäten (Philosophie, Jura, Medizin, Theologie) und den pädagogischen Unterbau einen universitären Zuschnitt erhalten. An der Antike orientierte lateinische Gedichte schmückten die Hochzeitsfeier (carmina epithalamia); die Leichenpredigten (laudationes funebres) auf bedeutende Bürgerinnen und Bürger erfreuten sich großer Beliebtheit und wurden vielfach über den Druck verbreitet. Der einflussreiche Bürgermeister und norddeutsche Politiker Heinrich Krefting (1520-1611) verfasste 1601/02 unter dem Namen „Discursus de reipublica Bremensi" den Entwurf einer städtischen Konstitution, die Elemente der antiken Mischverfassung mit den konkreten stadtstaatlichen Strukturen zu verbinden suchte.[21] Die stadtstaatliche Ordnung beruhte auf Bürgermeister (Proconsules), auf den Rat (Senatus) und auf die Beteiligung von Bürgergemeinschaften in unterschiedlichen Formen, deren jeweilige Kompetenzen abzustimmen waren.

Im Umkreis dieses antikisierenden Kultur- und Bildungshorizonts hat sich dann um 1600 auch die Gleichsetzung von Bremen mit dem beim kaiserzeitlichen Geographen Ptolemaios bezeugten Fabiranum vollzogen, eine Stadt, die dieser in das „nördliche Klima Germaniens" verlegt, auf der ptolemaischen Weltkarte zwischen Elbe und Weser nicht weit von der Nordsee gelegen. Eine Stadtchronik hält im Bild Bremen = Fabiranum fest.[22]

Der so behauptete Ursprung machte in Bremen Schule. So dichtete im genus eines antiken Stadtlobes der Gelehrte Urbanus Pierius (1546-1616) im Jahre 1609 ein „Elogium de Urbis Bremae antiquitate" und vermeldet dort:

Bremae est primevo Ptolemaei tempore nota
Brema est antiquis quae Fabirana fuit.
Und er fährt fort:
Brema fuit, Bremae cum nullus episcopus esset
Nulla nec hic cleri contio – Brema fuit
Brema fuit magnus cum Carolus ille sub egit
Saxones et populi militi fregit opes.[23]

---

[21] Henrici Krefftingii discursus de reipublica Bremensi conscriptus anno 1602 (SuUB brem.b.366), vorausgegangen Johann Esichs Discursus de reipublica Bremensi, Historiae Prodromus. Bremen 1598 (SuUB brem. a.157). Eine genaue Analyse der beiden Entwürfe steht noch aus. Zu Krefting: NDB 12, 1980, 131f.

[22] Ptolem. geogr. II 11,12. Zur Lokalisierung Wenskus 1994, 93. Die Abbildung bei Schwarzwälder 1995, 19.

[23] Urbanus Pierius (eigentlich Birnbaum), De urbis Bremae antiquitate consulumque et senatorum ordinae elogium, Bremen 1609 (SuUB Brem.C. 588), A3SQ. Zur Person Rudloff 2017, 241ff. Anm. 20.

Bremen als „Phabiranum" in der Dilich-Chronik, 1602

Bremens Geschichte reicht also bis in die römische Kaiserzeit zurück. Das Gemeinwesen bestand bereits, als es noch keinen Bischof und keine Kleriker gab. Es existierte, als Karl der Große die Macht der Sachsen brach und sie unterwarf.

Die Argumentation des Pierius, der ab 1599 Pastor an St. Ansgarii und ab 1608 Superintendent, oberster Repräsentant der protestantischen Bremer Kirche war, liegt klar zutage; Bremen stellt keine Schöpfung Karls und seiner Christianisierungspolitik mit der Einsetzung des Missionsbischofs Willehad dar, sondern besitzt eine ältere, nämlich römische städtische Tradition.

Dieser historische Verweis will erkennbar der Begründung einer bischöflichen Stadtherrschaft den Boden entziehen und zielt damit indirekt auf die Reichsunmittelbarkeit der Stadt, auf die Autonomie der Bürgergemeinde, die unter Führung des Rates seit dem 16. Jahrhundert faktisch, aber eben nicht rechtlich realisiert war.

Die Versicherung, dass Bremens Ursprung in grauer Vorzeit, lange vor dem christlichen Mittelalter gelegen habe, kehrt 1646 in der berühmten Assertio Libertatis wieder, der Bestätigung der „Reichsstandhaft" durch Kaiser Friedrich III. im sogenannten Linzer Diplom. Die Klärung durch die kaiserliche Reichskanzlei hat, so der Text,

„… onfehlbar befunden, daß die Statt Bremen von uhralten zeitten hero deß Hey. Röm. Reichs ohnmittelbahre freye Reichs-Statt gewesen und also Unß und dem Hey. Reich allein und ohne mittel untergehörig ist."[24]

Mit dem kaiserlichen Rescript gewann die Stadt ihre rechtliche Eigenständigkeit gegenüber dem Erzbischof und gegenüber Schweden, das sich im Dreißigjährigen Krieg in den Besitz des Herzogtums gesetzt hatte und gegen die Verselbständigung der Stadtgemeinde auch bei den Friedensverhandlungen in Osnabrück heftig opponierte.

Zur Anerkennung Bremens als freie Reichsstadt hat dabei freilich weniger der historische Rekurs als die enorme Summe von 50.000 Reichstalern verholfen, die der Rat nur unter größten

---

[24] Der Text nach Müller 1996, 22.

Schwierigkeiten aufbringen konnte.²⁵ Aber ohne die historisch-juristische Begründung wäre die Reichsstandhaft nicht zu vermitteln gewesen, ein Kapitel, das in die Geschichte von der Wirksamkeit fiktionaler Traditionen gehört: Bremen ist identisch mit der antiken Stadt Fabiranum.

VII.

Den Status einer freien Reichsstadt hat Bremen bis in die bundesrepublikanische Verfassung der Gegenwart hinein behalten können, ein Status, der in diversen historischen Situationen oft gefährdet war. Zur Zeit des Dreißigjährigen Krieges setzt der Humanist Martinus Pazar gegen die schlimmen und bedrohlichen Zeitläufe den ungestörten Fortgang des Unterrichts auf dem Gymnasium Illustre:

„*Brema potens variis petitur munc undique telis*
inuts dissidii glissit furialis Erinnys.
Nec tamen interea studiis melioribus ullae
injectae remorae: doctorum copia crescit."
„*Angegangen wird nun das mächtige Bremen von allen Seiten*
mit mannigfachen Geschossen.
Im Innern erstarkt Erinnys,
die Rasende, am Zwiespalt.
Aber dennoch gibt es in dieser Zeit für die höheren Studien
weder Hemmnis noch Zaudern: Es wächst die Schar der Gelehrten."²⁶

Man möchte gerne dieses Vertrauen auf die segensreiche Wirkung der humanistischen Studien in die Jetztzeit übertragen und hier im Norden auf die Einsicht von *docti viri*, von klugen Politikern hoffen. Die Bedrohung Bremens manifestiert sich gegenwärtig nicht in kriegerischen Aktionen, sondern in der möglichen Aufhebung seiner politischen Selbständigkeit. Als die Stadt im Jahre 2005 als Weltkulturerbe in die Liste der Unesco aufgenommen wurde, war für die Begründung neben dem imposanten baulichen Ensemble von Rathaus, Roland und Schütting (als Sitz der Kaufleute) etwas anderes entscheidend: das hinter dem architektonischen Ensemble greifbare republikanische Gemeinwesen, welches, „wie die antike Polis, eine societas civilis, eine auf der Basis der Gleichheit geordnete Rechtsgemeinschaft" als regulative Idee verwirklicht.²⁷

Diese Idee konnte sich auf antike Autoriäten, auf die römischen Republik mit ihrer legendären Formel SPQR stützen, auf Autoren wie Aristoteles und Cicero, wie Livius und Caesar.

Die Konstruktion einer antiken Herkunft zeigt mit Deutlichkeit die Faszinations- und Innovationskraft der antiken Staats- und Gesell-

---

²⁵ Müller 1996, 14ff. Anm. 26. Die historische Situation bei Otte 2017, 337f. Anm. 20.
²⁶ Frost – Knoll 1977.
²⁷ So Dilcher bei Elmshäuser 2017, 29 Anm. 13.

schaftsordnung in der frühen Neuzeit, die weit über den Stadtstaat hinaus Geltung besessen hat.[28]

Heute ruht die Tradition des Stadtstaates, ein durch und durch europäisches Vermächtnis, in Deutschland vor allem auf den Freien Hansestädten Bremen und Hamburg, für welche diese historisch gewordene Struktur nach wie vor identitätsstiftend wirkt. Auch wenn viele Zeitgenossen in ihnen einen Atavismus der bundesrepublikanischen Länderordnung sehen, ein survival, das man so schnell wie möglich überwinden sollte, bewahren sie doch Gestalt und Gestaltung eines autonomen Bürgerverbandes, eines, man möchte sagen: einzigartigen politischen Biotops, das ohne die Mäeutikdienste antiker (und mittelalterlicher Kultur) nicht so entstanden wäre, wie sie sich heute darstellt.

Bibliographie

Albrecht 1993	St. Albrecht, Das Bremer Rathaus im Zeichen städtischer Selbstdarstellung vor dem Dreißigjährigen Krieg, Marburg 1993.
Alpers 2010	K. Alpers, Lüneburg und die Antike, Lüneburg 2010.
Beckmann – Koch 1992	R. Beckmann – U. D. Koch, Die mittelalterlichen Glasmalereien in Lüneburg und den Heideklöstern, Berlin 1992.
Börtzler 1952	A. Börtzler, Lateinische Inschriften Bremens, Bremen 1952.
Bubke 2007	K. Bubke, Die Bremer Stadtmauer, Bremen 2007.
Claude 1972	D. Claude, Geschichte des Erzbistums Magdeburg I, Köln 1972.
Dilcher 2003	G. Dilcher, Gutachten zum Antrag der Bundesrepublik Deutschland an die UNESCO auf Anerkennung von Rathaus und Roland in Bremen als Weltkulturerbe, in: K. Elmshäuser u.a. (Hrgg.), Das Rathaus und der Roland auf dem Marktplatz zu Bremen, Bremen 2003, 16-33.
Ehmck – Schumacher 1862	D. R. Ehmck – H. A. Schumacher (Hgg.), Denkmäler der Geschichte und Kunst der Freien Hansestadt Bremen I, Bremen 1862.
Elmshäuser 2017	K. Elmshäuser (Hg.), Bremische Kirchengeschichte von der Reformation bis zum 18. Jahrhundert, Bremen 2017.
Elmshäuser – Kloft 2005	K. Elmshäuser – H. Kloft (Hrgg.), Der Stadtstaat-Bremen als Paradigma. Geschichte - Gegenwart – Perspektiven (= Jahrbuch der Wittheit zu Bremen 2005), Bremen 2005.
Elsmann 2005	Th. Elsmann, Religion – Bildung – geistige Kultur: Aspekte des Calvinismus in Bremen, in: Elmshäuser – Kloft 2005, 71-88.
Freyberger 2009	K. St. Freyberger, Das Forum Romanum, Mainz 2009².
Frost – Knoll 1977	D. Frost – G. Knoll, Gelegenheitsdichtung, Bremen 1977.
Gramatzki 1994	R. Gramatzki, Das Rathaus in Bremen, Bremen 1994.

---

[28] Die Statue des Aristoteles an der Westseite des gotischen Rathauses (zusammen mit Demosthenes und Cicero) ist die spätere Umwidmung eines mittelalterlichen Propheten, möglicherweise zu Beginn des 17. Jahrhunderts mit dem imposanten Renaissance-Ductus der Schauseite, Albrecht 1993, 37f. Anm. 14 (Foto: P. Heinitz). Zur Bedeutung des Aristoteles im Humanismus Wachenheim 2014, 61ff., s.v. Aristotelismus (Lit.).

Grossmann 1990	G. U. Grossmann, Renaissance im Land der Weser, Köln 1990.
Halfmann 2001	H. Halfmann, Städtebau und Bauherren im römischen Kleinasien, Tübingen 2001.
Hempel – Kloft 2004	G. Hempel – H. Kloft (Hrgg.), Der Roland und die Freiheit, Bremen 2004.
Isenman 2003	E. Isenmann, Ratsliteratur und städtische Ratsordnungen des späten Mittelalters und der frühen Neuzeit, in: P. Monnet – O. G. Oexle (Hrgg.), Stadt und Recht im Mittelalter, Göttingen 2003, 215-479.
Kloft 2017	H. Kloft, Die Makkabäer, Geschichte und Erinnerung, in: H. Beck u.a. (Hrgg.), Von Magna Graecia nach Asia Minor, Festschrift L.-M. Günther, Wiesbaden 2017, 349-364.
Kreft – Soenke 1986	H. Kreft – J. Soenke, Die Weserrenaissance, Hameln 1986^6.
Krefting 1980	H. Krefting, in: Neue deutsche Bibliographie XII, 1980, 731f. (Chr. Römer).
Losemann – Ruffing 2018	V. Losemann – K. Ruffing (Hrgg.), In solo barbarico, Das Seminar für Alte Geschichte an der Philipps-Universität Marburg, Münster-New York 2018.
Müller 1996	H. Müller, Das Linzer Diplom, Bremen 1996.
Otte 2017	H. Otte, Reichsstädtischer Protestantismus. Die evangelischen Kirchen 1648-1800, in: Elmshäuser 2017, 336-514.
Price 1984	S. R. F. Price, Rituals and Power, Cambridge 1984.
Rudloff 2017	O. Rudloff, Lutherische Reformation und reformierte Konfessionalisierung in Bremen 1522-1648, in: Elmshäuser 2017, 19-323.
Rüpke 2006	J. Rüpke, Die Religion der Römer, München 2006.
Schnur – Kößling 1984	H. C. Schnur – R. Kößling (Hrgg.), Galle und Honig, humanistische Epigramme, Leipzig 1984.
Schreiner – Meier 1994	K. Schreiner – U. Meier (Hrgg.), Stadtregiment und Bürgerfreiheit, Göttingen 1994.
Schubert 1995	E. Schubert, Sächsische Weltchronik, in: Lexikon des Mittelalters VII, 1995, 1242-1243.
Schwarzwälder 1995	H. Schwarzwälder, Geschichte der Freien Hansestadt Bremen I, Bremen 1995.
Schwarzwälder 2001	H. Schwarzwälder, Das große Bremen-Lexikon, Bremen 2001.
Von Lübtow 1955	U. von Lübtow, Das römische Volk, sein Staat und sein Recht, Frankfurt 1955.
Wachenheim 2014	M. Weichenmann, Aristotelismus, in: Der Neue Pauly, Suppl. 9, 2014, 61-71.
Wenskus 1994	R. Wenskus, Fabiranum, Reallexikon Germanische Alterstumskunde VIII, 1994, 93.
Wissowa 1912	G. Wissowa, Religion und Kultus der Römer, München 1912^2.

Kuzeyde Roma
Özet

Ren üzerindeki Xanten, Koblenz, Köln ve Mainz topluluklarından farklı olarak, merkezi ve kuzey Almanya'daki Ortaçağ kentlerinin orijinal bir Roma geçmişi bulunmamaktadır. Oysa kuzeydeki kentler, Hümanizm ve Rönesans sırasında kendilerini antik bir geleneğe yerleştirmek için pek çok yol aramışlardır. Bir Hanse (ticaret kentleri birliği) kenti olan Bremen, belediye binasının içini Latince deyiş ve alegorilerle süslemiştir (Iustitia, Sapientia, Virtus). Kent kapıları Romalı burjuva erdemlerine atıflar yapmaktadır. Yerel tarihçiler Hıristiyan piskoposların dönemi başlamadan çok önce yerleşimde bir Romalı kökeni bulmuşlardı. Antik kültür bugün hâlâ kent geleneğini karakterize etmektedir.

Anahtar Sözcükler: Halk tarihi, Roma tarihi, kent tarihi, tarih yazımı, Kuzey Almanya.

Rome in the North
Abstract

Unlike the communities on the Rhine: Xanten, Koblenz, Cologne and Mainz, the medieval cities in central and northern Germany do not have an original Roman past. Whereas during the Humanism and the Renaissance, cities in the north sought in many ways to place themselves in an ancient tradition. The Hanseatic city of Bremen adorned its city hall interiors with Latin sayings and allegories (Justitia, Sapientia, Virtus). The city gates referred to Roman bourgeois virtues. Local historians found a Roman origin in the community long before the reign of the Christian bishop. Ancient culture still characterizes the urban tradition today.

Keywords: Public History, Roman History, City History, Historiography, Northern Germany.

Eine Statuenbasis mit Ehreninschrift
für den Asklepiospriester P. Claudius Calpurnianus

Aygün EKİN MERİÇ* – Boris DREYER**

Seit nunmehr zwei Jahren wird am Theater von Nikaia unter der Grabungsleitung von Dr. Aygün Ekin Meriç von der Dokuz Eylül Universität mit großem Erfolg gegraben. Zu den Neufunden zählen auch Inschriften wie diejenige im September 2018 entdeckte Ehrung für einen Asklepiospriester.

Die Ehreninschrift wurde westlich des Theaters als ein Schlussstein gefunden (Abb. 2). Eine Inschrift befindet sich auf der Rundbasis mit Abakus, Scotia, Echinus und Halspartie. Die erste Zeile befindet sich oben auf dem Abakus, die zweite und dritte Zeile auf der Halspartie, die übrigen Zeilen darunter (Abb. 1). Die Maße der Basis, die oben Spuren für die Einlassung einer Statue (mit Resten einer Eisenverklammerung) enthält und die unten gebrochen ist (hier fehlen ca. 30 cm), betragen in der Höhe (max.): 59 cm, der Durchmesser ist ca. 41,5 cm. Die Buchstabenhöhe variiert zwischen 3 und 3,5 cm.

1   Ἀγαθῆι · τύχηι
    τὸν ἱερέα τοῦ Ἀσκληπιοῦ
    Π(όπλιον) · Κλαύδιον Καλπουρνιανὸν
    υἱὸν Π(οπλίου) Κλαυδίου Συλλιανοῦ
5   Νεικομήδους ἱερέως
    τοῦ μεγίστου αὐτοκράτορος
    Καίσαρος Ἁδριανοῦ Σεβαστοῦ
    [- - - - -]

Abb. 1

---

* Doç. Dr. Aygün Ekin Meriç, Dokuz Eylül University, Faculty of Literature, Department of Archaeology, İzmir, Turkey (aygunek@gmail.com).

** Prof. Dr. Boris Dreyer, Friedrich-Alexander-Universität Erlangen-Nürnberg, Deutschland (boris.dreyer@fau.de).

Für Hilfe und Unterstützung bei der Fertigstellung des Artikels danken wir Frau Nihal Kardoruk (Bursa), Mitarbeiterin der Grabung im Theater.

Übersetzung:

„Zu gutem Gelingen! Den Priester des Asklepios, Publius Claudius Calpurnianus, des Sohnes des Publius Claudius Syllianus Nikomedes, des Priesters des größten Imperator Caesar Hadrianus Augustus (ehrt ??)."

Kommentar:

In Nikaia gibt es einen Gaius Claudius Calpurnianus (nr. 2) in der Kaiserzeit: INikaia 1, nr. 205[1]. Weiter ist für das zweite Jahrhundert n.Chr. ein Titus Aurelius Calpurnianus Apollonides (als Prokurator) nachgewiesen[2]. Letztere Person ist nur Zeitgenosse. Der erste könnte zur Familie gehören, die sicherlich über einiges an Vermögen und über einen weitreichenden politischen Einfluss verfügte.

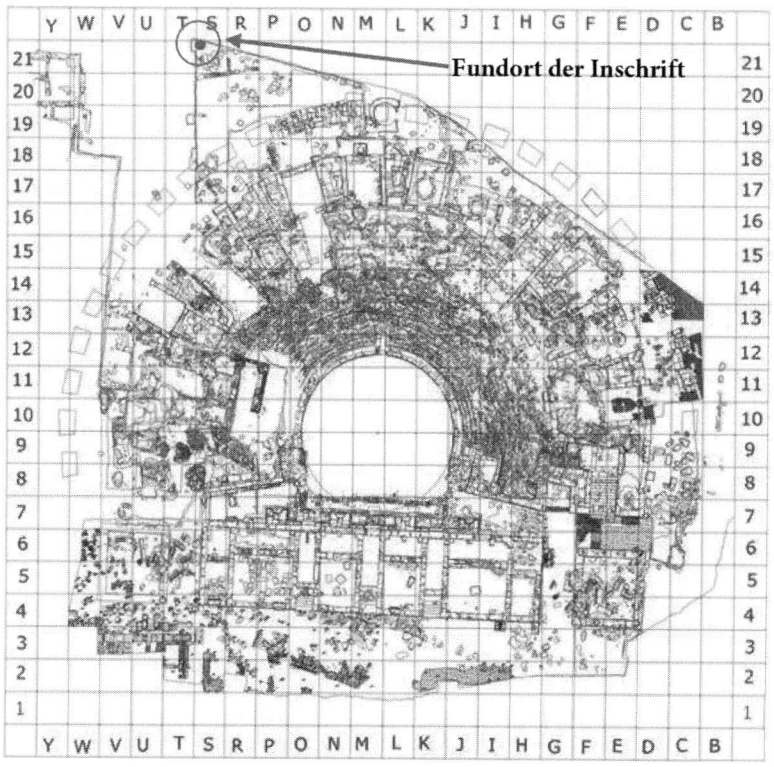

Abb. 2) *Plan des Theaters von Nikaia*

Der unbekannte Ehrende (Platz genug hätte für ihn auf der Ehrenbasis nach Z. 7 existiert) setzte dem Asklepiospriester[3] der Stadt ein Denkmal, dessen Bedeutung als Priester aus einer Familie mit einem im Kaiserkult erfolgreichen Verwandten deutlich betont wird: Der Vater, Claudius

---

[1] LGPN VA, s.v. Καλπουρνιανός (2), p. 240. Gaius Claudius Calpurnianus ist Eigentümer eines Gutes und verfügte über einen Oikonomos/Gutsverwalter. Vgl. Fernoux, 2004, 464-469, nr. 37-38 zu den Claudiern aus Nikaia (aus der Familie des Historikers Cassius Dio).

[2] LGPN VA, s.v. Καλπουρνιανός (1), p. 240; PIR A 1471; INikaia 1, nr. 58; ILS 8850; SEG 45, 985A, 18-19, SEG 45, 985B, 5-6; Fernoux 2004, 421-422, nr. 4.

[3] Zur Bedeutung des Gottes: Thraemer 1896, Sp. 1642-1697; Steger 2016. S.a. H. Boyana über Nikaia und den Kult des Asklepios in der Stadt, 2018; Şahin 2003, 14.

Syllianus[4] Nikomedes, ist Priester des „größten Imperator"[5] Caesar Hadrianus Augustus in der Stadt (gewesen).

Kaiser Hadrian hatte die Stadt und die Region nach einem Erdbeben persönlich besucht und Wiederaufbaumaßnahmen initiiert[6]. So mögen die Loyalitätsbekundungen für den Kaiser[7] und auch der Kult für Hadrian[8] Ausdruck einer echten Verbundenheit gewesen sein. In jedem Fall rückte der Mitbürger, der sich hier als Priester engagierte, wie der Vater des Geehrten, in den Mittelpunkt des politischen Geschehens und der Aufmerksamkeit in einer wieder aufgebauten Stadt. Die Position erlaubte auch den Einfluss auf die Besetzung anderer Priesterstellen, ggf. auch für die des Asklepios. Ein Priester des Asklepios – ansonsten, bes. in Kleinasien, sehr häufig anzutreffen (s. nur Pergamon) – ist in Nikaia inschriftlich hier das erste Mal belegt[9]. Wie er seine Position erlangte, ist nicht erschließbar, aber andere – besser belegte – Kulte in anderen Städten belegen „Querverbindungen" und damit Einfluss über Kultgrenzen hinweg[10].

Mit Stolz konnte man zumindest auf die familiäre Tradition von Priestern verweisen[11], was zur Vermutung führt, dass der Ehrende ein Familienmitglied, vielleicht der (älteste) Sohn, ggf. ein Priester, gewesen ist. Ob der Geehrte noch lebte, ist unsicher, doch ist zumindest der Verweis auf einen im hadrianischen Kaiserkult tätigen Großvater (?) aktuell. Das passt zur Schrift, die in die Mitte des 2. Jh. n.Chr. gehört.

Unglücklicherweise gibt es in Nikaia bislang keinen klaren Hinweis auf ein Heiligtum oder keine Überreste eines Tempels oder von Statuen, die Asklepios abbilden. Die angesprochenen archäologischen Ausgrabungen, die im Theater durchgeführt wurden, haben keine Funde zutage gefördert, die sich mit der Ehrung für den Asklepiospriester und mit dem von ihm betreuten Kult verbinden lassen.

---

[4] Der Name ist ein Patronymikon: der Name des Vaters des Claudius Nikomedes war Σύλλας (belegt in Nikaia I. Nikaia II 1303. Zu den Namen auf -ιανος s. Corsten 2010, 456-463.

[5] Eine seit Trajan geläufige Bezeichnung.

[6] INikaia I, 1; INikaia II 3, T 13, 15. Şahin 1978, 18-26, nr. 5 a und b; Şahin 2003, 9-10; 16. Aybek – Dreyer 2016, 12, 15-16, 28, 30.

[7] Şahin 1978, 19-20. INikaia I 29; 30; 30a; 32; 55 (ggf. dazu INikaia I 1 [Erlass über Wasserleitung]).

[8] Zum Kult für die Kaiser in Nikaia: INikaia I 64; vgl. nr. 116. Über den Kaiserkult s.a. ebd. I 60 und Şahin 1978, 23; Price 1984, z.B. 50-2 und 65-77 über die Bedeutung des Kaiserkultes seit Augustus in einer Wechselbeziehung zwischen Stadt und Kaiser; zu den Tempeln und Heiligtümern in Nikaia ebd. 266, nr. 99. Zu den Hadriantempeln s. Gülbay 2015, 29-30; Pergamon (p. 47), Sardis (p. 48), Smyrna (p. 50), Ephesus (p. 40), Miletus (p. 40).

[9] Asklepios selbst ist epigraphisch in Nikaia wahrscheinlich in der Weihung INikaia 1045 gemeint SEG 31, 1069.

[10] EDEN (http://wisski.cs.fau.de/eden/) nr. 100, Z. 1 (s.a. Dreyer – Engelmann 2009, 168, nr. 19, Z. 1); Aybek et al. 2018, 76-77, nr. b: Claudius Nikephoros ist unter den eponymen Arespriestern belegt und ist beim Krezimos-Kult „Hermas" gewesen. Innerhalb des Kultdienstpersonals wurden Positionen (mit Familienmitgliedern) kooptiert.

[11] EDEN (http://wisski.cs.fau.de/eden/) nr. 91, Z. 1-6 (s.a. Dreyer – Engelmann 2009, 172, nr. 11, Z. 1-6), und 101, 1-3 (s.a. Dreyer – Engelmann 2009, 172-173, nr. 20, Z. 1-3).

Eine Anzahl von Inschriften von Nikaia und der Nachbarschaft (Abb. 3) zeugen jedoch von einer etablierten Verehrung für Asklepios in der Region[12]:

1. Osmaneli / Lefke (INikaia 1041)
2. Gölpazarı /Aktaş (INikaia 1042)
3. Dereliköy, urspr. Köseler Mezarlığı (INikaia 1043)
4. Göynük / Boyacılar (INikaia 1044)
5. Gölpazarı / Kükürt (INikaia 1045)
6. Orhangazi / Pazarköy (Wiegand 1904, 273; INikaia 703[13])

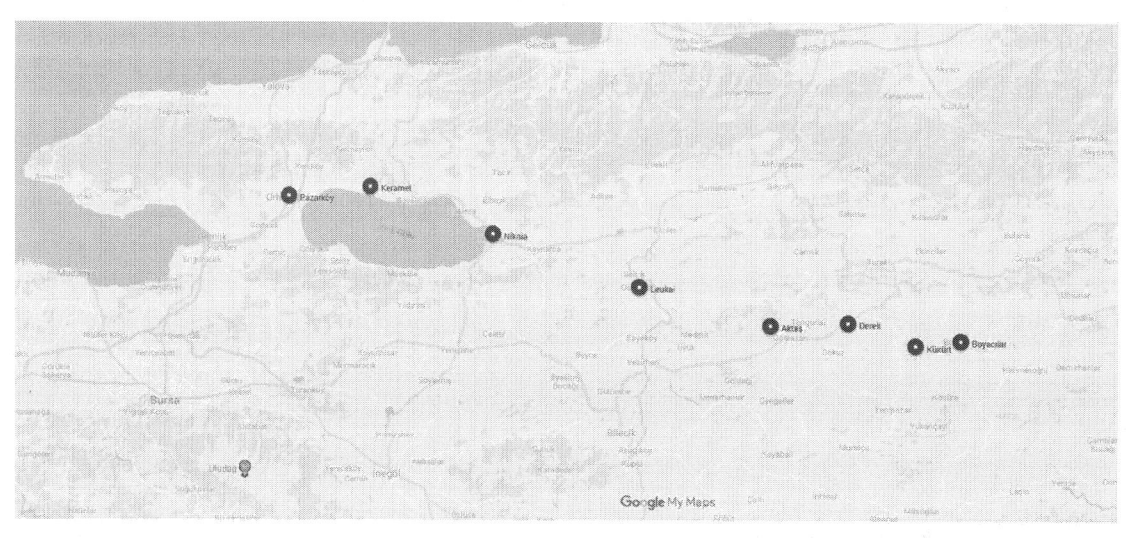

Abb. 3

Weiter ist Asklepios in Nikaia auf Münzen[14] der folgenden römischen Kaiser belegt:

— Antoninus Pius (138-161)
— Lucius Verus (161-169)
— Marcus Aurelius (161-180)
— Commodus (177-192)
— Caracalla (198-217)
— Severus Alexander (222-235)
— Tranquilina (238-244)
— Valerianus (253-260)

Die Kultstatue von Asklepios ist auf den kaiserzeitlichen Münzen zwischen Antonius Pius (168-161) und Valerianus (253-260) abgebildet. Die Fassade eines tetrastylen Tempels und die Kultstatue des Asklepios, die in der Mitte des Tempels steht, sind auf einer Münze der Zeit des Aurelius zu sehen. Deshalb ist angenommen worden, dass ein Tempel für Asklepios in Nikaia unter diesem Kaiser gebaut worden ist. Sein Ort ist gleichwohl unbekannt. Viele Münzen von Nikaia ab der Antoninischen Periode mit einem Abbild des Asklepios zeigen ihn in Gesellschaft mit

---

[12] Boyana 2018, 121-122.

[13] S.a. SEG 31, 1981, nr. 1069, 285-87, zu einigen der Inschriften.

[14] Boyana 2018, 123-128.

Hygieia[15], so dass man auf eine gemeinsame Verehrung schließen könnte. Vielleicht ist für die Thermalquellen bei Keramet ein Bezug zum Kult des Asklepios anzunehmen. Tatsächlich stammt eine Asklepios-Inschrift aus der Umgebung von Orhangazi/Pazarköy. Thermalquellen sind häufig mit Wundertaten oder Orakeln verbunden und dürfen als heilig gelten, wie es auch aus der Bedeutung des türkischen Ortsnahmen *Keramet* herzuleiten ist.

In Nikaia existierte ein Wettkampf mit der Bezeichnung Asklepieia, der zusammen mit den Pythia zu Ehren des Apollon und mit den Dionysia während des 2. und 3. nachchristlichen Jh. gefeiert wurde (Boyana 2018, 121-122).

Deshalb wird Asklepios ein wichtiger Gott in der Stadt Nikaia gewesen sein, der die Ehrung als „Retter" erfahren hat (Şahin 2003, S. 14). Möglicherweise – so hat S. Eyice angenommen (Eyice 1991, 9) – ist der Kult im Zuge einer Epidemie oder - darüber hinaus - nach einer Katastrophe (etwa nach einem Erdbeben wie dasjenige von 120 n.Chr.) begründet worden oder ist in diesem Zusammenhang aufgelebt.

Bibliographie

Aybek – Dreyer 2016	S. Aybek – B. Dreyer, Der Archäologische Survey von Apollonia am Rhyndakos beim Uluabat-See und in der Umgebung Mysiens, in der Nordwest-Türkei 2006–2010, Orient und Okzident 2, Berlin 2016.
Aybek et al. 2018	S. Aybek – B. Dreyer – C. Sponsel, Der Kultplatz des Zeus Krezimos in Metropolis in Ionien, Gephyra 15, 2018, 71-94.
Boyana 2018	H. Boyana, Nikaia Kenti ve Asklepios Kültü, in: Uluslararası Çoban Mustafa Paşa ve Kocaeli Tarihi-Kültürü Sempozyumu Bildirileri 4, Kocaeli Büyükşehir Belediyesi, 2018, 117-129.
Corsten 2010	T. Corsten, Names in -ιανος in Asia Minor. A preliminary study, in: E. Matthews – R. W. V. Catling – F. Marchand – M. Sasanow (edd.), Onomatologos. Studies in Greek personal names presented to Elaine Matthews, Oxford 2010, 456-463.
Dreyer – Engelmann 2009	B. Dreyer – H. Engelmann, Neue Dokumente zum Kult des Ares in Metropolis, ZPE 168, 2009, 161-176.
Eyice 1991	S. Eyice, İznik (Nicaea) Tarihçesi ve Eski Eserleri, İstanbul 1991.
Fernoux 2004	H. -F. Fernoux, Notables et élites des cités de Bithynie aux époques hellénistique et romaine, (IIIe s. av.-IIIe s. ap.J.-C.). Essai d'histoire sociale, Lyon 2004.
Gülbay 2015	O. Gülbay, Anadolu'da Hadrianus Dönemi İmar Faaliyetleri, İstanbul 2015.
LGPN VA	Th. Corsten – R. W. V. Catling – M. Ricl, A Lexicon of Greek Personal Names V A. Coastal Asia Minor: Pontos to Ionia, Oxford 2010.
Price 1984	S. R. F. Price, Rituals and Power. The Roman Imperial Cult in Asia Minor, Cambridge 1984.

---

[15] RPC IV [online: rpc.ashmus.ox.ac.uk], z.B. nr. 5878, 5879.

Steger 2016	F. Steger, Asklepios. Medizin und Kult, Stuttgart 2016.
Şahin 1978	S. Şahin, Bithynische Studien [Inschriften griechischer Städte in Kleinasien 7], Bonn 1978.
Şahin 1981	S. Şahin, Katalog der Antiken Inschriften des Museums von Iznik (Nikaia) / İznik Müzesi Antik Yazıtlar Kataloğu [Inschriften griechischer Städte in Kleinasien 10/1], Bonn 1981.
Şahin 2003	S. Şahin, İznik (Nicaea) in Hellenistic and Roman Periods, in: I. Akbaygil – H. İnalcık – O. Aslanapa (edd.), İznik throughout History, İstanbul 2003, 3-23.
Thraemer 1896	E. Thraemer, Asklepios 2, in: RE II/2, 1896, 1642-1697.

Asklepios rahibi P. Claudius Calpurnianus'un onurlandırma yazıtını taşıyan bir heykel kaidesi
Özet

Nikaia'da Doç. Dr. Aygün Ekin Meriç başkanlığında yürütülen Tiyatro kazılarında, kuzeybatı bölümde Asklepios rahibi Publius Claudius Calpurnianus'a ait yuvarlak kaide üzerinde bir onur yazıtı bulunmuştur. Onurlandırılan kişi İmparator Hadrianus'un rahibinin oğlu olup kentin tanınmış ailelerinden birine mensuptur. Hadrianus'un İ. S. 120 yılındaki depremden sonra yaptığı lütufkar yardımlar iyi bilinmektedir. Hadrianus rahibinin oğlu olan birisinin aynı zamanda Asklepios kültü rahibi olarak görev yapması pek yakışık almayabilirdi. Aile fertlerinden birinin bu heykel kaidesini diktirdiği düşünülebilir. Nikaia'da Asklepios rahibi olarak şimdiye kadar hiçbir buluntu ele geçmemiştir. Kült Nikaia için olduğu kadar bölge için de önemlidir. Asklepios bu yüzden "kurtarıcı" bir tanrı olarak, özellikle deprem gibi bir felaket sırasında önemli bir rol oynamıştır. Baba ile oğlun yakın ilişkisi gibi Hadrianus ile Asklepios rahibi zihnimizde İ. S. 120 yılındaki depreme odaklanmamızı sağlıyordu.

Anahtar Sözcükler: Nikaia, İznik, Asklepios rahibi, Hadrianus rahibi, İ. S. 120 depremi, "kurtarıcı" Asklepios.

A statue base with the honorary inscription of P. Claudius Calpurnianus, the priest of Asclepius
Abstract

In the northwest corner of the theatre-excavations under the leadership of Dr. Aygün Ekin Meriç in Nikaia a honorific round basis (originally with statue) for the Asclepius priest Publius Claudius Calpurnianus was detected. The person honoured was son of the priest of the ruler Hadrian and member of an influential family of the city. The role of Hadrian as a benefactor in rebuilding the city after the earthquake of 120 AD is well known. His priest may be crucial that his son was invested a priest of the Asclepius cult. A family member may also have erected the basis. A priest of Asclepios is not attested yet, in the city. The cult is important for the city and the region, though Asclepios, therefore, „a Saviour" god, probably played a significant role during a catastrophe like an earthquake. The close connection of father and son as well as of Hadrian and Asclepius priest focuses our minds on the earthquake of 120 AD.

Keywords: Nicaea, İznik, priest of Asclepius, priest of Hadrian, earthquake 120 AD, Asclepius "the saviour".

Innovationen und wirtschaftliche Entwicklung im Imperium Romanum

Helmuth SCHNEIDER*

> Johannes Nollés Schrift ‚Nundinae instituere et habere' (Hildesheim 1982) ist mit ihrer präzisen Interpretation und Kommentierung mehrerer Inschriften zu ländlichen Märkten in Afrika und in der Provinz Asia ein grundlegender Beitrag zur Analyse der Austauschbeziehungen und des regionalen Handels in der römischen Principatszeit. Deshalb widme ich diesen Artikel Herrn Professor Dr. Johannes Nollé, in der Hoffnung, dass die Ausführungen sein Interesse finden werden.

Die Mentalität der römischen Führungsschichten

Die Auffassung der älteren wissenschaftlichen Literatur, in der römischen Welt habe es nur geringe technische Fortschritte und wenige Innovationen von wirtschaftlicher Bedeutung gegeben,[1] kann nach den Forschungen von K. D. White, Ö. Wikander K. Greene und A. I. Wilson als widerlegt gelten.[2] Unter dieser Voraussetzung ist es notwendig, die Frage zu stellen, wie innovationsfähig die römische Gesellschaft gewesen ist, und Kontexte sowie Ursachen von Innovationen systematisch zu untersuchen. Bei einer Analyse von Innovationen in römischer Zeit ist deswegen zunächst auf die Rolle der römischen Führungsschichten und auf deren Mentalität einzugehen, weil in der althistorischen Forschung oft die ablehnende Haltung der Senatoren Neuerungen gegenüber, die als Bedrohung für die politische und soziale Ordnung empfunden worden seien, betont worden ist. Es bestand demnach in Rom eine deutliche Neigung, sich an den Exempla der Vergangenheit, an dem *mos maiorum*, der Sitte der Vorfahren, zu orientieren. Die tradierten sozialen und politischen Normen sollen in senatorischen Kreisen verbindlich für das politische und soziale Handeln gewesen sein.[3] Aufgrund solcher Überlegungen wurde angenommen, dass es in der römischen Gesellschaft insgesamt nur eine geringe Bereitschaft zu Innovationen im politischen, gesellschaftlichen, kulturellen oder wirtschaftlichen Bereich gegeben habe.

Gegen diese Sicht können allerdings Einwände erhoben werden. Es kann nicht übersehen werden, dass die Römer in vielen Bereichen auf neue Gegebenheiten pragmatisch reagierten und dabei fähig waren, auch technische Errungenschaften fremder Völker aufzugreifen und für sich zu nutzen. Dies gilt selbst für den politischen Bereich: Bereits Polybios hat die Auffassung geäußert, das politische System der römischen Republik sei nicht theoretischer Einsicht zu verdanken, sondern sei aus Krisen hervorgegangen, indem die Römer aus jeder schwierigen Lage die entsprechende Lehre zogen und dann das Bessere wählten.[4] In der Phase der außeritalischen Expansion waren die Römer gezwungen, mit der Einrichtung von Provinzen außerhalb Italiens

---

* Prof. Dr. Helmuth Schneider, Universität Kassel, Alte Geschichte, Nora Platiel-Str. 1, 34127 Kassel, Deutschland (helschne@uni-kassel.de).

[1] Finley 1965; Gille 1980, 170-195; Schneider 1992, 22-30, Greene 2008a.

[2] White 1984; Wikander 1984; Greene 2000; Wilson 2002.

[3] Diese Sicht findet ihren klassischen Ausdruck bei Cicero: Cic. rep. 5,1; Blösel 2000.

[4] Pol. 6,10. Vgl. auch Gehrke 2017, 537.

und der Gründung von Steuerpachtgesellschaften neue Formen der politischen Beherrschung eroberter Gebiete zu entwickeln. Cicero konnte aus diesem Grund in der Debatte über das *imperium* des Pompeius im Jahr 66 v. Chr. gegen das Argument führender Senatoren, es dürften keine Neuerungen eingeführt werden, darauf hinweisen, dass die Vorfahren im Kriege „neuen Umständen stets mit neuen Maßnahmen begegnet sind."[5]

Selbst die Politik der mittleren und späten römischen Republik erwies sich in vieler Hinsicht als innovationsfähig; es wurden neue gesetzliche Regelungen geschaffen, um Missstände abzuschaffen.[6] Hier ist vor allem auf die populare Politik hinzuweisen, die seit den Gesetzen der Gracchen immer wieder neue Vorschläge formulierte, um die Republik an neue politische, soziale und wirtschaftliche Erfordernisse anzupassen. Schließlich kulminierte diese Politik unter Augustus in der Schaffung eines staatsrechtlich neuen Systems, des Principats, das die alten Institutionen der Republik mit neuen Machtstrukturen verband.[7] Unter diesen historischen Voraussetzungen stellte Claudius 48 n. Chr. in einer Rede im Senat fest, im römischen Gemeinwesen habe es von Beginn an immer wieder Neuerungen gegeben.[8]

Mehrere Tatsachen belegen eine positive Einstellung der römischen Führungsschicht Innovationen gegenüber. Gerade im militärischen Bereich wurde technisches Wissen fremder Völker übernommen. Ein Beispiel hierfür war die Verwendung des spanischen Schwertes in den römischen Legionen; diese Waffe hatten die Römer während des Zweiten Punischen Krieges auf der Iberischen Halbinsel kennen gelernt und dann bereits im Krieg gegen Philipp V. eingesetzt.[9] Von erheblicher militärischer Bedeutung war die Ausrüstung der römischen Legionen mit Katapulten, die im 4. Jahrhundert v. Chr. zuerst in Syrakus entwickelt und in hellenistischer Zeit wesentlich verbessert worden waren. Gerade die Torsionskatapulte besaßen eine große Reichweite und eine hohe Durchschlagskraft. Der Einsatz der Katapulte im Krieg während der späten römischen Republik ist literarisch insbesondere für die Feldzüge Caesars in Gallien bezeugt; eine genaue Beschreibung dieser Waffe findet sich bei Vitruvius. Darüber hinaus gibt es neben archäologischen Funden von Metallteilen solcher Katapulte Abbildungen etwa auf der Traians-Säule.[10] Das Interesse der politischen Führungsschicht an der Entwicklung der Landwirtschaft in Italien geht aus dem Senatsbeschluss hervor, die Schriften des Karthagers Mago über die Landwirtschaft ins Lateinische übersetzen zu lassen. Auf diese Weise sollte römischen Großgrundbesitzern das Wissen der Karthager über die ertragsorientierte Gutswirtschaft zugänglich gemacht werden.[11]

---

[5] Cic. Manil. 60: *non dicam hoc loco maiores nostros semper in pace consuetudini, in bello utilitati paruisse, semper ad novos casus temporum novorum consiliorum rationes accommodasse.*

[6] Beispiel hierfür ist die *lex Villia annalis* des Jahres 180 v. Chr., ein Gesetz, das die Ämterlaufbahn regelte und so die Bewerbung sehr junger Senatoren um höhere Ämter ausschloss: Liv. 40.44,1.

[7] Eck 2006, 40-64.

[8] ILS 212, Z. 4-6: *sed illa potius cogitetis, quam multa in hac civitate novata sint, et quidem statim ob origine urbis nostrae in quod formas statusque res p(ublica) nostra diducta sit.*

[9] Pol. 6,23,6-7; Liv. 31,34,4-5.

[10] Baatz 1999; Moosbauer 2013. Vgl. Caes. Gall. 2,8,4; 4,25,1-2; 7,41,3; 7,81,5; 8,40,5; Vitr. 10,10-12; Tac. hist. 3,23. ann. 15,9,1.

[11] Ruffing 1999; Plin. nat. 18,22; Varro rust. 1,1,10.

Gerade auf dem Gebiet der Architektur und der Urbanistik wurden vom Senat und von den Senatoren neue Wege beschritten.¹² Bemerkenswert sind hier vor allem die Bauprogramme der Censoren in den Jahren 184, 179 und 174 v. Chr.; ihr Schwerpunkt lag auf der Errichtung von solchen Bauwerken, die der Förderung der Wirtschaft, der Versorgung der Bevölkerung mit Wasser und der öffentlichen Hygiene dienten. Im Jahr 184 v. Chr. wurden die *cloacae* gereinigt und neue *cloacae* auf dem Aventin angelegt, und Cato ließ am Forum eine Basilica errichten. Während der folgenden Censur 179 v. Chr. hat man einen Hafen am Tiber angelegt und die Pfeiler für eine neue Tiberbrücke gebaut sowie die Basilica Aemilia, einen Fischmarkt und mehrere *porticus* errichtet, während 174 v. Chr. die Censoren in Rom Straßen und einen Handelsplatz (*emporium*) pflastern und eine Treppe vom Tiber zum *emporium* bauen ließen.¹³ Eine Wasserleitung wurde 179 v. Chr. begonnen, konnte aber wegen des Einspruchs eines Senators, über dessen Besitzungen die Leitung geführt werden sollte, nicht vollendet werden.¹⁴ Die Stadt Rom erhielt durch diese Baumaßnahmen ein neues Gesicht, es wurde eine städtische Infrastruktur für den Handel und die Versorgung der Bevölkerung geschaffen.

Es ist auffallend, dass Bauwerke, die durch Verwendung von Marmor oder technisch wie auch ästhetisch ohne Vorbild waren, oft mit den Namen führender Senatoren verbunden waren. Wie Velleius Paterculus anmerkt, ließ Q. Metellus Macedonius (cos. 143) als erster einen Tempel aus Marmor errichten.¹⁵ Später gab M. Aemilius Lepidus (cos. 78) den Auftrag, in seinem Haus Schwellen aus numidischen Marmor zu legen.¹⁶ Neue Konstruktionsmerkmale weisen die im 2. Jahrhundert v. Chr. aus Stein errichteten Brücken über den Tiber auf: P. Cornelius Scipio und L. Mummius ließen während ihrer Censur im Jahre 142 v. Chr. die schon 179 v. Chr. für eine Brücke über den Tiber errichteten Pfeiler mit Bögen verbinden und schufen auf diese Weise die erste steinerne Bogenbrücke über den Tiber.¹⁷ Im Jahr 109 v. Chr., wurde während der Censur des M. Aemilius Scaurus der *pons Mulvius* gebaut, eine steinerne Brücke mit sechs Bögen, von denen die vier mittleren Bögen eine Spannweite von 18 Metern besaßen. Eine solche Brücke war für das 2. Jh. v. Chr. eine technische Meisterleistung, für die es kein Vorbild gab.¹⁸ Der Pons Fabricius aus dem Jahr 62 v. verbindet noch heute das Marsfeld mit der Tiberinsel; die Brücke hat zwei Bögen mit einer Spannweite von über 24 Metern.¹⁹ Die perfekte Beherrschung der Bogenkonstruktion selbst bei großen Bauwerken war die Voraussetzung für den Bau der *aqua Marcia* in den Jahren nach 144 v. Chr.; von den älteren Wasserleitungen und insbesondere von den griechischen Wasserleitungen unterschied die *aqua Marcia* sich durch die ca. neun Kilome-

---

¹² Coarelli 1977; Kolb 1995, 198-215; 250-271.

¹³ Liv. 39,44,5-7; 40,51,4-7; 41,27,5-8; Plin. nat. 36,102. Vgl. Freyberger 2012, 38-44; Kay 2014, 216-221.

¹⁴ Liv. 40,51,7.

¹⁵ Vell. 1,11,5.

¹⁶ Plin. nat. 36,49.

¹⁷ Liv. 40,51,4; Richardson 1992, 296-297; O'Connor 1993, 67-68. O'Connor nimmt an, dass die 179 v. Chr. errichteten Pfeiler eine Holzkonstruktion trugen, so wie es sie auch noch später gab. Zur Moselbrücke in Trier etwa vgl. O'Connor 1993, 141.

¹⁸ O'Connor 1993, 64-65.

¹⁹ Cass. Dio 37,45,3; Richardson 1992, 298; O'Connor 1993, 66.

ter lange Bogenstrecke vor der Stadt; die Leitung wurde auf diese Weise in großer Höhe in die Stadt geführt.[20]

Die Bogenkonstruktion fand aber nicht nur bei Bauten der Infrastruktur, sondern auch bei den Repräsentationsbauten im Zentrum Roms Anwendung. Das im Jahr 78 v. Chr. vollendete Tabularium besaß zum Forum Romanum hin eine Fassade, deren hervorstechendes Merkmal eine monumentale Arkadenreihe war. Die Aufsicht über den Bau hatte der Consul Q. Lutatius Catulus, der einer der führenden Anhänger Sullas war und wie M. Aemilius Scaurus von Cicero als geradliniger Optimat gerühmt wurde.[21] Bei dem Bau der Theater ging man in Rom im 1. Jahrhundert v. Chr. insofern vom griechischen Vorbild ab, als die Theaterbauten sich nicht mehr an einen Hügel anlehnten und der Zuschauerraum daher eine Fassade erhielt, die im Fall des unter Augustus gebauten Marcellus-Theaters aus zwei monumentalen Arkadenreihen bestand.[22]

Selbst in der Architektur der Tempel beschritten die Römer – teilweise in Anlehnung an hellenistische Vorbilder – unkonventionelle Wege; hervorragendes Beispiel hierfür ist neben dem Fortuna-Heiligtum von Praeneste das im 2. Jh. n. Chr. unter Hadrianus erneuerte Pantheon.[23] Dieser Tempel verbindet einen Kuppelbau aus *opus caementicium* mit einer Säulenhalle, die wie die Front eines griechischen Tempels einen Dreiecksgiebel besitzt. Neben den großen öffentlichen Bauten zeigt die Ausstattung privater Bauten, in welchem Ausmaß die Mitglieder der stadtrömischen Oberschicht und der lokalen Eliten sich für neue Formen des Wohnluxus interessierten. Hier ist nicht nur auf die entsprechenden Äußerungen von Plinius zu verweisen,[24] sondern vor allem auf die Wanddekoration und die Bodenmosaike größerer Häuser in Pompeii. In der Wandmalerei folgten in der späten Republik und im frühen Principat bis zur Zerstörung der Stadt 79 n. Chr. verschiedene Stile schnell aufeinander, und auch die Gestaltung der Gärten macht den Wandel im Wohnstil deutlich.[25]

Die römischen Führungsschichten standen neuen Stilrichtungen und bautechnischen Neuerungen in einem überraschenden Maße aufgeschlossen gegenüber. Die technischen Fortschritte in der späten Republik und in der frühen Principatszeit beschränkten sich aber nicht auf die Bereiche der Infrastruktur und der öffentlichen wie privaten Repräsentationsbauten, vielmehr ist auf relevante technische Fortschritte in der Wirtschaft und auf die Wahrnehmung solcher Fortschritte in der Fachliteratur zu verweisen.

---

[20] Frontin. aqu. 7; Adam 1984, 261-270.

[21] Dessau, ILS 35. 35a; Richardson 1992, 376-377; Hesberg 2005, 45; 120.

[22] Richardson 1992, 382-385. Abbildung: Ward-Perkins 1975, 64-65.

[23] Ward-Perkins 1975, 35-40; 133-142; Adam 1984, 200-202; Hesberg 2005, 22-23; 96.

[24] Plin. nat. 36,109-110. Vgl. Plin. nat. 17,1-6; 36,48-50.

[25] Strocka 2007; Wallace-Hadrill 1994, 17-61; Zanker 1995; Strocka 2007, 308 charakterisiert die Anfänge des Zweiten Stils als "revolutionary transformation of the solid First-Style system into an illusionistic play of infinite possibilities." Dieser Stil wird als "qualitative innovation" bewertet. Es handelte sich dabei nicht um ein regionales, auf den Golf von Neapel begrenztes Phänomen; Strocka nimmt an, dass der Zweite Stil sich gegen 100 v. Chr. in Rom durchgesetzt hat.

Innovationen in der Landwirtschaft und im Handwerk: Ein Überblick

Die Frage nach den technischen Innovationen in der römischen Wirtschaft beruht keineswegs nur auf modernen Erkenntnissen über den Zusammenhang von wirtschaftlicher und technischer Entwicklung,[26] sondern entspricht vielmehr auch den Wahrnehmungshorizonten griechischer und römischer Autoren, die bereits neue Geräte oder Verfahren erwähnt haben. Da die antiken Texte oft über die Einführung solcher Neuerungen oder über die Übernahme von technischen Errungenschaften aus anderen Regionen berichten,[27] können die Ursachen und Wirkungen solcher Innovationen auf der Basis von zeitgenössischen Aussagen und aufgrund der archäologischen Funde systematisch dargestellt und untersucht werden. Bei dem folgenden kurzen und keineswegs vollständigen Überblick über technische Neuerungen, die wirtschaftlich von Relevanz waren, ist zunächst auf die Landwirtschaft einzugehen, die in der Antike ohne Zweifel der wichtigste Wirtschaftssektor war: Einerseits war die Mehrzahl der arbeitenden Menschen im Agrarbereich tätig, um sich selbst und die städtische Bevölkerung mit Agrarerzeugnissen – sowohl mit Lebensmitteln als auch mit Rohstoffen wie Wolle oder Flachs – zu versorgen, andererseits hatte die Landwirtschaft einen erheblichen Anteil am gesamten Sozialprodukt der römischen Gesellschaft.[28] Überdies beruhten der Reichtum und die soziale Stellung der römischen Führungsschichten vor allem auf Landbesitz; ihre großen Güter produzierten neben anderen Erzeugnissen vor allem Wein und Olivenöl für regionale und überregionale Märkte und erwirtschafteten hohe Erträge.

Es ist deswegen nicht überraschend, dass gerade in der Konstruktion der Pressen für die Erzeugung von Wein und Olivenöl, die im antiken Mittelmeerraum zu den Grundnahrungsmitteln gehörten, erhebliche Fortschritte zu konstatieren sind. Da es kaum möglich war, die Effizienz der Weinlese oder der Olivenernte zu steigern, kam der Installation von Pressen und Ölmühlen sowie deren Verbesserung eine hohe Bedeutung zu. Beachtenswert sind vor allem die Aussagen über die Weinpressen bei Plinius, der einzelne Neuerungen nennt und ungefähr datiert:

„Manche pressen mit einzelnen Keltern, besser ist es aber mit zwei, mag jede davon auch noch so groß sein. Es kommt hierbei auf die Länge, nicht auf die Dicke [des Pressbalkens] an. Die großen pressen besser. Die Alten zogen sie mit Stricken, Riemen und Hebebäumen nieder. Vor etwa hundert Jahren hat man die griechischen Keltern erfunden, bei denen ein Gewinde am Pressbalken durch eine Schraubenmutter geht; auf der einen Seite ist eine Säule am Pressbaum befestigt, bei der anderen ein Steinkasten, der sich mit dem Pressbaum emporhebt, eine Einrichtung, die man für sehr nützlich erachtet. Vor 22 Jahren hat man die Erfindung gemacht, mit kleinen Pressen, einer weniger großen Kelter und einem in der Mitte errichteten kürzeren

---

[26] Walter 2007.

[27] Als ein Beispiel soll hier der Katalog von Erfindungen bei Plin. nat. 7,191-209 erwähnt werden. Vgl. ferner nat. 18,172 (Räderpflug); 18,296 (Gallisches Mähgerät); 18,317 (Weinpressen). Vitruvius erwähnt ebenfalls neue technische Entwicklungen oder Erfindungen, so etwa die Verwendung des *opus caementicium* in der Bautechnik (Vitr. 2,6. 5,12), die Wassermühle (10,5) oder die Archimedische Schraube (10,6). Zur Spätantike vgl. Aug. civ. 22,24. Vgl. ferner Greene 2008b, 804-809.

[28] White 1970; Bowman – Wilson 2013b, 1.

Pressbaum [zu arbeiten], wobei über die Trester gelegte runde Scheiben mit ihrem ganzen Gewicht drücken und man über die Presse noch schwere Gewichte anbringt."[29]

Voraussetzung für die Konstruktion der Schraubenpresse war die Erfindung der Schraube, die zu den Errungenschaften der hellenistischen Mechanik gehört.[30] Erst mit Hilfe der Schraube gelang es in augusteischer Zeit, einen Typ der Weinpresse zu entwickeln, der in den Weinbaugebieten Europas bis zum Beginn der Industrialisierung weitgehend unverändert eingesetzt wurde. Am Pressbalken war am vorderen Ende eine Schraubenmutter angebracht; die große hölzerne Schraube selbst konnte in dem Muttergewinde gedreht werden, an ihrem unteren Ende war ein Gewicht befestigt, das durch Drehung der Schraube gehoben wurde. Das Gewicht zog dann den Pressbalken kontinuierlich herab, bis es den Boden berührte, und wurde dann wiederum durch Drehung der Schraube gehoben. Die Schraubenpresse war wesentlich effizienter als die ältere Seilwindenpresse, bei der es noch notwendig war, mit Muskelkraft durch Drehen der Seilwinde den Pressbalken herabzuziehen, während bei der Schraubenpresse die Schwerkraft des Steinkastens auf den Pressbalken einwirkte. Eine Weiterentwicklung dieser Form der Schraubenpresse stellte eine Presse dar, bei der die Schraube in einem festen Holzrahmen angebracht war. Durch Drehung der Schraube nach unten konnte ein direkter Druck auf das Pressgut ausgeübt werden.[31]

Beim Dreschen, einem wichtigen Arbeitsvorgang nach der Getreideernte, wurden üblicherweise Tiere über das auf der Tenne liegende Getreide getrieben, um so das Korn aus den Ähren auszutreten;[32] seit dem 1. Jahrhundert v. Chr. verwendete man hierfür auch Dreschschlitten, die aus einem größeren, an der unteren Seite mit Spitzen aus Stein oder Eisen versehenen Brett bestanden, das durch ein Gewicht belastet und von zwei Ochsen über die ausgebreiteten Ähren gezogen wurde. Das *plostellum poenicum*, das nach Varro vornehmlich in *Hispania citerior* eingesetzt worden ist und wahrscheinlich auf ein karthagisches Gerät zurückzuführen ist, hatte Achsen, die mit gezähnten Scheiben versehen waren, und wurde ebenfalls von Ochsen über das Getreide gezogen.[33]

Für Innovationen im Handwerk bietet die Keramikproduktion ein gutes Beispiel; technische Neuerungen bewirkten bei der Herstellung reliefverzierter Keramik, der *Terra sigillata*, eine tiefgreifende Veränderung des Herstellungsprozesses und gleichzeitig eine erhebliche Steigerung der Produktivität. Durch die Verwendung von Formschüsseln wurde der Arbeitsprozess in mehrere hoch spezialisierte Arbeitsschritte zerlegt: Stempelschneider stellten Punzen mit den Reliefs her; die Punzen wurden in die Formschüsseln eingedrückt, so dass sie das Dekor in Negativform aufwiesen. Anschließend wurden die Formschüsseln gebrannt. Der Töpfer übernahm die fertige Formschüssel, zentrierte sie auf der Töpferscheibe und zog auf der schnell rotierenden Scheibe die Gefäßwand hoch. Damit war die Arbeit des Töpfers wesentlich vereinfacht, denn Form und Dekor des Gefäßes waren vorgegeben; es entfiel damit die Notwendigkeit, das vom Töpfer geformte Gefäß in einem weiteren Arbeitsgang zu verzieren. Wenn das Gefäß beim

---

[29] Plin. nat. 18,317. Vgl. ferner die Ausführungen bei Heron, Mechanik 3,13-20; White 1984, 67-70.

[30] Heron, Mechanik 2,5.

[31] Heron, Mechanik 3,20. Vgl. auch Marzano 2013.

[32] Varro rust. 1,52,2; Colum. 2,20,3-5; Anth. Gr. 9,301.

[33] Varro rust. 1,52,1; Colum. 2,20,4; White 1970, 184-186.

Trocknen geschrumpft war, wurde es der Formschüssel entnommen. Die Formschüsseln konnten mehrmals verwendet werden, so dass die Töpfer in der Lage waren, identische Gefäße in größerer Zahl zu produzieren. Die Verwendung von Formschüsseln bedeutete eine Standardisierung sowohl des Herstellungsprozesses als auch der Erzeugnisse, die der Töpfer nicht mehr frei gestaltete; auf diese Weise entstand in den römischen Töpferzentren eine Serienproduktion.[34] Die gestiegene Produktivität beim Töpfern der Gefäße erforderte schließlich leistungsfähigere Brennöfen, die große Mengen von Gefäßen und Schalen aufnehmen konnten. In La Graufesenque in Südfrankreich wurde ein Töpferofen ausgegraben, der mehr als vier Meter breit war und eine Höhe von etwa drei Metern hatte. Es wurden an diesem Ort Listen gefunden, auf denen bis zu 30.000 Gefäße verzeichnet waren, die von den Töpfern zum Brennen eingeliefert worden sind.[35]

Zwei Erfindungen hatten zur Folge, dass Glas, das in Mesopotamien und Altägypten bekannt war, aber nur zur Herstellung von kleinen, farbigen Gefäßen oder Glasperlen verwendet wurde, in großem Umfang als Material für die Herstellung von Trinkgefäßen, Schalen sowie Flaschen genutzt werden konnte: Im 1. Jahrhundert v. Chr. wurde in Syrien die Glasmacherpfeife erfunden und die Technik des Glasblasens entwickelt; zugleich gelang es, ein farbloses und lichtdurchlässiges Glas herzustellen. Bereits in augusteischer Zeit existierten Glasmacherwerkstätten in der Stadt Rom, Luxusgefäße aus Glas machten Trinkbechern aus Gold und Silber Konkurrenz. Die Glasmacher erwiesen sich als überaus erfindungsreich, wenn es darum ging, Gefäße zu schaffen, die aufgrund ihrer faszinierenden ästhetischen Wirkung hohe Preise erzielten. Dies trifft etwa auf die Kameogläser und die spätantiken Diatretgläser zu. Kameogläser hatten eine tiefblaue Gefäßwand und eine zweite, weiße Glasschicht, in die ein Relief eingeschnitten war, während die Diatretgläser aus einem inneren Becher und einem gläsernen Maschennetz bestehen, das den Becher umgibt. Die Diatretgläser sind bei Martialis und außerdem archäologisch für das späte 1. Jahrhundert n. Chr. bezeugt.[36] Wie die zahlreichen Wandgemälde in Pompeii, auf denen Schalen und Gefäße aus Glas dargestellt sind, zeigen, übten Gefäße aus durchsichtigem, farblosen Glas auf die römische Oberschicht eine große Faszination aus. Die vielfältigen neuen Möglichkeiten des Werkstoffs Glas fanden demnach rasch eine weite Akzeptanz in der römischen Gesellschaft.[37]

Das Fensterglas veränderte die Architektur privater und öffentlicher Gebäude; Glasfenster ließen das Tageslicht in die Innenräume und schützten gleichzeitig vor einer ungünstigen Witterung. Die großen Thermen der Principatszeit sind ohne Fensterglas nicht denkbar, und auch andere repräsentative Bauten wiesen zunehmend große Fensterfronten auf. Vom geschützten Innenraum her konnte man in die Landschaft blicken, die Trennung von Haus und umgebener Landschaft wurde dadurch tendenziell aufgehoben.[38]

---

[34] Brown 1976; Garbsch 1982; Peacock 1982; Jackson – Greene 2008; Fulford – Durham 2013.

[35] Vernhet 1981; Marichal 1988, 113-221; 250-259.

[36] Price 1976; Harden 1987; Newby – Painter 1991; Saldern 2004, 623-637; Stern 2008; Plin. nat. 36,189-199; Strabon 16,2,25; Petron. 50,7-51,6; Mart. 12,70,9.

[37] Naumann-Steckner 1991.

[38] Plin. epist. 2,17,4-5; 5,6,29; Saldern 2004, 200-202.

Während für die römische Glasherstellung die Verwendung neuer technischer Verfahren charakteristisch war, ist für andere Handwerkszweige eine Verbesserung alter Geräte oder die Übernahme neuer Geräte aus anderen Bereichen der Wirtschaft zu konstatieren. In der Textilherstellung erleichterte ein neuer Webstuhl die Arbeit; der römische Webstuhl besaß – im Gegensatz zu älteren Webstühlen mit einem Tuchbaum und Kettfäden, die durch Gewichte straff gezogen wurden – sowohl einen Tuchbaum als auch einen Garnbaum. Der Schussfaden wurde nun nicht mehr nach oben, sondern nach unten angeschlagen, so dass im Sitzen gewebt werden konnte. Der beim Weben notwendige Kraftaufwand war dadurch erheblich reduziert worden.[39] Es ist bezeichnend, dass in Herculaneum und Pompeii die Schraubenpresse, die sich zuvor in der Landwirtschaft beim Pressen von Oliven bewährt hatte, nun zum Pressen von Tuch verwendet wurde.[40] Ein Techniktransfer lag also für das römische Handwerk durchaus im Bereich des Möglichen. Auf den ersten Blick wenig bedeutsam scheint die Verwendung der seit dem 1. Jahrhundert v. Chr. bezeugten Schnellwaage in den Läden der Handwerker zu sein; das Wiegen der Ware wurde durch diesen Typ der Waage jedoch wesentlich erleichtert, weil das umständliche Hantieren mit den Gewichten entfiel. Das Gewicht der Ware konnte an einer Skala abgelesen werden, der Vorgang des Verkaufs ging auf diese Weise schneller vonstatten. Da die Waagen geeicht waren, war das Wiegen für den Käufer transparenter geworden.[41]

Im Bauhandwerk stellte die Verwendung des *opus caementicium* eine entscheidende Neuerung dar, die bei Vitruvius und Cassius Dio Beachtung fand und die einen tiefgreifenden Wandel der römischen Architektur zur Folge hatte. Der Gussmörtel, dessen Grundstoff Puteolanerde vulkanischen Ursprungs war, wurde beim Mauerbau oder bei der Errichtung von Gewölben oder Kuppeln in eine Verschalung gegossen; nach dem Trocknen und der Abnahme der Verschalung besaß das Mauerwerk ein so hohe Festigkeit, dass es möglich war, große Innenräume durch Gewölbe zu überdachen und dabei auf Stützen zu verzichten. Zunächst verwendete man *opus caementicium* bei der Errichtung von Nutzbauten, seit der frühen Principatszeit aber zunehmend auch bei der Errichtung repräsentativer Bauwerke. Herausragendes Beispiel dieser neuen Architektur ist das Pantheon, dessen Kuppel einen Durchmesser von 43,30 Metern hat und damit größer ist als die Kuppel der Peterskirche in Rom (42 Meter) oder des Doms von Florenz (42,30 Meter).[42] Die Verwendung des *opus caementicium* als Baustoff hat deutliche Auswirkungen auch auf den Hafenbau besessen, wie etwa die Erweiterung des Hafens von Puteoli durch eine große Mole oder der Bau des Hafens von Caesarea belegt.[43] Bei der Errichtung von Großbauten wurden Krane eingesetzt, die mit einem Flaschenzug und einem von Menschen bewegten Tretrad ausgestattet waren; es war so möglich, mit relativ geringer Kraft schwere Lasten zu heben.[44]

---

[39] Wild 2008, 470-474.

[40] Moeller 1976, 25-27.

[41] Vitr. 10,3,4. Abbildung auf dem Grabrelief eines Fleischers: Zimmer 1982, Nr. 2; ILS 8629-8632; Weiß 2001.

[42] Vitr. 2,6; Cass. Dio 48,51,3-4. Vgl. ferner Vitr. 5,12,2; Ward-Perkins 1975, 97-102; 133-144; Adam 1984, 192-211; Mogetta 2015.

[43] Vitr. 5,12; Puteoli: Strab. 5,4,6; Anth. Gr. 7,379; 9,708. Zu Caesarea vgl. Oleson – Branton 1992, 49-67.

[44] Vitr. 10,2,1-10; Heron, Mechanik 3,2-5; Landels 1978, 84-98. Vgl. Zimmer 1982, Nr. 82 und 83.

Die Schifffahrt auf dem Mittelmeer wurde durch den Ausbau der Häfen gefördert,[45] der Schiffbau passte sich gleichzeitig an die neuen Herausforderungen an: In der Principatszeit wurden Schiffe mit einer hohen Ladekapazität gebaut, die sich auch für die Hochseeschifffahrt eigneten. Es war möglich, mit solchen Schiffen von der Südküste Arabiens über den Indischen Ozean direkt nach Indien zu fahren. Um die Windkraft besser nutzen zu können, wurden Schiffe mit drei Masten gebaut; gleichzeitig wurde die Takelage verbessert; neben dem Rahsegel wurde das Lateinsegel eingeführt, das in der Küstenschifffahrt eine Rolle spielte.[46]

Eine der bedeutendsten technischen Innovationen der gesamten Antike war ohne Zweifel die Nutzung der Wasserkraft im Mühlenwesen. Sieht man von der Nutzung der Windkraft in der Seefahrt und der Schwerkraft bei den von Plinius beschriebenen Schraubenpressen einmal ab, beruhte die Arbeit in der Produktion und im Gütertransport ausschließlich auf der menschlichen und tierischen Muskelkraft, wobei mechanische Instrumente wie der Hebel, die Schraube oder die Rolle den Kraftaufwand bei bestimmten Arbeiten reduziert haben.[47]

Die Getreidemühle zeigt in exemplarischer Weise, welche Folgen technische Innovationen in der Antike für einen Arbeitsvorgang hatten, der unverzichtbar für die Versorgung der Bevölkerung mit dem Grundnahrungsmittel Brot war.[48] In Griechenland wurde die primitive, wenig effiziente Schiebemühle, mit der Frauen das Getreide mahlten, von der Olynthischen Mühle abgelöst, die einen Trichter, durch den die Getreidekörner kontinuierlich zwischen die Mühlsteine rutschen konnten, und einen Hebel zur Bewegung des oberen Mühlsteins besaß. Beides erhöhte die Produktivität der Mühle gegenüber der älteren Schiebemühle. In römischer Zeit gelang es mit der Konstruktion der Pompeianischen Rotationsmühle, die menschliche Arbeitskraft durch die tierische Muskelkraft zu ersetzen: Pferde oder Esel drehten mit einer extremen Körperbiegung und mit verbundenen Augen auf engstem Raum voranschreitend den oberen Mühlstein.[49]

Die Wassermühle, die bereits von Vitruvius beschrieben worden war, ersetzte in der Principatszeit beim Getreidemahlen die Arbeitskraft von Menschen oder Tieren und leitete über zur Nutzung einer Naturkraft im Produktionsprozess. Bei der Wassermühle handelt es sich um eine komplexe Installation: Die Rotation des vertikalen Wasserrades, das als Antrieb dient, wird über ein Winkelgetriebe mit Zahnrädern auf den Mühlstein, den Arbeitsteil der Mühle, übertragen.[50] Die vom Tier angetriebene Rotationsmühle, die im städtischen Raum in den Bäckereien installiert war, wurde in der Antike keineswegs verdrängt: im Preisedikt des Diocletianus aus dem Jahr 301 n. Chr. werden neben der Wassermühle noch die von Pferden oder Eseln bewegte Rotationsmühle und die Handmühle aufgeführt.[51] In den ländlichen Regionen der nordwestlichen

---

[45] Blackman 2008; Schmidts – Vučetič 2015; Wawrzinek 2016, 71-88; Ostia: Cass. Dio 60,11,1-5; Centumcellae: Plin. epist. 6,31,15-17; Ancona: ILS 298.

[46] Casson 1971; McGrail 2008.

[47] Heron, Mechanik 2,1-5; Cotterell – Kamminga 1990, 74-101.

[48] Moritz 1958; White 1984, 63-67.

[49] Vgl. Anth. Gr. 9,19-21; Apul. met. 9,13,1-2. Vgl. die Abbildungen bei Zimmer 1982, Nr. 18-25.

[50] Vitr. 10,5,2; Moritz 1958, 131-139; Wikander 2008, 141-152; Spain 2008.

[51] Edict. Diocl. 15,52-55.

Provinzen wurde jedoch eine beachtliche Zahl von Wassermühlen archäologisch nachgewiesen.[52]

Die Römer waren durchaus in der Lage, größere Anlagen zu errichten, in denen die Wasserkraft effizient genutzt wurde. Bei Arelate (Arles in Südfrankreich) existierte an einem Hang ein in der Zeit des Traianus errichteter Mühlenkomplex, der das Wasser von einem Aquädukt erhielt und insgesamt 16 Mühlräder hatte. In Rom erhielten die Mühlen am Abhang des Ianiculum ebenfalls Wasser aus einem Aquädukt; ein Erlass aus dem Jahr 398 verbot es, dieses Wasser für andere Zwecke als dem Mahlen von Getreide zu nutzen.[53] Eminent folgenreich war eine in einer Notsituation der Gotenkriege erfolgte Maßnahme des Belisarios; als die Goten bei der Belagerung Roms im Jahr 537 die Wasserzufuhr für die Wassermühlen am Ianiculum unterbrachen, ließ Belisarios an den Tiberbrücken Wassermühlen auf Schiffen installieren. Damit konnte sich die Mühle ohne Probleme an den wechselnden Wasserstand des Flusses anpassen.[54] Solche Schiffsmühlen existierten auf dem Tiber bis zum 19. Jahrhundert, sie erwiesen sich in den größeren europäischen Städten des Späten Mittelalters und der Frühen Neuzeit als unentbehrlich für das Mahlen von Getreide. Die mittelalterliche Mühlentechnik reicht so bis in die römische Zeit zurück.

In der Spätantike wurde die Wasserkraft außerdem für das Schneiden von Marmor eingesetzt. Dazu war es notwendig, die Rotation des Wasserrades in die hin- und hergehende Bewegung der Marmorsäge umzuwandeln, ein Mechanismus, der für einen Nebenfluss der Mosel und für Kleinasien nachgewiesen ist; Grund für den Einsatz solcher Marmorsägen in der Moselgegend während des 4. Jahrhunderts war sicherlich der repräsentative Ausbau der Residenz Trier.[55]

Ein weiterer Aspekt der technischen und zivilisatorischen Entwicklungen im Imperium Romanum verdient Beachtung: Durch die Expansion Roms und durch die Einrichtung von Provinzen in West- und Mitteleuropa fanden die zivilisatorischen Errungenschaften der griechisch-römischen Welt auf der Iberischen Halbinsel, in Gallien, im rechtsrheinischen Germanien, in den nördlich der Alpen und südlich der Donau gelegenen Regionen sowie in Britannien eine rasche Verbreitung. Dieser wesentlich von Rom gesteuerte Prozess bedeutete die vollständige Übernahme des im mediterranen Raum existierenden technischen Standards; wesentliches Moment dieser Anpassung war die Urbanisierung.[56] Es handelte sich hierbei aber eben nicht um Erfindungen und Innovationen, sondern um einen umfassenden Techniktransfer, der die betroffenen Gebiete jedoch tiefgreifend verändert hat. Daneben hat es aber auch immer wieder

---

[52] Wikander 1984.

[53] Leveau 1996; Wikander 2008, 149-150. Die Mühlen am Ianiculum: Cod. Theod. 14,15,4; Prok. BG 1,19,8-10.

[54] Prok. BG 1,19,8-27.

[55] Auson. Mos. 361-364. Vgl. ferner Ritti – Grewe – Kessener 2007; Wikander 2008, 150-151. Zum Schneiden von Marmor vgl. Plin. nat. 36,47; 36,50-51. Ein Mechanismus für die Umwandlung der Rotationsbewegung in eine hin- und hergehende Bewegung wurde bereits im Automatentheater Herons, das auf Philon von Byzanz zurückgeht, beschrieben (peri automatopoietikes 24), die Nutzung im Wirtschaftsleben setzte aber erst mit der wassergetriebenen Marmorsäge ein.

[56] Dieser Prozess wird in klassischer Weise von Tac. Agr. 21 beschrieben. Vgl. auch Cass. Dio 56,18,2; Strab. 3,2,15.

technische Errungenschaften gegeben, die keine Verbreitung im Imperium Romanum fanden, sondern regional begrenzt blieben. Dies gilt gerade für Gallien.

Regional begrenzte Innovationen: Gallien

Gallien war seit dem 1. Jahrhundert n. Chr. eine Region, die von zwei unterschiedlichen Entwicklungen geprägt worden ist: Nach der Eroberung durch Caesar und der Einrichtung der gallischen Provinzen gründeten die Römer Städte, die meist die für eine römische Stadt charakteristischen Bauwerke und Strukturen wie das Straßensystem, Forum, Circus, Theater und Wasserleitung aufwiesen, es wurden wie in Italien Fernstraßen angelegt, die eine Verbindung zu den Legionsstandorten am Rhein und zum Mittelmeerraum herstellten. Die Centuriation strukturierte die ländlichen Gebiete. Es kam zur Übernahme des Weinbaus zunächst im Süden; zur Zeit des Ausonius prägten dann Weinberge die Landschaft an der Mosel, und die Wein- und Olivenpressen entsprachen dem Standard in Italien.[57] Die in Süd- und Mittelgallien gelegenen Töpfereien, die teilweise von den Werkstätten in Arezzo gegründet worden waren, produzierten nach deren Vorbild Terra Sigillata für lokale und überregionale Märkte. Damit verwandelte sich das keltische Gallien in eine weitgehend von der römischen Zivilisation geprägte Region. Gleichzeitig aber gab es in den gallischen Provinzen eigenständige technische Entwicklungen, die im Mittelmeerraum keine Verbreitung fanden.

Plinius geht an mehreren Stellen auf die agrartechnischen Neuerungen in den gallischen Provinzen und in der Provinz Raetia ein und führt sie zum Teil auf naturräumliche Gegebenheiten zurück.[58] So erwies sich der einfache, in Griechenland und Italien übliche Pflug, der den Boden nur aufriss, aber nicht wendete, für das Pflügen der schweren Böden, die sich erheblich von den leichten Böden im mediterranen Raum unterschieden, als wenig geeignet. Aus diesem Grund setzte man einen Räderpflug ein, der von mehreren Ochsengespannen gezogen wurde. Die Pflugschar war so breit, dass der Boden gewendet wurde.[59]

Das gallische Mähgerät erleichterte in Nordgallien und *Germania inferior* die Getreideernte deutlich. Ein Tier, meist wohl ein Esel oder ein Pferd, schob einen vorn geöffneten Kasten, der an den Schmalseiten Räder hatte und an der Vorderseite mit einer Reihe Greifzähne ausgestattet war, über das Feld; das Tier ging zwischen den hinten angebrachten Stangen. Die Ähren wurden beim Voranschreiten von den Halmen abgerissen und fielen in den Kasten.[60] Die archäologischen Zeugnisse lassen vermuten, dass das gallische Mähgerät in einer eng umgrenzten Region, in den ländlichen Gegenden an der Straße zwischen Durocotorum (Reims) und Confluentes (Koblenz), verbreitet war; Plinius hebt hervor, dass das Gerät bei Ernten auf den großen Landgütern in Gallien eingesetzt wurde.[61] Es gibt verschiedene Ansätze zu einer Erklärung für diesen Tatbestand: B. D. Shaw weist in seiner umfassenden Analyse aller Zeugnisse vor allem auf die Eigenschaften des Getreides hin: „The crop that the reaping machine was designed to harvest,

---

[57] Brun 1986, 59-136.

[58] Plin. nat. 18,172 (Räderpflug); 18,296-297 (Gallisches Mähgerät).

[59] Shaw 2013, 122.

[60] Plin. nat. 18,296; Pall. agric. 7,2,3-4; Shaw 2013, 93-120. Vgl. Colum. 2,20,3: Ernte mit Mähgabeln oder Kämmen; hiervon ist die Konstruktion des gallischen Mähgerätes vielleicht angeregt worden.

[61] Shaw 2013, 110.

probably spelt, was well adapted to the peculiar stripping action of its teeth, and vice versa."[62] Es ist ferner denkbar, dass das gallische Mähgerät auch auf lokale Traditionen in der Ernte zurückging, denn die Reihe der Zähne an der Vorderseite wirkte ähnlich wie der bei Plinius erwähnte Handkamm, mit dem in Gallien Hirse geerntet wurde; Columella erklärt, dass diese Methode des Erntens auch bei dünn gesätem Getreide möglich war.[63] Die Verhältnisse in Gallien, ein Mangel an Arbeitskräften in der Erntezeit und eine Witterung, die eine rasche Durchführung der Ernte notwendig macht,[64] haben wahrscheinlich die Konstruktion und den Einsatz des gallischen Mähgerätes begünstigt. Außerdem berichtet Plinius, dass in Gallien beim Heuschnitt größere Sicheln als in Italien verwendet wurden.[65]

Der Räderpflug und das Mähgerät waren nicht die einzigen Innovationen im römischen Gallien: Daneben sind auch Veränderungen in der Transporttechnik zu erkennen, die durch eine größere Zahl von Reliefs für Gallien gut dokumentiert sind.[66] In den nordwestlichen Provinzen stand die römische Verwaltung vor der Aufgabe, große Binnenräume politisch und wirtschaftlich zu erschließen. Zu diesem Zweck wurde der Straßen- und Brückenbau in den Provinzen forciert und so ein Straßensystem geschaffen, das nur geringe Steigungen und selten enge Kurven aufwies; das Pflaster verhinderte bei starken Regenfällen ein Einsinken von Zugtieren und Rädern.[67] Unter diesen Bedingungen hat sich die Anschirrung von Pferden im Transportwesen in größerem Umfang durchgesetzt; die Reliefs zeigen von Pferden gezogene schwere Wagen mit zwei Achsen und Speichenrädern, wobei das Joch durch eine neue Form der Anschirrung ersetzt wurde. Wie ein Relief zeigt, war es sogar möglich geworden, zwei Paar Pferde hintereinander anzuschirren; auf einigen Reliefs ist ein vor einem zweirädrigen Wagen angespanntes Pferd zu sehen, das zwischen den Stangen geht. Die Differenz zwischen Gallien und der mediterranen Welt wird deutlich bei einem Vergleich zwischen den schweren Wagen mit Speichenrädern auf den Straßen Galliens und den von Ochsen gezogenen Karren mit den massiven Scheibenrädern, wie sie etwa auf dem Sarkophag des Lucius Annius Octavius Valerianus oder auf den Mosaiken in der Villa Piazza Armerina auf Sizilien dargestellt werden.[68]

Eine andere Neuerung im Transportwesen der nordwestlichen Provinzen und auch Norditaliens war die Verwendung von Holzfässern anstelle der im mediterranen Raum gebräuchlichen Amphoren als Flüssigkeitscontainer; sicherlich hängt dies mit dem Holzreichtum Galliens und der hochentwickelten Technik der Holzbearbeitung bei den Galliern zusammen. Große Weinfässer wurden mit Pferd und Wagen über Land transportiert. Ein Vorteil der Holzfässer bestand darin, dass sie über kurze Distanzen gerollt werden konnten, also nicht wie Amphoren getragen wer-

---

[62] Shaw 2013, 141. Vgl. 138.

[63] Plin. nat. 18,297; Colum. 2,20,3; Shaw 2013, 139.

[64] Vgl. dazu Colum. 2,201-2 zur Notwendigkeit, das Getreide auch im mediterranen Raum zeitig und schnell zu ernten. Gegenüber Italien hat sich der Zeitpunkt der Ernte allerdings verschoben; vgl. Shaw 2013, 117-120.

[65] Plin. nat. 18,261; Shaw 2013, 123-129.

[66] White 1984, 127-140; Raepsaet 2002.

[67] Quilici 2008. Zum Ausbau des Straßennetzes in Gallien unter Augustus vgl. Strab. 4,6,11.

[68] Raepsaet 2002; Raepsaet 2008; Relief aus Langres; Abb. bei White 1984, 130. Reliefs mit Einspännern, Abb. bei Schneider 1991, 250. Der Sarkophag des Lucius Annius Octavius befindet sich im Vatikan. Eine Zeichnung der Reliefs: Rostovtzeff 1957, 196.

den mussten, was beim Beladen von Schiffen ohne Zweifel eine Erleichterung der Arbeit mit sich brachte.[69]

Die Flüsse wurden in Gallien für die Binnenschifffahrt genutzt, wobei es typisch war, dass die Boote bei Fahrten stromaufwärts getreidelt wurden; Menschen zogen hier den Treidelkahn. Für die Flussschiffe sind auch neue Konstruktionsmerkmale feststellbar: Aus Köln stammt ein Relief mit der Darstellung eines Rheinschiffes mit einem Hecksteuerruder. Die Bauweise veränderte sich ebenfalls; bei den Booten am Rhein wurden anders als im Mittelmeerraum Eisennägel verwendet, um die Planken an den Spanten zu befestigen.[70]

Die Summe der in antiken Texten erwähnten oder durch archäologische Funde belegten Innovationen in den verschiedenen Bereichen der Wirtschaft und in den verschiedenen Regionen des Imperium Romanum lässt das Bild einer Gesellschaft entstehen, die Neuerungen keineswegs ablehnte, sondern eher über ein erhebliches Innovationspotential verfügte. Unter diesen Voraussetzungen ist zu fragen, ob wirtschaftliche Erwägungen, etwa der Wunsch, möglichst hohe Erträge und Einkommen zu erzielen, Einfluss auf Investitionen und Innovationen hatten und wie Innovationen beurteilt wurden.

Gewinnstreben, Investitionen und Innovationen im Agrarbereich

Es fehlen eindeutige Zeugnisse darüber, welche wirtschaftlichen Ziele in römischer Zeit mit Investitionen und Innovationen verbunden waren. Die ausführlichste Berechnung von Kosten, Erträgen und Gewinn, das Kapitel über den Weinbau bei Columella, geht auf Innovationen nicht ein, sondern berechnet die Kosten und Erträge einer Weinpflanzung und vergleicht den erzielten Gewinn mit dem im Geldverleih sowie in anderen Zweigen der Landwirtschaft.[71] Römische Gutsbesitzer waren primär an hohen Einnahmen interessiert, zugleich besaßen sie ein ausgeprägtes Kostenbewusstsein. Materieller Erfolg in der Landwirtschaft beruhte nach Meinung der Agrarschriftsteller neben dem Wissen und der Erfahrung des Landbesitzers auf zwei Faktoren, auf Arbeit und den Einsatz guter Geräte.[72] Varro nennt in seiner Aufzählung der Voraussetzungen für ein ertragsreiches Wirtschaften ausdrücklich die Gerätschaften und widmet dementsprechend dem *instrumentum* längere Ausführungen.[73]

Welchen Wert ein Großgrundbesitzer auf den Kauf und die sachgemäße Installation von neuen Geräten legte, zeigen die Abschnitte über Weinpressen und über das *trapetum* bei Cato.[74] Detailreich werden die Einzelteile und die Konstruktion von Weinpressen und der Ölmühle (*trape-*

---

[69] Norditalien: Strab. 5,1,8; 5,1,12; Plin. nat. 14,132; 16,50. Berühmt ist das Trierer Relief von einem Moselschiff, das Weinfässer geladen hat: Abb. bei Schneider 1991, Abb. 110. Transport eines großen Weinfasses mit einem Wagen: Relief aus Langres, Abb. bei White 1984, 133. Vgl. ferner ein Mainzer Relief, das zeigt, wie ein Schiff mit Weinfässern beladen wird: Schneider 1991, Abb. 116. Beladen eines Schiffes mit einer Amphore: Mosaik aus Ostia, Abb. bei White 1984, 154.

[70] Pferdehirt 1995, 26-36. Vgl. die Abbildungen Schneider 1991, Abb. 111-113.

[71] Colum. 3,3; Duncan-Jones 1974, 33-59.

[72] Wissen und Erfahrung des Gutsbesitzers: Varro rust. 1,1,11; 1,5,3; 1,18,8. Columella erwähnt zu Beginn seiner Ausführungen prägnant *prudentia rei, facultas inpendendi, voluntas agendi* (Colum. 1,1,1).

[73] Varro rust. 1,5,3; 1,22 (*instrumentum mutum*). Vgl. Colum. 1,8,8.

[74] Cato agr. 18-22.

tum) beschrieben, wobei auch genaue Arbeitsanweisungen gegeben werden; so soll ein Schmied alle Eisenteile an der Ölmühle anbringen. Cato listet im Abschnitt über den Drehbaum (*cupa*) die Kosten für Herstellung und Installation auf; die Arbeit des Schmiedes kostet 60 Sesterzen, das benötigte Blei kann für 4 Sesterzen gekauft werden und die Herstellung des Drehbaums sowie die damit zusammenhängenden Arbeiten werden mit 8 Sesterzen berechnet, zusammen sind nach Cato also 72 Sesterzen aufzuwenden. Nicht berücksichtigt werden dabei die Hilfskräfte (*adiutores*).

Das Kostenbewusstsein Catos findet seinen Ausdruck gerade in der Aufstellung der Kosten für eine Ölmühle. Cato bietet hier eine Alternative: Im nähergelegenen Suessa beträgt der Preis für das *trapetum* 400 Sesterzen und 50 Pfund Öl, die am Schluss in Sesterzen umgerechnet werden. Hinzu kommen die Kosten für die Montierung (40 HS), der Transport für sechs Tage und sechs Fuhrleute (172 HS), für den Drehbaum (72 Sesterzen) und schließlich für das Öl (25 HS), insgesamt also 729 Sesterzen. In Pompeii kann das gesamte *trapetum* für 384 Sesterzen gekauft werden, dafür sind aber die Kosten für den Transport wesentlich höher; sie betragen 280 Sesterzen, hinzu kommt der Aufbau der Ölmühle auf dem Gut mit 60 Sesterzen. Der Gesamtpreis liegt in diesem Fall bei 724 Sesterzen. Darüber hinaus gibt Cato noch den Preis für zwei Läufersteine an, die für eine alte Ölmühle als Ersatz für untauglich gewordene Läufersteine erworben werden. Die können in Rufri Maceriae oder in Pompeii für 180 Sesterzen gekauft werden, wobei für die Installation 30 Sesterzen aufzuwenden sind.[75]

Es gibt keinen Hinweis drauf, dass Cato aufgrund dieser Investitionen eine Steigerung der Erträge oder des Gewinns erwartete. Ferner bleibt unklar, ob es sich bei der beschriebenen Ölpresse und Ölmühle um das damals in Mittelitalien übliche Inventar eines Landgutes oder um neue Geräte handelte. Columella hält eine hinreichende Anzahl von Geräten für notwendig, um zu verhindern, dass die Sklaven ihre Arbeit wegen fehlender Geräte oder Werkzeuge unterbrechen. Obwohl er der Ausstattung eines Landgutes mit Gerätschaften für den Ackerbau und die Erzeugung von Wein und Olivenöl größere Aufmerksamkeit widmete, geht er auf Verbesserungen und technische Neuerungen nicht ein.[76] Die Geräte zum Auspressen der Oliven werden aufgeführt und in Hinsicht auf ihre Effizienz verglichen, aber Neuerungen werden nicht erwähnt.[77]

Unter den römischen Autoren ist es vor allem Plinius, der auf Innovationen eingeht. In dem Abschnitt über die Pressen gibt er einen Überblick über die zeitliche Abfolge der verschiedenen Typen der Weinpresse; ausdrücklich wird gesagt, dass die *antiqui*, Menschen früherer Zeiten, die Seilwindenpresse verwendeten, dass dann vor einhundert Jahren (also in augusteischer Zeit) die Schraubenpresse und zuletzt vor 22 Jahren die kleine Schraubenpresse erfunden (*inventa/inventum*) worden sei. Den Vorteil der kleinen Schraubenpresse sieht Plinius darin, dass sie auch in einem kleineren Kelterhaus aufgestellt werden kann. Die Entwicklung der Pressen in der römischen Landwirtschaft hat Plinius auf diese Weise kurz, aber präzise nachgezeichnet.[78] Im Fall des Räderpfluges spricht Plinius davon, dass dieses Gerät erst kurze Zeit zuvor erfunden

---

[75] Cato agr. 22.

[76] Colum. 1,8,8; 11,1,20; 12,52,9.

[77] Colum. 12,52,6-7. Vgl. 12,51,2.

[78] Plin. nat. 8,317. Zum Text vgl. oben Anm. 21. Vitruvius (Vitr. 6,6,3) weiß zwar, dass bei dem Bau eines Kelterhauses für eine Seilwindenpresse mehr Platz benötigt wird als für eine Schraubenpresse, geht auf diesen Sachverhalt aber nicht näher ein.

worden sei (*non pridem inventum*). Der Nutzen dieses Pfluges besteht nach Ansicht von Plinius darin, dass er beim Pflügen eines neuen Ackers ganze Rasenstücke wendet; es konnte dann sogleich gesät werden, das Jäten des Ackers entfiel. Allerdings mussten vor diesem Pflug mehrere Paar Ochsen angespannt werden.[79]

Heron gibt eindeutige Kriterien an, um die verschiedenen Pressen zu bewerten. Seiner Ansicht nach werden die Unfallgefahren, die im Betrieb der Pressen gegeben sind, durch die Schraubenpresse deutlich reduziert.[80] Die Arbeit wird ferner erleichtert durch ein Galeagra genanntes Holzgerüst, das die zuvor gebräuchlichen Netze und Körbe ersetzt und das Pressgut aufnimmt.[81] Die Schraubenpresse, bei der durch Drehen der Schrauben direkt Druck auf das Pressgut ausgeübt wird, ist kleiner als die Pressen mit einem langen Pressbaum; wie Heron betont, ist sie leicht zu handhaben, sie kann überdies mit geringem Aufwand transportiert und an jedem beliebigen Ort aufgestellt werden.[82]

Eine bemerkenswerte Feststellung des Plinius verweist für die Frage, welche Geräte oder Verfahren bei der Ernte eingesetzt werden, auf die Größe der Ernten und das Arbeitskräftepotential: „*ritus diversos magnitudo facit messium et caritas operarum.*"[83] Palladius hat diese Sicht in der Spätantike wiederholt und angemerkt, das Mähgerät ersetze die Arbeit von Menschen durch einen einzigen Ochsen und verkürze die Erntezeit.[84] Indirekt nimmt Palladius damit an, dass das Gallische Mähgerät eine erheblich höhere Produktivität hatte als die konventionellen Erntemethoden mit der Sichel.

Eine Ersparnis an Arbeit oder an Zeit (*maioris conpendii*) wird nach Plinius in Gallien bei der Heuernte durch die Verwendung einer größeren Sichel erzielt.[85] Der Einsatz von Dreschschlitten beim Dreschen des Getreides hängt nach Columella wiederum von der verfügbaren Zahl an Arbeitstieren ab. Die Empfehlung, einen Dreschschlitten zu nutzen, gibt Columella nur unter der Bedingung, dass zu wenig Ochsen vorhanden sind, sonst soll das Korn auf der Tenne durch Pferde oder Ochsen ausgetreten werden. Aus der höheren Arbeitsleistung der Dreschschlitten folgt also keineswegs ein Vorschlag für einen generellen Einsatz dieses Gerätes.[86]

Es ist ein auffallender Tatbestand, dass Vitruvius die Wassermühle exakt beschreibt und technisch überzeugend als ein Gerät, das dieselben Komponenten wie das Wasserschöpfrad aufweist, einordnet,[87] mit keinem Wort auf dessen Bedeutung für die Wirtschaft und die Arbeitswelt eingeht. Zuerst hat ein Dichter in einem Epigramm die Wassermühle gerühmt, weil sie die menschliche Muskelkraft ersetzte und so die Frauen von einer Arbeit befreite,[88] die aus antiker wie auch aus heutiger Sicht nur als monoton und körperlich anstrengend bezeichnet werden

---

[79] Plin. nat. 18,172.

[80] Heron, Mechanik 3,15.

[81] Heron, Mechanik 3,16.

[82] Heron, Mechanik 3,19.

[83] Plin. nat. 18,300. Vgl. Shaw 2013, 129.

[84] Pall. agric. 7,2,2; 7,2,4. Shaw 2013, 107-109.

[85] Plin. nat. 18,261.

[86] Colum. 2,20,4. Vgl. auch die Bemerkungen von Varro rust. 1,52.

[87] Vitr. 10,5,2: '*Eadem ratione etiam versantur hydraletae, in quibus eadem sunt omnia.*'

[88] Anth. Gr. 9,418. Das Epigramm stammt aus augusteischer Zeit.

kann.⁸⁹ Nach Palladius ist die Verbindung der Bäder mit einer Wassermühle nützlich, weil die Mühle mit den Abwässern angetrieben werden konnte. Auf diese Weise war es möglich, Getreide ohne tierische oder menschliche Arbeit zu mahlen.⁹⁰

Die Frage, welche Erträge in der Landwirtschaft erzielt werden konnten, bestimmte die Diskussion über die Hoftierhaltung (*pastio villatica*), die bei Cato nur eine geringe Rolle gespielt hatte⁹¹ und der Varro als einem eigenen Zweig der Gutswirtschaft ein ganzes Buch seiner Schrift über die Landwirtschaft gewidmet hat.⁹² Hier werden Motive und Interessenlage von Großgrundbesitzern wie selten sonst transparent, denn die Dialogform dieser Schrift gibt Varro die Gelegenheit, einerseits Gutsbesitzer die Vorteile der *pastio villatica* erläutern zu lassen und andererseits die Reaktion der Gesprächspartner, ebenfalls Gutsbesitzer, die aber mit der Hoftierhaltung nicht vertraut waren, zu schildern. In diesem Gespräch werden die Erträge einiger Landgüter genau angegeben, um die ökonomische Überlegenheit der *pastio villatica* durch einen Vergleich mit der konventionellen Villenwirtschaft zu erweisen; bemerkenswert sind vor allem die Äußerungen des Senators Q. Axius, der selbst ein Gutsbesitzer war, der aber über keine Kenntnisse der *pastio villatica* verfügte.

Das Gespräch beginnt mit einer Diskussion über ein Gut des M. Seius bei Ostia;⁹³ Der Augur Appius Claudius will dieses Landgut kaufen, obgleich es weder mit Anlagen für die Erzeugung von Wein und Olivenöl noch mit Gemälden oder Statuen ausgestattet ist.⁹⁴ Es wird zwischen der Viehzucht (*pastio agrestis*) und der Hoftierhaltung (*pastio villatica*) unterschieden, die zuvor nur von Mago und seinem griechischen Übersetzer Cassius Dionysios, allerdings unzusammenhängend und unsystematisch behandelt worden war, Texte, die M. Seius gelesen zu haben scheint.⁹⁵ Die *pastio villatica* war zu dem Zeitpunkt des Gespräches⁹⁶ noch nicht lange in Italien eingeführt, stellte demnach innerhalb der Landwirtschaft eine Neuerung dar. Auf dem Landgut des Seius wurden große Scharen von Gänsen, Hühnern, Tauben, Kranichen, Pfauen gehalten, außerdem Siebenschläfer, Fische, Keiler und anderes Jagdwild. Im Kern handelte es sich um eine Geflügelzucht, die durch die Haltung von kleinen Säugetieren wie den Siebenschläfern, durch Fischteiche und Wildgehege ergänzt wurde.⁹⁷

Das wichtigste Argument, das bereits zu Beginn des Gespräches zugunsten der *pastio villatica* vorgebracht wird, sind deren Erträge, die höher sein sollen als die Erträge ganzer Besitzungen.⁹⁸ Um dieses Argument zu erhärten, wird die Aussage des Verwalters zitiert, dass auf dem Gut des M. Seius im Jahr mehr als 50.000 Sesterzen erwirtschaftet werden. Als Axius sein Erstaunen über diese Summe zum Ausdruck bringt, wird ihm ein Beispiel für die Erträge der Geflügelzucht

---

⁸⁹ Die klassische Formulierung findet sich bei Hom. Od. 20,105-119.

⁹⁰ Pall. agric. 1,41: '*sine animalium vel hominum labore frumenta frangatur.*'

⁹¹ Cato agr. 89-90 (Geflügelmast).

⁹² Varro rust. 3. Vgl. Diederich 2007, 352-364.

⁹³ Varro rust. 3,2,7. Zu M. Seius vgl. Cic. off. 2,58. M. Seius war 74 v. Chr. Aedil gewesen.

⁹⁴ Varro rust. 3,2,7-8.

⁹⁵ Varro rust. 3,2,13.

⁹⁶ Vgl. zum Zeitpunkt des Dialoges Flach 2002, 29-33.

⁹⁷ Varro rust. 3,2,14.

⁹⁸ Varro rust. 3,2,13.

präsentiert: Ein Landgut an der *via Salaria* verkaufte für ein Festessen 5000 Drosseln zu einem Stückpreis von 12 Sesterzen; die Einnahme des Gutes betrug also aus diesem einen Verkauf 60.000 Sesterzen, damit zweimal soviel wie das Landgut des Axius bei Reate einbrachte. Als Axius an einen Scherz glaubt, wird ihm ein weiteres Beispiel genannt: Auf dem Landgut des Lucius Abuccius bei Alba wird mit dem Ackerbau weniger als mit der *pastio villatica* erwirtschaftet; als Beträge werden 10.000 Sesterzen für die Feldwirtschaft und 20.000 Sesterzen für die Hoftierhaltung genannt.[99]

Erträge und Preise werden im einzelnen für die Pfauenzucht aufgeführt; so wird Aufidius Lurco erwähnt, dessen Pfauenzucht 60.000 Sesterzen im Jahr einbrachte. M. Seius ließ Küken großziehen und verkaufte sie zu einem Preis von 200 Sesterzen das Stück. Nachdem Hortensius bei einem Festessen aus Anlass seiner Aufnahme in das Kollegium der Auguren als Geflügel das Fleisch von Pfauen auftragen ließ, wurden der Pfau als Speise und die Pfauenzucht schnell Mode, und die Preise schnellten in die Höhe: Eier wurden für 20 Sesterzen und Pfauen selbst für 200 Sesterzen verkauft. Eine Herde von einhundert Pfauen konnte unter diesen Voraussetzungen einen Ertrag von 40.000 Sesterzen im Jahr einbringen, L. Abuccius rechnete so mit einem Ertrag von 60.000 Sesterzen.[100]

Tauben wurden ebenfalls in großer Zahl gehalten; für ein Taubenhaus werden 5000 Tauben genannt. Auch in diesem Fall erwähnt Varro hohe Preise: 200 Sesterzen für ein Taubenpaar von schöner Färbung und aus guter Zucht und 1000 Sesterzen für außergewöhnliche Exemplare.[101] Große Herden von Gänsen besaßen Scipio Metellus und M. Seius.[102] Zuletzt findet sich auch eine Angabe zur Imkerei; Varro berichtet über zwei Brüder, die nur einen kleinen Hof erbten, dann aber Bienenstöcke aufstellten und auf dem Feld Thymian und Klee säten. Sie konnten den auf diese Weise gewonnenen Honig für 10.000 Sesterzen verkaufen.[103]

Den Abschluss des dritten Buches bilden die Ausführungen über die Fischteiche. Während Varro bislang nur die Erträge und Preise erwähnt, werden an dieser Stelle Erträge und Kosten gegenübergestellt. Prononciert meint Axius, dass die mit Salzwasser gefüllten *piscinae* der *nobiles*, der führenden Senatoren, eher die Geldbörse des Besitzers leeren als dass sie diese anfüllen, denn die Kosten für die Anlage solcher Teiche und für ihren Unterhalt seien extrem hoch. Hier wird das Beispiel des C. Lucilius Hirrus angeführt, der zwar 12.000 Sesterzen einnimmt, aber diese Einnahmen wiederum für das Futter ausgibt. Aufwand und Ertrag stehen so ökonomisch gesehen in keinem vernünftigen Verhältnis. Wie der Fall des Q. Hortensius zeigt, waren die reichen Besitzer der Teiche für Seefische auch nicht primär an hohen Erträgen interessiert, sie betrachteten ihre Fische weniger als eine ökonomische Investition, sondern vielmehr als einen kultivierten Zeitvertreib. Das schließt nicht aus, dass im Einzelfall große Mengen Fisch zu Festessen geliefert werden konnten oder dass Villen, die über große Fischteiche verfügten, beim Verkauf hohe Preise erzielten. So soll Hirrus seine Villa für 4 Mio. Sesterzen verkauft haben.[104]

---

[99] Varro rust. 3,2,14-17.
[100] Varro rust. 3,6.
[101] Varro rust. 3,7.
[102] Varro rust. 3,10,1.
[103] Varro rust. 3,16,10-11.
[104] Varro rust. 3,17,2-9.

Die Fischteiche stellen eine Lektion in ökonomischen Denken dar: Die Erträge müssen in Relation zu den Kosten gesehen werden; unter diesem Gesichtspunkt sind kostenaufwendige Teiche für Seefische ökonomisch nicht sinnvoll, im Gegensatz zu den Fischteichen für Süßwasserfische. In der Dichtung werden derartige sinnlose Investitionen im Agrarbereich, die Luxusbedürfnisse befriedigen, aber keine Erträge bringen, verspottet:

Der firmanische Landbesitz, Mentula, gilt nicht zu Unrecht
Für ein kostbares Gut, schließt er doch Herrliches ein:
Vogelfang, alle Fische und Wiesen, Felder und Tiere –
Aber umsonst, der Ertrag wird durch die Kosten verzehrt.[105]

Zusammenfassend muss festgestellt werden, dass in den Texten über Innovationen in der Landwirtschaft kein Versuch unternommen wird, den durch neue Geräte oder Verfahren erzielten Produktivitätszuwachs quantitativ zu erfassen. Cato beschreibt die teuren Pressen und das *trapetum* exakt und gibt auch Preise an, es werden jedoch keine Erwartungen, die an solche Investitionen gestellt werden, formuliert. Bei Plinius ist ein Interesse an technischen Neuerungen im Agrarbereich erkennbar, die Frage nach den Kosten und der Produktivität wird allerdings nicht ansatzweise diskutiert. Immerhin werden die Vorteile einiger Geräte genannt: Heron weist auf die Verringerung von Unfallgefahren durch die Schraubenpresse hin, und das gallische Mähgerät spart nach Palladius menschliche Arbeitskraft ein. Erst in der Darstellung der *pastio villatica* wird klar formuliert, dass in diesem neuen Zweig der Landwirtschaft höhere Erträge erzielt werden können als in der traditionellen Gutswirtschaft, aber es wird keine Relation zwischen den Erträgen und den Kosten in beiden Zweigen der Landwirtschaft hergestellt. Es gab zweifellos Innovationen in der römischen Landwirtschaft, es fehlte jedoch das Bewusstsein von der Bedeutung eines Prozesses permanenter Innovationen. Die Antike besaß noch nicht das auf die Zukunft gerichtete Pathos der Philosophie von Francis Bacon oder von René Descartes, die Auffassung nämlich, dass die Vermehrung des Wissens und die damit verbundenen zivilisatorischen Fortschritte zur Wohlfahrt der Menschheit beitragen könnten.

Die *res publica* und die *societates*: Der Bergbau

Mit der Eroberung der an der Mittelmeerküste gelegenen Regionen der Iberischen Halbinsel im Zweiten Punischen Krieg und der Einrichtung der hispanischen Provinzen erlangte die römische Republik den Zugriff auf die ehemals karthagischen Bergwerke und auf die größten und ertragreichsten Metallvorkommen des Mittelmeerraumes.[106] Mit der Einnahme von Carthago Nova, wo Silber abgebaut wurde, begann fast gleichzeitig die Prägung des *denarius*, der im 2. und 1. Jahrhundert v. Chr. die wichtigste römische Silbermünze war.[107] Die Römer waren gewillt, ihre Herrschaft auf der Iberischen Halbinsel auch gegen den offenen Widerstand der einheimischen Bevölkerung zu behaupten. Ihre wirtschaftlichen Interessen finden signifikanten Ausdruck in den Maßnahmen des Consuls M. Porcius Cato, der unmittelbar nach Befriedung

---

[105] Catull. 114.

[106] Diod. 5,35,1; Strab. 3,2,8-3,2,11; 3,2,14; 3,4,2; Plin. nat. 3,30; 4,112; 33,36; 37,20. Vgl. Davies 1935, 94. Ähnlich Craddock 2008, 95. Zu einem Silberbergwerk der Karthager, das jeden Tag 300 Pfund Silber (ca. 98 Kilogramm; das entspricht einer Jahresproduktion von über 35.000 Kilogramm oder 35 Tonnen) geliefert haben soll, vgl. Plin. nat. 33,96-97.

[107] Wolters 1999, 13-21.

der Provinz Hispania citerior 195 v. Chr. eine neue Besteuerung der Eisen- und Silberbergwerke einführte, wodurch der Reichtum der Provinz ständig angewachsen sein soll.[108] In der folgenden Zeit intensivierten die Römer den Abbau von Metallen, zunächst vor allem von Kupfer und Silber. Welche Bedeutung der Silberbergbau für die römischen Finanzen hatte, verdeutlicht die Bemerkung des Polybios, die Silberbergwerke allein bei Carthago Nova, in denen 40.000 Menschen arbeiteten, hätten der Republik im 2. Jahrhundert täglich 25.000 Denare eingebracht, was auf das Jahr umgerechnet 9,125 Mio. Denaren oder ca. 34 Tonnen Silber entspricht, eine Angabe, die einen ungefähren Eindruck von dem Umfang der Edelmetallförderung in den spanischen Provinzen vermittelt.[109]

Die Ausbeutung der Metallvorkommen und die Gewinnung von Edelmetallen auf der Iberischen Halbinsel war in der Zeit der Republik und des frühen Principats mit einer großen Zahl technischer Innovationen verbunden.[110] Zunächst betrifft dies das System der Stollen; im Gegensatz zur älteren Vorgehensweise, bei der zahlreiche Schächte in geringer Entfernung voneinander abgeteuft wurden und die Stollen entsprechend nur eine geringe Länge aufwiesen, haben die Römer umfangreiche Stollensysteme geschaffen. Dabei erreichten sie Tiefen von über 100 Metern.[111] Die Förderung von Erz mit mechanischen Hilfsmitteln, vor allem mit der Seilwinde, scheint weit verbreitet gewesen zu sein.[112] Da in den römischen Bergwerken auf der Iberischen Halbinsel Edelmetalle unter dem Grundwasserspiegel abgebaut wurden, war eine effiziente Wasserhaltung erforderlich.[113] Zu diesem Zweck wurde in der Zeit der Republik die Archimedische Schraube eingesetzt. Es handelte sich hierbei um einen Techniktransfer, denn dieses Wasserschöpfgerät ersetzte zunächst im hellenistischen Ägypten den Schaduf bei der Bewässerung von Feldern. Durch die Kombination mehrerer solcher Geräte war es möglich, das Grubenwasser zum Ausgang der Bergwerke zu leiten.[114] Eine größere Effizienz als die Archimedische Schraube hatten die großen Wasserschöpfräder, die einen Durchmesser von über vier Metern erreichten. Im südspanischen Bergwerk Rio Tinto waren solche Wasserschöpfräder in acht Paaren aufgestellt, so dass das Wasser hier um ca. 29 Meter gehoben werden konnte. Da es nicht möglich war, diese großen Schöpfräder durch die engen Stollen zum Platz ihrer Aufstellung zu

---

[108] Liv. 34,21,7. Vgl. die Erwähnung von Metallvorkommen bei Cato: Gell. 2,22,29: *Sunt in his regionibus ferrareae, argentifodinae pulcherrimae.* Badian 1972, 32-33.

[109] Strab. 3,2,10. Der Denar hatte ein Gewicht von 3,8g; 9,125 Mio. Denare hatten dementsprechend ein Gewicht von ca. 34.600 Kilogramm oder 34,6 Tonnen. Zu den Bergwerken von Riotinto vgl. Jones 1980.

[110] Healy 1978; Wood 1987; Domergue 1990; Healy 1999, 271-346; Domergue 2008; Pérez Macías – Schattner 2013, 251-252; Schneider 2013.

[111] Eine Übersicht bietet Domergue 1990, 430-432.

[112] Domergue 1990, 414-417; 432-433; Domergue 2008, 114-115.

[113] Healy 1978, 93-100; Landels 1978, 58-70; Domergue 1990, 433-460; Domergue 2008, 120-128; Pérez Macías – Schattner 2013, 251: "The most important innovation was the ability to drain water from the mines." Die römischen Wasserschöpfräder, die von Menschen angetrieben wurden, waren wesentlich effizienter als die Methode der Karthager, das Wasser über eine Distanz von mehr als 2000 Metern durch eine Menschenkette aus dem Berg herauszuschaffen: Plin. nat. 33,96-97.

[114] Diod. 5,37,3; Strab. 3,2,9; Vitr. 10,6.

bringen, hat man sie so konstruiert, dass sie in ihre Einzelteile zerlegt und im Bergwerk wieder zusammengesetzt werden konnten.[115]

Auch bei der Aufbereitung der Erze und bei der Verhüttung haben die Römer neue Techniken entwickelt, die etwa für den Bergwerksdistrikt von Carthago Nova belegt sind.[116] Für die Verhüttung von Silbererzen hat man Schmelzöfen mit hohen Schornsteinen gebaut, um die als giftig geltenden Abgase in großer Höhe in die Luft abzuleiten.[117]

In dieser Zeit kam es auch zu weitreichenden organisatorischen Veränderungen im Bergbau auf der Iberischen Halbinsel. Die Bergwerke wurden nicht direkt von Amtsträgern der Republik verwaltet, sondern an *publicani* verpachtet, die Gesellschaften (*societates publicorum*) bildeten. Diese Gesellschaften nahmen auch in anderen Bereichen öffentliche Aufgaben wahr und machten dabei zum Teil große Gewinne. Die Republik wiederum konnte durch das Pachtsystem ohne größeren Verwaltungsapparat ständig sichere hohe Einkünfte erzielen.[118] Mit den *publicani* sollen auch zahlreiche Italiker nach Spanien gekommen sein, um in den Bergwerken tätig zu werden.[119] Ein weiteres neues Element im spanischen Bergbau war der massenhafte Einsatz von Sklaven, die von den *publicani* für die Arbeit in den Bergwerken gekauft wurden.[120]

Nach Diodor hat der Betrieb der Bergwerke durch die *societates* zur Folge gehabt, dass Gewinn und Gewinnstreben den spanischen Bergbau immer stärker prägten. Die *societates* waren in der Lage, für die Pacht der Bergwerke große Geldbeträge aufzubringen; für ein Bleibergwerk in der Provinz Baetica nennt Plinius eine Summe von 1,02 Mio. Sesterzen.[121] Die Erwartung hoher Einnahmen führte zu umfangreichen Investitionen; die *publicani* installierten etwa, wenn es sich als notwendig erwies, aufwendige Schöpfgeräte zur Wasserhaltung in den Bergwerken.[122] Die Anlage der Stollensysteme führt Diodor ebenfalls auf das Gewinnstreben der Publicanen und auf den Einsatz der Sklaven im Bergbau zurück.[123]

Der ausführliche Bericht Diodors über die römischen Bergwerke auf der Iberischen Halbinsel legt einen engen Zusammenhang zwischen den technischen Innovationen einerseits und den organisatorischen Veränderungen sowie dem Gewinnstreben der Pachtgesellschaften andererseits nahe. Hinzu kam das Interesse der römischen Republik am spanischen Silber, das in großen Mengen für die Prägung der Denare gebraucht wurde. Die Zahl der geprägten Denare stieg nach etwa 150 v. Chr. stark an; eine Geldemission in diesem Umfang ist ohne die spanischen Silberbergwerke kaum denkbar.[124]

---

[115] Vitr. 10,4,3. Zu Rio Tinto vgl. Wood 1987, 621.

[116] Strab. 3,2,10.

[117] Strab. 3,2,8.

[118] Badian 1972, 31-34.

[119] Diod. 5,36,3-4.

[120] Diod. 5,36,4; 5,38,1. Zu den Sklaven im römischen Bergbau vgl. Domergue 1990, 335-366.

[121] Diod. 5,35,1; 5,36,3 (φιλοκερδίαν); 5,36,4; 5,37,2-3; 5,38,1; 5,38,3. Zur Höhe der Pacht von Bleibergwerken vgl. Plin. nat. 34,165: Die *societates* bezahlten als Pacht für ein Bergwerk in der Provinz Baetica im Jahr 255.000 Denare (1,02 Mio HS). Ein anderes Bergwerk wurde für 400.000 Sesterzen verpachtet.

[122] Diod. 5,37,3.

[123] Diod. 5,36,4.

[124] Wolters 1999, 37-44.

In der augusteischen Zeit gewann Gold für die römische Münzprägung erheblich an Bedeutung. Bereits während der Bürgerkriege nach der Ermordung Caesars wurden mehrere Serien von Goldmünzen geprägt; im Principat stellte der *aureus*, der den Wert von 25 Denaren oder 100 Sesterzen besaß, neben dem Denar die wichtigste römische Münze aus Edelmetall dar. Durch die Prägung von Goldmünzen stieg die Geldmenge im Imperium Romanum stark an. Richard Duncan-Jones hat den Wert des Münzgeldes für die Zeit des frühen Principats auf ca. 20 Milliarden Sesterzen geschätzt, wobei 12 Milliarden Sesterzen auf Goldmünzen und 6 Milliarden Sesterzen auf Silbermünzen entfielen; auch Elio Lo Cascio nimmt an, dass die Goldmünzen im frühen Principat insgesamt einen erheblich höheren Wert hatten als die Silbermünzen.[125]

Auch wenn es nicht möglich ist, die für die Emission von Goldmünzen jährlich benötigte Menge Gold ungefähr zu schätzen, kann doch das Gold, das in Form von Münzen in Umlauf war, annäherungsweise quantitativ erfasst werden: Ein Wert von 12 Milliarden Sesterzen hätte 120 Mio. *aurei* entsprochen, die bei einem Gewicht des *aureus* von ca. 7,8 Gramm zusammen ca. 936.000 Kilogramm (= 936 Tonnen) gewogen hätten. Es ist möglich, dass deutlich weniger *aurei* im Umlauf waren, aber es ist kaum mit weniger als ca. 60 Mio. *aurei* zu rechnen, die immerhin noch ein Gewicht von insgesamt ca. 468 Tonnen gehabt hätten. Auch im Fall der Goldmünzen muss mit einem Schwund der Münzen im Geldumlauf gerechnet werden. Allein schon deswegen benötigte das römische Gemeinwesen für die Prägung der *aurei* große Mengen an Gold, denn mit Sicherheit reichte es nicht aus, für die Prägung neuer *aurei* ältere Goldmünzen, die als Steuer eingezogen wurden, einzuschmelzen und das so gewonnene Gold zu nutzen. Es entspricht diesen Voraussetzungen, dass unter Augustus der Goldabbau im Nordwesten der Iberischen Halbinsel sofort nach der Eroberung dieser Region einsetzte.[126]

Die Verfahren bei der Goldgewinnung in Nordwestspanien sind allein schon aufgrund der Dimension des Abbaus beeindruckend. Gold fand sich in dieser Region meist in sekundären Lagerstätten, die einen extrem geringen Goldanteil aufweisen. Die Römer haben deswegen neue Methoden entwickelt, um die metallhaltigen Erden abbauen und Gold gewinnen zu können. Über diese Aktivitäten liegt eine ausführliche, wahrscheinlich auf eigener Anschauung beruhende Beschreibung des Plinius vor, die durch die genaue archäologische Analyse dieses Bergbaugebietes bestätigt worden ist. In dem Gebiet, in dem Gold vermutet wurde, haben die Römer über weite Strecken Stollen gegraben, wobei man im Gestein einzelne Stützen stehen ließ. Wurden diese Stützen zuletzt nacheinander weggeschlagen, konnte ein ganzer Berg zum Einsturz gebracht werden. Zum Ort dieses künstlich herbeigeführten Bergsturzes wurde in offenen Kanälen, die im Hochgebirge unter schwierigsten Umständen – teilweise an senkrechten Felswänden – angelegt worden waren, Wasser geleitet, das in großen Bassins aufgefangen und gespeichert worden war. Wenn diese Bassins geöffnet wurden, stürzten die Wassermassen auf das Erdreich und schwemmten es mit sich fort; in der Ebene konnten dann die goldhaltigen Erd- und Steinbrocken aufgefangen und das Gold vom übrigen Erdreich getrennt werden. Die Auswirkungen

---

[125] Duncan-Jones 1994, 168-170; Lo Cascio 2008, 162.

[126] Flor. epit. 2,33,60. Zum Krieg im Nordwesten der Iberischen Halbinsel vgl. Curchin 1991, 52-53. Curchin hält es durchaus für möglich, dass ein Motiv für den Krieg die geplante Ausbeutung der Goldvorkommen in der Region war: „Yet it is difficult to believe that Augustus did not have his eyes on the rich mineral resources of the north-west, from which the natives had long been producing gold torques, bracelets, diadems and other jewellery."

dieser Form der Goldgewinnung auf die Landschaft sind vor allem in Las Medulas noch heute gut sichtbar.[127] Die Folgen des Goldabbaus für die Landschaft hat Plinius mit der Bemerkung angedeutet, die bei der Trennung des Goldes von dem nicht goldhaltigen Material fortgeschwemmte Erde habe bereits Spanien weit in das Meer vorgeschoben.[128]

Für das starke römische Interesse am Bergbau in den spanischen Provinzen ist bezeichnend, dass ein *procurator* der Provinz *Hispania Tarraconensis*, C. Plinius, im Nordwesten der Iberischen Halbinsel präsent war; er kannte den römischen Tagebau aufgrund eigener Anschauung und konnte ihn präzise beschreiben.[129] Darüber hinaus bietet Plinius eine wahrscheinlich genaue Angabe zu den Erträgen des römischen Tagebaus in Asturia, Gallaecia und Lusitania: In diesen Regionen sollen pro Jahr 20.000 Pfund Gold gewonnen worden sein, also umgerechnet 6.549 Kilogramm (= 6,549 Tonnen).[130]

Entscheidende Ursache für die technischen Innovationen im römischen Bergbau – sowohl in den Silberbergwerken in den Gebieten an der Mittelmeerküste als auch im Tagebau im nordwestlichen Spanien – waren ohne Zweifel die ökonomischen Interessen Roms: Der hohe Bedarf an Silber und seit augusteischer Zeit auch an Gold für die römische Münzprägung gab einen wesentlichen Impuls zu den technischen und organisatorischen Neuerungen im römischen Bergbau auf der Iberischen Halbinsel.

Konsum, Luxus und Innovationen

Wie W. Jongman überzeugend darlegen konnte, übertraf das gesamte Einkommen der städtischen Führungsschichten im Imperium Romanum aufgrund der hohen Zahl der Städte und damit entsprechend auch der Decurionen in nennenswertem Umfang die Einkünfte der Senatoren und der Equites, die individuell jeweils über einen wesentlich größeren Reichtum verfügten als die meisten Angehörigen der städtischen Eliten, aber rein zahlenmäßig auch eine wesentlich kleinere soziale Schicht bildeten.[131] Von Belang war aber nicht allein die Höhe der Kaufkraft der sozialen Eliten, sondern insbesondere auch deren Konsumverhalten, das entscheidend von zwei Faktoren geprägt war: Die römische Gesellschaft war einerseits streng hierarchisch gegliedert, andererseits existierte gerade auch innerhalb der Führungsschichten eine bemerkenswerte soziale Mobilität. Unter diesen Bedingungen bestand eine klare Vorstellung darüber, dass soziale Distinktion neben Reichtum und politischem Erfolg auch die Aneignung bestimmter, fest definierter Prestigegüter zur Voraussetzung hatte. Sozialer Status beruhte somit in hohem Maß auf demonstrativem Konsum, und Prestigegüter dienten dazu, sich unteren Schichten gegenüber abzugrenzen, die wiederum gerade danach strebten, durch Erwerb und Besitz von Luxusprodukten ihren sozialen Rang aufzuwerten. Damit entstand in der späten Republik und im frühen

---

[127] Plin. nat. 33,70-78; Lewis – Jones 1970; Bird 1972; Bird 1984; Domergue 2008, 139-142; Schneider 2013.

[128] Plin. nat. 33,76.

[129] Plin. nat. 33,70-78; Bird 1984. Bird glaubt, dass die Aussage des Plinius über die Wirkung des Bergsturzes (nat. 33,73) auf eigener Erfahrung beruht.

[130] Plin. nat. 33,78 20.000 Pfund Gold entsprachen 800.000 *aurei* (40 *aurei* pro Pfund Gold) mit einem Wert von 80 Mio. Sesterzen.

[131] Jongman 2007, 611; 616.

Principat eine Dynamik im Konsumverhalten, die erhebliche Rückwirkungen auf die Produktion in der Landwirtschaft und im Handwerk und auf den Handel mit Luxusgütern hatte.[132]

Das Stadthaus eines Angehörigen der Oberschicht kann exemplarisch den Zusammenhang von materiellem Aufwand und sozialem Status verdeutlichen: Wenn Cicero normativ feststellt, *dignitas*, Würde, solle durch ein standesgemäßes Haus betont werden, aber nicht durch ein Haus erworben werden, dann wird hier immerhin auf ein Verhalten verwiesen, das dieser Norm widerspricht.[133] In der Architekturtheorie wird ebenfalls das Haus in Beziehung zur sozialen Stellung seines Besitzers gesetzt.[134] Dass bei der Errichtung von Stadthäusern oder Landvillen die Tendenz bestand, den Bauluxus prominenter Persönlichkeiten nachzuahmen, hat bereits Cicero gesehen.[135] Das Streben nach Distinktion zeitigte im Hausbau ein eindeutiges Ergebnis, das Plinius prägnant beschrieben hat: „Wie bei den gründlichsten Schriftstellern feststeht, gab es unter dem Konsulat des M. Lepidus und Q. Catulus (78 v. Chr.) zu Rom kein schöneres Haus als das des Lepidus selbst; doch nahm es, beim Hercules, 35 Jahre später nicht die hundertste Stellung ein."[136] Die Steigerung von Aufwand und Luxus bei der Ausgestaltung der Bäder demonstriert Seneca durch den Vergleich der Villa Scipios mit den Häusern seiner Gegenwart.[137] Welche Dynamik der Hausbau in der späten Republik dadurch erhielt, dass reiche Römer, die nicht der senatorischen Führungsschicht angehörten, durch den Bau eines pompösen Hauses die Dignität der politischen Elite zu erlangen, zeigt der Fall des Mamurra, der sich als *praefectus fabrum* unter Caesar in Gallien immens bereichert hatte und sein Haus auf dem Caelius als erster mit Marmorplatten verkleiden ließ.[138]

Die *naturalis historia* des Plinius stellt geradezu ein Kompendium des Luxus und der Moden in Rom dar und bietet dabei vielfältige Hinweise auf das Konsumverhalten der sozialen Elite; in nahezu allen Abschnitten seiner Enzyklopädie der Natur erwähnt Plinius die Herstellung und den Konsum von Luxusprodukten.[139] Zum standesgemäßen Lebensstil der Senatoren gehörte insbesondere der Besitz von Tafelsilber, das in vielen Fällen mehrere Pfund schwer war.[140] Für Gefäße aus Silber sollen bis zu 6000 HS je Pfund bezahlt worden sein;[141] der Senator L. Licinius Crassus (cos. 95) soll zwei silberne Trinkgefäße mit einem Wert von 100.000 HS besessen haben.[142] Bei Festessen wurde das Tafelsilber den Gästen demonstrativ auf einer Anrichte präsen-

---

[132] Wagner-Hasel 2002; Mayer 2012, 22-60; Maschek 2018, 174-226.

[133] Cic. off. 1,138-140. Zu den Häusern von Senatoren in der Principatszeit vgl. Eck 2010.

[134] Vitr. 6,5.

[135] Cic. off. 1,140.

[136] Plin. nat. 36,109. Übersetzung von R. König. Vgl. 17,1-6: Haus des L. Licinius Crassus (cos. 95 v. Chr.), der sechs Säulen aus hymettischem Marmor in dem Atrium aufstellen ließ. 36,49: Haus des M. Aemilius Lepidus (cos. 78 v. Chr.).

[137] Sen. epist. 86,4-13.

[138] Plin. nat. 36, 48.

[139] Zu Plinius vgl. Wagner-Hasel 2002, 326.

[140] Stein-Hölkeskamp 2005, 146-154.

[141] Plin. nat. 33,147. Das Pfund Silber entsprach im römischen Geldsystem 84 Denaren (336 HS); bei einem Preis von 6000 HS spielt also der künstlerische Wert der Gefäße eine weitaus größere Rolle als der reine Materialwert.

[142] Plin. nat. 33,147.

tiert.¹⁴³ Kostbare Möbel wie die Tische aus nordafrikanischem Zitrusholz kamen in der späten Republik in Mode; für solche Tische wurden Preise bis zu 1,2 Mio Sesterzen bezahlt. In diesem Zusammenhang erwähnt Plinius auch den Schmuck der Frauen, die mit dem Verweis auf diese Tische die männliche Kritik am Tragen von Perlen beantworten.¹⁴⁴ Frauen, die der Familie des Princeps angehörten, trugen demonstrativ in der Öffentlichkeit Perlen von außergewöhnlichen Wert, so Lollia Paulina, die auch bereit war, den Preis ihres Schmuckes, 40 Mio. Sesterzen, durch Rechnungen zu belegen.¹⁴⁵ Bemerkenswert ist die Aussage des Plinius, es sei für die Frauen eine Frage der Ehre (*gloria*), Perlen am Finger oder an den Ohren zu tragen, und selbst ärmere Frauen wünschten dies in der Meinung, Perlen übernähmen in der Öffentlichkeit für die Frauen die Aufgabe eines Lictors, dessen eigentliche Funktion es war, den Consuln auf der Straße den Weg freizumachen.¹⁴⁶ Die Mode, Perlen zu tragen, war in Rom spät aufgekommen; zur Zeit Sullas fingen die Frauen an, Perlen als Schmuck zu verwenden, in großem Stil hat sich dies aber erst unter Augustus durchgesetzt.¹⁴⁷

Ein anderes Beispiel für den im frühen Principat zunehmenden Luxuskonsum ist die Verwendung kostbarer Salben, die Plinius für überflüssig hält, da sie – anders als Perlen und Edelsteine – auf die Haut aufgetragen sich schnell verflüchtigten und nur dazu dienten, durch ihren Duft im Moment andere anzulocken.¹⁴⁸ Aus dem Gespinst von Schmetterlingen wurden leichte, als *bombycina* bezeichnete Stoffe verfertigt; Plinius meint, auf diese Weise sei es möglich geworden, dass Frauen durch Kleider entblößt würden. Derartige Gewänder wurden im Sommer sogar von Männern getragen, was für Plinius ein Indiz dafür ist, dass die Sitten sich vollständig verändert haben.¹⁴⁹ Klassisches Statussymbol in Rom war der goldene Fingerring, dem Plinius in dem Buch über die Metalle längere Ausführungen widmet.¹⁵⁰ Daneben war der Speiseluxus ein wichtiges Thema bei Plinius; ein Katalog erfasst Weine verschiedener Qualität aus Italien und aus anderen Ländern;¹⁵¹ in der späten Republik wurden griechische Weine aus Chios und Lesbos bevorzugt, daneben traten dann italienische Weine wie der berühmte Falerner, und es gibt auch Nachrichten darüber, dass einzelne reiche Römer wie Hortensius große Mengen Wein lagerten.¹⁵²

Der Wandel im Lebensstil der sozialen und politischen Elite wurde in der zeitgenössischen Literatur wahrgenommen und meist mit moralphilosophischen Argumenten kritisiert. Varro, der über die Bauten und Anlagen auf den Landgütern spricht, stellt fest, diese seien in dem früheren

---

[143] Cic. Verr. 2,4,33.

[144] Plin. nat. 13,91-99. Cicero soll einen derartigen Tisch zu einem Preis von 500.000 Sesterzen gekauft haben.

[145] Plin. nat. 9,117.

[146] Plin. nat. 9,114.

[147] Plin. nat. 9,123.

[148] Plin. nat. 13,20. Dasselbe Argument erscheint auch 9,124 in Bezug auf purpurgefärbte Stoffe, die sich mit jeder Stunde abnutzten, während Perlen ein nahezu unvergänglicher Besitz sind und vererbt oder verkauft werden konnten.

[149] Plin. nat. 11,76; 11,78.

[150] Plin. nat. 33,8-34.

[151] Plin. nat. 14, 59-76.

[152] Plin. nat. 14, 94-97.

Stadium von der alten Sparsamkeit (*frugalitas antiqua*), in der Gegenwart vom Luxus (*luxuria*) geprägt.¹⁵³ Bei Plinius finden sich zahlreiche Hinweise auf die Veränderungen in der Lebensweise und im Konsumverhalten; diese Entwicklung resultierte nach Plinius aus dem wachsenden Reichtum der Elite, die immer stärker am Gelderwerb interessiert war.¹⁵⁴ Plinius hat seine Sicht der Entwicklung eindrücklich formuliert: „So begann beim Hercules, der sinnliche Genuss zu leben, das Leben selbst aber hat aufgehört".¹⁵⁵

Ein direkter Zusammenhang zwischen Luxuskonsum und Innovationen war in den Aktivitäten des Sergius Orata gegeben, der in der Zeit um 100 v. Chr. Behälter erfunden haben soll, in denen Austern gezüchtet werden konnten. Als Motiv nennt Plinius Gewinnstreben (*avaritia*); mit der Austernzucht soll Sergius Orata große Einkünfte erzielt haben. Außerdem begann er, verschiedene Arten von Meeresfischen in Salzwasserbecken zu halten. Wie Plinius berichtet, hat Sergius Orata auch die beheizbaren Bäder erfunden, mit denen er Landhäuser ausstattete, die er nach dem Umbau schnell wieder verkaufte.¹⁵⁶

Eine der folgenreichsten Innovationen der römischen Welt korreliert mit dem Bestreben der Senatoren, öffentliche Gebäude, die ihren Namen trugen, und standesgemäße Stadthäuser für sich zu errichten: Das *opus caementicium*, der Gussmörtel, wurde nach neueren Forschungen gegen Mitte des 2. Jahrhunderts v. Chr. im Zuge von Bauvorhaben römischer Senatoren verwendet. Als Beispiele hierfür werden die *porticus Metelli*, das von Cicero erwähnte Stadthaus des Cn. Octavius (cos. 165) sowie die von diesem errichtete *porticus Octavia* genannt.¹⁵⁷

Die große Nachfrage nach einem mit Reliefs verzierten Geschirr, das sich an dem Vorbild getriebener Gefäße aus Edelmetall orientierte,¹⁵⁸ hat zweifellos die Herausbildung von Töpfereien, die Terra Sigillata herstellten, begünstigt; damit waren jene Schichten, die sich ein Tafelsilber nicht leisten konnten, in der Lage, ein ihren ästhetischen Ansprüchen genügendes Geschirr zu erwerben. Obgleich es im Hellenismus Vorläufer der Terra Sigillata gab, ist die Etablierung der großen Werkstätten insbesondere in Arezzo und im Süden Galliens als eine Entwicklung zu

---

¹⁵³ Varro rust. 3,3,6. Vgl. zur Ablehnung von Süßwasserfischen beim Gastmahl: Varro rust. 3,3,9. Vgl. ferner Iuv. 5,92-106.

¹⁵⁴ Plin. nat. 9,64-68 (Fisch); 14,1-9 (Weinbau); 14,91-97 (Wein); 18,107-108 (Bäcker in Rom); 19,49-56 (Gartenbau); 33,133-135; 33,139-150 (Besitz an Silber); 36,109-110 (Stadthaus); Auch Seneca stellt oft die vorbildliche Lebensweise in der Vergangenheit den inakzeptablen Sitten der Gegenwart gegenüber: Sen. epist. 55; 56; 86; 90,34-46; 122; 123. Vgl. ferner Val. Max. 9,1,5.

¹⁵⁵ Plin. nat. 14,6. *Ergo, Hercules, voluptas vivere coepit, vita ipsa desiit*.

¹⁵⁶ Plin. nat. 9,168; Val. Max. 9,1,1. Vgl. ferner Cic. de orat. 1,178; Varro rust. 3,3,10; Colum. 8,16,5; Bartels 2001. Bei den *pensiles balineas* (Plin. nat. 9,168) handelt es sich um Bäder mit einer Hypokaustenheizung, die in Griechenland bereits für das 3. Jahrhundert, in Italien aber erst für das späte 2. Jahrhundert nachgewiesen ist und hier vielleicht auf eine Initiative des Sergius Orata zurückgeht. Zu den Bädern vgl. Vitr. 5,10; Adam 1984, 288-290.

¹⁵⁷ *porticus Metelli*: Vell. 1,11,5; Mogetta 2015, 14-16. Haus des Octavius: Cic. off. 1,138. Häuser am Palatin: Mogetta 2015, 24-26. *porticus Octavia*: Vell. 2,1,2; Plin. nat. 34,13 (korinthische Kapitelle aus Bronze); Richardson 1992, 317. Es ist signifikant, dass Velleius den Bau der *porticus* im Zusammenhang mit dem privaten Luxus erwähnt und eine Beziehung zwischen öffentlicher *magnificentia* und privater *luxuria* herstellt. Ähnlich Vell. 1,11,5.

¹⁵⁸ Garbsch 1982, 8.

bewerten, die mit erheblichen technischen Innovationen verbunden war.[159] Ähnliches ist in der Glasherstellung zu beobachten. Auch hier gab der Bedarf an hochwertigen Gefäßen Impulse für die Einrichtung neuer Produktionsstätten und für technische Neuerungen; gerade in diesem Bereich wurden mit dem Kameoglas und den Diatretgläsern kostbare Produkte für eine kaufkräftige Elite geschaffen.[160]

Zusammenfassung

Der Blick auf die Innovationen vor allem in der Wirtschaft, aber auch in anderen Bereichen der römischen Gesellschaft, offenbart zwei Seiten der römischen Zivilisation: Neben einem ausgeprägten Sinn für politische und familiäre Traditionen, einer Beachtung überlieferter Werte, einer Argumentation, die sich in vielen Fällen auf die *maiores* bezieht, und einem von *exempla* geprägten politischen Denken existierte eine große Bereitschaft, Neuerungen einzuführen, wenn diese die Leistungsfähigkeit des politischen und sozialen Systems steigerten oder im privaten Bereich den sozialen Rang und die Distinktion einer Familie oder eines einzelnen Politikers Ausdruck verliehen.

Technische Innovationen wurden von antiken Autoren wie Vitruvius, Heron oder Plinius wahrgenommen und positiv bewertet; allerdings waren die Römer nicht in der Lage, ihren wirtschaftlichen Effekt, die Steigerung der Produktivität, quantitativ zu erfassen. Dabei sollte aber nicht übersehen werden, dass die technischen Innovationen für die Wirtschaft, das Transportwesen, die Architektur und die Infrastruktur tiefgreifende Folgen hatten; sie sind keineswegs als marginal einzuschätzen, denn sie hatten in der Landwirtschaft und im Handwerk eine steigende Produktivität zur Folge. Die trugen einerseits zu steigenden Gewinnen der Großgrundbesitzer und andererseits zu einer Verbesserung der Versorgung der Bevölkerung mit Agrarprodukten und Handwerkserzeugnissen bei. Die technischen Innovationen waren daher ohne Zweifel neben der unter Augustus beginnenden lang dauernden Friedensperiode, die den Bewohnern des Mittelmeerraumes eine beispiellose äußere und innere Sicherheit garantierte, eine unabdingbare Voraussetzung jener Urbanität, die im Zeitalter des Principats von einem weit verbreiteten Wohlstand und einem hohen ästhetischen Niveau der materiellen Kultur geprägt war.[161]

Bibliographie

Adam 1984	J. -P. Adam, La construction romaine. Materiaux et techniques, Paris 1984.
Baatz 1999	D. Baatz, Katapult, in: DNP 6, 1999, 340-343.
Badian 1972	E. Badian, E. Publicans and Sinners. Private enterprise in the service of the Roman Republic, Oxford 1972.
Bartels 2001	J. Bartels, Sergius Orata, C., in: DNP 11, 2001, 456.
Bird 1972	D. G. Bird, The Roman Gold Mines of North-West Spain, Bonner Jahrbücher 172, 1972, 36-64.
Bird 1984	D. G. Bird, Pliny and the Gold Mines of the North-West of the

---

[159] Brown 1976; Peacock 1982, 114-128.
[160] Saldern 2004, 157-474.
[161] Mayer 2012.

	Iberian Peninsula, in: T. F. C. Blagg – R. F. J. Jones - S. J. Keay (eds.), Papers in Iberian Archaeology (BAR International Series 193), Oxford 1984, 341-368.
Blackman 2008	D. J. Blackman, Sea Transport, Part 2: Harbors, in: Oleson 2008, 638-670.
Blösel 2000	W. Blösel, Die Geschichte des Begriffs mos maiorum von den Anfängen bis zu Cicero, in: B. Linke – M. Stemmler (Hg.), Mos maiorum. Untersuchungen zu den Formen der Identitätsstiftung und Stabilisierung in der römischen Republik, Stuttgart 2000, 25-97.
Bowman – Wilson 2013a	A. Bowman – A. Wilson (eds), The Roman Agricultural Economy. Organization, Investment, and Production, Oxford 2013.
Bowman – Wilson 2013b	A. Bowman – A. Wilson, Introduction: Quantifying Roman Agriculture, in: A. Bowman – A. Wilson (eds.), The Roman Agricultural Economy. Organization, Investment, and Production, Oxford 2013, 1-32.
Brown 1976	D. Brown, Pottery, in: Strong – Brown 1976, 75-91.
Brun 1986	J.-P. Brun, L'Oléiculture antique en Provence. Les huileries du département du Var, Paris 1986.
Burmeister et al. 2013	S. Burmeister – S. Hansen – M. Kunst – N. Müller-Scheeßel (eds.), Innovative Technologies and Social Change in Prehistory and Antiquity, Rahden 2013.
Casson 1971	L. Casson, Ships and Seamanship in the Ancient World, Princeton 1971.
Coarelli 1977	F. Coarelli, Public Building in Rome between the Second Punic War and Sulla, BSR 45, 1977, 1-23.
Cotterell – Kamminga 1990	B. Cotterell – J. Kamminga, Mechanics of Pre-industrial Technology, Cambridge 1990.
Craddock 2008	P. T. Craddock, Mining and Metallurgy, in: Oleson 2008, 93-120.
Curchin 1991	L. A. Curchin, Roman Spain. Conquest and Assimiliation, London 1991.
Davies 1935	O. Davies, Roman Mines in Europe, Oxford 1935.
Diederich 2007	S. Diederich, Römische Agrarhandbücher zwischen Fachwissenschaft, Literatur und Ideologie, Berlin 2007.
Dobbins – Foss 2007	J. J. Dobbins – P. W. Foss (eds.), The World of Pompeii, London 2007.
Domergue 1990	C. Domergue, Les mines de la Péninsule Ibérique dans l'antiquité romaine, Rom 1990.
Domergue 2008	C. Domergue, Les mines antiques. La production des métaux aux époques grecque et romaine, Paris 2008.
Duncan-Jones 1974	R. Duncan-Jones, The Economy of the Roman Empire. Quantitative Studies, Cambridge 1974.

Duncan-Jones 1994	R. Duncan-Jones, Money and government in the Roman Empire, Cambridge 1994.
Eck 2006	W. Eck, Augustus und seine Zeit, 4. Aufl, München 2006.
Eck 2010	W. Eck, Cum dignitate otium. Senatorische Häuser im kaiserzeitlichen Rom, in: W. Eck, Monument und Inschrift. Gesammelte Aufsätze zur senatorischen Repräsentation in der Kaiserzeit, Berlin 2010, 207-239.
Finley 1965	M. I. Finley, Technical Innovation and Economic Progress in the Ancient World, EHR 18, 1965, 29-45.
Flach 2002	D. Flach (Hg.), Marcus Terentius Varro. Gespräche über die Landwirtschaft, Buch 3, Darmstadt 2002.
Freyberger 2012	K. S. Freyberger, Das Forum Romanum. Spiegel der Stadtgeschichte des antiken Rom, Darmstadt ²2012.
Fulford – Durham 2013	M. Fulford – D. Durham (eds.), Seeing Red. New Economic and Social Perspectives on Terra Sigillata, London 2013.
Garbsch 1982	J. Garbsch, Terra Sigillata. Ein Weltreich im Spiegel seines Luxusgeschirrs, München 1982.
Gehrke 2017	H. -J. Gehrke, Die Welt der klassischen Antike, in: H. -J. Gehrke (Hg.), Frühe Zivilisationen. Vor 600, Harvard Geschichte der Welt. Band 1, München 2017, 417-596.
Gille 1980	B. Gille, Les mécaniciens grecs. La naissance de la technologie, Paris 1980.
Greene 2000	K. Greene, Technical Innovation and Economic Progress in the Ancient World: M. I. Finley reconsidered, EHR 53, 2000, 29-59.
Greene 2008a	K. Greene, Historiography and Theoretical Approaches, in: Oleson 2008, 62-90.
Greene 2008b	K. Greene, Inventors, Invention, and Attitudes toward Innovation, in Oleson, 2008, 800-818.
Harden 1987	D. B. Harden, Glass of the Caesars, Milano 1987.
Harris 2008	W. V. Harris, The Nature of Roman Money, in: W. V. Harris (ed.), The Monetary Systems of the Greeks and Romans, Oxford 2008, 174-207.
Healy 1978	J. F. Healy, Mining and Metallurgy in the Greek and Roman World, London 1978.
Healy 1999	J. F. Healy, Pliny the Elder on Science and Technology, Oxford 1999.
Hesberg 2005	H. von Hesberg, Römische Baukunst, München 2005.
Jackson – Greene 2008	M. Jackson – K. Greene ‚Ceramic production', in: Oleson 2008, 496-519.
Jones 1980	G. D. B. Jones, The Roman Mines at Riotinto, JRS 70, 1980, 146-165.

Jongman 2007	W. M. Jongman, The early Roman empire: Consumption, in: Scheidel – Morris – Saller 2007, 592-618.
Kay 2014	Ph. Kay, Rome's Economic Revolution, Oxford 2014.
Kolb 1995	F. Kolb, Rom. Geschichte der Stadt in der Antike, München 1995.
Landels 1978	J. G. Landels, Engineering in the Ancient World, London 1978.
Leveau 1996	Ph. Leveau, The Barbegal water mill in its environment: archaeology and the economic and social history of antiquity, JRA 9, 1996, 137-153.
Lewis – Jones 1970	P. R. Lewis – G. D. B. Jones, Roman Gold-Mining in North-West Spain, JRS 60, 1970, 169-185.
Lo Cascio 2008	E. Lo Cascio, The Function of Gold Coinage in the Monetar Economy of the Roman Empire, in: W. V. Harris (ed.), The Monetary Systems of the Greeks and Romans, Oxford 2008, 160-173.
Marichal 1988	R. Marichal, Les graffites de La Graufesenque, Paris 1988.
Marzano 2013	A. Marzano, Capital Investment and Agriculture: Multi-Press Facilities from Gaul, the Iberian Peninsula, and the Black Sea Region, in: Bowman – Wilson 2013a, 107-141.
Maschek 2018	D. Maschek, Die römischen Bürgerkriege. Archäologie und Geschichte einer Krisenzeit, Darmstadt 2018.
Mayer 2012	E. Mayer, The Ancient Middle Classes. Urban Life and Aesthetics in the Roman Empire 100 BCE-250 CE, Cambridge Mass. 2012.
McGrail 2008	S. McGrail, ‚Sea Transport, Part 1: Ships and Navigation', in: Oleson 2008, 606-637.
Moeller 1976	W. O. Moeller, The Wool Trade of Ancient Pompeii, Leiden 1976.
Mogetta 2015	M. Mogetta, A New Date for Concrete in Rome, JRS 105, 2015, 1-40.
Moosbauer 2013	G. Moosbauer, Torsionsgeschütze. Antike Wunderwaffen, in: Pöppelmann – Deppmeyer – Steinmetz 2013, 242-248.
Moritz 1958	L. A. Moritz, Grain-Mills and Flour in Classical Antiquity, Oxford 1958.
Naumann-Steckner 1991	F. Naumann-Steckner, Depictions of Glass in Roman Wall Paintings, in: Newby – Painter 1991, 86-98.
Newby – Painter 1991	M. Newby – K. Painter (eds.), Roman Glass. Two Centuries of Art and Invention, London 1991.
O'Connor 1993	C. O'Connor, Roman Bridges, Cambridge 1993.
Oleson 2008	J. P. Oleson (ed.), The Oxford Handbook of Engineering and Technology in the Classical World, Oxford 2008.
Oleson – Branton 1992	J. P. Oleson – G. Branton, The technology of King Herod's harbour, in: R. L. Vann (ed.), Caesarea Papers. Straton's Tower, Herod's Harbour, and Roman and Byzantine Caesarea, Ann Arbor 1992, 49-67.

Peacock 1982	D. P. S. Peacock, Pottery in the Roman world: An Ethnoarchaeological Approach, London 1982.
Pérez Macías – Schattner 2013	J. A. Pérez Macías – Th. G. Schattner, Retaining and Renewing. The Roman Municipium Munigua in the light of technical developments in mining in the Hispanic Southwest, in: Burmeister et al. 2013, 241-260.
Pferdehirt 1995	B. Pferdehirt, Das Museum für antike Schiffahrt. Ein Forschungsbereich des Römisch-Germanischen Zentralmuseums, Mainz 1995.
Pöppelmann – Deppmeyer – Steinmetz 2013	H. Pöppelmann – K. Deppmeyer – W. -D. Steinmetz (eds.), Roms vergessener Feldzug. Die Schlacht am Harzhorn, Darmstadt 2013.
Price 1976	J. Price, Glass, in: Strong – Brown 1976, 110-125.
Quilici 2008	L. Quilici, ‚Land Transport, Part 1: Roads and Bridges', in: Oleson 2008, 551-579.
Raepsaet 2002	G. Raepsaet, Attelages et techniques de transport dans le monde gréco-romain, Bruxelles 2002.
Raepsaet 2008	G. Raepsaet, 'Land Transport, Part 2: Riding, Harnesses, and Vehicles', in: Oleson 2008, 580-605.
Richardson 1992	L. Richardson jr., A New Topographical Dictionary of Ancient Rome, Baltimore 1992.
Ritti – Grewe – Kessener 2007	T. Ritti – K. Grewe – P. Kessener, A relief of a water-powered stone saws mill on a sarcophagus at Hierapolis and its implications, JRA 20, 2007, 139-163.
Rostovtzeff 1957	M. Rostovtzeff, The Social and Economic History of the Roman Empire, Oxford 1957.
Ruffing 1999	K. Ruffing, Mago 12, in: DNP 7, 1999, 702-703.
Saldern 2004	A. von Saldern, Antikes Glas (Handbuch der Archäologie), München 2004.
Scheidel – Morris – Saller 2007	W. Scheidel – I. Morris – R. P. Saller (eds.), The Cambridge Economic History of the Greco-Roman World, Cambridge 2007.
Schmidts – Vučetič 2015	Th. Schmidts – M. M. Vučetič (Hg.), Häfen im 1. Millenium AD. Bauliche Konzepte, Herrschaftliche und religiöse Einflüsse, Mainz 2015.
Schneider 1991	H. Schneider, Die Gaben des Prometheus. Technik im antiken Mittelmeerraum zwischen 750 v. Chr. und 500 n. Chr., in: W. König (ed.), Propyläen Technikgeschichte vol. 1, Landbau und Handwerk 750 v. Chr.-1000 n. Chr., Berlin 1991, 19-313.
Schneider 1992	H. Schneider, Einführung in die antike Technikgeschichte, Darmstadt 1992.
Schneider 2013	H. Schneider, Tertia ratio opera vicerit Gigantum: Innovations in Roman Mining on the Iberian Peninsula, in: Burmeister et al. 2013, 261-271.

Shaw 2013	B. D. Shaw, Bringing in the Sheaves. Economy and Metaphor in the Roman World, Toronto 2013.
Spain 2008	R. Spain, Power and Performance of Roman Water-Mills. Hydro-Mechanical Analysis of Vertical-Wheeled Water-Mills (BAR 1786), Oxford 2008.
Stein-Hölkeskamp 2005	E. Stein-Hölkeskamp, Das römische Gastmahl. Eine Kulturgeschichte, München 2005.
Stern 2008	E. M. Stern, Glass production, in: Oleson 2008, 520-547.
Strocka 2007	V. M. Strocka, Domestic decoration: painting and the „Four Styles", in: Dobbins – Foss 2007, 302-322.
Strong – Brown 1976	D. Strong – D. Brown (eds.), Roman Crafts, London 1976.
Vernhet 1981	A. Vernhet, Un four de La Graufesenque (Aveyron): La cuisson des vases sigillés, Gallia 39, 1981, 25-43.
Wagner-Hasel 2002	B. Wagner-Hasel, Verschwendung und Politik in Rom. Überlegungen zur politischen Semantik des Luxuskonsums in der späten Republik und frühen Kaiserzeit, Historische Anthropologie 10, 2002, 325-353.
Wallace-Hadrill 1994	A. Wallace-Hadrill, Houses and Society in Pompeii and Herculaneum, Princeton 1994.
Walter 2007	R. Walter (ed.), Innovationsgeschichte, Stuttgart 2007.
Ward-Perkins 1975	J. B. Ward-Perkins, Architektur der Römer, Stuttgart 1975.
Wawrzinek 2016	Chr. Wawrzinek, Tore zur Welt. Häfen in der Antike, Darmstadt 2016.
Weiß 2001	P. Weiß, Schnellwaage, in: DNP 11, 2001, 200-204.
White 1970	K. D. White, Roman Farming, London 1970.
White 1984	K. D. White, Greek and Roman Technology, London 1984.
Wikander 1984	Ö. Wikander, Exploitation of water-power or technical stagnation?, Lund 1984.
Wikander 2008	Ö. Wikander, Sources of Energy and Exploitation of Power, in: Oleson 2008, 136-157.
Wild 2008	J. P. Wild, ‚Textile production', in: Oleson 2008, 465-482.
Wilson 2002	A. Wilson, Machines, Power and the Ancient Economy, JRS 92, 2002, 1-32.
Wolters 1999	R. Wolters, Nummi Signati. Untersuchungen zur römischen Münzprägung und Geldwirtschaft, München 1999.
Wood 1987	A. Wood, Mining, in: J. Wacher (ed.), The Roman World, London 1987, 611-634.
Zanker 1995	P. Zanker, Pompeji. Stadtbild und Wohngeschmack, Mainz 1995.
Zimmer 1982	G. Zimmer, Römische Berufsdarstellungen, Berlin 1982 (= Archäologische Forschungen 12).

Roma İmparatorluğu'nda yenilikler ve ekonomik gelişim
Özet

Roma toplumunun özellikle ekonomide olmak üzere değişik alanlarındaki yenilikleri ele alındığında Roma uygarlığının iki yönü öne çıkmaktadır: Güçlü bir politik ve ailevi gelenekler anlayışına ve geleneksel değerlere duyulan saygıya ek olarak, politik ve sosyal sistemin etkinliğini artırmaları gerektiğinde yeniliğe de büyük bir istekleri vardı. Böylelikle res publica asaleti ya da özel ortamlarda ailenin sosyal statüsü yükselmekteydi. Orta ve geç Roma Cumhuriyeti'nin politikaları bile birçok yönden yenilikçi olduğunu kanıtlamıştır; Özellikle Gracchi yasaları, cumhuriyeti yeni siyasi, sosyal ve ekonomik ihtiyaçlara uyarlamak için defalarca yeni teklifler formüle ettiği için oluşan popüler politikayı vurgulamamız gerekir. Son olarak, Augustus Dönemi'nde bu politika, Cumhuriyet'in eski kurumlarını yeni güç yapılarıyla birleştiren yeni bir anayasal sistemin oluşturulması ile doruk noktasına ulaştı. Teknik yenilikler Vitruvius, Heron veya Plinius gibi antik yazarlar tarafından dikkate alındı ve olumlu olarak değerlendirildi. Ancak Romalılar yarattıkları ekonomik etkilerin ve üretimdeki artışın boyutunu ölçemiyorlardı. Ekonomi, ulaşım, mimarlık ve altyapı için teknik yeniliklerin büyük sonuçları olduğu göz ardı edilmemelidir. Romalılar hiçbir şekilde marjinal olarak kabul edilmemelidir, çünkü tarım ve el sanatlarında üretkenliği artırmışlar, böylece de bir yandan büyük toprak sahiplerinin kazançlarının artmasına, diğer yandan da tarım ve el sanatları ürünlerinin halka arzının büyütülmesine katkıda bulunmuşlardır. Özellikle altyapı alanında, örneğin su temininde, nüfusun refahı üzerinde olumlu etkileri olmuştur. Bu nedenle teknik yenilikler Augustus Dönemi'nde başlayıp Akdeniz'deki halka eşi görülmemiş bir dış ve iç güvenlik garantisi veren uzun barış sürecine ek olarak, hiç şüphesiz Principatus Dönemi'nde kentliliğin yaygın refah ve yüksek estetik standartlarla karakterize edildiği vazgeçilmez bir ortam sağlamıştı.

Anahtar Sözcükler: Antik teknik, Roma İmparatorluğu, teknolojik gelişmeler.

Innovation and economic development in the Roman Empire
Abstract

A look at the innovations, especially in the economy, but also in other areas of Roman society, reveals two sides of Roman civilization: In addition to a strong sense of political and family traditions and a respect of traditional values there was a great willingness to innovate if they were to increase the efficiency of the political and social system, thereby increasing the dignity of the res publica or, in the private sphere, the social rank of a family. Even the policies of the middle and late Roman republic proved in many ways to be innovative; In particular, we should point out the popular policy that since the laws of the Gracchi has repeatedly formulated new proposals to adapt the republic to new political, social and economic needs. Finally, under Augustus, this policy culminated in the creation of a constitutionally new system, the Principate, which combined the old institutions of the Republic with new power structures. Technical innovations were perceived and positively valued by ancient authors such as Vitruvius, Heron or Pliny; however, the Romans were unable to quantify their economic effect, the increase in productivity. However, it should not be overlooked that the technical innovations for the economy, transport, architecture and infrastructure had profound consequences; they are by no means to be considered as marginal, because they increased productivity in agriculture and crafts, thereby contributing on the one hand to increasing profits of large landowners and on the other hand to improving the supply of agricultural products and craft products to the population. Especially in the field of infrastructure, for example in the water supply, they had positive effects on the welfare of the population. The technical innovations were therefore undoubtedly in addition to the long period of peace beginning under Augustus, which guaranteed to the inhabitants of the Mediterranean an unprecedented external and internal security, an indispensable condition of that urbanity, which in the Principate's time was characterized by widespread prosperity and high aesthetic standards the material culture was characterized.

Keywords: Ancient technics, Roman Empire, innovations.

Was macht Skylla im lydischen Hinterland?
Zu einer Homonoia-Prägung von Philadelpheia und Smyrna

Katharina MARTIN*

„Um eine Vorstellung davon zu gewinnen, welche Assoziationen bestimmte Münzen bei den Menschen, die sie als Geld verwendeten, hervorgerufen haben könnten", müsse man „das historische Umfeld und mögliche Traditionen bestimmter Themen und Darstellungen … erhellen", und „selbst bei den Zeitgenossen des städtischen Geldes haben wir mit mehr oder weniger großen Interpretationsspielräumen zu rechnen", schreibt Johannes Nollé kürzlich in einem Beitrag über Münzen mit dem Bildnis des Okeanos[1]. Prägekontexte und das kulturhistorische Umfeld, lokale Bild- und Erzähltraditionen gilt es zu ergründen, um Erklärungen für einzelne Motive und ganze Bildprogramme zu finden. Auf diesem Gebiet hat sich Nollé in den letzten Jahren und Jahrzehnten immer wieder hervorgetan, hat lokale Mythen und fast vergessene Geschichten und damit einen Fundus an in der Antike geläufigen Erinnerungen ausgegraben, mit dem sich auch für uns heute scheinbar sperrige Bilder und Motive erklären lassen. Damit hat er Kolleginnen und Kollegen wie auch einer breiten Öffentlichkeit eine ganz neue Sicht auf antike Lebenswelten eröffnet und ihnen (mir auch!) wie nebenbei auch die Welt der Numismatik nahegebracht. Und dies tat und tut er in klaren und schön gesetzten Worten, ohne sich in gestelzten dem Zeitgeist geschuldeten Begrifflichkeiten zu verlieren. Um ein sperriges Münzbild geht es auch im Folgenden: Rätselhaft erscheint die Präsenz der Skylla auf einer Lokalbronze im lydischen Philadelpheia, einer Stadt im kleinasiatischen Hinterland, die 2017 aus dem Handel bekannt wurde (Abb. 1)[2]. Es handelt sich um eine sogenannte pseudo-autonome Prägung, eine kaiserzeitliche Münze ohne Kaiserbildnis, die die Eintracht (OMONOIA) der Stadt mit der ionischen Metropole Smyrna feiert:

Philadelpheia in Lydien, Æ 8,56 g; 6 h; 25mm

Vs. ΔΗΜΟC Φ[Ι]ΛΑΔΕΛΦΕΩΝ ΝΕΩ. Nackte Büste des jugendlichen Demos nach r. mit Binde im Haar und einem Gewandbausch am linken Schulteransatz; seine Haare fallen im Nacken in langen Strähnen herab und oberhalb der Stirn wölbt sich eine *anastolé*.

Rs. Κ·CΜΥΡ·Γ·Ν-Ε-Ω·ΟΜΟ. Skylla in Frontalansicht mit Blick nach rechts. Der weibliche Oberkörper läuft nach hinten in zwei langen fisch- oder seeschlangenartigen Schwänzen und nach vorne in zwei Hundeprotomen aus; in der ausholenden rechten Hand hält Skylla ein Steuerruder, mit der linken greift sie einen der Gefährten des Odysseus an den Haaren. Nach links hin versucht ein weiterer Seemann zu fliehen, wird aber vom linken der beiden Hunde gerissen.

---

* Katharina Martin, Heinrich-Heine-Universität Düsseldorf / Alte Geschichte, Universitätsstraße 1, 40225 Düsseldorf, Deutschland (katharina.martin@hhu.de).

[1] So Nollé 2018, 187.

[2] Nomos AG, Auktion 15 (22.10.2017) Nr. 165.

Die Münze gehört in eine Serie von Homonoiamünzen, die alle das Bildnis des lokalen Demos, der Personifikation des Volkes von Philadelpheia, auf der Vorderseite zeigen[3]; alle Münzen dieser Serie, auch die hier vorliegende Skyllaprägung, verwenden denselben Vorderseitenstempel. Auffällig bei dieser Serie ist unter anderem, dass die Legenden von Vorder- und Rückseite zusammenzulesen sind, angezeigt durch καὶ, das beide Seiten verbindet: ΔΗΜΟC ΦΙΛΑΔΕΛΦΕΩΝ ΝΕΩ(κορῶν) Κ(αὶ)·CΜΥΡ(ναίων)·Γ·Ν-Ε-Ω(κορῶν)·ΟΜΟ(νοία); außerdem hat man auf der Rückseite auf das meist übliche Miteinander zweier oder mehrerer Städtevertreter[4] zugunsten einer Zentralfigur verzichtet.

Abgesehen von dieser pseudo-autonomen Serie, die wohl in das frühe 3. Jahrhundert n. Chr. zu datieren ist[5], gibt Philadelpheia wiederholt, bereits in der Zeit von Commodus, dann unter Caracalla und schließlich unter Gordian III. Münzen heraus, die die Eintracht mit Smyrna feiern. Als einzige hat die gordianische Emission ein smyrnäisches Pendant[6]. Im Folgenden wird nicht der konkrete Anlass der Homonoiaserie hinterfragt, sondern nur die Frage nach der Funktion des Münzbildes auf der Rückseite gestellt.

Die Auswahl von Skylla als Motiv für eine Homonoiaprägung setzt die Assoziation von Skylla mit einer der beiden Städte, also ihre Funktion als städtische Repräsentantin voraus. Dies wirft Fragen nach der Zuordnung und Funktion der Figur auf. Philadelpheia liegt in einer fruchtbaren Landschaft nahe des Kogamis (dieser erscheint personifiziert auch auf Münzen), an der Verbindungsstraße zwischen Mäander- und Hermostal[7] – ein gewisser Wasserbezug ist also gegeben, mehr aber nicht. Smyrna ist eine Hafenstadt am Mittelmeer, und Skylla ist klar ein Meerwesen, doch wird sie traditionell weit weg von Kleinasien in der Meerenge zwischen Rhegion und Messina verortet[8]. Ihre Präsenz auf einer Münze aus Philadelpheia im Inneren Lydiens verwundert daher, hier scheint der Interpretationsspielraum groß.

---

[3] Zur Vorderseite Martin 2013 II, 107 f. Philadelpheia 5a-b und 6a-b. Die Vorderseite ist stempelgleich mit BMC Lydia Nr. 116-118; SNG von Aulock Nr. 3067; SNG München Nr. 435-436.

[4] Das illustrieren die vielen Beispiele im Katalog von Franke – Nollé 1997; allgemein dazu bereits Franke 1987, 90; Klose 1987, 45; Kampmann 1996, 1-3; das diffizile Spiel von Positionierung und Interaktion der verschiedenen Städtevertreter diskutieren Nollé – Nollé 1994. Eine weitere Homonoiaprägung Philadelpheias mit einer ionischen Metropole (diesmal mit der Provinzhauptstadt Ephesos) behandelt Nollé 2006, 73-83 (= Franke – Nollé 1997, 175 Nr. 1729-1731 = RPC IX Nr. 722). Auch hier folgen die Figuren auf der Rückseite nicht dem „Zwei-Städtevertreter-Prinzip", sondern Iphigenie, ihr Bruder Orest und ihr Vetter Pylades bringen das Kultbild der Artemis in einen Tempel. So wird hier das Moment einer Kulteinrichtung durch Mitglieder der Atreïdenfamilie illustriert, das für beide Städte gleichermaßen in Anspruch genommen werden kann und somit eine Syngeneia der beiden Poleis begründet (ebd. 78-81).

[5] Franke – Nollé 1997, 177-179 und Martin 2013 II, 107 ordnen die pseudo-autonomen Münzen in die Zeit von Caracallas Alleinherrschaft (211-217 n. Chr.) ein; Einschätzung im Auktionskatalog: ca. 215-230 n. Chr.; Klose 1987, 50 datiert die Emission in seine „4. Phase" und damit in die Spätzeit (244-268 n. Chr.).

[6] Franke – Nollé 1997, 174 (Übersicht) und 176-180; RPC VII,1 Nr. 267-269; zu ergänzen durch Mottet 2002, 25 f. = RPC VII,1 Nr. 269A; s. auch die Tabelle bei Klose 1987, 49 f.

[7] Magie 1950, 124 f.; s. auch http://nomisma.org/id/philadelpheia_lydia.

[8] So z. B. bei Thuk. 4,24,5, der zwar nicht Skylla, wohl aber Charybdis explizit nennt; Verg. Aen. 3,414-423 beschreibt die Klippen am Bruch zwischen Unteritalien und Sizilien; auch Palaiphatos 20 (περὶ Σκύλλης) sieht ihren Ursprung im tyrrhenisches Meer. Vgl. Stilp 2011, 10; Govers Hopman 2012, 135 und 168.

Skylla auf Münzen

Skylla gilt als Tochter des Meergottes Phorkys, die von Kirke, Amphitrite oder Poseidon in ein Meerungeheuer verwandelt wurde[9]. Am bekanntesten sind die Erzählungen, in denen ihr Odysseus, die Argonauten oder Aeneas nur unter großer Gefahr entkommen[10]. Aitiologisch basiert die Figur auf einer Naturgewalt, auf gefährlichen Klippen, die eine Schiffspassage nahezu unmöglich erscheinen lassen: „Denn auf der einen Seite tauchte in der Ferne der schroffe Felsen der Skylla auf, auf der anderen toste ohne Unterlass der sprudelnde Schlund der Charybdis"[11]; nach Palaiphatos ist sie eine Art Personifikation von Piratentum[12] – in beiden Fällen stellt sie eine existenzbedrohliche Gefahr für die Schifffahrt dar.

Die gestaltgewordene Skylla mit ihrem weiblichen Oberkörper, der in Fischschwänzen ausläuft und an dessen Hüfte mehrere Hundeprotome hervorspringen, ist literarisch und im Bild selbst vielfach überliefert, in der Vasenmalerei, Relief- oder Kleinkunst[13]. Als Helmzier oder Beiwerk mit klar apotropäischer Funktion begegnet Skylla auch auf Münzen, insbesondere im Bereich Unteritalien und Sizilien[14]. Sie kann mit Wasserwesen (mit Fischen, Tintenfischen, Muscheln),

---

[9] Harder 2001, 641 mit den literarischen Nachweisen; ausführlich zur Genealogie Waser 1894, 23-32.

[10] Vgl. Hom. Od. 12,201-259 (Kirkes Ratschläge geleiten Odysseus); Apoll. Rhod. 4,825-832 und 4,920-955 (auf Wunsch der Hera hilft Thetis den Argonauten); Aeneas kann sie umgehen (Verg. Aen. 3,429-432 und 683-689). Auch Ov. Met. 14,70-77 handelt kurz das Zusammentreffen mit Odysseus und Aeneas' Ausweichen ab.

[11] So Apoll. Rhod. 4,922 f. (Übers. R. Glei – S. Natzel-Glei). Ovid erklärt die gefährlichen Klippen als Ergebnis einer zweiten Verwandlung: Das Mädchen Skylla wird von Kirke zunächst in ein Ungeheuer (Ov. Met. 14,60-67), dann versteinert in die Klippen verwandelt (Ov. Met. 14,73 f.). Zu einem derartigen „rationalizing the monster" Govers Hopman 2012, 186-194.

Das Ineinandergreifen von Skylla und Charybdis wird gelegentlich mit Ebbe und Flut in Verbindung gebracht, dazu bereits Waser 1894, 13 f., der Skylla auch als „Verkörperung der Gefahren einer Meerenge oder noch allgemeiner der Ausdruck für die elementare Gewalt der grausen Meerflut, die an Felsen und Klippen haust …" beschreibt (ebd. 22).

[12] Palaiphatos 20 (περὶ Σκύλλης) erklärt, dass ein tyrrhenisches Piratenschiff namens Skylla den Mythos ausgelöst habe; die Erzählung um ein (halb-)menschengestaltiges Seeungeheuer mit Hundeköpfen sei erst darum herum konstruiert worden. Dies nimmt Andreae 1988, 114 f. auf und vermutet als Assoziation des antiken Betrachters „er dachte bei Skylla an Piraten". Siehe auch Andreae 1999, 215 und Lukan 6, 421-422.

[13] z. B. Verg. Aen. 3,426-428: „vorn ist Menschengestalt, mit schönem Busen ein Mädchen bis zum Schoß, dann aber mit grausigem Leibe ein Seetier, am Delphinenschwanz mit Seewolfsbauche verwachsen" (Übers. J. Götte); Palaiphatos 20 (περὶ Σκύλλης): „eine wilde Frau bis zum Nabel, von dort an seien ihr Hundeköpfe gewachsen, der übrige Körper sei der einer Schlange gewesen" (Übers. K. Brodersen); Themistios or. 22 (p. 279b, ed. Dindorf): „… Jungfrau, von der Hüfte aber sogleich in Hunde auslaufend, die furchterregend sind und grauenvoll" (Übers. B. Hebert).

Bereits Waser 1894, hat 78-129 (Kap. IV und im katalogartigen Anhang, S. 130-142) eine Zusammenstellung der Bildwerke geliefert; aktueller bei Jentel 1997, 1137-1145; zur Ikonografie auch Andreae 1982, 50-54.

[14] Die Belege hat Whybrew 2015, 27-29 Kap. 2.2.3 zusammengestellt: Thourioi, Eleia/Hyele, Herakleia, Tarent, Metapont (Vorkommen); S. 48-55 Kap. 1.1.3 (Mythos und Darstellungen in der Kunst etc.).

aber auch mit Felsbrocken werfen oder mit dem Steuerruder ausholen[15]. So erscheint sie hier meist als Übel abwehrender Helmschmuck der Athena. Das Ruder als Attribut weist auf ihren Charakter als Meerwesen und zeigt ihre Macht über Schiffe und Seeleute; ihr aggressiver Habitus wirkt apotropäisch[16].

Als zentrales alleiniges Münzmotiv dagegen sind Nachweise deutlich überschaubarer und in Einzelemissionen über eine insgesamt lange Zeitspanne verteilt[17]. Der früheste Beleg stammt aus Kyzikos (Abb. 2); hier sind nur einige wenige Exemplare überliefert. Es handelt sich um Elektronstatere aus der ersten Hälfte des fünften Jahrhunderts v. Chr., die ein nach links gerichtetes weibliches Meerwesen mit Fischschwanz zeigen; zwei Hundeköpfe an den Schultern weisen die Figur eindeutig als Skylla aus, wenngleich die Hunde mehr als erklärendes Beiwerk dienen denn als elementarer Part der Figur[18]. Das Parasemon der Stadt, der Thunfisch, ist zweifach vorhanden, einer im Abschnitt, einen weiteren hält sie in der Hand; der Stempelschneider spielt mit den Bildern und vermischt inhaltliche Aussage (Thunfisch als Wurfgeschoss der Skylla) mit nützlicher Information (Thunfisch als Erkennungszeichen der Prägestätte).

Weit entfernt, im sizilischen Akragas und in Syrakus, wo ihre Präsenz nicht verwundert, verdrängt Skylla als auffallend großes Beizeichen fast die eigentlichen Motive der Tetradrachmen im späten fünften Jahrhundert v. Chr.: In Akragas (Abb. 3) ist sie ebenfalls nach links gerichtet und weist zwei antithetisch an der Hüfte ansetzende Hundeprotome auf, ihr Schwanz ist mit Stacheln versehen; in Syrakus weist sie mit den Hunden nach rechts, hält einen Dreizack geschultert und wird von Fisch und Delphin begleitet[19].

Regelmäßige Emissionen mit Skylla als eigenständigem lokal beziehungsweise regional identitätsstiftendem Motiv folgen im späten fünften / frühen vierten Jahrhundert v. Chr. in einigen Städten in Unteritalien: An der kampanischen Küste prägt Kyme (Cumae) in der Zeit ca. 420–385 v. Chr. Didrachmen mit einer Skylla mit gezacktem Kamm am Schwanz und zwei antithetischen Hundeköpfen an den Schultern, weitere Hundeprotomen wachsen ihr aus der Hüfte und streben nach rechts (Abb. 4)[20]. Weiter im Landesinnern verwendet Allifae für seine Obolen eine ähnliche Skylla (Abb. 5): Ausgerichtet nach rechts hat auch sie zwei Hundeköpfe an ihrer Schulter und auch an

---

[15] Tuchelt 1967, 181.

[16] Beide Aspekte, das Aggressive und das übelabwehrend Schützende, gehören zum ambivalenten Wesen der Skylla, dazu die Untersuchung von Stilp 2011.

[17] Münzbeispiele bei Imhoof-Blumer – Keller 1889, 74 f. Nr. 1-7 Taf. XIII; s. auch Waser 1894, 99-103.

[18] Datierung ca. 460-400 v. Chr. (Boston, MFA, Inv. 04.282 = Baldwin Brett 1955 I, 195 Nr. 1495 Taf. 74; St. Petersburg = von Fritze 1912, 13 Nr. 175 Taf. V, 23)

[19] Zu Akragas: Hoover 2012, 30 Nr. 82; Westermark 2018, 168-171 Nr. 531-535 Taf. 35 unterscheidet drei Rs.-Stempel. Gelegentlich wird auch das Beizeichen auf Hemilitren als Skylla bezeichnet, hierbei handelt es sich jedoch um einen Muschelhorn blasenden Triton, worauf bereits Waser 1894, 107 hingewiesen hatte; s. dazu auch CNS I 177 Kommentar zu Nr. 48. Auch in Syrakus nimmt Skylla auf Tetradrachmen der Stempelschneider Euth-, Eumenes und Phrygillos (Hoover 2012, 357 Nr. 1334; Fischer-Bossert 2017, 225-227 Nr. 46-48 Taf. XII-XIII) viel Raum ein, durch ihre Positionierung klar im Abschnitt wird hier die Funktion als Beizeichen deutlicher als in Akragas.

[20] Nachweise Kyme: Hoover 2018, 187 Nr. 430; Rutter 2000, 67 Nr. 534 Taf. 9 (420-385 v. Chr.); Skylla kann nach rechts oder links gewandt sein.

ihrem Schwanz verläuft ein gezackter Rückenkamm, ihr fehlen aber weitere Hunde an der Hüfte[21]. In Skylletion findet sich ein Bezug zu Skylla schon im Ortsnamen; in der Zeit ca. 344–336 v. Chr. werden hier Bronzemünzen herausgegeben mit einer nach links gerichteten Skylla (Abb. 6); ihr wachsen zwei mächtige Hundeprotomen aus der Hüfte[22]. Wie in Akragas wird auch hier den Hunden eine starke Präsenz zugewiesen, sie nehmen etwa ein Drittel der Gesamtfigur ein.

Erst viel später nimmt Sextus Pompeius in den 30er Jahren des ersten Jahrhunderts v. Chr. in einer Serie imperatorischer Denare mit Skylla Bezug auf seine sizilischen Kampagnen[23]. Während auf einem Denar (RRC 511/2) der Hinweis eher versteckt in Form der Hundeköpfe am Seetropaeum erscheint, zeigt der andere Denar (RRC 511/4) eine aggressive Skylla in schräger Vorderansicht, die mit einem Steuerruder in den erhobenen Händen zum Schlag ausholt, drei Hunde preschen aus ihrem Unterleib vor und füllen den unteren Teil des Münzbildes aus (Abb. 7). Diese frontal ausgerichtete Darstellung erinnert schon an die Wiedergabe auf unserer noch deutlich späteren Homonoiaprägung.

In der Kaiserzeit bleibt Skylla auf wenige Ausnahmeprägungen beschränkt; so gibt die römische Kolonie Korinth in antoninischer und severischer Zeit gelegentlich Münzen mit Architekturmotiven heraus, auf denen Skylla städtische Brunnenanlagen schmückt (Abb. 8)[24]. Hier wird ihre Funktion auf ein rein dekoratives Wasserwesen reduziert. Vergleichbares findet sich im dritten

---

[21] Hoover 2018, 162 Nr. 357-358; Rutter 2000, 62 Nr. 460-461 Taf. 7 (Vs. Apollon) und Nr. 462 (Vs. Athena). Er weist auf die Lage im Inland ebenso hin wie auf die gute Verbindung nach Kyme und ans Meer „which could easily be reached from the Volturnus river". Die Spanne der Datierungen in der Literatur reicht von ca. 400-350 v. Chr. (SNG Copenhagen Nr. 295-297 oder SNG München Nr. 131) bis ca. 325-275 v. Chr. (Rutter 2000 und Hoover 2018).

Auf den zeitgleichen Bronzen findet sich ein Meerwesen nach links, das meist als Skylla bezeichnet wird (BMC Italy 74 Nr. 8; SNG München Nr. 132; Rutter 2000, 63 Nr. 464; Hoover 2018, 164 Nr. 361); wie in Akragas aber handelt es sich um einen Triton mit Ruder (möglicherweise Glaukos, den Geliebten der Skylla?).

[22] Hoover 2018, 493 Nr. 1722 (Mitte 4. Jh. v. Chr.); Rutter 2000, 192 Nr. 2565 Taf. 41 (drittes Viertel des 4. Jhs. v. Chr.). CNS III 319 f. weist diese Prägungen einem sizilischen Skylletion zu bzw. Söldnern im zentralen Nordsizilien, in der Nähe des heutigen Scillezio (Provinz Palermo); s. die Diskussion bei Hoover 2018, 493, der zugunsten von Skylletion in Bruttium entscheidet.

[23] RRC Nr. 511/2 (Seetropaeum mit Hundeprotomen) und 511/4 (Skylla mit Hundeprotomen und Steuerruder); s. bereits Waser 1894, 107 und auch den Kommentar zum Typ bei Bendschus – Feuser 2014, Nr. 609241. Die Datierung und damit der konkrete Anlass sind umstritten, nach RRC: 42-40 v. Chr., Woytek 1995, 79-94 datiert später, auf 37/36 v. Chr.

[24] So findet sich Skylla mit Hundeprotomen als Brunnenschmuck auf einem Felsen, der die Quelle Peirene anzeigt. Der Typ, den bereits Waser 1894, 108 nennt, wird geprägt unter Antoninus Pius (RPC IV Temp. Nr. 3528), Marc Aurel (RPC IV Temp. Nr. 9643), Lucius Verus (RPC IV Temp. Nr. 5171 und 10626), Commodus (RPC IV Temp. Nr. 9512, 10627 und 10810), Iulia Domna (Lanz, Auktion 121 [22. November 2004] Nr. 462) oder Plautilla (Peus, Auktion 366 [29.11.2000] Nr. 453). In der Zeit von Lucius Verus (RPC IV Temp. Nr. 9494) und Septimius Severus (Price – Trell 1977, 80 f. mit Abb. 139-139A) kann der Brunnen mit Skylla auch in einer architektonischen Rahmung wiedergegeben werden. Unter Septimius Severus sitzt die Quellnymphe Peirene neben dem Brunnen mit Skylla (BMC Corinth 86 Nr. 655 Taf. XXI,17 = Price – Trell 1977, 80 f. mit Abb. 138).

Jahrhundert weit entfernt im kilikischen Tarsos: Unter Caracalla zeigen Bronzemünzen ein Meerwesen als architektonisches Beiwerk des städtischen Nymphäums, das in der Literatur mehrfach als Skylla benannt ist[25]. Alle überlieferten Stücke lassen aber meines Erachtens nur eine allgemeine Deutung als „Meerwesen" zu, da insbesondere Hunde nicht erkennbar sind. Die einzigen gesicherten kaiserzeitlichen Skylladarstellungen erscheinen hier in Tarsos unter Pupienus (Abb. 9) und Gordian III.[26]: in Frontalansicht mit Ruder und insgesamt vier vorpreschenden Hunden erinnert dieser Typ wieder an die Denare des Pompeius.

Skylla und Odysseus

Unsere Homonoiamünze aus Philadelpheia dagegen zeigt Skylla nicht losgelöst vom mythischen Kontext, einfach nur als Meerwesen, als apotropäisches oder illustratives Beiwerk, sondern schildert ein konkretes Aufeinandertreffen von Mensch und Seeungeheuer – eine Szenerie, die außer auf spätantiken Kontorniaten (Abb. 10)[27] in der Münzprägung nicht bekannt ist. Wohl am nachhaltigsten ist uns diese Konfrontation in der Odyssee überliefert[28], von der es diverse Reflexe in der bildenden Kunst gibt. So ist dieses Moment sehr eindrücklich in der monumentalen Skyllaskulptur aus Sperlonga umgesetzt[29]. Um den Strudeln der Charybdis zu entgehen, musste Odysseus nahe an Skylla vorbeifahren. Dabei kalkulierte er personelle Verluste ein, die ihren Ausdruck in der Ergreifung von zweien seiner Gefährten finden: Während einer der Hunde einen Seemann beißt, greift Skylla selbst den Steuermann an den Haaren[30]. Unabhängig davon, ob diese monumentale plastische Wiedergabe auf ein griechisches, eventuell rhodisches Bildwerk zurückgeht oder eine genuin italische Schöpfung ist[31], belegt die Gruppe, dass in römischer Zeit diese Bildfassung bekannt und geläufig ist für ein Moment aus dem Odysseusmythos.

---

[25] Als Giebelmotiv: SNG von Aulock Nr. 6016 („Thalassa"); SNG Levante Nr. 1045 und SNG Levante Suppl. Nr. 265 („Scylla"); SNG Paris II Nr. 1505 („Scylla") und Price – Trell 1977, 226 Abb. 511 (unbenannt).

[26] Als Einzelmotiv in Tarsos unter Gordian III.: BMC Cilicia 215 Nr. 268; SNG Righetti 1682; SNG Paris II Nr. 1690; SNG Levante Nr. 1125; unter Pupienus: SNG Tübingen Nr. 4576; SNG Pfalz VI Nr. 1387-1388; SNG Paris II Nr. 1633 (mit Ruder, allerdings friedfertiger und ohne die aggressiven Hunde); dazu auch Waser 1894, 109, der die Präsenz der Skylla hier im Osten damit begründet, dass man sich in Kilikien „darauf kaprizierte, unteritalische und sizilische Münztypen nachzuahmen".

[27] Alföldi – Alföldi-Rosenbaum 1976, 8 Nr. 27 Taf. 9, 3-6; 10 Nr. 35-36 Taf. 12,5-8; 11 Nr. 39 Taf. 13,4-8 (Vs. Alexander); 21 Nr. 73 Taf. 25,5-6 (Vs. Roma); 53 f. Nr. 179 Taf. 63,9-65,5 (Vs. Nero); 118-121 Nr. 359-360 Taf. 146,2-149,11; 124 Nr. 367-368 Taf. 153,5-154,7; 129 Nr. 382 Taf. 159,6; 130 Nr. 384 Taf. 160,9-161,2; 131 Nr. 390 Taf. 162,6-163,1 (Vs. Trajan).

Die Nachweise zeigen, dass Skylla auf den spätantiken Kontorniaten durchaus häufig vorkommt, es können fünf Stempel unterschieden werden: Alföldi – Alföldi Rosenbaum 1990, 156 f. Nr. 83-86 (N. Forsyth – E. Alföldi Rosenbaum); s. auch Mittag 1999, 110 f. 295 f. Nr. 83-86 Taf. 22.

[28] Odysseus' Zusammentreffen mit Skylla wird von Hom. Od. 12, 201-259 überliefert; Beschreibung und Warnung vor Skylla durch Kirke bei Hom. Od. 12,85-126.

[29] Vgl. Andreae 1982, 103-120, 156-163; Andreae – Conticello 1987; Andreae 1988, bes. 76-94 mit Abb. 15-17, 19-24; Andreae 1999, 205-215 mit Abb. zu Kat.-Nr. 78; Jentel 1997, 1142 Nr. 57 Taf. 790.

[30] Zum Verlust von sechs seiner Männer Hom. Od. 12,109 f. und 12,245-257; zum Bildmotiv: Andreae 1982, 50; Andreae 1999, 206.

[31] Ridgway 2000, 78-86, bes. 80 fasst den Forschungsstand zusammen.

Es ist die „kleine" Variante, die aus der Villa Hadriana bei Tivoli stammt und die durch diverse Replikenfragmente breiter überliefert ist[32], die typologisch in ihrer Frontalität und Gesamtkomposition fast vollständig dem Homonoia-Münzbild aus Philadelpheia entspricht.

Skylla in Kleinasien

Sicher nach Kleinasien zuzuweisende Bildbelege der Skylla sind selten, was nicht verwundert, da ihre naturräumliche Verortung in Unteritalien weit entfernt ist und hier kein Lokal- oder Regionalbezug vorliegt. Dennoch findet sich eine unterlebensgroße, aber durchaus bedeutende Figur im Museum von Afyon. In ihr erkannte man eine verkleinerte Replik der bekannten Sperlonga-Skylla, die man daher für die Rekonstruktion der monumentalen Gruppe nutzte[33]. Gabriele Schmitz vermutet hinter dem Fragment rein dekorativen Charakter[34], wie wir ihn beispielsweise im architektonischen Rahmen eines Nymphäums fassen können. Im karischen Bargylia, einer Hafenstadt am Mittelmeer, haben sich Teile einer hellenistischen Skyllafigur erhalten, die einen weiblichen Torso zeigt, der in drei Hundeprotome ausläuft. Hier handelt es sich hier um Bestandteile eines Grabbaus[35]; ihre Funktion hier im Sepulkralkontext scheint rein apotropäisch zu sein.

Figuralschmuck auf einem Pfeilerkapitell in Magnesia am Mäander zeigt eine Skylla in Konfrontation mit Seeleuten; es mag sich um Odysseus' Gefährten handeln, auch wenn die Szenerie hier symmetrisch dekorativ und weniger gewalttätig wirkt; die Menschen schwimmen, zum Teil kopfüber (als Ausdruck dafür, dass sie bereits verstorben sind?), werden aber weder von Skylla noch von den Hunden direkt angegriffen[36]. Ein Tonmodel aus Didyma zeigt Skylla in deutlich aggressiverer Haltung[37]; sie erinnert typologisch deutlich an die Skylla aus der Villa Hadriana und an unser Münzbild der Homonoia-Serie.

---

[32] Andreae 1957, 316; Tuchelt 1967, 193 Nr. 74; Andreae 1982, 225-244 (hadrianische Kopie eines hellenistischen Originals, s. ebd. 231 und 240); Jentel 1997, 1143 Nr. 58; Andreae 1974, 82 grenzt die Tivoli-Gruppe als die „kleine" ab und stellt 81 f. in der ausführlichen Anm. 48 zahlreiche Replikenfragmente zusammen; nach Andreae 1982, 229 f. besteht zumindest die Möglichkeit, dass viele dieser Fragmente letztlich aus Tivoli stammen.

[33] Zur Figur in Afyon, Inv. 1875: Schmitz 1992, 117-123 Taf. 12-13; Jentel 1997, 1142 Nr. 57a (1. Jh. n. Chr.); der Fundort liegt in der Nähe des phrygischen Amorion; meist findet sich in der Literatur der Hinweis, die Figur stamme aus dem Steinbruch von Dokimeion – beides noch deutlich weiter im Landesinneren als Philadelpheia. Zu ihrer Nutzung für die Rekonstruktion in Sperlonga u. a. Andreae 1999, 205.

[34] Schmitz 1992, 122 f.; ebd. Anm. 34 hält sie eine Produktion für den Export für möglich, sodass ein kleinasiatischer Aufstellungs- oder Funktionskontext möglicherweise gar nicht intendiert war.

[35] Sog. Scylla Tomb, heute im British Museum, Inv. 1865,1212.4; dazu u. a. Jentel 1997, 1144 Nr. 74 Taf. 791 (ca. 200-150 v. Chr.). Zu Scylla im Grabkontext auch Stilp 2011, 15-17.

[36] Bingöl 1992, 418-423 verortet die Szenerie in den Mythos um Aeneas. Zum Kapitell auch Jentel 1997, 1141 Nr. 49 Taf. 788 (römisch).

[37] Ausführlich Tuchelt 1967, 173-189 Taf. 17 (erste Hälfte 2. Jh. v. Chr.); Andreae 1982, 231 mit Abb.; Andreae 1988, 103 mit Abb. 30; zum Vorbildcharakter des Models für die Skulptur in der Villa Hadriana ebd. 240 f.

Literarisch ist ein Tafelbild des Androkydes aus Kyzikos überliefert, das Skylla zeigt[38]. Dass das Gemälde in der Heimatstadt des spätklassischen Malers (und damit in einer Hafenstadt am Marmarameer, die eine Elektronmünze mit Skylla geprägt hat, s.o.) zu verorten ist, ist weder gesichert noch wahrscheinlich.

Die wohl bedeutendste Skulptur in Kleinasien, eine Bronzegruppe mit Schiff, die Skylla zeigt, wie sie „die von der Charybdis ausgeworfenen Menschen frißt, und es ist Odysseus, den sie mit der Hand am Kopf festhält"[39] (dieses „handgreifliche" Motiv findet sich hier wie in Sperlonga, der Villa Hadriana, auf den Kontorniaten oder auf unserer Münze), ist ebenfalls nur literarisch überliefert. Bis zum Ende der mittelbyzantinischen Zeit steht sie auf der Spina des Hippodroms von Konstantinopel und wird oftmals als Vorbild für die Sperlongagruppe verstanden[40].

Belege für Skylla in Kleinasien sind also vorhanden, aber die Anzahl bleibt überschaubar. Es handelt sich um Kunstwerke, um dekorative Architektur- oder Bauelemente, die „Mythos" höchstens als Genre verwenden; nirgends aber zeigen diese kleinasiatischen Beispiele aus den Bereichen Skulptur, Malerei und Numismatik echten identitätsstiftenden Lokalbezug, wie man ihn für eine Instrumentalisierung im Münzbild der Homonoiaserie vermuten sollte.

Skylla als Synonym für Homer?

Nicht nachweisbar heißt nicht, dass es einen Lokalbezug nicht gegeben hat, aber aus dem Negativbefund heraus zu argumentieren, ist problematisch. Ein anderer Zugang zur Frage nach der Funktion des Münzbildes scheint erfolgversprechender, denn unbestritten ist, dass man Skylla für das Münzbild bewusst ausgewählt hat.

Die formale Struktur der Homonoiaserie, zu der auch die Skyllamünze gehört, zeigt, dass die Repräsentanten der beiden beteiligten Städte offenbar auf die beiden Münzseiten verteilt sind. Für die ausgebende Stadt Philadelpheia steht auf der Vorderseite der lokale Demos, der zwar im Bild ganz unspezifisch erscheint, aber durch die Beischrift klar identifiziert ist. Auf den Rückseiten der Serie finden sich eine thronende Kybele[41], eine Stadttyche mit Statuetten der beiden smyrnäischen Nemeseis[42] und eben Skylla. Bei den erstgenannten ist der Bezug zu Smyrna klar: Kybele ist (als

---

[38] Plut. symp. 4,2,3 und 4,4,2; Athen. 8,341a. Beiden Autoren geht es mehr um die naturalistisch gemalten die Skylla umgebenden Fische als um Skylla selbst; auf das konkrete Motiv und die Gesamtkomposition des Bildes kann aus den Passagen nicht geschlossen werden; dazu auch Waser 1894, 112 f.; Jentel 1997, 1144 Nr. 85 (ca. 420-370 v. Chr.).

[39] Patria Kontantinupoleos II 77 (ed. Preger) (= Hebert 1989, Q 3, hier in der Übersetzung von Berger 1988, 546); vermutlich ist in der Anthologie Graeca IX 755 (= Hebert 1989, Q 5) dieselbe Gruppe gemeint. Erst bei der Plünderung Konstantinopels durch die Kreuzfahrer im Jahre 1204 wurde sie zerstört, eingeschmolzen und zu Münzgeld (!) ausgeprägt.

Zusammenstellungen von Texten, die entweder konkrete Skyllagruppen bzw. allgemein die gängige Ikonografie überliefern, finden sich bei Tuchelt, 1967, 189; Andreae – Conticello 1987, 24 f. ausführliche Anm. 57; Hebert 1989, 6-8 Q2-5.

[40] z. B. von Andreae 1982, 160; Andreae – Conticello 1987, 24-26; Andreae 1988, 107-111; Hebert 1989, 5; Andreae 1999, 205, 388.

[41] Franke – Nollé 1997, 177 f. Nr. 1745-1762; 178 Nr. 1770-1780; Martin 2013 II, 107 f. Philadelpheia 5a-b.

[42] Franke – Nollé 1997, 178 Nr. 1763-1769; Martin 2013 II, 108 Philadelpheia 6a-b.

Meter Sipylene) vielfach im Typenspektrum von Smyrna präsent, ebenso die beiden Nemeseis, die zu den ältesten Gottheiten vor Ort gehören und Alexander den Großen im Traum zur Neugründung der Stadt bewogen haben[43]. Ohne dass sie selbst in der ionischen Hafenstadt eine Rolle spielt, steht aber offenbar auch Skylla für Smyrna.

Smyrna ist bekannt dafür, dass die Stadt sich als Geburtsort Homers (...αὐτοῦ πατρίδα...)[44] versteht, ihm ein Heiligtum eingerichtet hat und in hellenistischer Zeit Münzen mit dem Bildnis der sitzenden Homers mit schräg gehaltenem Zepter und Buchrolle herausgibt, deren antiker Rufname „Homereia" von Strabon überliefert ist (Abb. 11)[45]. Dazu gehören unter diversen Magistraten herausgegebene (seltenere) Drachmen sowie massenhaft produzierte Bronzemünzen vom Wert eines Obol[46]. Eine Vereinnahmung des Dichters und eine deutliche Identifizierung über ihn über das Medium Münze ist also nachweisbar. Allerdings bricht die Prägung der „Homereia" in der Kaiserzeit ab; nur noch einmal, in severischer Zeit, zeigt eine Serie pseudo-autonomer Münzen den sitzenden Dichter (Abb. 12)[47].

---

[43] Beide Gottheiten erscheinen sowohl als städtische Repräsentanten auf Vorderseiten als auch ganzfigurig auf Rückseiten, z. T. auch auf diversen Homonoiaprägungen.

Zu Kybele: Klose 1987, 25 f.; 130 f. Nr. 12-19; 145 f. Nr. 75-87; 169-171 Nr. 1-14 (Vs.) oder 139 Nr. 1-6; 221 f. Nr. 1-20; 234 Nr. 19-33; 242 f. Nr. 1-24; 254 f. Nr. 1-3; 255 Nr. 6; 258 Nr. 14; 263 Nr. 2-3; 265 f. Nr. 4-5; 266 Nr. 9-11; 269 Nr. 9-14; 270 Nr. 17; 272 Nr. 2-4; 295 Nr. 21; 297 Nr. 3; 315 Nr. 4; 318-320 Nr. 15-29 (Rs.).

Smyrnäische Homonoia-Münzen mit Kybele: Klose 1987, 330 Nr. 8-14 (mit Laodikeia); 330 f. Nr. 15-16 und 332 Nr. 2-4 (mit Nikomedeia); 334 Nr. 16-18 (mit Athen); 336 Nr. 32-36 (mit Sparta); 340 f. Nr. 6-7 (mit Pergamon).

Zur einfachen oder doppelten Nemesis: Klose 1987, 28-30, 135-138 Nr. 62-114; 146 Nr. 88-94 (Vs.); 147 Nr. 1-14; 152 Nr. 24; 162 Nr. 1-3; 184 Nr. 1; 185 Nr. 5-8; 186 Nr. 1-3; 187 f. Nr. 7-10; 189 Nr. 1; 190 Nr. 1-2; 191 f. Nr. 9-10; 194 f. Nr. 2-4; 197 f. Nr. 1-15; 203 Nr. 45-48; 228-230 Nr. 1-35; 239 Nr. 11; 241 f. Nr. 1-3; 255 Nr. 7; 261 Nr. 12-17; 263 Nr. 1-2; 265 Nr. 2 und 3; 268 Nr. 2-4; 273 f. Nr. 4-9; 277 Nr. 24-26 Nr. 4-9; 279 Nr. 39; 280 Nr. 42 und 43; 282 Nr. 51-52; 289 Nr. 30; 291-293 Nr. 1-15; 298 f. Nr. 8; 305 Nr. 1; 306 f. Nr. 6-7; 308 Nr. 14; 315 Nr. 3; 317 f. Nr. 8-14 (Rs.).

Die Traumszene unter Marc Aurel: Klose 1987, 257 f. Nr. 1-13 (= RPC IV Temp. Nr. 239 und 3087) unter Gordian III.: Klose 1987, 308 Nr. 15 (= RPC VII,1 Nr. 310) oder unter Philipp I.: Klose 1987, 313 Nr. 1.

Smyrnäische Homonoia-Münzen mit (meist) beiden Nemeseis: Klose 1987, 327 f. Nr. 1-4; 333 f. Nr. 14-15 und 334 f. Nr. 19-26 (mit Athen); 328 Nr. 5-6 (mit Sparta); 328 f. 1-4 und 331 Nr. 1-2 (mit Laodikeia); 331 Nr. 1; 337 Nr. 2-3 (mit Nikomedeia); 339 Nr. 1; 340 Nr. 5; 343 Nr. 18 und 19 (mit Pergamon).

[44] Strab. 12,3,27 (p. 554); ähnlich auch Cic. pro Archias 19.

[45] Im Kontext der baulichen Ausstattung von Smyrna beschreibt Strab. 14,1,37 (p. 646) auch das Homerheiligtum mit dem Xoanon, nebenbei werden auch die Münzen erwähnt; zu diesen auch Esdaile 1912, 305-307; Heyman 1982 und Klose 1987, 34.

[46] Zu den gängigen Drachmen: Milne 1912, 277-298; zu einem wohl etwas früheren Typ ohne Magistratsnamen mit Homer in anderer Haltung: Milne 1921, 143 f. und Heyman 1982, 166-169 Type II.

Zu den Bronzen: Esdaile 1912, 306 (α); Milne 1927 und Milne 1928 und subsumiert sie jeweils unter „Type J"; Heyman 1982, 162-166 Type I.

[47] Esdaile 1912, 306 (Smyrna β); Heyman 1982, 170-173 Type IV; Klose 1987, 35, 181 f. V1-2, R1-2, Taf. 11 („Zweier", zur Datierung auf ca. 198-202 n. Chr. ebd. 82).

Deutlich wird, dass Homer im *kaiserzeitlichen* Typenrepertoire Smyrnas keine größere Bedeutung zukommt. Gleichzeitig bleibt die Überlieferung, dass die Stadt als einer der Geburtsorte Homers gehandelt wird, im Bewusstsein der Zeitgenossen ebenso verankert wie die Präsenz des Homerheiligtums im Stadtbild.

In diesem Zusammenhang sollte kurz ein Münztyp aus Laodikeia am Lykos erwähnt werden, der ebenfalls eine Homonoia mit Smyrna feiert und auf der Rückseite zwei langgewandete Demoi als Städtevertreter zeigt, die vor dem Schriftzug ΟΜΗΡΟΣ im Handschlag vereint stehen[48]. Die von Dietrich Klose etablierte Lesung von ὅμηρος als „Sicherheit, Pfand", was den in der Legende genannten Magistraten Zenon zum „Bürgen" der guten Beziehung der beiden Städte macht, hat sich zwar in der Forschung durchgesetzt[49], doch erscheint mir die Verwendung dieses sonst auf Münzen nie (es sei denn als Benennung Homers[50]) verwendeten Begriffs in einer Homonoiaprägung speziell mit der Homerstadt Smyrna mehr als ein Zufall, sondern ein ganz bewusstes Wortspiel zu sein.

Es scheint naheliegend, dass die antiken Zeitgenossen in Kleinasien das Münzbild einer Skylla im Kampf mit Seeleuten mit der Episode aus der Odyssee und daher – auf den zweiten Blick – dann mit dem Dichter Homer selbst assoziieren, auch wenn die übliche bildliche Darstellungsweise der konkreten Beschreibung Skyllas in der Odyssee gar nicht entspricht, die längst eine ikonografische Eigendynamik durchlaufen hat[51]. Einer Stadt wie Smyrna, deren Bindung an den Dichter im kollektiven Gedächtnis der Zeit außer Frage steht, eine der anschaulichsten Figuren aus dem homerischen Sagenkreis als Repräsentantin für eine Homonoiaprägung zuzuweisen, ist durchaus konsequent und spricht zudem von einer gewissen Originalität.

Bibliographie

Alföldi – Alföldi-Rosenbaum 1976	A. Alföldi – E. Alföldi-Rosenbaum, Die Kontorniat-Medaillons (AMuGS 6) Teil 1, Berlin 1976.
Alföldi – Alföldi-Rosenbaum 1990	A. Alföldi – E. Alföldi-Rosenbaum, Die Kontorniat-Medaillons (AMuGS 6) Teil 2, Berlin 1990.
Andreae 1957	B. Andreae, Archäologische Funde und Grabungen im Bereich der Soprintendenzen von Rom 1949-1956/57, AA 1957, 110-358.

---

[48] Heyman 1982, 169 f. Type III (Homer und Muse); Klose 1984; Klose 1987, 53; RPC I Nr. 2928 und Martin 2013 II 206 f. Laodikeia 5 mit Anm. 269 (zwei Demoi).

[49] Zur Lesung der Legende Klose 1984, 3; Franke 1987, 91; Klose 1987, 35 und 53.

[50] Eine Reihe von kaiserzeitlichen Beispielen mit ΟΜΗΡΟC als Benennung Homers findet sich bei Esdaile 1912, 306 (Smyrna β); 307 f. (Chios α-γ); 311 f. (Cyme α-β); 312 (Nikaia α-γ); 317 f. (Amastris α-θ); 321 (Melos). In Ios wird der Genitiv ΟΜΗΡΟΥ verwendet, s. Esdaile 1912, 315 f. (Ios α-θ). Zu Amastris auch Nollé 2013, 34 f.

[51] Bei Hom. Od. 12,85 besitzt „Skylla (...) zwölf mißgestaltete Füße und sechs Hälse dazu, ganz überlange, auf jedem sitzt ein grausiger Kopf, darin drei Reihen von Zähnen" (Übers. A. Weiher). Dass Text- und Bildtraditionen auseinanderlaufen, formuliert später auch Themistios or. 22 (p.279b, ed. Dindorf): „Ich habe, glaube ich, oft ein Bild der Skylla gesehen, nicht so, wie Homer sie beschreibt..." (Übers. nach Hebert), s. dazu auch Tuchelt 1967, 176; Andreae 1982, 50-54; ausführlich Stilp 2011, bes. 3-10.

Andreae 1974	B. Andreae, Die römischen Repliken der mythologischen Skulpturengruppen von Sperlonga, in: AntPl XIV, 1974, 61-108, bes. 81-87 (Die Skyllagruppe).
Andreae 1982	B. Andreae, Odysseus. Archäologie des europäischen Menschenbildes, Frankfurt 1982.
Andreae 1988	B. Andreae, Laokoon und die Gründung Roms (Kulturgeschichte der antiken Welt 39), Mainz 1988.
Andreae 1999	B. Andreae, Odysseus. Mythos und Erinnerung. Ausstellung im Haus der Kunst, 1. Oktober 1999 bis 9. Januar 2000, Mainz 1999.
Andreae – Conticello 1987	B. Andreae – B. Conticello, Skylla und Charybdis. Zur Skylla-Gruppe von Sperlonga (Abhandlungen der Geistes- und Sozialwissenschaftlichen Klasse / Akademie der Wissenschaften und der Literatur Mainz), Stuttgart 1987.
Baldwin Brett 1955	A. Baldwin Brett, Catalogue of Greek Coins, Boston 1955.
Bendschus – Feuser 2014	T. Bendschus – S. Feuser, Bilder und Vorstellungen römischer Hafenanlagen. Gattungsübergreifende Dokumentation und kontextualisierte Analyse römischer Hafenanlagen (abgeschlossen 2014), Onlinekatalog abrufbar unter https://arachne.uni-koeln.de/drupal/?q=de_DE/node/ 370.
Berger 1988	A. Berger, Untersuchungen zu den Patria Konstantinupoleos (Poikila Byzantina 8), Bonn 1988.
Bingöl 1992	O. Bingöl, Das Skyllakapitell von Magnesia am Mäander, in: H. Fronning u. a. (Hrsg.), Kotinos. Festschrift für Erika Simon, Mainz 1992, 418-423.
Esdaile 1912	K. A. Esdaile, An Essay towards the Classification of Homeric Coin Types, JHS 32, 1912, 298-325.
Fischer-Bossert 2017	W. R. Fischer-Bossert, Coins, Artists and Tyrants. Syracuse in the Time of the Peloponnesian War (Numismatic Studies 33), New York 2017.
Franke 1987	P. R. Franke, Zu den Homomoia-Münzen Kleinasiens, in: E. Olshausen (Hrsg.), Stuttgarter Kolloquium zur historischen Geographie des Altertums 1, Bonn 1987, 81-102.
Franke – Nollé 1997	P. R. Franke – M. K. Nollé, Die Homonoia-Münzen Kleinasiens und der thrakischen Randgebiete (Saarbrücker Studien zur Alten Geschichte und Archäologie 10), Saarbrücken 1997.
Fritze 1912	H. v. Fritze, Die Elektronprägung von Kyzikos. Eine chronologische Studie, Nomisma 7, 1912, 1-38.
Govers Hopman 2012	M. Govers Hopman, Scylla: Myth, Metaphor, Paradox, Cambridge 2012.
Harder 2001	R. E. Harder, DNP XI, 2001, 641, s. v. Skylla.
Hebert 1989	B. Hebert, Schriftquellen zur hellenistischen Kunst. Plastik, Malerei und Kunsthandwerk der Griechen vom vierten bis zum zweiten Jahrhundert (Grazer Beiträge Suppl. 4), Horn-Graz 1989.

Heyman 1982	C. Heyman, Homer on Coins from Smyrna, in: S. Scheers (Hrsg.), Studia Paulo Naster oblata (Numismatica Antica, Orientalia Lovaniensia analecta 12), Leiden 1982, 161-174.
Hoover 2012	O. D. Hoover, Handbook of Coins of Sicily (including Lipara). Civic, Royal, Siculo-Punic, and Romano-Sicilian Issues. Sixth to First Centuries, Lancaster u. a. 2012.
Hoover 2018	O. D. Hoover, Handbook of Coins of Italy and Magna Graecia. Sixth to First Centuries BC, Lancaster u. a. 2018.
Imhoof-Blumer – Keller 1889	F. Imhoof-Blumer – O. Keller, Tier- und Pflanzenbilder auf Münzen und Gemmen des klassischen Altertums, Leipzig 1889.
Jentel 1997	M.-O. Jentel, LIMC VIII, 1997, 1137-1145, s. v. Skylla 1.
Klose 1984	D. O. A. Klose, Homer - ΟΜΗΡΟΣ, SchwMüBl 133, 1984, 1-3.
Klose 1987	D. O. A. Klose, Die Münzprägung von Smyrna in der römischen Kaiserzeit (AMuGS 10), Berlin 1987.
Magie 1950	D. Magie, Roman Rule in Asia Minor to the End of the Third Century after Christ, Princeton 1950.
Martin 2013	K. Martin, Demos. Boule. Gerousia. Personifikationen städtischer Institutionen auf kaiserzeitlichen Münzen aus Kleinasien (EUROS 3), Bonn 2013.
Milne 1921	J. G. Milne, Silver Drachma of Smyrna, NumChron Ser. 5,1, 1921, 143-144.
Milne 1927	J. G. Milne, The Autonomous Coinage of Smyrna (Section II), NumChron Ser. 5,7, 1927, 1-107.
Milne 1928	J. G. Milne, The Autonomous Coinage of Smyrna (Section III), NumChron Ser. 5,8, 1928, 131-171.
Mittag 1999	F. P. Mittag, Alte Köpfe in neuen Händen. Urheber und Funktion der Kontorniaten (Antiquitas Reihe 3, 38), Bonn 1999.
Mottet 2000/2002	Ph. Mottet, Eine unedierte Homonoia-Prägung von Philadelpheia in Lydien aus der Zeit Gordians III., SchwMüBl 50/52, 2000-2002, 25-26.
Nollé 2006	J. Nollé, Beiträge zur kleinasiatischen Münzkunde und Geschichte 1. Homonoia zwischen Philadelpheia und Ephesos, Gephyra 2, 2005 (2006), 73-83.
Nollé 2013	J. Nollé, Dichter, Flussgott. Wie ein kleine Stadt Anspruch auf Homer erhebt, Archäologie weltweit 1, 2013, 34-35.
Nollé 2018	J. Nollé, Okeanos auf Münzen. Überlegungen zu den Hintergründen eines seltenen Münzbildes, in: M. Fuchs (Hrsg.), Ahoros. Gedenkschrift für Hugo Meyer, Wien 2018, 183-216.
Nollé – Nollé 1994	J. Nollé – M. K. Nollé, Vom feinen Spiel städtischer Diplomatie. Zu Zeremoniell und Sinn kaiserzeitlicher Homonoia-Feste, ZPE 102, 1994, 241-261.
Price – Trell 1977	M. J. Price – B. L. Trell, Coins and their Cities. Architecture on the Coins of Greece, Rome, and Palestine, London 1977.

Ridgway 2000	B. S. Ridgway, The Sperlonga Sculptures. The Current State of Research, in: N. T. de Grummond – B. S. Ridgway (Hrsg.), From Pergamon to Sperlonga. Sculpture and Context (Hellenistic Culture and Society 34), Berkeley u. a. 2000, 78-91.
Schmitz 1992	G. Schmitz, Eine weibliche Statuette im Museum von Afyon, AMS 8, 1992, 117-123.
Stilp 2011	F. Stilp, Scylla l'ambivalente, RA 51,1, 2011, 3-26.
Tuchelt 1967	K. Tuchelt, Skylla. Zu einem neugefundenen Tonmodell aus Didyma, IstMitt 17, 1967, 173-194.
Waser 1894	O. Waser, Skylla und Charybdis in der Literatur und Kunst der Griechen und Römer. Mythologisch-archäologische Monographie, Phil. Diss. Zürich 1894.
Westermark 2018	U. Westermark, The Coinage of Akragas, c. 510-406 BC I-II, Uppsala 2018.
Whybrew 2015	D. S. Whybrew, Die Helmdekoration mythologischer Gestalten auf den Münzen der griechischen Poleis Italiens und Siziliens. Überlegungen zu Motivik und semantischem Gehalt, unpubl. Masterarbeit Münster 2015.
Woytek 1995	B. Woytek, MAG PIVS IMP ITER. Die Datierung der sizilischen Münzprägung des Sextus Pompeius, JNG 45, 1995, 79-94.

Lydia Hinterlantı'nda Skylla Ne Arıyor?
Philadelphia ve Smyrna'nın Bir Homonoia Sikkesi Üzerine
Özet

Lydia'nın bir kenti olan Philadelphia'ya ait şimdiye kadar bilinmeyen tipteki bir sikkenin arka yüzünde Skylla betimlenmiştir. Bu betimleme aynı zamanda Smyrna ile yapılan bir homonoia anlaşmasının varlığına da işaret etmektedir. Skylla Yunanistan'ın doğusunda basılan sikkelerde nadiren görülmektedir. Sikke ikonografisinde aktif ve agresif bir şekilde ve de iki deniz canlısına saldırı anında görülen bir Skylla betimi ise tekildir. Yani burada dekoratif bir süsleme unsuru betimlenmemiş, aksine Odyseia'dan bilinen bir mitten somut bir an resme dönüştürülmüştür. Bu betimleme tipolojik olarak Tivoli'deki Villa Hadriana'da bulunan Skylla heykelinin sahnesel motifi ile aynıdır. Philadelphia sikkesinde bu sahne Smyrna'nın temsilcisi olarak Homeros'u betimlemektedir.

Anahtar Sözcükler: Roma eyalet sikkesi, Homonoia konusu, sikke ikonografisi, Odysseia.

What does Scylla do in the hinterland of Lydia?
On a homonoia coin of Philadelphia and Smyrna
Abstract

So far unknown a coin type from Lydian Philadelphia illustrates Scylla on its reverse and alludes to the city's concord (Homonoia) with Smyrna. In the Greek east Scylla is rarely depicted on coins, never at all there is an operating figure, attacking aggressively two sailors as illustrated on the new coin in question. Thus as coin type Scylla is not just a decorative element, but we are confronted with a narrative scene from Homeric Odyssey. Typologically the motif is known from a sculpture in the Hadrianic villa near Tivoli. On the Philadelphian coin the scene seems to refer to Homer as representative for Smyrna.

Keywords: Roman Provincial coin, Homonoia issue, coin iconography, Odyssey.

Abb. 1) *Homonoia-Prägung von Philadelpheia und Smyrna*
(Nomos AG, Auktion 15 [22.10.2017] Nr. 165)

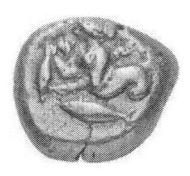

Abb. 2) *Elektronstater aus Kyzikos*
(Numismatik Lanz, Auktion 147 [2.11.2009] Nr. 93)

Abb. 3) *Tetradrachme aus Akragas*
(Fritz Rudolf Künker GmbH & Co KG, Auktion 124
[16.3.2007] Nr. 7847, Foto: Lübke & Wiedemann KG
Stuttgart)

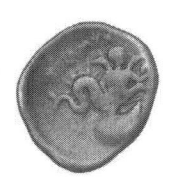

Abb. 4) *Didrachme aus Kyme*
(Münzkabinett des Kunsthistorischen Museums Wien, Inv.
GR 1437; Foto: Margit Redl)

Abb. 5) *Obol aus Allifae*
(NAC, Auktion O [13.5.2004] Nr. 1011)

Abb. 6) *Æ aus Skylletion*
(Peus, Auktion 371 [24.4.2002] Nr. 68)

Abb. 7) *Denar des Sextus Pompeius*
(American Numismatic Society, Inv. 1937.158.343,
http://numismatics.org/collection/1937.158.343,
Bildrechte nach CC BY-NC 4.0)

Abb. 8) *Bronzemünze aus Korinth*
(Münzkabinett der Staatlichen Museen zu Berlin,
Objektnummer 18215294; Foto: Reinhard Saczewski,
https://ikmk.smb.museum/object?id=18215294)

Abb. 9) *Großbronze aus Tarsos*
(Leu, Webauktion 7-1 [23.2.2019] Nr. 4766613l)

Abb. 10) *Spätantiker Kontorniat*
(Münzkabinett des Kunsthistorischen Museums Wien,
Inv. RÖ 32500; Foto: Photoatelier, KHM)

Abb. 11) „Homereion" aus Smyrna
(Münzsammlung des Archäologischen Instituts der
Universität Münster, Inv. M 1141, Foto: Robert Dylka)

Abb. 12) *Bronzemünze aus Smyrna*
(Münzkabinett der Staatlichen Museen zu Berlin,
Objektnummer 18200630; Foto: Reinhard Saczewski,
https://ikmk.smb.museum/object?id=18200630)

New Inscriptions from the Museum of Bursa

N. Eda AKYÜREK ŞAHİN* – Hüseyin UZUNOĞLU**

In this contribution we present some new ancient Greek inscriptions from the Bursa Museum. Of the 36 artefacts, the first four are dedications, while the remaining examples are funerary stones. Six funerary stelai do not bear any inscriptions, nevertheless they are included in the article. After having been produced in the local ateliers, these uninscribed stones were presumably never sold to the customers and they were never employed as funerary stones. Some of the inscribed artefacts in the article (nos. 21-25) have been recently been published by E. Laflı and H. Bru (2016) without having obtained any permission from the museum directory, whereas we were invited and officially given the authorisation to record all inscriptions housed in the museum. We have therefore decided to re-publish them and made corrigenda to their texts where needed. The provenance of some of the artefacts is unfortunately unknown, but in general they were brought to the museum from Bursa province and its environs, such as from the districts of Nilüfer, İnegöl, Orhaneli, Harmancık, Keles, Gemlik, Karacabey and Orhangazi, as well as from the province of Yalova. The ex-votos are offered to Meter Taurene, Men Tauropoleites, Zeus Kersoullos and Apollon. The first two deities are not known in the region of Mysia, Bithynia or the surroundings and their epitheta imply that their places of worship are to be found in the south-southwest of Asia Minor. These dedications might have found their way to the Bursa museum probably through confiscation consequent from the illegal activities of the smugglers of antiquities.

The funerary stones presented in the article have diverse forms, i.e. sarcophagus, prismatic and cylindirical altar, stele with banquet scenes, and stele on altar, which indicate a rich typology in terms of funerary monuments. The inscriptions engraved on them also contribute to enriching

---

* Prof. Dr. Nalan Eda Akyürek Şahin, Akdeniz Üniversitesi, Edebiyat Fakültesi, Eskiçağ Dilleri ve Kültürleri Bölümü, Antalya, Turkey (edasahin@akdeniz.edu.tr).

** Dr. Hüseyin Uzunoğlu, Akdeniz Üniversitesi, Edebiyat Fakültesi, Eskiçağ Dilleri ve Kültürleri Bölümü, Antalya, Turkey (huseyinuzunoglu@gmail.com).

We, foremost, thank Mrs. Ebru Dumlupınar, the current director of the Bursa Museum as well as Mr. Enver Sağır and Mr. Sinan Özdizbay, the ex-directors of the museum for giving me (N. Eda Akyürek Şahin) permission to work on the epigraphic material for many years, as well as the archaeologists, Mrs. Koncagül Hançer, Mrs. Gökçen Ovacık Şeker and Mr. Selçuk Çaprak. My work in the museum is still ongoing and a comprehensive corpus including all the new material is in progress. We are grateful to Prof. Dr. Johannes Nollé (Munich) and to two anonymous reviewers for their insightful comments and suggestions. Needless to say, all remaining errors are ours. We further thank T. Michael P. Duggan (Antalya) for improving the English of this paper.

Ergün Laflı and Hadrien Bru have published some inscriptions from the museum without permission (2016), which are re-published here and some of them have been corrected and improved. Cf. also some inscribed stamps which were also published in an unauthorized way by Ergün Laflı and Maurizio Buora, Un Possibile Stampo per Anfore e Altri Stampi per Pane di età Mediobizantina dal Museo di Bursa, Le Iscrizioni con Funzioni Didascalico-Esplicativa: Committente, Destinatario, Contenuto e Descrizione dell'-Oggetto nell' Instrumentum Inscriptum. Atti del Vi Incontro Instrumenta Inscripta, Aquileia (26-28 Marzo 2015), Trieste 2016, 351-358.

the onomastics of the Mysia and Bithynia regions. However humble they may seem, these funerary inscriptions still provide some interesting information concerning, e.g., a freedman (no. 5), a new phyle called Protinia (no. 10) and a posthumous honouring of a woman doctor (no. 11). The inscriptions to a large extent date to the Roman Imperial Period, but there are also a few Hellenistic examples (no. 13, 19, 24, 25).

Dedications

1. Dedication to Meter Taurene and Men Tauropeleites

A small votive stele of marble; kept on public display inside the museum.

Inv. No.: 2013/58; findspot unknown. After being smuggled to İnegöl, the stele was seized there and transported to the museum following the judicial process. Dimensions: H.: 51 cm; W.: 38 cm (base); 35 cm (top); 20 cm (dowel); D.: 6,5-7 cm; Lh.: 1-3 cm.

The stele is broken at the top and the head of the goddess is missing due to this break. On the shaft of the stele the seated Meter figure on a throne is depicted; the throne is flanked by a lion on either side. The goddess holds a patera in her right hand and a tympanon (tambourine) in her left hand. She wears a chiton with a himation over it. Her feet are visible out of her long dress and she rests them on a rectangular footstool. Below this scene an untidy Greek inscription of five lines is carved. The stele has a somewhat thick and high dowel.

    Μητρόδωρος Ἐπι-
2   τυνχάνοντος
    Μητρὶ Ταυρηνῇ καὶ
4   Μηνὶ Ταυροπολείτῃ
    εὐχήν.

Metrodoros, son of Epitynchanon, (fulfilled) his vow to Meter Taurene and Men Tauropoleites.

L. 3-4: Μητρὶ Ταυρηνῇ καὶ Μηνὶ Ταυροπολείτῃ. Up to now, a mother goddess worshipped with this epithet seems to be unknown. Yet, the epithet of Taurene attached to the goddess Ma occurs once in the territory of Hadrianoi in Pisidia, see Milner 1998, 70-71, no. 155: [. θε]ᾷ Μᾷ Ταυρη[νῇ (?)]. Our new inscription indicates that the restoration by Milner of that dedication is more plausible than that made by G. E. Bean (1959, 95, no. 43) who tentatively suggested Taurelatis or Tauregetis. It is also very possible that Meter Metaurene testified in Pisidia is in close relation with the Meter Taurene of our inscription. For Meter Metaurene see SEG 6, 619; Talloen 2015, 60 and 248. It is highly probable that both epitheta were derived from the Taurus mountains, and this is also supported by the fact that Meter is known as a goddess of the mountains, i.e. Meter Oreia, see Akın 2016 who compiled and evaluated all the evidence in Asia Minor (yet she doesn't mention Meter Metaurene in her work). Although it is not surprising that this cult is attested in Pisidia which is crossed by the western Taurus range, its occurence in Bithynia is rather astonishing. The inventory states that the artefact was transported from İnegöl, but its exact provenance is not recorded. Given the fact that the Bursa Museum houses numerous monuments of various provenances which found their way there as a result of smuggling (see for example Uzunoğlu 2019), it is not improbable that this stele originated from an area near the Western Taurus. That the god Men to whom this ex-voto is also offered bears the epithet of Tauropoleites gains a particular significance. To date, it is attested only once in Oinoanda as a designation of Ares, see Heberdey – Kalinka 1897, 53-54, no. 76: Θόας Δ[ωσί]θεος | θεῷ Ἄρῃ Ταυ|ροπολείτῃ, whereas the lunar god Men doesn't seem to have possessed this epithet according to our current knowledge. For all the known epitheta of Men, see Lane 1976, 67-80. Höfer (1916-1924, 137) claims that the epithet of Tauropoleites in the Oinoanda inscription is associated with the Carian city of Tauropolis mentioned in Stephanus of Byzantium (s.v. Ταυρόπολις· πόλις Καρίας. τὸ ἐθνικὸν Ταυροπολίτης). Although the exact location of that city has not been pinpointed to date, a passage in Constantinus Porphyrogennetos (*de Them.* 14) implies that it must be located somewhere in the Lycian-Carian borderland, see Ruge 1934, 33-34. So, although not certainly, it is possible that the provenance of our stele was somewhere in the mountainous area in the south-west Taurus Mountains. Nevertheless, one cannot rule out the possibility that the epithet is simply derived from the word ταῦρος (= bull) or is somehow associated with the Iphigenia mythos, as is the case for Artemis Tauropoulos, see Nollé 2009.

It is highly probable that Metrodoros, who is named after the mother goddess, considered her as his guardian goddess. Thus this inscription provides a good example for the relation of the theophoric name-bearers with their patron deities.

For the examples of the juxtaposition of Meter and Men, see Lane 1976, 81-83.

Date: Roman Imperial Period

2. Dedication to Zeus Kersoullos

Column of grey marble. Inv. No.: 3051; findspot: unknown. Dimensions: H.: 189 cm; Diameter: (top) 25 cm, (below) 34 cm; Lh.: 2,2-3,5 cm.

The thin and long votive column has some partial breaks and cracks. On the rear part there are deep scratches. Otherwise well preserved, the column bears a Greek dedicatory inscription of eight lines. Some letters are barely legible due to erosion-abrasion.

[Ἀγα]θῇ τύχῃ·
2 Δι[ὶ Κ]ε[ρ]σούλλῳ
Ἀπολλώνιος Ἀσκλη-
4 πιάδου Ἀνκυρανὸς
κώμης Ἀοριασσης
6 ἀνέστησεν κατ' ἐπιταγήν,
προφητεύσαντος
8 Ῥούφου μυστάρχου.

With good fortune!
Apollonios, son of Asklepiades,
a citizen of Ankyra, from the
village of Aoriasse, dedicated
(this column) to Zeus
Kersoullos, in accordance with
a command, when the mystarch
Rufus was the prophet.

L. 2: Δι[ὶ] Κερ[σ]ούλλῳ. Schwertheim (IHadrianoi, p. 4) is of the opinion that Zeus Kersoullos was a god of agriculture and fertility, given the assumption that his epithet Κερσος is of Thracian origin and means "field, farmland", yet Schwabl (1993, 334) is not entirely convinced by his assertion. For Κερσος and its meanings, see also Detschew 1957, 242; cf. also Dunst 1971. For the cult in general, see Çaçu 2005.

Zeus Kersoullos has been attested 12 times in the territory of Hadrianoi in Mysia and both the number of these inscriptions and their contents apparently reveal that the god had a sancutary there which functioned as an oracle centre (see below). These inscriptions have been discovered in the villages of Akçapınar, Belenören and Haydar situated in close proximity to each other between Orhaneli (ancient Hadrianoi) and the district of Keles. This may indicate that the sanctuary must have stood in their neighbourhood. The findspot of our inscription is unknown, but it is very probable that it has the same provenance. Apart from these, the other dedications to Zeus Kersoullos are documented in the villages of Şehriman and Derecik, ca. 70 km north-west of the sanctuary. In the case of the inscription recorded in the village of Dağdibi, ca. 20 km north of the sanctuary, it is not clear whether it is related with the cult of Zeus Kersoullos. The god is mentioned as Zeus Kersoullos Olympios in an inscription found in the territory of Aizanoi, but it is rather to be associated with the principal Zeus cult in the city because it is again closely linked with the cult in the territory of Hadrianoi, see Lehmler – Wörrle 2006, 81. The Aizanoi inscription confirms Schwertheim (1989, 253) who previously suggested that Zeus Kersoullos should be identified with the Zeus Olympios attested in some passages of Aelius Aristides. Cf. also Schwabl 1993, 334, fn. 14, and Battistoni – Rothenhöfer 2013, 108. All the epigraphic evidence concerning Zeus Kersoullos is given in an appendix below.

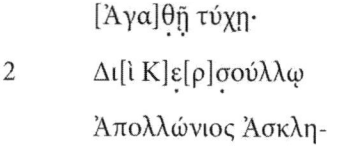

L. 4-5: The dedicant Apollonios was apparently a citizen of Ankyra who resided in the village of Aoriasse. Till now, no information on this village is available. Given the geographical proximity, Ankyra is most likely to be identified with the city in Mysia Abbaitis, not in Galatia. A similar case can also be observed in IHadrianoi, no. 4 where a certain Attalos, a citizen of Aizanoi and resident of the village of Olgeizeos (Ἄτταλος Ἀττάλου Αἰζανείτης οἰκῶν ἐν Ὀλγειζηῳ) made a dedication to Zeus Kersoullos (given as Kersoussos in the inscription). Schwertheim accepted with reservation that the village of Olgeizos was located in the Aizanitis, but this has been rejected by Lehmler and Wörrle (2006, 81) on the grounds that the dedicant possessed the right of residence as a metoikos and they assert that the village must have been within the territory of Hadrianoi. It is less likely that this can also be applied to our case, since we don't have the 'οἰκῶν ἐν' structure and we may therefore suggest that the village of Aoriasse was situated somewhere within the boundaries of Ankyra. The god is also attested on the coins of Kaisareia Germanike (Ripollès et al. 2015, 99) implying that the fame of this local cult surpassed Hadrianoi and extended to several places such as Ankyra, Aizanoi, and to Kaisareia Germanike.

In fact, it is not certain to which city's territory the sanctuary of Zeus Kersoullos belonged. The reason for this ambiguity lies in the fact that a Bithyniarch is attested in a fragmentary inscription dated to 146/7 or 155/6 A.D. and discovered in the village of Baraklı, lying approximately 10 km northeast of Akçapınar village, where the sanctuary is located (Battistoni – Rothenhöfer 2013, 110-114, no. 1; SEG 61, 1013; SEG 63, 1024: [ἔτου]ς θ' ἐπὶ Αὐτοκράτορος τὸ β' Καί| [σαρος] Τ(ί-του) Αἰλίου Ἀδριανοῦ Ἀντωνίνου Σεβαστοῦ | Ε[ὐσε]βοῦς καὶ Αὐρηλίου Οὐήρου Καίσαρος χρυσοφο|ροῦντος βιθυνιάρχου κτλ.). Moreover, the citizens of Prusa ad Olympum offered a dedication to Zeus Kersoullos in Tazlaktepe, a quarter of Akçapınar village (Battistoni – Rothenhöfer 2013, 128-129, no. 31 = SEG 63, no. 1026). F. Battistoni and P. Rothenhöfer hesitatingly deduced from the above mentioned evidence that Baraklı and the area around the Zeus Kersoullos sanctuary belonged to the territory of Prusa ad Olympum in Bithynia instead of Hadrianoi in Mysia, see Battistoni – Rothenhöfer 2013, 103-104. Even though T. Corsten, on the other hand, accepts that the reference to a Bithyniarch is not expected there, he doesn't agree with them, recalling the case of Aur. Mindius Mattidianus Pollio of Ephesos who served as Bithyniarch three times (I.Ephesos 627 LL. 17/18), see SEG 61, 1013 and SEG 63, 1024.

L. 6: ἀνέστησεν: Even though it is not said in the inscription what is offered to the god, it is obviously a column. This is explicitly stated in four other Zeus Kersoullos dedications as ἀνέσ|τησα τὸν κείονα (see in the appendix nos 6-8-10-13). In one inscription, a παραστάς and a golden τύπωμα worthy of 100 denaria is dedicated to the god (no. 1) as well as a βωμός in another (no. 3).

The expression κατὰ ἐπιταγήν occurs particularly in Bithynia and Mysia regions. For this formula see Nock 1925, 95-98; Pleket 1981, 154 and 158.

L. 7: προφητεύσαντος. The *prophetes* was responsible for proclaiming the god's responses in the sanctuary. When its verb form προφητεύω is used in a genitivus absolutus-construction like προφητεύοντος or προφητεύσαντος τοῦ δεῖνα, it usually has the function of a dating formula. The prophets attested around Hadrianoi were listed by Battistoni – Rothenhöfer 2013, 107-108. The existence of the prophets provides the most tangible evidence that we here deal with an oracular sanctuary, and this is also supported by yet another inscription discovered in the village of Akçapınar which tells us that a certain Gauros received πιστοὺς λόγους from a prophet, see IHadrianoi, no. 24: Γαῦρος προφητῶν εἰλό|μην πιστοὺς λόγους καὶ ἐπέ|γραψα νίκην Καίσαρος καὶ ἄ[λ]|λους θεῶν κτλ. Schwertheim translated the line ἐπέγραψα ... ἄ[λ]λους θεῶν as "he inscribed

… the other (words) of the gods", and accordingly argued that the prophecy was given in this shrine not by one single (i.e. Zeus) but by various other gods. On the other hand, H. Schwabl (1993, 337-338) draws attention to the fact that ἐπιγράφω means not only "to inscribe" but also "to depict, portray etc." and by restoring the line as "ἐπέγραψα … κἄ[θ]λους θεῶν", he provided a new translation: "Gauros portrayed … the war of the gods" and concluded that the oracular sanctuary is merely related with Zeus because this line concerns rather the Gigantomachy which resulted in the victory of Zeus. It is also confirmed by the fact that the majority of the dedicatory inscriptions found at Akçapınar and its environs are associated with Zeus Kersoullos.

The sanctuary in Hadrianoi was obviously not as famous as Didyma or Claros and it was possibly one of the local or regional oracular centres in Asia mentioned in a passage of Lucian (*de dea Syria* 36), see IHadrianoi, p. 22. We don't have a large number of epigraphic records regarding the office of prophetes and this term appears to be restricted mainly to Mysia, Bithynia, Phrygia, and Lydia, see Robert, OMS I, 421-422. For some examples, see SEG 59, 1416 [Apollonia ad Rhyndacum]; IKalchedon, nos. 7, 19, 42, 61; TAM V,1, 535 [Maionia]; TAM V,2, 1411 [Magnesia ad Sipylum]; ILaodikeia am Lykos, no. 67; MAMA IX, 60 [Aizanitis]; Onur 2011, 337-338.

L. 8: μυστάρχου. Mystarches, who presided over the mysteries, are rarely recorded in the epigraphical evidence. Most of the occurences in Asia Minor are from Kyzikos, a city lying not so far from the area in question, see e.g. CIG II 2, 3662; 3663A. As far as we know, there are only two examples apart from Kyzikos, see IPrusa ad Olympum I, no. 52; IKlaudiu Polis, no. 65. While one of its equivalents μυστηριάρχης is attested only in Kyzikos and Nikomedia (see CIG II 2, 3666 [Kyzikos]; Şahin 1974, 34 = TAM IV, 262 [Nikomedia], ἀρχιμύστης is documented much more frequently and over a much wider geography, see Waldmann 1978, 1309-1315. It is striking that Rufus served both as a prophet and a mystarch at the same time. Rufus is named without a patronymic.

Date: Roman Imperial Period

Appendix: Documents relating to Zeus Kersoullos

1. IHadrianoi, no. 1 (second half of the 1st cent. A.D.)

ἀγαθῇ τύχῃ· | Μᾶρκος Οὔπιες | Καιλιανὸς Μηγι|ανὸς Δὶ Κερ[σο]ύλ|λῳ τὴν παραστά|δαν ἐκ τῶ | εἰδίων·| ἀνέστη[σε δὲ] καὶ δῶρ[α] | τόγαν, δακτύλιον | χρύσεον σὺν ὄσσ<ο>ις δύ|ω, ἀσπίδαν, δόρυ· εὐ|χαριστῖ τῷ κυρίῳ | Δὶ κατὰ πάσας εὐ|χάς·| ἀνέθηκε δὲ | καὶ τύπωμα | χρύσεον ἀπὸ | δηναρίων | ἑκατόν.

2. IHadrianoi, no. 2 (2nd cent. A.D.)

Θάλαμος Μενεκράτους Διὶ | Κερσούλλῳ εὐχήν.

3. IHadrianoi, no. 3 = Battistoni – Rothenhöfer 2013, 122-123, no. 17 = SEG 63, no. 1027 (2nd cent. A.D.)

[Ἀσκ]ληπιάδης Μελ[ε]|[ά]γ[ρ]ου κατ' ἐπιταγὴν | Διὶ Κερσούλλῳ ὑπέρ τε | ἑαυτοῦ καὶ Χρυσ[ίο]υ τῆ|ς συνβίου καὶ τῶν υἱῶ|ν τὸν βωμὸν ἀνέσ|τησεν. | Λειβηνός.

4. IHadrianoi, no. 4 (2nd cent. A.D.)

Ἄτταλος | Ἀττάλου | Αἰζανείτης | οἰκῶν ἐν | Ὀλγειζηῳ | ἐκ τῶν ἰδίων | Διὶ Κερσούσσῳ | εὐχήν.

5. IHadrianoi, no. 5 (1st cent. A.D.)

[--- Διὶ] | Κερσούλλ[ῳ]· | ἐπιμελησ[α]|μένων Γα<ί>|ου Αὐδίου | καὶ Μηνᾶς | καὶ Γάειος.

6. IHadrianoi, no. 6 (2nd cent. A.D.)

ἀγαθῇ τύχῃ· | Διὶ Κερσούλλῳ Ἀρτᾶς | Ἀριστοκράτους Πλανη|νὸς μετὰ τῆς συνβίου | Ἀμμίας καὶ τῶν τέκνων | Ἀπφᾶ καὶ Ἀριστοκράτους καὶ | Ἀρτᾶ καὶ Χρυσογόνου ἀνέσ|τησα τὸν κείονα ἐκ τῶν ἰδίων· | προφητεύσαντος Ἀπολ|λωνίου Ἐπιθυμήτου.

7. IHadrianoi, no. 7 (2nd-3rd cent. A.D.)

ἀγαθῇ τύχῃ· Κ[---]|δωξης Διὶ Κερ[σούλλῳ εὐχήν].

8. IHadrianoi, no. 8 (3rd cent. A.D.)

ἀγαθῇ τύχῃ· | Αὐρήλιοι Ὀνήσι|μος Φίλωνος | Ελλη[-----]ου | κα[ὶ] Ἀλέξανδ[ρ]ος [Ἀπ]ο[λ]|λων[ίου] κατὰ ἐπιταγὴν | Διὸς Κερσούλ|λου τὸν κεί|[ο]να καὶ τὸν ἀν{δ}|δριάντην | ἀνέστησαν | ἐκ τῶν ἰδίων.

9. Battistoni – Rothenhöfer 2013, 129, no. 32 = SEG 63, no. 1031 (2nd-3rd cent. A.D.)

Ο[...]ος Α[...]ος | [ἔ]στρωσε [.]ΑΝ[..]Σ[- | Διὶ Κ]ερσούλλῳ.

10. Battistoni – Rothenhöfer 2013, 128-129, no. 31 = SEG 63, no. 1026 = AE 2013, no. 1467 (113/114 A.D.)

Ἔτους ι[.]΄, [ἐπὶ Αὐτ]οκράτορο[ς] | Κέσαρος Σεβαστοῦ Γερμανικοῦ | Δακικοῦ κατὰ ἐπιταγὴν Διὶ Κερ|σούλλῳ ὑπὲρ τῆς Καίσαρος νίκης | Ἀσκληπιάδης κὲ Παπᾶς οἱ Παπᾶ |το[ῦ?] ΕΑΝΟ[.], πολῖτε Προυσα(έ)ων ἀνέσ|τησα[ν τ]οὺς κίονας ὑπὲρ ἑαυτῶν |[καὶ τῶν] γονέων κ[αὶ τέκνων αὐ]-| τῶν ἐκ{κ} τοῦ ἰδίου.

11. Battistoni – Rothenhöfer 2013, 124, no. 19 = SEG 63, no. 1029 (2nd-3rd cent. A.D.)

Ἀγαθῇ τύχῃ· | Διὶ Κερσούλλῳ | Ἀπο[λλ]ώνιος κ(ὲ) Ἀπολ[- -] | κ(ὲ) Διονύσιος οἱ Διονυ[σίου] | [.]ΙΣΤΗΝ[.]ΝΟΙ ἐκ τῶν ἰδίων | κατὰ ἐπιταγὴν προφητεύ|σαντος Διοφάνου Τειμοθέου.

12. Battistoni – Rothenhöfer 2013, 124-125, no. 20 = SEG 63, no. 1030; AE 2013, no. 466 (2nd-3rd cent. A.D.)

[Μ]αρκία Ὀμ[- - | Διὶ] Κερσούλλῳ [- - -]

13. Battistoni – Rothenhöfer 2013, 123-124, no. 18 = SEG 63, no. 1028 (2nd-3rd cent. A.D.)

⟦Ἀγαθῇ τύχῃ· | Κλέανδρο[ς - 4-5 -] | [πόλεως Ἁδ[ρι]ανῆς | Διὶ Κερσούλλῳ τὸν | κείονα ἀνέσ-τ[η]σα | ἐκ τῶν ἰδίων, [προφη]|τεύσα[ντος] Ἀπολλω|νίου Ἐπιθυμήτου⟧

14. Akyürek Şahin 2010, 273-274 = Jones 2012, 233-236 = SEG 59, no. 1418 (2nd-3rd cent. A.D.)

Ζεὺς Ἀναβα|τηνὸς Διὶ Κερ|σούλλῳ ν ἀνέσ|τησεν.

15. IHadrianoi, no. 21 (?)

ἀγα[θῇ τύχῃ]· Γεμέ[λλος ---|---]ραιου [---]|[---]ρου Σο[---|---] Διὸς Κ[ερσούλλου |---]ΟΠΟΛΥ[---|---]ΥΡΟΥΟ[---|---]εὐχὴν π[---]|ΕΙΣΙΧΝΟ[---]|ΒΕΙΟΙΣΟ[---]|ΜΟΣΔΟ[---|---]ΟΣΜ[---|---]ΤΥ[---]

16. Lehmler – Wörrle 2006, 79-82 no. 137 = SEG 56, no. 1436 (Aizanoi-Early Imperial Period).

A. [--] Διεὶ Ὀλυνπίῳ Κερσούλλῳ εὐχὴν οἱ εἰε[ροὶ Ἀπολ]λώνιος Μητρ[- - - - σὺν τοῖς υἱοῖς - - ca. 14 - -] | καὶ Ἀπολλωνίῳ καὶ οἱ λοιποὶ ἕκαστος παρ᾽ ἑαυτοῦ Μητρόδωρος Μητροδ[ώρου, - - ca. 18 - - | - - - - - - - ca. 21 - - - - - - - - - - - - -] Τρυφωνιανὸς Τ[ρ]ύφων[ο]ς, [- - - - - - - ca. 38- - - - - -] | Ἀρτεμίδωρος Τείμωνος, Ζήνων Ἀπολλωνίου, Φί(λ)ιππος Φιλέρωτος Λέων, Μένανδρος β΄, Ἀσκληπιάδης Τροφίμου.

Cf. also IHadrianoi, no. 36; SGO II, no. 08/08/03 (2nd-3rd cent. A.D.)

3. Dedication to a God (Zeus Kersoullos?)

Marble block stone; no inventory number yet given; findspot unknown. Dimensions: H.: 106 cm; W.: 66 cm; D.: 23 cm; Lh.: 1,3-3,5 cm.

Carved block with a thick frame. Broken at the right. The profile presumably continued on the broken missing part. Damaged in all parts, in particular on the moulding. A Greek inscription of six lines is carved in the upper part of the framed area. The inscription is carelessly carved but intact.

Ἀγαθῇ τύχῃ· Ἀντιγέν-
2 ης Ἀσκληπίδου καὶ Ἀφ[ί]α
    ἀνέστησαν ἐκ τῶν ἰδίων
4 τὸν σηκὸν τῷ θεῷ προ-
    φυτεύσαντος Ἀριστοκρά-
6 του εἱερέος.

With good fortune! Antigenes, son of Asklepides, and Aphia, dedicated this sekos (shrine?) to the god at their own expense, when the priest Aristokrates was the prophet.

L. 4: τὸν σηκόν: The term bears chiefly two meanings: It is primarily a double-storey family tomb (see Kubińska 1968, 114-116; Mitchell 1977, 90), but it also designates a sacred enclosure, shrine or a cella, see LSJ, s.v.; Ginouvès 1998, 39, who claims that this word means only the cella/naos and not the whole temple.

The authors Pollux and Ammonius explain the distinction between naos and sekos in a way that the former pertains to the gods, while the latter is employed for the heros, see Pollux, *Onom.* I. 6: οἱ μὲν γὰρ ἀκριβέστεροι σηκὸν τὸν τῶν ἡρώων λέγουσιν, οἱ δὲ ποιηταὶ καὶ τὸν τῶν θεῶν; Ammonius, *diff.* 396: ναὸς καὶ σηκὸς διαφέρει. ὁ μὲν γὰρ ναός ἐστι θεῶν, ὁ δὲ σηκὸς ἡρώων. Nevertheless, it is beyond any doubt that according to the wording of this inscription the sekos is dedicated to a god. As already emphasized above, many dedications to Zeus Kersoullos in this area manifest evidence of the existence of the god's sanctuary. Furthermore, Battistoni and Rothenhöfer argued that there must have been another shrine of an unknown god around Baraklı village, apart from that of Zeus Kersoullos in Akçapınar village and its surroundings. That we don't know the actual findspot of this artefact and that the god's name is not clearly expressed in the inscription poses a difficulty to us in determining to which sanctuary this term related.

For the occurrences of the term in Asia Minor relating to a sanctuary, see Mitchell 1977, 89-90, no. 31 = SEG 27, 851 [Ankyra]; ISmyrna II.1, no. 726.

τῷ θεῷ. It presumably meant Zeus (Kersoullos), the dominant god worshipped in the region (see above). However, the fact that some other male deities such as Dionysos and Apollon are also attested and that there is no iconographic element on the artefact prevents us from claiming anything with certainty concerning the identity of the god, see IHadrianoi, no. 12; Battistoni – Rothenhöfer 2013, 122, no. 16. For instance, ἡ θεός in Ihadrianoi, no. 16 could have been securely identified with Hygiea due to the snake figures carved below the inscribed field. Cf. a similar case in Battistoni – Rothenhöfer 2013, 119-120, no. 12.

L. 4-5: προφυτεύσαντος = προφητεύσαντος. The stonecutter apparently carved upsilon instead of eta. For the office of prophetes, cf. above. It is a strong indication that this stone was also brought to the museum from the same area.

L. 6: εἱερέος: ἱερέως. That the prophets are mentioned with another title at the same time is not prevalent and seemingly attested only above no. 2 (as mystarches) and here as priest. In Didyma, for example, the cult was headed by a prophet, never by a hiereus, contrary to Delphi, where the cultic inscriptions always refer to a hiereus, see Fontenrose 1988, 46. For the priests who are also called prophets, cf. Callan 2010, 40.

Date: Roman Imperial Period

3a. Marble bomos. Copied in the village of Baraklı, Keles/Bursa in 2006 by Mr. Ayhan Çaçu who is working as a school teacher there. We haven't seen the inscription itself but deciphered it from the hand-copy and the photos taken by Çaçu. We thank him very much for sharing the inscription with us. The current whereabouts of the bomos remains unknown.

	Ἀγαθῇ τύχῃ·	With good fortune!
2	Μητρόδω-	Metrodoros, son of Menios
	ρος Μηνίου	(and) Euraion Neiketes
4	Εὐραίων	(dedicated this to?)
	Νεικήτης δυσ-	in fulfillment of a vow
6	κόλων και-	due to? the unpleasant times
	ρῶν ὑπὲρ τ-	for the sake of their own
8	ῶν ἰδίων	(family members)
	[- - - - - - - -]	when N.N., son of T...
10	εὐχήν, προφ-	was the prophet.
	ητεύσαντος Τ- - -]	
	- - - - - - - - - -	

L. 4: Εὐραίων has to date never been attested, but we cannot be sure if this reading is accurate because the first letters are extremely dubious. If we preferred beta, for example, instead of a rho, we would then have the name Eubaion, which has indeed few occurrences (albeit geographically distant), see LGPN I, 171 s.v. and II, 163 s.v.

L. 5-7: The position of δυσκόλων καιρῶν in the genitive plural without any preposition before it, is bizarre. Epigraphically, this expression is rare and not attested in any dedicatory context. It only occurs in an Attic decree (IG II², no. 682, l. 33: περιστάντων τεῖ πόλει καιρῶν δυσκόλων), in two honorific decrees from Sestos and Stratonikeia (ISestos, no. 1, l. 54 γυμνασιαρχῆσαι ὑπέμεινεν ἐν καιροῖς δυσκόλοις; IStratonikeia I, no. 16, l. 13-14: τετελεκότα καὶ πρυτανείαν καὶ γραμματείαν ἐν δυσκόλοις καιροῖς ἐπὶ ὠφελίᾳ τῆς πόλεως) and in one honorific inscription from Lydia (TAM V,2 no. 942, l. 8-9: σειτωνήσαντα ἐν καιρῷ δυσκόλῳ;). The most plausible explanation for our case is that the dedicants were probably farmers and after having been affected negatively by the meteorological conditions (drought or conversely flood/hail), they made this vow to the god. Yet again we don't know whether it was offered to Zeus Kersoullos who is thought to be a god of fertility and agriculture (see above no. 2), but if our interpretation were correct, this would be a strong possibility.

L. 9: In the copy of Çacu, there is a space in line 9. We couldn't read anything on the photo, but it is highly possible that the name of the god must have stood there in the dative case.

Date: Roman Imperial Period

4. Dedication to a God

A marble altar fragment; kept in the garden of the Bursa Museum. No inventory number yet given. Findspot: Zindan Kapısı in Bursa. Dimensions: H: 35 cm; W: 31 cm; D: 23,5 cm; Lh.: missing.

The altar is broken at the top and below. Crown and base are missing. Shaft also broken into two parts and heavily damaged. An inscription of seven lines is neatly carved.

	Ἀπόλ[λωνι?..]-	Polyainos,
2	ραίῳ τὸν βωμὸν	son of Akylas,
	κατὰ ἐπιταγὴν	together with his wife
4	ἀνέστησεν Πο-	dedicated this bomos

	λύαινο[ς] Ἀκύλου	on (divine) command,
6	μετὰ τ[ῆ]ς γυναι-	to Apollon?.. raios.
	κός.	

L. 1-2: Ἀπόλ[λωνι?..]ραίῳ = Ἀπόλ[λωνι? Ἀκ?]ραίῳ. Neither the restoration of Apollon nor that of his epithet Akraios is certain, but if it were the case, this would be the first document in which Apollon is attested with the epithet of Akraios. Akraios is mainly related with Zeus, but the third letter in the first line, i.e. an omicron, doesn't let us make a reconstruction as Διὶ Ἀκραίῳ. As far as we could determine, Akraios was also applied to Men once, see Drew-Bear 1978, 31, no. 5. One can also suggest the epithet Agoraios, which is not infrequently attested for Zeus, as well as for other deities such as Dionysos and Hermes.

L. 3: For κατὰ ἐπιταγήν see above no. 2.

Date: Roman Imperial Period

Funerary Inscriptions

5. Funerary inscription of Ekgle(k)tos?

A marble sarcophagus with grey veins. Kept in the garden of the museum. No inventory number yet given. Unearthed in the course of highway construction at Çaylı/Nilüfer. Dimensions: H.: 77 cm; W.: 237 cm; D.: 21 cm; Lh.: 2,5 cm.

Only the facade of this half-fabricated garland sarcophagus is preserved, unfortunately the rest is missing. In the middle of the chest there is a rectangular tabula ansata containing an inscription of four lines.

	Ἐκγλετε Ἀρ-	*Ekgle(k)tos,*
2	τέμωνος ἀ-	*freedman of*
	πελεύθε-	*Artemon,*
4	ρε χαῖρε.	*farewell!*

L. 1: As far as we know, there is no further evidence for Ἔκγλετος, but we can be sure that either Ἔκγλεκτος (IGUR II, no. 495) or a far more attested name Ἔκλεκτος/Ἔγλεκτος is meant here, see LGPN VA, 132 s.v.; Anderson et al. 1910, 194 (for Ἔγλεκτος). Cf. below no. 24 where the deceased is mentioned also in the vocative case.

This is yet another example for the Proconnesian half-fabricated garland sarcophagus which was quite prevalent in Asia Minor in the 2nd and 3rd centuries A.D., see Asgari 1977 and Koch – Sichtermann 1982, 484-497. For a similar sarcophagus discovered in Mudanya (Apameia Myrleia in Bithynia) which today is also kept in the garden of the Bursa Museum, see IApameia-Pylai, 37 no. 27 A pl. 1.

Date: Roman Imperial Period

6. Funerary bomos of Asklepiodote

Marble bomos. Kept in the garden of the museum. No inventory number yet given. Unearthed in the course of Buski (Bursa Water and Sewage Administration) works in İnegöl (Çitli). Dimensions: H.: 132 cm; W.: 63 cm (crown); 48-52 cm (shaft); 71-72 cm (base); D.: 53 cm (crown); 43-44 cm (shaft); 55 cm (base); Lh.: 3-4 cm.

The bomos is defaced at the top and has small breaks. On the sides of the shaft some breaks are also visible. Upper moulding decorated with corner acroteria. Low base undecorated. A carelessly carved inscription of four lines begins from the moulding.

  Λούκιος Μάρκου
2 ζῶν ἑαυτῷ καὶ Ἀσκλη-
  πιοδότῃ, Νεννεος
4 τῇ ἑαυτοῦ.

Lucius, son of Marcus, (constructed this bomos) in his lifetime, for himself and for Asklepiodote, daughter of Nennis, his own (wife).

L. 3: Νεννεος. Nennis (gen. Nennios) is attested once in Cilicia, see Dagron – Feissel 1987, no. 11 A 2, l. 40 = LGPN VB, 312 s.v. In this inscription ι appears as ε, cf. Brixhe 1987, 51: „*Les inscriptions anatoliennes fournissent bon nombre d'échanges entre E (AI) et I (EI, H, Y) devant /a, o, u, e/.*"

L. 4: In the end of the line, γυναικί is expected following τῇ ἑαυτοῦ.

Date: Roman Imperial Period

7. Funerary bomos of Eutychides

Marble bomos. Placed in the garden of the museum. No inventory number yet given. Findspot unknown. Confiscated by the police from smugglers near Söğüt Mah., Orhaneli/Bursa. Dimensions: H: 84 cm; W: 37,5 cm; D: 30 cm; Lh: 2,5-3 cm.

Except for some small damages, the altar is generally well-preserved. It has a low base and crown. On the upper front face there is an inscription of five lines. Guidelines applied to prevent the lines from becoming uneven are visible. Beneath the inscription the high relief of a large wreath.

     Αὐρ. Δωρὶς σὺν τοῖς τέ-
  2 κνοις Ἐλπιδηφόρῳ
     κὲ Εὐτυχίδῃ ἀνδρὶ γλυ-
  4 κυτάτῳ Εὐτυχίδῃ μνή-   *the forms*
     μης   χάριν.   *of eta*

Aur(elia) Doris (constructed this altar) with her children Elpidephoros and Eutychides to her sweetest husband Eutychides, in memory.

L. 1: Apart from this inscription, the name of Δωρίς occurs only once in Bithynia and Mysia, see Şahin – Onur 2010, 35-36, no. 10. In Greek mythology, she was the mother of the sea nymphs known as the Nereids. For the name, cf. also Brixhe 1991, 20.

L. 2: Ἐλπιδηφόρῳ. For the name, see LGPN VA, 154 s.v. It is also documented in a funerary inscription found in Balıkesir, see Tanrıver 2013, 54 no. 50.

L. 3-4: For Εὐτυχίδης see LGPN VA, 185 s.v.

Date: After 212 A.D. (Constitutio Antoniniana).

8. Funerary Inscription of Chreste

Marble altar fragment. Kept in the garden of the museum. No inventory number yet given. Findspot: Harmancık/Bursa. Dimensions: H: 83 cm; W.: 45-52 cm; D.: 38 cm; Lh.: 2-2,5 cm.

Broken at the top and below. The remaining shaft is also broken into two pieces in the middle. Base missing. The crown is heavily damaged. The inscription of four lines carved on the shaft is hardly legible in the broken parts. Below the inscription there are some figures in relief depicting objects possibly of a woman but they cannot be certainly identified due to their defaced surfaces, except for the circular object, most probably a mirror with a handle.

    Ἑρμᾶς Μενεσθέο[ς]
2   Χρήστῃ τῇ συνβίῳ
    [ἐ]κ τῶν ἰδίων αὐτ[οῦ]
4   ΜΗΣΜΗΣ χάριν.

Hermas, son of Menestheus, (constructed this altar) to his wife Chreste at his own expense, in memory.

L. 1: Μενεσθέος = Μενεσθέως. For the name see LGPN VA, 297-298 s.v.

L. 4: ΜΗΣΜΗΣ: What is meant is obviously μνήμης. Cf. MAMA VII, no. 15 where the editors write in minuscule transcription μήσμης and state that the form may be μνήμης.

For a similiar altar both in terms of its typology and the objects sculpted, see IHadrianoi, 101 no. 152 pl. 25.

Date: Roman Imperial Period

9. Funerary Inscription

Altar of white marble, now in the garden of the museum. Inv. no: 2009/159. Findspot: Yazıbaşı village/Keles/Bursa. Dimensions: H.: 71 cm; W.: 37 cm; D.: 32,5 cm; Lh.: 3 cm.

The altar is cut on all sides and corners, possibly for making it suitable for a secondary use. Both the crown and the base are chiseled away and do not longer exist. Thereby, the inscription was damaged at the top and on both sides.

[3-4].Ο.ΛΕΙ[3-4]
2 [. .] Παπιανο[ῦ?. .]
   [. . .] αὐτοῦ γυ[ν .]
4 [. . .]Ι·Ι·Α Ἀρτεμι[. .]
   [. .]ου συνβίῳ Σ[. .]
6 [. . .]δεως μνήμ[ης]
   χάριν.

L. 2: Παπιανο[ῦ. The name is very likely Παπιανός.

L. 4: [. . .]Ι·Ι·Α. Possibly a woman's name ending in -a stood in this line. Ἀρτεμι[. . . .]. A name Ἀρτεμίδωρος *vel sim* is expected here.

Date: Roman Imperial Period

10. Funerary bomos of Aurelius Stachys, his wife Secunda and their children

A cylindrical bomos of marble; placed in the garden of the museum. Inv. no: 2016/24. Findspot: Gemlik (Kios)/Bursa. Dimensions: H.: 91-93,5 cm; Diameter: 57 cm; Lh.: 3-4 cm.

The bomos has mouldings on the crown and one moulding on the base. The base is partly broken. The monument is quite abraded and shows many cracks. An inscription of nine lines is carved on the shaft.

	Αὐρήλιος Στάχυς
2	Ἀσκληπιοδότου
	φυλῆς Πρωτινίας
4	φύλαρχος, ζῶν ἑαυτῷ
	κατεσκεύσα τὸ μην-
6	μῖον καὶ τῇ γλυκυτάτῃ
	μου γυνεκὶ Σεκούν-
8	δᾳ καὶ τοῖς γλυκυτά-
	τοις μου τέκνυς.

I, Aurelius Stachys, son of Asklepiodotos, the phylarch of the phyle of Protinia, constructed (this funerary bomos) during lifetime for myself and for my sweetest wife Secunda and for my sweetest children.

L. 1: For Στάχυς see LGPN V A, 409 s.v. Till now this name appears not to have been attested in Bithynia.

L. 3: φυλῆς Πρωτινίας. Based on an ephebian list dated to 108/9 A.D., it is thought that Kios had at least 10 phylai, see IKios, no. 16. See also Kunnert 2012, 80-81. However, so far we know only one of them: IKios, no. 37 and 77 (φυλὴ Ἡρακλεωτίς). The phyle Herakleotis was named after the mythical founder of the city, Herakles. With this new inscription, the number of the phylai documented increased to two. We don't have any knowledge regarding this phyle, and what the word or name Protinia signifies remains unknown.

L. 4: For the office of φύλαρχος see Kunnert 2012, 261-267. Stachys used instead of the grammatically required ἐμαυτῷ the form for the third person, ἑαυτῷ.

L. 5-6: κατεσκεύσα = κατεσκεύασα. τὸ μηνμῖον = τὸ μνημεῖον.

L. 7: γυνεκί = γυναικί.

L. 9: τέκνυς = τέκνοις.

Date: After 212 A.D. (Constitutio Antoniniana)

11. Posthumous honorary inscription of Fabia Fabula

Cylindrical column of white marbe, now in the garden of the museum. Till now no inventory number was given to it. Findspot unknown. Dimensions: H.: 68 cm; Diameter: 43 cm; Lh.: 2,5-4 cm.

The column is evenly cut off at the top and below. No crown or base is preserved. An inscription of six lines is carved on the shaft.

	ὁ δῆμος	The people
2	Φαβίαν	(honoured)
	Φάβουλαν	Fabia Fabula,
4	εἰατρείνην	the doctor (the midwife?)
	ζήσασαν	having lived
6	κοσμίως.	decently.

L. 1: For other posthumous honors paid to the deceased in Prusa ad Olympum, see IPrusa ad Olympum I, nos. 26-31.

L. 3: The latin cognomen of Φάβουλα (= Fabul(l)a) has not, as far as we could determine, been recorded in Asia Minor to date. Yet, both Fabulla and its female version prevail in the western Roman Empire, see Kajanto 1965, 170. Cf. Schulze 1991, 176, 461. At the end of the line, it seems that the stonemason carved a sigma at first and then converted it to a ny.

L. 4: εἰατρείνην = ἰατρίνην. In Greek and Roman antiquity, the doctors were overwhelmingly male, but there were, though rarely, also female doctors. It is commonly thought that they were mostly confined to the speciality of obstetrics and gynecology, but we simply don't have enough sources to determine if they were also active in any other medical field, see Samama 2003, 15-16. For other female doctors attested in Asia Minor see Samama 2003, nos. 188 (Pergamon); 280 (Tlos); 304 (Kios); 320 (Ankyra); 324 (Neoclaudiopolis); 329 (Adada); 342 (Lycaonia); 354 (Seleucia ad Calycadnum); 358 (Korykos); İplikçioğlu et al. 2007, no. 32 = SEG 57, 1486 (Termessos). For a useful study that evaluates all the Latin and ancient Greek epigraphic and literary evidence for female doctors, see Cilliers – Retief 1999, 47-65. See also Flemming 2007, 257-259; Laes 2011, 154-162. It is worth noting that we know an ἀρχιατρίνη who should not have been restricted to birth assistance, cf. Robert 1964, 177.

L. 6: κοσμίως is frequently seen in the funerary inscriptions of Prusa ad Olympum, see IPrusa ad Olympum I, p. 75; Uzunoğlu 2015, 405.

Date: Roman Imperial Period

12. Funerary inscription of Maxima

Altar-like stele of whitish marble. Kept in the garden of the museum. No inventory number yet given. Findspot unknown. Dimensions: H.: 90 cm; W.: 30 cm; D.: 15 cm; Lh.: 1-1,3 cm.

The crown of the altar-like stele is decorated with high corner acroteria. A horizontal moulding is seen above the crown and its upper part is partly broken. A carefully carved inscription of seven line is on the shaft of the stele.

	Μ(ᾶρκος)· Δομίτις ⚫	M(arcus) Domiti(o)s
2	Στερτίννις	Stertinni(o)s
	Ἀρισταίνετος	Aristainetos
4	Μαξίμα Λόγγου	(constructed this tomb)
	τῇ γλυκυτάσῃ sic.	for his sweetest wife
6	συμβίῳ τὸ	Maxima, daughter of
	μνημεῖον.	Longus.

L. 1: Δομίτις = Δομίτιος.

L. 2: Στερτίννις = Στερτίννιος. For the -nn gemination in *nomina gentilicia* see Solin 2004, 176.

L. 3-5: For Ἀρισταίνετος see LGPN VA, 61 s.v. The omicron in Ἀρισταίνετος, the second omicron in Λόγγου and the eta in γλυκυτάσῃ (for γλυκυτάτῃ) were carved much smaller in order to save space and to avoid the spreading of names over two lines.

Date: Roman Imperial Period

13. Funerary Inscription

Marble stele; kept in the garden of the museum. Inv. no: 9642. Findspot unknown. Dimensions: H.: 71 cm; W.: 50 cm; D.: 17 cm; Lh.: 1,5-2,5 cm.

Broken above. Pediment entirely missing. The monument appears to have had various panels on which miscellaneous sceneries were pictured. Amongst them, only the lowermost panel is fully preserved; only the lower section of the panel above is preserved. The forelegs of a horse are probably seen in this broken panel, but the depiction on the right is unclear. In the lower panel, a hunter fighting a bear that had stood up straight with his spear is depicted.

Below is seen a dog attacking the bear. Beneath the panel there is a carelessly carved inscription of four lines. The right portion of the inscribed area is weathered and the letters are barely legible. For bears in Bithynia cf. Robert 1948, 90.

	Τορκοσινιης Διλιποριος	*Torkosinies,*
2	ἐπέστησεν δὲ τὸ ΣΙΠΣ[..]	*son of Diliporis*
	ὁ γαμβρὸς αὐτοῦ δὲ ΣΕΠΤΙΟ[..]	*set (this) up. His son-in-law - - -*
4	Διδιπεους. χαῖρε.	*son of Didipes - - - - - -. Farewell!*

L. 1: Τορκοσινιης is hitherto unattested but there is no doubt that this is also a Thracian name as are the other names in the inscription. For the Thracian personal names beginning with Torc, see Dana 2014, 374-375. For the other Thracian name Διλίπορις see Dana 2014, 131-132. Cf. also Mitchell 1978, 122.

L. 2: ΣΙΠΣ[..]. unclear. Possibly a term relating to a grave should be expected in this line.

L. 3: ΣΕΠΤΙΟ[..]. Also not clear.

L. 4: Διδιπης is most likely a Thracian personal name that is not documented to date. Some Thracian names beginning with Did- such as Didis, Didas, Didila etc. are recorded, see Dana 2014, 128-129. Detschew underscores that the names beginning with Did- are not confined to the Thracians, but also appear in Phyrgian onomastics. On Thracian names in Bithynia and the onomastics of the indigenous people of north-western Asia Minor in general see Özlem-Aytaçlar 2010, 506-529 = Özlem-Aytaçlar 2012, 63-113 (in Turkish).

For a very similar relief attested in the north of Myra (Muskar/Belören) see Zahle 1979, 306-309. See also Özdilek 2008, 238 and 246 fig. 4; Özdilek – Çevik 2009, 286 and 289 fig. 5 and 13.

Date: Late Hellenistic, probably 1st cent. B.C.

14. Funerary inscription of Ammia

Marble stele, now in the garden of the museum. Inv. no: 9040. Findspot unknown. Dimensions: H.: 87 cm; W.: 44-55 cm; D.: 21-23 cm; Lh.: 2-2,5 cm.

The pediment of the stele is broken and missing. A carved niche is on the front side of the stele, and the bust of a woman is depicted inside it. Her dress, hair and face are partly damaged. The folds of the woman's chiton are worked elaborately. Beneath the bust an inscription of two lines is carved.

   Αμμια Μνασέου, γυνὴ δὲ
2 Μενεστράτου· χαῖρε.

Ammia, daughter of Mnaseas, wife of Menestratos. Farewell!

L. 1: Αμμια is a Lallname, frequently attested in Phrygia, but also prevalent in the whole of Asia Minor, see Zgusta 1964, § 57.16. For the occurrences in Bithynia, see LGPN VA, 24 s.v. For Μνασέας, see LGPN VA, 319 s.v.

Date: Roman Imperial Period

15. Funerary inscription of Alexandris

Marble stele. Kept in the garden of the museum. No inventory number yet given. Findspot: İnegöl/Bursa; Dimensions: H.: 80 cm; W.: 43,5 cm; D.: 7 cm; Lh.: 2,5-3 cm.

Broken above and below. Pediment and base missing. Otherwise complete. On the shaft two large wreaths are worked in low relief. The pair of wreaths were formed from bay leaves and were tied with ribbons. Beneath them is carved an inscription of five lines.

	Ἀλεξανδρὶς	Alexandris,
2	Μάρκου,	daughter of Marcus
	γυνὴ δὲ Βάσσου·	wife of Bassus,
4	ἐτῶν	having lived
	ιε'.	for 15 years.

L. 1: In Asia Minor, Ἀλεξανδρίς is a poorly attested female name, see LGPN VB, 17 s.v.; LGPN VC, 14 s.v. Alexandris was apparently married when she was at the age of 15. Although it may seem that this is an early age for marriage, we have some other examples for so young brides from both Bithynia and its adjacent region Phrygia, see for example below no. 21: the funerary inscription of Fabia Rufa. Similarly in Prusa ad Olympum, the funerary inscription of a certain Soteris records that she had been married for 7 years when she passed away in the age of 20, which means that she was married at the age of 13, see IPrusa ad Olympum I, no. 165. In fact, in a funerary epigram from the territory of Amorion in Phrygia an even earlier marriage age is recorded. According to this text, the deceased woman was married at the age of 11 to her husband, see MAMA VII, 258 = SGO III, no. 16/43/04. Thonemann (2013, 134-135) asserts that the average marriage age in Phrygia was around 16. For the age at first marriage, see also Saller 1994, 25-41; Scheidel 2007, 389-402.

L. 2: There are the traces of erasure under the name of Marcus, indicating that something else was carved here erroneously and then replaced with the correct one. On the erased spot the last two letters, possibly an omicron and upsilon are still visible.

Date: Roman Imperial Period

16. Funerary inscription of Tiberius Claudius Phillys

Marble stele placed in the garden of the museum. No inventory number yet given. Findspot unknown. Dimensions: H.: 67 cm; W.: 36 cm; D.: 6,5 cm; Lh.: 1; 4; 6 cm.

Broken above, and pediment missing. At the top the lower part of a wreath is visible. Two four-leaf rosettes on each side are carved below the wreath, and two ribbons of the wreath are placed between the rosettes. Below them an inscription of six lines inside a tabula ansata is carved.

Τι. Κλαύδ-
2 ιος Φίλλυς
Κλαυδίου Φίλ-
4 λυ παιδευ-
τοῦ υἱὸς ἐτῶν
6 ιε΄.

Ti(berius) Claudius Phillys, son of the teacher Claudius Phillys, having lived for 15 years.

L. 2-4: Φίλλυς has been hitherto only once attested in Bithynia, see LGPN VA, 451 s.v. Cf. also Robert, OMS VI, 57-69 who provides an extensive survey of the names terminating in -υς. (for Φίλλυς see in particular p. 59, fn. 15).

L. 4-5: παιδευτοῦ. The father of the deceased boy was a teacher. From one posthumous honorary inscription in the Bursa Museum we know of another teacher, see IPrusa ad Olympum I, no. 1009. Even though Th. Corsten, referring to Robert – Robert 1948, 89-91, states that *paideutes* is rarely attested in the epigraphic record, plenty of *paideutai* are known from both Asia Minor and the ancient world in general. The evidence even suggests that they formed associations, see Paz de Hoz 2015. For *paideutes*, see also Paz de Hoz 2007, 309-310. Cf. also Del Corso 2007, 141-190.

Date: Roman Imperial Period

17. Funerary Inscription of Tatia

Marble stele, now in the garden of the museum. Inv. no: 2016/26. Findspot: Kestel/Bursa. Dimensions: H.: 86 cm; W.: 50 cm; D.: 7 cm; Lh.: 3-4 cm.

The surface of the stele with its triangular pediment is strongly weathered. The monument possibly stayed in the water for a long time so that the marble has totally lost its smoothness. The top of its middle acroterium is broken off. The middle part of the base is also lost. A star-like rosette of six leaves is placed in the pediment. On the shaft a panel in which a wreath, two star-like rosettes and some objects symbolising female activities such as a mirror with handle, a comb, a wool basket, a spindle and a distaff are depicted. An inscription of four lines is carved beneath the relief-field. Due to the outbreak the last line is hardly legible.

Π. Ἀκίλιος Τατιᾳ γυναι-
2 κί, θυγατρὶ δὲ Διωγένο[υς]
[το]ῦ καὶ Χρυσίου, ζήσασῃ με[γα-]
4 [λο]πρ[- - - - -]ΚΡΙΔ[- - - - -]
- - - - - - - - - - - - - - - - - - -

P(ublius) Acilius (or Pakilios set this stele up) for Tatia, daughter of Diogenes alias Chrysios, having lived generously? - - - -

L. 1: The name of the person who constructed the funerary stone is not very clear on the stone. It is either Pakilios (for this name see LGPN I, 357 s.v.) or much more likely P(ublius) Acilius. The nomen gentilicium Acilius is once attested in Mysia, see LGPN VA, 14 s.v.

L. 2: Διωγένους = Διογένους.

L. 3: The name Χρύσιος seems hitherto unattested.

L. 3-4: με[γαλο]πρ[- - It is probable that we deal here with the adjective of μεγαλοπρεπής, -ές (= generous, benevolent), which may indicate that the deceased Tatia was a munificent person when she was alive.

Date: Roman Imperial Period

18. Funerary Inscription of Paideros

Whitish marble stele, now in the garden of the museum. Inv. no: 2009/69. Findspot: Kestel/Bursa. Dimensions: H.: 117 cm; W.: 42-51 cm; D.: 15-16 cm; Lh.: 2 cm.

Slightly broken at the top left corner. Its surface is weathered and has plenty of small damages and scratches. Triangular pediment decorated with acroteria and a central rosette. In the panel beneath the pediment a large wreath is flanked at either side by a rosette. In the second panel three standing figures are depicted. It is clear from their garments that the figure on the right is a woman and the one on the left a man. A male child is standing between them. A barely legible inscription of six lines is carved beneath this panel.

[Π]αιδαίρως
2 Φιλαργύρου υἱ-
ός· ἐτῶν ς′ or ζ′. 
4 Φιλάργυρος καὶ Ἀσ-
τρατίῃ τῷ αὐτῶν τέκνῳ
6 Παιδέρωτι τὸ μνῆμα.

Paideros, son of Philargyros, having lived for 6 (or 7 years). Philargyros and Astratie? (constructed) this memorial for their child Paideros.

L. 1 and 6: Παιδαίρως = Παιδέρως. The name is commonly attested, see LGPN VA, 353. It is worth mentioning that the name is written differently in the beginning and at the end.

L. 2: Φιλάργυρος is poorly attested in Mysia, see LGPN VA, 446 s.v.

L. 3: ἐτῶν ς′ or ζ′.

L. 4-5: The reading of the letters after Astra- is dubious. For Astrateia, see Pape – Benseler 1884, 164. It is possible that the woman originally comes from an area where still some Ionic pronounciation had survived.

Date: Roman Imperial Period

19. Funerary inscription of Demetrios and Mainia?

Fragment of a marble stele, placed in the garden of the museum. Till now no inventory number was given. Findspot unknown. Dimensions: H.: 43 cm; W.: 51 cm; D.: 13 cm; Lh.: 1,5 cm.

Broken above and below. Base and pediment missing. The stele is seemingly decorated with panels, yet only the middle one is preserved. Inside the remaining panel an elaborately worked banquet scene is depicted. The deceased reclines on a couch and holds a wreath in his hand. His wife in the pudicitia pose is sitting in front of him. Behind the woman there is a servant girl, depicted in a smaller scale. Another servant is dealing with some objects (oinochoe?) on a table visible behind the man. A partly damaged inscription of two lines is written beneath this secenery. Only paws belonging possibly to an eagle have remained from the upper panel. Having at least 3 panels, this stele might belong to the group of "Stockwerkstelen" (Cremer 1991, 27-31).

Δημήτριος Ποσειδωνίου, γυνὴ
2   Μαινία, χ[α]ίρε ᵛ τε.

Demetrios, son of Poseidonios,
(and his) wife Mainia, farewell!

L. 2: Μαινία is not listed in any volume of LGPN, but there are at least two occurrences of this name, both in Argeia, IG IV, 620 and 647. It is not to be ruled out that the first iota is simply a scratch and the name is far more attested Μανία.

Date: Due to the relatively small letters as well as because of its belonging to the group of stelai with storeys (Stockwerkstele), that were prevalent in the Late Hellenistic Period, this monument should presumably be dated into the Late Hellenistic or Early Imperial Period.

20. Funerary Inscription

Fragment of a marble stele; kept in the garden of the museum. No inventory number is yet given.

Findspot: Doğla village/Karacabey/Bursa. Dimensions: H.: 59 cm; W.: 61 cm; D.: 12 cm; Lh.: 2,5-3 cm.

Broken above and below. Pediment almost entirely lost. A banquet scene is depicted. The man reclines on a couch; on either side he is accompanied by a female figure. Probably the woman on the right of the man is his wife, while the one on the left could be his daughter. The small boy in front of the man may be his son. Beside him a tripod table with fruits is placed. Below the woman on the right a servant is visible. Beneath the scene a fragmentary inscription of two lines is preserved.

[- - - - - Ἀρι]στοκράτου τοῦ   ... son of Aristokrates

2   [- - - - - - - - -]τρὸς αὐτοῦ   - - - - - - his- - - -

- - - - - - - - - - - - - - - - - - - -

L. 2: - -]τρός can be restored as perhaps πα]τρός, μη]τρός or θυγα]τρός.

Date: Roman Imperial Period

21. Funerary Inscription of Diogenes and Fabia Rufa

Marble stele, now in in the garden of the museum. Inv. no: 2016/23. Findspot: Çitli village/İnegöl/Bursa. Dimensions: H.: 181 cm; W.: 72 cm (top); 77 cm (below); D.: 13 cm (top); 20 cm (below); Lh.: 1; 3; 4,5 cm. Dim. of the block on which the stele stands: H.: 32 cm; W.: 94 cm; D: 22 cm.

Ed.: Laflı – Bru 2016, 110-111 no. 9. Cf. Taeuber 2016, 288-290.

The big stele was found together with the large and heavy block which served as its base. Today, it is not placed on this block, but on the floor. It is broken above, and there are many small breaks and scratches on it. It is decorated with a triangular pediment, in which a wool basket, a box-like object and two small figures being probably scent bottles are sculptured. The right corner acroterion is broken. Beneath the pediment two laurel wreaths are depicted. In the bottom section of the stele a large, now empty niche is cut out. Above the niche two small rosettes are carved as a kind of decoration. Between the niche and the laurel wreaths an inscription of 6 lines is written on a large tabula ansata, however, further 5 lines, the beginning of the epitaph, are not very elegantly placed above the tabula, and finally the last line of this epitaph is carved below the tabula. It is very likely that the first 5 rows were added when the tabula was already described.

χαίρε-
τε πα-
ροδῖτα[ι].

Διογένης Διογένου ζήσας
κοσμίω<ς> ἔτη ξ, ὧδε ἀττεταῖ.

Διογένης Τειμο-
[θέ]ου τῇ ἑαυτοῦ γυ-
ναικὶ συνβιωσάσῃ ἔτ-
η ͦιβ′ͦ Φαβίᾳ Ῥούφᾳ ἐτει-
λέττησεν ἐτῶν κε′ ἀνέ-
στησεν τὴν ἰστήλην μνή-
μης χάριν.

Greetings wayfarers!

Diogenes, son of Diogenes, having lived for 60 years decently. Alas!

Diogenes, son of Teimotheos, set up this stele in memory for his wife Fabia Rufa that lived together with him for 12 years and died at the age of 25.

L. 2-3: τ{ε}᾽Επαφροδίτα Laflı – Bru.

L. 5: ζῴδεα ΠΕΤΑ[---] Laflı – Bru; ἀπίετα[ι] Taeuber. The last letter in κοσμίως is carved as epsilon on the stone. Before kappa is seen another letter or a leaf motif but cannot be understood because of the break. For κοσμίως, see above no. 11.

ὧδε ἀττεταῖ. ἀττεταῖ is very likely to be understood as ἀτταταῖ. This interjection, employed exclusively in the poetic texts expressing pain and vexation has never been epigraphically attested. According to Nordgren (2015, 108-110), it has been recorded 11 times in total, 9 occurences in Aristophanes, 2 in Sophocles. Instead of ἀτταταῖ, we usually come across αἰαῖ (Nordgren 2015, 130-133; Yıldız 2019, p. 588) or φεῦ in the funerary epigrams.

L. 8: συμβιωσάσῃ ἔτη ͦιβ′ͦ: Fabia Rufa apparently married Diogenes at the age of 13. For marriage at an early age cf. above no. 15.

L. 9-10: ἔτη ο′ ΗΒΟ ..... ΕΤΕΣΛΕΤΤΗΣΕΝΕΤ[?]Ν Laflı – Bru. <ἠ>ἐτελε<ύ>τησεν Taeuber.

ἐτελεύτησεν was pronounced ἐτελέϝτισεν; probably by assimilation the form ἐτελέττησεν came into being. At the end of line 9 a letter (either iota or sigma) may be read, but in reality it was a breakage in the stone. ἐτῶν is carved as being ΕΤΙΥΝ on the stone.

L. 11: For the prothetic ἰ- of ἰστήλην see Dieterich 1898, 34; Brixhe 1987, 115-116.

Date: Roman Imperial Period

22. Funerary Inscription of Gaius Murius Valens, Muria Prima and their son Rufus

Marble stele, now in the garden of the museum; till now without inventory number given. Findspot: Karadere Mevkii/İnegöl/Bursa. Dimensions: H.: 122 cm; W.: 69 cm; D.: 15 cm; Lh.: 3,5-4 cm.

Ed. Laflı – Bru 2016, 111-112 no. 10.

The upper part above the pediment is broken off. The niche below is also largely broken, and the base is not preserved. The lower portions of two wreaths are seen on either side of the pediment. A Gorgo head whose face is damaged, is placed in the pediment. In the panel beneath the pediment there are three standing figures, which are presumably to identify with mother, father and son mentioned in the inscription. Beneath the panel an inscription with six lines is carved. Inside the niche area *a falx arboraria* (pruning hook), a comb and a spindle? are depicted.

    Γ(αίῳ) Μουρίῳ Οὐάλεντι
2 καὶ Μουρίᾳ Πρείμᾳ ζῶ-
    σιν καὶ Ῥούφῳ υἱῷ αὐτῶν
4 ζήσαντι ἔτη ⸎ κβ′
    τὴν στήλην ἀνέστη-
6 σε Μάρκελλα ἡ θυγάτηρ.

The daughter Marcella set this stele up for G(aius) Murius Valens and Muria Prima while still living and for their son, having lived 25 years.

L. 1: Γ(αίῳ) Μούνῳ Οὐαλεντίῳ Laflı – Bru.

L. 1-2: In Latin inscriptions both Murius and Murrius are well attested, cf. CIL V, 2245; CIL VIII, 27512; Schulze 1991, 196 and 424.

L. 2: Μουνᾳ Laflı – Bru.

L. 3: υἱῷ Laflı – Bru.

Date: Roman Imperial Period

23. Funerary Inscription of Rhadamanthys

Marble stele, now housed in the Bursa Museum. Inv. No: 2014-65. Found during the excavation of a football field by the Directorate of Technical Works of İnegöl Municipality at İnegöl/Bursa. Dimensions: H.: 124 cm; W.: 67-70 cm; D.: 14-17 cm; Lh.: 2-2,5 cm.

Ed. Laflı – Bru 2016, 112-113 no. 11.

The central acroterion, a big part from the right corner with half the acroterion, and the lower right corner of the stele are broken off. A triangular pediment is sculpted in flat relief on the stone surface. Inside this pediment a large wreath is placed, and outside of the gable two small rosettes are depicted on both sides. An inscription of one line is written on the pediment's bottom profile. On the shaft of the stele there is a large niche, in which an papyrus scroll, a kalamotheke, and a diptychon are depicted. χαῖρε is inscribed on the scroll. The bowllike cavity on the niche's bottom may have been used for libations.

Ῥαδάμανθυς Μενεκράτου

2 χαῖ-

ρε.

Rhadamanthys, son of Menekrates, farewell!

L. 1: Ῥαδάμανθυς: As far as we know, this is the first attestation of this heroic name in Asia Minor. For the name, see LGPN II, 390 s.v.; LGPN IIIA, 384 s.v. Cf. the phyle Rhadamanthis in Kaunos, which is named after the hero, Marek 2006, no. 64.

Date: Roman Imperial Period

24. Funerary Inscription of Hipparchos

Marble stele. Kept in the garden of the museum. No inventory number given yet. Findspot: Kurtul village/Gemlik/Bursa. Dimensions: H.: 89 cm; W.: 29 cm; D.: 8,5 cm; Lh.: 2 cm.

Ed: Laflı – Bru 2016, 113 no. 12.

Slim and tall stele; segment pediment in which a facing eagle with spread wings sets about devouring a serpent whose tail the bird retains with his right claw. The upper margin of the stele is now damaged, but we provide a photo which was taken when the monument was still intact. The stele consists of two panels. The first one shows a banquet scene: The man reclines on a couch and holds a wreath in his right hand, attended by his seated wife in front of him and by a servant girl who is standing behind the woman and is carrying a basket. Behind the man a male servant dealing with the objects on the table is depicted. It is interesting to see that in this composition the table is not a tripod but rather has four legs; it is placed not in the centre but on the edge. In the other panel a man seated on a stool is sculpted. Opposite to him a second man standing and putting his left foot on a footrest is shown. Beneath this panel an inscription of two lines is carved.

Ἵππαρχε Βίαντος
2   χαῖρε.

Hipparkhos, son of Bias, farewell!

L. 1: Ἵππαρχε. Cf. above no. 5 which also records the name of the deceased in the vocative case. For Βίας, see LGPN VA, 101 s.v.

Date: Late Hellenistic.

In Bursa Museum, there is yet another stele in whose pediment is similarly filled with an eagle fighting against a snake (Inv. no. 9049). For the same motif, cf. also IPrusa ad Olympum, no. 80 (found at Hamzabey village near İnegöl). See also Rodríguez Pérez 2010, 1-18.

25. Funerary inscription of Charmides

Marble stele, placed in the garden of the museum. Inv. no: 3193. Findspot: Dağkadı village/Karacabey/Bursa. Dimensions: H.: 87 cm; W.: 61 cm; D.: 21 cm; Lh.: 1,5-2 cm.

Ed: Laflı – Bru 2016, 114-115 no. 14.

Base and pediment of this rectangular stele are not preserved. Upper part moulded; on the shaft there are two panels. The upper panel contains a scene in which a man seated on a stool holds a roll. His feet are rested on a low footstool. His garment is richly folded. In front of the man a male child holding a roll is standing. This composition presumably depicts a teacher and his pupil or student. Inside the panel traces of the original colours are preserved. Beneath the first panel an inscription of one line is inscribed. The second panel shows a man riding his horse; behind him a servant holding a thin rod.

Χαρμίδου τοῦ Διονυσοδώρου.

(The stele of) Charmides, son of Dionysodoros.

Date: Late Hellenistic

Uninscribed Stelai

26. Funerary stone

Marble stele; kept in the garden of the museum. Inv. no: 3186. Findspot: Gönen/Balıkesir. Dimension not recorded.

Neither pediment nor base of this rectangular stele are preserved. It contains two panels. All the figures are heavily abraded so that many details are lost. The upper panel shows a banquet scene in which two men reclining on a couch are accompanied by two women on either side. The women depicted in the pudicitia pose are sitting on stools. On the central table fruits are depicted. The panel below is smaller and centered. Inside the panel a woman riding a horse is sculpted, a stableboy who is leading the horse and a female figure behind the horse are represented.

Date: 2.-3. cent. A.D.

27. Funerary stone

Marble stele; kept in the garden of the museum. Till now no inventory number is given. Findspot: Turşucu village (Gedelek Mahallesi)/Orhangazi/Bursa. Dimensions: H.: 77 cm; W.: 103-113 cm; D.: 12-45 cm.

Only the frontside of this somewhat rough stone block is hewn. The top of the stele is roughly smoothed and there are 3 dowel holes, indicating that the stele was placed in an architectural construction. The front face is worked in the form of two adjacent stelai with acroteria and triangular pediments. Inside both pediments rosettes are depicted. The niche on the right was left blank, in the left niche a *falx arboraria* and a bunch of grapes are carved in relief.

A single rosette is above each niche on the outer side. On the inner side between both niches a bunch of grapes with a pigeon on either side is carved.

Date: Roman Imperial Period

28. Funerary stone

Marble stele; now in the garden of the museum. Inv. no: 2018/13. Findspot unknown. Dimensions: H.: 53 cm; W.: 33 cm; D.: 7 cm.

This small rectangular stele has a low triangular pediment and no base. On the shaft a typical banquet scene is pictured. The man reclining on a couch holds a wreath in his right hand. In front of him a woman in the pudicitia pose is sitting. In front of the kline a tripod table with fruits is placed. To the right of the tripod, in the right corner a tiny male servant and opposite in the left corner a tiny female servant are ready for serving their masters.

Date: Roman Imperial Period

29. Funerary stone

Marble stele, now in the garden of the museum. Till now no inventory number was distributed to it. Findspot: Karacabey/Bursa. Dimensions: H.: 61 cm; W.: 40 cm; D.: 16 cm.

The rectangular stele has no pediment and base. A banquet scene is depicted on the stele. A man is reclining on a couch, whereas in front of him a woman in the pudicitia pose is seated. In front of the kline a tripod table with fruits is placed. To the right of the tripod a small male servant preparing wine for drinking is standing besides a krater. In the opposite corner, next to the lady of the house, a small female servant is waiting for her commands.

Date: Roman Imperial Period

30. Funerary stone

Marble stele; kept in the garden of the museum; without inventory number. Findspot: Tirilye/Mudanya/Bursa. Dimensions: H.: 87 cm; W.: 50 cm; D.: 10 cm.

The stele is complete and has a triangular pediment elaborately decorated with corner and top acroteria and a base having small breaks. Inside the pediment is a four-leaf rosette flanked by tendrils which fill the gable's corners form the pediment's decoration. The rectangular panel below shows a rich variety of depictions. A large wreath with great ribbons is placed in the the middle of the composition; inside the wreath a great hand mirror signalises that the monument is intended to be the tomb stone for a woman. The upper corners are filled with rosettes. In the lower corners a large basket filled with wool, a spindle and a distaff are sculpted. Above the basket is a double-sided comb is placed. All these items indicate that this stele was designed for a woman. Beneath the inset panel a large, but blank tabula ansata is carved out.

Date: Roman Imperial Period

31. Funerary stone

Marble stele; now in the garden of the museum. Inv. no: 2016/25; Findspot: İnegöl/Bursa. Dimensions: H.: 140 cm; W.: 51 cm; D.: 15 cm. Date: Roman Imperial Period

This tall stele is broken above; there are many breaks on the whole surface. The upper portion of the triangular pediment is damaged. In the pediment a somewhat clumsily hewn four-leaf rosette and beneath it two ribboned wreaths are carved out. Beneath the pediment a large, but blank tabula ansata is placed. Between a niche which took up the stele's lowest part and the tabula ansata a diptychon, a book roll, and a kalamotheke are depicted. In the niche there are some items belonging to a woman, a mirror with handle, a comb, a perfume flask, a chest-like object and some other objects unidentifiable because of the hole. The hole cut in the niche below was probably made to enable it to be used to face a water source.

Date: Roman Imperial Period

Monuments not preserved in the Bursa Museum

32. Funerary inscription of Lakaina

Marble stele. Findspot unknown. Currently housed in the Directorate of Technical Works at Gemlik Municipality (Gemlik [Kios]/Bursa). Dimensions: H.: 62 cm; W.: 42-44 cm; D.: 11-14 cm; Lh.: 2-4 cm.

The surface of the stele with triangular pediment is slightly weathered. Otherwise complete. The base is not preserved. The corner acroteria show floral decorations. In the middle of the pediment a small rosette is visible. In a rectangular panel a mirror, a wool basket, a spindle and a distaff are carved out. An inscription of five lines is written beneath the panel.

    Λάκαινα, Νεικίου
2 καὶ Ἀφροδείτης
    θυγατήρ, γύνη δὲ
4 Λ. Ὀρφίου Φήλεικος
    ἐτῶν κγ′. χαῖρε.

Lakaina, daughter of Neikias and Aphrodite, wife of L(ucius) Orfius Felix, having lived for 23 years. Farewell!

L. 1: To date, Λάκαινα appears to have been attested twice, one example in Ionia and the other in Lydia, see LGPN VA, 263 s.v.

L. 2: For the theophoric name Aphrodite in Asia Minor cf. LGPN VA, 93 s.v.; VB, 79 s.v.; VC, 80 s.v.; Herrmann – Malay 2007, 42-43, no. 26.

L. 4: There are at least 2 occurrences of this name in a list of *prytaneis* in Kyzikos, see Mordtmann 1881, 42, no. 1b, L. 3; Lolling 1888, 304, AIII, L. 26.

Φῆλειξ = Ψῆλιξ.   Date: Roman Imperial Period

33. Funerary Inscription of Eia

Marble stele. Findspot unknown. Currently kept in the Directorate of Technical Works at Gemlik Municipality (Gemlik [Kios]/Bursa). Dimensions: H.: 57 cm; W.: 38-42 cm; D.: 13 cm; Lh.: 2,5-3 cm.

Slightly broken at the top left corner and at the bottom. The left side is damaged and gives the impression that it had submerged in water for a considerable time. Inside the triangular pediment a small rosette is cut out. Beneath the pediment a rectangular panel in which a seated girl holding an unidentifiable object in her right hand is depicted. She puts her feet on a footstool. In the right of the panel a large mirror with handle, a spindle and a distaff are sculpted. Below there is an insciption of five lines.

Τυραννίων καὶ Ἀριστώ
2   ζῶντες καὶ φρονεῦν-
    τες κατεσκεύα-
4   σαν τὸ μνημεῖον Ει-
    ᾳ τῷ τέκνῳ. χαῖρε.

Tyrannion and Aristo, still living and clear-minded, constructed this tomb for their child Eia. Farewell!

L. 1: For Τυραννίων, see LGPN VA, 439 s.v. This name, together with Τυράννιον, Τυρράνιον, and Τυρρανίων seem to be restricted to Ionia and Pontos.

For Ἀριστώ, see LGPN VB, 58 s.v. Apart from this, the name has only been attested twice in Asia Minor (Caria and Cilicia Pedias).

L. 3-4: κατεσκεύασαν. The first sigma of the verb was first inscribed as a classical four-bar sigma but then converted into a square form.   Date: Roman Imperial Period

34. Funerary Monument of Phoibion and Teimothea

White marble bomos with a stele on its front side. Discovered in the necropolis area in the Çiftlikköy excavations in Yalova. Its dimensions are unrecorded. The archaeologist Funda Ünal, who was working in the Bursa Museum, conducted the excavations and unearthed this and the following monument. We sincerely thank her for the photos, relevant information about the monuments, and finally for the permission to publish these monuments. The memorial consists of a bomos and a stele placed on it. The crown of the bomos has corner acroteria, between which a small Medusa/Gorgo head is placed. An inscription of seven lines is written on the shaft of the altar. The stele has a triangular pediment. In the rectangular panel beneath the pediment a banquet scene is represented. A man reclining on a couch holds a wreath in his right hand, and a woman in the pudicitia pose is sitting on a stool. A small figure in front of the woman may be identified as one of their two children or as a servant. The table in front of the couch seems to have been left unfinished.

Αὐρ. Τειμοθέα Δείου ζῶ-
2 σα ἑαυτῇ τὸ μνημεῖον κατεσκεύασα καὶ τῷ ἑαυ<τ>ῆς
4 ἀνδρὶ Φοιβίωνι Δείου ζήσαντι ἔτ(η) ν΄ μνήμης χά-
6 ριν μετὰ τῶν τέκνων [Ε]ὐ-
τύχους καὶ Τειμοθέας.

I, Aur(elia) Teimothea, daughter of Deios (or Deias), while still living have constructed this memorial for myself and for my husband Phoibion, son of Deios (or Deias), who lived 50 years, in remembrance of him. I did this together with my children Eutykhes and Teimothea.

L. 1 and 4: Δείου. Both Δεῖος (Dios) and Δειάς (Dias) are possible here. Although the father of the wife and the father of her husband have the same name, there is no reason to believe that the both Dios/Dias are identical and that the persons buried were siblings. The phenomenon of brother-sister marriages is almost entirely confined to Lycia in Roman Asia Minor, see Thonemann 2017, 155-156. Cf. Yıldız 2018, 410.

L. 4: Φοιβίων is not yet attested in Bithynia but is recorded twice in Mysia, see LGPN VA, 457 s.v.

This type of funerary monument is peculiar to Yalova (ancient Pylai). In almost all examples, a small Gorgo/Medusa head is depicted between the acroteria. For similar examples, see Pfuhl – Möbius 1979, p. 463 nos. 1922, 1923, 1978, 1979 and pl. 277; IApameia-Pylai, p. 163-168 (p. 163 no. 198 fn. 1); p. 111-112 no. 106 and 107, pl. 3 and p. 154-156 no. 141-143 (= Mansel 1933, no. 1-2); Baz – Seçkin 2013, p. 394-396 nos. 6-7 fig. 7-8 (and possibly no. 8 and 9 fig. 9-10).

Date: After 212 A.D. (Constitutio Antoniniana).

35. Funerary Bomos

Fragment of a white marble bomos. Discovered in an area close to the excavation site in course of the Çiftlikköy excavations above mentioned. Dimensions unrecorded.

The monument seems to be similar to the before discussed memorial. The stele and the lower portion of the bomos shaft are broken off and missing. The Medusa head between the acroteria is preserved. Only two lines from the inscription have remained intact.

Φιλώτας Φιλώτα

2   ΤΗΣΑΞΤΙ[..]Τ[..]

Philotas, son of Philotas - - - - - -

L. 2: ΤΗ ΣΑΞΤΙ[. .]: Possibly a woman's name is inscribed here, but it cannot be exactly determined because of the abrasion of the letters.

Date: Roman Imperial Period

36. Inscription fragment

Marble block; discovered in the late antique wall during the excavations in Zindankapı District (Pınarbaşı mahallesi). The inscribed block was apparently reused in the wall. Dimensions: H.: 75 cm; W.: 1,51 cm; D.: can't be measured; Lh.: 9-20 cm.

Broken at the left side and at the bottom; heavily damaged. Only a few letters from the Greek inscription are preserved. The script is irregular, and the second line is painted in a different colour. The dowel hole on the surface suggests that the stone had already before undergone a second usage. Some carvings above the first line of the inscription either belong to a decoration or to a different type of script.

[- --] ΙΟΥΛ[- - -]

2   ΟΜ

L. 1: ΙΟΥΛ[- - -]. A personal name (Ἰούλιος/Ἰουλία etc.) is possible but we can't say anything for sure since it is very fragmentary.

Date: Roman Imperial Period

Index of Personal Names

Ἀκίλιος? 17
Ἀκύλας 4
Ἀλεξανδρίς 15
Αμμια 14
Ἀντιγένης 3
Ἀπολλώνιος 2
Ἀρισταίνετος 12
Ἀριστοκράτης 3, 20
Ἀριστώ 33
Ἀρτέμων 5
Ἀσκληπιάδης 2
Ἀσκληπίδης 3
Ἀσκληπιοδότη 6
Ἀσκληπιόδοτος 10
Ἀστρατίη 18
Αὐρ. 7, 10, 34
Αὐρήλιος Στάχυς 10
Αφια 3
Ἀφροδείτη 32
Βάσσος 15
Βίας 24
Γ(άιος) Μούριος Οὐάλης 22
Δεῖος or Δειάς 34
Δημήτριος 19
Διδιπης 13
Διλίπορις 13
Διογένης 17, 21
Διονυσόδωρος 25
Δομίτις 12
Δωρίς 7
Εια 33
Ἔκγλε(κ)τος? 5
Ἐλπιδήφορος 7
Ἐπιτυνχάνων 1

Ἑρμᾶς 8
Εὐραίων 3a
Εὐτυχίδης 7
Εὐτύχης 34
Ἵππαρχος 24
Κλαύδιος 16
Λάκαινα 32
Λόγγος 12
Λ. Ὄρφιος Φῆλειξ 32
Λούκιος 6
Μ(ᾶρκος) Δομίτις Στερτίννι(ο)ς Ἀρισταίνετος 12
Μαινια? 19
Μαξίμα 12
Μάρκελλα 22
Μᾶρκος 6, 12, 15
Μενεκράτης 23
Μενεσθεύς 8
Μενέστρατος 14
Μήνιος 3a
Μητρόδωρος 1, 3a
Μνασέας 14
Μουρία Πρείμα 22
Μούριος 22
Νεικήτης 3a
Νεικίας 32
Νεννεος 6
Ὄρφιος 32
Οὐάλης 22
Παπιανός? 9
Παιδαίρως 18
Παιδέρως 18
Π(όπλιος) Ἀκίλιος? 17
Πακίλιος? 17

Πολύαινος 4
Ποσειδώνιος 19
Ῥαδάμανθυς 23
Ῥοῦφος 2, 22
Σεκοῦνδα 10
Στάχυς 10
Στερτίννι(ο)ς 12
Τατια 17
Τειμοθέα 34
Τειμόθεος 21
Τι(βέριος) Κλαύδιος Φίλλυς 16
Τορκοσινιης 13
Τυραννίων 33
Φαβία Ῥούφα 21
Φαβία Φάβουλα 11
Φῆλειξ 32
Φιλάργυρος 18
Φίλλυς 16
Φιλώτας 35
Φοιβίων 34
Φύλαρχος 10
Χαρμίδης 25
Χρήστη 8
Χρύσιος 17

Fragments
Ἀρτεμι[. .] 9
ΙΟΥΛ[- - -] 36
ΣΕΠΤΙΟ[. .] 13
[. . .]Ι·Ι·Α 9
[. . .]δεως 9

Bibliography

AE	L'Année épigraphique.
Akın 2016	Y. Akın, Küçük Asya'da Dağ ve Mağara Tanrıları. Meter Oreia Kültü ve İlgili Yazıtlar, in: N. Eda Akyürek Şahin – M. E. Yıldız – H. Uzunoğlu (ed.), Eskiçağ Yazıları 8 [Akron 10], 143-203, İstanbul 2016.
Akyürek Şahin 2010	N. E. Akyürek Şahin, Zwei neue Inschriften für Hosios kai Dikaios, Olba 18, 2010, 267-280.
Akyürek Şahin – Onur 2010	N. E. Akyürek Şahin – F. Onur, Neue Grabinschriften im Museum von Bursa, Gephyra 7, 2010, 23-39.
Anderson et al. 1910	J. G. C. Anderson – F. Cumont – H. Grégoire, Studia Pontica: Recueil des inscriptions grecques et latines du Pont et de l'Arménie III, Brussels 1910.
Asgari 1977	N. Asgari, Die Halbfabrikate kleinasiatischer Girlandensarkophage und ihre Herkunft, Archäologischer Anzeiger, 1977, 329-380.
Battistoni – Rothenhöfer 2013	F. Battistoni – P. Rothenhöfer, Inschriften aus dem Raum Keles und Orhaneli (Provinz Bursa, Türkei), EA 46, 2013, 101-165.
Baz – Seçkin 2013	F. Baz – S. Seçkin, Neue Grabinschriften aus Pylai in Bithynien, Olba 21, 2013, 387-404.
Bean 1959	G. E. Bean, Notes and Inscriptions from Pisidia. Part I, Anatolian Studies 9, 1959, 67-117.
Brixhe 1987	C. Brixhe, Essai sur le grec anatolien au début de notre ère, nouvelle édition, Nancy 1987.
Brixhe 1991	C. Brixhe, Corpus des inscriptions dialectales de Pamphylie. Supplément III, in: P. Goukovsky – C. Brixhe (ed.), Hellènika Symmikta. Histoire, archéologie, épigraphie, Nancy 1991, 15-27.
Callan 2010	T. Callan, Prophecy and Oracles, in: M. Gagarin – E. Fantham (ed.), The Oxford Encyclopedia of Ancient Greece and Rome, Vol. I, Oxford 2010, 39-41.
CIG	Corpus Inscriptionum Graecarum.
Cilliers – Retief 1999	L. Cilliers – F. P. Retief, Die helende hand: die rol van die vrou in die antieke geneeskunde, Acta Classica 42,1, 1999, 47-65.
Cremer 1991	M. Cremer, Hellenistisch-römische Grabstelen im nordwestlichen Kleinasien 1. Mysien (Asia Minor Studien 4,1), Bonn 1991.
Çaçu 2005	A. Çaçu, Zeus Kersoullos. 1. Burza Turizm Sempozyumu, 30 Eylül - 2 Ekim, Bursa 2005, 453-468.
Dagron – Feissel 1987	G. Dagron – D. Feissel, Inscriptions de Cilicie, Paris 1987.
Dana 2014	D. Dana, Onomasticon Thracicum (OnomThrac): Répertoire des noms indigènes de Thrace, Macédoine Orientale, Mésies, Dacie et Bithynie, Athens 2014.

Del Corso 2007	L. Del Corso, Le pratiche scolastiche nelle testimonianze epigrafiche di età ellenistica, in: J. A. Fernández Delgado – F. Pordomingo – A. Stramaglia (eds.), Escuela y literatura en Grecia antigua. Actas del simposio internacional Universidad de Salamanca, 17-19 noviembre de 2004, Cassino 2007, 141-190.
Detschew 1957	D. Detschew, Die thrakischen Sprachreste, Wien 1957.
Dieterich 1898	K. Dieterich, Untersuchungen zur Geschichte der griechischen Sprache, Leipzig 1898.
Drew-Bear 1978	Th. Drew-Bear, Nouvelles Inscriptions de Phrygie, Zutphen 1978.
Dunst 1971	G. Dunst, Κερσης, Chiron 1, 1971, 107-109.
Flemming 2007	R. Flemming, Women, Writing and Medicine in the Classical World, Classical Quarterly 57, 2007, 257-279.
Fontenrose 1988	J. Fontenrose, Didyma. Apollo's Oracles, Cults and Companions, Berkeley-Los Angeles-London 1988.
Ginouvès 1998	R. Ginouvès, Dictionnaire méthodique de l'architecture grecque et romaine. Tome III. Espaces architecturaux, bâtiments et ensembles, Roma 1998.
Heberdey – Kalinka 1897	R. Heberdey – E. Kalinka, Bericht über zwei Reisen im südwestlichen Kleinasien, Vienna 1897.
Herrmann – Malay 2007	P. Herrmann – H. Malay, New Documents from Lydia (Österr. Akad. Wiss., Phil.-hist. Kl., Denkschr. 340, Erg. zu den TAM 24), Vienna 2007.
Höfer 1916-1924	O. Höfer, s.v. Tauropoleites, in: W. H. Roscher (ed.), Ausführliches Lexikon der griechischen und römischen Mythologie V: T, Leipzig 1916-1924, 137.
IApameia-Pylai	Th. Corsten, Die Inschriften von Apameia (Bithynien) und Pylai (IK 32), Bonn 1987.
IHadrianoi	E. Schwertheim, Die Inschriften von Hadrianoi und Hadrianeia (IK 33), Bonn 1987.
IKalchedon	R. Merkelbach, Die Inschriften von Kalchedon (IK 20), Bonn 1980.
IKlaudiu Polis	F. Becker-Bertau, Die Inschriften von Klaudiu Polis (IK 31), Bonn 1986.
IKios	Th. Corsten, Die Inschriften von Kios (IK 29), Bonn 1985.
ILaodikeia am Lykos	Th. Corsten, Die Inschriften von Laodikeia am Lykos, Teil I (IK 49), Bonn 1997.
IPrusa ad Olympum I	Th. Corsten, Die Inschriften von Prusa ad Olympum, Teil I (IK 39), Bonn 1991.
IPrusa ad Olympum II	Th. Corsten, Die Inschriften von Prusa ad Olympum II (IK 40), Bonn 1993.
ISestos	J. Krauss, Die Inschriften von Sestos und der thrakischen Chersones (IK 19), Bonn 1980.

ISmyrna II.1	G. Petzl, Die Inschriften von Smyrna, Teil II.1 (IK 24,1), Bonn 1987.
IStratonikeia I	M. Çetin Şahin, Die Inschriften von Stratonikeia, Teil I: Panamara (IK 21), Bonn 1981.
İplikçioğlu et al. 2007	B. İplikçioğlu – G. Çelgin – A. V. Çelgin, Epigraphische Forschungen in Termessos und seinem Territorium IV, Vienna 2007.
Jones 2012	C. P. Jones, Zeus Anabatênos and Zeus Kersoullos, ZPE 180, 2012, 233-236.
Kajanto 1965	I. Kajanto, The Latin Cognomina, Helsinki 1965.
Koch – Sichtermann 1982	G. Koch – H. Sichtermann, Römische Sarkophage (Handbuch der Archäologie), München 1982.
Kubińska 1968	J. Kubińska, Les monuments funéraires dans les inscriptions grecques de l'Asie Mineure, Warsaw 1968.
Kunnert 2012	U. Kunnert, Bürger unter sich. Phylen in den Städten des kaiserzeitlichen Ostens, Basel 2012.
Laes 2011	C. Laes, Midwives in Greek inscriptions in Hellenistic and Roman Antiquity, ZPE 2011, 154-162.
Laflı – Bru 2016	E. Laflı – H. Bru, Inscriptions et monuments funéraires gréco-romains d'Anatolie occidentale, Anatolia Antiqua 24, 2016, 103-116.
Lane 1976	E. L. Lane, Corpus Monumentorum Religionis Dei Menis. Vol. III: Interpretations and Testimonia, Leiden 1976.
Lehmler – Wörrle 2006	C. Lehmler – M. Wörrle, Neue Inschriften aus Aizanoi IV: Aizanitica Minora II, Chiron 36, 2006, 45-111.
LGPN II	M. J. Osborne – S. G. Byrne, A Lexicon of Greek Personal Names II. Attica, Oxford 1994.
LGPN IIIA	P. M. Fraser – E. Matthews, A Lexicon of Greek Personal Names III A. The Peloponnese, Western Greece, Sicily and Magna Graecia, Oxford 1997.
LGPN VA	Th. Corsten – R. W. V. Catling – M. Ricl, A Lexicon of Greek Personal Names VA. Coastal Asia Minor: Pontos to Ionia, Oxford 2010.
LGPN VB	J. -S. Balzat – R. W. V. Catling – É. Chiricat – F. Marchand, A Lexicon of Greek Personal Names, Vol. V.B. Coastal Asia Minor: Caria to Cilicia, Oxford 2013.
LGPN VC	J. -S. Balzat – R. W. V. Catling – É. Chiricat – Th. Corsten, A Lexicon of Greek Personal Names, Vol. VC: Inland Asia Minor, Oxford 2018.
Lolling 1888	H. G. Lolling, Inschrift aus Kyzikos, MDAI 13, 1888, 304-309.

MAMA VII	W. M. Calder, Monuments from Eastern Phrygia (MAMA VII), Manchester 1956.
MAMA IX	B. Levick – St. Mitchell – J. Potter – M. Waelkens, Inscriptions from Aezani and the Aezanitis (MAMA IX), London 1988.
Mansel 1933	A. M. Mansel, Yalova'da Bulunan İki Mezar Taşı, Türk Arkeoloji Dergisi 1, 1933, 113-120.
Marek 2006	Ch. Marek, Die Inschriften von Kaunos (Vestigia. Beiträge zur Alten Geschichte 65), Munich 1965.
Milner 1998	N. P. Milner, An Epigraphical Survey in the Kibyra-Olbasa Region Conducted by A. S. Hall (Regional Epigraphic Catalogues of Asia Minor 3), Ankara 1998.
Mitchell 1977	St. Mitchell, R.E.C.A.M. Notes and Studies No.1: Inscriptions of Ancyra, AS 27, 1977, 63-103.
Mitchell 1978	St. Mitchell, Onomastic survey of Mysia and the Asiatic shore of the Propontis, in: Pulpudeva. Semaines philippopolitaines de l'histoire et de la culture thrace 2, Plovdiv, 4-19 octobre 1976, Sofia 1978, 119-127.
Mordtmann 1881	J. H. Mordtmann, Zur Epigraphik von Kyzikos, MDAI 6, 1881, 40-55.
Nock 1925	A. D. Nock, Studies in the Graeco-Roman Beliefs of the Empire, JHS 45, 1925, 84-101.
Nollé 2009	J. Nollé, Die taurische Artemis im Tauros: Zeugnisse und Überlegungen zum Artemiskult von Termessos in Pisidien, in: O. Tekin (Hrsg.), Ancient History, Numismatics and Epigraphy in the Mediterranean World. Studies in memory of Clemens E. Bosch and Sabahat Atlan and in honour of Nezahat Baydur, İstanbul 2009, 275-289.
Nordgren 2015	L. Nordgren, Greek Interjections. Syntax, Semantics and Pragmatics, Berlin-Boston 2015.
Onur 2011	F. Onur, New inscriptions from Hadrianoi pros Olympon (Mysia), Olba 19, 2011, 331-348.
Özlem-Aytaçlar 2010	P. Özlem-Aytaçlar, An Onomastic Survey of the Indigenous Population of North-western Asia Minor, in: R. W. V. Catling – F. Marchand (edd.), Onomatologos. Studies in Greek Personal names presented to Elaine Matthews, Oxford 2010, 506-529.
Özlem-Aytaçlar 2012	P. Özlem-Aytaçlar, Kuzeybatı Küçük Asya'nın Yerel Halklarının Onomastiği Üzerine Bir Araştırma, in: N. E. Akyürek Şahin – B. Takmer – F. Onur (edd.), Akron 1. Eskiçağ Yazıları 1, Antalya 2012, 63-113.
Özdilek 2008	B. Özdilek, Neapolis Nekropolleri Üzerine Bir Ön-Rapor, in: II.-IV. Ulusal Arkeoloji Araştırmalar Sempozyumu, Anadolu/

	Anatolia, Ek Dizi No. 2/Supplement Series Nr. 2, Ankara 2008, 235-252.
Özdilek – Çevik 2009	B. Özdilek – N. Çevik, New Discoveries in Rural North East Lycia: Scenes of Daily Life on Roman Rural Sarcophagi, in: Ç. Özkan Aygün (ed.), SOMA 2007. Proceedings of the XI Symposium on Mediterranean Archaeology, Istanbul Technical University, 24-29 April 2007 (BAR International Series 1900), 2009, 284-290.
Pape – Benseler 1884	W. Pape - G. E. Benseler, Wörterbuch der griechischen Eigennamen, Vol. 2, Braunschweig 1884.
Paz de Hoz 2007	M. Paz de Hoz, Testimonios epigráficos sobre la educación griega de época imperial, in: J. A. Fernández Delgado – F. Pordomingo – A. Stramaglia (eds.), Escuela y literatura en Grecia antigua. Actas del simposio internacional Universidad de Salamanca, 17-19 noviembre de 2004, Cassino 2007, 307-332.
Paz de Hoz 2015	M. Paz de Hoz, Associations of Physicians and Teachers in Asia Minor: Between Private and Public, in: V. Gabrielsen- Ch. A. Thomsen (eds.), Private Associations and the Public Sphere: Proceedings of a Symposium held at the Royal Danish Academy of Sciences and Letters, 9-11 September 2010, Copenhagen 2015, 92-121.
Pfuhl – Möbius 1979	E. Pfuhl – H. Möbius, Die ostgriechischen Grabreliefs II, Mainz 1979.
Pleket 1981	H. W. Pleket, Religious history as the history of mentality: the ‹believer› as servant of the deity in the Greek World, in: H. S. Versnel (ed.), Faith, Hope and Worship, Leiden 1981, 152-192.
Ripollès et al. 2015	P. P. Ripollès – A. Burnett – M. Amandry – I. Carradice – M. S. Butcher, Roman Provincial Coinage. Consolidated Supplement III, 2015 (https://rpc.ashmus.ox.ac.uk/supp/rpc_cons_supp_1-3.pdf- Access: 08.03.2019).
Robert 1948	L. Robert, Hellenica V, Paris 1948.
Robert – Robert 1948	L. Robert – J. Robert, Hellenica, Recueil d'épigraphie, de numismatique et d'antiquités grecques publié par L. Robert. Vol. VI. Inscriptions grecques de Lydie, Paris 1948.
Robert 1964	L. Robert, L'édition et l'index commenté des épitaphes, in: N. Fıratlı, Les stèles funéraires de Byzance gréco-romaine, Paris 1964, 131-189.
Robert, OMS I	L. Robert, Opera Minora Selecta. Épigraphie et antiquités grecques, Tome I, Amsterdam 1969.
Robert, OMS VI	L. Robert, Opera Minora Selecta. Épigraphie et antiquités grecques, Tome VI, Amsterdam 1989.
Rodríguez Pérez 2010	D. Rodríguez Pérez, Contextualizing Symbols: «the Eagle and the Snake» in the Ancient Greek World, Boreas 33, 2010, 1-18.

Ruge 1934	W. Ruge, s.v. Tauropolis (3), in: RE VA, 1, 1934, 33-34.
Saller 1994	R. P. Saller, Patriarchy, Property and Death in the Roman Family, Cambridge 1994.
Samama 2003	E. Samama, Les médecins dans le monde grec: sources épigraphiques sur la naissance d'un corps médical, Geneva 2003.
Scheidel 2007	W. Scheidel, Roman Funerary Commemoration and the Age at First Marriage, Classical Philology 102,4, 2007, 389-402.
Schulze 1991	W. Schulze, Zur Geschichte lateinischer Eigennamen, mit einer Berichtigungsliste zur Neuausgabe von Olli Salomies, Hildesheim 1991.
Schwabl 1993	H. Schwabl, Zum Kult des Zeus in Kleinasien, in: G. Dobesch – G. Rehrenböck (Hrsg.), Die epigraphische und altertumskundliche Erforschung Kleinasiens: Hundert Jahre Kleinasiatische Kommission der Österreichischen Akademie der Wissenschaften. Akten des Symposiums vom 23. bis 25. Oktober 1990, Vienna 1993, 329-338.
Schwertheim 1989	E. Schwertheim, Die Heimat des Aelius Aristides, in: H. -J. Drexhage – J. Sünske (ed.), Migratio et commutatio: Studien zur alten Geschichte und deren Nachleben: Thomas Pekáry zum 60. Geburtstag am 13. September 1989 dargebracht von Freunden, Kollegen und Schülern, St. Katharinen 1989, 249-257.
SGO II	R. Merkelbach – J. Stauber, Steinepigramme aus dem griechischen Osten II. Die Nordküste Kleinasiens (Marmarameer und Pontos), München-Leipzig 2001.
SGO III	R. Merkelbach – J. Stauber, Steinepigramme aus dem griechischen Osten III. Der ferne Osten und das Landesinnere bis zum Tauros, München-Leipzig 2001.
Solin 2004	H. Solin, Analecta epigraphica CCXVI-CCXXII, Arctos XXXVIII, 2004, 163-205.
Şahin 1974	S. Şahin, Neufunde von antiken Inschriften in Nikomedeia (İzmit) und in der Umgebung der Stadt, Münster 1974.
Talloen 2015	P. Talloen, Cult in Pisidia. Religious Practice in Southwestern Asia Minor from Alexander the Great to the Rise of Christianity, Turnhout 2015.
TAM V,1	P. Herrmann, Tituli Asiae Minoris V: Tituli Lydiae linguis Graeca et Latina conscripti, Fasc. 1: nos. 1-825, Regio septentrionalis ad occidentem vergens, Vienna 1981.
TAM V,2	P. Herrmann, Tituli Asiae Minoris V: Tituli Lydiae linguis Graeca et Latina conscripti, Fasc. 2: nos. 826-1414, Regio septentrionalis ad occidentem vergens, Vienna 1989.
Tanrıver 2013	C. Tanrıver, Mysia'dan Yeni Epigrafik Buluntular, İzmir 2013.

Taeuber 2016	H. Tauber, Zu einer Grabstele aus İnegöl (Bursa), in: Adnotationes Epigraphicae VII, Tyche 31, 2016, 285-290.
Thonemann 2013	P. Thonemann, Households and families in Roman Phrygia, in: P. Thonemann (ed.), Roman Phrygia. Culture and Society, Cambridge 2013, 124-142.
Thonemann 2017	P. Thonemann, Close-Kin Marriage in Roman Anatolia, The Cambridge Classical Journal 63, 2017, 143-166.
Uzunoğlu 2015	H. Uzunoğlu, Bursa Müzesi'nden Ölü Ziyafeti Sahneli Yeni Mezar Stelleri, Olba 23, 397-415.
Uzunoğlu 2019	H. Uzunoğlu, Phrygia'dan Bir Grup Yeni Mezar Steli, Mediterranean Journal of Humanities IX/1, 2019, in print.
Waldmann 1978	H. Waldmann, Ein Archimystes in Sagalassos, in: M. de Boer - T. A. Edridge (ed.), Hommages à Maarten J. Vermaseren, Volume 3, Leiden 1978, 1309-1315.
Yıldız 2018	M. E. Yıldız, Tlos'tan İki Yeni Mezar Yazıtı, Olba XXVI, 2018, 405-414.
Yıldız 2019	M. E. Yıldız, Epigramm auf die verstorbene Moschion. Eine neue Grabstele aus dem Territorium von Miletupolis in Mysien, in: M. Nollé – P. M. Rothenhöfer – G. Schmied-Kowarzik – H. Schwarz – H. Ch. von Mosch (eds.), Panegyrikoi Logoi. Festschrift für Johannes Nollé zum 65. Geburtstag, Bonn 2019, 583-590.
Zahle 1979	J. Zahle, Lykische Felsgräber mit Reliefs aus dem 4. Jahrhundert v. Chr. JbDAI 94, 1979, 245-346.
Zgusta 1964	L. Zgusta, Kleinasiatische Personennamen, Prag 1964.

Bursa Müzesi'nden Yeni Yazıtlar
Özet

Bu makalede Bursa müzesindeki bir grup Eski Yunanca yazıtlı yeni eser tanıtılmaktadır. Burada yayımlanan 36 eserin ilk 4 tanesi adak, geriye kalan eserler ise mezar taşıdır. Mezar taşlarından altı tanesinde (no. 26-31) yazıt yoktur, fakat bu eserlerin de bilim dünyasında tanınması için makaleye onlar da alınmıştır. Bu yazıtsız eserler olasılıkla atölyelerde üretilmiş ve hiç bir zaman bir müşteriye satılmamış ve mezar taşı olarak kullanılmamıştır. Mezar yazıtlarından bazıları (no. 21-25) Laflı ve Bru (2016) tarafından müzede bizim çalışmamıza rağmen ve müzeden izinsiz biçimde daha önce yayımlanmıştır. Bu yazıtların bazıları tarafımızdan burada düzeltilmiştir. Makalede bazılarının buluntu yerleri bilinmemekle birlikte eserlerin genellikle Bursa ve çevresinde bulundukları görülmektedir. Buluntu yerleri olarak Bursa'da Nilüfer, İnegöl, Orhaneli, Harmancık, Keles, Gemlik, Karacabey, Orhangazi ve Mudanya ilçeleri ile Yalova ili görülmektedir. Adak yazıtları bize Meter Taurene, Men Tauropoleites, Zeus Kersoullos ve Apollon gibi tanrıların isimlerini vermektedir. İlk iki tanrı Mysia bölgesinde tapınım gören tanrılardan değildirler ve kültlerini olasılıkla Küçük Asya'nın güney batı bölgelerinde aramak gerekmektedir.

Makalede tanıtılan mezar taşlarının ise lahit, prizma biçimli altar, silindir altar, stel, ölü yemeği sahneli stel ve de altar üzerinde stel olarak karşımıza çıktığı görülmektedir. Zengin bir mezar taşı tipolojisi vardır. Buradaki yazıtlar da Mysia bölgesinin onomastiği hakkında bilgilerimizi zenginleştirmektedir. Basit de olsa mezar yazıtlarından bir azatlı (no. 5), Protinia isimli bir phyle (no. 10), bir demos'un bir kadın doktoru onurlandırması (no. 11), bir öğretmen (no. 16) gibi bilgiler de edinilmektedir. Yazıtlar büyük oranda Roma İmparatorluk Dönemi'nin 2. ve 3. yüzyıllarına aittir. Ancak olasılıkla Hellenistik Dönem'e ait birkaç yazıt da vardır (no. 13, 19, 24, 25).

Yazıtların çevirileri şöyledir:

1. Epitynkhanon'un oğlu Metrodoros (bunu) Meter Taurene ve Men Tauropoleites için adak olarak (sundu).

2. Hayırlı uğurlu olsun! Asklepiades'in oğlu, Aoriasse köyünden Ankyra vatandaşı Apollonios (bu sütunu tanrının) emri uyarınca, gizli ayinlerin başkanı Rufus'un kâhinlik (profetlik) yaptığı sırada Zeus Kersoullos'a adadı.

3. Hayırlı uğurlu olsun! Asklepides oğlu Antigenes ve Aphia bu sekos'u (kutsal yeri?) masraflarını kendileri karşılayarak rahip Aristokrates'in kâhinlik (profetlik) yaptığı sırada tanrıya adadılar.

3a. Hayırlı uğurlu olsun! Menios'un oğlu Metrodoros (ve) Euraion Neiketes kötü mevsimler (nedeniyle?) ve kendileri için adağı - - - - - - - - kâhinlik (profetlik) yaptığı sırada (sundular).

4. Apollon? [Ak]raios? için bu altarı (tanrının) emri uyarınca Akylas'ın oğlu Polyainos eşi ile beraber dikti.

5. Artemon'un azatlısı ey Ekgle(k)tos, elveda!

6. Marcus'un oğlu Lucius (bu altarı) yaşarken kendisi için ve kendi (eşi) Nennis'in kızı Asklepiodote için (yaptırdı).

7. Aur(elia) Doris çocukları Elpidephoros ve Eutykhides ile beraber biricik kocası Eutykhides için anısı nedeniyle (bu altarı dikti).

8. Menestheus oğlu Hermas eşi Khreste için onun anısı nedeniyle (bu mezarı) parasını kendisi ödeyerek (yaptırdı).

9. Papianus'un? oğlu - - - - - - - - ve onun karısı - - -ia Artemi- - - kocası/karısı - - -des'in oğlu/kızı S- - - - için anısı nedeniyle (bu mezarı yaptırdı).

10. Ben Asklepiodotos'un oğlu, Protinia phylesi'nden phylarkhos Aurelius Stakhys hayattayken bu mezarı kendim için ve biricik eşim Secunda ve biricik çocuklarım için yaptırdım.

11. Demos (insanlar) mütevazı bir şekilde hayat sürmüş olan kadın doktor (ebe?) Fabia Fabula'yı (ölümünden sonra onurlandırdı).

12. Bu mezarı, M(arcus) Domiti(o)s Stertinni(o)s Aristainetos pek tatlı hayat arkadaşı Longus'un kızı Maxima için (yaptırdı).

13. Dilıporis'in oğlu Torkosinies - - - - - - yaptırdı. Onun damadı Didipes'in oğlu - - - - - -. Elveda!

14. Mnaseas'ın kızı, Menestratos'un ise eşi Ammia. Elveda!

15. Marcus'un kızı, Bassus'un ise eşi 15 yaşındaki Aleksandris için.

16. Öğretmen Claudius Phillys'ün oğlu 15 yaşındaki Tiberius Claudius Phillys için.

17. P(ublius) Acilius (veya Pakilios) bir ismi de Khrysios olan Diogenes'in kızı olan eşi, cömert? Tatia için hayattayken - - - (bu mezarı yaptırdı).

18. Philargyros'un oğlu 6 (veya 7) yaşındaki Paideros için. Philargyros ve Astratie? kendi oğulları Paideros için bu mezarı (yaptırdılar).

19. Poseidonios'un oğlu Demetrios (ve) eşi Mainia?. Elveda!

20. Aristokrates'in oğlu - - - - - - onun - - -

21. Selam ey yoldan geçen! Örnek biçimde 60 yıl yaşam sürmüş olan Diogenes'in oğlu Diogenes; vah ki ne vah! Teimotheos'un oğlu Diogenes 12 yıl birlikte yaşam sürdüğü kendi eşi Fabia Rufa için; (ki) o 25 yaşını tamamladı; (bu) steli hatırası nedeniyle yaptırdı.

22. Henüz hayatta olan G(aius) Murius Valens ve Muria Prima için ve onların oğulları 22 yıl yaşamış olan Rufus için. (Bu) steli kızları Marcella yaptırdı.

23. Menekrates'in oğlu Rhadamanthys. Elveda!

24. Bias'ın oğlu ey Hipparkhos, elveda!

25. Dionysodoros'un oğlu Kharmides.

32. Neikias ve Aphrodite'nin kızları, L(ucius) Orfius Felix'in ise eşi, 23 yaşındaki Lakaina. Elveda!

33. Tyrannion ve Aristo yaşarken ve akılları yerindeyken (bu) mezarı çocukları Eia için yaptırdılar. Elveda!

34. Ben, Deios'un (veya Deias'ın) kızı Aur(elia) Teimothea henüz hayatta iken kendim için ve 50 sene yaşayan kocam Deios (veya Deias) oğlu Phoibion'un hatırası nedeniyle bu mezar anıtını çocuklarım Eutykhes ve Teimothea ile birlikte yaptırdım.

35. Philotas'ın oğlu Philotas - - - - - -

36. Fragman.

Anahtar sözcükler: Bursa Müzesi, adak ve mezar yazıtları, Meter Taurene, Men Tauropeleites, Zeus Kersoullos, prophetes, kadın doktor, paideutes.

New Inscriptions from the Museum of Bursa
Abstract

In this contribution we introduce some new ancient Greek inscriptions from the Bursa Museum. Of the 36 artefacts, the first four are dedications, while the remaining are funerary stones. Six funerary stelai do not bear any inscriptions. The provenance of some artefacts unfortunately remain unknown, but in general they were brought to the museum from Bursa province and its environs such as the districts of Nilüfer, İnegöl, Orhaneli, Harmancık, Keles, Gemlik, Karacabey and Orhangazi, as well as from the province of Yalova. The ex-votos are offered to Meter Taurene, Men Tauropoleites, Zeus Kersoullos and Apollon. The funerary inscriptions are humble, but apart from contributing to the already rich onomastics of Bithynia Mysia, they also provide some interesting information, such as concerning a freedman (no. 5), a new phyle called Protinia (no. 10), the posthumous honouring of a woman doctor (no. 11), and, a teacher (no. 16). The inscriptions mostly date to the Roman Imperial Period, but there are also a few Hellenistic examples (nos. 13, 19, 24, 25).

Keywords: Bursa Museum, ex-votos and funerary inscriptions, Meter Taurene, Men Tauropeleites, Zeus Kersoullos, prophetes, female doctor, paideutes.